Physics of Impurities in Quantum Gases

Physics of Impurities in Quantum Gases

Editors

Simeon Mistakidis
Artem Volosniev

MDPI • Basel • Beijing • Wuhan • Barcelona • Belgrade • Manchester • Tokyo • Cluj • Tianjin

Editors
Simeon Mistakidis
Harvard & Smithsonian
USA

Artem Volosniev
IST Austria
Austria

Editorial Office
MDPI
St. Alban-Anlage 66
4052 Basel, Switzerland

This is a reprint of articles from the Special Issue published online in the open access journal *Atoms* (ISSN 2218-2004) (available at: https://www.mdpi.com/journal/atoms/special_issues/Physics_Impurities_QuantumGases).

For citation purposes, cite each article independently as indicated on the article page online and as indicated below:

LastName, A.A.; LastName, B.B.; LastName, C.C. Article Title. *Journal Name* **Year**, *Volume Number*, Page Range.

ISBN 978-3-0365-4873-9 (Hbk)
ISBN 978-3-0365-4874-6 (PDF)

© 2022 by the authors. Articles in this book are Open Access and distributed under the Creative Commons Attribution (CC BY) license, which allows users to download, copy and build upon published articles, as long as the author and publisher are properly credited, which ensures maximum dissemination and a wider impact of our publications.

The book as a whole is distributed by MDPI under the terms and conditions of the Creative Commons license CC BY-NC-ND.

Contents

About the Editors vii

Preface to "Physics of Impurities in Quantum Gases" ix

Magnus G. Skou, Thomas G. Skov, Nils B. Jørgensen and Jan J. Arlt
Initial Dynamics of Quantum Impurities in a Bose–Einstein Condensate
Reprinted from: *Atoms* 2021, 9, 22, doi:10.3390/atoms9020022 1

Francesco Scazza, Matteo Zaccanti, Pietro Massignan, Meera M. Parish and Jesper Levinsen
Repulsive Fermi and Bose Polarons in Quantum Gases
Reprinted from: *Atoms* 2022, 10, 55, doi:10.3390/atoms10020055 11

Hiroyuki Tajima, Junichi Takahashi, Simeon I. Mistakidis, Eiji Nakano, and Kei Iida
Polaron Problems in Ultracold Atoms: Role of a Fermi Sea across Different Spatial Dimensions and Quantum Fluctuations of a Bose Medium
Reprinted from: *Atoms* 2021, 9, 18, doi:10.3390/atoms9010018 41

Luis A. Peña Ardila
Ultra-Dilute Gas of Polarons in a Bose–Einstein Condensate
Reprinted from: *Atoms* 2022, 10, 29, doi:10.3390/atoms10010029 67

Galyna Panochko, Volodymyr Pastukhov
Static Impurities in a Weakly Interacting Bose Gas
Reprinted from: *Atoms* 2022, 10, 19, doi:10.3390/atoms10010019 77

Georgios M. Koutentakis, Simeon I. Mistakidis and Peter Schmelcher
Pattern Formation in One-Dimensional Polaron Systems and Temporal Orthogonality Catastrophe
Reprinted from: *Atoms* 2022, 10, 3, doi:10.3390/atoms10010003 89

Miguel Angel Bastarrachea-Magnani, Jannie Thomsen, Arturo Camacho-Guardian and Georg Morten Bruun
Polaritons in an Electron Gas—Quasiparticles and Landau Effective Interactions
Reprinted from: *Atoms* 2021, 9, 81, doi:10.3390/atoms9040081 119

Morris Brooks, Mikhail Lemeshko, Douglas Lundholm and Enderalp Yakaboylu
Emergence of Anyons on the Two-Sphere in Molecular Impurities
Reprinted from: *Atoms* 2021, 9, 106, doi:10.3390/atoms9040106 135

Chiara D'Errico, and Marco G. Tarallo
One-Dimensional Disordered Bosonic Systems
Reprinted from: *Atoms* 2021, 9, 112, doi:10.3390/atoms9040112 147

Ofir E. Alon
Fragmentation of Identical and Distinguishable Bosons' Pairs and Natural Geminals of a Trapped Bosonic Mixture
Reprinted from: *Atoms* 2021, 9, 92, doi:10.3390/atoms9040092 161

Panagiotis Giannakeas and Chris H. Greene
Asymmetric Lineshapes of Efimov Resonances in Mass-Imbalanced Ultracold Gases
Reprinted from: *Atoms* 2021, 9, 110, doi:10.3390/atoms9040110 187

Koushik Mukherjee, Soumik Bandyopadhyay, Dilip Angom, Andy M. Martin and Sonjoy Majumder
Dynamics of the Creation of a Rotating Bose–Einstein Condensation by Two Photon Raman Transition Using a Laguerre–Gaussian Laser Pulse
Reprinted from: *Atoms* **2021**, *9*, 14, doi:10.3390/atoms9010014 . . . . **203**

About the Editors

Simeon Mistakidis

Simeon Mistakidis is an ITAMP postdoctoral fellow at Harvard University working on engineering entanglement-based processes and magnetic phenomena appearing in many-body multicomponent systems ranging from quasiparticles and droplets to long-range settings. He obtained his master's degree in theoretical physics in the sector of Nuclear and Particle Physics at the National and Kapodistrian University of Athens, Greece. He then moved to the University of Hamburg as an exchange student to complete his master's and PhD studies in Atomic Molecular and Optical Physics, where he received a scholarship to serve as a graduate exchange visiting student assistant and, afterwards, the PhD Scholarship Hamburgisches Gesetz zur Förderung des wissenschaftlichen und künstlerischen Nachwuchses. His research was devoted to studying the correlated nonequilibrium quantum dynamics of many-body atomic systems with a particular emphasis on excitation processes in optical lattices, pattern formation and the physics of polarons. Following his PhD (with summa cum laude), he received the Lenz-Ising Award presented to outstanding junior scientists. He has co-authored more than 60 scientific publications and serves as a reviewer for more than 20 international journals and a topic editor for 2 of these journals.

Artem Volosniev

Artem Volosniev is a postdoctoral researcher at the Institute of Science and Technology Austria primarily interested in strongly correlated quantum systems as well as in the theory of quantum simulations and engineering. In 2010, he graduated from V. N. Karazin Kharkiv National University (Ukraine). In 2013, he was awarded his PhD degree in theoretical physics from Aarhus University (Denmark). After a brief postdoc in Aarhus, he held a temporary research position at TU Darmstadt (Germany). His research there was supported by the Humboldt Foundation and by the DFG (German Research Foundation). In 2018, he was awarded a Marie Curie (ISTplus) fellowship to continue his research in Austria.

Preface to "Physics of Impurities in Quantum Gases"

Systems with impurities have served as motivation for establishing some of the most important concepts in quantum physics, chemistry and materials science in the last century. Nowadays, the fundamentals of these concepts are being tested using cold-atom setups.

In this Special Issue, we present a few recent studies that examine the properties of impurities in quantum gases, fundamental properties and universal aspects of quasiparticles and other related many-body phenomena. Particular focus is placed on the Fermi and Bose polarons.

We would like to cordially thank the contributing authors for their original research and review articles. We are grateful to Ms. Lauren Liu for providing assistance in the preparation of the Special Issue. We hope that this book will help to shape our understanding of systems with impurities and pave the way for future endeavors.

Simeon Mistakidis and Artem Volosniev
Editors

Article

Initial Dynamics of Quantum Impurities in a Bose–Einstein Condensate

Magnus G. Skou *, Thomas G. Skov, Nils B. Jørgensen and Jan J. Arlt

Center for Complex Quantum Systems, Department of Physics and Astronomy, Aarhus University, Ny Munkegade 120, DK-8000 Aarhus, Denmark; tg.skov@phys.au.dk (T.G.S.); nilsbyg@hotmail.com (N.B.J.); arlt@phys.au.dk (J.J.A.)
* Correspondence: magnus.skou@phys.au.dk

Abstract: An impurity immersed in a medium constitutes a canonical scenario applicable in a wide range of fields in physics. Though our understanding has advanced significantly in the past decades, quantum impurities in a bosonic environment are still of considerable theoretical and experimental interest. Here, we discuss the initial dynamics of such impurities, which was recently observed in interferometric experiments. Experimental observations from weak to unitary interactions are presented and compared to a theoretical description. In particular, the transition between two initial dynamical regimes dominated by two-body interactions is analyzed, yielding transition times in clear agreement with the theoretical prediction. Additionally, the distinct time dependence of the coherence amplitude in these regimes is obtained by extracting its power-law exponents. This benchmarks our understanding and suggests new ways of probing dynamical properties of quantum impurities.

Keywords: Bose–Einstein condensates; impurity dynamics; ramsey interferometry; polarons

Citation: Skou, M.G.; Skov, T.G.; Jørgensen, N.B.; Arlt, J.J. Initial Dynamics of Quantum Impurities in a Bose–Einstein Condensate. *Atoms* 2021, 9, 22. https://doi.org/10.3390/atoms9020022

Academic Editors: Mistakidis Simeon and Artem Volosniev

Received: 26 February 2021
Accepted: 23 March 2021
Published: 27 March 2021

Publisher's Note: MDPI stays neutral with regard to jurisdictional claims in published maps and institutional affiliations.

Copyright: © 2021 by the authors. Licensee MDPI, Basel, Switzerland. This article is an open access article distributed under the terms and conditions of the Creative Commons Attribution (CC BY) license (https://creativecommons.org/licenses/by/4.0/).

1. Introduction

The behavior of interacting quantum impurities is a problem of significant scientific and technological importance. Initial theoretical studies by Landau and Pekar [1] showed that a crystal lattice dresses electrons to form quasiparticles coined polarons. This intuitive model is highly successful and now serves as a basis for understanding complex condensed matter systems [2]. The concept of polarons is thus central for important technologies such as organic semiconductors [3] and high-temperature superconductors [4].

The initial dynamics of an impurity is especially intriguing. It sheds light on the intrinsic link between two-body and many-body correlations, and is key to understanding the eventual formation of a polaron. Due to the fast evolution times in most materials, this evolution has eluded observation until recently. With the advent of quantum gases, this is no longer the case since their low densities allow for long interrogation times in pure and controllable environments. Based on these systems, the spectral response and dynamical evolution of an impurity in a Fermi gas have been explored in great theoretical and experimental detail [5–13]. The mobile Bose polaron, which resembles the solid-state problem closely, has been studied spectroscopically [14–17] and its behavior has been investigated in a one-dimensional Bose gas [18,19]. However, the formation dynamics of the Bose polaron in a three-dimensional gas has remained unclear.

Here we present recent experiments, which succeed in investigating the dynamics of impurities in a Bose–Einstein condensate (BEC). This evolution of the impurities can be resolved using an interferometric sequence. The first pulse in this sequence creates an imbalanced superposition state, which evolves under the influence of interactions in the system. The second pulse then allows a measurement of the coherence between the initial state and the evolved impurity state [20]. The dynamics of the impurity can be separated into three regimes, as illustrated in Figure 1, depending on the interaction strength and the evolution time. The initial dynamics at all interaction strengths is governed by two-body scattering between the impurity and the condensate. For short times, the two-body scattering is unitarity-limited causing the coherence to evolve universally [21]. For weak interactions, this is followed by a regime of two-body weak coupling dynamics which depends on the scattering length between the impurity state and medium state. For longer times, the dynamical behavior transitions into a regime where many-body correlations govern the evolution. For strong interactions, this regime is entered directly from universal dynamics.

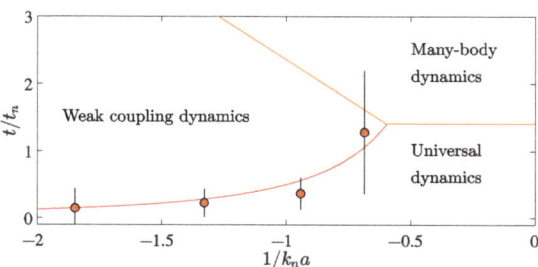

Figure 1. Regimes of impurity dynamics. Characteristic regimes of impurity dynamics as a function of the inverse interaction strength $1/k_n a$ (see text) and the evolution time t/t_n (see text). Solid lines indicate predicted transitions between the dynamical regimes. Red data points are experimentally extracted transition times and errors correspond to fit uncertainties. A similar figure was presented in Ref. [20].

This dynamical evolution was initially investigated in Ref. [20] where all three regimes were observed. Furthermore, the transition times between the regimes were obtained showing clear agreement with theoretical predictions. In this paper, we extend the analysis of the experimental observations to provide a deeper understanding of the two regimes of universal and weak coupling dynamics illustrated in Figure 1. Specifically, we discuss the transition time between them and consider the functional behavior of the coherence in the two regimes.

The paper is structured as follows. In Section 2, the experiment is briefly presented including the interferometric sequence. This is followed by the discussion of a theoretical model in Section 3. In Section 4, this model is compared with experimental observations of the coherence amplitude and phase evolution for weak and unitary interactions. The transition between the two regimes is discussed in Section 5. Finally, in Section 6 the dependence of the dynamical evolution on interaction strength is presented.

2. Experimental Details

The experiment was performed using a quantum gas of ^{39}K. The production of ^{39}K BECs has been presented in detail in Refs. [14,22] and only the relevant steps for investigating impurity dynamics are outlined here.

The experiments are based on a ^{39}K BEC in the hyperfine state $|F=1, m_F = -1\rangle$ held in an optical dipole potential with an average condensate density of $n_B = 0.9 \times 10^{14}$ cm^{-3}. This determines the system energy scale $E_n = \hbar^2 k_n^2/2m$ through the wave number $k_n = (6\pi^2 n_B)^{1/3}$ and importantly sets the relevant timescale $t_n = \hbar/E_n = 4\,\mu$s. We employ a second hyperfine state $|F=1, m_F = 0\rangle$ as the impurity state. The interaction strength between the two states is characterized by the dimensionless parameter $1/k_n a$, where a is the interstate scattering length. This scattering length can be tuned by the magnetic field via a Feshbach resonance located at 113.8 G [23,24]. The medium scattering length is $a_B \approx 9 a_0$, where a_0 is the Bohr radius, and is approximately constant for the applied magnetic fields

An interferometric sequence consisting of two radio-frequency (rf) pulses is employed, which allows us to populate an impurity state and probe the subsequent dynamics. Similar interferometric investigations have previously explored impurity dynamics in a Fermi gas [8,9] and motional coherence of fixed impurities in a BEC [25,26]. The rf pulses are resonant with the atomic transition and their short duration of 0.5 µs allows the dynamics to be well resolved. The first rf pulse quenches the system into a superposition of the impurity state and the medium state corresponding to a ∼5% population in the former, which ensures vanishing interaction between the impurites [20]. The system then evolves for a variable time t, in which the phase of the coherence advances and the coherence amplitude decays due to interactions between the two states. Finally, a second rf pulse probes the system with a variable phase φ. Subsequently, the atoms are held in the dipole trap for an additional 2 ms where three-body losses remove two medium atoms for each impurity. Thus, only medium atoms remain whose number is inversely proportional to the number of impurity atoms after the second rf pulse. After free expansion the remaining number of the medium state atoms is measured through absorption imaging.

This resulting atom number depends sinusoidally on the probe phase and for each evolution time t we perform a fit $\mathcal{N}(\varphi) = N_0 - \mathcal{A}\cos(\varphi - \varphi_C)$. Here, the amplitude $\mathcal{A}$ corresponds to the extent to which the coherence is preserved and φ_C corresponds to the phase acquired during the evolution time t. Thus, we obtain the amplitude $|C(t)| = |\mathcal{A}(t)/\mathcal{A}(0)|$ and the phase φ_C of the coherence for each chosen interaction strength and evolution time. Example measurements of the coherence amplitude and phase are shown in Figure 2 for weak and unitary interactions (Slight differences in the data with respect to Ref. [20] arise due to an improved calibration of the imaging system.). These measurements clearly display how the coherence of the system evolves as time progresses between the two rf pulses.

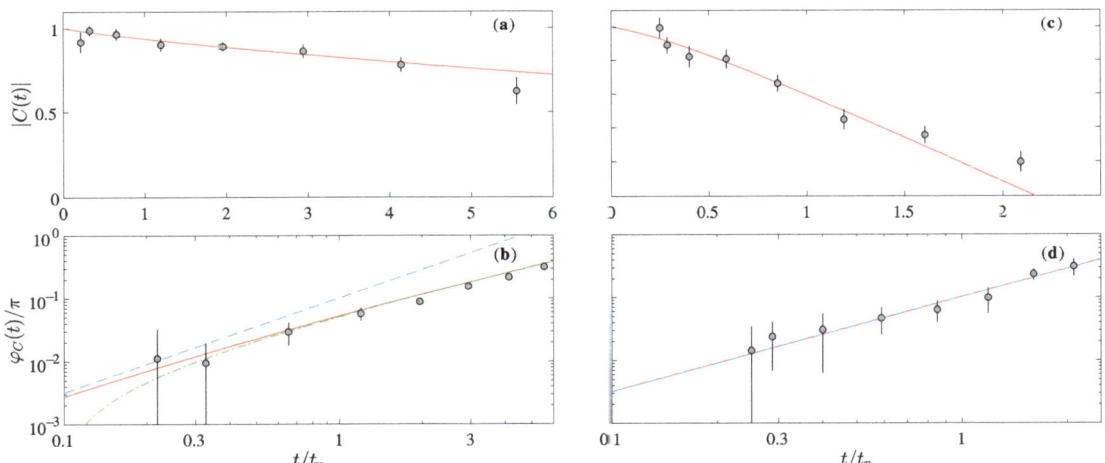

Figure 2. Two-body dynamics at weak and unitary interaction strengths. The coherence amplitude (top row) and phase evolution (bottom row) at $1/k_n a = -1.8$ (**a,b**) and $1/k_n a = 0.01$ (**c,d**). The corresponding data were previously presented in Ref. [20]. Equation (1) is shown as a solid red line and the two limits in Equation (2) are shown as a dashed blue line and a dash-dotted green line for the universal and the weak coupling dynamics, respectively. Note that the universal description coincides with the general two-body model in panel (**d**). The errors correspond to fit uncertainties.

3. Two-Body Regimes of Dynamical Evolution

In the following section we briefly outline the theoretical description of the dynamical regimes which we compare with our experimental results. A short-time theoretical prediction can be obtained from the spectral function of the impurity. This describes the impurity in the frequency-domain and generally contains a polaron ground state and a continuum of excited states. Though the exact spectral function at arbitrary interaction strength has no general solution, the tail of excited states at high frequencies has previously been investigated in detail [27]. Due to the intrinsic link between frequency-domain and time-domain behavior, the Fourier transform of this high-frequency solution yields the coherence for the initial two-body dynamics. For low medium-medium scattering length, it can be expressed as [20]

$$C(t) \simeq 1 - i\frac{E_{\mathrm{mf}}t}{\hbar} + \frac{2}{3\pi}(k_n|a|)^3 \left[1 - \frac{2}{\sqrt{\pi}} e^{it/t_a} \Gamma\left(\frac{3}{2}, i\frac{t}{t_a}\right)\right], \quad (1)$$

where Γ is the incomplete gamma function, $E_{\mathrm{mf}} = 4\pi\hbar^2 n_B a/m$ is the mean-field energy and $t_a = ma^2/\hbar$ is the timescale set by the medium-impurity scattering length a. The coherence amplitude and phase can be examined using the coherence in the small-angle approximation. Thus, to the lowest order, the experimentally measured amplitude and phase correspond to the real and imaginary part of Equation (1).

Remarkably, this two-body prediction is exact for any interaction strength from weak to strong interactions [20]. Furthermore, it is possible to simplify Equation (1) in the following limits

$$C(t) = \begin{cases} 1 - (1-i)\frac{16}{9\pi^{3/2}}\left(\frac{t}{t_n}\right)^{3/2} & t \ll t_a \\ 1 - iE_{\mathrm{mf}}t/\hbar - (1+i)\left(\frac{t}{t_w}\right)^{1/2} & t \gg t_a \end{cases} \quad (2)$$

where $t_w = m/32\pi\hbar n_B^2 a^4$. The long-time limit of the equation is valid to second order in the impurity-medium scattering length a, and it can be extended to include a third-order correction [20]. Furthermore, it clearly demonstrates two distinct regimes. At short times $t \ll t_a$ the high-frequency scattering is limited by the density and the coherence evolves with an interaction independent timescale t_n and an exponent of 3/2. For longer times $t \gg t_a$, this transitions into weak coupling dynamics marked by the appearance of the mean-field energy, the interaction dependent timescale t_w, and the exponent 1/2.

These power laws reflect the behavior of the scattering cross section $\sigma(k) = 4\pi a^2/[1 + (ka)^2]$ in the two regimes [20]. In a simple picture, it governs the collision rate, which we assume to equal the rate of decoherence $\dot{C}(t) \sim -n_B \sigma v$. At a given time t during the evolution after the first rf pulse, the characteristic energy associated with decoherence is $E \sim \hbar/t$, which sets the wave number $k \sim \sqrt{m/\hbar t}$ and collisional velocity $v \sim \sqrt{\hbar/mt}$. For short times $t \ll t_a$, the cross section is unitary-limited $\sigma \sim 1/k^2 \sim \hbar t/m$. By integrating the corresponding rate of decoherence we obtain $C(t) \sim (t/t_n)^{3/2}$, which precisely reflects the universal limit of Equation (2). In contrast, for longer times $t \gg t_a$ the cross section is dominated by the scattering length as $\sigma \sim a^2$. Integrating the decoherence rate here yields the weak coupling limit $C(t) \sim (t/t_w)^{1/2}$. The timescale t_a is therefore key in describing which regime governs the dynamical evolution of the system.

4. Coherence Amplitude and Phase Evolution

Based on the experiment described in Section 2, it is possible to observe the evolution of an impurity state by monitoring the coherence amplitude $|C|$ and phase φ_C. Here we compare such measurements with the theoretical prediction from Section 3. Examples of measured coherence amplitude and phase are shown in Figure 2 for weak and resonant interactions with the general two-body description (Equation (1)) for all panels and with its limits (Equation (2)) for the phase.

For both data sets, the coherence amplitude decreases as function of evolution time, driven by the dynamical scattering events. This shows that the impurity state evolves and loses coherence with the initial state (To compare the experimental observations with this prediction, the coherence amplitude is normalized by fitting Equation (1) with an overall amplitude within t_n.) at a rate which increases for large interaction strengths as expected.

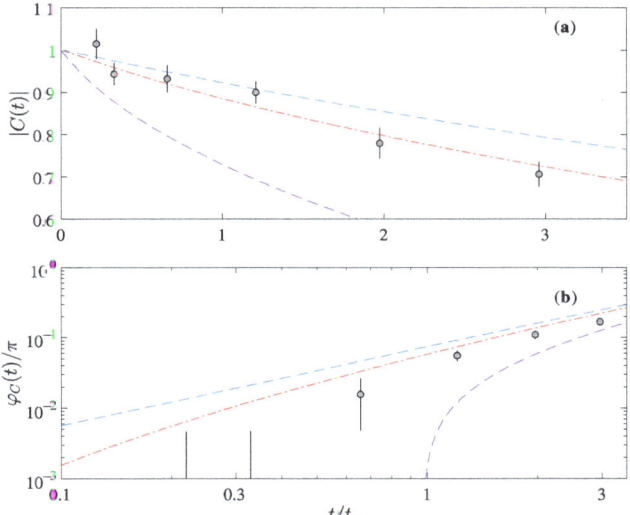

Figure 3. Transition from universal to weak coupling dynamics. (**a**) The coherence amplitude and (**b**) phase evolution at $1/k_n a = -1.3$ (circles) with Equation (1) as a dash-dotted line for its fitted value $t_a = 0.2 t_n$ (red) and as dashed lines using two additional values $0.05 t_n$ (purple) and $0.5 t_n$ (blue). The errors correspond to fit uncertainties.

The coherence amplitude in the upper panels of Figure 2 is affected by additional decoherence processes which all contribute to its gradual decay. To accurately model the experiment, we therefore include effects stemming from the inhomogeneous density distribution, the lifetime of the impurity and shot-to-shot magnetic field fluctuations in our theoretical description. The dephasing due to the inhomogeneous density distribution is accounted for by integration of the coherence over the density distribution of the BEC. This is modeled in the Thomas–Fermi limit using a parabolic density profile. The lifetime of the impurity due to recombination was measured independently and included by multiplying the coherence with an exponential decay. The lifetime ranges from $\sim 7 t_r$ at unitarity to $\sim 42 t_n$ at weak interaction strengths. The shot-to-shot magnetic field fluctuations were also measured independently and incorporated in the theoretical description of the coherence. This was achieved by multiplying the coherence with the integrated distribution of phases caused by the slight differences in the magnetic field at each experimental repetition. Since the temperature of the cloud was ~ 50 nK, the corresponding thermal timescale $\hbar/k_B T \sim 38 t_n$ is beyond the accessible regime of impurity dynamics and thus thermal effects are negligible. The resulting two-body prediction is illustrated in Figure 2 and clearly agrees with the data for short times. Since no fitting parameters are employed, the excellent agreement of the prediction and observations highlights that the theory captures the dynamical behavior of the system exceedingly well.

The lower panels of Figure 2 show the evolution of the coherence phase as a function of time, where a faster evolution is observed for larger interaction strengths. Since the experimental decoherence mechanisms primarily influence the coherence amplitude, the phase is better suited to observe the power-law behavior of the coherence evolution. It is therefore plotted in a double logarithmic fashion (Note that the coherence phase cannot be reliably extracted for long evolution times due to the vanishing coherence amplitude.). The imaginary part of Equation (1) is also shown in the lower panels of Figure 2 in good agreement with the observations. To gain further insight, we show the limits of Equation (2) as well. For weak interactions (Figure 2b) the transition from two-body universal dynamics to weak coupling dynamics occurs almost immediately and the $\sim t^{1/2}$ limit of Equation (2) captures the entire observed phase evolution. At unitarity, the universal dynamics extends to much longer evolution times and thus the $\sim t^{3/2}$ limit of Equation (2) coincides with Equation (1) and agrees with the experimental observations.

In general, it is remarkable how well the measured coherence amplitude and phase at short times agree with Equation (1) considering the wide span of interaction strengths from weak to unitary. Moreover, our result shows that the limits of Equation (2) are valid and allow a clear distinction of the two regimes. This consolidates our understanding of the initial two-body dynamics and validates the theoretical prediction.

5. Transition from Universal to Weak Coupling Dynamics

Equation (2) shows that the transition between the universal and the weak coupling regime is given by t_a, which sets an important timescale of the dynamics and motivates its experimental investigation. In the following we show that the transition time can be extracted from the observations with a model-dependent fit and discuss the fitted results as function of interaction strength.

The transition time t_a appears in the general short-time prediction Equation (1) as an interaction dependent timescale. We therefore fit Equation (1) simultaneously to the coherence amplitude and phase evolution with t_a as the only free parameter to extract the transition between the two regimes. Importantly, we only fit the initial data of each set since Equation (1) is only valid in the limit of short times. The fitted timescales at four interaction strengths are shown in Figure 1a together with the predicted transition times between the dynamical regimes. The extracted transition time increases for stronger interactions indicating an extended evolution time of universal dynamics. Moreover, the timescale is in clear agreement with the predicted value of t_a.

Remarkably, the fitted value and its error are small compared with the dynamical timescale t_n. Since the duration of the probing pulses is $0.5\,\mu s \sim 0.1 t_n$, it is not immediately clear that such small timescales can be extracted experimentally. To illustrate the feasibility, a fit at $1/k_n a = -1.3$ is shown in Figure 3, which yields an extracted transition time of $0.2(2)t_n$ in agreement with the predicted value of $t_a = 0.3 t_n$. Additionally, two lines are shown where $t_a = 0.05 t_n$ and $0.5 t_n$. This figure thus clarifies that t_a affects the functional shape of the coherence at times much larger than its own value. Therefore, even small differences in t_a cause large discrepancies when compared with the experimental observation, which is most pronounced for the coherence amplitude Figure 3a.

We thus demonstrate that a transition time can be extracted experimentally in agreement with theoretical predictions. For sufficiently large interaction strengths $|1/k_n a| \lesssim 0.5$, a transition to weak coupling dynamics is not observable, since the many-body regime is entered directly.

6. Two-Body Exponent and Time Constant

The limits given by Equation (2) show that the universal and weak coupling regime display distinctively different functional behavior corresponding to power-law exponents $3/2$ and $1/2$, respectively. We now turn our attention to the investigation of this functional difference by fitting such a power law to the coherence amplitude and observing its dependence on the interaction strength.

The two limits of the two-body prediction in Equation (2) are especially simple for the coherence amplitude and follow the form $1 - (t/t_c)^\beta$. For weak coupling dynamics $\beta = 1/2$ and t_c is interaction dependent whereas for universal dynamics $\beta = 3/2$ and t_c is constant. By fitting a power law to the coherence amplitude within the regimes of two-body dynamics, the fitted values of β and t_c can indicate the functional behavior at the chosen interaction strength.

The fitted exponents and time constants are shown in Figure 4 together with the weak coupling and universal values. For low interaction strengths β agrees with the prediction of weak coupling dynamics. At stronger interactions it slowly increases and reaches $3/2$ at unitarity in agreement with the universal prediction. The fitted time constant t_c initially decreases for increasing interaction strength and qualitatively follows the behavior of the predicted timescale t_w of weak coupling dynamics. However, for strong interaction strengths, where t_w diverges, t_c remains finite and connects with the universal value of $\sim 2.1 t_n$. The error bars correspond to symmetric fit uncertainties and the apparent asymmetry is due to the logarithmic scale.

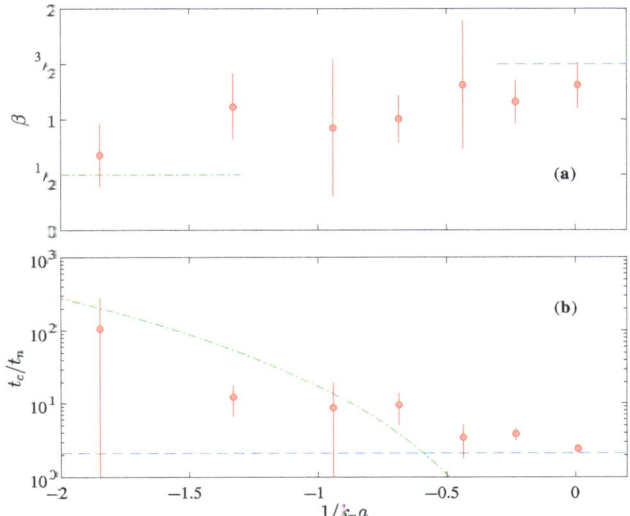

Figure 4. Characteristic exponent and time constant. By fitting a power law $1 - (t/t_c)^\beta$ to the coherence amplitude, we obtain the characteristic exponent (**a**) and time constant (**b**) at various interaction strengths. The theoretically predicted exponent and time constants for universal and weak coupling dynamics are shown as a dashed blue line and a dash-dotted green line, respectively. The errors correspond to fit uncertainties.

The experimental observations in the transition region between weak and unitary interactions are influenced by the behavior of both two-body regimes. Therefore, the specific values of β and t_c bear no physical meaning and are a consequence of fitting a single time dependence to the data when both weak coupling and universal dynamics are present. Nonetheless, at weak and unitary interactions the fitted power law is dominated by either one of the two-body regimes and we observe a smooth connection between the two in the transition region.

7. Conclusions

The results presented here provide a detailed investigation of the initial two-body dynamics of a quantum impurity in a BEC. The impurity dynamics has previously been studied [20], and here we have extended the analysis of the initial universal and subsequent weak coupling dynamics and the transition between them.

An interferometric sequence was used to measure the coherence of the system quenched into a superposition of an impurity state and a medium state. The evolution of the coherence was predicted by a rigorous short-time model, which showed a universal and a weak coupling regime with distinct exponents and timescales. A direct comparison between the experimental observations and the two-body theoretical prediction confirmed the validity of the model.

The transition between the two regimes was analyzed at four interaction strengths yielding transition times in clear agreement with the theoretical prediction as shown in Figure 1. Additionally, the transition was investigated by fitting a power law to the coherence amplitude, revealing how the exponent and time constant change from weak coupling to universal dynamics for increasing interaction strength.

These investigations improve our understanding of the fundamental properties of quasiparticles. By comparing interferometric observations at long evolution times to earlier spectroscopic results [14–17] a complete model for the Bose polaron in both time and frequency-domain can be obtained. Furthermore, the experimental methods may be expanded to help elucidate exotic phenomena such as transport processes [28,29] or dynamical formation of bipolarons [30].

Author Contributions: Conceptualization, M.G.S., T.G.S., N.B.J. and J.J.A.; methodology, M.G.S.; software, M.G.S.; validation, M.G.S., T.G.S., N.B.J. and J.J.A.; formal analysis, M.G.S.; investigation, M.G.S., T.G.S., N.B.J. and J.J.A.; resources, J.J.A.; data curation, M.G.S.; writing—original draft preparation, M.G.S.; writing—review and editing, M.G.S., T.G.S., N.B.J. and J.J.A.; visualization, M.G.S.; supervision, J.J.A.; project administration, J.J.A.; funding acquisition, J.J.A. All authors have read and agreed to the published version of the manuscript.

Funding: This work has been supported by the Danish National Research Foundation through the Center of Excellence "CCQ" (Grant agreement no.: DNRF156).

Institutional Review Board Statement: Not applicable.

Informed Consent Statement: Not applicable.

Data Availability Statement: The data that support the findings of this study are available from the corresponding author upon reasonable request.

Acknowledgments: We thank K. K. Nielsen, A. Camacho-Guardian, T. Pohl, and G. M. Bruun for helpful discussions.

Conflicts of Interest: The authors declare no conflict of interest.

References

1. Landau, L.D.; Pekar, S.I. Effective mass of a polaron. *Zh. Eksp. Teor. Fiz.* **1948**, *18*, 419–423.
2. Devreese, J.T.; Alexandrov, A.S. Fröhlich polaron and bipolaron: Recent developments. *Rep. Prog. Phys.* **2009**, *72*, 066501. [CrossRef]
3. Gershenson, M.E.; Podzorov, V.; Morpurgo, A.F. Colloquium: Electron. Transp. Single-Cryst. Org. *Rev. Mod. Phys.* **2006**, *78*, 973–989. [CrossRef]
4. Dagotto, E. Correlated electrons in high-temperature superconductors. *Rev. Mod. Phys.* **1994**, *66*, 763–840. [CrossRef]
5. Schirotzek, A.; Wu, C.H.; Sommer, A.; Zwierlein, M.W. Observation of Fermi polarons in a tunable Fermi liquid of ultracold atoms. *Phys. Rev. Lett.* **2009**, *102*, 230402. [CrossRef] [PubMed]
6. Kohstall, C.; Zaccanti, M.; Jag, M.; Trenkwalder, A.; Massignan, P.; Bruun, G.M.; Schreck, F.; Grimm, R. Metastability and coherence of repulsive polarons in a strongly interacting Fermi mixture. *Nature* **2012**, *485*, 615–618. [CrossRef]
7. Koschorreck, M.; Pertot, D.; Vogt, E.; Fröhlich, B.; Feld, M.; Köhl, M. Attractive and repulsive Fermi polarons in two dimensions. *Nature* **2012**, *485*, 619–622. [CrossRef]
8. Cetina, M.; Jag, M.; Lous, R.S.; Walraven, J.T.M.; Grimm, R.; Christensen, R.S.; Bruun, G.M. Decoherence of Impurities in a Fermi Sea of Ultracold Atoms. *Phys. Rev. Lett.* **2015**, *115*, 135302. [CrossRef]
9. Cetina, M.; Jag, M.; Lous, R.S.; Fritsche, I.; Walraven, J.T.; Grimm, R.; Levinsen, J.; Parish, M.M.; Schmidt, R.; Knap, M.; et al. Ultrafast many-body interferometry of impurities coupled to a Fermi sea. *Science* **2016**, *354*, 96–99. [CrossRef] [PubMed]
10. Scazza, F.; Valtolina, G.; Massignan, P.; Recati, A.; Amico, A.; Burchianti, A.; Fort, C.; Inguscio, M.; Zaccanti, M.; Roati, G. Repulsive Fermi Polarons in a Resonant Mixture of Ultracold ^{6}Li Atoms. *Phys. Rev. Lett.* **2017**, *118*, 083602. [CrossRef]
11. Schmidt, R.; Knap, M.; Ivanov, D.A.; You, J.S.; Cetina, M.; Demler, E. Universal many-body response of heavy impurities coupled to a Fermi sea: A review of recent progress. *Rep. Prog. Phys.* **2018**, *81*, 024401. [CrossRef]
12. Yan, Z.; Patel, P.B.; Mukherjee, B.; Fletcher, R.J.; Struck, J.; Zwierlein, M.W. Boiling a Unitary Fermi Liquid. *Phys. Rev. Lett.* **2019**, *122*, 093401. [CrossRef]
13. Darkwah Oppong, N.; Riegger, L.; Bettermann, O.; Höfer, M.; Levinsen, J.; Parish, M.M.; Bloch, I.; Fölling, S. Observation of Coherent Multiorbital Polarons in a Two-Dimensional Fermi Gas. *Phys. Rev. Lett.* **2019**, *122*, 193604. [CrossRef]
14. Jørgensen, N.B.; Wacker, L.; Skalmstang, K.T.; Parish, M.M.; Levinsen, J.; Christensen, R.S.; Bruun, G.M.; Arlt, J.J. Observation of Attractive and Repulsive Polarons in a Bose-Einstein Condensate. *Phys. Rev. Lett.* **2016**, *117*, 055302. [CrossRef] [PubMed]
15. Hu, M.G.; Van de Graaff, M.J.; Kedar, D.; Corson, J.P.; Cornell, E.A.; Jin, D.S. Bose Polarons in the Strongly Interacting Regime. *Phys. Rev. Lett.* **2016**, *117*, 055301. [CrossRef]
16. Peña Ardila, L.A.; Jørgensen, N.B.; Pohl, T.; Giorgini, S.; Bruun, G.M.; Arlt, J.J. Analyzing a Bose polaron across resonant interactions. *Phys. Rev. A* **2019**, *99*, 063607. [CrossRef]

17. Yan, Z.Z.; Ni, Y.; Robens, C.; Zwierlein, M.W. Bose polarons near quantum criticality. *Science* **2020**, *368*, 190–194. [CrossRef] [PubMed]
18. Catani, J.; Lamporesi, G.; Naik, D.; Gring, M.; Inguscio, M.; Minardi, F.; Kantian, A.; Giamarchi, T. Quantum dynamics of impurities in a one-dimensional Bose gas. *Phys. Rev. A* **2012**, *85*, 023623. [CrossRef]
19. Meinert, F.; Knap, M.; Kirilov, E.; Jag-Lauber, K.; Zvonarev, M.B.; Demler, E.; Nägerl, H.C. Bloch oscillations in the absence of a lattice. *Science* **2017**, *356*, 945–948. [CrossRef]
20. Skou, M.G.; Skov, T.G.; Jørgensen, N.B.; Nielsen, K.K.; Camacho-Guardian, A.; Pohl, T.; Bruun, G.M.; Arlt, J.J. Non-equilibrium quantum dynamics and formation of the Bose polaron. *Nat. Phys.* **2021**. [CrossRef]
21. Parish, M.M.; Levinsen, J. Quantum dynamics of impurities coupled to a Fermi sea. *Phys. Rev. B* **2016**, *94*, 184303. [CrossRef]
22. Wacker, L.J.; Jørgensen, N.B.; Birkmose, D.; Winter, N.; Mikkelsen, M.; Sherson, J.; Zinner, N.; Arlt, J.J. Universal Three-Body Physics in Ultracold KRb Mixtures. *Phys. Rev. Lett.* **2016**, *117*, 163201. [CrossRef]
23. Lysebo, M.; Veseth, L. Feshbach resonances and transition rates for cold homonuclear collisions between ^{39}K and ^{41}K atoms. *Phys. Rev. A* **2010**, *81*, 032702. [CrossRef]
24. Tanzi, L.; Cabrera, C.R.; Sanz, J.; Cheiney, P.; Tomza, M.; Tarruell, L. Feshbach resonances in potassium Bose-Bose mixtures. *Phys. Rev. A* **2018**, *98*, 062712. [CrossRef]
25. Scelle, R.; Rentrop, T.; Trautmann, A.; Schuster, T.; Oberthaler, M.K. Motional Coherence of Fermions Immersed in a Bose Gas. *Phys. Rev. Lett.* **2013**, *111*, 070401. [CrossRef] [PubMed]
26. Rentrop, T.; Trautmann, A.; Olivares, F.A.; Jendrzejewski, F.; Komnik, A.; Oberthaler, M.K. Observation of the Phononic Lamb Shift with a Synthetic Vacuum. *Phys. Rev. X* **2016**, *6*, 041041. [CrossRef]
27. Braaten, E.; Kang, D.; Platter, L. Short-Time Operator Product Expansion for rf Spectroscopy of a Strongly Interacting Fermi Gas. *Phys. Rev. Lett.* **2010**, *104*, 223004. [CrossRef]
28. Sommer, A.; Ku, M.; Zwierlein, M.W. Spin transport in polaronic and superfluid Fermi gases. *New J. Phys.* **2011**, *13*, 055009. [CrossRef]
29. Bardon, A.B.; Beattie, S.; Luciuk, C.; Cairncross, W.; Fine, D.; Cheng, N.S.; Edge, G.J.A.; Taylor, E.; Zhang, S.; Trotzky, S.; et al. Transverse Demagnetization Dynamics of a Unitary Fermi Gas. *Science* **2014**, *344*, 722–724. [CrossRef] [PubMed]
30. Camacho-Guardian, A.; Peña Ardila, L.A.; Pohl, T.; Bruun, G.M. Bipolarons in a Bose-Einstein Condensate. *Phys. Rev. Lett.* **2018**, *121*, 013401. [CrossRef]

Review

Repulsive Fermi and Bose Polarons in Quantum Gases

Francesco Scazza [1,2,3,*], Matteo Zaccanti [2,3,*], Pietro Massignan [4,*], Meera M. Parish [5,6,*] and Jesper Levinsen [5,6,*]

1. Department of Physics, University of Trieste, 34127 Trieste, Italy
2. Istituto Nazionale di Ottica del Consiglio Nazionale delle Ricerche (CNR-INO), 50019 Sesto Fiorentino, Italy
3. European Laboratory for Nonlinear Spectroscopy (LENS), University of Florence, 50019 Sesto Fiorentino, Italy
4. Departament de Física, Universitat Politècnica de Catalunya, Campus Nord B4-B5, 08034 Barcelona, Spain
5. School of Physics and Astronomy, Monash University, Victoria 3800, Australia
6. ARC Centre of Excellence in Future Low-Energy Electronics Technologies, Monash University, Victoria 3800, Australia

* Correspondence: francesco.scazza@units.it (F.S.); zaccanti@lens.unifi.it (M.Z.); pietro.massignan@upc.edu (P.M.); meera.parish@monash.edu (M.M.P.); jesper.levinsen@monash.edu (J.L.)

Abstract: Polaron quasiparticles are formed when a mobile impurity is coupled to the elementary excitations of a many-particle background. In the field of ultracold atoms, the study of the associated impurity problem has attracted a growing interest over the last fifteen years. Polaron quasiparticle properties are essential to our understanding of a variety of paradigmatic quantum many-body systems realized in ultracold atomic gases and in the solid state, from imbalanced Bose–Fermi and Fermi–Fermi mixtures to fermionic Hubbard models. In this topical review, we focus on the so-called repulsive polaron branch, which emerges as an excited many-body state in systems with underlying attractive interactions such as ultracold atomic mixtures, and is characterized by an effective repulsion between the impurity and the surrounding medium. We give a brief account of the current theoretical and experimental understanding of repulsive polaron properties, for impurities embedded in both fermionic and bosonic media, and we highlight open issues deserving future investigations.

Keywords: Fermi polarons; Bose polarons; repulsive interactions; metastable quasiparticles; quasiparticle lifetime; mediated interactions; repulsive Fermi gas; ultracold atomic mixtures

1. Introduction

Understanding the fate of an impurity particle immersed within a complex medium represents a paradigmatic problem in quantum physics [1], encompassing a variety of physical scenarios and spanning an enormous range of energies: from ultracold atomic gases [2–4], helium liquids [5,6] and solid-state materials [7–10], all the way up to nuclear and quark matter [11–13]. The interest in such $(N+1)$ many-body systems is two-fold: on the one hand, a primary goal is to characterize how the interactions with the surrounding bath turn the impurity particle into a *quasiparticle* with modified static and dynamical properties, such as a renormalized energy, a finite lifetime and an effective mass. On the other hand, understanding how the bare particle is effectively *dressed* by its environment provides important information about the nature of the medium itself, since the impurity can act as a microscopic, local probe for both the excitations and the collective properties of the surrounding material.

Importantly, a common set of ideas and technical tools can be applied to investigate the impurity problem in seemingly disparate setups, the investigation of one system yielding information on another. In particular, the so-called Fermi polaron—a mobile quantum impurity embedded in a degenerate Fermi gas—has been successfully investigated and characterized both in ultracold atomic mixtures [14–29] and in atomically thin semiconductors [30,31], using a single theoretical framework and relying on similar experimental methods. This has recently stimulated much cross-fertilization between the two fields (see, e.g., Ref. [32] in this Special Issue). In addition, the original polaron scenario of a

single electron interacting with phonons in a crystal [7] has now been extended to quantum impurities immersed in a Bose–Einstein condensate—the so-called Bose polaron [33–37].

Ultracold atoms represent a particularly appealing playground for the exploration of impurity physics, both in and out of equilibrium, owing to their versatility, their clean and isolated nature, as well as their accessible time and length scales. Initiated with the investigation of the highly-polarized limit of resonantly interacting Fermi gases across the BCS-BEC crossover, and the observation of the so-called attractive Fermi polaron [14,15], over the last decade a series of groundbreaking experiments have renewed the interest in the $(N+1)$ problem within the field of quantum gases. These have already enabled the characterization of the quasiparticle properties of impurity atoms embedded within both Fermi [14–29] and Bose [34–38] environments, for various impurity-to-medium particle mass ratios, and encompassing not only systems in three dimensions (3D), but also two- [17,18,26] and one-dimensional [33,39,40] environments. Combining the exquisite control over interatomic interactions enabled by magnetic Feshbach resonances [41] with advanced spectroscopic tools [42,43], quantum gases allow one to prepare both impurity and medium particles in single, well-defined quantum states, and to probe quasiparticle properties with unparalleled accuracy, down to the single-atom level.

As a non-trivial and quite general result, the detailed comparison between experiment and theory has demonstrated that most quasiparticle properties can be accurately modeled, even in the strong coupling regime, using theoretical methods which are much simpler than those required for a quantitative description of balanced atomic mixtures. For instance, excellent agreement between theory and experiment has been demonstrated for the ground-state properties of a highly imbalanced Fermi mixture, owing to the almost exact cancellation of a large set of high-order Feynman diagrams [44,45], and the agreement even extends to the non-equilibrium evolution of impurities immersed in an ultracold Fermi gas following an interaction quench [22,46]. Simple theories for strongly interacting many-body systems are rare, and the $(N+1)$ problem therefore provides an important testbed for improving our understanding of more complex states of highly correlated matter. In particular, the study of the extremely polarized case of a single impurity provides accurate information for systems that feature a sizable concentration of minority particles, the impurity limit exhibiting some of the critical points of the full phase diagram, whose topology we can thus learn about by investigating highly polarized systems [47].

In this topical review article, we focus on a specific kind of impurity quasiparticle, termed the *repulsive polaron*, discussing experimental and theoretical progress in the understanding of its highly non-trivial nature from a cold-atom perspective. Originally introduced to characterize the Stoner instability [48] of a gas of itinerant fermions towards a ferromagnetic state [3,49,50], the repulsive polaron concept is nowadays generically employed to denote any impurity particle dressed by strong repulsive interactions with a surrounding (either fermionic or bosonic) medium. While for genuine impurity-medium interparticle repulsion, e.g., the one originating from Coulomb or hard-sphere interaction potentials, the repulsive polaron represents the ground state of the $(N+1)$-system, in the case of van der Waals interactions relevant for cold atomic gases [41] such repulsive quasiparticles connect to an excited energy branch of the many-body spectrum (see Figure 1). This is due to the fact that any short-ranged repulsion with a scattering length exceeding the interaction range inherently requires an underlying weakly-bound molecular level into which the system may decay, thereby making the repulsive polaron metastable. As a consequence, repulsive quasiparticles in ultracold atomic mixtures represent both a theoretical and experimental challenge, which has stimulated over the last decade an intense debate about the nature of the repulsive branch, with even its existence being questioned [51]. On the other hand, this has triggered the rapid development of new theoretical methods and experimental probes, able to trace in real time the quasiparticle formation, decay and decoherence [22,28,37,46,52–58].

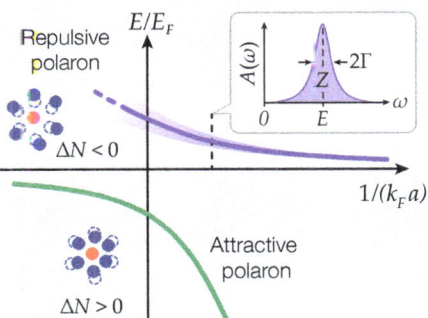

Figure 1. Quasiparticle spectrum as a function of interaction strength $1/(k_F a)$. Attractive (green) and repulsive (purple) polaron energy branches. The shaded area centered around the repulsive polaron energy represents the quasiparticle spectral width Γ. For widths comparable to its energy, the repulsive polaron ceases to be a well defined *coherent* quasiparticle (dashed line ending). In the case of a fermionic medium, the attractive polaron also stops being well defined at sufficiently large $1/(k_F a)$, where it undergoes a sharp transition to a dressed molecule quasiparticle [59]. On the other hand, the ground state of the Bose polaron spectrum does not feature a single-impurity transition. Inset: impurity spectral function $A(\omega)$ at zero momentum for $\omega > 0$, i.e., a vertical cut through the repulsive polaron spectrum at fixed interaction strength. The center of the polaron spectral function denotes the polaron energy E, while its half width at half maximum and area relate to the quasiparticle width Γ and residue Z, respectively.

Here, we provide a concise overview of the recent advances in this research field. Our discussion will concentrate on the most widely explored scenario of three-dimensional systems; for impurity problems in lower dimensions, we refer the interested reader to already available review articles by Levinsen and Parish [4] and by Mistakidis et al. [60], which focus on two- and one-dimensional systems, respectively. The remainder of the paper is organized as follows: in Section 2, we outline the theoretical basis for the treatment of single-impurity problems in ultracold bosonic and fermionic atomic media; in Section 3, we introduce the main experimental probes of polaron quasiparticle properties, especially focusing on the metastable repulsive branch; in Section 4, we discuss the origin of the repulsive polaron quasiparticle lifetime, reconciling different interpretations for the quasiparticle damping mechanisms found in the literature; finally, in Section 5, we discuss the emergence of long-range impurity-impurity interactions mediated by the medium, thereby linking polaron physics to that of bosonic and fermionic atomic mixtures.

2. Fermi and Bose Polarons

We begin by introducing the problem of a single impurity in a quantum medium and providing an overview of the basic theoretical concepts. Our focus will be on the case of short-range interactions between the impurity and medium particles, which is appropriate for dilute quantum gases. For concreteness, we will restrict our attention to three-dimensional (3D) systems, since this is the situation for most of the cold-atom experiments that have been performed thus far. However, the phenomenology of the repulsive polaron branch is similar in two dimensions [28], and thus our discussion is also relevant to exciton polarons in atomically thin semiconductors [30].

2.1. Theoretical Description

In this review, we will assume that the medium consists of identical particles of mass m_{med} which are in thermal equilibrium at a temperature T and chemical potential μ. The medium can, for instance, correspond to an ideal Fermi gas or a weakly interacting Bose gas. It is governed by a Hamiltonian $\hat{H}_{\text{med}}$ which, in the two cases, is given by either:

$$\hat{H}_{\text{Fermi}} = \sum_{\mathbf{k}} (\epsilon_{\mathbf{k}}^{\text{med}} - \mu) \hat{f}_{\mathbf{k}}^{\dagger} \hat{f}_{\mathbf{k}}, \qquad (1)$$

where the creation operator $\hat{f}_{\mathbf{k}}^{\dagger}$ satisfies the usual fermionic commutation relations, or

$$\hat{H}_{\text{Bose}} = \sum_{\mathbf{k}} (\epsilon_{\mathbf{k}}^{\text{med}} - \mu) \hat{b}_{\mathbf{k}}^{\dagger} \hat{b}_{\mathbf{k}} + \sum_{\mathbf{k}\mathbf{k}'\mathbf{q}} V_B(\mathbf{q}) \hat{b}_{\mathbf{k}+\mathbf{q}}^{\dagger} \hat{b}_{\mathbf{k}'-\mathbf{q}}^{\dagger} \hat{b}_{\mathbf{k}'} \hat{b}_{\mathbf{k}}, \qquad (2)$$

with the bosonic creation operator $\hat{b}_{\mathbf{k}}^{\dagger}$. The single-particle dispersion in the medium is $\epsilon_{\mathbf{k}}^{\text{med}} = |\mathbf{k}|^2/2m_{\text{med}} \equiv k^2/2m_{\text{med}}$ at momentum $\mathbf{k}$. To be able to directly compare results for the two cases, we will define a Fermi wave vector $k_F = (6\pi^2 n)^{1/3}$ and Fermi energy $E_F = k_F^2/2m_{\text{med}}$ in terms of the density n of the bath, independent of the medium statistics (k_F and E_F are often labeled k_n and E_n in the Bose polaron literature). In Equation (2) for a bosonic medium, we have introduced a boson interaction potential V_B which is assumed to be of short range and characterized by a scattering length a_B which is positive and small, $0 < n a_B^3 \ll 1$, to ensure the stability of the Bose gas. Here and throughout this review we use units where the volume, Boltzmann's constant k_B and the reduced Planck's constant $\hbar$ are all set to one.

Including the impurity degree of freedom as well as the impurity-medium interactions, we therefore have the total Hamiltonian:

$$\hat{H} = \hat{H}_{\text{med}} + \sum_{\mathbf{k}} \epsilon_{\mathbf{k}} \hat{c}_{\mathbf{k}}^{\dagger} \hat{c}_{\mathbf{k}} + \sum_{\mathbf{k},\mathbf{q}} V(\mathbf{q}) \hat{\rho}_{\mathbf{q}} \hat{c}_{\mathbf{k}+\mathbf{q}}^{\dagger} \hat{c}_{\mathbf{k}}. \qquad (3)$$

Here, $\hat{c}_{\mathbf{k}}^{\dagger}$ is the impurity creation operator and $\epsilon_{\mathbf{k}} = k^2/2m$ is the impurity kinetic energy, with m the impurity mass. The bosonic operator $\hat{\rho}_{\mathbf{q}}$ corresponds to medium density operators, and takes the form $\hat{\rho}_{\mathbf{q}} = \sum_{\mathbf{k}} \hat{f}_{\mathbf{k}-\mathbf{q}}^{\dagger} \hat{f}_{\mathbf{k}}$ or $\hat{\rho}_{\mathbf{q}} = \sum_{\mathbf{k}} \hat{b}_{\mathbf{k}-\mathbf{q}}^{\dagger} \hat{b}_{\mathbf{k}}$ depending on the statistics of the medium. Note that we treat the impurity within the canonical ensemble, where we have a fixed number of impurities (one impurity in this case), while we use the grand canonical ensemble for the medium.

We have written the impurity-medium interactions in the Hamiltonian (3) in terms of a generic finite-range potential $V(\mathbf{q})$, which can in principle describe an actual repulsive interaction such as a soft-sphere potential, as well as the short-range attractive interactions that are the main focus of this review. Importantly, regardless of whether $V(\mathbf{q})$ is attractive or repulsive, the low-energy scattering amplitude between an impurity and a medium atom at relative momentum $\mathbf{k}$ can be cast in the *universal* form[1]

$$f_s(\mathbf{k}) = -\frac{1}{1/a + ik}, \qquad (4)$$

where a is the s-wave scattering length. This allows us to employ pseudo-potentials for the impurity-medium interactions that simplify calculations and expose the universal physics.

In the following, we take $V(\mathbf{q}) = g$, where the constant g is the coupling strength, and we introduce an ultraviolet cutoff Λ—effectively corresponding to the (inverse) range of the potential—on the relative collision momenta in all two-body scattering processes. We then use the low-energy scattering amplitude in Equation (4) to relate the physical parameter a to the "bare" parameters of the model, g and Λ, yielding the relation,

$$\frac{1}{g} = \frac{m_r}{2\pi a} - \sum_{\mathbf{k}}^{\Lambda} \frac{1}{\epsilon_{\mathbf{k}} + \epsilon_{\mathbf{k}}^{\text{med}}} = \frac{m_r}{2\pi a} - \frac{m_r}{2\pi^2} \Lambda, \qquad (5)$$

where $m_r = (1/m + 1/m_{\text{med}})^{-1}$ is the reduced mass. Here, we immediately see that for repulsive interactions $g > 0$, we have the constraint $\pi/\Lambda > a > 0$, where π/Λ mimics the

14

range of a repulsive potential. Thus, in this case, the scattering length a is always positive, and it has an upper limit set by the range of the potential itself.

In the case of ultracold atomic gases where the underlying van der Waals interactions are attractive, there are no such restrictions on the scattering length and it can be freely tuned to both positive and negative values by varying an external magnetic field. In particular, in the vicinity of a broad Feshbach resonance [41], the scattering length a can be enhanced to greatly exceed any other length scale in the problem, attaining the regime of unitarity-limited interactions with negligible contribution from finite-range corrections. When the scattering length is positive, there exists a shallow bound state between the impurity and a particle from the medium, with binding energy $\varepsilon_b = 1/2m_r a^2$, corresponding to the pole of the scattering amplitude $f_s(\mathbf{k})$ given by Equation (4), at $k = i/a$ [62].

2.2. Quasiparticle Properties

The interactions between the impurity and the medium lead to excitations of the medium, and consequently the state corresponding to the bare impurity on top of an unperturbed bath is no longer an eigenstate of the system Hamiltonian. As illustrated in Figure 1, the resulting impurity *quasiparticle* has modified properties such as energy, mass, and residue (squared wave function overlap with the non-interacting state), and likewise the quasiparticle can acquire a finite lifetime. We now outline how these formally appear in the theory.

The quasiparticle properties at temperature $T = 1/\beta$ are all encoded in the retarded impurity Green's function,

$$\mathcal{G}(\mathbf{p}, t) = -i\Theta(t)\, \text{tr}\!\left[\hat{\rho}_{\text{med}} \hat{c}_\mathbf{p}(t) \hat{c}_\mathbf{p}^\dagger(0)\right], \tag{6}$$

which is written in terms of the time-dependent impurity operator $\hat{c}_\mathbf{p}(t) = e^{i\hat{H}t} \hat{c}_\mathbf{p} e^{-i\hat{H}t}$. Here, $\hat{\rho}_{\text{med}} = e^{-\beta \hat{H}_{\text{med}}} / \text{tr}\!\left[e^{-\beta \hat{H}_{\text{med}}}\right]$ is the medium density matrix and the trace is over the eigenstates of the medium in the absence of the impurity. In a time-independent system, it is convenient to introduce the impurity Green's function as a function of frequency via the Fourier transform,

$$G(\mathbf{p}, \omega) = \int dt\, e^{i\omega t} \mathcal{G}(\mathbf{p}, t). \tag{7}$$

This satisfies the Dyson equation:

$$G(\mathbf{p}, \omega) = G_0(\mathbf{p}, \omega) + G_0(\mathbf{p}, \omega) \Sigma(\mathbf{p}, \omega) G(\mathbf{p}, \omega) = \frac{1}{G_0(\mathbf{p}, \omega)^{-1} - \Sigma(\mathbf{p}, \omega)}, \tag{8}$$

in terms of the impurity self energy Σ and the bare impurity propagator $G_0(\mathbf{p}, \omega) = 1/(\omega - \epsilon_\mathbf{p} + i0)$, where the infinitesimal factor $+i0$ shifts the pole slightly into the lower half plane.

The impurity self energy allows us to extract the quasiparticle properties [63]. In particular, the presence of a quasiparticle is related to a pole of the Green's function, and in the vicinity of this pole we have:

$$G(\mathbf{p}, \omega) \simeq \frac{Z}{\omega - E - p^2/2m^* + i\Gamma}, \tag{9}$$

for small momenta. Here, the energy E, residue Z, effective mass m^*, and damping rate Γ are related to the self energy as outlined in Table 1. The quasiparticle properties manifest themselves in the spectral function, defined from the Green's function as:

$$A(\mathbf{p}, \omega) = -\frac{1}{\pi} \text{Im}[G(\mathbf{p}, \omega)], \tag{10}$$

which is one of the key experimental observables of quantum impurity physics (see Figure 1).

Table 1. Quasiparticle properties of an impurity in a medium. The quasiparticle energy E is found as the solution of a transcendental equation, and serves as an input into the remaining expressions. The expressions for m^*, C and ΔN involve Z since, for a general parameter λ, one has $\partial_\lambda E = \partial_\lambda \text{Re}[\Sigma(0,E)] + \partial_E \text{Re}[\Sigma(0,E)]\partial_\lambda E$, so that $\partial_\lambda E = Z \partial_\lambda \text{Re}[\Sigma(0,E)]$.

Quasiparticle Property	Symbol	Relation to Self Energy
Energy	E	$E = \text{Re}[\Sigma(0,E)]$
Residue	Z	$Z = \left(1 - \left.\frac{\partial \text{Re}[\Sigma(0,\omega)]}{\partial \omega}\right|_{\omega=E}\right)^{-1}$
Effective mass	m^*	$m^* = \frac{m}{Z}\left(1 + \left.\frac{\partial \text{Re}[\Sigma(\mathbf{p},E)]}{\partial \epsilon_p}\right|_{p=0}\right)^{-1}$
Damping	Γ	$\Gamma = -Z \text{Im}[\Sigma(0,E)]$
Contact	C	$\frac{C}{8\pi m_r} = \frac{\partial E}{\partial(-1/a)} = Z\frac{\partial \text{Re}[\Sigma(0,E)]}{\partial(-1/a)}$
Particles in dressing cloud	ΔN	$\Delta N = -\frac{\partial E}{\partial \mu} = -Z\frac{\partial \text{Re}[\Sigma(0,E)]}{\partial \mu}$.

In addition to the above properties, which are familiar from Fermi liquid theory, the quasiparticles are also characterized by quantities that encode the impurity-medium correlations. Of particular interest is the impurity Tan contact [64,65],

$$C = 8\pi m_r \frac{\partial E}{\partial(-1/a)}, \tag{11}$$

which is related to the probability of a medium particle being close to the impurity. This contact governs the occupation at large momenta [64] and, when the polaron energy E corresponds to the ground-state energy at zero temperature, it is a thermodynamic quantity that plays a role in various thermodynamic properties [64,66]. The impurity contact can also be a thermodynamic variable at finite temperature, but in this case it should be defined from the free energy rather than the polaron energy [67].

Another quantity of interest is the number of bath particles in the impurity dressing cloud [68]

$$\Delta N = -\frac{\partial E}{\partial \mu}, \tag{12}$$

defined as the number of particles that must be added to the medium in order to keep its chemical potential (i.e., the medium density far away from the impurity) fixed when the impurity is inserted into the system.

The energy, the contact and the number of particles in the dressing cloud are actually tightly linked, as can be shown by a simple argument based on dimensional analysis [63,69]. Since the polaron energy is independent of the chosen unit of length, we must have $E(T,a,n,R) = \lambda^{-2} E(T\lambda^2, a/\lambda, n\lambda^3, R/\lambda)$ for arbitrary scaling factor $\lambda > 0$. Here, R represents an extra length scale which may influence the energy, such as a_B in the case of Bose polarons, or the effective range at narrow Feshbach resonances. Taking $dE/d\lambda = 0$ and setting $\lambda = 1$, we obtain:

$$E = \left(T\partial_T - \frac{a}{2}\partial_a + \frac{3n}{2}\partial_n - \frac{R}{2}\partial_R\right)E. \tag{13}$$

For a broad Feshbach resonance at $T = 0$, this yields

$$\Delta N = -\frac{1}{E_F}\left[\frac{C}{16\pi m_r a} + E\right] \text{ (Fermi)}; \quad \Delta N = -\frac{2}{3\mu}\left[\frac{C}{16\pi m_r a} + E + \frac{a_B}{2}\frac{\partial E}{\partial a_B}\right] \text{ (Bose)}, \tag{14}$$

in the case of Fermi [70] and Bose polarons. These expressions differ due to the additional length scale a_B in the Bose gas and the density scaling of each chemical potential, which is $\mu = E_F$ and $\mu = 4\pi a_B n/m_{\text{med}}$ for Fermi and Bose media, respectively. Moreover, the additional term in the Bose case can be regarded as a three-body contact [71] involving the impurity and two bosons[2]. As a direct consequence of Equation (14), the energy of attractive Fermi polarons at the unitary point (where a diverges) satisfies $\Delta N = -E/E_F$. In general, we define C and ΔN from the impurity self energy, as displayed in Table 1, such that we can apply these relationships to arbitrary quasiparticles with a finite lifetime—e.g., the repulsive polaron—not just those that correspond to an eigenstate.

2.2.1 Limit of Weak Interactions

In the limit of weak impurity-medium interactions $k_F|a| \ll 1$, one can apply perturbation theory to obtain exact analytical expressions for the quasiparticle properties. Here, the scattering length a can be either positive or negative, corresponding to repulsive or attractive polarons, respectively. Most notably, the behavior up to order $(k_F a)^2$ is universal and independent of the microscopic details of the interactions for both Fermi and Bose polarons. Indeed, the perturbative expressions at this order are even insensitive to whether the underlying interactions are attractive or repulsive.

Table 2 summarizes the perturbative results up to $\mathcal{O}(a^2)$ or to the lowest non-vanishing order for both types of polarons, where, for simplicity, we specialize to the case of an impurity of the same mass as the medium particles and we take T to be smaller than the interaction energy shift such that it has no effect at this order. In the case of the Fermi polaron, the perturbative expansion was first carried out by Bishop [72]. For the Bose polaron, the expansion was first considered by Novikov and Ovchinnikov [73] and requires $|a|/\xi \ll 1$ and $a^2/(a_B\xi) \ll 1$, where we assume that the Bose medium is condensed with $\xi = 1/\sqrt{8\pi n a_B}$ the condensate healing length (note that the Bose polaron expansion has been carried out to even higher order in a—for details, see Ref. [74]). From Table 2 we see that, apart from Γ and the number of particles in the dressing cloud, the leading order behavior is the same, i.e., the statistics of the medium only enters at higher order. However, already beyond leading order, there are intriguing differences between the two cases. While the expressions for the correction to, e.g., the energy and the contact look quite different, they take a similar form when formulated in terms of the compressibility of the two media. For instance, relating the 2nd order term to the respective speeds of sound, $c_F = k_F/(\sqrt{3}m)$ and $c_B = 1/(\sqrt{2}m\xi)$, we find that the correction to the energy is comparable: $\frac{3}{2\pi}k_F a \approx 0.8 m a c_F$ and $\frac{8\sqrt{2}}{3\pi}\frac{a}{\xi} \approx 1.7 m a c_B$.

Table 2. Perturbation theory results for quasiparticle properties in the case $m = m_{\text{med}}$, evaluated up to 2nd order in the impurity-medium scattering length. The result for the damping rate Γ refers to the repulsive polaron in the case where we have short-range attractive impurity-medium interactions (see Section 4).

	Fermi Polaron	Bose Polaron
E	$\frac{\varepsilon\pi n a}{m}\left(1 + \frac{3}{2\pi}k_F a\right)$ [72]	$\frac{4\pi n a}{m}\left(1 + \frac{8\sqrt{2}}{3\pi}\frac{a}{\xi}\right)$ [73]
Z	$1 - \frac{2}{\pi^2}(k_F a)^2$ [75]	$1 - \frac{2\sqrt{2}}{3\pi}\frac{a^2}{a_B\xi}$ [74]
m^*/m	$1 + \frac{2}{3\pi^2}(k_F a)^2$ [72]	$1 + \frac{16\sqrt{2}}{45\pi}\frac{a^2}{a_B\xi}$ [76]
Γ	$\frac{8(k_F a)^4}{9\pi^3}E_F$ [28]	$\frac{4\pi n a^2}{3m\xi}$, if $a = a_B$
C	$16\pi^2 n a^2\left(1 + \frac{3}{\pi}k_F a\right)$	$16\pi^2 n a^2\left(1 + \frac{16\sqrt{2}}{3\pi}\frac{a}{\xi}\right)$
ΔN	$-\frac{2}{\pi}k_F a - \frac{4}{\pi^2}(k_F a)^2$ [77]	$-\frac{a}{a_B} - \frac{4\sqrt{2}}{\pi}\frac{a^2}{a_B\xi}$

2.2.2 Strong-Coupling Polarons

Going beyond the limit of weak impurity-medium interactions, the polaron problem generally becomes analytically intractable and one must turn to approximation methods. In particular, the metastable repulsive branch in the strong-coupling regime where $|k_F a| \gtrsim 1$ has been tackled with a wide variety of methods. For the Fermi polaron, these include variational methods [28,46,54,78], diagrammatic Monte Carlo [51], diagrammatic methods

(T-matrix, many-body T-matrix and beyond) [77,79–82], virial expansion [80], functional renormalization group [83], and functional determinants [55]. In the case of the Bose polaron, the repulsive branch has been investigated using diagrammatic methods [84,85], variational methods [35,86–88], quantum Monte Carlo [38,89,90], virial expansion [91], and functional renormalization group [92,93]. We will briefly discuss the variational method in Section 4; however an in-depth discussion of the other methods is beyond the scope of this review.

3. Experimental Probes

We now provide a brief description of the techniques used to probe and characterize quasiparticle properties in current experiments with ultracold atoms, and we discuss how the available experimental measurements compare with existing theories. This short overview focuses on the metastable repulsive polaron state, and mainly addresses the case of a fermionic medium, where the most advanced experimental protocols have been developed and already exploited successfully.

The most well-established experimental protocol for probing quasiparticles in ultracold atomic mixtures is radio-frequency (RF) spectroscopy [42]. In the last decade, RF spectroscopy has been the technique of choice to precisely address a variety of properties in ultracold atom experiments [43]. It has permitted the first direct observation of both attractive [14] and repulsive [16,17] Fermi polarons, and since then it has been exploited extensively in both Fermi and Bose polaron studies [18,23,25,29,34–36]. RF spectroscopy involves two internal (hyperfine) states of the impurity atoms which are coupled by an oscillating RF field. Because of its long wavelength, the RF field is essentially uniform over the sub-millimeter scale of atomic samples, and RF photon absorption transfers a negligible momentum to the atoms. The two coupled impurity states are chosen so as to feature different interaction strengths with the surrounding medium, which may in turn be composed of a third hyperfine state of the same atomic species or an entirely different atomic species.

In the case of the so-called *injection* spectroscopy, a weak RF pulse transfers impurities from a (nearly) non-interacting state to another state featuring strong interactions with the medium particles. To perform spectroscopy at varying interaction strength, the impurity-medium scattering length a is tuned by means of a Feshbach resonance [41]. Within the linear response regime, the RF signal is given by (see, e.g., Refs. [94,95]):

$$I_{\text{inj}}(\omega) \propto \sum_{\mathbf{p}} n_{\mathbf{p}} A(\mathbf{p}, \epsilon_{\mathbf{p}} + \omega). \tag{15}$$

Here, $n_{\mathbf{p}}$ is the initial momentum distribution function of the impurities, $A(\mathbf{p}, \omega)$ is the impurity spectral function given by Equation (10), and we measure the frequency ω from the bare transition frequency between the initial and final hyperfine states. Since the RF pulse has a finite duration, in order to describe the experimental spectral response, Equation (15) has to be convoluted with a filter function whose width is inversely proportional to the duration of the RF pulse. To maintain a direct correspondence between the experimentally recorded spectrum and the impurity spectral function, care must be taken to operate sufficiently close to the linear response regime, as well as to work with sufficiently low impurity concentrations and sample temperatures. Otherwise, for instance, the first moment of the experimental RF signal may significantly deviate from the quasiparticle energy [16,38].

Injection spectroscopy allows one to probe the entire many-body spectrum of strongly interacting impurities, since it addresses both the ground and the excited states of the impurity-medium Hamiltonian [see Equation (3)]. Indeed, repulsive Fermi polarons have been revealed by injection spectroscopy (see Figure 2), first in a highly imbalanced, heteronuclear Fermi mixture [16] and subsequently in a homonuclear spin mixture [23]. Similarly, injection RF spectroscopy of mobile impurities immersed in a Bose-Einstein condensate has allowed the observation of repulsive Bose polarons [34,35]. This RF spectroscopy technique has been recently extended to the optical domain [26], exploiting the clock transition and tunable clock state interactions in alkaline-earth-like atoms [96,97].

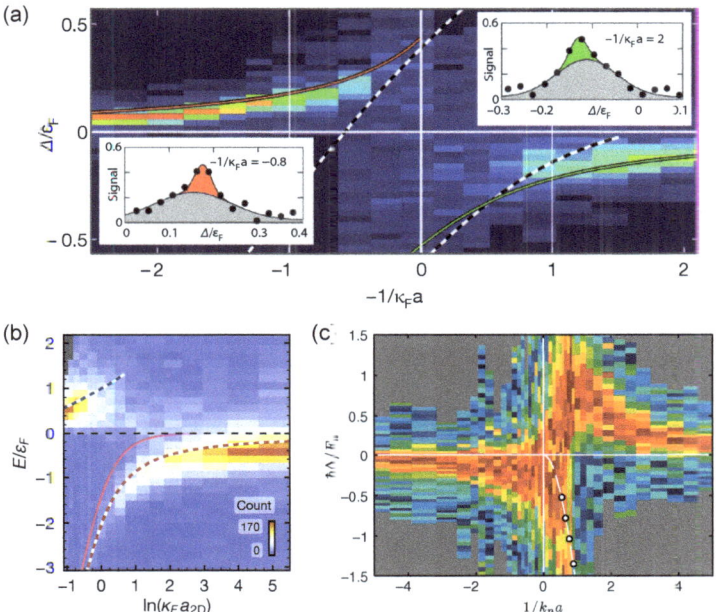

Figure 2. Experimental RF injection spectroscopy of impurities immersed in different media: (**a**) a three-dimensional (3D) Fermi gas [16], (**b**) a two-dimensional (2D) Fermi gas [26] and (**c**) a 3D Bose-Einstein condensate [35]. For the 3D and 2D fermionic backgrounds, the impurity-medium interaction strength is encoded by the dimensionless parameters $1/k_F a$ and $\log(k_F a_{2D})$, and are tuned via a narrow Feshbach resonance [16] and an orbital Feshbach resonance [26], respectively. The vertical energy scale is normalized to E_F and the zero corresponds to the frequency of the atomic RF transition in the absence of the medium. The repulsive polaron energy branch is clearly visible in all cases at positive RF detuning, ceasing to be well defined upon approaching unitarity-limited interactions from the repulsive side, i.e. $a > 0$ or $\ln(k_F a_{2D}) < 0$. Panel (**a**) is adapted from Ref. [16], panel (**b**) from Ref. [26], and panel (**c**) from Ref. [35].

The opposite protocol, where a strongly interacting state is flipped into a non-interacting state, is termed *ejection* spectroscopy, and has been extensively used to probe the ground state of strongly interacting mixtures with arbitrary population imbalance [43]. While ejection spectroscopy in general depends on the initial occupation of states in the strongly interacting system, it simplifies in the case of a very low impurity concentration, where the impurities are uncorrelated and the distribution function in Equation (15) reduces to a Boltzmann distribution. There, the ejection and injection spectra are directly related via [98]

$$I_{ej}(\omega) = e^{\beta\omega} e^{\beta\Delta F} I_{inj}(-\omega), \quad (16)$$

in terms of the difference in free energy between the interacting and the non-interacting impurity, ΔF. The exponential prefactor suppresses the repulsive branch at positive energies, which clearly illustrates why ejection spectroscopy is ideally suited to investigations of ground-state properties.

The impurity RF response encapsulates a variety of essential information about polaronic states [3]. Most importantly, when the spectrum contains a well-defined quasiparticle, i.e., a coherent excitation of the medium, the main contribution to the spectral function stems from the quasiparticle pole [see Equation (9)], and thus the mean and the width of the RF signal $I_{inj}(\omega)$ yield a measure of the mean quasiparticle energy $E + \langle p^2 \rangle / 2m^*$ and quasiparticle width Γ, respectively (see also the inset of Figure 1). Ejection spectroscopy additionally allows one to extract the contact C of the attractive polaron [25,27,36,43,67], which is encoded in the high-frequency tail of the RF signal [99]. RF spectra have been successfully employed to extract the quasiparticle energies of both attractive and repulsive (Bose and Fermi) polarons as a function of the impurity-medium interaction strength [14,16,17,23,29,34,35] and temperature [25,36]. Experimental results for the energies of repulsive Fermi and Bose polarons at the lowest achieved temperatures in homonuclear mixtures are shown in Figure 3, where they are also compared to existing theories. Note that, while the energy of Fermi polarons depends only on a single parameter (up to second order, only on $k_F a$), the energy of Bose polarons depends additionally on a/ξ [100]. Future spectroscopic studies in homogeneous Bose and Fermi gases could resolve the remaining discrepancies between available measurements performed with harmonically trapped samples and calculations at fixed density.

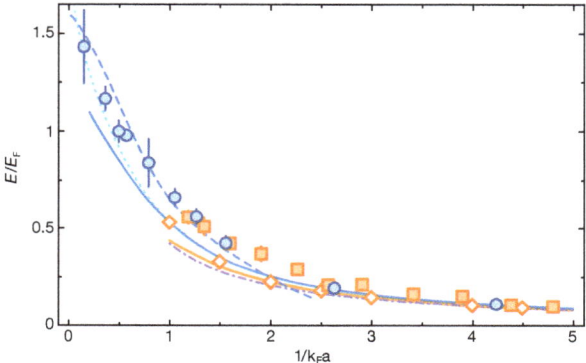

Figure 3. Energy of repulsive Fermi polarons (blue symbols and lines) and Bose polarons (orange symbols and lines) in the equal-mass case. RF spectroscopy experimental data are taken from Ref. [23] (filled blue circles) and Ref. [38] (filled orange squares). We also display theoretical results obtained by a non self-consistent T-matrix approach [77] (solid blue line), functional renormalization group [83] (dashed blue line) and a variational wavefunction [78] (dotted light blue line) for the repulsive Fermi polaron, and by the truncated basis method (TBM) [35] (solid orange line) and fixed-node diffusion QMC [38] (empty orange diamonds) for the repulsive Bose polaron. The mean-field prediction $E = 4\pi n a/m \equiv E_F \frac{4}{3\pi} k_F a$ (purple dot-dashed line) coincides for the Bose and Fermi polarons.

The quasiparticle width can also be obtained from the RF spectra within linear response, although a precise extraction becomes increasingly difficult as the quasiparticle spectral peak becomes either narrow or broad with respect to the polaron energy. Here, there are strong distinctions between the attractive and repulsive branches, and between Fermi and Bose polarons. In the latter Bose polaron case, the attractive polaron quasiparticle with a finite residue remains the ground state at all interaction strengths, and hence the quasiparticle width Γ always vanishes at zero temperature. However, for the Fermi polaron, the attractive polaron is the many-body ground state only for $1/k_F a$ up to the so-called polaron-molecule transition [59,101,102]. At finite temperature, the attractive polaron width in the RF signal is simply linked to the impurity-medium collision rate [25,103]. Conversely, the metastable repulsive polaron retains a finite lifetime even for a zero-momentum impurity, which for weak coupling is governed by a many-body dephasing mechanism rather than by the decay to lower-lying attractive states (see below and Section 4).

The polaron effective mass is rather challenging to probe, as it requires one to access the polaron dispersion relation, i.e., to probe the spectral response at different impurity momenta [see Equation (9)]. An effective spectroscopic technique relies on the fact that, due to the enhanced effective mass of polarons $m^* > m$, a moving polaron transferred into a final non-interacting state, or vice versa, will have a RF response peak that varies with the impurity momentum. For the case of fermionic impurities, one can effectively adjust the mean impurity momentum by simply varying the impurity concentration, while still remaining within the highly polarized limit. Indeed, owing to the Pauli exclusion principle, at low but finite temperatures the mean impurity momentum will progressively increase, moving from the (small) thermal value in the limit of vanishing concentration to the (larger) one set by the Fermi momentum of the minority component, which starts building its own Fermi sea for higher concentration. This effect has been successfully exploited, both in ejection and injection RF spectroscopy, to yield estimates of the attractive and repulsive Fermi polaron effective mass [14,23] (see Figure 4). Although it has not been demonstrated thus far, the same method could be in principle employed in Bose polaron experiments dealing with fermionic impurities [34,36]. However, such a strategy cannot be applied to Bose or Fermi polarons that are realized using bosonic minority particles [29,35]. Furthermore, a general drawback of this technique is that it is *a priori* difficult to disentangle the measurement of the quasiparticle effective mass from the possible impact of weak polaron-polaron interactions, that are expected to become progressively more relevant as the impurity concentration is increased.

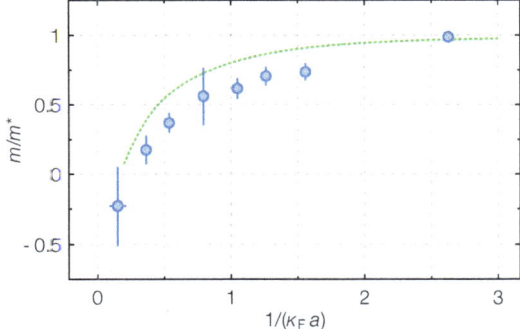

Figure 4. Effective mass of the repulsive Fermi polaron in the equal-mass case: experimental results (blue circles) and theoretical results from a *T*-matrix approach (dotted green line) [77]. Experimentally, m^* is observed to diverge and to even turn negative when approaching the unitary limit, compatibly with a thermodynamic instability of the repulsive polaron Fermi liquid [102,104] at strong coupling. The remaining deviation between theory and experimental data may result from higher-order particle-hole excitations not taken into account in the calculation, as well as from weak polaron–polaron interactions which are neglected in the experimental extraction of m/m^*. The figure is adapted from Ref. [23].

Momentum-resolved ejection spectroscopy has also been exploited in a highly polarized spin mixture in 2D to directly measure the impurity energy dispersion curve as a function of momentum, yielding an estimate of the attractive Fermi polaron mass [17]. Experimental measurements of the Bose polaron effective mass are presently lacking. Novel Raman spectroscopic techniques [27] could be exploited to study the impurity spectral response upon imparting an adjustable momentum to the impurities, both in the case of fermionic and bosonic media. This may allow one to perform two-photon injection spectroscopy and extract the effective mass of repulsive polarons.

The injection and ejection RF spectroscopic probes which we have considered thus far are suited to precisely access quasiparticle spectral properties, as they are well resolved in energy. However, they cannot be exploited to track the formation of quasiparticles in real time, because they lack the time resolution necessary to monitor the rapid build-up of the polaron dressing cloud. Conversely, dynamical probes such as many-body Ramsey interferometry are well adapted to this scope [46,52–55], and have indeed enabled the experimental observation of the formation (and the decoherence) of both Fermi and Bose polarons [22,37], with the long-time value of the Ramsey contrast being connected to the quasiparticle residue [22,54]. It has also been shown that coherently driving Rabi oscillations between the two impurity states involved in the RF spectroscopy protocol is a powerful complementary technique to probe the polaron quasiparticle properties [28,54]. In particular, the residue Z is directly connected to the Rabi frequency Ω normalized to the bare Rabi frequency Ω_0 [16], which is obtained by performing Rabi oscillations in the absence of the medium. Indeed, $\sqrt{Z}$ essentially quantifies the wavefunction overlap between the polaron state and the bare, non-interacting impurity, and one finds that $Z \simeq (\Omega^2 + \Gamma^2)/\Omega_0^2$ as long as $\Gamma \lesssim \sqrt{Z}\Omega_0$ [28]. This connection affords an alternative route to estimating the quasiparticle residue from the area of the coherent spectral response [14,25,36], a method which is extremely challenging once the coherent quasiparticle resonance approaches the onset of the molecular continuum.

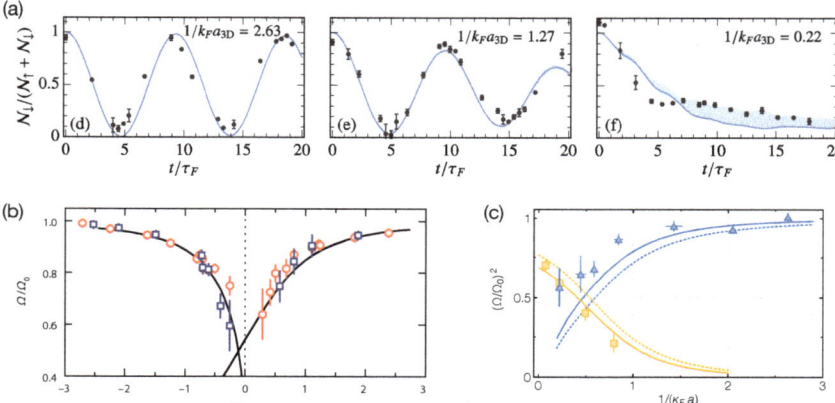

Figure 5. Rabi oscillations between non-interacting and strongly interacting impurity states in a fermionic medium. (**a**) Points are experimental measurements, while lines denote theoretical predictions based on a variational ansatz with no free parameters [28]. Shaded regions allow for experimental parameter uncertainties. (**b**,**c**) Normalized Rabi frequency extracted from experimental Rabi oscillations (symbols) in mass-imbalanced [in (**b**)] [16] and equal-mass [in (**c**)] [23] mixtures are compared to theoretical predictions for $\sqrt{Z}$ [in (**b**)] and Z [in (**c**)] (lines), obtained with a T-matrix method [16,23,77]. Solid lines in panel (**c**) take into account the effect of small initial-state interactions. Panel (**a**) is adapted from Ref. [28], panel (**b**) from Ref. [16], and panel (**c**) from Ref. [23].

Rabi oscillations have allowed experiments to obtain the quasiparticle residue of attractive and repulsive Fermi polarons [16,23,26] (see Figure 5). By contrast, the extension of such a method to bosonic media is currently lacking. While this technique appears to be potentially well-suited also to investigate the Bose polaron properties in two-species mixtures [34,36], it cannot be directly applied to single-species experiments [35] where the impurity particles are created upon transferring atoms from the host condensate—prepared in a certain hyperfine state—into another atomic level. Theoretically, it has recently been shown that the damping rate of Rabi oscillations can be essentially identified with the quasiparticle damping rate Γ for coherent quasiparticles with $\Gamma \lesssim \sqrt{Z}\Omega_0$ [28]. Thus, if the repulsive branch is both present and remains coherent, valuable information on the lifetime of repulsive polarons may be extracted from the damping rate of Rabi oscillations in experiment. As shown in panel (a) of Figure 6, the measured damping rate of Rabi oscillations of impurities in a Fermi gas is found to be in excellent agreement with the quasiparticle damping rate Γ obtained from a finite-temperature variational calculation containing a single particle-hole excitation [28,46,98]—see Section 4 for a detailed discussion of this approach.

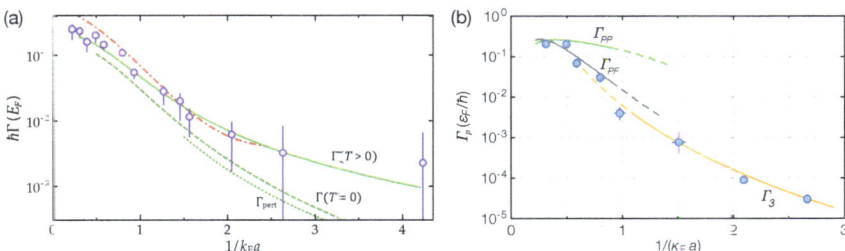

Figure 6. Stability of the repulsive Fermi polaron in the equal-mass, broad-resonance case. (**a**) Decoherence rate Γ of the repulsive Fermi polaron. (**b**) Population decay rate Γ_p of the repulsive branch to lower-lying states. Circles are experimental data points from Ref. [23], obtained by measuring: (**a**) the damping rate of Rabi oscillations on the repulsive polaron, or (**b**) the relaxation of the upper branch measured via a double-pulse experiment. In panel (**a**), lines denote the quasiparticle spectral width Γ calculated with a variational method [28,46,98] at $T=0$ (dashed, green) and $T=0.13\,E_F$ (solid, green), with functional renormalization group (red, dot-dashed) [83], and at the first non-vanishing order in perturbation theory, $\Gamma_{\text{pert}} = \frac{8(k_F a)^4}{9\pi^3} E_F$ [28] (dotted, green—see Table 2). In panel (**b**), lines denote the upper branch decay rate predicted by considering polaron-to-polaron recombination (green) [77], polaron-to-free particle recombination (grey) [23], and three-body molecular recombination (yellow) [105]. Panel (**b**) is adapted from Ref. [23].

In order to quantify the stability of the repulsive branch against relaxation to lower-lying attractive states, double-pulse sequences have been employed to directly address the repulsive branch de-population rate Γ_p [16,17,23,26,29] (see Figure 6b). This technique is weakly sensitive to momentum, because it requires fast π-pulses with large Rabi frequency $\Omega \sim E_F$, thus coupling to all impurities in the medium irrespective of their kinetic energy. Theoretical calculations of the upper branch population decay rate Γ_p, based on variants of T-matrix techniques including two and three particle processes, match well with experimental measurements in Fermi-Fermi and Fermi-Bose mixtures at a narrow Feshbach resonance with heavy impurities for all couplings [16,29] and in the strongly-interacting region at a broad resonance in the mass-balanced case [23]. For the equal-mass, broad-resonance case [23] at weaker couplings $1/k_F a \gtrsim 1$ the measured repulsive branch decay rate was instead found to match well with the predicted rate of recombination into dimers via three-body processes, Γ_3 [105], as expected in the spin-balanced regime of a Fermi mixture [56,106]. Future theory approaches beyond the one particle-hole approximation for Fermi polarons may succeed in describing the trend of Γ_p for an extended range of couplings in the equal-mass, universal broad-resonance case.

To conclude, in a fermionic medium with $1/k_F a \gtrsim 1$, the repulsive branch decay rate Γ_p is generally significantly smaller than the quasiparticle width Γ (see Figure 6), in both mass-imbalanced and mass-balanced scenarios [16,23], thereby showing that the lifetime of repulsive Fermi polarons is mostly limited by decoherence processes (see also Section 4). Future experiments with repulsive fermionic impurities immersed in a Bose medium, possibly realized by mass-imbalanced mixtures with reduced three-body losses [107], could further address the important question of the stability of repulsive Bose polarons.

4. Repulsive Quasiparticle Stability

The repulsive polaron quasiparticle is challenging to investigate theoretically, since it is a metastable object in quantum gases where the underlying short-range interactions are attractive. In particular, there has been much debate about what controls the stability of the quasiparticle, as encoded by the quasiparticle damping rate Γ in Equation (9) [16,21,23,28,77,83]. As discussed in Section 3, Γ directly manifests itself in the damping of Rabi oscillations and in the broadening of the quasiparticle peak in the spectral function. However, the quasiparticle damping rate has turned out to be far from trivial to calculate even in the weak-coupling limit [23,28].

In this section, we will focus on the case of an impurity at rest, such that we can exclude any spectral broadening due to momentum relaxation [21,103], where the polaron lowers its momentum via collisions. To gain insight into the quasiparticle stability, let us start with the non-interacting impurity-medium system at $T=0$ and then imagine gradually increasing the scattering length a from zero, such that we adiabatically populate the repulsive branch. In the weak-coupling limit $k_F a \ll 1$ (Table 2), the behavior of the metastable repulsive polaron up to order a^2 is indistinguishable from that of the purely repulsive case, resembling an infinitely long-lived quasiparticle in the ground state. However, as we further increase the strength of the interactions, the metastable polaron develops a non-zero Γ, in contrast to the purely repulsive ground-state polaron. If we assume that Γ is dictated by the decay into the attractive branch at negative energies (as it was initially assumed [16,77]), then we can estimate its leading order behavior in a from calculations of three-body recombination involving the impurity and two medium particles. This yields the scaling a^6 for the Fermi polaron case [105] and a^4 for the Bose polaron when $a = a_B$ [108], which can be understood from the fact that the population decay rate Γ_p in this limit must scale as n^2 in the Bose case and $E_F n^2$ in the Fermi polaron case. However, an alternative mechanism for the quasiparticle damping has recently been proposed [28], whereby the repulsive polaron loses its coherence by coupling to the many-body continuum at positive energies, as illustrated in Figure 7. Crucially, this *many-body dephasing* enters at a lower power of a (see Table 2) and thus dominates Γ at weak coupling. This is consistent with experimental observations in Figure 6, as discussed in Section 3.

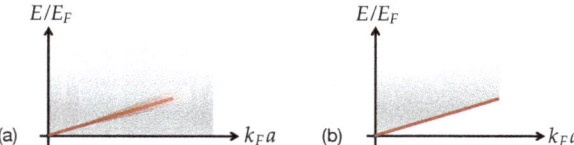

Figure 7. Behavior of repulsive polarons for underlying attractive interactions (**a**) and purely repulsive interactions (**b**). In the former case, the polaron is embedded in a continuum (grey shading) at positive energies, thus resulting in broadening with increasing $k_F a$. By contrast, in the latter case, the continuum lies above the polaron energy and the polaron has an infinite lifetime.

As we approach strong interactions, we eventually expect both many-body dephasing and relaxation to the lower branch to determine the repulsive polaron lifetime. In this regime, the repulsive polaron becomes increasingly ill-defined and it is quite challenging to calculate the associated quasiparticle properties. Indeed, as illustrated in Figure 8, different state-of-the-art calculations give inconsistent results for the spectral function in the case of the Fermi polaron, clearly indicating the need for future work. In particular, we see that the theories even disagree on the shape of the repulsive polaron peak at unitary, as well as yielding different results for the peak position and width.

In the following, we will delve further into one particular method, namely the variational method, since this describes many-body dephasing within the upper branch and provides a particularly intuitive way of accounting for excitations of the medium. We will also show how the case of purely repulsive interactions results in a ground-state polaron with $\Gamma = 0$ in this approach. Finally, we will examine the special case of an infinitely heavy impurity, since it admits an exact solution that serves as a useful reference point for the repulsive polaron, even though the quasiparticle residue Z vanishes in this case.

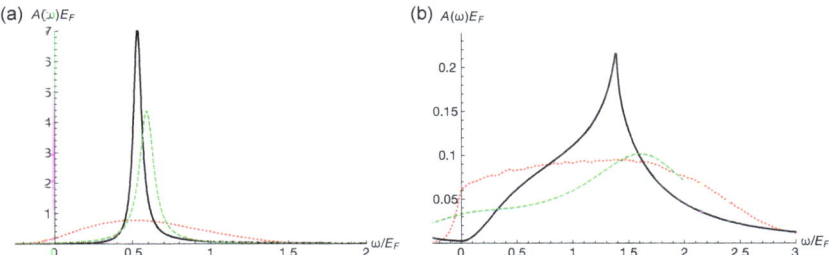

Figure 8. Spectral function $A(\omega) \equiv A(0,\omega)$ of the Fermi polaron for $m = m_{\text{med}}$ and $T = 0$, calculated using a T-matrix formalism [77] (black, solid), functional renormalization group [83] (green, dashed), and diagrammatic Monte Carlo [51] (red, dotted), where in the latter case, we display the maximally smooth solution [51]. We show the results for slightly different values of $1/k_F a \approx 1$ (**a**), and for $1/k_F a = 0$ (**b**).

4.1. Variational Description of Attractive and Repulsive Polarons

The basic idea of the variational method is to construct a variational form of the time-dependent impurity operator and then use this to approximate the impurity Green's function (6). In particular, it has proved remarkably fruitful to consider "truncated" operators with up to one or two excitations of the medium [28,46,88,98]. For the Fermi polaron, the simplest form we can write down for the zero-momentum impurity operator is [46]:

$$\hat{c}_0(t) \simeq \alpha_0(t)\,\hat{c}_0 + \sum_{\mathbf{k},\mathbf{q}} \alpha_{\mathbf{k}\mathbf{q}}(t)\,\hat{f}_{\mathbf{q}}^\dagger \hat{f}_{\mathbf{k}} \hat{c}_{\mathbf{q}-\mathbf{k}}, \qquad (17)$$

where the time-dependent complex functions $\alpha_j(t)$ are variational parameters. Equation (17) can be regarded as the operator version of the variational wave function originally introduced by F. Chevy for the attractive Fermi polaron [109]. However, unlike the original Chevy ansatz which only describes the attractive polaron ground state, the time-dependent variational operator can capture all the interacting impurity states at arbitrary temperature. In particular, the variational operator becomes exact in the high-temperature limit, where it becomes equivalent to the leading order contribution to the virial expansion [46].

Similarly, the operator in the case of the Bose polaron has the form [88]:

$$\hat{c}_0(t) \simeq \alpha_0(t)\,\hat{c}_0 + \sum_{\mathbf{q}} \alpha^{\mathbf{q}}(t)\,\hat{b}_{\mathbf{q}}^\dagger \hat{c}_{\mathbf{q}} + \sum_{\mathbf{k}} \alpha_{\mathbf{k}}(t)\,\hat{b}_{\mathbf{k}} \hat{c}_{-\mathbf{k}} + \sum_{\mathbf{k},\mathbf{q}} \alpha_{\mathbf{k}}^{\mathbf{q}}(t)\,\hat{b}_{\mathbf{q}}^\dagger \hat{b}_{\mathbf{k}} \hat{c}_{\mathbf{q}-\mathbf{k}} + \dots, \qquad (18)$$

where we have only explicitly written the terms with up to one excitation of the medium. Note that this differs slightly from the Fermi polaron case, since the second and third terms in Equation (18) describe bosons being scattered into and out of the condensate, respectively. In principle, we could obtain the exact impurity operator by including an infinite number of possible excitations. However, in practice, this is only feasible for special cases such as the infinitely heavy impurity in a non-interacting quantum gas.

To proceed, we consider the "error operator" $\hat{\epsilon}(t) = i\partial_t \hat{c}_0(t) - [\hat{c}_0(t), \hat{H}]$, which quantifies how well the approximate time-dependent impurity operator satisfies the Heisenberg equation of motion. We then construct the error quantity $\Delta(t) \equiv \text{tr}[\hat{\rho}_{\text{med}}\hat{\epsilon}(t)\hat{\epsilon}^\dagger(t)]$, which we minimize with respect to $\partial_t \alpha_j^*(t)$ in order to obtain the differential equations for the parameters $\alpha_j(t)$. Specializing to the Fermi polaron and taking the stationary condition $\alpha_j(t) = \alpha_j e^{-i\omega t}$, we finally obtain the coupled set of equations

$$\omega\alpha_0 = gn\alpha_0 + g\sum_{\mathbf{k},\mathbf{q}}^{\Lambda}(1-n_{\mathbf{k}})n_{\mathbf{q}}\alpha_{\mathbf{kq}}$$

$$\omega\alpha_{\mathbf{kq}} = \left[\epsilon_{\mathbf{q}-\mathbf{k}} + \epsilon_{\mathbf{k}}^{\text{med}} - \epsilon_{\mathbf{q}}^{\text{med}} + gn\right]\alpha_{\mathbf{kq}} + g\alpha_0 + g\sum_{\mathbf{k}'}^{\Lambda}(1-n_{\mathbf{k}'})\alpha_{\mathbf{k}'\mathbf{q}} - g\sum_{\mathbf{q}'}^{\Lambda}n_{\mathbf{q}'}\alpha_{\mathbf{kq}'},$$
(19)

where we have used the simplified impurity–medium interaction defined by Equation (5), and we have the Fermi–Dirac distribution for the medium particles,

$$n_{\mathbf{k}} = \text{tr}\left[\hat{\rho}_{\text{med}}\hat{f}_{\mathbf{k}}^{\dagger}\hat{f}_{\mathbf{k}}\right] = \frac{1}{1+e^{\beta(\epsilon_{\mathbf{k}}^{\text{med}}-\mu)}}.$$
(20)

For the case of purely repulsive interactions, Equation (5) requires $g > 2\pi a/m_r > 0$, and we can see in Equation (19) that all the single-particle impurity energies are shifted upwards by gn, the Born approximation of the interaction energy. Furthermore, gn corresponds to an upper bound on the repulsive polaron energy in the ground state since $E \leq \langle 0|\hat{c}_0\hat{H}\hat{c}_0^{\dagger}|0\rangle = gn$, where $|0\rangle$ is the state of the undisturbed medium at zero temperature. Therefore, the lowest energy solution to Equation (19) at zero temperature will always lie below the onset of the scattering continuum, and thus the variational approach yields a ground-state repulsive polaron with an infinite lifetime (see Figure 7). This energy gap between the polaron ground state and the onset of the continuum is an artifact of the approximation (similar to what was found for the attractive polaron [104]), since an exact theory with an infinite number of particle-hole excitations will contain excited polaronic states with energies arbitrarily close to the ground-state energy. Note that Equation (19) correctly yields the mean-field energy $E \simeq 2\pi a n/m_r$ in the limit $n \to 0$, which one can show by making use of Equation (5).

For attractive impurity-medium interactions, we can take the limit $g \to 0^-$ and still have a well-defined scattering length a, provided we also take $\Lambda \to \infty$. This corresponds to the case of a zero-range potential, which is a reasonable description for a dilute atomic gas where all the relevant length scales are much greater than the range of the van der Waals interactions. In this case, Equation (19) is equivalent to the non-self-consistent T-matrix approach [46,110], where the impurity self energy $\Sigma = g\sum_{\mathbf{k},\mathbf{q}}^{\Lambda}(1-n_{\mathbf{k}})n_{\mathbf{q}}\alpha_{\mathbf{kq}}/\alpha_0$ corresponds to

$$\Sigma(0,\omega) = \sum_{\mathbf{q}}n_{\mathbf{q}}\left[\frac{m_r}{2\pi a} - \sum_{\mathbf{k}}\left(\frac{1-n_{\mathbf{k}}}{\omega-\epsilon_{\mathbf{q}-\mathbf{k}}-\epsilon_{\mathbf{k}}^{\text{med}}+\epsilon_{\mathbf{q}}^{\text{med}}+i0} + \frac{1}{\epsilon_{\mathbf{k}}+\epsilon_{\mathbf{k}}^{\text{med}}}\right)\right]^{-1}.$$
(21)

In contrast to purely repulsive interactions, we see here that there is no shift of the single-particle impurity energies and thus the self energy acquires an imaginary part when $\omega > 0$. For Bose polarons above the BEC critical temperature, the self energy has the same form as Equation (21), where the Fermi distributions are instead replaced by Bose distributions, and we have $1 + n_{\mathbf{k}}$ rather than $1 - n_{\mathbf{k}}$ in Equation (21).

We can determine the lifetime of the metastable repulsive Fermi polaron in the weak-coupling limit by expanding Equation (21) in a and computing the lowest order contribution to the imaginary part [28]. This yields, for arbitrary temperature,

$$\Gamma \simeq -\text{Im}[\Sigma(0,E)] = \pi\left(\frac{2\pi a}{m_r}\right)^2\sum_{\mathbf{k},\mathbf{q}}n_{\mathbf{q}}(1-n_{\mathbf{k}})\delta\left(E-\epsilon_{\mathbf{q}-\mathbf{k}}-\epsilon_{\mathbf{k}}^{\text{med}}+\epsilon_{\mathbf{q}}^{\text{med}}\right) \quad \text{(Fermi)}.$$
(22)

Here, we see how Γ is derived from the many-body continuum of states at positive energies, which is qualitatively distinct from the process of relaxation to lower energy states. Taking $T=0$, $m=m_{\text{med}}$ and using the lowest order energy $E = 4\pi a n/m$ then gives the expression for Γ in Table 2. We stress that this imaginary contribution arising from many-body dephasing is not canceled by third-order diagrams involving self-energy insertions [74], since these only yield real terms.

The quasiparticle damping rate of the repulsive Bose polaron can be obtained in a similar manner, yielding the zero-temperature expression:

$$\Gamma \simeq \pi n \left(\frac{2\pi a}{m_r}\right)^2 \sum_{\mathbf{k}} \frac{\epsilon_{\mathbf{k}}^{\text{med}}}{E_{\mathbf{k}}} \delta(E - \epsilon_{\mathbf{k}} - E_{\mathbf{k}}) \quad \text{(Bose)}, \tag{23}$$

where the Bogoliubov dispersion $E_{\mathbf{k}} = \sqrt{\epsilon_{\mathbf{k}}^{\text{med}}(\epsilon_{\mathbf{k}}^{\text{med}} + 2\mu)}$, and we have used the second-order self energy in Ref. [74]. In this case, Γ depends on both the boson–boson and impurity-boson interactions. However, if we consider the special case where $a_B = a$ and $m = m_{\text{med}}$, we obtain the simple expression in Table 2.

Finally, let us contrast the quasiparticle decoherence process described in this section with the standard Fermi liquid picture. There, the dominant mechanism for quasiparticle damping is momentum relaxation, which at low temperatures yields a lifetime proportional to $1/T^2$ [25], and at zero temperatures to $1/p^4$ [103,111] for attractive Fermi polarons. However, the repulsive polaron has a finite lifetime at zero momentum, even in the absence of any decay into lower-lying excitations (such as attractive polarons, dressed molecules and tightly-bound dimers). In this sense, the repulsive polaron defies the standard Fermi liquid picture, which predicts that the lifetime should diverge at the impurity "Fermi surface" ($k = 0$) [111].

4.2. The Case of an Infinitely Heavy Impurity

A useful reference system is that of an infinitely heavy impurity, which could in principle be approximately realized in cold-atom experiments by pinning the impurity atoms in tight traps. Remarkably, this problem affords analytic expressions for the spectral function when the medium is an ideal gas. Most notably, the Fermi polaron in the limit $m/m_{\text{med}} \to \infty$ experiences the celebrated Anderson's orthogonality catastrophe [112], where the impurity ground states with and without interactions with the surrounding fermionic bath are orthogonal, i.e., the quasiparticle residue $Z = 0$, and the spectrum features a power-law singularity, as quantified by the threshold behavior

$$A(\omega) \sim \theta(\omega - \omega_0)(\omega - \omega_0)^{\alpha - 1}. \tag{24}$$

Here, the power law coefficient $\alpha = \delta(k_F)^2/\pi^2$ is related to the impurity-fermion scattering phase shift $\delta(k) = -\tan^{-1}(ka)$ evaluated at the Fermi surface, and the repulsive branch of the spectrum starts at: $\omega_0 = -\int_0^{E_F} dE\, \delta(\sqrt{2mE})/\pi$.

More recently, the case of an infinitely heavy impurity in an ideal Bose gas has also been investigated [113]. This is, of course, a highly singular limit. Even for a finite impurity mass, the lack of compressibility of the ideal Bose gas implies that $Z = 0$ for the ground state [87,100,114,115] and that the ground-state energy itself becomes ill defined for $a \geq 0$. This highlights the crucial role played by boson-boson interactions in stabilizing the system [116]. Despite this, the ideal Bose polaron spectrum remains well-defined, and in the case of an infinitely heavy impurity it can be obtained from an analytic solution of the impurity time evolution [113]. The analysis of Ref. [113] demonstrated a threshold behavior of the repulsive branch, valid when $0 < k_F a \ll 1$,

$$A(\omega) \sim \theta(\omega - \omega_0)(\omega - \omega_0)^{-3/2} \exp\left(-\frac{8\pi n^2 a^4}{m(\omega - \omega_0)}\right), \tag{25}$$

where $\omega_0 = 2\pi a n/m$. As in the Fermi case, the spectral function contains a power law, but in this case there is a strong suppression of spectral weight associated with low-energy excitations, preventing the power-law singularity.

The behavior in the two cases is illustrated in Figure 9. One major difference is that the Fermi case features a spectral gap between the attractive and repulsive branches when $a > 0$, whereas the Bose case instead has a strongly suppressed weight between the branches.

Away from the resonance, the repulsive branches look reasonably similar; however as we approach the resonance, the behavior is remarkably different. We emphasize that in both the Fermi and Bose cases the problem is integrable, and completely determined by the solution of the two-body problem involving the impurity and a particle from the medium. Therefore, there is no analog of three-body recombination, and hence the population decay rate Γ_p is identically 0. Likewise, our argument for the many-body dephasing relied on the existence of a well-defined quasiparticle that is pushed up into a scattering continuum, and thus also does not apply in either case. These points illustrate the strong qualitative differences between the mobile and the fixed impurity for properties beyond the impurity energy.

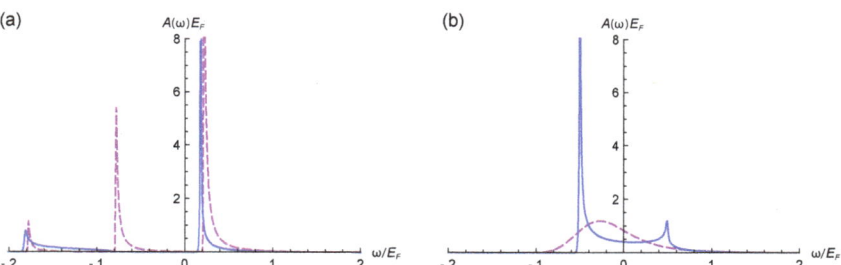

Figure 9. Spectral function of an infinitely heavy impurity in an ideal Fermi gas at $T = 0.01\, E_F$ (blue, solid) [52] or an ideal Bose gas at $T = 0$ [113] (purple, dashed). We show the result for $1/k_F a = 1$ (**a**) and $1/k_F a = 0$ (**b**). On the left, the two attractive peaks in the Bose case are due to single or double occupation of the impurity-boson bound state.

5. Beyond the Impurity Limit: Induced Interactions and Instabilities

5.1. Polaron-Polaron Induced Interactions

When considering more than one impurity, the problem becomes significantly more complex at low temperatures where there are correlations between impurities. On the one hand, the statistics of the impurities starts to play a role. On the other, a variety of thermodynamic phases exist for the various components, which may be normal or condensed, mixed or phase-separated, *etc*. Below we will treat separately the different cases which arise depending on the statistics of the bath and the impurities.

5.1.1. Bosonic Impurities in a Fermi Sea

The energy density of a gas containing $N_\downarrow$ bosonic impurities immersed in a bath of $N_\uparrow \gg N_\downarrow$ ideal fermions may be written as [117]:

$$\mathcal{E}(n_\uparrow, n_\downarrow) = \frac{3}{5} E_F n_\uparrow + E_\downarrow n_\downarrow + \frac{1}{2} F n_\downarrow^2. \tag{26}$$

The various terms represent, in order, the (purely kinetic) energy of the unperturbed Fermi sea, the energy of isolated polarons, and the contribution due to *polaron–polaron* interactions. We have omitted the mean kinetic energy of the impurities, which is negligible when cold bosonic impurities are considered.

The effective interaction F between Landau quasiparticles can be split into two contributions: $F = g_1 + F_x$. The first is the direct interaction, $g_1 = 4\pi a_{11}/m_\downarrow$, where a_{11} is the scattering length between bare impurities (and we assume $|k_F a_{11}| \lesssim 1$). The second term instead describes an exchange contribution, mediated by particle-hole excitations of the Fermi sea.

To obtain an explicit expression for the exchange interaction term, we follow the simple derivation outlined in Refs. [118,119]. An $\uparrow$ atom and a $\downarrow$ polaron interact with a coupling constant g_x given by:

$$g_x = \frac{\partial^2 \mathcal{E}}{\partial n_\uparrow \partial n_\downarrow} = \frac{\partial \mu_\uparrow}{\partial n_\downarrow} = \frac{\partial \mu_\downarrow}{\partial n_\uparrow}. \tag{27}$$

Here and in the following, derivatives with respect to the density of a component will be taken at fixed density of the other. To second order in g_x, the polaron-polaron interaction is then given by:

$$\mathcal{E}^{(2)} = -\frac{g_x^2}{V^3} \sum_{\mathbf{k},\mathbf{p},\mathbf{q}} \frac{(1-n^\uparrow_{\mathbf{k+q}})(1+n^\downarrow_{\mathbf{p-q}})n^\downarrow_{\mathbf{p}}n^\uparrow_{\mathbf{k}}}{\epsilon^{\text{med}}_{\mathbf{k+q}} + \epsilon^*_{\mathbf{p-q}} - \epsilon^*_{\mathbf{p}} - \epsilon^{\text{med}}_{\mathbf{k}}}, \tag{28}$$

where $n^\uparrow_{\mathbf{k}}$ and $n^\downarrow_{\mathbf{p}}$ indicate, respectively, Fermi and Bose distribution functions, since we are assuming bosonic impurities in a Fermi bath, and we have introduced the polaron dispersion $\epsilon^*_{\mathbf{p}} = p^2/2m^*$. The exchange contribution to Landau's polaron–polaron interaction is then obtained by differentiating with respect to the distribution functions of the two quasiparticles,

$$F_x = \frac{\delta^2 \mathcal{E}^{(2)}}{\delta n^\downarrow_{\mathbf{p-q}} \delta n^\downarrow_{\mathbf{p}}}, \tag{29}$$

where both $\mathbf{p}$ and $\mathbf{q}$ are assumed to be vanishingly small. Performing the functional derivatives one finds:

$$F_x = -\frac{g_x^2}{V} \left(\sum_{\mathbf{k}} \frac{n^\uparrow_{\mathbf{k}} - n^\uparrow_{\mathbf{k+q}}}{\epsilon^{\text{med}}_{\mathbf{k+q}} - \epsilon^{\text{med}}_{\mathbf{k}}} \right)_{q \to 0} = -g_x^2 L, \tag{30}$$

where L is the so-called Lindhard function[3], which at zero temperature coincides with the density of states at the Fermi surface $\mathcal{N} = \left(\frac{\partial n_\uparrow}{\partial \mu_\uparrow}\right) = \frac{3n_\uparrow}{2E_F}$. Collecting the above results, at zero temperature we obtain:

$$F_x = -g_x^2 \mathcal{N} = -\left(\frac{\partial \mu_\uparrow}{\partial n_\downarrow}\right)^2 \frac{\partial n_\uparrow}{\partial \mu_\uparrow} = -\left[-\frac{\left(\frac{\partial \mu_\uparrow}{\partial n_\downarrow}\right)}{\left(\frac{\partial \mu_\uparrow}{\partial n_\uparrow}\right)}\right]^2 \frac{\partial \mu_\uparrow}{\partial n_\uparrow}. \tag{31}$$

To simplify this expression, we use the *triple product rule* $\left(\frac{\partial x}{\partial y}\right)_z \left(\frac{\partial y}{\partial z}\right)_x \left(\frac{\partial z}{\partial x}\right)_y = -1$ to find:

$$-\left(\frac{\partial \mu_\uparrow}{\partial n_\downarrow}\right)_{n_\uparrow} \bigg/ \left(\frac{\partial \mu_\uparrow}{\partial n_\uparrow}\right)_{n_\downarrow} = \frac{\partial n_\uparrow}{\partial n_\downarrow}\bigg|_{\mu_\uparrow} = \Delta N, \tag{32}$$

where ΔN is the number of bath particles in the dressing cloud of an impurity introduced in Equation (12). The latter expression shows that the induced quasiparticle interaction for bosonic impurities may be compactly written as

$$F_x = -\frac{(\Delta N)^2}{\mathcal{N}}. \tag{33}$$

This final result highlights the power and beauty of *Fermi liquid theory*: to derive the effective interaction we have used perturbation theory to describe the *weak* interaction mediated by the bath between two *quasi*-particles. The strong-coupling effects which generate the quasiparticles themselves are fully taken into account in Equation (33) by means of ΔN, a quantity which must be computed using a suitable theory describing the strongly coupled $N + 1$ problem (like those described in the earlier sections of this work). As such, Equation (33) holds for arbitrarily strong impurity-bath interaction strength provided there are no instabilities or transitions that invalidate the use of Fermi liquid theory.

Very recent measurements targeting locally-large concentrations of bosonic impurities in a Fermi bath showed a trend compatible with this Fermi liquid prediction [29,121], but more accurate observations are needed to clearly pinpoint the phenomenon. Indeed, multiple issues render the measurements complicated in the case of a Bose–Fermi mixture. First, the relevant Feshbach resonances featured a relatively small magnetic field width, so that magnetic field instabilities generated large error bars. Second, the bosonic component is highly compressible, so that the density distributions can vary rapidly before and after the "injection". Indeed, for repulsive Bose–Fermi interactions, the mixture is highly unstable towards phase-separation [117,122,123]. On the other hand, the absence of Pauli blocking in the minority component means that it is possible to create mixtures featuring large local concentrations of impurities. As such, Bose–Fermi mixtures represent a very favorable setting for studying polaron–polaron induced interactions.

5.1.2. Fermionic Impurities in a Fermi Sea

When a fermionic bath hosts distinguishable fermionic impurities, the energy density may be written as:

$$\mathcal{E}(n_\uparrow, n_\downarrow) = \frac{3}{5} E_F n_\uparrow + \mathcal{E}_{\text{kin}\downarrow} + E_\downarrow n_\downarrow + \frac{1}{2} F n_\downarrow^2. \quad (34)$$

A number of differences are present with respect to the discussion of bosonic impurities given in the previous Section 5.1.1:

i. There is no direct interaction between identical fermionic impurities (i.e., $F = F_x$).
ii. Pauli pressure dictates that impurities form their own Fermi sea, with Fermi energy $E_{F\downarrow} = (n_\downarrow/n_\uparrow)^{2/3}(m/m^*)E_F$. The corresponding contribution $\mathcal{E}_{\text{kin}\downarrow} = \frac{3}{5} E_{F\downarrow} n_\downarrow$ to the energy density can be sizable, and this indeed permitted a direct measurement of the effective mass m^* of the polarons via injection RF spectroscopy in Ref. [23].
iii. Correspondingly, final states available to the interacting impurities are "Pauli blocked", rather than "Bose enhanced", so that in the numerator of Equation (28) one needs to replace $(1 + n_{\mathbf{p-q}}^\downarrow)$ by $(1 - n_{\mathbf{p-q}}^\downarrow)$, where $n_{\mathbf{k}}^\downarrow$ is now a Fermi distribution function. As a consequence, the functional derivative with respect to the distribution functions of the minority particles in Equation (29) leads to an overall sign change in the exchange interaction term for fermionic impurities, which ultimately becomes repulsive and reads:

$$F_x = \frac{(\Delta N)^2}{\mathcal{N}}. \quad (35)$$

Despite intense efforts, experiments on Fermi–Fermi mixtures have so far proved unable to unambiguously detect the presence of induced polaron–polaron interactions. Indeed, reported measurements remain compatible within the experimental uncertainties with a description in terms of uncorrelated quasiparticles up to sizable concentrations of impurities [14,23]. Somewhat unexpectedly, the contribution $Fn_\downarrow^2/2$ due to induced interactions between quasiparticles disappears from the equation of state when one switches from the canonical description used above to a grand-canonical formulation [124]. In the latter case, the equation of state for the mixture gives a pressure which is the sum of the pressures of an ideal gas of fermions and an ideal gas of polarons, with no interaction terms. The apparent contradiction is resolved by realizing that the polaron energy is actually a function of the majority chemical potential $\mu_\uparrow$, so that the two pressures are effectively coupled. A careful calculation shows that the correct interaction term $\propto Fn_\downarrow^2$ is recovered when switching back to the canonical ensemble. A grand-canonical description is the appropriate one when extracting thermodynamic quantities from *in-situ* measurements on trapped gases, as performed for example in Ref. [125] following the proposal of Ref. [126], but a canonical description is generally needed to describe RF experiments or QMC calculations, where a controlled number of impurities is present in the system. The induced interaction term between polarons was indeed retained and shown to be important when analyzing state-of-the-art QMC calculations, and a complete phase diagram featuring the various possible phases arising in zero temperature Fermi–Fermi mixtures was derived in Ref. [127].

5.1.3. Bosonic Media

A bosonic bath is highly compressible, due to the absence of the large Fermi pressure. As a consequence, all bath particles condense in the same physical state at low temperatures, and the kinetic energy is negligible. On the other hand, the bath bosons experience a mutual direct (mean field) interaction. The energy density of the mixture may therefore be written as:

$$\mathcal{E}(n_\uparrow, n_\downarrow) = \frac{2\pi a_B}{m} n_\uparrow^2 + \mathcal{E}_{\text{kin}\downarrow} + E_\downarrow n_\downarrow + \frac{1}{2} F n_\downarrow^2, \qquad (36)$$

irrespective of the impurity statistics, where $\mathcal{E}_{\text{kin}\downarrow} = \frac{3}{5} E_{F\downarrow} n_\downarrow$ in the case of fermionic impurities, while it vanishes for bosonic impurities. Even though the fundamental excitations in the bath are Bogoliubov modes, rather than particle-hole excitations, a calculation similar to that developed above leads to an identical result [119,128],

$$F_x = \mp g_x^2 \frac{\partial n_\uparrow}{\partial \mu_\uparrow} = \mp \frac{(\Delta N)^2}{\mathcal{N}} \qquad (37)$$

(with $-$ for bosonic impurities and $+$ for fermionic ones), the only difference being that here $\mathcal{N} = \partial n_\uparrow / \partial \mu_\uparrow = m_{\text{med}}/(4\pi a_B)$.

5.2. Ferromagnetic and Pairing Instabilities in Fermi–Fermi Mixtures

As mentioned in the introduction, a major motivation for studying the impurity problem is the fact that understanding quasiparticle properties of the polarized system provides important insight into the more challenging phase diagram of its population-balanced counterpart [47]. This holds true especially for the repulsive Fermi polaron, that was first considered [49,50] in connection with the physics of itinerant ferromagnetism of a repulsive Fermi gas, originally introduced by E. Stoner in his textbook model [48]. Repulsive polarons indeed constitute the building blocks of a repulsive Fermi liquid, which in turn represents the paramagnetic state of a two-component Fermi mixture with short-ranged inter-species repulsion.

For a hypothetical, genuine two-body repulsive potential, a knowledge of the energy E of repulsive polarons as a function of the interaction strength suffices to determine the emergence of a ferromagnetic instability in the $(N+1)$-particle system [3,49,50]. This can be understood if one considers a bath of spin-↑ electrons, interacting with a spin-↓ electron impurity via a screened, short-range Coulomb repulsion. As long as the polaron energy does not exceed the Fermi energy E_F of the surrounding bath, the spin-down quasiparticle embedded in the fermionic medium is energetically favored, and the system is in the Fermi liquid, paramagnetic state. Instead for $E > E_F$, the system becomes unstable towards a fully ferromagnetic phase, as it is now energetically convenient for the impurity electron to flip its spin, resulting in a polarized Fermi gas of $N+1$ spin-↑ particles: in this latter case, the energy cost of adding one spin-↑ electron to the medium is lower than the energy cost associated with a strong impurity-bath repulsion. In contrast with the case of electrons in solids, where only the total electron population is fixed, in ultracold gases the two pseudospin numbers, $N_\uparrow$ and $N_\downarrow$, are generally fixed separately. As a result, the total "magnetization" $N_\uparrow - N_\downarrow$ is constrained by the two initial spin populations at which the gas is prepared. Yet, the same energetic argument applies [3], and for $E > E_F$ ferromagnetism appears in this case as an instability of the repulsive Fermi liquid towards the formation of spatially separated, polarized domains of spin-↑ or spin-↓ particles (see Figure 10).

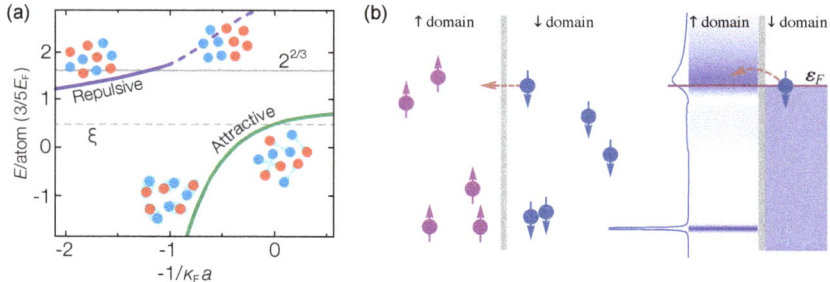

Figure 10. Ferromagnetic instability of a repulsive balanced Fermi mixture. (**a**) The energy of the upper (purple) and lower (green) many-body branches is illustrated, corresponding to a net repulsive and attractive interaction, respectively. The ground state is a paired phase, featuring a mean energy per particle $E = \frac{3}{5}\xi E_F$ at $1/k_F a = 0$, where $\xi \approx 0.37$ is the Bertsch parameter [129]. The repulsive Fermi liquid may undergo a ferromagnetic phase transition beyond a critical interaction strength along the upper branch, where a spin-segregated state is energetically favored. For an equal-mass, balanced mixture at $T = 0$, this occurs when the mean energy per particle of the mixed, paramagnetic state exceeds that in a non-interacting Fermi gas, namely $E = \frac{3}{5} E_F$, by a factor $2^{2/3}$. (**b**) Illustration of the stability condition for spin-polarized domains. A spin-↓ fermion can tunnel across a spin domain wall, thereby becoming a repulsive quasiparticle within the spin-↑ domain. On the right, the energy levels available to the fermion are represented. If a well defined repulsive polaron exists and its energy overcomes the Fermi energy, i.e., $E > E_F$, tunneling through the interface is suppressed and the domain wall is energetically stable. Panel (**b**) is adapted with permission from Ref. [130].

Such a seemingly simple scenario becomes richer and more complex once one considers the short-ranged attractive potentials relevant for a realistic description of the interaction between two ultracold atoms. As discussed in the previous sections, the presence of a lower-lying energy branch, connected with the existence of a weakly-bound molecular level below the two-body scattering threshold [41], makes repulsive polarons acquire a quasiparticle decay rate even at $T = 0$. As a consequence, ferromagnetism inherently competes with the tendency of the system to relax into the many-body ground state. Around the interaction strength $k_F a \sim 1$ relevant for ferromagnetism to develop, the spin-imbalanced ground state corresponds to phase separation between a superfluid of dimers and a spin-polarized Fermi gas [127,131]. Therefore, here the attractive branch can be safely regarded as a paired state where all impurity particles are bound to a partner of the host gas [14].

In this framework, the importance of a proper interpretation of the polaron spectral width Γ thus becomes clear: If Γ was exclusively linked to the population decay rate of the repulsive Fermi liquid [3], one would expect the repulsive branch to become ill-defined at strong repulsion, and the physics of Stoner's model to be inaccessible with such systems, since ferromagnetic correlations would be completely forestalled by attractive ones (such as pairing) [132]. Instead, in agreement with the recent theoretical analysis [28] outlined in Section 4, experimental pursuits have provided convincing evidence for the metastability of the repulsive branch even at strong coupling [16,23,26]. In particular, a short but finite time window was identified within which the instability of the repulsive Fermi gas towards a magnetically correlated state could be observed. Spectroscopic studies on ^{6}Li mixtures in the impurity limit indeed revealed well-defined quasiparticles even at very large repulsion, where E exceeds the Fermi energy of the bath while m^* diverges, indicating both an energetic and thermodynamic instability of the repulsive Fermi liquid state beyond critical interactions [23].

Studies of spin-dynamics in a repulsive Fermi gas initialized in two spin domains separated by a sharp domain wall [133] further allowed the characterization of the ferromagnetic behavior of the system, including the experimental determination of the metastable region in the temperature-interaction plane. This was linked to the softening of the spin-dipole mode, in quantitative agreement with theory models [134,135] that completely neglect pairing correlations. Finally, later works based on time-resolved pump-probe spectroscopic techniques succeeded in tracing the out-of-equilibrium dynamics of two-component balanced spin mixtures [56]. For this, fermions were selectively brought to strong repulsion along the upper branch of a Feshbach resonance, quickly enough to avoid undergoing substantial dynamics during the preparation itself, starting essentially from the paramagnetic Fermi liquid state. The rapid growth of short-range anti-correlations between repulsive quasiparticles was observed beyond critical interactions, demonstrating that concurrent pairing processes could be initially overcome. These studies [56], paralleled also by spin-density noise correlation measurements and monitoring of other macroscopic observables [136], led to the discovery of an unpredicted, emergent heterogeneous phase: a quantum emulsion where paired and unpaired fermions macroscopically coexist, while featuring microscale phase separation. In turn, this observation links the physics of the repulsive Fermi gas to certain strongly correlated electron materials, where competing order parameters coexist in nanoscale phase separation [137,138].

6. Concluding Remarks

Repulsive mixtures of ultracold atoms, both within and beyond the impurity limit, feature a very rich and intriguing phenomenology. In particular, owing to the metastability of the upper many-body branch, quantum mixtures are ideally suited to investigate the competition between exotic metastable quantum phases arising from repulsive (anti-)correlations and pairing phenomena. Indeed, in the case of Fermi–Fermi mixtures, the upper branch population decays on a timescale significantly slower than that set by quasiparticle decoherence, which has enabled experiments to gain important insights into aspects of Stoner's model [48] and the magnetic properties of itinerant fermionic particles [56,103,136]. Similarly, dilute Bose mixtures allow one to investigate the interplay between attractive and repulsive inter- and intra-species interactions, potentially leading to the emergence of quantum droplets [139] as one increases the minority density from the impurity limit. The presence of the concurrent pairing instability further enriches these scenarios, triggering non-trivial dynamics over longer timescales. In the Fermi case, this led to the emergence of unpredicted heterogeneous many-body states [56,136].

In future experiments, it would be interesting to explore the transport properties of such spatially inhomogeneous, slowly relaxing states, and to probe their emergence in box-like potentials [140], weak optical lattices [141,142] or lower dimensions [143,144]. For instance, quantum gas microscopes [145] could uniquely explore the competition between antiferromagnetic ordering, favored by the underlying lattice structure, and quantum emulsions of itinerant fermions. Further, the realization of such rich scenarios opens up exciting possibilities to dynamically create elusive phases of magnetized superfluidity [146,147] and to spontaneously attain mesoscopic magnetic impurities within strongly interacting superfluids [148].

The study of imbalanced quantum mixtures also paves the way for the observation of a crucially missing milestone in the experimental demonstration of the Fermi liquid paradigm in ultracold atoms, namely, polaron-polaron interactions. This can, for instance, be achieved by embedding highly-compressible bosonic impurities in a large Fermi sea as realized in a recent experiment [29]. The interactions are predicted to be even stronger between Bose polarons, since a dilute bosonic bath is highly compressible and can more easily convey excitations [128].

In the future, Bose and Fermi polaron studies with ultracold gases could be extended to the case where the motion of the impurity and/or the medium is confined within a lattice potential [53], possibly in reduced dimensions and in the presence of engineered site-resolved disorder [149]. For a comprehensive modeling of such scenarios, an essential preliminary step is to derive *ab initio* the effective interaction parameters associated with two atoms interacting strongly in an optical lattice potential, extending previous three-dimensional calculations [150]. The probing techniques discussed in this review could also find potential applications in the investigation of magnetic polarons [151–153], i.e., charge excitations moving within a magnetic background where they become dressed and acquire renormalized quasiparticle properties [10,154]. In particular, such excitations emerge in fermionic Hubbard models from the interplay between charge and spin [155], as observed by experiments [152,153]. These recent observations have attracted much interest [156–158], since the dynamics of magnetic polarons in doped Mott insulators may explain the behavior of certain strongly correlated materials such as high-temperature superconductors [159].

The phenomenology of the 3D polarons described in this review largely carries over to the case of two-dimensional systems. In this context, a promising new platform for polaron physics, complementary to cold-atom settings, is that of doped atomically thin semiconductors [30]. These effectively realize a two-dimensional Bose–Fermi mixture where excitons (bound electron-hole pairs) play the role of impurities in a Fermi sea of electrons, and these systems are directly analogous to experiments on 2D Fermi polarons in cold atomic gases [17,26], and can be modeled in a similar fashion [160]. However, this new platform introduces a number of new experimental knobs such as direct control of medium density via external gating, strong Rabi coupling of impurities to light in a microcavity [30], and strong magnetic fields that Landau-quantize the electronic medium [161,162]. Two-dimensional semiconductor microcavities also hold promise for realizing Bose polarons using exciton polaritons as the medium [163]. If the impurities are themselves polaritons one may obtain enhanced photon-photon correlations, while doped systems may foster new forms of induced electron pairing [164].

In conclusion, the quantum impurity problem in ultracold quantum gases represents a rare example of a strongly interacting many-body system for which it has been possible to achieve a remarkable agreement between theory and experiment, for a wide range of both static and dynamic properties. All fundamental advances in the topic have been driven by a close synergy between theory and experiment, leading to the development of approaches with broad applicability. Yet, as discussed in this review, many open questions still remain, with the emergence of new platforms further challenging our understanding and making polaron physics an extremely vital field of research.

Author Contributions: Conceptualization, F.S., M.Z., P.M., M.M.P. and J.L.; writing—original draft preparation, F.S., M.Z., P.M., M.M.P. and J.L.; writing—review and editing, F.S., M.Z., P.M., M.M.P. and J.L. All authors have read and agreed to the published version of the manuscript.

Funding: F.S. acknowledges funding from the European Research Council (ERC) under the European Union's Horizon 2020 research and innovation programme (Grant Agreement no. 949438). M.Z. acknowledges funding from the ERC through grant no. 637738 PoLiChroM and from the Italian MIUR through the FARE grant no. R168HMHFYM. P.M. was supported by grant PID2020-113565GB-C21 funded by MCIN/AEI/10.13039/501100011033, by EU FEDER Quantumcat, by the National Science Foundation under Grant No. NSF PHY-1748958, and by the *ICREA Academia* program. J.L. and M.M.P. acknowledge support from the Australian Research Council Centre of Excellence in Future Low-Energy Electronics Technologies (CE170100039). J.L. and M.M.P. are also supported through the Australian Research Council Future Fellowships FT160100244 and FT200100619, respectively, and J.L. furthermore acknowledges support from the Australian Research Council Discovery Project DP210101652.

Institutional Review Board Statement: Not applicable.

Informed Consent Statement: Not applicable.

Data Availability Statement: No new data were created or analyzed in this study. Data sharing is not applicable to this article.

Acknowledgments: The authors would like to thank Luis Peña Ardila for providing the data from Ref. [38], Olga Goulko for providing the data from Ref. [51], Richard Schmidt for providing the data from Ref. [83], Moritz Drescher for providing data from Ref. [113], and Haydn Adlong and Weizhe Liu for providing additional data for Figure 9. We also thank Haydn Adlong, Georg Bruun, Frédéric

Chevy, Tilman Enss, Weizhe Liu, Brendan Mulkerin, Alessio Recati, Giacomo Roati, and Richard Schmidt for insightful discussions.

Conflicts of Interest: The authors declare no conflict of interest.

Notes

1. More generally, the s-wave scattering amplitude takes the form $f(k) = 1/(k \cot \delta(k) - ik)$ in terms of the two-body scattering phase shift $\delta(k)$. For a low-energy collision at relative momentum k, this may be expanded as $k \cot \delta(k) = -a^{-1} + r_e k^2/2 + \ldots$, where a is the scattering length and r_e is the effective range. A Feshbach resonance is classified as *narrow* if the effective range plays a relevant role (e.g., if $|r_e| \gtrsim 1/k_F$ in a many-body problem), while it is termed *broad* when this may be safely neglected. Broad resonances are accurately described by the *single-channel* Hamiltonian introduced in this section, while to investigate narrow resonances one needs to employ a more sophisticated two-channel model [3,61].
2. Since the derivative of energy with respect to the Bose-Bose scattering length acts on the impurity energy, this term necessarily involves the impurity and two bosons.
3. We follow here the sign convention used in Ref. [120], but note that other sources define the Lindhard function with the opposite sign.

References

1. Mahan, G. *Many-Particle Physics*; Kluwer Academic/Plenum Publishers: New York, NY, USA, 2000.
2. Chevy, F.; Mora, C. Ultra-cold polarized Fermi gases. *Rep. Progr. Phys.* **2010**, *73*, 112401. [CrossRef]
3. Massignan, P.; Zaccanti, M.; Bruun, G.M. Polarons, dressed molecules and itinerant ferromagnetism in ultracold Fermi gases. *Rep. Progr. Phys.* **2014**, *77*, 034401. [CrossRef]
4. Levinsen, J.; Parish, M.M. Strongly interacting two-dimensional Fermi gases. *Annu. Rev. Cold Atoms Mol.* **2015**, *3*, 1–75.
5. Bardeen, J.; Baym, G.; Pines, D. Effective Interaction of ^{3}He Atoms in Dilute Solutions of ^{3}He in ^{4}He at Low Temperatures. *Phys. Rev.* **1967**, *156*, 207–221. [CrossRef]
6. Lemeshko, M.; Schmidt, R. Molecular Impurities Interacting with a Many-particle Environment: From Ultracold Gases to Helium Nanodroplets. In *Cold Chemistry: Molecular Scattering and Reactivity Near Absolute Zero*; Royal Society of Chemistry London, UK, 2018; pp. 444–495. [CrossRef]
7. Landau, L.D.; Pekar, S.I. Effective mass of a polaron. *Zh. Eksp. Teor. Fiz.* **1948**, *18*, 419.
8. Fröhlich, H. Electrons in lattice fields. *Adv. Phys.* **1954**, *3*, 325–361. [CrossRef]
9. Feynman, R.P. Slow Electrons in a Polar Crystal. *Phys. Rev.* **1955**, *97*, 660–665. [CrossRef]
10. Alexandrov, A.S.; Devreese, J.T. *Advances in Polaron Physics*; Springer: Berlin, Germany, 2010; Volume 159.
11. Klimov, V.V. Spectrum of Elementary Fermi Excitations in Quark Gluon Plasma. *Sov. J. Nucl. Phys.* **1981**, *33*, 934–935.
12. Weldon, H.A. Dynamical holes in the quark-gluon plasma. *Phys. Rev. D* **1989**, *40*, 2410–2420. [CrossRef]
13. Nakano, E.; Iida, K.; Horiuchi, W. Quasiparticle properties of a single α particle in cold neutron matter. *Phys. Rev. C* **2020**, *102*, 055802. [CrossRef]
14. Schirotzek, A.; Wu, C.H.; Sommer, A.; Zwierlein, M.W. Observation of Fermi Polarons in a Tunable Fermi Liquid of Ultracold Atoms. *Phys. Rev. Lett.* **2009**, *102*, 230402. [CrossRef] [PubMed]
15. Nascimbène, S.; Navon, N.; Jiang, K.J.; Tarruell, L.; Teichmann, M.; McKeever, J.; Chevy, F.; Salomon, C. Collective Oscillations of an Imbalanced Fermi Gas: Axial Compression Modes and Polaron Effective Mass. *Phys. Rev. Lett.* **2009**, *103*, 170402. [CrossRef] [PubMed]
16. Kohstall, C.; Zaccanti, M.; Jag, M.; Trenkwalder, A.; Massignan, P.; Bruun, G.M.; Schreck, F.; Grimm, R. Metastability and coherence of repulsive polarons in a strongly interacting Fermi mixture. *Nature* **2012**, *485*, 615–618. [CrossRef] [PubMed]
17. Koschorreck, M.; Pertot, D.; Vogt, E.; Fröhlich, B.; Feld, M.; Köhl, M. Attractive and repulsive Fermi polarons in two dimensions. *Nature* **2012**, *485*, 619–622. [CrossRef] [PubMed]
18. Zhang, Y.; Ong, W.; Arakelyan, I.; Thomas, J.E. Polaron-to-Polaron Transitions in the Radio-Frequency Spectrum of a Quasi-Two-Dimensional Fermi Gas. *Phys. Rev. Lett.* **2012**, *108*, 235302. [CrossRef]
19. Wenz, A.N.; Zürn, G.; Murmann, S.; Brouzos, I.; Lompe, T.; Jochim, S. From Few to Many: Observing the Formation of a Fermi Sea One Atom at a Time. *Science* **2013**, *342*, 457–460. [CrossRef] [PubMed]
20. Ong, W.; Cheng, C.; Arakelyan, L.; Thomas, J.E. Spin-Imbalanced Quasi-Two-Dimensional Fermi Gases. *Phys. Rev. Lett.* **2015**, *114*, 110403. [CrossRef]
21. Cetina, M.; Jag, M.; Lous, R.S.; Walraven, J.T.M.; Grimm, R.; Christensen, R.S.; Bruun, G.M. Decoherence of Impurities in a Fermi Sea of Ultracold Atoms. *Phys. Rev. Lett.* **2015**, *115*, 135302. [CrossRef]
22. Cetina, M.; Jag, M.; Lous, R.S.; Fritsche, I.; Walraven, J.T.M.; Grimm, R.; Levinsen, J.; Parish, M.M.; Schmidt, R.; Knap, M.; et al. Ultrafast many-body interferometry of impurities coupled to a Fermi sea. *Science* **2016**, *354*, 96–99. [CrossRef]
23. Scazza, F.; Valtolina, G.; Massignan, P.; Recati, A.; Amico, A.; Burchianti, A.; Fort, C.; Inguscio, M.; Zaccanti, M.; Roati, G. Repulsive Fermi Polarons in a Resonant Mixture of Ultracold ^{6}Li Atoms. *Phys. Rev. Lett.* **2017**, *118*, 083602. [CrossRef]
24. Mukherjee, B.; Yan, Z.; Patel, P.B.; Hadzibabic, Z.; Yefsah, T.; Struck, J.; Zwierlein, M.W. Homogeneous Atomic Fermi Gases. *Phys. Rev. Lett.* **2017**, *118*, 123401. [CrossRef] [PubMed]

25. Yan, Z.; Patel, P.B.; Mukherjee, B.; Fletcher, R.J.; Struck, J.; Zwierlein, M.W. Boiling a Unitary Fermi Liquid. *Phys. Rev. Lett.* **2019**, *122*, 093401. [CrossRef] [PubMed]
26. Darkwah Oppong, N.; Riegger, L.; Bettermann, O.; Höfer, M.; Levinsen, J.; Parish, M.M.; Bloch, I.; Fölling, S. Observation of Coherent Multiorbital Polarons in a Two-Dimensional Fermi Gas. *Phys. Rev. Lett.* **2019**, *122*, 193604. [CrossRef]
27. Ness, G.; Shkedrov, C.; Florshaim, Y.; Diessel, O.K.; von Milczewski, J.; Schmidt, R.; Sagi, Y. Observation of a Smooth Polaron-Molecule Transition in a Degenerate Fermi Gas. *Phys. Rev. X* **2020**, *10*, 041019. [CrossRef]
28. Adlong, H.S.; Liu, W.E.; Scazza, F.; Zaccanti, M.; Oppong, N.D.; Fölling, S.; Parish, M.M.; Levinsen, J. Quasiparticle Lifetime of the Repulsive Fermi Polaron. *Phys. Rev. Lett.* **2020**, *125*, 133401. [CrossRef]
29. Fritsche, I.; Baroni, C.; Dobler, E.; Kirilov, E.; Huang, B.; Grimm, R.; Bruun, G.M.; Massignan, P. Stability and breakdown of Fermi polarons in a strongly interacting Fermi-Bose mixture. *Phys. Rev. A* **2021**, *103*, 053314. [CrossRef]
30. Sidler, M.; Back, P.; Cotlet, O.; Srivastava, A.; Fink, T.; Kroner, M.; Demler, E.; Imamoglu, A. Fermi polaron-polaritons in charge-tunable atomically thin semiconductors. *Nat. Phys.* **2017**, *13*, 255–261. [CrossRef]
31. Wang, G.; Chernikov, A.; Glazov, M.M.; Heinz, T.F.; Marie, X.; Amand, T.; Urbaszek, B. Colloquium: Excitons in atomically thin transition metal dichalcogenides. *Rev. Mod. Phys.* **2018**, *90*, 021001. [CrossRef]
32. Bastarrachea-Magnani, M.A.; Thomsen, J.; Camacho-Guardian, A.; Bruun, G.M. Polaritons in an Electron Gas—Quasiparticles and Landau Effective Interactions. *Atoms* **2021**, *9*, 81. [CrossRef]
33. Catani, J.; Lamporesi, G.; Naik, D.; Gring, M.; Inguscio, M.; Minardi, F.; Kantian, A.; Giamarchi, T. Quantum dynamics of impurities in a one-dimensional Bose gas. *Phys. Rev. A* **2012**, *85*, 023623. [CrossRef]
34. Hu, M.G.; Van de Graaff, M.J.; Kedar, D.; Corson, J.P.; Cornell, E.A.; Jin, D.S. Bose Polarons in the Strongly Interacting Regime. *Phys. Rev. Lett.* **2016**, *117*, 055301. [CrossRef] [PubMed]
35. Jørgensen, N.B.; Wacker, L.; Skalmstang, K.T.; Parish, M.M.; Levinsen, J.; Christensen, R.S.; Bruun, G.M.; Arlt, J.J. Observation of Attractive and Repulsive Polarons in a Bose-Einstein Condensate. *Phys. Rev. Lett.* **2016**, *117*, 055302. [CrossRef] [PubMed]
36. Yan, Z.Z.; Ni, Y.; Robens, C.; Zwierlein, M.W. Bose polarons near quantum criticality. *Science* **2020**, *368*, 190–194. [CrossRef] [PubMed]
37. Skou, M.G.; Skov, T.G.; Jørgensen, N.B.; Nielsen, K.K.; Camacho-Guardian, A.; Pohl, T.; Bruun, G.M.; Arlt, J.J. Non-equilibrium quantum dynamics and formation of the Bose polaron. *Nat. Phys.* **2021**, *17*, 731–735. [CrossRef]
38. Peña Ardila, L.A.; Jørgensen, N.B.; Pohl, T.; Giorgini, S.; Bruun, G.M.; Arlt, J.J. Analyzing a Bose polaron across resonant interactions. *Phys. Rev. A* **2019**, *99*, 063607. [CrossRef]
39. Palzer, S.; Zipkes, C.; Sias, C.; Köhl, M. Quantum Transport through a Tonks-Girardeau Gas. *Phys. Rev. Lett.* **2009**, *103*, 150601. [CrossRef] [PubMed]
40. Meinert, F.; Knap, M.; Kirilov, E.; Jag-Lauber, K.; Zvonarev, M.B.; Demler, E.; Nägerl, H.C. Bloch oscillations in the absence of a lattice. *Science* **2017**, *356*, 945–948. [CrossRef] [PubMed]
41. Chin, C.; Grimm, R.; Julienne, P.; Tiesinga, E. Feshbach resonances in ultracold gases. *Rev. Mod. Phys.* **2010**, *82*, 1225–1286. [CrossRef]
42. Torma, P. Physics of ultracold Fermi gases revealed by spectroscopies. *Phys. Scr.* **2016**, *91*, 043006. [CrossRef]
43. Vale, C.J.; Zwierlein, M. Spectroscopic probes of quantum gases. *Nat. Phys.* **2021**, *17*, 1305–1315. [CrossRef]
44. Combescot, R.; Giraud, S. Normal State of Highly Polarized Fermi Gases: Full Many-Body Treatment. *Phys. Rev. Lett.* **2008**, *101*, 050404. [CrossRef]
45. Van Houcke, K.; Werner, F.; Rossi, R. High-precision numerical solution of the Fermi polaron problem and large-order behavior of its diagrammatic series. *Phys. Rev. B* **2020**, *101*, 045134. [CrossRef]
46. Liu, W.E.; Levinsen, J.; Parish, M.M. Variational Approach for Impurity Dynamics at Finite Temperature. *Phys. Rev. Lett.* **2019**, *122*, 205301. [CrossRef] [PubMed]
47. Parish, M.M.; Marchetti, F.M.; Lamacraft, A.; Simons, B.D. Finite-temperature phase diagram of a polarized Fermi condensate. *Nat. Phys.* **2007**, *3*, 124–128. [CrossRef]
48. Stoner, E. Atomic moments in ferromagnetic metals and alloys with non-ferromagnetic elements. *Philos. Mag.* **1933**, *15*, 1018–1034. [CrossRef]
49. Pilati, S.; Bertaina, G.; Giorgini, S.; Troyer, M. Itinerant Ferromagnetism of a Repulsive Atomic Fermi Gas: A Quantum Monte Carlo Study. *Phys. Rev. Lett.* **2010**, *105*, 030405. [CrossRef]
50. Chang, S.Y.; Randeria, M.; Trivedi, N. Ferromagnetism in the upper branch of the Feshbach resonance and the hard-sphere Fermi gas. *Proc. Nat. Acad. Sci. USA* **2011**, *108*, 51–54. [CrossRef]
51. Goulko, O.; Mishchenko, A.S.; Prokof'ev, N.; Svistunov, B. Dark continuum in the spectral function of the resonant Fermi polaron. *Phys. Rev. A* **2016**, *94*, 051605. [CrossRef]
52. Goold, J.; Fogarty, T.; Lo Gullo, N.; Paternostro, M.; Busch, T. Orthogonality catastrophe as a consequence of qubit embedding in an ultracold Fermi gas. *Phys. Rev. A* **2011**, *84*, 063632. [CrossRef]
53. Knap, M.; Shashi, A.; Nishida, Y.; Imambekov, A.; Abanin, D.A.; Demler, E. Time-Dependent Impurity in Ultracold Fermions: Orthogonality Catastrophe and Beyond. *Phys. Rev. X* **2012**, *2*, 041020. [CrossRef]
54. Parish, M.M.; Levinsen, J. Quantum dynamics of impurities coupled to a Fermi sea. *Phys. Rev. B* **2016**, *94*, 184303. [CrossRef]
55. Schmidt, R.; Knap, M.; Ivanov, D.A.; You, J.S.; Cetina, M.; Demler, E. Universal many-body response of heavy impurities coupled to a Fermi sea: A review of recent progress. *Rep. Progr. Phys.* **2018**, *81*, 024401. [CrossRef] [PubMed]

56. Amico, A.; Scazza, F.; Valtolina, G.; Tavares, P.E.S.; Ketterle, W.; Inguscio, M.; Roati, G.; Zaccanti, M. Time-Resolved Observation of Competing Attractive and Repulsive Short-Range Correlations in Strongly Interacting Fermi Gases. *Phys. Rev. Lett.* **2018**, *121*, 253602. [CrossRef] [PubMed]
57. Khan, M.M.; Terças, H.; Mendonça, J.T.; Wehr, J.; Charalambous, C.; Lewenstein, M.; Garcia-March, M.A. Quantum dynamics of a Bose polaron in a *d*-dimensional Bose-Einstein condensate. *Phys. Rev. A* **2021**, *103*, 023303. [CrossRef]
58. Seetharam, K.; Shchadilova, Y.; Grusdt, F.; Zvonarev, M.B.; Demler, E. Dynamical Quantum Cherenkov Transition of Fast Impurities in Quantum Liquids. *Phys. Rev. Lett.* **2021**, *127*, 185302. [CrossRef]
59. Prokof'ev, N.; Svistunov, B. Fermi-polaron problem: Diagrammatic Monte Carlo method for divergent sign-alternating series. *Phys. Rev. B* **2008**, *77*, 020408. [CrossRef]
60. Mistakidis, S.I.; Volosniev, A.G.; Barfknecht, R.E.; Fogarty, T.; Busch, T.; Foerster, A.; Schmelcher, P.; Zinner, N.T. Cold atoms in low dimensions—A laboratory for quantum dynamics. *arXiv* **2022**, arXiv:2202.11071.
61. Timmermans, E.; Tommasini, P.; Hussein, M.; Kerman, A. Feshbach resonances in atomic Bose–Einstein condensates. *Phys. Rep.* **1999**, *315*, 199–230. [CrossRef]
62. Sakurai, J.J.; Tuan, S.F. *Modern Quantum Mechanics*; Addison-Wesley Reading: Boston, MA, USA, 1985.
63. Fetter, A.L.; Walecka, J.D. *Quantum Theory of Many-Particle Systems*; Dover: New York, NY, USA, 2003.
64. Tan, S. Energetics of a strongly correlated Fermi gas. *Ann. Phys.* **2008**, *323*, 2952–2970. [CrossRef]
65. Tan, S. Large momentum part of a strongly correlated Fermi gas. *Ann. Phys.* **2008**, *323*, 2971–2986. [CrossRef]
66. Braaten, E.; Platter, L. Exact Relations for a Strongly Interacting Fermi Gas from the Operator Product Expansion. *Phys. Rev. Lett.* **2008**, *100*, 205301. [CrossRef] [PubMed]
67. Liu, W.E.; Shi, Z.Y.; Levinsen, J.; Parish, M.M. Radio-Frequency Response and Contact of Impurities in a Quantum Gas. *Phys. Rev. Lett.* **2020**, *125*, 065301 [CrossRef] [PubMed]
68. Massignan, P.; Pethick, C.J.; Smith, H. Static properties of positive ions in atomic Bose-Einstein condensates. *Phys. Rev. A* **2005**, *71*, 023606. [CrossRef]
69. Werner, F. Virial theorems for trapped cold atoms. *Phys. Rev. A* **2008**, *78*, 025601. [CrossRef]
70. Massignan, P. Polarons and dressed molecules near narrow Feshbach resonances. *Europhys. Lett.* **2012**, *98*, 10012. [CrossRef]
71. Braaten, E.; Kang, D.; Platter, L. Universal Relations for Identical Bosons from Three-Body Physics. *Phys. Rev. Lett.* **2011**, *106*, 153005. [CrossRef]
72. Bishop, R. On the ground state of an impurity in a dilute fermi gas. *Ann. Phys.* **1973**, *78*, 391. [CrossRef]
73. Novikov, A.; Ovchinnikov, M. A diagrammatic calculation of the energy spectrum of quantum impurity in degenerate Bose–Einstein condensate. *J. Phys. Math. Theor.* **2009**, *42*, 135301. [CrossRef]
74. Christensen, R.S.; Levinsen, J.; Bruun, G.M. Quasiparticle Properties of a Mobile Impurity in a Bose-Einstein Condensate. *Phys. Rev. Lett.* **2015**, *115*, 160401. [CrossRef]
75. Trefzger, C.; Castin, Y. Polaron residue and spatial structure in a Fermi gas. *EPL* **2013**, *101*, 30006. [CrossRef]
76. Casteels, W.; Wouters, M. Polaron formation in the vicinity of a narrow Feshbach resonance. *Phys. Rev. A* **2014**, *90*, 043602. [CrossRef]
77. Massignan, P.; Bruun, G.M. Repulsive polarons and itinerant ferromagnetism in strongly polarized Fermi gases. *EPJ D* **2011**, *65*, 83–89. [CrossRef]
78. Cui, X.; Zhai, H. Stability of a fully magnetized ferromagnetic state in repulsively interacting ultracold Fermi gases. *Phys. Rev. A* **2010**, *81*, 041602. [CrossRef]
79. Tajima, H.; Uchino, S. Many Fermi polarons at nonzero temperature. *New J. Phys.* **2018**, *20*, 073048. [CrossRef]
80. Mulkerin, B.C.; Liu, X.J.; Hu, H. Breakdown of the Fermi polaron description near Fermi degeneracy at unitarity. *Ann. Phys.* **2019**, *407*, 29–45. [CrossRef]
81. Tajima, H.; Takahashi, J.; Mistakidis, S.I.; Nakano, E.; Iida, K. Polaron Problems in Ultracold Atoms: Role of a Fermi Sea across Different Spatial Dimensions and Quantum Fluctuations of a Bose Medium. *Atoms* **2021**, *9*, 18. [CrossRef]
82. Hu, H.; Liu, X.J. Fermi polarons at finite temperature: Spectral function and rf spectroscopy. *Phys. Rev. A* **2022**, *105*, 043303. [CrossRef]
83. Schmidt, R.; Enss, T. Excitation spectra and rf response near the polaron-to-molecule transition from the functional renormalization group. *Phys. Rev. A* **2011**, *83*, 063620. [CrossRef]
84. Rath, S.P.; Schmidt, R. Field-theoretical study of the Bose polaron. *Phys. Rev. A* **2013**, *88*, 053632. [CrossRef]
85. Guenther, N.E.; Massignan, P.; Lewenstein, M.; Bruun, G.M. Bose Polarons at Finite Temperature and Strong Coupling. *Phys. Rev. Lett.* **2018**, *120*, 050405. [CrossRef]
86. Li, W.; Das Sarma, S. Variational study of polarons in Bose-Einstein condensates. *Phys. Rev. A* **2014**, *90*, 013618 [CrossRef]
87. Shchadilova, Y.E.; Schmidt, R.; Grusdt, F.; Demler, E. Quantum Dynamics of Ultracold Bose Polarons. *Phys. Rev. Lett.* **2016**, *117*, 113002. [CrossRef] [PubMed]
88. Field, B.; Levinsen, J.; Parish, M.M. Fate of the Bose polaron at finite temperature. *Phys. Rev. A* **2020**, *101*, 013623. [CrossRef]
89. Peña Ardila, L.A.; Giorgini, S. Impurity in a Bose-Einstein condensate: Study of the attractive and repulsive branch using quantum Monte Carlo methods. *Phys. Rev. A* **2015**, *92*, 033612. [CrossRef]
90. Peña Ardila, L.A.; Astrakharchik, G.E.; Giorgini, S. Strong coupling Bose polarons in a two-dimensional gas. *Phys. Rev. Research* **2020**, *2*, 023405. [CrossRef]

91. Sun, M.; Zhai, H.; Cui, X. Visualizing the Efimov Correlation in Bose Polarons. *Phys. Rev. Lett.* **2017**, *119*, 013401. [CrossRef]
92. Grusdt, F.; Seetharam, K.; Shchadilova, Y.; Demler, E. Strong-coupling Bose polarons out of equilibrium: Dynamical renormalization-group approach. *Phys. Rev. A* **2018**, *97*, 033612. [CrossRef]
93. Isaule, F.; Morera, I.; Massignan, P.; Juliá-Díaz, B. Renormalization-group study of Bose polarons. *Phys. Rev. A* **2021**, *104*, 023317. [CrossRef]
94. Punk, M.; Zwerger, W. Theory of rf-Spectroscopy of Strongly Interacting Fermions. *Phys. Rev. Lett.* **2007**, *99*, 170404. [CrossRef] [PubMed]
95. Massignan, P.; Bruun, G.M.; Stoof, H.T.C. Twin peaks in rf spectra of Fermi gases at unitarity. *Phys. Rev. A* **2008**, *77*, 031601. [CrossRef]
96. Scazza, F.; Hofrichter, C.; Höfer, M.; De Groot, P.C.; Bloch, I.; Fölling, S. Observation of two-orbital spin-exchange interactions with ultracold SU(N)-symmetric fermions. *Nat. Phys.* **2014**, *10*, 779. [CrossRef]
97. Höfer, M.; Riegger, L.; Scazza, F.; Hofrichter, C.; Fernandes, D.R.; Parish, M.M.; Levinsen, J.; Bloch, I.; Fölling, S. Observation of an Orbital Interaction-Induced Feshbach Resonance in ^{173}Yb. *Phys. Rev. Lett.* **2015**, *115*, 265302. [CrossRef]
98. Liu, W.E.; Shi, Z.Y.; Parish, M.M.; Levinsen, J. Theory of radio-frequency spectroscopy of impurities in quantum gases. *Phys. Rev. A* **2020**, *102*, 023304. [CrossRef]
99. Braaten, E.; Kang, D.; Platter, L. Short-Time Operator Product Expansion for rf Spectroscopy of a Strongly Interacting Fermi Gas. *Phys. Rev. Lett.* **2010**, *104*, 223004. [CrossRef] [PubMed]
100. Guenther, N.E.; Schmidt, R.; Bruun, G.M.; Gurarie, V.; Massignan, P. Mobile impurity in a Bose-Einstein condensate and the orthogonality catastrophe. *Phys. Rev. A* **2021**, *103*, 013317. [CrossRef]
101. Punk, M.; Dumitrescu, P.T.; Zwerger, W. Polaron-to-molecule transition in a strongly imbalanced Fermi gas. *Phys. Rev. A* **2009**, *80*, 053605. [CrossRef]
102. Combescot, R.; Giraud, S.; Leyronas, X. Analytical theory of the dressed bound state in highly polarized Fermi gases. *Europhys. Lett.* **2009**, *88*, 60007. [CrossRef]
103. Bruun, G.M.; Recati, A.; Pethick, C.J.; Smith, H.; Stringari, S. Collisional Properties of a Polarized Fermi Gas with Resonant Interactions. *Phys. Rev. Lett.* **2008**, *100*, 240406. [CrossRef]
104. Trefzger, C.; Castin, Y. Impurity in a Fermi sea on a narrow Feshbach resonance: A variational study of the polaronic and dimeronic branches. *Phys. Rev. A* **2012**, *85*, 053612. [CrossRef]
105. Petrov, D.S. Three-body problem in Fermi gases with short-range interparticle interaction. *Phys. Rev. A* **2003**, *67*, 010703. [CrossRef]
106. Sanner, C.; Su, E.J.; Huang, W.; Keshet, A.; Gillen, J.; Ketterle, W. Correlations and Pair Formation in a Repulsively Interacting Fermi Gas. *Phys. Rev. Lett.* **2012**, *108*, 240404. [CrossRef] [PubMed]
107. Chen, X.Y.; Duda, M.; Schindewolf, A.; Bause, R.; Bloch, I.; Luo, X.Y. Suppression of Unitary Three-Body Loss in a Degenerate Bose–Fermi Mixture. *Phys. Rev. Lett.* **2022**, *128*, 153401. [CrossRef]
108. Braaten, E.; Hammer, H.W. Universality in few-body systems with large scattering length. *Phys. Rep.* **2006**, *428*, 259–390. [CrossRef]
109. Chevy, F. Universal phase diagram of a strongly interacting Fermi gas with unbalanced spin populations. *Phys. Rev. A* **2006**, *74*, 063628. [CrossRef]
110. Combescot, R.; Recati, A.; Lobo, C.; Chevy, F. Normal State of Highly Polarized Fermi Gases: Simple Many-Body Approaches. *Phys. Rev. Lett.* **2007**, *98*, 180402. [CrossRef] [PubMed]
111. Pines, D.; Noziéres, P. *Theory of Quantum Liquids: Normal Fermi Liquids*; Addison-Wesley: New York, NY, USA, 1966.
112. Anderson, P.W. Infrared Catastrophe in Fermi Gases with Local Scattering Potentials. *Phys. Rev. Lett.* **1967**, *18*, 1049. [CrossRef]
113. Drescher, M.; Salmhofer, M.; Enss, T. Quench Dynamics of the Ideal Bose Polaron at Zero and Nonzero Temperatures. *Phys. Rev. A* **2021**, *103*, 033317. [CrossRef]
114. Yoshida, S.M.; Endo, S.; Levinsen, J.; Parish, M.M. Universality of an Impurity in a Bose-Einstein Condensate. *Phys. Rev. X* **2018**, *8*, 011024. [CrossRef]
115. Mistakidis, S.I.; Katsimiga, G.C.; Koutentakis, G.M.; Busch, T.; Schmelcher, P. Quench Dynamics and Orthogonality Catastrophe of Bose Polarons. *Phys. Rev. Lett.* **2019**, *122*, 183001. [CrossRef]
116. Levinsen, J.; Ardila, L.A.P.n.; Yoshida, S.M.; Parish, M.M. Quantum Behavior of a Heavy Impurity Strongly Coupled to a Bose Gas. *Phys. Rev. Lett.* **2021**, *127*, 033401. [CrossRef]
117. Viverit, L.; Pethick, C.J.; Smith, H. Zero-temperature phase diagram of binary boson-fermion mixtures. *Phys. Rev. A* **2000**, *61*, 053605. [CrossRef]
118. Yu, Z.; Zöllner, S.; Pethick, C.J. Comment on "Normal Phase of an Imbalanced Fermi Gas". *Phys. Rev. Lett.* **2010**, *105*, 188901. [CrossRef] [PubMed]
119. Yu, Z.; Pethick, C.J. Induced interactions in dilute atomic gases and liquid helium mixtures. *Phys. Rev. A* **2012**, *85*, 063616. [CrossRef]
120. Pethick, C.; Smith, H. *Bose–Einstein Condensation in Dilute Gases*; Cambridge University Press: Cambridge, UK, 2008.
121. DeSalvo, B.J.; Patel, K.; Cai, G.; Chin, C. Observation of fermion-mediated interactions between bosonic atoms. *Nature* **2019**, *568*, 61–64. [CrossRef] [PubMed]

122. Lous, R.S.; Fritsche, I.; Jag, M.; Lehmann, F.; Kirilov, E.; Huang, B.; Grimm, R. Probing the Interface of a Phase-Separated State in a Repulsive Bose–Fermi Mixture. *Phys. Rev. Lett.* **2018**, *120*, 243403. [CrossRef] [PubMed]
123. Huang, B.; Fritsche, I.; Lous, R.S.; Baroni, C.; Walraven, J.T.M.; Kirilov, E.; Grimm, R. Breathing mode of a Bose-Einstein condensate repulsively interacting with a fermionic reservoir. *Phys. Rev. A* **2019**, *99*, 041602. [CrossRef]
124. Mora, C.; Chevy, F. Normal Phase of an Imbalanced Fermi Gas. *Phys. Rev. Lett.* **2010**, *104*, 230402. [CrossRef]
125. Nascimbène, S.; Navon, N.; Jiang, K.J.; Chevy, F.; Salomon, C. Exploring the thermodynamics of a universal Fermi gas. *Nature* **2010**, *463*, 1057–1060. [CrossRef]
126. Ho, T.L.; Zhou, Q. Obtaining the phase diagram and thermodynamic quantities of bulk systems from the densities of trapped gases. *Nat. Phys.* **2010**, *6*, 131–134. [CrossRef]
127. Pilati, S.; Giorgini, S. Phase Separation in a Polarized Fermi Gas at Zero Temperature. *Phys. Rev. Lett.* **2008**, *100*, 030401. [CrossRef]
128. Camacho-Guardian, A.; Bruun, G.M. Landau Effective Interaction between Quasiparticles in a Bose-Einstein Condensate. *Phys. Rev. X* **2018**, *8*, 031042 [CrossRef]
129. Zwerger, W. *The BCS-BEC Crossover and the Unitary Fermi Gas*; Springer Science & Business Media: Berlin/Heidelberg, Germany, 2011; Volume 836.
130. Ngampruetikorn, V. *Low-Dimensional Fermi Gases: From Few to Many-Body Physics*; Ph.D. Thesis, University of Cambridge, Cambridge, UK, 2015.
131. Parish, M.M.; Adlong, H.S.; Liu, W.E.; Levinsen, J. Thermodynamic signatures of the polaron-molecule transition in a Fermi gas. *Phys. Rev. A* **2021**, *103* 023312. [CrossRef]
132. Pekker, D.; Babadi, M.; Sensarma, R.; Zinner, N.; Pollet, L.; Zwierlein, M.W.; Demler, E. Competition between Pairing and Ferromagnetic Instabilities in Ultracold Fermi Gases near Feshbach Resonances. *Phys. Rev. Lett.* **2011**, *106*, 050402. [CrossRef] [PubMed]
133. Valtolina, G.; Scazza, F.; Amico, A.; Burchianti, A.; Recati, A.; Enss, T.; Inguscio, M.; Zaccanti, M.; Roati, G. Exploring the ferromagnetic behaviour of a repulsive Fermi gas through spin dynamics. *Nat. Phys.* **2017**, *13*, 704–709. [CrossRef]
134. Recati, A.; Stringari, S. Spin Fluctuations, Susceptibility, and the Dipole Oscillation of a Nearly Ferromagnetic Fermi Gas. *Phys. Rev. Lett.* **2011**, *106*, 080402. [CrossRef]
135. Grochowski, P.T.; Karpiuk, T.; Brewczyk, M.; Rzkażewski, K. Unified Description of Dynamics of a Repulsive Two-Component Fermi Gas. *Phys. Rev. Lett.* **2017**, *119*, 215303. [CrossRef]
136. Scazza, F.; Valtolina, G.; Amico, A.; Tavares, P.E.S.; Inguscio, M.; Ketterle, W.; Roati, G.; Zaccanti, M. Exploring emergent heterogeneous phases in strongly repulsive Fermi gases. *Phys. Rev. A* **2020**, *101*, 013603. [CrossRef]
137. Dagotto, E.; Burgy, J.; Moreo, A. Nanoscale phase separation in colossal magnetoresistance materials: Lessons for the cuprates? *Solid State Commun.* **2003**, *126*, 9–22. [CrossRef]
138. Dagotto, E. Complexity in Strongly Correlated Electronic Systems. *Science* **2005**, *309*, 257–262. [CrossRef]
139. Petrov, D.S. Quantum Mechanical Stabilization of a Collapsing Bose–Bose Mixture. *Phys. Rev. Lett.* **2015**, *115*, 155302. [CrossRef]
140. Navon, N.; Smith, R.P.; Hadzibabic, Z. Quantum gases in optical boxes. *Nat. Phys.* **2021**, *17*, 1334–1341. [CrossRef]
141. Pilati, S.; Zintchenko, I.; Troyer, M. Ferromagnetism of a Repulsive Atomic Fermi Gas in an Optical Lattice: A Quantum Monte Carlo Study. *Phys. Rev. Lett.* **2014**, *112*, 015301. [CrossRef] [PubMed]
142. Zintchenko, I.; Wang, L.; Troyer, M. Ferromagnetism of the repulsive atomic Fermi gas: Three-body recombination and domain formation. *EPJ B* **2016**, *89*, 180. [CrossRef]
143. Conduit, G.J. Itinerant ferromagnetism in a two-dimensional atomic gas. *Phys. Rev. A* **2010**, *82*, 043604. [CrossRef]
144. Cui, X.; Ho, T.L. Ground-state ferromagnetic transition in strongly repulsive one-dimensional Fermi gases. *Phys. Rev. A* **2014**, *89*, 023611. [CrossRef]
145. Gross, C.; Bloch, I. Quantum simulations with ultracold atoms in optical lattices. *Science* **2017**, *357*, 995–1001. [CrossRef]
146. Casalbuoni, R.; Nardulli, G. Inhomogeneous superconductivity in condensed matter and QCD. *Rev. Mod. Phys.* **2004**, *76*, 263–320. [CrossRef]
147. Fukushima, K.; Hatsuda, T. The phase diagram of dense QCD. *Rep. Progr. Phys.* **2010**, *74*, 014001. [CrossRef]
148. Magierski, P.; Tüzemen, B.; Wlazłowski, G. Spin-polarized droplets in the unitary Fermi gas. *Phys. Rev. A* **2019**, *100*, 033613. [CrossRef]
149. Hu, H.; Wang, A.B.; Yi, S.; Liu, X.J. Fermi polaron in a one-dimensional quasiperiodic optical lattice: The simplest many-body localization challenge. *Phys. Rev. A* **2016**, *93*, 053601. [CrossRef]
150. Büchler, H.P. Microscopic Derivation of Hubbard Parameters for Cold Atomic Gases. *Phys. Rev. Lett.* **2010**, *104*, 090402. [CrossRef] [PubMed]
151. Ashida, Y.; Schmidt, R.; Tarruell, L.; Demler, E. Many-body interferometry of magnetic polaron dynamics. *Phys. Rev. B* **2018**, *97*, 060302. [CrossRef]
152. Koepsell, J.; Vijayan, J.; Sompet, P.; Grusdt, F.; Hilker, T.A.; Demler, E. Salomon, G.; Bloch, I.; Gross, C. Imaging magnetic polarons in the doped Fermi–Hubbard model. *Nature* **2019**, *572*, 358–362. [CrossRef]
153. Ji, G.; Xu, M.; Kendrick, L.H.; Chiu, C.S.; Brüggenjürgen, J.C.; Greif, D.; Bohrdt, A.; Grusdt, F.; Demler, E.; Lebrat, M.; et al. Coupling a Mobile Hole to an Antiferromagnetic Spin Background: Transient Dynamics of a Magnetic Polaron. *Phys. Rev. X* **2021**, *11*, 021022. [CrossRef]

154. Kane, C.L.; Lee, P.A.; Read, N. Motion of a single hole in a quantum antiferromagnet. *Phys. Rev. B* **1989**, *39*, 6880–6897. [CrossRef]
155. Grusdt, F.; Kánasz-Nagy, M.; Bohrdt, A.; Chiu, C.S.; Ji, G.; Greiner, M.; Greif, D.; Demler, E. Parton Theory of Magnetic Polarons: Mesonic Resonances and Signatures in Dynamics. *Phys. Rev. X* **2018**, *8*, 011046. [CrossRef]
156. Grusdt, F.; Bohrdt, A.; Demler, E. Microscopic spinon-chargon theory of magnetic polarons in the $t-J$ model. *Phys. Rev. B* **2019**, *99*, 224422. [CrossRef]
157. Blomquist, E.; Carlström, J. Unbiased description of magnetic polarons in a Mott insulator. *Commun. Phys.* **2020**, *3*, 172. [CrossRef]
158. Nielsen, K.K.; Bastarrachea-Magnani, M.A.; Pohl, T.; Bruun, G.M. Spatial structure of magnetic polarons in strongly interacting antiferromagnets. *Phys. Rev. B* **2021**, *104*, 155136. [CrossRef]
159. Lee, P.A.; Nagaosa, N.; Wen, X.G. Doping a Mott insulator: Physics of high-temperature superconductivity. *Rev. Mod. Phys.* **2006**, *78*, 17–85. [CrossRef]
160. Efimkin, D.K.; MacDonald, A.H. Many-body theory of trion absorption features in two-dimensional semiconductors. *Phys. Rev. B* **2017**, *95*, 035417. [CrossRef]
161. Efimkin, D.K.; MacDonald, A.H. Exciton-polarons in doped semiconductors in a strong magnetic field. *Phys. Rev. B* **2018**, *97*, 235432. [CrossRef]
162. Smoleński, T.; Cotlet, O.; Popert, A.; Back, P.; Shimazaki, Y.; Knüppel, P.; Dietler, N.; Taniguchi, T.; Watanabe, K.; Kroner, M.; et al. Interaction-Induced Shubnikov–de Haas Oscillations in Optical Conductivity of Monolayer $MoSe_2$. *Phys. Rev. Lett.* **2019**, *123*, 097403. [CrossRef] [PubMed]
163. Levinsen, J.; Marchetti, F.M.; Keeling, J.; Parish, M.M. Spectroscopic Signatures of Quantum Many-Body Correlations in Polariton Microcavities. *Phys. Rev. Lett.* **2019**, *123*, 266401. [CrossRef] [PubMed]
164. Cotleţ, O.; Zeytinoğlu, S.; Sigrist, M.; Demler, E.; Imamoğlu, A. Superconductivity and other collective phenomena in a hybrid Bose–Fermi mixture formed by a polariton condensate and an electron system in two dimensions. *Phys. Rev. B* **2016**, *93*, 054510. [CrossRef]

Article

Polaron Problems in Ultracold Atoms: Role of a Fermi Sea across Different Spatial Dimensions and Quantum Fluctuations of a Bose Medium

Hiroyuki Tajima [1,*], Junichi Takahashi [2], Simeon I. Mistakidis [3], Eiji Nakano [1] and Kei Iida [1]

1 Department of Mathematics and Physics, Kochi University, Kochi 780-8520, Japan; e.nakano@kochi-u.ac.jp (E.N.); iida@kochi-u.ac.jp (K.I.)
2 Department of Electronic and Physical Systems, Waseda University, Tokyo 169-8555, Japan; takahashi.j@aoni.waseda.jp
3 Center for Optical Quantum Technologies, Department of Physics, University of Hamburg, Luruper Chaussee 149, 22761 Hamburg, Germany; smistaki@physnet.uni-hamburg.de
* Correspondence: hiroyuki.tajima@riken.jp

Citation: Tajima, H.; Takahashi, J.; Mistakidis, S.I.; Nakano, E.; Iida, K Polaron Problems in Ultracold Atoms: Role of a Fermi Sea across Different Spatial Dimensions and Quantum Fluctuations of a Bose Medium. *Atoms* 2021, 9, 18. https://doi.org/10.3390/atoms9010018

Received: 19 January 2021
Accepted: 3 March 2021
Published: 9 March 2021

Publisher's Note: MDPI stays neutral with regard to jurisdictional claims in published maps and institutional affiliations.

Copyright: © 2021 by the authors. Licensee MDPI, Basel, Switzerland. This article is an open access article distributed under the terms and conditions of the Creative Commons Attribution (CC BY) license (https://creativecommons.org/licenses/by/4.0/).

Abstract: The notion of a polaron, originally introduced in the context of electrons in ionic lattices, helps us to understand how a quantum impurity behaves when being immersed in and interacting with a many-body background. We discuss the impact of the impurities on the medium particles by considering feedback effects from polarons that can be realized in ultracold quantum gas experiments. In particular, we exemplify the modifications of the medium in the presence of either Fermi or Bose polarons. Regarding Fermi polarons we present a corresponding many-body diagrammatic approach operating at finite temperatures and discuss how mediated two- and three-body interactions are implemented within this framework. Utilizing this approach, we analyze the behavior of the spectral function of Fermi polarons at finite temperature by varying impurity-medium interactions as well as spatial dimensions from three to one. Interestingly, we reveal that the spectral function of the medium atoms could be a useful quantity for analyzing the transition/crossover from attractive polarons to molecules in three-dimensions. As for the Bose polaron, we showcase the depletion of the background Bose-Einstein condensate in the vicinity of the impurity atom. Such spatial modulations would be important for future investigations regarding the quantification of interpolaron correlations in Bose polaron problems.

Keywords: polaron; impurity; spectroscopy of quasiparticles; interpolaron correlations; quantum depletion; ultracold atoms; Bose–Einstein condensate; Fermi degenerate gases

1. Introduction

The quantum many-body problem, which is one of the central issues of modern physics, is encountered in various research fields such as condensed matter and nuclear physics. The major obstacle that prevents their adequate description stems from the presence of many degrees-of-freedom as well as strong correlations. The polaron concept, which was originally proposed by S. I. Pekar and L. Landau [1,2] to characterize electron properties in crystals, provides a useful playground for understanding related nontrivial many-body aspects of quantum matter and interactions. For instance, a key advantage of the polaron picture is that, under specific circumstances, it enables the reduction of a complicated many-body problem to an effective single-particle or a few-body one with renormalized parameters. In the last decade, the polaron concept has been intensively studied for two-component ultracold mixtures, where a minority component is embedded in a majority one (host) and becomes dressed by the low-energy excitations of the latter forming a polaron. Indeed, ultracold atoms, owing to the excellent controllability of the involved system parameters, are utilized to quantitatively determine polaron properties, as has been demonstrated in a variety of relevant experimental efforts. These include, for instance, the measurement of the quasiparticle excitation spectra [3–12], monitoring the quantum dynamics of impurities [13,14], the observation of a phononic Lamb shift [15], the estimation of relevant thermodynamic quantities [16,17], the identification of medium induced interactions [18,19], and polariton properties [20–22].

Polarons basically appear in two different types, namely, Fermi and Bose polarons where the impurity atoms are immersed in a Fermi sea and a Bose-Einstein condensate (BEC) respectively. Both cases are experimentally realizable by employing a mixture of atoms residing in different hyperfine states or using distinct isotopes. The impurity-medium interaction strength can be flexibly adjusted with the aid of Feshbach resonances [23], and as such strong interactions between the impurity and the majority atoms can be achieved. Due to this non-zero interaction, the impurities are subsequently dressed by the elementary excitations of their background atoms, leading to a quasi-particle state that is called the polaron. In that light, the polaron and more generally the quasiparticle generation is inherently related to the build-up of strong entanglement among the impurities and their background medium [24–26]. Moreover, since various situations such as mass-imbalanced [5], low-dimensional [6], and multi-orbital [11] ultracold settings can be realized, atomic polarons can also be expected to be quantum simulators of quasiparticle states in nuclear physics [27–31]. Recently, a Rydberg Fermi polaron has also been discussed theoretically [32].

The single-particle character of polarons has been intensively investigated theoretically in the past few years by using different approaches [33–50] ranging from variational treatments [33–36] to diagrammatic Monte-Carlo simulations [42–47]. Interestingly, a multitude of experimental observations regarding polaronic excitations have been well described based on theoretical frameworks relying on the single-polaron ansatz [3,4,10]. However, it is still a challenging problem and highly unexplored topic how many polaron systems behave, especially during their nonequilibrium dynamics. While the single-polaron analysis clarifies the mechanism of polaron formation via the dressing from the surrounding majority cloud, the many-polaron study is dedicated to the question of how polarons interact with each other through the exchange of the excitations of their host. Therefore, the background medium plays a crucial role in understanding many-polaron physics. In this sense, the concept of induced interpolaron interactions has attracted a tremendous attention [51–61]. For instance, in recent experiments, the sizable shift of the effective scattering length due to the fermion-mediated interaction has been observed in Fermi polaron systems [18,19]. The corresponding impact on the medium atoms due to the presence of strong impurity-bath correlations is under active investigation [55]. In the case of Bose polarons [7–9,13–15,62–67], the influence of the impurities on their environment (BEC) is more pronounced when compared to Fermi polarons due to the absence of the Pauli blocking effect. Characteristic examples, here, constitute the self-localization [68–73] and temporal orthogonality catastrophe [24] phenomena as well as complex tunneling [74–77] and emergent relaxation processes [60,78]. They originate from the presence of the impurity which imprints significant deformations to its environment when the interaction between the subsystems is finite.

In this work, we first provide a discussion on the role of the background atoms in many-polaron problems that are tractable in ultracold atom settings. Particularly, we present diagrammatic approaches to Fermi polaron systems and elaborate on how mediated two- and three-body interpolation interactions are consistently taken into account within these frameworks [55,56]. Importantly, a comparison of the Fermi polaron excitation spectral function in three dimensions (3D) and at finite temperatures is performed among different variants of the diagrammatic T-matrix approach. Namely, the usual T-matrix approach (TMA) which is based on the self-energy including the repeated particle-particle scattering processes consisting of bare propagators [79,80], the extended T-matrix approach (ETMA) where the bare propagator in the self-energy is partially replaced [81–83], and the self-consistent T-matrix approach where all the propagators in the self-energy consist of dressed ones [84,85] are employed. We reveal how medium-induced interactions are involved in these approaches and examine their effects in mass-balanced Fermi polaron settings realized, e.g., in ^{6}Li atomic mixtures. Subsequently, we discuss the polaron excitation spectrum in two (2D) and one (1D) spatial dimensions. The behavior of the spectral function of the host and the impurities at strong impurity-medium interactions is exemplified. Finally, the real-space Bogoliubov approach to Bose polarons in 3D is reviewed. The latter allows us to unveil the condensate deformation due to the presence of the impurity and appreciate the resultant quantum fluctuations [86]. We argue that the degree of the quantum depletion of the condensate decreases (increases) for repulsive (attractive) impurity-medium interactions, a result that is associated with the deformation of its density distribution. This is in contrast to homogeneous setups where the depletion increases independently of the sign of the interaction.

This work is organized as follows. In Section 2, we present the model Hamiltonian describing ultracold Fermi polarons in 3D. For the Fermi polaron, we consider uniform systems and develop the concept of the diagrammatic T-matrix approximation. After explaining the ingredients of the diagrammatic approaches in some detail, we clarify how mediated two- and three-body interactions are incorporated in these approaches. The behavior of the resultant polaron spectral function at finite temperatures and impurity concentrations in three-, two-, and one-dimensions is discussed. In Section 3, we utilize the real-space mean-field formulation for Bose polarons and expose the presence of quantum depletion for the three-dimensional trapped Bose polaron at zero temperature. In Section 4, we summarize our results and provide future perspectives. For convenience, in what follows, we use $k_B = \hbar = 1$.

2. Fermi Polarons

2.1. T-Matrix Approach to Fermi Polaron Problems

Here we explain the concept of many-body diagrammatic approaches to Fermi polarons, namely, settings referring to the situation where fermionic impurity atoms are immersed in a uniform Fermi gas. Since such a two-component Fermi mixture mimics spin-1/2 electrons, we denote the bath component as $\sigma = B = \uparrow$ and the impurity one by $\sigma = I = \downarrow$. Note that these are standard conventions without loss of generality. The model Hamiltonian describing this system reads

$$H = \sum_{p,\sigma} \xi_{p,\sigma} c^\dagger_{p,\sigma} c_{p,\sigma} + g \sum_{p,p',q} c^\dagger_{p+q/2,\uparrow} c^\dagger_{-p+q/2,\downarrow} c_{-p'+q/2,\downarrow} c_{p'+q/2,\uparrow}, \quad (1)$$

where $\xi_{p,\sigma} = p^2/(2m_\sigma) - \mu_\sigma$ is the kinetic energy minus the chemical potential μ_σ, and m_σ is the atomic mass of the σ component. The parameters $c_{p,\sigma}$ and $c^\dagger_{p,\sigma}$ refer to the annihilation and creation operators of a σ component fermion, respectively, possessing momentum p.

We measure the effective coupling constant g of the contact-type interaction between two different component fermions by using the low-energy scattering parameter, namely, the scattering length a. In 3D, it is known [87] that the coupling constant g_{3D} and the scattering length a are related via

$$\frac{m_r}{2\pi a} = \frac{1}{g_{3D}} + \frac{m_r \Lambda}{\pi^2}, \quad (2)$$

with $m_r^{-1} = m_\uparrow^{-1} + m_\downarrow^{-1}$ being the reduced mass. In this expression, the momentum cutoff Λ is introduced to avoid an ultraviolet divergence in the momentum summation of the Lippmann–Schwinger equation expressed in momentum space. This allows us to achieve the effective short-range interaction of finite range $r_e \propto 1/\Lambda$. Similarly, the relevant relations in 2D and 1D read [88]

$$a_{2D} = \frac{1}{\Lambda} e^{-\frac{\pi}{m_r g_{2D}}}, \quad \text{and} \quad a_{1D} = \frac{1}{m_r g_{1D}}, \quad (3)$$

respectively, where g_{2D} and g_{1D} are the coupling constants in 2D and 1D.

First, we introduce a thermal single-particle Green's function [89]

$$G_\sigma(\mathbf{p}, i\omega_n) = \frac{1}{i\omega_n - \xi_{\mathbf{p},\sigma} - \Sigma_\sigma(\mathbf{p}, i\omega_n)}, \quad (4)$$

where $\omega_n = (2n+1)\pi T$ is the fermion Matsubara frequency introduced within the finite-temperature T formalism and $n \in \mathbb{Z}$ [89]. The effect of the impurity-medium interaction is taken into account in the self-energy $\Sigma_\sigma(\mathbf{p}, i\omega_n)$. The excitation spectrum $A_\downarrow(\mathbf{p}, \omega)$ of a Fermi polaron can be obtained via the retarded Green's function $G_\downarrow^R(\mathbf{p}, \omega) = G_\downarrow(\mathbf{p}, i\omega_n \to \omega + i\delta)$ (where δ is a positive infinitesimal) through analytic continuation [89]. In particular, it can be shown that

$$A_\downarrow(\mathbf{p}, \omega) = -\frac{1}{\pi} \mathrm{Im} G_\downarrow^R(\mathbf{p}, \omega). \quad (5)$$

Experimentally, this quantity can be monitored by using a radio-frequency (rf) spectroscopy scheme where the atoms are transferred from their thermal equilibrium state to a specific spin state which interacts with the medium [90]. Indeed, the reverse rf response $I_r(\omega)$ [10] and the ejection one $I_e(\omega)$ [16] are given by

$$I_r(\omega) = 2\pi \Omega_{\mathrm{Rabi}}^2 \sum_{\mathbf{p}} f(\xi_{\mathbf{p},i}) A_\downarrow(\mathbf{p}, \omega + \xi_{\mathbf{p},\downarrow}) \quad (6)$$

and

$$I_e(\omega) = 2\pi \Omega_{\mathrm{Rabi}}^2 \sum_{\mathbf{p}} f(\xi_{\mathbf{p},\downarrow} - \omega) A_\downarrow(\mathbf{p}, \xi_{\mathbf{p},\downarrow} - \omega), \quad (7)$$

respectively. Here, $\xi_{\mathbf{p},i}$ represents the kinetic energy of the initial state in the reverse rf scheme. In Equations (6) and (7), Ω_{Rabi} is the Rabi frequency.

Importantly, the self-energy $\Sigma_\uparrow(\mathbf{p}, i\omega_n)$ of the background plays an important role in describing the mediated interpolaron interactions. This fact will be evinced below and it is achieved by expanding $\Sigma_\uparrow(\mathbf{p}, i\omega_n)$ with respect to G_σ and G_σ^0. The chemical potentials μ_σ are kept fixed by imposing the particle number conservation condition obeying

$$N_\sigma = T \sum_{\mathbf{p}, i\omega_n} G_\sigma(\mathbf{p}, i\omega_n). \quad (8)$$

Moreover, in the remainder of this work, we define the impurity concentration as follows

$$x = \frac{N_\downarrow}{N_\uparrow}. \quad (9)$$

Additionally, within the TMA [34,54] the self-energy $\Sigma_\sigma(\mathbf{p}, i\omega_n)$ of the σ component reads

$$\Sigma_\sigma(\mathbf{p}, i\omega_n) = T \sum_{\mathbf{q}, i\nu_\ell} \Gamma(\mathbf{q}, i\nu_\ell) G_{-\sigma}^0(\mathbf{q} - \mathbf{p}, i\nu_\ell - i\omega_n), \quad (10)$$

where $\Gamma(\mathbf{q}, i\nu_\ell)$ is the many-body T-matrix, as diagrammatically shown in Figure 1a, with the boson Matsubara frequency $i\nu_\ell = 2\ell\pi T$ ($\ell \in \mathbb{Z}$). Here, $G_\sigma^0(\mathbf{p}, i\omega_n) = (i\omega_n - \xi_{\mathbf{p},\sigma})^{-1}$ is the bare thermal single-particle Green's function. Furthermore, by adopting a ladder approximation illustrated in Figure 1d, the T-matrix $\Gamma(\mathbf{q}, i\nu_\ell)$ is given by

$$\Gamma(\mathbf{q}, i\nu_\ell) = \frac{g}{1 + g\Pi(\mathbf{q}, i\nu_\ell)}, \quad (11)$$

where

$$\Pi(\boldsymbol{q}, i\nu_\ell) = T \sum_{\boldsymbol{p}, i\omega_n} G^0_\uparrow(\boldsymbol{p}+\boldsymbol{q}, i\omega_n + i\nu_\ell) G^0_\downarrow(-\boldsymbol{p}, -i\omega_n) \qquad (12)$$

is the lowest-order particle-particle bubble. The latter describes a virtual particle-particle scattering process associated with the impurity-medium interaction g which is replaced by g_{3D}, g_{2D}, and g_{1D} in 3D, 2D, and 1D, respectively. Note that in Equation (10) the impurity-impurity interaction is not taken into account.

The extended T-matrix approach (ETMA) [55] constitutes an improved approximation that allows us to take the induced polaron-polaron interactions into account in a self-consistent way. In this method, as depicted in Figure 1b we include higher-order correlations by replacing the bare Green function G^0 in Equation (10) with the dressed one G_σ. Namely

$$\Sigma^E_\sigma(\boldsymbol{p}, i\omega_n) = T \sum_{\boldsymbol{q}, i\nu_\ell} \Gamma(\boldsymbol{q}, i\nu_\ell) G_{-\sigma}(\boldsymbol{q}-\boldsymbol{p}, i\nu_\ell - i\omega_n). \qquad (13)$$

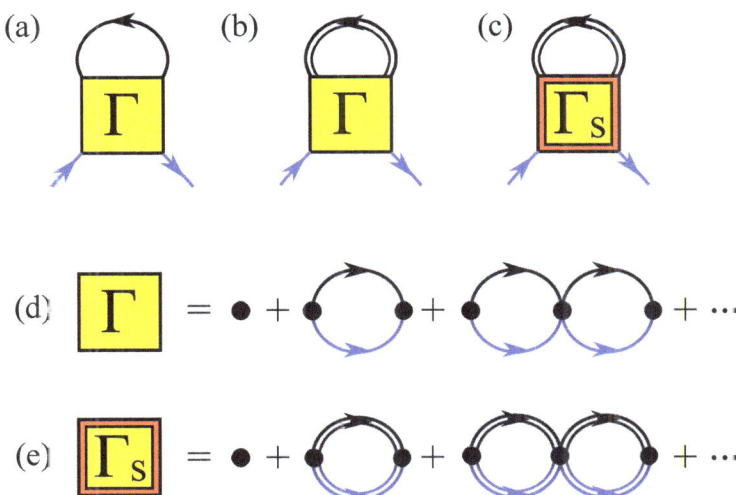

Figure 1. Feynman diagrams for (**a**) the T-matrix approach (TMA), (**b**) the extended T-matrix approach (ETMA), and (**c**) the self-consistent T-matrix approach (SCTMA). Γ and Γ_S are the many-body T-matrices, whose perturbative expansions are shown schematically in (**d**,**e**), consisting of bare and dressed propagators G^0_σ and G_σ, respectively. While in TMA, all the lines in the self-energy (**a**) consist of G^0_σ, they are replaced with G_σ partially (upper loop of (**b**)) in ETMA and fully in SCTMA (**c**) (see also (**e**) where G^0_σ is replaced by G_σ compared to (**d**)), respectively.

Importantly, the TMA and ETMA approaches are equivalent to each other in the single-polaron limit i.e., $x \to 0$, where the self-energy of the fermionic medium $\Sigma^E_\uparrow$ (capturing the difference between $G^0_\uparrow$ and $G_\uparrow$ in Equations (10) and (13), respectively) is negligible. Additionally, at zero temperature, these two treatments coincide with the variational ansatz proposed by F. Chevy [33]. Recall that $\mu_\uparrow = E_F$ and $\mu_\downarrow = E_P^{(a)}$ at $T = 0$ and $x \to 0$, where $E_F = p_F^2/(2m_\uparrow)$ denotes the Fermi energy of the majority component atoms while $E_P^{(a)}$ corresponds to the attractive polaron energy.

Proceeding one step further, it is possible to construct the so-called self-consistent T-matrix approach (SCTMA) [56,91,92] which deploys the many-body T-matrix Γ_S composed of dressed propagators as schematically shown in Figure 1e. In particular, the corresponding T-matrix is given by

$$\Gamma_S(q, i\nu_\ell) = \frac{g}{1 + g\Pi_S(q, i\nu_\ell)}, \tag{14}$$

where

$$\Pi_S(q, i\nu_\ell) = T \sum_{p, i\omega_n} G_\uparrow(p + q, i\omega_n + i\nu_\ell) G_\downarrow(-p, -i\omega_n), \tag{15}$$

which describes a scattering process denoted by $G_\uparrow$ and $G_\downarrow$, of the dressed medium atoms with the impurities and the dressed ones (polarons), respectively. This is in contrast to Equation (12) obtained in ETMA and consisting of G_σ^0 which represents the impurity-medium scattering process of only the bare atoms. Using this T-matrix, we can express the SCTMA self-energy Σ_σ^S (see also Figure 1c) as

$$\Sigma_\sigma^S(p, i\omega_n) = T \sum_{q, i\nu_\ell} \Gamma_S(q, i\nu_\ell) G_{-\sigma}(q - p, i\nu_\ell - i\omega_n). \tag{16}$$

We note that within the ETMA, the impurity self-energy $\Sigma_\downarrow^E$ (Equation (11)) can be rewritten as

$$\Sigma_\downarrow^E(p, i\omega_n) = T \sum_{q, i\nu_\ell} \Gamma(q, i\nu_\ell) \Big[G_\uparrow^0(q - p, i\nu_\ell - i\omega_n)$$
$$+ G_\uparrow^0(q - p, i\nu_\ell - i\omega_n) \Sigma_\uparrow(q - p, i\nu_\ell - i\omega_n) G_\uparrow(q - p, i\nu_\ell - i\omega_n) \Big]$$
$$\equiv \Sigma_\downarrow(p, i\omega_n) + \delta\Sigma_\downarrow(p, i\omega_n), \tag{17}$$

with the higher-order correction $\delta\Sigma_\downarrow(p, i\omega_n)$ beyond the TMA being

$$\delta\Sigma_\downarrow(p, i\omega_n) = T^2 \sum_{q, q', i\nu_\ell, i\nu_{\ell'}} \Gamma(q, i\nu_\ell) \Gamma(q', i\nu_{\ell'}) G_\uparrow^0(q - p, i\nu_\ell - i\omega_n) G_\uparrow(q - p, i\nu_\ell - i\omega_n)$$
$$\times G_\downarrow(q' - q + p, i\nu_{\ell'} - i\nu_\ell + i\omega_n)$$
$$\equiv T \sum_{p', i\omega_{n'}} V_{\text{eff}}^{(2)}(p, i\omega_n, p', i\omega_{n'}; p, i\omega_n, p', i\omega_{n'}) G_\downarrow(p', i\omega_{n'}). \tag{18}$$

In this expression, $V_{\text{eff}}^{(2)}(p_1, i\omega_{n_1}, p_2, i\omega_{n_2}; p_1', i\omega_{n_1'}, p_2', i\omega_{n_2'})$ represents the induced impurity-impurity interaction (diagrammatically shown in Figure 2a) with incoming and outgoing momenta and frequencies $\{p_i, i\omega_{n_i}\}$ and $\{p_i', i\omega_{n_i'}\}$, respectively, where $i = 1, 2$. It reads

$$V_{\text{eff}}^{(2)}(p_1, i\omega_{n_1}, p_2, i\omega_{n_2}; p_1', i\omega_{n_1'}, p_2', i\omega_{n_2'}) = \delta_{p_1 + p_2, p_1' + p_2'} \delta_{n_1 + n_2, n_1' + n_2'}$$
$$\times T \sum_{q, i\nu_\ell} \Gamma(q, i\nu_\ell) \Gamma(q + p_2 - p_1', i\nu_\ell + i\omega_{n_2} - i\omega_{n_1'}) G_\uparrow^0(q - p_1, i\nu_\ell - i\omega_{n_1}) G_\uparrow^0(q - p_1', i\nu_\ell - i\omega_{n_1'}). \tag{19}$$

Here, $\delta_{i,j}$ is the Kronecker delta imposing the energy and momentum conservation in the two-body scattering.

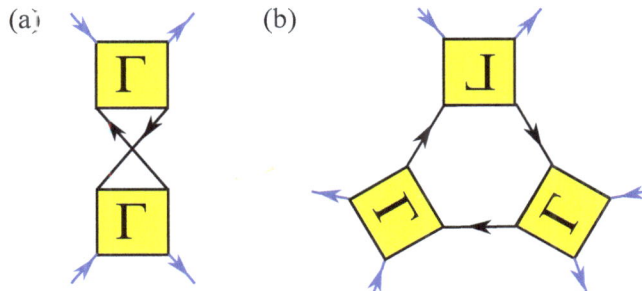

Figure 2. Feynman diagrams for induced (**a**) two- and (**b**) three-body interactions $V_{\text{eff}}^{(2,3)}$ among polarons. The arrows represent the direction of momentum and energy transfer in each propagator.

The self-energy $\Sigma_\downarrow^S$ of the impurities within the SCTMA involves a contribution of induced three-impurity correlations due to the dressed pair propagator $\Sigma_\downarrow^c$. The latter can again be decomposed as

$$\Sigma_\downarrow^S(p, i\omega_n) \equiv \Sigma_\downarrow^E(p, i\omega_n) + \delta\Sigma_\downarrow'(p, i\omega_n), \qquad (20)$$

where

$$\begin{aligned}\delta\Sigma_\downarrow'(p, i\omega_n) &= T \sum_{q, i\nu_\ell} [\Gamma_S(q, i\nu_\ell) - \Gamma(q, i\nu_\ell)] G_\uparrow(q-p, i\nu_\ell - i\omega_n) \\ &= T \sum_{q, i\nu_\ell} \Gamma_S(q, i\nu_\ell) \Gamma(q, i\nu_\ell) \Phi(q, i\nu_\ell) G_\uparrow(q-p, i\nu_\ell - i\omega_n).\end{aligned} \qquad (21)$$

Here we defined

$$\begin{aligned}\Phi(q, i\nu_\ell) &= \Pi_S(q, i\nu_\ell) - \Pi(q, i\nu_\ell) \\ &= T \sum_{p, i\omega_n} \left[G_\uparrow(p+q, i\omega_n + i\nu_\ell) G_\downarrow(-p, -i\omega_n) - G_\uparrow^0(p+q, i\omega_n + i\nu_\ell) G_\downarrow^0(-p, -i\omega_n) \right] \\ &\simeq T \sum_{p, i\omega_n} \left[G_\uparrow^0(p+q, i\omega_n + i\nu_\ell) \right]^2 \Sigma_\uparrow^S(p+q, i\omega_n + i\nu_\ell) G_\downarrow^0(-p, -i\omega_n),\end{aligned} \qquad (22)$$

which represents the difference between the Π and Π_S, namely, the medium-impurity and the medium-polaron propagators. In the last line of Equation (22), we assumed that $G_\uparrow \simeq G_\uparrow^0$ and $\Sigma_\downarrow^S \simeq 0$. Thus, one can find a three-body correlation effect beyond the ETMA as shown in Figure 2b and captured by

$$\delta\Sigma_\downarrow'(p, i\omega_n) \simeq T \sum_{p', i\omega_{n'}} V_{\text{eff}}^{(3)}(p, i\omega_n, p', i\omega_{n'}, p'', i\omega_{n''}; p', i\omega_{n'}, p, i\omega_n, p'', i\omega_{n''}) \\ \times G_\downarrow(p', i\omega_{n'}) G_\downarrow^0(p'', i\omega_{n''}), \qquad (23)$$

where $V_{\text{eff}}^{(3)}(p_1, i\omega_{n_1}, p_2, i\omega_{n_2}, p_3, i\omega_{n_3}; p_1', i\omega_{n_1'}, p_2', i\omega_{n_2'}, p_3', i\omega_{n_3'})$ is the induced three-polaron interaction term. Its explicit form reads

$$\begin{aligned}
V_{\text{eff}}^{(3)}(p_1, i\omega_{n_1}, p_2, i\omega_{n_2}, p_3, i\omega_{n_3}; p'_1, i\omega_{n'_1}, p'_2, i\omega_{n'_2}, p'_3, i\omega_{n'_3}) &= \delta_{p_1+p_2+p_3, p'_1+p'_2+p'_3} \delta_{n_1+n_2+n_3, n'_1+n'_2+n'_3} \\
&\times T \sum_{q, i\nu_\ell} \Gamma(q, i\nu_\ell) \Gamma(q + p_3 - p'_1, i\nu_\ell + i\omega_{n_3} - i\omega_{n'_1}) \Gamma(q + p'_2 - p_1, i\nu_\ell + i\omega_{n'_2} - i\omega_{n_1}) \\
&\times G_\uparrow^0(q - p'_1, i\nu_\ell - i\omega_{n'_1}) G_\uparrow^0(q - p_1, i\nu_\ell - i\omega_{n_1}) G_\uparrow^0(q - p'_1 + p_3 - p'_3, i\nu_\ell - i\omega_{n'_1} + i\omega_{n_3} - i\omega_{n'_3}).
\end{aligned} \quad (24)$$

From the above discussion, it becomes evident how the medium-induced two-body and three-body interpolaron interactions are included in the ETMA and the SCTMA treatments. Recall that in the TMA the interpolaron interaction is not taken into account. Even so, observables such as thermodynamic quantities (e.g., particle number density) and spectral functions obtained via rf spectroscopy can in principle provide indications of the effect of interpolaron interactions through $\Sigma_\sigma(p, i\omega_n)$.

2.2. Spectral Response of Fermi Polarons

In the following, we shall present and discuss the behavior of the spectral function of Fermi polarons for temperatures ranging from zero to the Fermi temperature of the majority component as well as for different spatial dimensions from three to one. For simplicity, we consider a mass-balanced fermionic mixture i.e., $m_\uparrow = m_\downarrow \equiv m$. The latter is experimentally relevant for instance by considering two different hyperfine states, e.g., $|F = 1/2, m_F = +1/2\rangle$ and $|F = 3/2, m_F = -3/2\rangle$ of ^{6}Li. In this notation, F and m_F are the total angular momentum and its projection, respectively, of the specific hyperfine state [10] at thermal equilibrium.

2.2.1. Three-Dimensional Case

The resultant spectral function $A_\sigma(p = 0, \omega)$ of the fermionic medium ($\sigma = \uparrow$) and the impurities ($\sigma = \downarrow$) is depicted in Figure 3 as a function of the single-particle energy ω. Here, we consider a temperature $T = 0.3 T_F$, impurity concentration $x = 0.1$, and impurity-medium interaction at unitarity, i.e., $(p_F a)^{-1} = 0$. The Fermi temperature is $T_F = p_F^2/(2m_\uparrow)$ and the Fermi momentum p_F. Evidently, the spectral function of the majority component (Figure 3a) exhibits a peak around $\omega + \mu_\uparrow = 0$ in all three diagrammatic approaches introduced in Section 2. The sharp peak around $\omega + \mu_\uparrow = 0$ corresponds to the spectrum of the bare medium atoms given by $A(p, \omega) = \delta(\omega - \xi_{p,\uparrow})$ at $p = 0$. This indicates that the imprint of the impurity-medium interaction on the fermionic host is negligible for such small impurity concentrations $x = 0.1$; see also the discussion below. Indeed, the renormalization of $\mu_\uparrow$ (which essentially evinces the backaction on the majority atoms from the impurities) in the ETMA at unitarity is proportional to x [55] and in particular

$$\frac{\mu_\uparrow}{E_F} = 1 - 0.526 x. \quad (25)$$

It can be shown that in the weak-coupling limit, this shift is given by the Hartree correction $\Sigma_\uparrow^H = \frac{4\pi a}{m} N_\downarrow$ [89]. However, at the unitarity limit presented in Figure 3, such a weak-coupling approximation cannot be applied and therefore the factor 0.526 in Equation (25) originates from the existence of strong correlations between the majority and the minority component atoms.

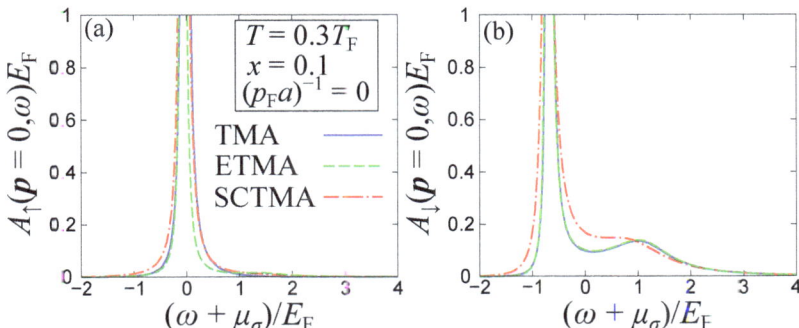

Figure 3. Zero-momentum spectral functions $A_\sigma(p=0,\omega)$ of (**a**) the majority (medium) and (**b**) the minority (impurities) fermions for varying energy ω at unitarity, $(p_F a)^{-1} = 0$. We consider a temperature $T = 0.3 T_F$ and an impurity concentration $x = 0.1$. The solid, dashed, and dash-dotted lines represent the results of the TMA, ETMA, and SCTMA approaches respectively. While $A_\uparrow(p=0,\omega)$ is almost the same among the three approaches, $A_\downarrow(p=0,\omega)$ within the SCTMA experiences a sizable difference compared to the response obtained in the TMA and the ETMA approaches.

The corresponding polaronic excitation spectrum is captured by $A_\downarrow(p=0,\omega)$ (Figure 3b) having a dominant peak at $\omega + \mu_\downarrow = -E_P^{(a)}$ where $E_P^{(a)}$ is the attractive polaron energy. Notice here that since this peak is located at negative energies it indicates the formation of an attractive Fermi polaron. This observation can be understood from the fact that in the absence of impurity-medium interactions, the bare-particle pole, namely, the position of the pole of the bare retarded single-particle Green's function $G_\downarrow^{0,R}(p=0,\omega) = (\omega + i\delta + \mu_\downarrow)^{-1}$, occurs at $\omega + \mu_\downarrow = 0$. Moreover, the attractive polaron energy $E_P^{(a)}$ (being of course negative) is defined by the self-energy shift as $E_P^{(a)} = \Sigma_\downarrow(0, E_P^{(a)})$. Thus, one can regard the deviation of the position of the peak from $\omega + \mu_\downarrow = 0$ as the attractive polaron energy $E_P^{(a)}$, since it is given by $A_\downarrow(p=0,\omega) \sim \delta(\omega + \mu_\downarrow - E_P^{(a)})$. Recall that, in general, for finite temperatures T and impurity concentrations x, $\mu_\downarrow \neq E_P^{(a)}$ holds in contrast to the single-polaron limit at $T=0$ [55]. Additionally, a weak amplitude peak appears in $A_\downarrow(p=0,\omega)$ at positive energies $\omega \simeq E_F$. It stems from the metastable upper branch of the impurities, where excited atoms repulsively interact with each other. This peak becomes sharper at positive scattering lengths away from unitarity. Indeed, for positive scattering lengths, the quasi-particle excitation called a repulsive Fermi polaron emerges [25].

Figure 4a presents the polaron spectral function $A_\downarrow(p=0,\omega)$ with respect to the interaction parameter $(p_F a)^{-1}$ obtained within the ETMA method at $T = 0.03 T_F$ and $x = O(10^{-4})$. From the position of the poles of $G_\downarrow^R(p=0,\omega)$, one can extract two kinds of polaron energies, namely, $E_P^{(a)}$ and $E_P^{(r)}$ corresponding to the attractive and the repulsive polaron energies, respectively. The interaction dependence of these energies is provided in Figure 4b. $E_P^{(r)}$ approaches the Hartree shift $\Sigma_\downarrow^H = \frac{4\pi a}{m} N_\uparrow$ without the imaginary part of the self-energy (being responsible for the width of the spectra) and finally becomes zero [25]. Indeed, the spectrum in Figure 4a shows that the peak of the repulsive polaron at $\omega + \mu_\downarrow > 0$ becomes sharper when increasing $(p_F a)^{-1}$, indicating the vanishing imaginary part of the self-energy. On the other hand, $E_P^{(a)}$ decreases with increasing $(p_F a)^{-1}$ as depicted by the position of the low-energy peak (where $\omega + \mu_\downarrow < 0$) in Figure 4a. Eventually, the attractive polaron undergoes the molecule transition as we discuss below. Another important issue here is that in the strong-coupling regime the attractive polaron undergoes the transition to the molecular state with increasing impurity-bath attraction [93]. Although this transition was originally predicted to be of first-order, recent experimental and theoretical studies showed an underlying crossover behavior and coexistence between polaronic and molecular states [17]. We note that in the case of finite impurity concentrations, a BEC of molecules can appear at low temperatures; see also Equations (26) and (27) below. It is also a fact that the interplay among a molecular BEC, thermally excited molecules, and polarons may occur at finite temperatures [94]. In the calculation of the attractive polaron energy $E_P^{(a)}$ for different coupling strengths (Figure 4b), however, we do not encounter the molecular BEC transition identified by the Thouless criterion [95]

$$1 + g\Pi(\mathbf{q} = \mathbf{0}, i\nu_\ell = 0) = 0. \quad (26)$$

In particular, in the strong-coupling limit, from Equation (26) combined with the particle number conservation (Equation (8)) the BEC temperature T_{BEC} of molecules satisfies [96]

$$T_{\text{BEC}} \simeq 2\pi \left(\frac{x}{12\pi^2 \zeta(3/2)} \right)^{\frac{2}{3}} T_F, \quad (27)$$

where $\zeta(3/2) \simeq 2.612$ is the zeta function. Since we consider a small impurity concentration $x = O(10^{-4})$ here, $T = 0.03 T_F$ is far above $T_{\text{BEC}} \propto x^{\frac{2}{3}}$.

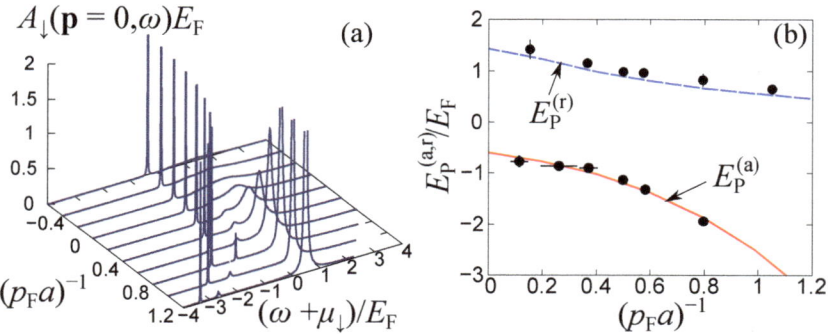

Figure 4. (a) Polaron spectral function $A_\downarrow(\mathbf{p} = \mathbf{0}, \omega)$ for several coupling strengths $(p_F a)^{-1}$. The spectrum is calculated within the ETMA at temperature $T = 0.03 T_F$ and impurity concentration $x = O(10^{-4})$ [55]. Panel (b) represents the attractive and repulsive polaron energies, namely, $E_P^{(a)}$ and $E_P^{(r)}$, respectively, as a function of $(p_F a)^{-1}$. The polaron energies have been extracted from the peak position of $A_\downarrow(\mathbf{p} = \mathbf{0}, \omega)$, that is, the pole of $G_\downarrow^R(\mathbf{p} = \mathbf{0}, \omega)$. The experimental data of Ref. [10] are plotted in black circles for direct comparison with the theoretical predictions.

According to the above-description, induced polaron-polaron interactions are mediated by the host atoms, which are taken into account within the ETMA and the SCTMA methods as explicated in Section 2, are weak in the present mass-balanced fermionic mixture. These finite temperature findings are consistent with previous theoretical works [51–53] predicting a spectral shift of the polaron energy $\Delta E = F E_{\text{FG}} x$ with $F = 0.1 \sim 0.2$ at $T = 0$ (where E_{FG} is the ground-state energy of a non-interacting single-component Fermi gas at $T = 0$) as well as the experimental observations of Ref. [4]. On the other hand, the presence of induced polaron–polaron interactions in the repulsive polaron scenario cannot be observed experimentally [10], a result that is further supported by recent studies based on diagrammatic approaches [55].

Furthermore, the spectral deviations between the TMA and the ETMA treatments represent the effect of induced two-body interpolaron interactions in the attractive polaron case. However, in our case there is no sizable shift between the spectral lines predicted in these approaches (Figure 3b). Indeed, the induced two-body energy is estimated to be of the order of $10^{-3} E_{\text{FG}}$ at $x = 0.1$. The induced three-body interpolaron interaction, which is responsible for the difference among the ETMA and the SCTMA results, exhibits a sizable effect on the width of the polaron spectra. We remark that at $T = 0.3T_F$ and $x = 0.1$ (Figure 3b) although the minority atoms basically obey the Boltzmann statistic, since their temperature is higher than the Fermi degenerate temperature $T_{F,\downarrow} = \frac{(6\pi^2 N_\downarrow)^{\frac{2}{3}}}{2m}$ [55] namely $T = 0.3T_F \simeq 1.39T_{F,\downarrow}$, effects of the strong medium-impurity interaction on the polaron spectra are present manifesting for instance as a corresponding broadering. Although the SCTMA treatment tends to overestimate the polaron energy, the observed full-width-at-half maximum (FWHM) of the rf spectrum given by $2.71(T/T_F)^2$ [16] can be well reproduced by this approach. The latter gives $2.95(T/T_F)^2$ whereas the FWHM in ETMA is $1.61(T/T_F)^2$ [56]. We should also note that the decay rate related to the FWHM for repulsive polarons as extracted using TMA (and simultaneously ETMA) agree quantitatively with the experimental result of Ref. [10]. For the attractive polaron, the quantitative agreement between the experiment and these diagrammatic approaches is broken at high temperatures. For instance, the recent experiment of Ref. [16] showed that the transition from polarons to the Boltzmann gas occurs at $T \simeq 0.75T_F$ [16], while the prediction of the diagrammatic approaches is above T_F [56]. Besides the fact that such polaron decay properties may be related to multi-polaron scattering events leading to many-body dephasing [12], they are necessary for further detailed polaron investigations at various temperatures and interaction strengths that facilitate the understanding of the underlying physics of the observed polaron-to-Boltzmann-gas transition.

The dependence of the polaron spectra $A_\downarrow(p,\omega)$ on the energy and the momentum of the impurities is illustrated in Figure 5 for $T = 0.2T_F$, $x = 0$, and $(p_F a)^{-1} = 0$. To infer the impact of the multi-polaron correlations on the spectrum we explicitly compare $A_\downarrow(p,\omega)$ between the ETMA and the SCTMA methods. As it can be seen, $A_\downarrow(p,\omega)$ exhibits a sharp peak which is associated with the attractive polaron state and shows an almost quadratic behavior for increasing momentum of the impurities. It is also apparent that the SCTMA spectrum (Figure 5b) at low momenta is broadened when compared to the ETMA one (Figure 5a) due to the induced beyond two-body interpolation correlations, e.g., three-body ones. At small impurity momenta, the spectral peak of the attractive Fermi polaron within the present model as described by Equation (1), is generally given by

$$A_\downarrow(p,\omega) \simeq Z_a \delta\left(\omega + \mu_\downarrow - \frac{p^2}{2m_a^*} - E_P^{(a)}\right), \quad (28)$$

where Z_a and m_a^* are the quasiparticle residue [25] and the effective mass of the attractive polaron, respectively. At unitarity it holds that $Z_a \simeq 0.8$, $m_a^* \simeq 1.2m$, and $E_P^{(a)} \simeq -0.6E_F$ within the zero-temperature and single-polaron limits [34]. The behavior of these quantities has been intensively studied in current experiments [3,4,10] and an adequate agreement has been reported using various theories. For instance, Chevy's variational ansatz (being equivalent to the TMA at $T = 0$ and $x \to 0$) [33,34] gives $Z_a = 0.78$, $m_a^* = 1.17m$, and $E_P^{(a)} = -0.6066E_F$. More recently, the functional renormalization group [39] predicts $Z_a = 0.796$ and $E_P^{(a)} = -0.57E_F$, while according to the diagrammatic Monte Carlo method [47] $E_P^{(a)} = -0.6157E_F$. In this sense, nowadays, the corresponding values of these quantities can be regarded as important benchmarks, especially for theoretical approaches. It is also worth mentioning that higher-order diagrammatic approximations such as the SCTMA do not necessarily lead to improved accuracy in terms of the values of relevant observables. In particular, a detailed comparison between the predictions of the TMA and the SCTMA has been discussed in Ref. [54] demonstrating that the former adequately estimates the experimentally observed polaron energy whereas the SCTMA overestimates its magnitude in the strong-coupling regime. Moreover, the diagrammatic Monte Carlo method based on bare Green's functions in self-energies exhibits a better convergence behavior compared to the ones employing dressed Green's functions due to the approximate cancellation of higher-order diagrams [44]. As such, the partial inclusion of higher-order diagrams by replacing the bare Green's functions with the dressed ones may lead to overestimating the molecule-molecule and the polaron-molecule scattering lengths in the strong-coupling regime [56].

As we demonstrated previously (see Figure 3), besides the fact that the spectral response within the SCTMA method is broader compared to the one obtained in the ETMA, the two spectra feature a qualitatively similar behavior. Indeed, both approaches evince that the spectra beyond $p = p_F$ are strongly broadened. Recall that in this region of momenta the atoms of the majority component, which form the Fermi sphere, cannot follow the impurity atoms. This indicates that the dressed polaron state ceases to exist due to the phenomenon of the Cherenkov instability [97,98], where the polaron moves faster than the speed of sound of the medium and consequently it becomes unstable against the spontaneous emission of elementary excitations of the medium. Such a spectral broadening can also be observed in mesoscopic spin transport measurements [99] and may also be related to the underlying polaron-Boltzmann gas transition [16] since the contribution of high-momentum polarons can be captured in rf spectroscopy due to the thermal broadening of the Fermi distribution function in Equation (7) at high temperatures. Moreover, the momentum-resolved photoemission spectra would reveal these effects across this transition.

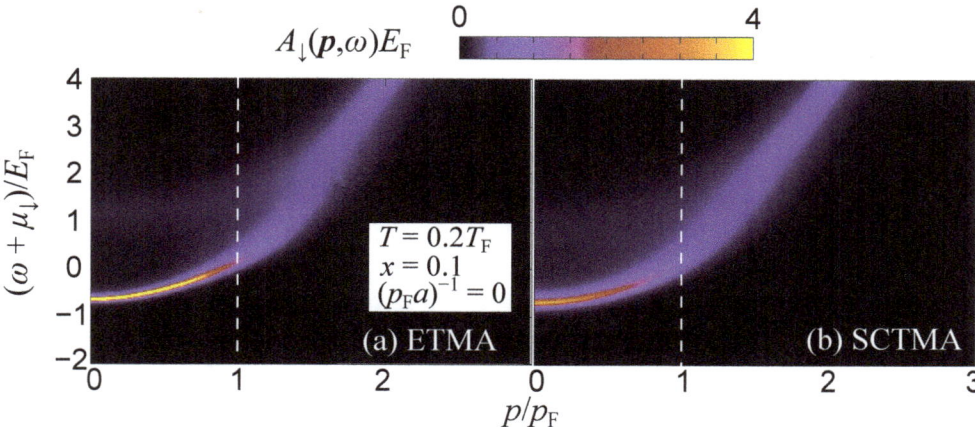

Figure 5. Polaron spectral function $A_\downarrow(p,\omega)$ as a function of the momentum p and the energy ω of the impurities at temperature $T = 0.2T_F$, impurity concentration $x = 0.1$, and interaction $(p_F a)^{-1} = 0$. $A_\downarrow(p,\omega)$ is calculated within (**a**) the ETMA and (**b**) the SCTMA approaches. The vertical dashed line marks the Fermi momentum $p = p_F$ of the medium. While the two approaches predict qualitatively similar spectra with a sharp peak at low momenta and broadening above $p = p_F$, the SCTMA result (**b**) shows a relatively broadened peak at low momenta compared to the ETMA one (**a**).

We remark that the medium spectral function $A_\uparrow(p,\omega)$ is also useful to reveal the properties of strong-coupling polarons in the case of finite temperature and impurity concentration. Figure 6 presents $A_\uparrow(p,\omega)$ for various impurity-medium couplings $((p_F a)^{-1} = -0.4, 0, 0.4, 0.7,$ and $1.0)$ at $T = 0.4T_F$ and $x = 0.1$. At $(p_F a)^{-1} = -0.4$ and $(p_F a)^{-1} = 0$, $A_\uparrow(p = 0,\omega)$ features a single peak at $\omega + \mu_\uparrow = 0$. On the other hand, at intermediate couplings $(p_F a)^{-1} = 0.4$ and $(p_F a)^{-1} = 0.7$, besides a dominant spectral maximum a second peak appears around $\omega + \mu_\uparrow = E_F$. The latter evinces the backaction from the repulsive polaron because the inset of Figure 6 shows that the repulsive polaron is located around $\omega + \mu_\uparrow \simeq E_F$. Moreover, at $(p_F a)^{-1} = 1$, another peak emerges in the low-energy region ($\omega + \mu_\uparrow \simeq -3E_F$). This low-energy peak elucidates the emergence of two-body molecules with the binding energy given by $E_b = 1/(ma^2)$ due to the strong impurity-medium attraction. Concluding, the spectral function of the medium atoms can provide us with useful information for the recently observed smooth crossover from polarons to molecules [17]. Notice also that spectral and thermodynamic signatures of the polaron-molecule transition have been recently reported within a variational approach [100], while the associated molecule-hole continuum can be captured using the TMA method [101].

In the following, we shall elaborate on the behavior of the spectral function of lower dimensional Fermi polarons solely within the TMA approach. The latter provides an adequate description of the polaron formation in our case since the induced interpolaron interaction [59,60] is weak in the considered mass-balanced system.

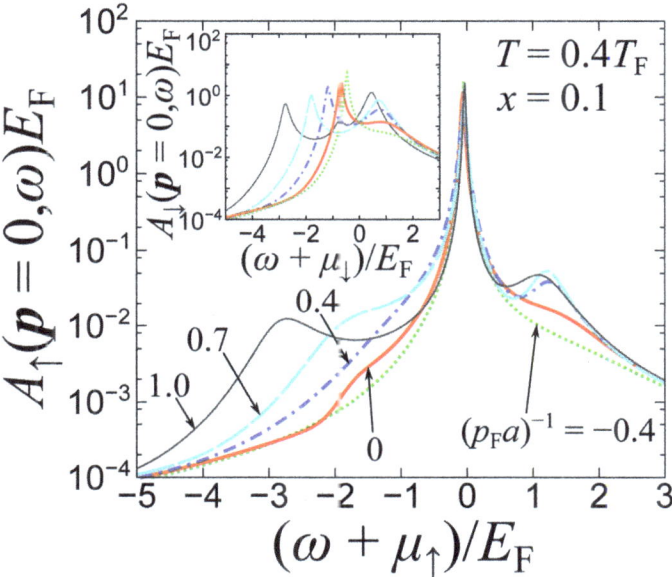

Figure 6. Spectral function of the medium $A_\uparrow(p=0,\omega)$ within the ETMA approach at zero momentum of the impurity and for different impurity-medium couplings $(p_F a)^{-1} = -0.4, 0, 0.4, 0.7,$ and 1.0. The temperature and the impurity concentration are given by $T = 0.4T_F$ and $x = 0.1$, respectively. The inset shows the corresponding impurity spectral functions $A_\downarrow(p=0,\omega)$. While the sharp peak at $\omega + \mu_\uparrow \simeq 0$ in $A_\uparrow(p=0,\omega)$ is associated with the bare state, the small amplitude side peaks at positive $(\omega + \mu_\uparrow \simeq E_F)$ and negative energies $(\omega + \mu_\downarrow \simeq -3E_F$ for the case with $(p_F a)^{-1} = 1)$ originate from the backaction due to the impurities.

2.2.2. Spectral Response of Fermi Polarons in Two-Dimensions

In two spatial dimensions, the attractive impurity-medium effective interaction $g_{2D} < 0$ is always accompanied by the existence of a two-body bound state whose energy scales as $-1/(ma_{2D}^2)$ [102]. Simultaneously, the repulsive polaron branch appears at positive energies [25] in addition to the attractive one located at negative energies. This phenomenology is similar to the case of a positive impurity-bath scattering length in 3D [101]. To elaborate on the typical spectrum of 2D Fermi polarons below we employ a homogeneous Fermi mixture characterized by an impurity concentration $x = 0.1$, temperature $T = 0.3T_F$, and a typically weak dimensionless coupling parameter $\ln(p_F a_{2D}) = 0.4$ where a_{2D} is the 2D scattering length introduced in Equation (3). The spectral response of both the fermionic background $(A_\uparrow(p,\omega))$ and the impurities $(A_\downarrow(p,\omega))$ for varying momenta and energies of the impurities within the TMA approach is depicted in Figure 7. We observe that the small impurity concentration, i.e., $x = 0.1$, leads to the non-interacting dispersion of the spectrum of the majority component given by $A_\uparrow(p,\omega) \simeq \delta(\omega - \xi_{p,\uparrow})$; see Figure 7a. In this case, therefore, the medium does not experience any backaction from the impurities. Importantly, one can indeed identify a sizable backaction on the medium in the case of a larger impurity concentration and smaller impurity-medium 2D scattering length as shown in Figure 7(b1,b2) where $T = 0.3T_F$, $x = 0.3$, and $\ln(p_F a_{2D}) = 0$. Moreover, since the repulsive interaction in the excited branch of the impurities ($\omega + \mu_\downarrow \simeq E_F$) is relatively strong, the impurity excitation spectrum at positive energies ($\omega + \mu_\downarrow > 0$) is largely broadened. We note that the stable repulsive polaron branch can be found in the case of small a_{2D}. It also becomes evident that the impurity spectrum in 2D is largely broadened beyond $p = p_F$ as compared to the 3D spectral response (Figure 5). Simultaneously, the intensity of the metastable impurity excitation in the repulsive branch becomes relatively strong in both the 2D and 3D cases. This result implies that fast-moving impurities do not dress the medium atoms and occupy the non-interacting excited states in such high-momentum regions.

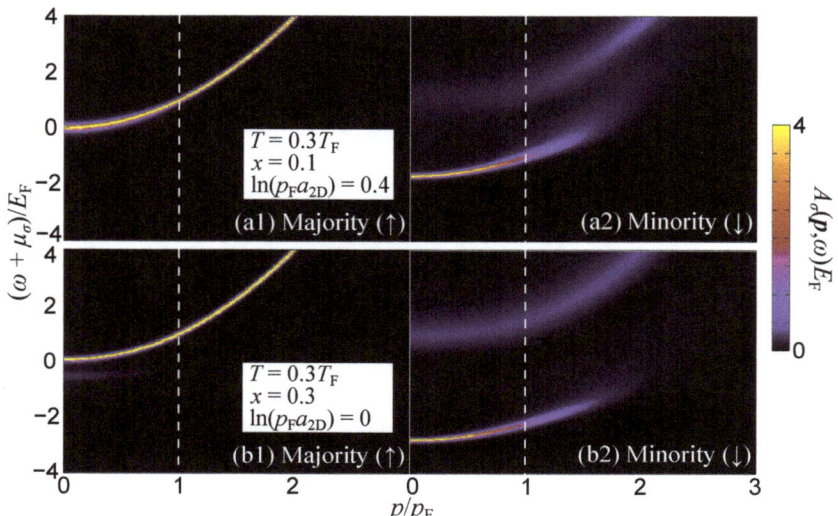

Figure 7. Spectral function $A_\sigma(p, \omega)$ of the Fermi (**a1**) medium and (**a2**) impurities in two-dimensions for different momenta and energies of the impurities. We consider a temperature $T = 0.3T_F$, impurity concentration $x = 0.1$, and dimensionless coupling parameter $\ln(p_F a_{2D}) = 0.4$. The vertical dashed line indicates the Fermi momentum $p = p_F$ of the majority component atoms. While the majority component (**a**) exhibits a sharp peak with quadratic dispersion $\omega + \mu_\uparrow = p^2/(2m)$, the minority atoms (**b**) form the attractive polaron at negative energies ($\omega + \mu_\downarrow < 0$) and a broadened peak associated with the repulsive impurity branch at positive energies ($\omega + \mu_\downarrow > 0$). For comparison, we provide the spectral functions of the medium (**b1**) and the impurities (**b2**) in the case of $T = 0.3T_F$, $x = 0.3$ and $\ln(p_F a_{2D}) = 0$. Evidently, the feedback on the medium from the impurities is enhanced in the low-momentum region ($p \simeq 0$).

2.2.3. Fermi Polarons in One-Dimension

In one spatial dimension the quasiparticle notion is somewhat more complicated as compared to the higher-dimensional case. Interestingly, various experiments are nowadays possible to realize 1D ensembles and thus probe the properties of the emergent quasi-particles. Below, we provide spectral evidences of 1D Fermi polarons and in particular calculate the respective $A_\sigma(p, \omega)$ (Figure 8) for the background fermionic medium and the minority atoms within the T-matrix approach including the Hartree correction. The system has an impurity concentration $x = 0.326$, it lies at temperature $T = 0.157T_F$, and the 1D dimensionless coupling parameter for the impurity-medium attraction is $(p_F a_{1D})^{-1} = 0.28$ in Figure 8(a1,a2). For comparison, we also provide $A_\sigma(p, \omega)$ in Figure 8(b1,b2) for the repulsive interaction case $(p_F a_{1D})^{-1} = -0.55$ with system parameters $x = 0.264$ and $T = 0.598T_F$. We remark that the impurity-medium attraction is considered weak herein such that the induced interpolaron interactions are negligible. In this sense, we do not expect significant deviations when considering the ETMA or even the SCTMA approaches.

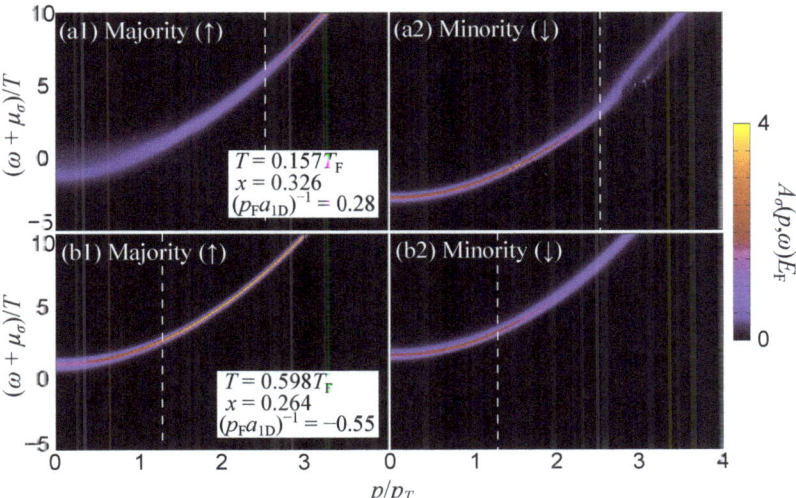

Figure 8. Spectral function $A_\sigma(p,\omega)$ of the fermionic (**a1**) background and (**a2**) impurity atoms of concentration $x = 0.326$ with an attractive medium-impurity interaction for varying momenta and energies of the impurities in one-dimension. The system is at temperature $T = 0.157T_F$ and dimensionless coupling parameter $(p_F a_{1D})^{-1} = 0.28$. $p_T = \sqrt{2mT}$ is the momentum scale associated with the temperature T. The vertical dashed line marks the Fermi momentum $p = p_F$ of the background atoms. The majority component (**a1**) is largely broadened due to the backaction from the impurities in the low-momentum region ($p \lesssim p_T$). On the other hand, the minority component (**a2**) exhibits a sharp peak in the low-momentum region below $p = p_F$ and it is broadened above $p = p_F$. For comparison, we show the (**b1**) medium and (**b2**) impurity spectral functions in the case of repulsive medium-impurity interaction characterized by $(p_F a_{1D})^{-1} = -0.55$, where the temperature and the impurity concentraion are given by $T = 0.598T_F$ and $x = 0.264$. Although the impurity quasiparticle peak in the low-energy region ($\omega + \mu_\downarrow \simeq 0$) is shifted upward, the tendency of a spectral broadening is similar to the attractive case.

It is also important to note here that in sharp contrast to higher spatial dimensions, the coupling constant g_{1D} does not vanish when $\Lambda \to \infty$ in the renormalization procedure; see Section 2.1. Thus, we take the Hartree shift $\Sigma^H_\sigma = g_{1D} N_{-\sigma}$ into account in the building block of the self-energy diagrams [103]. This treatment is not necessary in the single-polaron limit since $\Sigma^H_\uparrow \to 0$ and $\Sigma^H_\downarrow \to g_{1D} T \sum_{p,i\omega_n} G^0_\uparrow(p, i\omega_n)$ (which is included in the TMA self-energy) when $x \to 0$. The non-vanishing coupling constant in 1D plays an important role in the emergence of induced interpolaron interactions as it has been recently demonstrated, e.g., in Refs. [61,104,105]. The polaronic excitation properties obtained within the TMA approach show an excellent agreement with the results of the thermodynamic Bethe ansatz [106]. The latter provides an exact solution in 1D and in the single-polaron limit at $T = 0$ [102,107]. From these results, it is found that there is no transition but rather a crossover behavior between polarons and molecules. As it can be seen by inspecting Figure 8(a1) the spectrum of the majority component is affected by the scattering with the impurities. This is attributed to the relatively large impurity concentration x considered here. In particular, $A_\uparrow(p,\omega)$ is broadened at low momenta below $p = p_F$. On the other hand, the spectral response of the impurities in Figure 8(a2) exhibits a sharp peak associated with the attractive polaron below $p = p_F$ and it becomes broadened above $p = p_F$. Apparently, the curvature of the position of the polaron peak corresponding to the effective mass (curvature of the dispersion) is changed around this value of the momentum. Similar broadening effects of sharp peaks can be found even in the case of repulsive impurity–medium interaction shown in Figure 8(b1,b2). However, the low-energy sharp peak (corresponding to the repulsive polaron) in the impurity spectrum (Figure 8(b2)) is shifted to larger energies as a consequence of the impurity–medium repulsion.

3. Bose Polarons

In this section, we shall discuss the Bogoliubov theory of trapped Bose polaron systems in real space [86,108,109]. The reason for focusing on a real-space Bogoliubov theory is to elaborate on the deformation of the BEC medium in the presence of an impurity. Indeed, the interaction between the impurity and the medium bosons leads to significant inhomogeneities of the density distribution of the background which cannot be described within a simple Thomas–Fermi approximation. Such a modification of the boson distribution causes, for instance, enhanced phonon emission [61,78]. Moreover, in cold atom experiments the background bosons and the impurity are generally trapped. Considering the impact of inhomogeneity that naturally arises in trapped systems, therefore, we treat the Bose polaron in real space without plane wave expansion because the momentum is not a good quantum number. Below, we review the description of a Bose polaron in trapped 3D systems at zero temperature using the Bogoliubov theory and elaborate on the ground state properties. We remark that our analysis, to be presented below, is applicable independently of the shape of the external potential while for simplicity herein we consider the case of a harmonic trap.

In particular, we consider a 3D setting where a single atomic impurity is trapped in an external harmonic potential denoted by $V_I(r)$ and is embedded in a BEC medium that is also trapped in an another harmonic potential $V_B(r)$ whose center coincides with that of $V_I(r)$. Hereafter, we use units in which $\hbar = 1$. This system is described by the following model Hamiltonian

$$\hat{H} = \int d^d \mathbf{r}\, \hat{\psi}^\dagger(\mathbf{r}) \left[-\frac{\nabla^2}{2m_I} + V_I(\mathbf{r}) \right] \hat{\psi}(\mathbf{r}) + g_{IB} \int d^d \mathbf{r}\, \hat{\phi}^\dagger(\mathbf{r}) \hat{\phi}(\mathbf{r}) \hat{\psi}^\dagger(\mathbf{r}) \hat{\psi}(\mathbf{r}) \\ + \int d^d \mathbf{r}\, \hat{\phi}^\dagger(\mathbf{r}) \left[-\frac{\nabla^2}{2m_B} + V_B(\mathbf{r}) + g_{BB} \hat{\phi}^\dagger(\mathbf{r}) \hat{\phi}(\mathbf{r}) \right] \hat{\phi}(\mathbf{r}). \tag{29}$$

Here, $\hat{\phi}$ and $\hat{\psi}$ are the field operators of the bosonic medium and the impurity, respectively. $m_{I(B)}$ is the mass of the impurity atom (the medium bosons) and μ is the chemical potential of the medium bosons. The effective couplings g_{IB} and g_{BB} refer to the impurity-boson and boson-boson interaction strengths, respectively.

3.1. Bogoliubov Theory for Bose Polaron Problems

First, we calculate the expectation value of the Hamiltonian in terms of the single-impurity state $|\text{imp}\rangle = \hat{a}_{\text{imp}}^\dagger |0\rangle_{\text{imp}}$ in order to integrate out the impurity's degree-of-freedom

$$\hat{\mathcal{H}}_B = \int d^d \mathbf{r}\, \psi^*(\mathbf{r}) \left[-\frac{\nabla^2}{2m_I} + V_I(\mathbf{r}) \right] \psi(\mathbf{r}) \\ + \int d^d \mathbf{r}\, \hat{\phi}^\dagger(\mathbf{r}) \left[-\frac{\nabla^2}{2m_B} + V_B(\mathbf{r}) + g_{IB} |\psi(\mathbf{r})|^2 + g_{BB} \hat{\phi}^\dagger(\mathbf{r}) \hat{\phi}(\mathbf{r}) \right] \hat{\phi}(\mathbf{r}), \tag{30}$$

where $\hat{a}_{\text{imp}}$ denotes the annihilation operator of an impurity in the ground state; $\psi(r)$ is the corresponding wave function that can be determined self-consistently by Equation (35). In this way, we have obtained the effective Hamiltonian for the medium bosons, in which the bosons experience an effective potential constructed by the external trap and the density of the impurity $g_{IB}|\psi(r)|^2$. Since we have set the temperature to zero in the present study, we have to assume that the medium bosons possess a condensed part, the so-called order parameter or the macroscopic wavefunction, when using perturbation theory. It is known [87,110,111] that when BEC occurs, the vacuum expectation value of the field operator $\hat{\phi}$ leads to a non-zero function which is used as an order parameter, i.e., $\langle \hat{\phi}(\mathbf{r}) \rangle_b = \phi(\mathbf{r})$, where $\langle \cdots \rangle_b$ means $_b\langle 0| \cdots |0\rangle_b$. The vacuum $|0\rangle_b$ is determined from the effective Hamiltonian (30) within the Bogoliubov theory to the second order of fluctuations. This is equivalent to splitting the operator as $\hat{\phi} = \phi + \hat{\varphi}$, where $\langle \hat{\varphi} \rangle_b = 0$. Substituting this into the Hamiltonian of Equation (30) and expressing it in terms of the different orders of $\hat{\varphi}$, we can readily obtain the expansion $\hat{\mathcal{H}}_B \simeq \mathcal{H}^{(0)} + \mathcal{H}^{(1)} + \mathcal{H}^{(2)}$ because the number of the non-condensed bosons is significantly smaller than that of the condensed ones at zero temperature and weak couplings. In this expression, the individual contributions correspond to

$$\mathcal{H}^{(0)} = \int d^d\mathbf{r}\, \psi^* \left[-\frac{\nabla^2}{2m_I} + V_I \right] \psi + \int d^d\mathbf{r}\, \phi^* \left[-\frac{\nabla^2}{2m_B} + V_B + g_{IB}|\psi|^2 + \frac{g_{BB}}{2}|\phi|^2 - \mu \right] \phi, \quad (31)$$

$$\mathcal{H}^{(1)} = \int d^d\mathbf{r}\, \hat{\varphi}^\dagger \left[-\frac{\nabla^2}{2m_B} + V_B + g_{IB}|\psi|^2 + g_{BB}|\phi|^2 - \mu \right] \phi + h.c., \quad (32)$$

$$\mathcal{H}^{(2)} = \frac{1}{2} \int d^d\mathbf{r}\, \begin{pmatrix} \hat{\varphi}^\dagger & \hat{\varphi} \end{pmatrix} \begin{pmatrix} \mathcal{L} & \mathcal{M} \\ \mathcal{M}^* & \mathcal{L}^* \end{pmatrix} \begin{pmatrix} \hat{\varphi} \\ \hat{\varphi}^\dagger \end{pmatrix}, \quad (33)$$

where $\mathcal{L}(\mathbf{r}) = -\frac{\nabla^2}{2m_B} + V_B(\mathbf{r}) + g_{IB}|\psi(\mathbf{r})|^2 + 2g_{BB}|\phi(\mathbf{r})|^2 - \mu$, and $\mathcal{M}(\mathbf{r}) = g_{BB}\phi^2(\mathbf{r})$. Note that we assume the weakly interacting limit of the medium to ensure the BEC dominating condition and thus g_{BB} is adequately small such that the perturbation theory is valid. In the above expansion we ignore the contributions stemming from the third- and fourth-order terms in the field operator assuming that they are negligible for the same reason.

Subsequently, let us derive the corresponding equations of motion that describe the Bose-polaron system. From the Heisenberg equation, the bosonic field operator $\hat{\varphi}$ satisfies $i\partial_t \langle \hat{\varphi} \rangle_b = \langle [\hat{\varphi}, \hat{\mathcal{H}}^{(1)} + \hat{\mathcal{H}}^{(2)}] \rangle_b = 0$ in the interaction picture. Accordingly, it is possible to retrieve the celebrated Gross-Pitaevskii equation describing the BEC background

$$\left[-\frac{\nabla^2}{2m_B} + V_B(\mathbf{r}) + g_{IB}|\psi(\mathbf{r})|^2 + g_{BB}|\phi(\mathbf{r})|^2 - \mu \right] \phi(\mathbf{r}) = 0. \quad (34)$$

We remark that here, for simplicity, we consider the stationary case where the condensate is time-independent. Next, by following the variational principle for ψ namely $\delta \langle \mathcal{H}_B \rangle_b / \delta \psi^* = 0$, we arrive at the Schrödinger equation for the impurity wavefunction

$$\left[-\frac{\nabla^2}{2m_I} + V_I(\mathbf{r}) + g_{IB}|\phi(\mathbf{r})|^2 + g_{IB} n_{ex}(\mathbf{r}) \right] \psi(\mathbf{r}) = 0, \quad (35)$$

where $n_{ex}(\mathbf{r}) = \langle \hat{\varphi}^\dagger(\mathbf{r}) \hat{\varphi}(\mathbf{r}) \rangle_b$ is the density of the non-condensed bosons in vacuum, the so-called *quantum depletion*.

To evaluate this expectation value, we need the ground state $|0\rangle_b$ of the Hamiltonian that can be obtained by the diagonalization of Equation (33). Namely, $H^{(2)} = \sum_n E_n \hat{b}_n^\dagger \hat{b}_n$ is achieved using the following field expansion $\hat{\varphi}(\mathbf{r}) = \sum_n \left[\hat{b}_n u_n(\mathbf{r}) + \hat{b}_n^\dagger v_n^*(\mathbf{r}) \right]$. Here the complete set $\{u_i, v_i\}$ satisfies the following system of linear equations being the so-called Bogoliubov-de Gennes (BdG) equations [112,113]

$$\begin{pmatrix} \mathcal{L}(\mathbf{r}) & \mathcal{M}(\mathbf{r}) \\ -\mathcal{M}^*(\mathbf{r}) & -\mathcal{L}(\mathbf{r}) \end{pmatrix} \begin{pmatrix} u_n(\mathbf{r}) \\ v_n(\mathbf{r}) \end{pmatrix} = E_n \begin{pmatrix} u_n(\mathbf{r}) \\ v_n(\mathbf{r}) \end{pmatrix}. \quad (36)$$

We remark that the BdG equations are commonly used in mode analysis of condensates. In this context, the real eigenvalues constitute the spectrum, while the complex eigenvalues unveil the dynamically unstable modes of the condensate [114,115]. More precisely, if complex eigenvalues exist then the Hamiltonian can not be expressed in the above-mentioned diagonal form in terms of the annihilation/creation operators. As such, the dynamically unstable situation is beyond the scope of the present description. By using this expansion, we can calculate the vacuum expectation, e.g., $n_{\text{ex}}(\mathbf{r}) = \sum_n |v_n(\mathbf{r})|^2$. For the numerical calculations, to be presented below, the total number of bosons N_B is conserved, i.e.,

$$N_B = N_0 + N_{\text{ex}}, \quad \text{with} \quad N_0 = \int d^d \mathbf{r} \, |\phi(\mathbf{r})|^2 \text{ and } N_{\text{ex}} = \int d^d \mathbf{r} \, n_{\text{ex}}(\mathbf{r}). \tag{37}$$

This condition is achieved by tuning the chemical potential μ of the bosonic medium. Notice that N_{ex} becomes non-zero due to thermal fluctuations at finite temperature, while in the ultracold regime it can be finite due to the presence of quantum fluctuations, otherwise termed quantum depletion [116]. We also remark that all of the above Equations (34)–(36) need to be solved simultaneously. The above-described treatment will be referred to in the following as the real-space formulation of the Bose-polaron problem.

3.2. Quantum Depletion around a Bose Polaron

Since N_B is fixed (Equation (37)), the number of condensed particles N_0 changes due to the existence of N_{ex}. This is a quantum effect that occurs even at zero temperature, and it is called quantum depletion [111]. We need to clarify that the term quantum depletion refers to the beyond mean-field corrections for the description of the bosonic ensemble. In the following, we shall investigate the effect of an impurity on the quantum depletion of the medium bosons at zero temperature. Indeed, the quantum depletion is a measurable quantum effect that is included in Equation (35) and its quantification makes it possible to evaluate the backaction of the impurity on the medium condensate.

A commonly used external confinement in cold atom experiments is the harmonic potential. As such, here, we consider that the traps of the impurity and the bosonic medium are spherically symmetric, namely,

$$V_B(r) = \frac{1}{2} m_B \omega_B^2 r^2 \quad \text{and} \quad V_I(r) = \frac{1}{2} m_I \omega_I^2 r^2. \tag{38}$$

Accordingly, the order parameter of the BEC and the impuritys' wave function have spherically symmetric forms, and therefore the underlying BdG eigenfunctions are separable with the help of spherical harmonics as

$$\phi(\mathbf{r}) = \phi(r), \quad \psi(\mathbf{r}) = \psi(r), \quad \begin{Bmatrix} u_{n_r \ell m}(\mathbf{r}) \\ v_{n_r \ell m}(\mathbf{r}) \end{Bmatrix} = \begin{Bmatrix} \mathcal{U}_{n_r \ell}(r) \\ \mathcal{V}_{n_r \ell}(r) \end{Bmatrix} Y_{\ell m}(\theta_1, \theta_2), \tag{39}$$

where $r = |\mathbf{r}|$. Here, (n_r, ℓ, m) denote the radial, azimuthal, and magnetic quantum numbers, respectively.

As a further simplification, we consider the situation where ω_I is sufficiently larger than ω_B, namely, the impurity is more tightly confined than the medium bosons. As such, the order parameter ϕ of the condensate changes much more gradually with respect to the spatial change of the impurity's wave function ψ. Since the impurity's wave function is relatively narrow compared to the condensate and the impurity-medium interaction is weak, the impurity essentially experiences to a good approximation an almost flat (homogeneous) environment. This also means that trap effects are not very pronounced in this case. In this sense, ϕ can be regarded as being constant and the impurity's wave function can be well approximated by a Gaussian function i.e., $\psi(r) \simeq \left(\frac{\pi}{m_I \omega_I}\right)^{-\frac{3}{4}} \exp(-\frac{m_I \omega_I}{2} r^2)$. We remark that in the presence of another external potential, e.g., a double-well, one naturally needs to employ another appropriate initial wavefunction ansatz for the impurity. To experimentally realize such a setting it is possible to consider a ^{40}K Fermi impurity immersed in a ^{87}Rb BEC, where $m_I/m_B \simeq 0.460$. For the medium we employ a total number of bosons $N_B = 10^5$ and the ratio of the strength of the trapping potentials $\omega_I/\omega_B = 10$ with $\omega_B = 20 \times 2\pi$ Hz [9]. Moreover, for the boson-boson and impurity-boson interactions, we utilize the values $1/(a_{BB}n_B^{1/3}) = 100$ and $1/(a_{IB}n_B^{1/3}) = \pm 1$ with $n_B = N_B / \left(\frac{4\pi}{3}d_B^3\right)$ and $d_B = \sqrt{m_B \omega_B}$.

To reveal the backaction of the impurity on the bosonic environment we provide the corresponding ground state density profiles of the condensed and the depleted part of the bath in Figure 9a,c, respectively. In the case of $g_{IB} > 0$ ($g_{IB} < 0$), the condensate experiences an additional potential hump (dip) at the location of the impurity and eventually it seems to be slightly repelled from (pulled towards) the impurity as shown in Figure 9b, where the deformation of the radial profile of the condensate from the case of zero impurity-medium interactions is provided. Moreover, in order to appreciate the role of the quantum depletion of the BEC environment we illustrate its depletion density in the absence and in the presence of the impurity in Figure 9b,d, respectively. Apparently, the degree of the quantum depletion decreases (increases) (Figure 9d) for $g_{IB} > 0$ ($g_{IB} < 0$), a phenomenon that is accompanied by the deformation of the condensate density. The effect of the impurity on the quantum depletion of the condensate is summarized in the Table 1. Inspecting the latter we can deduce that the quantum depletion decreases (increases) when the interaction is repulsive (attractive). This is a non-trivial result caused by the presence of the trap since in a uniform system [117–119] the depletion always increases irrespectively of whether the interaction is positive or negative.

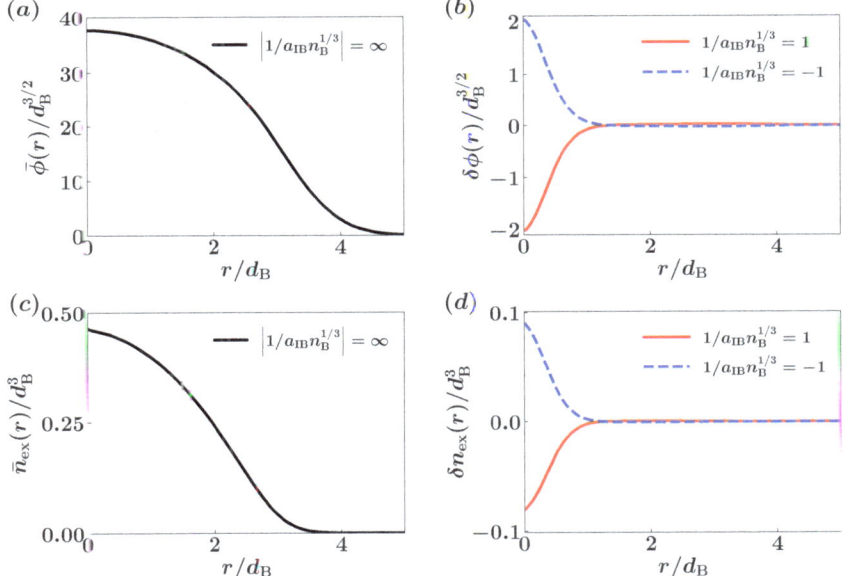

Figure 9. Radial profiles of (a) the order parameter $\bar{\phi}(r) = \phi(r; g_{IB} = 0)/\sqrt{N_0/4\pi}$ and (c) the density of depletion $\bar{n}_{ex}(r) = n_{ex}(r; g_{IB} = 0)$ in the absence of an impurity. Differences of the radial profiles of (b) the order parameter $\delta\Phi(r) = (\phi(r; g_{IB}) - \phi(r; g_{IB} = 0))/\sqrt{N_0/4\pi}$ and (d) the density of depletion $\delta n_{ex}(r) = n_{ex}(r; g_{IB}) - n_{ex}(r; g_{IB} = 0)$ in the presence of an impurity from the result depicted in (a) and (c), respectively.

Table 1. The number of depletion N_{ex} and its deviation $\delta N_{\text{ex}} = 4\pi \int dr\, r^2 \delta n_{\text{ex}}(r)$ from the case of zero impurity-medium interaction. It is evident that degree of depletion increases (decreases) for attractive (repulsive) interactions.

$1/(a_{\text{IB}} n_{\text{B}}^{1/3})$	∞	$+1$	-1
N_{ex}	24.244	24.220	24.270
δN_{ex}	0	-2.361×10^{-2}	2.584×10^{-2}

4. Conclusions

In this work, we have discussed the existence and behavior of Fermi and Bose polarons that can be realized in ultracold quantum gases focusing on their backaction on the background medium. We have explicated three different diagrammatic approaches applicable to Fermi polarons in the homogeneous case. These include the TMA, the ETMA, and the SCTMA frameworks, where the ETMA considers induced two-body interpolaron interactions and the SCTMA includes two- and three-body ones. Importantly, we have explicitly derived the mediated two- and three-body interpolaron correlation effects as captured within the different diagrammatic approaches. Although these induced interactions are weak in the considered mass-balanced Fermi polaron systems, our framework can be applied to various settings such as mass-imbalanced Fermi polaron systems. Using this strong-coupling approach, we analyze the spectral response of the Fermi polaron in one-, two-, and three- spatial dimensions at finite temperature. It has been shown that the spectral function of the minority component exhibits a sharp polaron dispersion in the low-momentum region but it is broadened for higher momenta. Moreover, we argue that the spectral response reflects the character of majority atoms forming a Fermi sphere while a strong interaction between the majority and the minority atoms induces a two-body bound state between a medium atom and an impurity particle. The presence of this two-body bound state becomes more important in lower dimensions.

Next, we present the mean-field treatment of trapped Bose polarons in three-dimensions and analyze the role of quantum depletion identified by the deformation of the background density within the framework of Bogoliubov theory of excitations. A systematic investigation of the latter enables us to deduce that the repulsive (attractive) impurity-medium interaction, giving rise to repulsive (attractive) Bose polarons, induces a decreasing (increasing) condensate depletion captured by the deformation of the density distribution of the host. This effect is a consequence of the presence of the external confinement since for a homogeneous background the quantum depletion increases independently of the sign of the impurity-medium interaction. Therefore, this result is considered as a particular feature of the trapped system.

Our investigation opens up the possibility for further studies on various polaron aspects. In particular, the effect of finite temperatures and the impurity concentration on the 2D Fermi polaron spectral response is expected to play a significant role close to the Berezinskii-Kosterlitz-Thouless transition of molecules [120]. Moreover, systems characterized by highly mass-imbalanced components, e.g., heavy polarons, provide promising candidates for the realization of more pronounced polaron-polaron induced interactions. However, the treatment of these settings will most probably require a more sophisticated approach including for instance three-body correlations between the atoms of the medium. Additionally, the investigation of finite sized systems at non-zero temperatures in the dimensional crossover from 3D to 2D as it has been reported e.g., in Ref. [121] but in the ultracold and single-polaron limits offers an interesting perspective for forthcoming endeavors. Furthermore, the comparison of the predictions of our methodology to treat the effect of quantum fluctuations in Bose polaron settings with other approaches based also on the mean-field framework [118,119] is certainly of interest. Finally, the backaction of the impurities on the medium when considering dipolar interactions between the medium atoms may affect the density collapse of the medium at strong impurity-medium attractions [122] and thus provides another intriguing prospect.

Author Contributions: Conceptualization, H.T., J.T., S.I.M., E.N. and K.I.; methodology, H.T. and J.T.; software H.T. and J.T.; validation, H.T. and J.T.; formal analysis, H.T. and J.T.; investigation, H.T. and J.T.; resources, H.T. and J.T.; data curation, H.T. and J.T.; writing—original draft preparation, H.T. and J.T.; writing—review and editing, H.T., J.T., S.I.M., E.N. and K.I.; visualization, H.T. J.T., S.I.M., E.N. and K.I.; supervision, E.N. and K.I. All authors have read and agreed to the published version of the manuscript.

Funding: This research was funded by a Grant-in-Aid for JSPS fellows (Grant No. 17J03975) and for Scientific Research from JSPS (Grants No. 17K05445, No. 18K03501, No. 18H05406, No. 18H01211, and No. 19K14619).

Institutional Review Board Statement: Not applicable.

Informed Consent Statement: Not applicable.

Data Availability Statement: All data discussed in this study are available within the article.

Acknowledgments: The authors thank K. Nishimura, T. Hata, K. Ochi, T. M. Doi, and S. Tsutsui for useful discussion. S.I.M. gratefully acknowledges financial support in the framework of the Lenz-Ising Award of the University of Hamburg.

Conflicts of Interest: The authors declare no conflict of interest.

References

1. Pekar, S.I. Local quantum states of electrons in an ideal ion crystal. *Zhurnal Eksperimentalnoi I Teoreticheskoi Fiziki* **1946**, *16*, 341.
2. Landau, L.D.; Pekar, S.I. Effective mass of a polaron. *Zhurnal Eksperimentalnoi I Teoreticheskoi Fiziki* **1948**, *18*, 418.
3. Nascimbène, S.; Navon, N.; Jiang, K.J.; Tarruell, L.; Teichmann, M.; McKeever, J.; Chevy, F.; Salomon, C. Collective Oscillations of an Imbalanced Fermi Gas: Axial Compression Modes and Polaron Effective Mass. *Phys. Rev. Lett.* **2009**, *103*, 170402. [CrossRef]
4. Schirotzek, A.; Wu, C.-H.; Sommer, A.; Zwierlein, M.W. Observation of Fermi Polarons in a Tunable Fermi Liquid of Ultracold Atoms. *Phys. Rev. Lett.* **2009**, *102*, 230402. [CrossRef] [PubMed]
5. Kohstall, C.; Zaccanti, M.; Jag, M.; Trenkwalder, A.; Massignan, P.; Bruun, G.M.; Schreck, F.; Grimm, R. Metastability and Coherence of Repulsive Polarons in a Strongly Interacting Fermi Mixture. *Nature* **2011**, *485*, 615. [CrossRef]
6. Koschorreck, M.; Pertot, D.; Vogt, E.; Fröhlich, B.; Feld, M.; Köhl, M. Attractive and repulsive Fermi polarons in two dimensions. *Nature* **2012**, *485*, 619. [CrossRef]
7. Hohmann, M.; Kindermann, F.; Gänger, B.; Lausch, T.; Mayer, D.; Schmidt, F.; Widera, A. Neutral Impurities in a Bose-Einstein Condensate for Simulation of the Fröhlich-Polaron. *EPJ Quantum Technol.* **2015**, *2*, 23. [CrossRef]
8. Jorgensen, N.B.; Wacker, L.; Skalmstang, K.T.; Parish, M.M.; Levinsen, J.; Christensen, R.S.; Bruun, G.M.; Arlt, J.J. Observation of Attractive and Repulsive Polarons in a Bose-Einstein Condensate. *Phys. Rev. Lett.* **2016**, *117*, 055302. [CrossRef] [PubMed]
9. Hu, M.-G.; Van de Graaff, M.J.; Kedar, D.; Corson, J.P.; Cornell, E.A.; Jin, D.S. Bose Polarons in the Strongly Interacting Regime. *Phys. Rev. Lett.* **2016**, *117*, 055301. [CrossRef] [PubMed]
10. Scazza, F.; Valtolina, G.; Massignan, P.; Recati, A.; Amico, A.; Burchianti, A.; Fort, C.; Inguscio, M.; Zaccanti, M.; Roati, G. Repulsive Fermi Polarons in a Resonant Mixture of Ultracold ^{6}Li Atoms. *Phys. Rev. Lett.* **2017**, *118*, 083602. [CrossRef]
11. Oppong, N.D.; Riegger, L.; Bettermann, O.; Höfer, M.; Levinsen, J.; Parish, M.M.; Bloch, I.; Fölling, S. Observation of Coherent Multiorbital Polarons in a Two-Dimensional Fermi Gas. *Phys. Rev. Lett.* **2019**, *122*, 193604. [CrossRef] [PubMed]
12. Adlong, H.S.; Liu, W.E.; Scazza, F.; Zaccanti, M.; Oppong, N.D.; Fölling, S.; Parish, M.M.; Levinsen, J. Quasiparticle Lifetime of the Repulsive Fermi Polaron. *Phys. Rev. Lett.* **2020**, *125*, 133401. [CrossRef] [PubMed]
13. Catani, J.; Lamporesi, G.; Naik, D.; Gring, M.; Inguscio, M.; Minardi, F.; Kantian, A.; Giamarchi, T. Quantum Dynamics of Impurities in a One-Dimensional Bose Gas. *Phys. Rev. A* **2012**, *85*, 023623. [CrossRef]
14. Scelle, R.; Rentrop, T.; Trautmann, A.; Schuster, T.; Oberthaler, M.K. Motional Coherence of Fermions Immersed in a Bose Gas. *Phys. Rev. Lett.* **2013**, *111*, 070401. [CrossRef] [PubMed]
15. Rentrop, T.; Trautmann, A.; Olivares, F.A.; Jendrzejewski, F.; Komnik, A.; Oberthaler, M.K. Observation of the Phononic Lamb Shift with a Synthetic Vacuum. *Phys. Rev. X* **2016**, *6*, 041041. [CrossRef]
16. Yan, Z.; Patel, P.B.; Mukherjee, B.; Fletcher, R.J.; Struck, J.; Zwierlein, M.W. Boiling a Unitary Fermi Liquid. *Phys. Rev. Lett.* **2019**, *122*, 093401. [CrossRef]
17. Ness, G.; Shkedrov, C.; Florshaim, Y.; Diessel, O.K.; von Milczewski, J.; Schmidt, R.; Sagi, Y. Observation of a smooth polaron-molecule transition in a degenerate Fermi gas. *Phys. Rev. X* **2020**, *10*, 041019. [CrossRef]
18. DeSalvo, B.J.; Patel, K.; Cai, G.; Chin, C. Observation of fermion-mediated interactions between bosonic atoms. *Nature* **2019**, *568*, 61. [CrossRef]
19. Edri, H.; Raz, B.; Matzliah, N.; Davidson, N.; Ozeri, R. Observation of Spin-Spin Fermion-Mediated Interactions between Ultracold Bosons. *Phys. Rev. Lett.* **2020**, *124*, 163401. [CrossRef]
20. Peyronel, T.; Firstenberg, O.; Liang, Q.-Y.; Hofferberth, S.; Gorshkov, A.V.; Pohl, T.; Lukin, M.D.; Vuletić, V. Quantum nonlinear optics with single photons enabled by strongly interacting atoms. *Nature* **2012**, *488*, 57. [CrossRef]

21. Ningyuan J.; Georgakopoulos, A.; Ryou, A.; Schine, N.; Sommer, A. Simon, J. Observation and characterization of cavity Rydberg polaritons. *Phys. Rev. A* **2016**, *93*, 041802. [CrossRef]
22. Thompson, J.D.; Nicholson, T.L.; Liang, Q.-Y.; Cantu, S.H.; Venkatramani, A.V.; Choi, S.; Fedorov, I.A.; Viscor, D.; Pohl, T.; Lukin, M.D.; et al. Symmetry-protected collisions between strongly interacting photons. *Nature* **2017**, *542*, 206. [CrossRef] [PubMed]
23. Chin, C.; Grimm, R.; Julienne, P.; Tiesinga, E. Feshbach resonances in ultracold gases. *Rev. Mod. Phys.* **2010** *82*, 1225. [CrossRef]
24. Mistakidis, S.I.; Katsimiga, G.C.; Koutentakis, G.M.; Busch, T.H.; Schmelcher, P. Quench Dynamics and Orthogonality Catastrophe of Bose Polarons. *Phys. Rev. Lett.* **2019**, *122*, 183001. [CrossRef]
25. Massignan, P.; Zaccanti, M.; Bruun, G.M. Polarons, dressed molecules and itinerant ferromagnetism in ultracold Fermi gases. *Rep. Prog. Phys.* **2014**, *77*, 034401. [CrossRef]
26. Schmidt, R.; Knap, M.; Ivanov, D.A.; You, J.-S.; Cetina, M.; Demler, E. Universal many-body response of heavy impurities coupled to a Fermi sea: A review of recent progress. *Rep. Prog. Phys.* **2018**, *81*, 024401. [CrossRef] [PubMed]
27. Kutschera, M.; Wójcik, W. Proton impurity in the neutron matter: A nuclear polaron problem. *Phys. Rev. C* **1993**, *47*, 1077. [CrossRef]
28. Forbes, M.M.; Gezerlis, A.; Hebeler, K.; Lesinski, T.; Schwenk, A. Neutron polaron as a constraint on nuclear density functionals. *Phys. Rev. C* **2014**, *89*, 041301(R). [CrossRef]
29. Tajima, H.; Hatsuda, T.; van Wyk, P.; Ohashi, Y. Superfluid Phase Transitions and Effects Thermal Pairing Fluctuations in Asymmetric Nuclear Matter. *Sci. Rep.* **2019**, *9*, 18477. [CrossRef] [PubMed]
30. Nakano, E.; Iida, K.; Horiuchi, W. Quasiparticle properties of a single α particle in cold neutron matter. *Phys. Rev. C* **2020**, *102*, 055802. [CrossRef]
31. Vidana, I. Fermi polaron in low-density spin-polarized neutron matter. *arXiv* **2021**, arXiv:2101.02941.
32. Sous, J.; Sadeghpour, H.R.; Killian, T.C.; Demler, E.; Schmidt, R. Rydberg impurity in a Fermi gas: Quantum statistics and rotational blockade. *Phys. Rev. Res.* **2020**, *2*, 023021. [CrossRef]
33. Chevy, F. Universal phase diagram of a strongly interacting Fermi gas with unbalanced spin populations. *Phys. Rev. A* **2006**, *74*, 063628. [CrossRef]
34. Combescot, R.; Recati, A.; Lobo, C.; Chevy, F. Normal State of Highly Polarized Fermi Gases: Simple Many-Body Approaches. *Phys. Rev. Lett.* **2007**, *98*, 180402. [CrossRef]
35. Combescot, R.; Giraud, S. Normal State of Highly Polarized Fermi Gases: Full Many-Body Treatment. *Phys. Rev. Lett.* **2008**, *101*, 050404. [CrossRef]
36. Cui, X.; Zhai, H. Stability of a fully magnetized ferromagnetic state in repulsively interacting ultracold Fermi gases. *Phys. Rev. A* **2010**, *81*, 041602(R). [CrossRef]
37. Bruun, G.M.; Massignan, P. Decay of Polarons and Molecules in a Strongly Polarized Fermi Gas. *Phys. Rev. Lett.* **2010**, *105*, 020403. [CrossRef] [PubMed]
38. Mathy, C.J.M.; Parish, M.M.; Huse, D.A. Trimers, Molecules, and Polarons in Mass-Imbalanced Atomic Fermi Gases. *Phys. Rev. Lett.* **2011**. *106*, 166404. [CrossRef]
39. Schmidt, R.; Enss, T. Excitation spectra and rf response near the polaron-to-molecule transition from the functional renormalization group. *Phys. Rev. A* **2011**, *83*, 063620. [CrossRef]
40. Trefzger, C.; Castin, Y. Impurity in a Fermi sea on a narrow Feshbach resonance: A variational study of the polaronic and dimeronic branches. *Phys. Rev. A* **2012**, *85*, 053612. [CrossRef]
41. Baarsma, J.E.; Armaitis, J.; Duine, R.A.; Stoof, H.T.C. Polarons in extremely polarized Fermi gases: The strongly interacting ^{6}Li-^{40}K mixture. *Phys. Rev. A* **2012**, *85*, 033631. [CrossRef]
42. Prokof'ev, N.; Svistunov, B. Fermi-polaron problem: Diagrammatic Monte Carlo method for divergent sign-alternating series. *Phys. Rev. B* **2008**, *77*, 020408(R). [CrossRef]
43. Prokof'ev, N.V.; Svistunov, B.V. Bold diagrammatic Monte Carlo: A generic sign-problem tolerant technique for polaron models and possibly interacting many-body problems. *Phys. Rev. B* **2008**, *77*, 125101. [CrossRef]
44. Vlietinck, J.; Ryckebusch J.; Van Houcke, K. Quasiparticle properties of an impurity in a Fermi gas. *Phys. Rev. B* **2013**, *87*, 115133. [CrossRef]
45. Kroiss, P.; Pollet, L. Diagrammatic Monte Carlo study of a mass-imbalanced Fermi-polaron system. *Phys. Rev. B* **2015**, *91*, 144507. [CrossRef]
46. Goulko, O.; Mishchenko, A.S.; Prokof'ev, N.; Svistunov, B. Dark continuum in the spectral function of the resonant Fermi polaron. *Phys. Rev. A* **2016**, *94*, 051605(R). [CrossRef]
47. Van Houcke, K.; Werner, F.; Rossi, R. High-precision numerical solution of the Fermi polaron problem and large-order behavior of its diagrammatic series. *Phys. Rev. B* **2020**, *101*, 045134. [CrossRef]
48. Kamikado, K.; Kanazawa, T.; Uchino, S. Mobile impurity in a Fermi sea from the functional renormalization group analytically continued to real time. *Phys. Rev. A* **2017**, *95*, 013612. [CrossRef]
49. Liu, W.E.; Shi, Z.-Y.; Parish, M.M.; Levinsen, J. Theory of radio-frequency spectroscopy of impurities in quantum gases. *Phys. Rev. A* **2020**, *102*, 023304. [CrossRef]
50. Liu, W.E.; Shi, Z.-Y.; Levinsen, J.; Parish, M.M. Radio-Frequency Response and Contact of Impurities in a Quantum Gas. *Phys. Rev. Lett.* **2020**, *125*, 065301. [CrossRef]

51. Pilati, S.; Giorgini, S. Phase Separation in a Polarized Fermi Gas at Zero Temperature. *Phys. Rev. Lett.* **2008**, *100*, 030401. [CrossRef] [PubMed]
52. Mora, C.; Chevy, F. Normal State of an Imbalanced Fermi Gas. *Phys. Rev. Lett.* **2010**, *104*, 230402. [CrossRef] [PubMed]
53. Giraud, S.; Combescot, R. Interaction between polarons and analogous effects in polarized Fermi gases. *Phys. Rev. A* **2012**, *85*, 013605. [CrossRef]
54. Hu, H.; Mulkerin, B.C.; Wang, J.; Liu, X.-J. Attractive Fermi polarons at nonzero temperatures with a finite impurity concentration. *Phys. Rev. A* **2018**, *98*, 013626. [CrossRef]
55. Tajima, H.; Uchino, S. Many Fermi polarons at nonzero temperature. *New J. Phys.* **2018**, *20*, 073048. [CrossRef]
56. Tajima, H.; Uchino, S. Thermal crossover, transition, and coexistence in Fermi polaronic spectroscopies. *Phys. Rev. A* **2019**, *99*, 063606. [CrossRef]
57. Tajima, H.; Takahashi, J.; Nakano, E.; Iida, K. Collisional dynamics of polaronic clouds immersed in a Fermi sea. *Phys. Rev. A* **2020**, *102*, 051302(R). [CrossRef]
58. Takahashi, J.; Tajima, H.; Nakano, E.; Iida, K. Extracting non-local inter-polaron interactions from collisional dynamics. *arXiv* **2020**, arXiv:2011.07911.
59. Mistakidis, S.I.; Volosniev, A.G.; Schmelcher, P. Induced correlations between impurities in a one-dimensional quenched Bose gas. *Phys. Rev. Res.* **2020**, *2*, 023154. [CrossRef]
60. Mistakidis, S.I.; Katsimiga, G.C.; Koutentakis, G.M.; Busch, T.; Schmelcher, P. Pump-probe spectroscopy of Bose polarons: Dynamical formation and coherence. *Phys. Rev. Res.* **2020**, *2*, 033380. [CrossRef]
61. Mukherjee, K.; Mistakidis, S.I.; Majumder, S.; Schmelcher, P. Induced interactions and quench dynamics of bosonic impurities immersed in a Fermi sea. *Phys. Rev. A* **2020**, *102*, 053317. [CrossRef]
62. Compagno, E.; De Chiara, G.; Angelakis, D.G.; Palma, G.M. Tunable Polarons in Bose-Einstein Condensates. *Sci. Rep.* **2017**, *7*, 2355. [CrossRef]
63. Sous, J.; Berciu, M.; Krems, R.V. Bipolarons bound by repulsive phonon-mediated interactions. *Phys. Rev. A* **2017**, *96*, 063619. [CrossRef]
64. Nakano, E.; Yabu, H.; Iida, K. Bose-Einstein-Condensate Polaron in Harmonic Trap Potentials in the Weak-Coupling Regime: Lee-Low-Pines–Type Approach. *Phys. Rev. A* **2017**, *95*, 023626. [CrossRef]
65. Watanabe, K.; Nakano, E.; Yabu, H. Bose Polaron in Spherically Symmetric Trap Potentials: Ground States with Zero and Lower Angular Momenta. *Phys. Rev. A* **2019**, *99*, 033624. [CrossRef]
66. Peña Ardila, L.A.; Jorgensen, N.B.; Pohl, T.; Giorgini, S.; Bruun, G.M.; Arlt, J.J. Analyzing a Bose polaron across resonant interactions. *Phys. Rev. A* **2019**, *99*, 063607. [CrossRef]
67. Peña Ardila, L.A.; Astrakharchik, G.E.; Giorgini, S. Strong coupling Bose polarons in a two-dimensional gas. *Phys. Rev. Res.* **2020**, *2*, 023405. [CrossRef]
68. Cucchietti, F.M.; Timmermans, E. Strong-Coupling Polarons in Dilute Gas Bose-Einstein Condensates. *Phys. Rev. Lett.* **2006**, *96*, 210401. [CrossRef] [PubMed]
69. Sacha, K.; Timmermans, E. Self-Localized Impurities Embedded in a One-Dimensional Bose-Einstein Condensate and Their Quantum Fluctuations. *Phys. Rev. A* **2006**, *73*, 063604. [CrossRef]
70. Kalas, R.M.; Blume, D. Interaction-Induced Localization of an Impurity in a Trapped Bose-Einstein Condensate. *Phys. Rev. A* **2006**, *73*, 043608. [CrossRef]
71. Bruderer, M.; Bao, W.; Jaksch, D. Self-trapping of impurities in Bose-Einstein condensates: Strong attractive and repulsive coupling. *EuroPhys. Lett.* **2008**, *82*, 30004. [CrossRef]
72. Boudjemâa, A. Self-localized state and solitons in a Bose-Einstein-condensate-impurity mixture at finite temperature. *Phys. Rev. A* **2014**, *90*, 013628. [CrossRef]
73. Sous, J.; Chakraborty, M.; Adolphs, C.P.J.; Krems, R.V.; Berciu, M. Phonon-mediated repulsion, sharp transitions and (quasi)self-trapping in the extended Peierls-Hubbard model. *Sci. Rep.* **2017**, *7*, 1169. [CrossRef]
74. Cai, Z.; Wang, L.; Xie, X.C.; Wang, Y. Interaction-induced anomalous transport behavior in one-dimensional optical lattices. *Phys. Rev. A* **2010** *81*, 043602. [CrossRef]
75. Theel, F.; Keiler, K.; Mistakidis, S.I.; Schmelcher, P. Many-body collisional dynamics of impurities injected into a double-well trapped Bose-Einstein condensate. *arXiv* **2020**, arXiv:2009.12147.
76. Keiler, K.; Mistakidis, S.I.; Schmelcher, P. Doping a lattice-trapped bosonic species with impurities: From ground state properties to correlated tunneling dynamics. *New J. Phys.* **2020**, *22*, 083003. [CrossRef]
77. Siegl, P.; Mistakidis, S.I.; Schmelcher, P. Many-body expansion dynamics of a Bose-Fermi mixture confined in an optical lattice. *Phys. Rev. A* **2018**, *97*, 053626. [CrossRef]
78. Mistakidis, S.I.; Grusdt, F.; Koutentakis, G.M.; Schmelcher, P. Dissipative correlated dynamics of a moving impurity immersed in a Bose–Einstein condensate. *New J. Phys.* **2019**, *21*, 103026. [CrossRef]
79. Strinati, G.C.; Pieri, P.; Röpke, G.; Schuck, P.; Urban, M. The BCS-BEC crossover: From ultra-cold Fermi gases to nuclear systems. *Phys. Rep.* **2018**, *738*, 1. [CrossRef]
80. Ohashi, Y.; Tajima, H.; van Wyk, P. BCS-BEC crossover in cold atomic and nuclear systems. *Prog. Part. Nucl. Phys.* **2020**, *111*, 103739. [CrossRef]

81. Kashimura, T.; Watanabe, R.; Ohashi, Y. Spin susceptibility and fluctuation corrections in the BCS-BEC crossover regime of an ultracold Fermi gas. *Phys. Rev. A* **2012**, *86*, 043622. [CrossRef]
82. Tajima, H.; van Wyk, P.; Hanai, R.; Kagamihara, D.; Inotani, D.; Horikoshi, M.; Ohashi, Y. Strong-coupling corrections to ground-state properties of a superfluid Fermi gas. *Phys. Rev. A* **2017**, *95*, 043625. [CrossRef]
83. Horikoshi, M.; Koashi, M.; Tajima, H.; Ohashi, Y.; Kuwata-Gonokami, M. Ground-State Thermodynamic Quantities of Homogeneous Spin-1/2 Fermions from the BCS Region to the Unitarity Limit. *Phys. Rev. X* **2017**, *7*, 041004. [CrossRef]
84. Haussmann, R. Crossover from BCS superconductivity to Bose-Einstein condensation: A self-consistent theory. *Z. Phys. B* **1993**, *91*, 291. [CrossRef]
85. Haussmann, R.; Rantner, W.; Cerrito, S.; Zwerger, W. THermodynamics of the BCS-BEC crossover. *Phys. Rev. A* **2007**, *75*, 023610. [CrossRef]
86. Takahashi, J.; Imai, R.; Nakano, E.; Iida, K. Bose Polaron in Spherical Trap Potentials: Spatial Structure and Quantum Depletion. *Phys. Rev. A* **2019**, *100*, 023624. [CrossRef]
87. Pethick, C.J.; Smith, H. *Bose-Einstein Condensation in Dilute Gases*; Cambridge University Press: Cambridge, UK, 2008.
88. Morgan, S.A.; Lee, M.D.; Burnett, K. Off-shell T matrices in one, two and three dimensions. *Phys. Rev. A* **2002**, *65*, 022706. [CrossRef]
89. Fetter, A.L.; Walecka, J.D. *Quantum Theory of Many-Particle Systems*; Dover: New York, NY, USA, 2003.
90. Törmä, P. Spectroscopies–Theory. In *Quantum Gas Experiments: Exploring Many-Body States*; Törmä, P., Sengstock, K., Eds.; Imperial College: London, UK, 2015.
91. Frank, B.; Lang, J.; Zwerger, W. Universal phase diagram and scaling functions of imbalanced Fermi gases. *J. Exp. Theor. Phys.* **2018**, *127*, 812. [CrossRef]
92. Pini, M.; Pieri, P.; Strinati, G.C. Fermi gas throughout the BCS-BEC crossover: Comparative study of *t*-matrix approaches with various degrees of self-consistency. *Phys. Rev. B* **2019**, *99*, 094502. [CrossRef]
93. Punk, M.; Dumitrescu, P.T.; Zwerger, W. Polaron-to-molecule transition in a strongly imbalanced Fermi gas. *Phys. Rev. A* **2009**, *80*, 053605. [CrossRef]
94. Cui, X. Fermi polaron revisited: Polaron-molecule transition and coexistence. *Phys. Rev. A* **2020**, *102*, 061301(R). [CrossRef]
95. Thouless, D.J. Perturbation theory in statistical mechanics and the theory of superconductivity. *Ann. Phys.* **1960**, *10*, 553. [CrossRef]
96. Liu, X.-J.; Hu, H. BCS-BEC crossover in an asymmetric two-component Fermi gas. *Europhys. Lett.* **2006**, *75*, 364. [CrossRef]
97. Grudst, F.; Seetharam, K.; Shchadilova, Y.; Demler, E. Strong-coupling Bose polarons out of equilibrium: Dynamical renormalization group approach. *Phys. Rev. A* **2018**, *97*, 033612.
98. Nielsen, K.; Peña Ardila, L.A.; Bruun, G.M.; Pohl, T. Critical slowdown of non-equilibrium polaron dynamics. *New J. Phys.* **2019**, *21*, 043014. [CrossRef]
99. Sekino, Y.; Tajima, H.; Uchino, S. Mesoscopic spin transport between strongly interacting Fermi gases. *Phys. Rev. Res.* **2020**, *2*, 023152. [CrossRef]
100. Parish, M.M.; Adlong, H.S.; Liu, W.E.; Levinsen, J. Thermodynamic signatures of the polaron-molecule transition in a Fermi gas. *Phys. Rev. A* **2021**, *103*, 023312. [CrossRef]
101. Schmidt, R.; Enss, T.; Pietilä, V.; Demler, E. Fermi polarons in two dimensions. *Phys. Rev. A* **2012**, *85*, 021602(R). [CrossRef]
102. Klawunn, M.; Recati, A. The Fermi-polaron in two dimensions: Importance of the two-body bound state. *Phys. Rev. A* **2011**, *84*, 033607. [CrossRef]
103. Tajima, H.; Tsutsui, S.; Doi, T.M. Low-dimensional fluctuations and pseudogap in Gaudin-Yang Fermi gas. *Phys. Rev. Res.* **2020**, *2*, 033441. [CrossRef]
104. Mistakidis, S.I.; Katsimiga, G.C.; Koutentakis, G.M.; Schmelcher, P. Repulsive Fermi polarons and their induced interactions in binary mixtures of ultracold atoms. *New J. Phys.* **2018**, *21*, 043032. [CrossRef]
105. Kwasniok, J.; Mistakidis, S.I.; Schmelcher, P. Correlated dynamics of fermionic impurities of an emsemble of fermions. *Phys. Rev. A* **2020**, *101*, 053619. [CrossRef]
106. Guan, X.-W.; Batchelor, M.T.; Lee, C. Fermi gases in one dimension: From Bethe ansatz to experiments. *Rev. Mod. Phys.* **2013**, *85*, 1633. [CrossRef]
107. Doggen, E.V.H.; Kinnunen, J.J. Energy and Contact of the One-Dimensional Fermi Polaron at Zero and Finite Temperature. *Phys. Rev. Lett.* **2013**, *111*, 025302. [CrossRef]
108. Lampo, A.; Charalambous, C.; García-March, M.Á.; Lewenstein, M. Non-Markovian Polaron Dynamics in a Trapped Bose-Einstein Condensate. *Phys. Rev. A* **2018**, *98*, 063630. [CrossRef]
109. Mistakidis, S.I.; Volosniev, A.G.; Zinner, N.T.; Schmelcher, P. Effective Approach to Impurity Dynamics in One-Dimensional Trapped Bose Gases. *Phys. Rev. A* **2019**, *100*, 013619. [CrossRef]
110. Pitaevskii, L.; Stringari, S. *Bose-Einstein Condensation*; Cambridge University Press: Cambridge, UK, 2003.
111. Dalfovo, F.; Giorgini, S.; Pitaevskii, L.P.; Stringari, S. Theory of Bose-Einstein Condensation in Trapped Gases. *Rev. Mod. Phys.* **1999**, *71*, 463. [CrossRef]
112. Bogoliubov, N.N. On the theory of superfluidity. *J. Phys.* **1947**, *11*, 32.
113. de Gennes, P.G. *Superconductivity of Metals and Alloys*; CRC Press: Boca Raton, FL, USA, 1966.

114. Katsimiga, G.C.; Mistakidis, S.I.; Bersano, T.M.; Ome, M.K.H.; Mossman, S.M.; Mukherjee, K.; Schmelcher, P.; Engels, P.; Kevrekidis, P.G. Observation and Analysis of Multiple Dark-Antidark Solitons in Two-Component Bose-Einstein Condensates. *Phys. Rev. A* **2020**, *102*, 023301. [CrossRef]
115. Katsimiga, G.C.; Mistakidis, S.I.; Schmelcher, P.; Kevrekidis, P.G. Phase Diagram, Stability and Magnetic Properties of Nonlinear Excitations in Spinor Bose-Einstein Condensates. *New J. Phys.* **2021**, *23*, 013015. [CrossRef]
116. Mueller, E.J.; Ho, T.L.; Ueda, M.; Baym, G. Fragmentation of bose-einstein condensates. *Phys. Rev. A* **2006**, *74* 033612. [CrossRef]
117. Shchadilova, Y.E.; Schmidt, R.; Grusdt, F.; Demler, E. Quantum Dynamics of Ultracold Bose Polarons. *Phys. Rev. Lett.* **2016**, *117*, 113002. [CrossRef] [PubMed]
118. Drescher, M.; Salmhofer, M.; Enss, T. Theory of a resonantly interacting impurity in a Bose-Einstein condensate. *Phys. Rev. Res.* **2020**, *2*, 032011(R). [CrossRef]
119. Guenther, N.-E.; Schmidt, R.; Bruun, G.M.; Gurarie, V.; Massignan, P. Mobile impurity in a Bose-Einstein condensate and the orthogonality catastrophe. *Phys. Rev. A* **2021**, *103*, 013317. [CrossRef]
120. Tempere, J.; Klimin, S.N.; Devreese, J.T. Effect of population imbalance on the Berezinskii-Kosterlitz-Thouless phase transition in a superfluid Fermi gas. *Phys. Rev. A* **2009**, *79*, 053637. [CrossRef]
121. Levinsen, J.; Baur, S.K. High-polarization limit of the quasi-two-dimensional Fermi gas. *Phys. Rev. A* **2012**, *86*, 041602(R). [CrossRef]
122. Nishimura, K.; Nakano, E.; Iida, K.; Tajima, H.; Miyakawa, T.; Yabu, H. The ground state of polaron in an ultracold dipolar Fermi gas. *arXiv* **2020**, arXiv:2010.15558.

Article

Ultra-Dilute Gas of Polarons in a Bose–Einstein Condensate

Luis A. Peña Ardila

Institut für Theoretische Physik, Leibniz Universität, 30167 Hannover, Germany; luis.ardila@itp.uni-hannover.de

Citation: Ardila, L.A.P. Ultra-Dilute Gas of Polarons in a Bose–Einstein Condensate. *Atoms* **2022**, *10*, 29. https://doi.org/10.3390/atoms10010029

Academic Editors: Simeon Mistakidis and Artem Volosniev

Received: 11 February 2022
Accepted: 27 February 2022
Published: 2 March 2022

Publisher's Note: MDPI stays neutral with regard to jurisdictional claims in published maps and institutional affiliations.

Copyright: © 2022 by the authors. Licensee MDPI, Basel, Switzerland. This article is an open access article distributed under the terms and conditions of the Creative Commons Attribution (CC BY) license (https://creativecommons.org/licenses/by/4.0/).

Abstract: We investigate the properties of a dilute gas of impurities embedded in an ultracold gas of bosons that forms a Bose–Einstein condensate (BEC). This work focuses mainly on the equation of state (EoS) of the impurity gas at zero temperature and the induced interaction between impurities mediated by the host bath. We use perturbative field-theory approaches, such as Hugenholtz–Pines formalism, in the weakly interacting regime. In turn, for strong interactions, we aim at non-perturbative techniques such as quantum–Monte Carlo (QMC) methods. Our findings agree with experimental observations for an ultra dilute gas of impurities, modeled in the framework of the single impurity problem; however, as the density of impurities increases, systematic deviations are displayed with respect to the one-body Bose polaron problem.

Keywords: polaron–polaron interaction; induced interaction; gas of impurities; quantum–Monte Carlo

1. Introduction

In a non-relativistic framework, interactions mediated by a scalar bosonic field are in general attractive in 3D. This paradigm maps into a system of impurities interacting with an ultra-cold bosonic gas. In the case of a single impurity, the problem is known as the Bose polaron problem. In solid state systems, polarons are relevant to describe specific properties in materials. For instance, understanding the motion of electrons in a polar crystal gives insight into how good a material conducts. Yet, a complete microscopical description of the problem is unfeasible due to the complexity and imperfections in solids. Landau and Pekar introduced the concept of polaron [1,2], to give an approximate good description of the many-body problem in terms of quasiparticles—a strongly correlated system maps into a weakly interacting gas of elementary excitations. Thus, the particles in the system are modeled as almost non-interacting particles with a renormalized energy and mass. This simplification yields that the latter problem is more trackable within analytical, yet robust, approaches. For instance, electrons in a polarizable lattice [3] and electrons in ^{3}He and ^{4}He have been prominent candidates to test Landau theory [4,5].

Besides the single-particle renormalization quantities, quasiparticles may interact among them because they are not in free space and ripples in the medium interfere, i.e., its host medium could mediate interactions. Restoring to the concept of adiabaticity—also in the heart of Landau's theory—one can consider a system of non-interacting particles at $t = 0$ and suddenly quench the interaction; thus, a one-to-one correspondence is established between particles and the low-energy excitations of the non-interacting system in the neighborhood of the Fermi surface and even yet-excited states are occupied, the interaction between quasiparticles is not negligible. In the case of bosons, the Pauli principle is no longer a constraint, and the interaction between bosonic quasiparticles are more significant with respect to its fermionic counterpart [6].

Detection of quasiparticles, as well as their experimental control, is achievable by using ultracold quantum gases. Impurities embedded in a degenerate quantum gas form either a Fermi polaron [7–13] or a Bose polaron [14–19] depending on the statistical nature of the host bath. In addition, tunability on the impurity–bath interaction [20,21] allows exploring the strongly interacting regime, inaccessible in the solid-state realm. Theoretically, the problem of a single impurity in a quantum gas have been addressed with several techniques such as mean-field, perturbation theory, renormalization group, modified Gross-Pitaevskii equation, variational ansatzes and field-theory approaches [22–36] and numerical approaches such as quantum Monte-Carlo methods [37–40]. Interestingly, the single-particle polaron problem agrees very well with experiments, where the number of impurities is on the order of five up to ten percent with respect to the total number of atoms of the host gas. A priori, one of the conclusions drawn from this observation is that the interaction between polarons appears to be negligible. Recently, it has been shown that polaron–polaron interaction can manifest only when the impurity–bath interaction is sizable in slow impurities [41]. The typical scenario is the strongly interacting regime where the scattering length is much larger than the interparticle distance between host atoms (the bath becomes more compressible favoring the effective interaction). In the particular case of two impurities, induced interactions are attractive, and bound-states known as bipolaron are expected to be formed [42–44]. Recently, the ground state properties of a gas of impurities in a BEC have been extracted from the structure factor of the impurity gas by using variational methods [45]. Strong induced interactions can also be manifested in the weakly interacting regime if the momentum of the impurity is resonant with a mode of the condensate [6], however, in this work we are interested in the case of slow polarons (momentum zero).

In this work, we turn our attention to the case of many impurities, where impurity statistics plays an important role. Here we investigate the ground state properties of bosonic impurities immersed in a Bose–Einstein condensate at zero temperature using perturbative approaches such as Hugenholtz–Pines for weak coupling. At the same time, QMC techniques are employed to study the strongly interacting regime. From an experimental point of view, a system of few impurities immersed in a quantum gas is more realistic than the case of a single one. Yet, there is an open question of whether the interactions between polarons are relevant for the different time scales in the system.

The article is organized as follows. In Section 2, we present the EoS for a multi-impurity system in the weakly interacting regime. Here we employ the Hugenholtz–Pines formalism, and we derive an expression for small polarization and coupling strength. Furthermore, we introduce the general form of the Jastrow wave function and the specific potentials used in QMC calculations. Section 3 discusses the results, and finally, conclusions are drawn in Section 4.

2. Methods

The system consists of a two-component quantum gas formed by bosons. The first component (host gas) is a Bose–Einstein condensate (BEC) characterized by a density n_1, while the second component is embedded into the host gas and is formed by atoms of density n_2 termed from now on, as impurities. The Hamiltonian in the second quantization of the system reads,

$$\mathcal{H} = \sum_{\mathbf{p}} \frac{\hat{\mathbf{P}}^2}{2m_I} \hat{c}_{\mathbf{p}}^\dagger \hat{c}_{\mathbf{p}} + \sum_{\mathbf{k}} \frac{\hbar^2 \mathbf{k}^2}{2m_B} \hat{a}_{\mathbf{k}}^\dagger \hat{a}_{\mathbf{k}} + \frac{1}{2V} \sum_{\mathbf{k},\mathbf{k}',\mathbf{q}} V_{11}(\mathbf{q}) \hat{a}_{\mathbf{k}+\mathbf{q}}^\dagger \hat{a}_{\mathbf{k}'-\mathbf{q}}^\dagger \hat{a}_{\mathbf{k}'} \hat{a}_{\mathbf{k}}$$
$$+ \frac{1}{2V} \sum_{\mathbf{k},\mathbf{k}',\mathbf{q}} V_{22}(\mathbf{q}) \hat{c}_{\mathbf{k}+\mathbf{q}}^\dagger \hat{c}_{\mathbf{k}'-\mathbf{q}}^\dagger \hat{c}_{\mathbf{k}'} \hat{c}_{\mathbf{k}} + \frac{1}{V} \sum_{\mathbf{k},\mathbf{k}',\mathbf{q}} V_{12}(\mathbf{q}) \hat{a}_{\mathbf{k}+\mathbf{q}}^\dagger \hat{c}_{\mathbf{k}'-\mathbf{q}}^\dagger \hat{c}_{\mathbf{k}'} \hat{a}_{\mathbf{k}} \quad , \quad (1)$$

the operators $\hat{c}_{\mathbf{p}}$ ($\hat{c}_{\mathbf{p}}^\dagger$) annihilate (create) an impurity atom of mass m_I and momentum $\mathbf{P}$, whereas $\hat{a}_{\mathbf{k}}$ ($\hat{a}_{\mathbf{k}}^\dagger$) annihilates (creates) a boson of mass m_B and momentum $\hbar \mathbf{k}$. The intra- and interspecies interactions are short-range and without loss of generality we consider the equal mass case $m_I = m_B = m$. The boson–boson and impurity–boson interaction terms can be written as $V_{11}(\mathbf{k}) = 4\pi \hbar^2 a_{11}/m$ and $V_{12}(\mathbf{k}) = 4\pi \hbar^2 a_{12}/m$ respectively; the impurity-impurity term reads $V_{22}(\mathbf{k}) = 4\pi \hbar^2 a_{22}/m$. Where a_{11}, a_{12} and a_{22} are the s-wave scattering lengths. In current experiments a_{22} is finite, however in order to disentangle an induced interaction effect form the bare impurity–impurity interactions we may consider the case $a_{22} = 0$, such as the case of bi-polarons [42,44].

2.1. Weakly Interacting Regime

In this section, we estimate the polaron energy for the gas of impurities interacting with a majority condensate. The system can be accurately described by using the Gross–Pitaevskii theory in the regime, where the coupling strength impurity–bath is small or comparable with the one of the host bath. For a large number of atoms in the condensate and slow-moving impurities, one writes the chemical potential of the mixture as:

$$\mu_1 = -\frac{\hbar^2 \nabla^2}{2m}\psi_1(\mathbf{r}) + g_{11}n_1(\mathbf{r}) + g_{12}n_2(\mathbf{r}) + V_{ext,1}(\mathbf{r}) + \mu_{LHY}^{(1)}(\psi_1(\mathbf{r}), \psi_2(\mathbf{r}))$$
$$\mu_2 = -\frac{\hbar^2 \nabla^2}{2m}\psi_2(\mathbf{r}) + g_{22}n_2(\mathbf{r}) + g_{12}n_1(\mathbf{r}) + V_{ext,2}(\mathbf{r}) + \mu_{LHY}^{(2)}(\psi_1(\mathbf{r}), \psi_2(\mathbf{r}))$$
(2)

Here, μ_2 is identified as the polaron energy in the weakly interacting regime and $V_{ext,i}$ is the external potential experienced by the components in the mixture. Components 1 and 2 can be chosen as two hyperfine states and one can safely use the same external potential. The beyond mean-field or Lee–Huang–Yang (LHY) contribution reads, $\mu_2^{LHY} = \partial_{n_2}\epsilon_{LHY}$, where ϵ_{LHY} is the density energy computed within the Hugenholtz–Pines formalism [46] and coincides with the results for the chemical potential in a two-component quantum mixture [47]. Thus, the polaron energy up to the second-order reads

$$\mu_2^{LHY} = \frac{32\sqrt{\pi}}{3\sqrt{2}}\left(n_1 a_{11}^3\right)^{3/2}\frac{\hbar^2}{ma_{11}^2}\sum_{\lambda=\pm} Q_\lambda^{3/2}\partial_{n_2}Q_\lambda,$$
(3)

with the term $Q_\pm = 1 + P\frac{a_{22}}{a_{11}} \pm \sqrt{\left(1 - P\frac{a_{22}}{a_{11}}\right)^2 + 4P\left(\frac{a_{12}}{a_{11}}\right)^2}$ and the polarization $P = n_2/n_1$. Computing explicitly the derivative in Equation (3) one has

$$\mu_2^{LHY} = \frac{32\sqrt{\pi}}{3\sqrt{2}}\frac{\hbar^2}{ma_{11}^2}(n_1 a_{11}^3)^{3/2}\sum_{\lambda=\pm} W_\lambda,$$
(4)

with the function W_λ defined as

$$W_\lambda = \frac{a_{22}}{a_{11}}Q_\lambda^{3/2}\left(1 + \lambda\frac{\left(P\frac{a_{22}}{a_{11}} - 1\right) + 2\frac{a_{12}^2}{a_{11}a_{22}}}{\sqrt{\left(1 - P\frac{a_{22}}{a_{11}}\right)^2 + 4P\left(\frac{a_{12}}{a_{11}}\right)^2}}\right).$$
(5)

The results derived so far are exact for a weakly interacting mixture and they coincide with [47]. The beyond-single impurity limit can be obtained by expanding out the energy in terms of P and keep, as well, the terms up to the second-order in the coupling strength $(a_{12}/a_{11})^2$; thus, the polaron energy reads

$$\mu_2 = \left[\mu_{single} + \frac{32\sqrt{\pi}}{3\sqrt{2}}\left(n_1 a_{11}^3\right)^{3/2}\left(\frac{a_{22}}{a_{11}}\right)F(P)\right]\frac{\hbar^2}{ma_{11}^2}$$
(6)

where the single polaron energy [25,37] in the weakly interacting regime is recovered

$$\mu_{single} = 4\pi n_1 a_{11}^3 \frac{a_{12}}{a_{11}}\left(1 + \frac{32}{3\sqrt{\pi}}(n_1 a_{11}^3)^{1/2}\frac{a_{12}}{a_{11}}\right)$$
(7)

and the function taking into account the effects of the impurity concentration is

$$F(P) = k_1 P + k_2 P^{3/2} + k_3 P^2,$$
(8)

where $k_1 = 8\sqrt{2}\left(\frac{a_{12}}{a_{11}}\right)^2$, $k_2 = 4\sqrt{2}\left(\frac{a_{22}}{a_{11}}\right)^{1/2}\left(\left(\frac{a_{22}}{a_{11}}\right) - \frac{5}{2}\left(\frac{a_{12}}{a_{11}}\right)^2\right)$ and $k_3 = 12\sqrt{2}\left(\frac{a_{22}}{a_{11}}\right)\left(\frac{a_{12}}{a_{11}}\right)^2$.
Note that, for $a_{22} = 0$, the interactions *vanishes* in the weakly interacting regime. If we consider $a_{11} = a_{22} = a$, the polaron energy reads, $\mu_2 = \mu_{single} + \frac{32\sqrt{\pi}}{3\sqrt{2}}\left(n_1 a^3\right)^{3/2} F(P)$,

$$F(P) = 8\sqrt{2}\left(\frac{a_{12}}{a}\right)^2 P + 4\sqrt{2}\left(1 - \frac{5}{2}\left(\frac{a_{12}}{a}\right)^2\right) P^{3/2} + 12\sqrt{2}\left(\frac{a_{12}}{a}\right)^2 P^2. \tag{9}$$

In the derivation of the previous equation it is important to highlight that results are reliable in weak coupling, namely $\sqrt{n_1 a_{11}^3}\frac{a_{12}}{a_{11}} \ll 1$ and small polarization, $M/N \ll 1$. In the strongly interacting regime, one expects a large condensate depletion because of the strong presence of impurities. Hence, we use non-perturbative methods, such as Monte Carlo techniques. The method implementation for a system of impurities is discussed in the next session.

2.2. Strongly Interacting Regime

In this section, we exclusively use QMC methods to compute the ground-state energy of a system of M impurities immersed in a bath of N bosonic atoms. In QMC simulations we use a box of size $L = (N/n_1)^{1/3} > \xi$, being $\xi = (8\pi n_1 a_{11})^{-1/2}$ the healing length of the bath. In addition, periodic boundary conditions are employed. The general Hamiltonian of the system reads

$$H = -\frac{\hbar^2}{2m}\left(\sum_{i=1}^{N}\nabla_i^2 + \sum_{\alpha=1}^{M}\nabla_\alpha^2\right) + \sum_{i<j}V_{11}(r_{ij}) + \sum_{\alpha<\beta}V_{22}(r_{\alpha\beta}) + \sum_{i=1}^{N}\sum_{\alpha=1}^{M}V_{12}(r_{i\alpha}), \tag{10}$$

and the previous Hamiltonian is written in a similar way to the one in Equation (1). However, we employ different model potentials in our definitions, corresponding to finite and short-range potentials. In particular, we use a hard-sphere potential where the radius of the sphere corresponds to the boson–boson and impurity–impurity scattering lengths, respectively. Instead, the impurity–boson potential is modeled by a square well for both attractive and repulsive interactions, namely $V(\mathbf{r}) = -V_0$ for $r \leq R_0$, being R_0 the range of the potential and $V(\mathbf{r}) = 0$ otherwise [37,48]. We fix the strength of the potential V_0 and the impurity–boson scattering length depends on the range of the potential via $a_{12} = R_0\left[1 - \frac{\tan\theta(R_0)}{\theta(R_0)}\right]$ with $\theta(R_0) = \sqrt{\frac{V_0}{\hbar^2/mR_0^2}}$. In addition, $r_{\alpha\beta} = |\mathbf{r}_\beta - \mathbf{r}_\alpha|$ and $r_{ij} = |\mathbf{r}_i - \mathbf{r}_j|$ is the intra-particle distance between impurities and bosons respectively. Whereas $r_{i\alpha} = |\mathbf{r}_i - \mathbf{r}_\alpha|$ is the interparticle distance between the impurity and the host bath component. The trial wave function for this system is written as the product,

$$\psi_T(\mathbf{R_1}, \mathbf{R_2}) = \Pi_{\alpha<\beta}f_1(r_{\alpha\beta})\Pi_{i<j}f_2(r_{ij})\Pi_i\Pi_\alpha f_{12}(r_{i\alpha}) \tag{11}$$

Here $\mathbf{R_1}$ and $\mathbf{R_2}$ represent the positions of the impurities and bosons, respectively. The Jastrow wave function is obtained by solving the two-body problem with the pairwise potentials aforementioned. Explicit expressions for the trial wave functions are widely discussed in references [37,48]. The local energy in QMC algorithms is defined as

$$E_L = -\frac{\hbar^2}{2m}\frac{\left(\nabla_{\mathbf{R_1}}^2 + \nabla_{\mathbf{R_2}}^2\right)\psi_T(\mathbf{R_1}, \mathbf{R_2})}{\psi_T(\mathbf{R_1}, \mathbf{R_2})} + \frac{V(\mathbf{R_1}, \mathbf{R_2})\psi_T(\mathbf{R_1}, \mathbf{R_2})}{\psi_T(\mathbf{R_1}, \mathbf{R_2})}, \tag{12}$$

here $\mathbf{R_1} = \{r_1, r_2, \cdots, r_N\}$ and $\mathbf{R_2} = \{s_1, s_2, \cdots, s_M\}$ are the position of the atoms of component 1 and component 2 respectively and $V(\mathbf{R_1}, \mathbf{R_2})$ is an external potential. By using the definition of the trial wave-function in Equation (11), the gradients in the previous equation can be computed explicitly,

$$\begin{aligned}\nabla^2_{\mathbf{R}_1}\psi_T(\mathbf{R}_1,\mathbf{R}_2) =\ & \Psi_2(\mathbf{R}_2)\left[\left(\nabla^2_{\mathbf{R}_1}\Psi_1(\mathbf{R}_1)\right)\Psi_{12}(\mathbf{R}_1\mathbf{R}_2)+\Psi_1(\mathbf{R}_1)\left(\nabla^2_{\mathbf{R}_1}\Psi_{12}(\mathbf{R}_1,\mathbf{R}_2)\right)\right.\\ & +\left. 2\nabla_{\mathbf{R}_1}\Psi_1(\mathbf{R}_1)\cdot\nabla_{\mathbf{R}_1}\Psi_{12}(\mathbf{R}_1,\mathbf{R}_2)\right]\end{aligned} \quad (13)$$

and

$$\begin{aligned}\nabla^2_{\mathbf{R}_2}\psi_T(\mathbf{R}_1,\mathbf{R}_2) =\ & \Psi_1(\mathbf{R}_1)\left[\left(\nabla^2_{\mathbf{R}_2}\Psi_2(\mathbf{R}_2)\right)\Psi_{12}(\mathbf{R}_1\mathbf{R}_2)+\Psi_2(\mathbf{R}_2)\left(\nabla^2_{\mathbf{R}_2}\Psi_{12}(\mathbf{R}_1,\mathbf{R}_2)\right)\right.\\ & +\left. 2\nabla_{\mathbf{R}_2}\Psi_2(\mathbf{R}_2)\cdot\nabla_{\mathbf{R}_2}\Psi_{12}(\mathbf{R}_1,\mathbf{R}_2)\right]\end{aligned} \quad (14)$$

and plugging into the local energy and rearranging terms one obtains

$$\begin{aligned}E_L = -\frac{\hbar^2}{2m}\Bigg\{&\frac{\nabla^2_{\mathbf{R}_1}\Psi_1(\mathbf{R}_1)}{\Psi_1(\mathbf{R}_1)}+\frac{\nabla^2_{\mathbf{R}_2}\Psi_2(\mathbf{R}_2)}{\Psi_2(\mathbf{R}_2)}+\frac{\left(\nabla^2_{\mathbf{R}_1}+\nabla^2_{\mathbf{R}_2}\right)\Psi_{12}(\mathbf{R}_1,\mathbf{R}_2)}{\Psi_{12}(\mathbf{R}_1,\mathbf{R}_2)}\\ &+2\frac{\nabla_{\mathbf{R}_1}\Psi_1(\mathbf{R}_1)}{\Psi_1(\mathbf{R}_1)}\cdot\frac{\nabla_{\mathbf{R}_1}\Psi_{12}(\mathbf{R}_1,\mathbf{R}_2)}{\Psi_{12}(\mathbf{R}_1,\mathbf{R}_2)}+2\frac{\nabla_{\mathbf{R}_2}\Psi_2(\mathbf{R}_2)}{\Psi_2(\mathbf{R}_2)}\cdot\frac{\nabla_{\mathbf{R}_1}\Psi_{12}(\mathbf{R}_1,\mathbf{R}_2)}{\Psi_{12}(\mathbf{R}_1,\mathbf{R}_2)}\Bigg\}+V(\mathbf{R}_1,\mathbf{R}_2)\end{aligned} \quad (15)$$

the local energy is finally obtained as

$$E_L = E_L^A(\mathbf{R}_1) + E_L^B(\mathbf{R}_2) + E_L^A(\mathbf{R}_1,\mathbf{R}_2) + E_L^B(\mathbf{R}_1,\mathbf{R}_2) + \mathbf{F}_1\cdot\mathbf{F}_{12} + \mathbf{F}_2\cdot\mathbf{F}_{21} + V(\mathbf{R}_1,\mathbf{R}_2) \quad (16)$$

with the local energies and quantum force terms written as

$$\begin{pmatrix} E_L^A(\mathbf{R}_1) & E_L^A(\mathbf{R}_1,\mathbf{R}_2) \\ E_L^B(\mathbf{R}_1,\mathbf{R}_2) & E_L^B(\mathbf{R}_2) \end{pmatrix} = -\frac{\hbar^2}{2m}\begin{pmatrix} \frac{\nabla^2_{\mathbf{R}_1}\Psi_1(\mathbf{R}_1)}{\Psi_1(\mathbf{R}_1)} & \frac{\nabla^2_{\mathbf{R}_1}\Psi_{12}(\mathbf{R}_1,\mathbf{R}_2)}{\Psi_{12}(\mathbf{R}_1,\mathbf{R}_2)} \\ \frac{\nabla^2_{\mathbf{R}_2}\Psi_{12}(\mathbf{R}_1,\mathbf{R}_2)}{\Psi_{12}(\mathbf{R}_1,\mathbf{R}_2)} & \frac{\nabla^2_{\mathbf{R}_2}\Psi_2(\mathbf{R}_2)}{\Psi_2(\mathbf{R}_2)} \end{pmatrix} \quad (17)$$

and

$$\begin{pmatrix} \mathbf{F}_1(\mathbf{R}_1) & \mathbf{F}_{12}(\mathbf{R}_1,\mathbf{R}_2) \\ \mathbf{F}_{21}(\mathbf{R}_1,\mathbf{R}_2) & \mathbf{F}_2(\mathbf{R}_2) \end{pmatrix} = -\frac{\hbar^2}{2m}\begin{pmatrix} 2\frac{\nabla_{\mathbf{R}_1}\Psi_1(\mathbf{R}_1)}{\Psi_1(\mathbf{R}_1)} & \frac{\nabla_{\mathbf{R}_1}\Psi_{12}(\mathbf{R}_1,\mathbf{R}_2)}{\Psi_{12}(\mathbf{R}_1,\mathbf{R}_2)} \\ \frac{\nabla_{\mathbf{R}_2}\Psi_{12}(\mathbf{R}_1,\mathbf{R}_2)}{\Psi_{12}(\mathbf{R}_1,\mathbf{R}_2)} & 2\frac{\nabla_{\mathbf{R}_2}\Psi_2(\mathbf{R}_2)}{\Psi_2(\mathbf{R}_2)} \end{pmatrix} \quad (18)$$

respectively. Thus, the EoS of the impurity gas is computed as,

$$\mu = E(M,N) - E(N). \quad (19)$$

Here, $E(N,M)$ is the ground state energy of the full system, whereas $E(N)$ depicts the energy of the host bosons. The "quantum force" can be used to build an alternative estimator to check the correct implementation of the trial wave function in a similar way to the single-impurity case [49]. In addition, to use the numerical method in the regime where the Bogoliubov theory breaks down, our numerical technique includes all possible correlations in the system and includes the critical role of the Bose–Bose interaction and the quantum nature of both impurities and bath [50], which ultimately defines the compressibility of the bath that is relevant for mediated interactions.

3. Results and Discussion

In this section, we compute the EoS μ of the impurity gas for weak and strong coupling using QMC methods and compare the polaron energy expansion in the Fröhlich regime. The latter is obtained within the Hugenholtz–Pines formalism and derived under the assumption that the depletion of the condensate is small enough to justify the use of the Bogoliubov approximation. In contrast, QMC techniques allow computing the accurately the polaron EoS within statistical uncertainly. This non-perturbative technique does not rely on the Bogoliubov approximation and it is suitable for describing the strongly interacting regime.

In Figure 1 we plot the total polaron energy (Equation (19)) as a function of the dimensionless coupling strength $1/(k_n a_{12})$ with $k_n = \left(6\pi^2 n_1\right)^{1/3}$. For a gas parameter, $n_1 a_{11}^3 = 10^{-5}$ we scan all the coupling strengths from the weak to the strong coupling regime. Comparison with the perturbative results in Section 2.1 is affordable in the weak coupling and low polarization limits. The polaron energy is computed for different polarizations ranging from $P = 0.05$ to $P = 0.15$. Note that current experiments in polaron physics with ultra-cold atoms rely on impurity polarization of the order of $P = 0.1$ or less and resemble our current case as the inter-species impurity–impurity scattering length is finite and repulsive. The latter is important to guarantee the mechanical stability of the system as P increases.

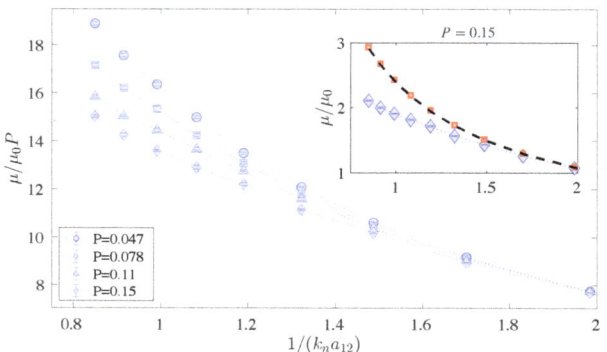

Figure 1. Total polaron energy μ (excited state) as a function of the coupling strength for different polarization $P = M/N$ in the weak and intermediate coupling. The gas parameter is taken to be $n a_{11}^3 = 10^{-5}$. Inset: comparison between perturbation theory and the QMC result for highest polarization $P = 0.15$. The red squares represents the theoretical results using perturbation theory in [37] (Subfigure adapted from [49]), whereas the black dashed line depicts the calculation in this work (see Equation (9)), here $a_{11} = a_{22}$. Error bars are smaller than the size symbol.

The single impurity regime holds for values of the coupling strength $|1/(k_n a_{12})| \gg 1$, yet deviations from this limit are displayed as both the impurity–boson coupling $(k_n a_{12})$ and the polarization increases. In fact, the analytical result obtained in Equation (6) is strictly valid for $|1/(k_n a_{12})| \gg 1$ and small polarization, i.e., $P \ll 1$. Higher correlations play an important role in the beyond mean-field regime and are captured by our numerical method. The bare polaron energy μ increases with the number of impurities, as similarly observed in [45]. The repulsive mean-field energy of the impurity gas $\sim g_{22} n_2$ is much larger than any attractive induced interaction mediated by the bath. The upwards shift of the energy agrees with recent results in reference [45]. For small polarization, for example, $P = 0.047$, the theory agrees reasonably with the numerical calculation up to values of $1/k_n a_{12} \ll 1$, noticeable as the polarization increases, the agreement between the perturbative approach and the simulations still prevails for larger values of $1/k_n a_{12}$. Up to a concentration near to the 15%, the critical value where no dependence is observed is around $1/(k_n a_{12}) \gg 1.4$ for these specific parameters. Similarly to the single-polaron case, the unitary limit is not reachable from this repulsive branch.

In Figure 2a, we compute the EoS, see Equation (19), for a system of a few impurities with a negative coupling strength a_{12} and null direct interacting between impurities $a_{22} = 0$. Similarly to Figure 1 where the EoS is normalized to the polarization at weak coupling, all lines overlap; however, in the strongly interacting regime, small deviations are presented, which are better displayed when the induced interaction is computed. In Figure 2a, the green symbols depict QMC calculations for the polaron energy in the single impurity case [19]. The polaron energy has a negligible dependence with the number of impurities for values of polarization $P < 0.1$ in current experiments [15], however by considering no net inter-impurity interaction as in the current calculation, the dependence appear to be considerable from values of polarization larger than the 5%. In experiments, a positive impurity-impurity interaction dominates over any residual interaction and the system is stable.

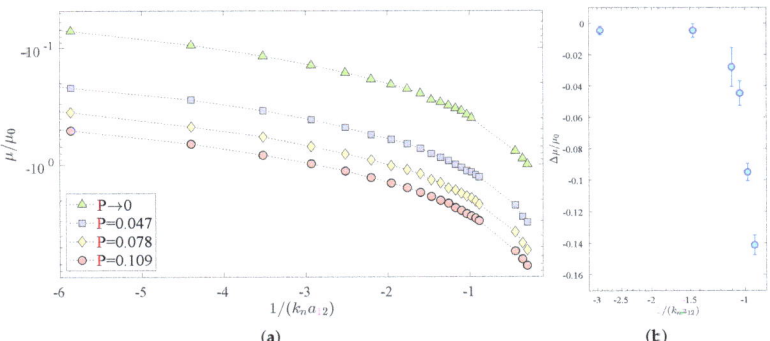

Figure 2. (a) EoS for polarons (ground-state) we added a and b for subfigure, please check. as a function of the number of impurities and coupling strength. Error bars are smaller than the size symbol. (b) Induced interaction for a ultra dilute gas of impurities computed as in Equation (20) for a polarization $P = 0.109$.

However, for $a_{22} = 0$, the system has two possibilities, either (i) the attractive induced interaction drives the impurity system into a collapse, for a large polarization—similarly to the case of a condensate with attractive interactions in a homogeneous space [51] or (ii) a few-particle bound-state such as multi-polaron can stabilize the system [52]. The reason is that impurities tend to attract to each other regardless of the sign of a_{12}. A naive way to understand the induced interaction is considering two impurities interacting with a homogeneous condensate. If $a_{12} > 0$, there is a local hole in the density, thus creating a local density depletion in the impurities neighborhood and therefore, the energy minimizes as the impurities get closer. Contrary, for $a_{12} < 0$, the local depletion caused by the impurity atoms creates a local bump and the energy is minimized as the two approaches the high-density regions. In the weakly interacting regime, the induced interaction corresponds to a Yukawa-type of interaction in 3D [42] or exponential trend in 1D [44,53]. A two-body impurity–impurity (bipolaron state) bound state always exist for $-1 < 1/k_n a_{12} < 0$, hence it may favor the formation of few-body bound states, akin to the case of ionic polarons [54,55] where a many-body bound state emerges from bound two-body correlations. In fact, from our calculations, higher concentrations of impurities may drive the system into clusterization. To compute the effective interaction, we calculate the ground-state energy of the whole system consisting of M impurities and N bosons, $E(M, N)$ with respect to the energy of the host bath in the absence of impurities, namely $\mu_M = E(M, N) - E(0, N)$, and compare it with the binding energy of the single polaron ($\mu_1 = E(1, N) - E(0, N)$). If polarons do not interact, $E(M, N)$ equals $ME(1, N)$, which is the typical case of weak coupling. Thus an attractive induced interaction appears when

$$\Delta \mu = E(M, N) - ME(1, N) + (M-1)E(0, N) < 0 \qquad (20)$$

In Figure 2b, we compute the induced interaction $\Delta \mu$ as a function of the coupling strength. As expected, the attractive induced interaction increases as a function of the coupling strength. In the weakly interacting regime, it is negligible, in stark contrast, to the strong coupling, where few-body bound states of impurities arise similar to the bi-polaron (in the case of two impurities). Although the induced interaction is relevant in the strongly interacting regime, there might be a critical number for the polarization where the system undergoes a dynamical collapse, similar to an ideal gas with underlying attractive interactions. Another interesting point is the attractive interaction between polarons that can compete with the direct repulsion between impurities which is set by imposing a positive a_{22} and the system may undergo into amorphous nucleation of impurities, forming thus an ultra dilute liquid of impurities. Both the transition and the role of impurity interaction need to be addressed carefully in the future. Additional quasi-particles properties such as the residue can be obtained by computing the limit at larges distances of the one-body density matrix of the impurity gas [54,56].

4. Conclusions

In this work, we have studied the role of an impurity gas in a Bose–Einstein condensate and the possibility of creating multipolaronic states. Our studies focused on the role of the impurity–bath and impurity–impurity interaction, which is the situation in current experiments of polarons and mixtures. The single polaron limit in the Fröhlich framework is recovered for very weak impurity–boson coupling and low polarization. The EoS of the polaron gas strongly depends on both the polarization and the impurity–boson couplings. In this work, we compute this equation for impurities in the ground state and excited state. In the former, multi-polaron states or few-body impurity states are expected to be formed in the neighborhood of the resonance. We explicitly compute the induced interaction and compare the results with mean field approaches in the weakly interacting regime. A significant problem arises in the strongly interacting regime as still remains a question on the stability of the impurity gas as interactions and polarization grow out of the impurity limit. Another exciting avenue, as an outlook, is the role of thermal fluctuations. Contrary to the single impurity case, statistics and temperature play essential roles. Finite temperature effect may favor the stabilization of the system against collapse [57]. In addition, both a non-negligible concentration of impurities and finite temperature effects may combine, changing the polaron properties drastically in comparison with the single impurity case at $T = 0$, as recently revealed for Fermi polarons [58]. Finally, another avenue is studying the role of the direct impurity–impurity interaction and its influence on forming a gas or liquid of polarons and the role of bosonic quasi-particles in the formation of self-bound structures [59–61].

Funding: This research was funded by the DFG Excellence Cluster QuantumFrontiers.

Institutional Review Board Statement: Not applicable.

Informed Consent Statement: Not applicable.

Data Availability Statement: The data that support the findings of this study are available from the corresponding author upon reasonable request.

Acknowledgments: I thank Cesar Cabrera and Arturo Camacho for fruitful discussions and for critical reading of the manuscript.

Conflicts of Interest: The author declares no conflict of interest.

References and Notes

1. Landau, L.D. Über Die Bewegung der Elektronen in Kristallgitter. *Phys. Z. Sowjetunion* **1933**, *3*, 644–645.
2. Landau, L.; Pekar, S. Effective mass of a polaron. *J. Exp. Theor. Phys.* **1948**, *18*, 419–423.
3. Feynman, R.P. Slow Electrons in a Polar Crystal. *Phys. Rev.* **1955**, *97*, 660–665. [CrossRef]
4. Devreese, J.; Peters, F. *Polarons and Excitons in Polar Semiconductors and Ionic Crystals*; Plenum Press: New York, NY, USA, 1984.
5. Baym, G.; Pethick, C. *Landau Fermi-Liquid Theory: Concepts and Applications*; Wiley-VCH: New York, NY, USA, 1991.
6. Camacho-Guardian, A.; Bruun, G.M. Landau Effective Interaction between Quasiparticles in a Bose-Einstein Condensate. *Phys. Rev. X* **2018**, *8*, 031042. [CrossRef]

7. Schirotzek, A.; Wu, C.H.; Sommer, A.; Zwierlein, M.W. Observation of Fermi Polarons in a Tunable Fermi Liquid of Ultracold Atoms. *Phys. Rev. Lett.* **2009**, *102*, 230402. [CrossRef]
8. Ngampruetikorn, V.; Levinsen, J.; Parish, M.M. Repulsive polarons in two-dimensional Fermi gases. *EPL Europhys. Lett.* **2012**, *98*, 30005. [CrossRef]
9. Koschorreck, M.; Pertot, D.; Vogt, E.; Fröhlich, B.; Feld, M.; Köhl, M. Attractive and repulsive Fermi polarons in two dimensions. *Nature* **2012**, *485*, 619–622. [CrossRef]
10. Kohstall, C.; Zaccanti, M.; Jag, M.; Trenkwalder, A.; Massignan, P.; Bruun, G.M.; Schreck, F.; Grimm, R. Metastability and coherence of repulsive polarons in a strongly interacting Fermi mixture. *Nature* **2012**, *485*, 615–618. [CrossRef]
11. Cetina, M.; Jag, M.; Lous, R.S.; Fritsche, I.; Walraven, J.T.; Grimm, R.; Levinsen, J.; Parish, M.M.; Schmidt, R.; Knap, M.; Demler, E. Ultrafast many-body interferometry of impurities coupled to a Fermi sea. *Science* **2016**, *354*, 96–99. [CrossRef]
12. Scazza, F.; Valtolina, G.; Massignan, P.; Recati, A.; Amico, A.; Burchianti, A.; Fort, C.; Inguscio, M.; Zaccanti, M.; Roati, G. Repulsive Fermi Polarons in a Resonant Mixture of Ultracold ^{6}Li Atoms. *Phys. Rev. Lett.* **2017**, *118*, 083602. [CrossRef]
13. Sidler, M.; Back, P.; Cotlet, O.; Srivastava, A.; Fink, T.; Kroner, M.; Demler, E.; Imamoglu, A. Fermi polaron-polaritons in charge-tunable atomically thin semiconductors. *Nat. Phys.* **2017**, *13*, 255–261. [CrossRef]
14. Catani, J.; Lamporesi, G.; Naik, D.; Gring, M.; Inguscio, M.; Minardi, F.; Kantian, A.; Giamarchi, T. Quantum dynamics of impurities in a one-dimensional Bose gas. *Phys. Rev. A* **2012**, *85*, 023623. [CrossRef]
15. Jørgensen, N.B.; Wacker, L.; Skalmstang, K.T.; Parish, M.M.; Levinsen, J.; Christensen, R.S.; Bruun, G.M.; Arlt, J.J. Observation of Attractive and Repulsive Polarons in a Bose-Einstein Condensate. *Phys. Rev. Lett.* **2016**, *117*, 055302. [CrossRef] [PubMed]
16. Hu, M.G.; Van de Graaff, M.J.; Kedar, D.; Corson, J.P.; Cornell, E.A.; Jin, D.S. Bose Polarons in the Strongly Interacting Regime. *Phys. Rev. Lett.* **2016**, *117*, 055301. [CrossRef] [PubMed]
17. Yan, Z.Z.; Ni, Y.; Robens, C.; Zwierlein, M.W. Bose polarons near quantum criticality. *Science* **2020**, *368*, 190–194. [CrossRef]
18. Camargo, F.; Schmidt, R.; Whalen, J.D.; Ding, R.; Woehl, G.; Yoshida, S.; Burgdörfer, J.; Dunning, F.B.; Sadeghpour, H.R.; Demler, E.; et al. Creation of Rydberg Polarons in a Bose Gas. *Phys. Rev. Lett.* **2018**, *120*, 083401. [CrossRef]
19. Peña Ardila, L.A.; Jørgensen, N.B.; Pohl, T.; Giorgini, S.; Bruun, G.M.; Arlt, J.J. Analyzing a Bose polaron across resonant interactions. *Phys. Rev. A* **2019**, *99*, 063607. [CrossRef]
20. Chin, C.; Grimm, R.; Julienne, P.; Tiesinga, E. Feshbach resonances in ultracold gases. *Rev. Mod. Phys.* **2010**, *82*, 1225–1286. [CrossRef]
21. Bloch, I.; Dalibard, J.; Zwerger, W. Many-body physics with ultracold gases. *Rev. Mod. Phys.* **2008**, *80*, 885–964. [CrossRef]
22. Tempere, J.; Casteels, W.; Oberthaler, M.K.; Knoop, S.; Timmermans, E.; Devreese, J.T. Feynman path-integral treatment of the BEC-impurity polaron. *Phys. Rev. B* **2009**, *80*, 184504. [CrossRef]
23. Grusdt, F.; Demler, E. New theoretical approaches to Bose polarons. *arXiv* 2015, arXiv:1510.04934.
24. Volosniev, A.G.; Hammer, H.W.; Zinner, N.T. Real-time dynamics of an impurity in an ideal Bose gas in a trap. *Phys. Rev. A* **2015**, *92*, 023623. [CrossRef]
25. Christensen, R.S.; Levinsen, J.; Bruun, G.M. Quasiparticle Properties of a Mobile Impurity in a Bose-Einstein Condensate. *Phys. Rev. Lett.* **2015**, *115*, 160401. [CrossRef] [PubMed]
26. Shchadilova, Y.E.; Schmidt, R.; Grusdt, F.; Demler, E. Quantum Dynamics of Ultracold Bose Polarons. *Phys. Rev. Lett.* **2016**, *117*, 113002. [CrossRef]
27. Levinsen, J.; Parish, M.M.; Bruun, G.M. Impurity in a Bose-Einstein Condensate and the Efimov Effect. *Phys. Rev. Lett.* **2015**, *115*, 125302. [CrossRef]
28. Lampo, A.; Charalambous, C.; García-March, M.A.; Lewenstein, M. Non-Markovian polaron dynamics in a trapped Bose-Einstein condensate. *Phys. Rev. A* **2018**, *93*, 063630. [CrossRef]
29. Lausch, T.; Widera, A.; Fleischhauer, M. Prethermalization in the cooling dynamics of an impurity in a Bose-Einstein condensate. *Phys. Rev. A* **2018**, *97*, 023621. [CrossRef]
30. Levinsen, J.; Parish, M.M.; Christensen, R.S.; Arlt, J.J.; Bruun, G.M. Finite-temperature behavior of the Bose polaron. *Phys. Rev. A* **2017**, *96*, 063622. [CrossRef]
31. Nielsen, K.K.; Ardila, L.A.P.; Bruun, G.M.; Pohl, T. Critical slowdown of non-equilibrium polaron dynamics. *New J. Phys.* **2019**, *21*, 043014. [CrossRef]
32. Liu, W.E.; Levinsen, J.; Parish, M.M. Variational Approach for Impurity Dynamics at Finite Temperature. *Phys. Rev. Lett.* **2019**, *122*, 205301. [CrossRef]
33. Drescher, M.; Salmhofer, M.; Enss, T. Real-space dynamics of attractive and repulsive polarons in Bose-Einstein condensates. *Phys. Rev. A* **2019**, *99*, 023601. [CrossRef]
34. Mistakidis, S.I.; Katsimiga, G.C.; Koutentakis, G.M.; Busch, T.; Schmelcher, P. Quench Dynamics and Orthogonality Catastrophe of Bose Polarons. *Phys. Rev. Lett.* **2019**, *122*, 183001. [CrossRef]
35. Mistakidis, S.I.; Grusdt, F.; Koutentakis, G.M.; Schmelcher, P. Dissipative correlated dynamics of a moving impurity immersed in a Bose–Einstein condensate. *New J. Phys.* **2019**, *21*, 103026. [CrossRef]
36. Massignan, P.; Yegovtsev, N.; Gurarie, V. Universal Aspects of a Strongly Interacting Impurity in a Dilute Bose Condensate. *Phys. Rev. Lett.* **2021**, *126*, 123403. [CrossRef] [PubMed]
37. Ardila, L.A.P.; Giorgini, S. Impurity in a Bose-Einstein condensate: Study of the attractive and repulsive branch using quantum Monte Carlo methods. *Phys. Rev. A* **2015**, *92*, 033612. [CrossRef]

38. Parisi, L.; Giorgini, S. Quantum Monte Carlo study of the Bose-polaron problem in a one-dimensional gas with contact interactions *Phys. Rev. A* **2017**, *95*, 023619. [CrossRef]
39. Bombín, R.; Cikojević, V.; Sánchez-Baena, J.; Boronat, J. Finite-range effects in the two-dimensional repulsive Fermi polaron. *Phys. Rev. A* **2021**, *103*, L041302. [CrossRef]
40. Grusdt, F.; Astrakharchik, G.E.; Demler, E. Bose polarons in ultracold atoms in one dimension: Beyond the Fröhlich paradigm. *New J. Phys.* **2017**, *19*, 103035. [CrossRef]
41. Slow impurities are defined as impurities with a momentum $P \ll mc$ where c is the speed of sound of the condensate a m is the mass of the impurity.
42. Camacho-Guardian, A.; Peña Ardila, L.A.; Pohl, T.; Bruun, G.M. Bipolarons in a Bose-Einstein Condensate. *Phys. Rev. Lett.* **2018**, *121*, 013401. [CrossRef]
43. Naidon, P. Two Impurities in a Bose–Einstein Condensate: From Yukawa to Efimov Attracted Polarons. *J. Phys. Soc. Jpn.* **2018**, *87*, 043002. [CrossRef]
44. Will, M.; Astrakharchik, G.E.; Fleischhauer, M. Polaron Interactions and Bipolarons in One-Dimensional Bose Gases in the Strong Coupling Regime. *Phys. Rev. Lett.* **2021**, *127*, 103401. [CrossRef]
45. Van Loon, S.; Casteels, W.; Tempere, J. Ground-state properties of interacting Bose polarons. *Phys. Rev. A* **2018**, *98*, 063631. [CrossRef]
46. Bisset, R.N.; Ardila, L.A.P.; Santos, L. Quantum Droplets of Dipolar Mixtures. *Phys. Rev. Lett.* **2021**, *126*, 025301. [CrossRef] [PubMed]
47. Petrov, D.S. Quantum Mechanical Stabilization of a Collapsing Bose-Bose Mixture. *Phys. Rev. Lett.* **2015**, *115*, 155302. [CrossRef] [PubMed]
48. Ardila, L.A.P.; Giorgini, S. Bose polaron problem: Effect of mass imbalance on binding energy. *Phys. Rev. A* **2016**, *94*, 063640. [CrossRef]
49. Ardila, L.A.P. Impurities in a Bose-Einstein Condensate Using Quantum Monte-Carlo Methods: Ground-State Properties. Ph.D. Thesis, University of Trento, Trento, Italy, 2015.
50. Levinsen, J.; Ardila, L.A.P.; Yoshida, S.M.; Parish, M.M. Quantum Behavior of a Heavy Impurity Strongly Coupled to a Bose Gas. *Phys. Rev. Lett.* **2021**, *127*, 033401. [CrossRef]
51. In trapped experiments the situation may be different since the high increase of the density to reduce the interaction energy may overcome the kinetic energy of the impuriy gas. The situation is completely analogous to attarctive particle is an harmonic potential, however in this case the trapping potential due to the deformation of the condensation sets a different scalings for the stability.
52. Santamore, D.; Timmermans, E. Multi-impurity polarons in a dilute Bose–Einstein condensate. *New J. Phys.* **2011**, *13*, 103029. [CrossRef]
53. Brauneis, F.; Hammer, H.W.; Lemeshko, M.; Volosniev, A.G. Impurities in a one-dimensional Bose gas: The flow equation approach. *SciPost Phys.* **2021**, *11*, 8. [CrossRef]
54. Astrakharchik, G.E.; Ardila, L.A.P.; Schmidt, R.; Jachymski, K.; Negretti, A. Ionic polaron in a Bose-Einstein condensate. *Commun. Phys.* **2021**, *4*, 94. [CrossRef]
55. Christensen, E.R.; Camacho-Guardian, A.; Bruun, G.M. Charged Polarons and Molecules in a Bose-Einstein Condensate. *Phys. Rev. Lett.* **2021**, *126*, 243001. [CrossRef]
56. Ardila, L.A.P.n.; Astrakharchik, G.E.; Giorgini, S. Strong coupling Bose polarons in a two-dimensional gas. *Phys. Rev. Res.* **2020**, *2*, 023405. [CrossRef]
57. Ospelkaus, C.; Ospelkaus, S.; Sengstock, K.; Bongs, K. Interaction-Driven Dynamics of ^{40}K–^{87}Rb Fermion-Boson Gas Mixtures in the Large-Particle-Number Limit. *Phys. Rev. Lett.* **2006**, *96*, 020401. [CrossRef] [PubMed]
58. Ness, G.; Shkedrov, C.; Florshaim, Y.; Diessel, O.K.; von Milczewski, J.; Schmidt, R.; Sagi, Y. Observation of a Smooth Polaron-Molecule Transition in a Degenerate Fermi Gas. *Phys. Rev. X* **2020**, *10*, 041019. [CrossRef]
59. Cabrera, C.R.; Tanzi, L.; Sanz, J.; Naylor, B.; Thomas, P.; Cheiney, P.; Tarruell, L. Quantum liquid droplets in a mixture of Bose-Einstein condensates. *Science* **2018**, *359*, 301–304. [CrossRef] [PubMed]
60. Semeghini, G.; Ferioli, G.; Masi, L.; Mazzinghi, C.; Wolswijk, L.; Minardi, F.; Modugno, M.; Modugno, G.; Inguscio, M.; Fattori, M. Self-Bound Quantum Droplets of Atomic Mixtures in Free Space. *Phys. Rev. Lett.* **2018**, *120*, 235301. [CrossRef] [PubMed]
61. Naidon, P.; Petrov, D.S. Mixed Bubbles in Bose-Bose Mixtures. *Phys. Rev. Lett.* **2021**, *126*, 115301. [CrossRef]

Article

Static Impurities in a Weakly Interacting Bose Gas

Galyna Panochko [1] and Volodymyr Pastukhov [2,*]

[1] Department of Optoelectronics and Information Technologies, Ivan Franko National University of Lviv, 107 Tarnavskyj Str., 79000 Lviv, Ukraine; gpanochko@gmail.com
[2] Department for Theoretical Physics, Ivan Franko National University of Lviv, 12 Drahomanov Str., 79000 Lviv, Ukraine
* Correspondence: volodyapastukhov@gmail.com

Abstract: We present a comprehensive discussion of the ground-state properties of dilute D-dimensional Bose gas interacting with a few static impurities. Assuming the short-ranged character of the boson-impurity interaction, we calculated the energy of three- and two-dimensional Bose systems with one and two impurities immersed.

Keywords: Bose polaron and bipolaron; effective field theory approach; induced interaction

1. Introduction

The problem of impurities in mediums formed by bosons is comprehensively studied in condensed matter physics. Even properties of a single atom immersed in the weakly interacting Bose gas change drastically [1–5]. Depending on the strength of the boson–impurity interaction, a number of physically distinct impurity phases can be realized, namely, the Bose-polaronic state [6–9] in various spatial dimensions, which is very similar to the free-particle one but with the modified, due to the presence of bath, kinematic characteristics; the molecular state [10,11], when the impurity captures one boson with the formation of a dimer; a set of the Efimov states [12–15] with the universal scaling behavior of energy levels, and higher-order conglomerates, [16–21] which involve a larger number of host atoms. Remarkably, some of these phases can be observed in experiments [22,23]. The experimental progress in the field of ultra-cold atomic gases has recently lead to the observation [24] of Bose polarons at finite temperatures. This experiment confirmed previous theoretical predictions [25–30] about the breakdown of the quasi-particle picture description of Bose polarons in a close vicinity of the Bose–Einstein condensation (BEC) point.

Recently, the problem of two impurities immersed in the dilute one and three-dimensional Bose gases has become a subject of extensive examination. Physically, this problem is substantially distinguishable from the single Bose polaron one due to the emergence of the induced effective interaction [31–34] between impurity particles. In 1D, the character of this interaction crucially depends on a sign of the boson–impurity coupling constant [35]; the effective attraction is found for positive couplings, while the induced repulsive potential is inherent for the negative interactions. While it increases, the induced attractive interaction between impurities leads to the formation of bipolarons [36] in the continuum and on the lattice [37] and even to the emergence of the two-polaron bound states [38]. In one-dimensional geometries with harmonic trapping, the induced interaction causes the clustering [39] of two initially non-interacting atoms and modifies their quench dynamics [40]. By switching the boson–impurity interaction in 3D dilute BEC with two impurities, the transition from weakly interacting through the Yukawa potential bipolarons to the Efimov trimer state was predicted in Ref. [41]. Recently, properties of a single polaron in 2D BEC have been discussed both analytically [42,43] and numerically [44,45]. The arbitrary D one-polaron case was considered in Ref. [46]. As far as we know, the problem of two Bose polarons in 2D Bose gas has never been discussed; therefore, the objective of this study

Citation: Panochko, G.; Pastukhov V. Static Impurities in a Weakly Interacting Bose Gas. *Atoms* **2022**, *10*, 19. https://doi.org/10.3390/atoms10010019

Academic Editors: Simeon Mistakidis and Artem Volosniev

Received: 30 September 2021
Accepted: 28 January 2022
Published: 8 February 2022

Publisher's Note: MDPI stays neutral with regard to jurisdictional claims in published maps and institutional affiliations.

Copyright: © 2022 by the authors. Licensee MDPI, Basel, Switzerland. This article is an open access article distributed under the terms and conditions of the Creative Commons Attribution (CC BY) license (https://creativecommons.org/licenses/by/4.0/).

was to make the first step toward the revealing of peculiarities of the bipolaron physics and the boson-induced effective interaction between impurities by considering the static limit. The absence of the impurity dynamics in this limit allows to find the exact solution of the problem in the dilute 1D Bose mediums both in one- [47] and two-particle [48,49] cases. In 3D, only a case of the ideal Bose gas [50,51] is the exactly tractable one, while the presence of a weak boson–boson interaction requires [52] a substantial numerical efforts.

2. Formulation
2.1. Model

The discussed model consists of the D-dimensional (here we focus on $D = 2, 3$ cases) Bose gas loaded in volume L^D (with the periodic boundary conditions imposed) with the weak interparticle interaction and microscopic number $\mathcal{N}$ of heavy (infinite-mass) impurities immersed in it. Heavy particles are supposed to be randomly placed in positions $\{\mathbf{r}_j\}$. In the following, we adopt the imaginary-time path-integral approach with Euclidean action

$$S = \int dx \psi^*(x) \{\partial_\tau - \varepsilon + \mu - \Phi(\mathbf{r})\} \psi(x) - \frac{g_{B,\Lambda}}{2} \int dx |\psi(x)|^4, \quad (1)$$

where $x = (\tau, \mathbf{r})$ denotes the "position" in $D+1$-dimensional space (and consequently $\int dx = \int_0^\beta d\tau \int_{L^D} d\mathbf{r}$), and the complex field $\psi(x)$ is periodic in τ with period β (which is the inverse temperature of the system). We also use the shorthand notations for bosonic dispersion $\varepsilon = -\frac{\hbar^2 \nabla^2}{2m}$ and the chemical potential μ that fixes average density n of Bose gas and for the term

$$\Phi(\mathbf{r}) = \sum_{1 \le j \le \mathcal{N}} g_{I,\Lambda} \delta_\Lambda(\mathbf{r} - \mathbf{r}_j), \quad (2)$$

that describes the interaction between Bose particles and impurities. The δ-like two-body potential is ill-defined in the higher ($D \ge 2$) dimensions, and therefore, in order to obtain any reasonable results one should adopt some renormalization scheme. The latter is typically realized by the implication of the ultraviolet cutoff Λ in all momentum summations and in the simultaneous rewriting of bare couplings $g_{B,\Lambda}$ and $g_{I,\Lambda}$ via the two-body vacuum binding energies ϵ_B and ϵ_I

$$g_{B,\Lambda}^{-1} = g_B^{-1} - \frac{1}{L^D} \sum_{\mathbf{k}} \frac{1}{2\varepsilon_k}, \quad (3)$$

$$g_{I,\Lambda}^{-1} = g_I^{-1} - \frac{1}{L^D} \sum_{\mathbf{k}} \frac{1}{\varepsilon_k}, \quad (4)$$

respectively, (from now on, we assume that all summations over the wave-vector $\mathbf{k}$ are restricted from the above $|\mathbf{k}| < \Lambda$). Such a "regularization" is already used in the definition of the point-like boson–impurity interaction potential, $\delta_\Lambda(\mathbf{r}) = \frac{1}{L^D} \sum_{|\mathbf{k}|<\Lambda} e^{i\mathbf{k}\mathbf{r}}$, in Equation (2). The "observable" couplings g_B and g_I are specified as follows

$$g_B^{-1} = -\frac{\Gamma(\frac{2-D}{2})}{(4\pi)^{\frac{D}{2}}} \left(\frac{m}{\hbar^2}\right)^{\frac{D}{2}} |\epsilon_B|^{\frac{D}{2}-1}, \quad (5)$$

$$g_I^{-1} = -\frac{\Gamma(\frac{2-D}{2})}{(2\pi)^{\frac{D}{2}}} \left(\frac{m}{\hbar^2}\right)^{\frac{D}{2}} |\epsilon_I|^{\frac{D}{2}-1}, \quad (6)$$

where $\Gamma(z)$ stands for the gamma function. Note that the bound states are only possible for positive g_Bs and g_Is, but it is convenient to parameterize negative couplings by the binding energies. By careful inspection of the $D \to 2$ limit, one can conclude that Equations (3)–(6)

provide a correct description of zero-range potentials even in the two-dimensional case. Moreover, the $D = 2$ pseudo-potential always provides the existence of one bound state.

The alternative method (see, for instance [53]) to deal with point-like interactions is to initially start from some "physical" (Gaussian, for instance) potentials and then relate the appropriate coupling constant to the s-wave scattering lengths a_B and a_I in the limit where the effective ranges are the smallest parameters with the dimension of length in the system. In the following, no restrictions are set on a magnitude of the boson–impurity interaction, while the Bose gas itself is expected to be extremely dilute.

2.2. Effective Field Theory Approach

The further analysis will be performed in a spirit of the effective field theory approach (see. for a review [54]), which is known to be extremely convenient for the many-boson systems. Particularly, this formulation automatically guarantees the implementation of the Hugenholtz–Pines theorem (which is a concrete manifestation of the Goldstone theorem) in every order of a loop expansion. Moreover, the effective field theory approach provides a non-perturbative predictions for the Bose gas thermodynamics. In the limit of weak boson–boson coupling, the loop expansion is identical to the perturbation theory in terms of characteristic small parameter $a_B^D n$. The main idea of the method relies on the separation of "classical" dynamics during the computations of the partition function by means of the path integral

$$\psi(x) = \psi_0(\mathbf{r}) + \tilde{\psi}(x), \quad \psi^*(x) = \psi_0^*(\mathbf{r}) + \tilde{\psi}^*(x), \tag{7}$$

where the introduced classical fields are determined by the minimization of the action (1): $\delta S_0 = \delta S[\psi_0^*, \psi_0] = 0$. Note that in general $|\psi_0(\mathbf{r})|^2$ should not be confused with the Bose condensate density. In the absence of impurities, $\Phi(\mathbf{r}) = 0$, the solution $\psi_0(\mathbf{r})$ is real and uniform. Putting a microscopic amount of heavy particles in the Bose condensate, we cannot principally change the character of this solution provided that $\psi_0(\mathbf{r})$ becomes only slightly non-uniform, i.e., $\int_{L^D} d\mathbf{r} |\psi_0(\mathbf{r})|^2 \propto L^D$. Of course, one may argue that the localized solutions $\psi_0(\mathbf{r})$ decrease the total energy by $\propto -\mathcal{N}|\epsilon_I|$, but any non-zero repulsion between bosons immediately increases the energy of the system by $\propto N^2 g_B / a_I^D$. Therefore, the collapsed BEC state [50] is not energetically preferable in the thermodynamic limit, where both the number of the repulsively interacting bosons N and the volume of the box L^D infinitely increase.

Performing the shift (7), we end up with the following effective action

$$S_{\text{eff}} = S_0 - \frac{1}{2} \int dx [\tilde{\psi}^*(x), \tilde{\psi}(x)] \hat{K} \begin{bmatrix} \tilde{\psi}(x) \\ \tilde{\psi}^*(x) \end{bmatrix}, \tag{8}$$

where only the Gaussian in the fluctuation fields part is explicitly written down. Here the 2×2 matrix operator $\hat{K}$ with elements

$$\begin{aligned} \hat{K}_{11} &= \varepsilon - \mu + \Phi(\mathbf{r}) + 2g_{B,\Lambda} |\psi_0(\mathbf{r})|^2 - \partial_\tau, \\ \hat{K}_{12} &= \hat{K}_{21}^* = g_{B,\Lambda} \psi_0^2(\mathbf{r}), \\ \hat{K}_{22} &= \varepsilon - \mu + \Phi(\mathbf{r}) + 2g_{B,\Lambda} |\psi_0(\mathbf{r})|^2 + \partial_\tau. \end{aligned} \tag{9}$$

is introduced. Taking into account the equation for $\psi_0(\mathbf{r})$

$$\left\{ \varepsilon - \mu + \Phi(\mathbf{r}) + g_{B,\Lambda} |\psi_0(\mathbf{r})|^2 \right\} \psi_0(\mathbf{r}) = 0, \tag{10}$$

and performing the Gaussian integration in (8), we finally obtain the grand potential of the Bose system with the impurities immersed

$$\Omega = -\frac{g_{B,\Lambda}}{2} \int_{L^D} d\mathbf{r} |\psi_0(\mathbf{r})|^4 + \frac{1}{2\beta} \text{Sp} \ln \hat{K} - \text{const}, \tag{11}$$

where Sp denotes the trace in the $D+1$ space. A constant term (counterterm) in (11) is most straightforwardly represented in the plane-wave basis const $=\frac{1}{2}\sum_{\mathbf{k}}\langle\mathbf{k}|\varepsilon-\mu+2g_{B,\Lambda}|\psi_0(\mathbf{r})|^2+\Phi(\mathbf{r})|\mathbf{k}\rangle$ but cannot be obtained by the functional integration and has to be written by hand [55] in order to resolve a standard normal-ordering routine. Consequently, the calculation of thermodynamics for "Bose gas + static impurities" reduces to finding a solution of Equation (10) and then, with $\psi_0(\mathbf{r})$ in hand, to the evaluation of the functional determinant. Note that by taking into account S_0 only, one reproduces the mean-field [56–61] description of the system generalized to $\mathcal{N}$ impurities in the static limit. In comparison to other Bose-polaron theories, the adopted approach takes into account the correct short-distance boson-impurity physics from the very beginning of the celebrated Bogoliubov treatment of dilute Bose condensates.

2.3. Limit of Dilute Bose Gas

In the general case, the above program, which can be realized to the very end in 1D [48] even at finite impurity masses [56,58,62], requires considerable numerical efforts in the higher dimensions, but the limit of weak inter-boson interaction can be handled more or less easily. Indeed, the intrinsic, for the dilute Bose gas, length-scale is represented by the coherence length $\xi=\frac{\hbar}{mc}$ (with $c=\sqrt{ng_B/m}$ being the sound velocity), which is large in comparison to the average distance between particles and to the boson–boson s-wave scattering length a_B. The magnitude of the boson–impurity interaction, in turn, is dictated by the boson–impurity s-wave scattering length a_I. So, if we additionally assume that $a_I \ll \xi$, the solution of Equation (10) can be immediately found $\psi_0(\mathbf{r})=\sqrt{\mu/g_{B,\Lambda}}\simeq\sqrt{n}$. In all other cases, we can apply the successive expansion in terms of the ψ_0-field "non-uniformity"

$$\psi_0(\mathbf{r})=\sqrt{\mu/g_{B,\Lambda}}\left\{1-\bar{\psi}_0^{(1)}(\mathbf{r})-\bar{\psi}_0^{(2)}(\mathbf{r})\dots\right\}, \quad (12)$$

where after the substitution in Equation (10) the dimensionless functions $\bar{\psi}_0^{(1)}(\mathbf{r})$, $\bar{\psi}_0^{(2)}(\mathbf{r})$ satisfy the following equations:

$$\{\varepsilon+2\mu+\Phi(\mathbf{r})\}\bar{\psi}_0^{(1)}(\mathbf{r})=\Phi(\mathbf{r}), \quad (13)$$

$$\{\varepsilon+2\mu+\Phi(\mathbf{r})\}\bar{\psi}_0^{(2)}(\mathbf{r})=3\mu\left(\bar{\psi}_0^{(1)}(\mathbf{r})\right)^2. \quad (14)$$

Note that the above approximate procedure does not require the boson–impurity interaction to be weak. Furthermore, by a naive dimensional analysis, it is easy to argue that both at the weak and strong couplings g_I, the contribution of the second-order correction $\bar{\psi}_0^{(2)}(\mathbf{r})$ in the thermodynamics of the system is much smaller than the one originating from $\bar{\psi}_0^{(1)}(\mathbf{r})$. Therefore, in our consideration below we fully focus on the first-order correction. However, even this simple approximation effectively sums up some infinite set of terms of the standard pertubation theory for a model with the uniform condensate [47]. Equation (13) with $\Phi(\mathbf{r})$ given by (2) can be solved for arbitrary $\mathcal{N}$ by means of the Fourier transformation

$$\bar{\psi}_0^{(1)}(\mathbf{r})=\sum_{1\le j\le\mathcal{N}}A_j\frac{1}{L^D}\sum_{\mathbf{k}}\frac{e^{i\mathbf{k}(\mathbf{r}-\mathbf{r}_j)}}{\varepsilon_k+2\mu}, \quad (15)$$

with $\varepsilon_k=\frac{\hbar^2k^2}{2m}$ and coefficients $A_j=\sum_{1\le i\le\mathcal{N}}T_{ji}(-2\mu)$, where matrix $T_{ji}(-2\mu)$ is introduced in Appendix A.

We can now proceed with the calculations of the functional determinant in (11). Taking into account the extreme diluteness of the Bose subsystem, it is enough to expand $\mathrm{Sp}\ln\hat{K}\simeq\mathrm{Sp}\ln\hat{K}^{(0)}+\mathrm{Sp}\left\{[\hat{K}^{(0)}]^{-1}\Delta\hat{K}\right\}$, where $\hat{K}^{(0)}$ is given by (9) but with $\psi_0(\mathbf{r})\to\sqrt{\mu/g_{B,\Lambda}}$ and $\Delta\hat{K}=\hat{K}-\hat{K}^{(0)}$. Following our previous discussion, we ignore in $\Delta\hat{K}$ all higher-order corrections except $\bar{\psi}_0^{(1)}(\mathbf{r})$. After this, the calculations are relatively simple, and at absolute zero we obtain the Ω-potential in the adopted approximation

$$\Omega \simeq -L^D \frac{\mu^2}{2g_{B,\Lambda}} + \frac{\mu}{g_{B,\Lambda}} \sum_{1 \leq j \leq \mathcal{N}} A_j$$
$$+ \frac{1}{2} \sum_{\mathbf{k}} \langle \mathbf{k} | \mathcal{E} - \varepsilon - \mu - \Phi(\mathbf{r}) | \mathbf{k} \rangle + \frac{1}{L^D} \sum_{\mathbf{k}} \left\{ 1 - \frac{\varepsilon_k + \mu/2}{E_k} \right\} \sum_{1 \leq j \leq \mathcal{N}} A_j, \quad (16)$$

where $\mathcal{E} = \sqrt{(\varepsilon + \Phi(\mathbf{r}))^2 + 2\mu(\varepsilon + \Phi(\mathbf{r}))}$ and $E_k = \sqrt{\varepsilon_k^2 + 2\mu\varepsilon_k}$ stands for the Bogoliubov spectrum of the "pure" Bose system. It should be noted that for dilute Bose systems the impact of the quantum fluctuations (terms with the summations over the wave-vector) to Ω is much smaller than the first two terms (the mean-field contributions). The last step to be performed in these calculations is to replace the bare couplings $g_{B,\Lambda}$ and $g_{I,\Lambda}$ via (3) and (4), respectively. This procedure provides the convergence of sums over the wave-vector in the last two terms of (16). Then, the trace in the third term of (16) can be computed (see Appendix A for details). With the well-defined grand potential, we can relate, by using the thermodynamic identity $n = -\frac{\partial}{\partial \mu} \frac{\Omega}{L^D}$, the chemical potential of the Bose system to its equilibrium density n. Performing these calculations, one must keep in mind that the presence of a microscopic number of impurities cannot principally change the properties of the system. So, if we denote (and appropriate grand potential Ω_B) the chemical potential of Bose gas without exterior particles by μ_B, the difference $\Delta \mu = \mu - \mu_B \propto \mathcal{N}/L^D$ should be small. Using this fact and $n = -\frac{\partial}{\partial \mu} \frac{\Omega_B}{L^D} - \frac{\partial}{\partial \mu} \frac{\Delta \Omega}{L^D}$, we can identify a small correction $\Delta \mu = -\frac{\partial \Delta \Omega}{\partial \mu_B} / \frac{\partial^2 \Omega_B}{\partial \mu_B^2}$. The latter formula allows to determine the energy that the Bose system gains when $\mathcal{N}$ impurities are immersed

$$\Delta E_\mathcal{N} = (\Omega - \Omega_B)|_{\mu \to \mu_B}, \quad (17)$$

which is an explicit manifestation of the well-known theorem about small corrections to the thermodynamic potentials.

3. Results

Before we proceed to describing our main results, it is necessary to analyze the case of "pure" bosons. Setting $\Phi(\mathbf{r}) = 0$ in (16) and calculating integrals, we obtain for density

$$n = \frac{\mu_B}{g_B} \left\{ 1 - \frac{\Gamma(D)}{\frac{D}{2}\Gamma^2(\frac{D}{2})} \left(\frac{\mu_B}{|\epsilon_B|} \right)^{\frac{D}{2}-1} \right\}, \quad (18)$$

which allows to obtain the expression for μ_B iteratively. For the weakly non-ideal three-dimensional bosons we find the well-known formula ($|\epsilon_B| = \frac{\hbar^2}{ma_B^2}$ in 3D)

$$\mu_B = \frac{4\pi\hbar^2 a_B n}{m} \left\{ 1 + \frac{32}{3\sqrt{\pi}} \sqrt{na_B^3} + \ldots \right\}. \quad (19)$$

Similarly, in the two-dimensional case we have the transcendental equation [63]

$$n = \frac{m\mu_B}{4\pi\hbar^2} \left\{ \ln \frac{|\epsilon_B|}{\mu_B} - 1 \right\}. \quad (20)$$

Being convinced that the limit of Bose gas without impurities is correctly reproduced by the adopted approach, we are ready to present our main results concerning the binding energy of one- and two-impurity atoms in the dilute three- and two-dimensional Bose gases.

3.1. 3D Case

In the 3D case, the general structure of the two-impurity binding energy in the dilute Bose gas ($n\xi^3 \ll 1$) can be represented as

$$\Delta E_2 = \Delta E_2^{(0)} \left[\varepsilon_1 \left(\frac{a_I}{\xi}; \frac{R}{\xi} \right) + \frac{1}{n\xi^3} \varepsilon_2 \left(\frac{a_I}{\xi}; \frac{R}{\xi} \right) + \ldots \right], \tag{21}$$

where $\Delta E_2^{(0)} = 2 g_I n$ is the contribution of the ideal Bose gas; a_I is the s-wave scattering length that parameterizes the (renormalized) two-body coupling $g_I = \frac{2\pi\hbar^2 a_I}{m}$; and R is the distance between two static particles. The first term in (21) has a simple analytic form

$$\varepsilon_1 \left(\frac{a_I}{\xi}; \frac{R}{\xi} \right) = \frac{\xi/a_I}{\xi/a_I - 2 + e^{-2R/\xi}/(R/\xi)}, \tag{22}$$

and originates purely from the mean-field correction to the grand potential (the second term in (16)), while $\varepsilon_2 \left(\frac{a_I}{\xi}; \frac{R}{\xi} \right)$ contains both the mean-field and purely quantum corrections. Note that in the formula for Ω only the one-loop corrections were taken into account, and a consistent consideration of the next to a leading order terms in series expansion over the small parameter $1/(n\xi^3)$ necessarily requires the calculation of the two-loop diagrams to the grand potential. By setting the distance between heavy particles R to infinity, one obtains from (21) the one-impurity limit. A typical behavior of functions $\varepsilon_{1,2} \left(\frac{a_I}{\xi}; \infty \right)$ is presented in Figure 1.

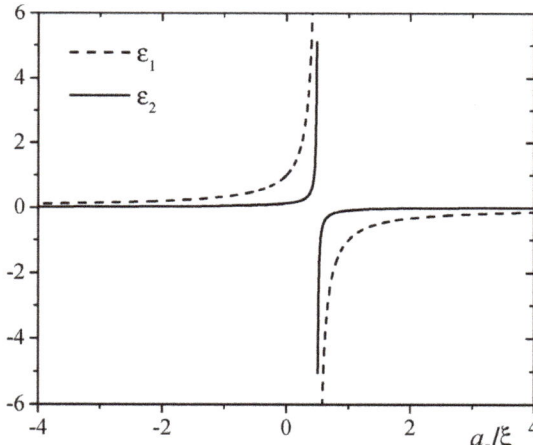

Figure 1. Dimensionless functions $\varepsilon_{1,2} \left(\frac{a_I}{\xi}; \infty \right)$ determining the one-impurity energy in 3D dilute Bose gas.

Let us recall that the problem considered here is the exactly solvable one, when the bosons are non-interacting. Therefore, it should be clearly understood that the presented results are accurate if the coherence length ξ is the largest parameter with the dimension of the length in the system. In order to reveal the interplay between regimes of very dilute $a_I/\xi \to 0$ Bose gas and intermediate boson–impurity interaction, we plotted in Figure 2 the binding energy of two heavy particles for the positive and negative s-wave scattering lengths a_I.

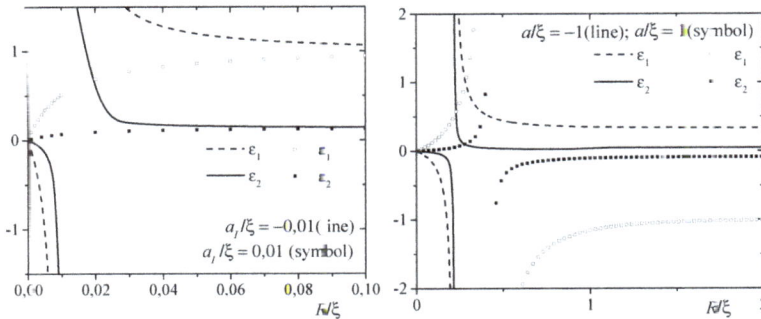

Figure 2. Mean-field and the first-order quantum corrections $\varepsilon_{1,2}\left(\frac{a_I}{\xi}; \frac{R}{\xi}\right)$ to the energy of 3D dilute Bose gas generated by two impurities for $\frac{a_I}{\xi} = \pm 0.01$ and $\frac{a_I}{\xi} = \pm 1$.

Comparing these findings to the ideal Bose gas results [50], we can observe similar patterns in the behavior of the systems at weak coupling: at positive a_I, the binding energy is the monotonic function of R, while at the negative boson–impurity scattering lengths both, $\varepsilon_{1,2}\left(-0.01; \frac{R}{\xi}\right)$ have a simple-pole singularity. When the interaction increases (see right panel in Figure 2) the mean-field and quantum corrections to the ground-state energy of 3D Bose gas possess an infinite discontinuities independently of a sign of a_I.

3.2. 2D Case

In general, the low-dimensional dilute Bose systems with static impurities are very peculiar. When the interaction between bosons is switched off, these systems are insensible to the boson–impurity interaction in their un-collapsed ground state, and therefore, the binding energy of the heavy particles requires a finite compressibility of the host system to be non-zero. This is a general result for the low-dimensional (1D and 2D) ideal Bose gases with impurities that is independent of the approximations made. Introducing the two-body s-wave scattering length a_I through the boson–impurity vacuum bound state energy $|\epsilon_I| = 2e^{-2\gamma}\hbar^2/(ma_I^2)$, we can write down the energy that the 2D Bose gas gains when two heavy particles are immersed in it

$$\Delta E_2 = 2\frac{2\pi\hbar^2 n}{m}\left[\varepsilon_1\left(\frac{a_I}{\xi}; \frac{R}{\xi}\right) + \frac{1}{n\xi^2}\varepsilon_2\left(\frac{a_I}{\xi}; \frac{R}{\xi}\right) + \ldots\right]. \quad (23)$$

As in the 3D case, the mean-field correction casts into a simple analytic form

$$\varepsilon_1\left(\frac{a_I}{\xi}; \frac{R}{\xi}\right) = \frac{1}{\ln\left(\frac{e^{-2\gamma}\xi^2}{a_I^2}\right) - 2K_0\left(\frac{2R}{\xi}\right)}, \quad (24)$$

$K_0(z)$ is the modified Bessel function of the second kind [64]. Note that in contrast to a 3D case, $\varepsilon_2\left(\frac{a_I}{\xi}; \frac{R}{\xi}\right)$ tends to zero (at least logarithmically) in the limit of ideal Bose gas ($\xi \to \infty$). At large distances R, Equation (23) gives the double binding energy of a single impurity, which is presented in Figure 3.

Particularly, these calculations clearly demonstrate the weakening of the role of quantum fluctuations in the formation of polarons in two-dimensional Bose systems. Actually, this observation [62] seems to be intrinsic for the low-dimensional systems in general.

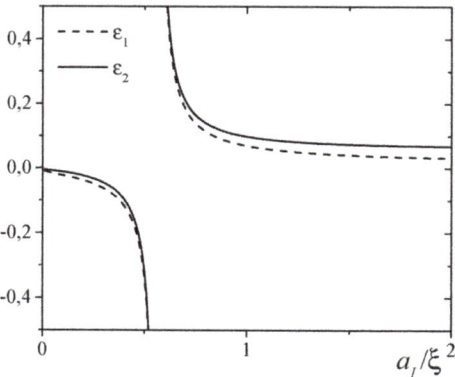

Figure 3. Dimensioless one-impurity binding energy terms $\varepsilon_{1,2}\left(\frac{a_I}{\xi};\infty\right)$ (see Equation (23)) in 2D case.

The numerical computations of the two-impurity energies (see Figure 4).

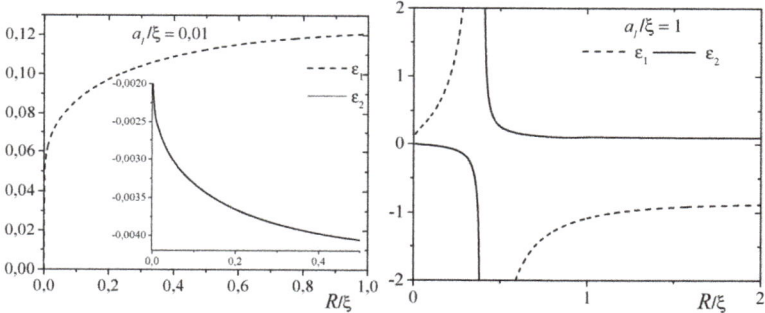

Figure 4. The two-impurity dimensionless binding energy corrections $\varepsilon_{1,2}\left(\frac{a_I}{\xi};\frac{R}{\xi}\right)$ in 2D dilute Bose gas.

The 2D Bose gas demonstrates qualitative similarity between the two- and three-dimensional cases. At weak boson–impurity interactions $a_I/\xi \ll 1$, where our effective field-theoretical formulation is supposed to make a quantitative predictions, the mean-field term $\varepsilon_1\left(\frac{a_I}{\xi};\frac{R}{\xi}\right)$ as well as the one that includes the quantum corrections $\varepsilon_2\left(\frac{a_I}{\xi};\frac{R}{\xi}\right)$ behave as monotonic functions of R. The interaction-induced effective two-body potential between static particles at large a_I/ξ always contains a singularity.

4. Conclusions

In summary, by means of the effective field theory formulation, we calculated the impurity-induced shifts to the ground-state energies of the two- and three-dimensional dilute Bose gases. Particularly, by taking into account the extreme diluteness of the host bosons, we proposed the approximate procedure that allows to calculate the properties of an arbitrary (microscopic) number of static impurities in terms of a characteristic small parameter $1/(n\xi^D)$ (where n and ξ are the density and the coherence length of bosons, respectively). The numerical calculations of the binding energies of two static impurities in dilute 2D and 3D Bose gases that were performed for a wide range of the boson–impurity interactions and distances between impurities has revealed the peculiarities of the medium-induced (Casimir) forces: (i) the two-body effective potential always demonstrates singular behavior at the distances between impurities comparable to the boson–impurity s-wave scattering lengths a_I; (ii) an impact of purely quantum corrections decreases with the lowering of a spatial dimensionality. Similar singularities are also intrinsic for the binding energy of a single impurity at $a_I \sim \xi$, which may signal [65] about the inapplicability of the adopted approximate treatment for calculations of the "classical" solution $\psi_0(\mathbf{r})$ in that region, where the full numerical solution to Equation (10) is required.

Author Contributions: Conceptualization, V.P.; methodology, G.P. and V.P.; software, G.P.; validation, G.P. and V.P.; formal analysis, G.P. and V.P.; investigation, G.P. and V.P.; resources, G.P. and V.P.; data curation, G.P. and V.P.; writing—original draft preparation, G.P. and V.P.; visualization, G.P.; supervision, V.P. All authors have read and agreed to the published version of the manuscript.

Funding: This research received no external funding.

Institutional Review Board Statement: Not applicable.

Informed Consent Statement: Not applicable.

Data Availability Statement: No new data were created or analyzed in this study.

Acknowledgments: We are indebted to Iryna Pastukhova for comments on the manuscript.

Conflicts of Interest: The authors declare no conflict of interest.

Appendix A

For completeness, in this section we give some details of the calculations not presented in the main text. Let us first start from the equation that determines the classical field $\psi_0(\mathbf{r})$. Explicitly writing down Equation (13), after the implementation of ansatz (15)

$$\sum_{1 \le j \le \mathcal{N}} A_j \delta_\Lambda(\mathbf{r} - \mathbf{r}_j) + \sum_{1 \le j \le \mathcal{N}} g_{I,\Lambda} \delta_\Lambda(\mathbf{r} - \mathbf{r}_j) \sum_{1 \le i \le \mathcal{N}} A_i \frac{1}{L^D} \sum_{\mathbf{k}} \frac{e^{i\mathbf{k}(\mathbf{r} - \mathbf{r}_i)}}{\varepsilon_k + 2\mu} = \sum_{1 \le j \le \mathcal{N}} g_{I,\Lambda} \delta_\Lambda(\mathbf{r} - \mathbf{r}_j),$$

and combining $j = i$ terms in double sum with the first term of equation, we obtain

$$A_j \left[\frac{1}{g_{I,\Lambda}} + \frac{1}{L^D} \sum_{\mathbf{k}} \frac{1}{\varepsilon_k + 2\mu} \right] + \sum_{1 \le i \ne j \le \mathcal{N}} \frac{1}{L^D} \sum_{\mathbf{k}} \frac{e^{i\mathbf{k}(\mathbf{r}_j - \mathbf{r}_i)}}{\varepsilon_k + 2\mu} A_i = 1.$$

The divergent sum in the square brackets is now regularized by the renormalization of a coupling constant (4), so the final result contains only observable g_I. One can easily recognize the square brackets as the boson–impurity two-body T-matrix

$$t_I^{-1}(\omega) = g_{I,\Lambda}^{-1} - \frac{1}{L^D} \sum_{\mathbf{k}} \frac{1}{\omega - \varepsilon_k},$$

and introducing auxiliary notations

$$\Delta_{ij}(\omega) = \frac{1}{L^D} \sum_{\mathbf{k}} \frac{e^{i\mathbf{k}(\mathbf{r}_i - \mathbf{r}_j)}}{\omega - \varepsilon_k},$$

we find the result for coefficients A_j announced in the main text

$$A_i = \sum_{1 \le j \le \mathcal{N}} T_{ij}(-2\mu), \qquad T_{ij}^{-1}(-2\mu) = \delta_{ij} t_I^{-1}(-2\mu) - \Delta_{ij}(-2\mu)(1 - \delta_{ij}).$$

For the calculation of the trace in the second term of (16), we used formal identity

$$\sum_{\mathbf{k}} \langle \mathbf{k}|\mathcal{E} - \varepsilon - \mu - \Phi(\mathbf{r})|\mathbf{k}\rangle = \int d\omega D(\omega)\left[\sqrt{\omega^2 + 2\mu\omega} - \omega - \mu\right],$$

$$D(\omega) = \sum_{\mathbf{k}} \langle \mathbf{k}|\delta(\omega - \varepsilon - \Phi(\mathbf{r})|\mathbf{k}\rangle.$$

The density of states $D(\omega)$ is easily calculated within the Green's function method [50]

$$D(\omega) = \sum_{\mathbf{k}}\left[\delta(\omega - \varepsilon_k) - \frac{1}{\pi}\text{Im}\frac{\langle \mathbf{k}|\mathcal{T}(\omega + i0)|\mathbf{k}\rangle}{(\omega + i0 - \varepsilon_k)^2}\right],$$

where the T-matrix $\mathcal{T}(\omega)$ characterizes the scattering of a single boson on $\mathcal{N}$ impurities

$$\langle \mathbf{q}|\mathcal{T}(\omega)|\mathbf{k}\rangle = \sum_{1 \le i,j \le \mathcal{N}} e^{-i\mathbf{q}\mathbf{r}_i} T_{ij}(\omega) e^{i\mathbf{k}\mathbf{r}_j}.$$

The calculations of $\langle \mathbf{k}|\mathcal{T}(\omega + i0)|\mathbf{k}\rangle$ in the density of states requires the knowledge of an explicit analytic formulas for the boson–impurity two-body T-matrix

$$t_I^{-1}(\omega) = \frac{\Gamma(\frac{2-D}{2})}{(2\pi)^{\frac{D}{2}}}\left(\frac{m}{\hbar^2}\right)^{\frac{D}{2}}\left[(-\omega)^{\frac{D}{2}-1} - |\epsilon_I|^{\frac{D}{2}-1}\right],$$

and a function $\Delta_{ij}(\omega) = \Delta_R(\omega)$ of distance $R = |\mathbf{r}_i - \mathbf{r}_j|$ between two impurities in arbitrary D

$$\Delta_R(\omega) = \frac{1}{(2\pi)^{\frac{D}{2}}}\frac{2mk_\omega^{D-2}}{\hbar^2}\frac{K_{\frac{D}{2}-1}(Rk_\omega)}{(Rk_\omega)^{\frac{D}{2}-1}},$$

where $k_\omega = \sqrt{2m(-\omega)}/\hbar$, and $K_\nu(z)$ is the modified Bessel function of the second kind [64].

References

1. Tempere, J.; Casteels, W.; Oberthaler, M.K.; Knoop, S.; Timmermans, E.; Devreese, J.T. Feynman path-integral treatment of the BEC-impurity polaron. *Phys. Rev. B* **2009**, *80*, 184504. [CrossRef]
2. Vlietinck, J.; Casteels, W.; Houcke, K.V.; Tempere, J.; Ryckebusch, J.; Devreese, J.T. Diagrammatic Monte Carlo study of the acoustic and the Bose–Einstein condensate polaron. *New J. Phys.* **2015**, *17*, 033023. [CrossRef]
3. Ardila, L.A.P.; Giorgini, S. Impurity in a Bose-Einstein condensate: Study of the attractive and repulsive branch using quantum Monte Carlo methods. *Phys. Rev. A* **2015**, *92*, 033612. [CrossRef]
4. Grusdt, F.; Shchadilova, Y.E.; Rubtsov, A.N.; Demler, E. Renormalization group approach to the Frohlich polaron model: Application to impurity-BEC problem. *Sci. Rep.* **2015**, *5*, 12124. [CrossRef] [PubMed]
5. Panochko, G.; Pastukhov, V.; Vakarchuk, I. Behavior of the impurity atom in a weakly-interacting Bose gas. *Cond. Matt. Phys.* **2017**, *20*, 13604. [CrossRef]
6. Astrakharchik, G.E.; Pitaevskii, L.P. Motion of a heavy impurity through a Bose-Einstein condensate. *Phys. Rev. A* **2004**, *70*, 013608. [CrossRef]
7. Novikov, A.; Ovchinnikov, M. A diagrammatic calculation of the energy spectrum of quantum impurity in degenerate Bose–Einstein condensate. *J. Phys. A Math. Theor.* **2009**, *42*, 135301. [CrossRef]
8. Christensen, R.S.; Levinsen, J.; Bruun, G.M. Quasiparticle Properties of a Mobile Impurity in a Bose-Einstein Condensate. *Phys. Rev. Lett.* **2015**, *115*, 160401. [CrossRef]
9. Panochko, G.; Pastukhov, V.; Vakarchuk, I. Impurity self-energy in the strongly-correlated Bose systems. *Int. J. Mod. Phys. B* **2018**, *32*, 1850053. [CrossRef]
10. Rath, S.P.; Schmidt, R. Field-theoretical study of the Bose polaron. *Phys. Rev. A* **2013**, *88*, 053632. [CrossRef]
11. Li, W.; Sarma, S.D. Variational study of polarons in Bose-Einstein condensate. *Phys. Rev. A* **2014**, *90*, 013618. [CrossRef]
12. Levinsen, J.; Massignan, P.; Parish, M.M. Efimov Trimers under Strong Confinement. *Phys. Rev. X* **2014**, *4*, 031020. [CrossRef]
13. Naidon, P.; Endo, S. Efimov physics: A review. *Rep. Prog. Phys.* **2017** *80*, 056001. [CrossRef]
14. Levinsen, J.; Parish, M.M.; Bruun, G.M. Impurity in a Bose-Einstein Condensate and the Efimov Effect. *Phys. Rev. Lett.* **2015**, *115*, 125302. [CrossRef] [PubMed]

15. Sun, M.; Zhai, H.; Cui, X. Visualizing the Efimov Correlation in Bose Polarons. *Phys. Rev. Lett.* **2017**, *119*, 013401. [CrossRef] [PubMed]
16. Wang, Y.; Laing, W.B.; Stecher, J.; Esry, B.D. Efimov Physics in Heteronuclear Four-Body Systems. *Phys. Rev. Lett.* **2012**, *108*, 073201. [CrossRef] [PubMed]
17. Casteels, W.; Tempere, J.; Devreese, J.T. Bipolarons and multipolarons consisting of impurity atoms in a Bose-Einstein condensate. *Phys. Rev. A* **2013**, *88*, 013613. [CrossRef]
18. Blume, D.; Yan, Y. Generalized Efimov Scenario for Heavy-Light Mixtures. *Phys. Rev. Lett.* **2014**, *113*, 213201. [CrossRef]
19. Shi, Z.Y.; Yoshida, S.M.; Parish, M.M.; Levinsen, J. Impurity-Induced Multibody Resonances in a Bose Gas. *Phys. Rev. Lett.* **2018**, *121*, 243401. [CrossRef] [PubMed]
20. Yoshida, S.M.; Shi, Z.Y.; Levinsen, J.; Parish, M.M. Few-body states of bosons interacting with a heavy quantum impurity. *Phys. Rev. A* **2018**, *98*, 062705. [CrossRef]
21. Blume, D. Few-boson system with a single impurity: Universal bound states tied to Efimov trimers. *Phys. Rev. A* **2019**, *99*, 013613. [CrossRef]
22. Jorgensen, N.B.; Wacker, L.; Skalmstang, K.T.; Parish, M.M.; Levinsen, J.; Christensen, R.S.; Bruun, G.M.; Arlt, J.J. Observation of Attractive and Repulsive Polarons in a Bose-Einstein Condensate. *Phys. Rev. Lett.* **2016**, *117*, 055302. [CrossRef] [PubMed]
23. Hu, M.-G.; de Graaff, M.J.V.; Kedar, D.; Corson, J.P.; Cornell, E.A.; Jin, D.S. Bose Polarons in the Strongly Interacting Regime. *Phys. Rev. Lett.* **2016**, *117*, 055301. [CrossRef] [PubMed]
24. Yan, Z.Z.; Ni, Y.; Robens, C.; Zwierlein, M.W. Bose polarons near quantum criticality. *Science* **2020**, *368*, 190. [CrossRef] [PubMed]
25. Levinsen, J.; Parish, M.M.; Christensen, R.S.; Arlt, J.J.; Bruun, G.M. Finite-temperature behavior of the Bose polaron. *Phys. Rev. A* **2017** *96*, 063622. [CrossRef]
26. Guenther, N.-E.; Massignan, P.; Lewenstein, M.; Bruun, G.M. Bose Polarons at Finite Temperature and Strong Coupling. *Phys. Rev. Lett.* **2018**, *120*, 050405. [CrossRef]
27. Pastukhov, V. Polaron in the dilute critical Bose condensate. *J. Phys. A Math. Theor.* **2018**, *51*, 195003. [CrossRef]
28. Liu, W.E.; Levinsen, J.; Paris, M.M. Variational Approach for Impurity Dynamics at Finite Temperature. *Phys. Rev. Lett.* **2019**, *122*, 205301. [CrossRef]
29. Field, B.; Levinsen, J.; Parish, M.M. Fate of the Bose polaron at finite temperature. *Phys. Rev. A* **2020**, *101*, 013623 [CrossRef]
30. Pascual, G.; Boronat, J. Quasiparticle Nature of the Bose Polaron at Finite Temperature. *Phys. Rev. Lett.* **2021**, *127*, 205301. [CrossRef]
31. Zinner, N.T. Efimov states of heavy impurities in a Bose-Einstein condensate. *Europhys. Phys. Lett.* **2013**, *101*, 60009. [CrossRef]
32. Zinner, N.T. Spectral flow of trimer states of two heavy impurities and one light condensed boson. *Europhys. Phys. J. D* **2014**, *68*, 216. [CrossRef]
33. Camacho-Guardian, A.; Ardila, L.A.P.; Pohl, T.; Bruun, G.M. Bipolarons in a Bose-Einstein Condensate. *Phys. Rev. Lett.* **2018**, *121*, 013401. [CrossRef] [PubMed]
34. Camacho-Guardian, A.; Bruun, G.M. Landau Effective Interaction between Quasiparticles in a Bose-Einstein Condensate. *Phys. Rev. X* **2018**, *8*, 031042. [CrossRef]
35. Brauneis, F.; Hammer, H.-W.; Lemeshko, M.; Volosniev, A.G. Impurities in a one-dimensional Bose gas: The flow equation approach. *SciPost Phys.* **2021**, *11*, 008. [CrossRef]
36. Petcovich, A.; Ristivojevic, Z. Mediated interaction between polarons in a one-dimensional Bose gas. *arXiv* **2021**, arXiv:2103.08772.
37. Pasek, M.; Orso, G. Induced pairing of fermionic impurities in a one-dimensional strongly correlated Bose gas. *Phys. Rev. B* **2019**, *100*, 245419. [CrossRef]
38. Will, M.; Astrakharchik, G.E.; Fleischhauer, M. Polaron Interactions and Bipolarons in One-Dimensional Bose Gases in the Strong Coupling Regime. *Phys. Rev. Lett.* **2021**, *127*, 103401. [CrossRef]
39. Dehkharghani, A.S.; Volosniev, A.G.; Zinner, N.T. Coalescence of Two Impurities in a Trapped One-dimensional Bose Gas. *Phys. Rev. Lett.* **2018**, *121*, 080405. [CrossRef]
40. Mistakidis, S.I.; Volosniev, A.G.; Schmelcher, P. Induced correlations between impurities in a one-dimensional quenched Bose gas. *Phys. Rev. Res.* **2020**, *2*, 023154. [CrossRef]
41. Naidon, P. Two Impurities in a Bose–Einstein Condensate: From Yukawa to Efimov Attracted Polarons. *J. Phys. Soc. Jpn.* **2018**, *87*, 043002. [CrossRef]
42. Pastukhov, V. Polaron in dilute 2D Bose gas at low temperatures. *J. Phys. B At. Mol. Opt. Phys.* **2018**, *51*, 155203. [CrossRef]
43. Isaule, F.; Morera, I.; Massignan, P.; Juliá-Díaz, B. Renormalization-group study of Bose polarons. *Phys. Rev. A* **2021**, *104*, 023317. [CrossRef]
44. Akaturk, E.; Tanatar, B. Two-dimensional Bose polaron using diffusion Monte Carlo method. *Int. J. Mod. Phys. B* **2019**, *33*, 1950238. [CrossRef]
45. Ardila, L.A.P.; Astrakharchik, G.E.; Giorgini, S. Strong coupling Bose polarons in a two-dimensional gas. *Phys. Rev. Res.* **2020**, *2*, 023405. [CrossRef]
46. Khan, M.M.; Tercas, H.; Mendonca, J.T.; Wehr, J.; Charalambous, C.; Lewenstein, M.; Garcia-March, M.A. Quantum dynamics of a Bose polaron in a d-dimensional Bose-Einstein condensate. *Phys. Rev. A* **2021**, *103*, 023303. [CrossRef]
47. Kain, B.; Ling, H.Y. Analytical study of static beyond-Frohlich Bose polarons in one dimension. *Phys. Rev. A* **2018**, *98*, 033610. [CrossRef]

48. Reichert, B.; Ristivojevic, Z.; Petkovic, A. The Casimir-like effect in a one-dimensional Bose gas. *New J. Phys.* **2019**, *21*, 053024. [CrossRef]
49. Reichert, B.; Ristivojevic, Z.; Petkovic, A. Field-theoretical approach to the Casimir-like interaction in a one-dimensional Bose gas. *Phys. Rev. B* **2019**, *99*, 205414. [CrossRef]
50. Panochko, G.; Pastukhov, V. Two- and three-body effective potentials between impurities in ideal BEC. *J. Phys A Math. Theor.* **2021**, *54*, 085001. [CrossRef]
51. Drescher, M.; Salmhofer, M.; Enss, T. Quench Dynamics of the Ideal Bose Polaron at Zero and Nonzero Temperatures. *Phys. Rev. A* **2021**, *103*, 033317. [CrossRef]
52. Levinsen, J.; Ardila, L.A.P.; Yoshida, S.M.; Parish, M.M. Quantum Behavior of a Heavy Impurity Strongly Coupled to a Bose Gas. *Phys. Rev. Lett.* **2021**, *127*, 033401. [CrossRef]
53. Volosniev, A.G.; Hammer, H.-W.; Zinner, N.T. Real-time dynamics of an impurity in an ideal Bose gas in a trap. *Phys. Rev. A* **2015**, *92*, 023623. [CrossRef]
54. Andersen, J.O. Theory of the weakly interacting Bose gas. *Rev. Mod. Phys.* **2004**, *76*, 599. [CrossRef]
55. Salasnich, L.; Toigo, F. Zero-point energy of ultracold atoms. *Phys. Rep.* **2016**, *640*, 1. [CrossRef]
56. Volosniev, A.G.; Hammer, H.-W. Analytical approach to the Bose-polaron problem in one dimension. *Phys. Rev. A* **2017**, *96*, 031601(R). [CrossRef]
57. Pastukhov, V. Mean-field properties of impurity in Bose gas with three-body forces. *Phys. Lett. A* **2019**, *383*, 2610. [CrossRef]
58. Panochko, G.; Pastukhov, V. Mean-field construction for spectrum of one-dimensional Bose polaron. *Ann. Phys.* **2019**, *409*, 167933. [CrossRef]
59. Hryhorchak, O.; Panochko, G.; Pastukhov, V. Mean-field study of repulsive 2D and 3D Bose polarons. *J. Phys. B At. Mol. Opt. Phys.* **2020**, *53*, 205302. [CrossRef]
60. Hryhorchak, O.; Panochko, G.; Pastukhov, V. Impurity in a three-dimensional unitary Bose gas. *Phys. Lett. A* **2020**, *384*, 126934. [CrossRef]
61. Massignan, P.; Yegovtsev, N.; Gurarie, V. Universal Aspects of a Strongly Interacting Impurity in a Dilute Bose Condensate. *Phys. Rev. Lett.* **2021**, *126*, 123403. [CrossRef] [PubMed]
62. Jager, J.; Barnett, R.; Will, M.; Fleischhauer, M. Strong-coupling Bose polarons in one dimension: Condensate deformation and modified Bogoliubov phonons. *Phys. Rev. Res.* **2020**, *2*, 033142. [CrossRef]
63. Mora, C.; Castin, Y. Ground State Energy of the Two-Dimensional Weakly Interacting Bose Gas: First Correction Beyond Bogoliubov Theory. *Phys. Rev. Lett.* **2009**, *102*, 180404. [CrossRef] [PubMed]
64. Abramowitz, M.; Stegun, I. *Handbook of Mathematical Functions with Formulas, Graphs, and Mathematical Tables*; US Government Printing Office: Washington, DC, USA, 1964.
65. Schmidt, R.; Enss, T. Self-stabilized Bose polarons. *arXiv* **2021**, arXiv:2102.13616.

Article

Pattern Formation in One-Dimensional Polaron Systems and Temporal Orthogonality Catastrophe

Georgios M. Koutentakis [1,2,*], Simeon I. Mistakidis [1,3] and Peter Schmelcher [1,2]

[1] Center for Optical Quantum Technologies, Department of Physics, University of Hamburg, Luruper Chaussee 149, 22761 Hamburg, Germany; smistaki@physnet.uni-hamburg.de (S.I.M.); pschmelc@physnet.uni-hamburg.de (P.S.)
[2] The Hamburg Centre for Ultrafast Imaging, University of Hamburg, Luruper Chaussee 149, 22761 Hamburg, Germany
[3] ITAMP, Center for Astrophysics | Harvard & Smithsonian, Cambridge, MA 02138, USA; symeon.mystakidis@cfa.harvard.edu
* Correspondence: gkoutent@physnet.uni-hamburg.de

Abstract: Recent studies have demonstrated that higher than two-body bath-impurity correlations are not important for quantitatively describing the ground state of the Bose polaron. Motivated by the above, we employ the so-called Gross Ansatz (GA) approach to unravel the stationary and dynamical properties of the homogeneous one-dimensional Bose-polaron for different impurity momenta and bath-impurity couplings. We explicate that the character of the equilibrium state crossovers from the quasi-particle Bose polaron regime to the collective-excitation stationary dark-bright soliton for varying impurity momentum and interactions. Following an interspecies interaction quench the temporal orthogonality catastrophe is identified, provided that bath-impurity interactions are sufficiently stronger than the intraspecies bath ones, thus generalizing the results of the confined case. This catastrophe originates from the formation of dispersive shock wave structures associated with the zero-range character of the bath-impurity potential. For initially moving impurities, a momentum transfer process from the impurity to the dispersive shock waves via the exerted drag force is demonstrated, resulting in a final polaronic state with reduced velocity. Our results clearly demonstrate the crucial role of non-linear excitations for determining the behavior of the one-dimensional Bose polaron.

Keywords: Bose polaron; pattern formation; temporal orthogonality catastrophe; Lee-Low-Pines transformation; mobile and immobile impurities

---

Citation: Koutentakis, G.M.; Mistakidis, S.I.; Schmelcher, P. Pattern Formation in One-Dimensional Polaron Systems and Temporal Orthogonality Catastrophe. *Atoms* **2022**, *10*, 3. https://doi.org/10.3390/atoms10010003

Academic Editor: Manuel Bautista

Received: 21 October 2021
Accepted: 23 December 2021
Published: 28 December 2021

Publisher's Note: MDPI stays neutral with regard to jurisdictional claims in published maps and institutional affiliations.

Copyright: © 2021 by the authors. Licensee MDPI, Basel, Switzerland. This article is an open access article distributed under the terms and conditions of the Creative Commons Attribution (CC BY) license (https://creativecommons.org/licenses/by/4.0/).

1. Introduction

Polaronic excitations constitute an ubiquitous class of quasi-particles, incorporating important ramifications in multiple branches of physics [1]. In material science polarons are encountered in several classes of technologically relevant materials, for instance, in He droplets [2,3], polar [4–8] or organic [9–11] semiconductors and transition metal oxides [12,13], while their broad relevance stretches even towards biophysics [14]. Their formation, properties and interactions are key elements in important phenomena such as the electric conductivity of polymers [15,16], the organic magnetoresistance [17], the Kondo effect [18] and even high-temperature superconductivity [19–24]. Therefore, it is not surprising that ultracold atoms, being one of the prime platforms for quantum simulation [25], have been employed for studying polaronic structures. In these systems, two different kinds of polaronic excitations have been experimentally realized to date. Namely, the Fermi polaron [26–31] referring to an impurity interacting with an extensive gas of fermionic atoms, and the Bose polaron [32–37], where the environment possesses a bosonic character. Accordingly, these systems have recently been a topic of intense theoretical study in the ultracold community especially regarding their stationary properties [38,39,39–63]. Lately, it has been argued that the ground state of the Bose polaron can be well-described in terms of a simple Gross-Pitaevskii mean-field type variational approach [55–65] herewith referred to as the Gross Ansatz (GA)[1]. The latter neglects all correlations except for the two-body bath-impurity ones.

The dynamics of the Bose polaron has also been actively explored [66–74,74–83]. Among the many different facets of the polaron dynamics, here we will focus on the phenomenon of temporal orthogonality catastrophe [58,79–83]. The latter occurs when an impurity is embedded into an adequately strongly repulsive Bose gas and is manifested by the rapid evolution of the system state towards a configuration orthogonal to the initial one, signifying the dynamical decay of the Bose polaron. In particular, the temporal orthogonality catastrophe has been extensively explored in the case of confined one-dimensional (1D) Bose gases, where an effective potential description, delineated by the bath density and impurity-medium coupling, has been found to be crucial for understanding the dynamical behavior of the system [72,76,77,80–85]. This potential is speculated to be the origin of the temporal orthogonality catastrophe, leading to the question of whether a similar mechanism appears in the homogeneous setting where the notion of the effective potential does not exist. Recent studies indicate that this actually might be the case [58,60,61]. One of our central objectives is thus to address this issue and reveal the origin of the temporal orthogonality catastrophe phenomenon for homogeneous Bose gases.

The main culprit for the manifestation of this phenomenon in homogeneous systems refers to the possible emission of non-linear waves by the Bose-Einstein Condensate (BEC). Importantly, over the past decades the Gross-Pitaevskii equation has proven to perfectly describe such non-linear excitations [86,87]. The relevant ones for the 1D setting refer, among others, to dark-solitons [88–90] and dispersive shock waves [91–94], which have been also realized experimentally [95–98]. In addition, numerous recent studies exemplified that these excitations also occur in the presence of interparticle correlations [73,98–105], albeit possessing a more involved behavior than their mean-field counterparts. In this context, it is crucial to answering whether such non-linear excitations contribute to the dynamics of the Bose polaron, a question which is further mandated by the similarity between the GA equations-of-motion and the Gross-Pitaevskii one.

In this work, we employ the GA formulation to examine the equilibrium and dynamical properties of the repulsive Bose polaron and its relation to non-linear pattern formation. After revisiting the ground state behavior of the Bose polaron [55–57,59], we focus on the equilibrium properties of a moving polaron, where we unveil the crossover from the polaronic to a dark-bright soliton regime. The above indicates a quite intriguing crossover of the impurity state which for weak interspecies repulsions and/or impurity momenta realizes a quasi-particle and in the opposite limit contributes to a collective excitation of the bosonic host. The comparison of the equilibrium results obtained through GA with the Multi-Layer Multi-Configuration Time-Dependent Hartree method for atomic mixtures (ML-MCTHDX) [106], verifies the exceptional accuracy of the former in describing the two-particle interspecies correlations of the system. In particular, the GA approach provides in this case almost identical results to the correlated ML-MCTDHX method for the energy, effective mass, and bath-impurity correlations of the Bose polaron, while it overestimates the polaronic residue.

We subsequently explore the dynamical response of the system within GA, by employing interspecies interaction quenches from zero to a finite repulsive coupling. Here, the temporal orthogonality catastrophe is exhibited for all initial impurity momenta, as long as the bath-impurity interactions are sufficiently stronger than the intraspecies bath ones, a phenomenon that generalizes the results reported in the confined scenario [79–83]. Interestingly, we show for the first time that this mechanism is related to the formation of dispersive shock wave structures associated with the short-range character of the bath-impurity potential. Note that independently shock wave formation has been demonstrated after the collision of two polaronic clouds immersed in a Fermi medium [107]. In all cases, the post quench state of the system corresponds to a Bose polaron, accompanied by two dispersive shock wave excitations traveling away from the impurity and having a velocity equal to the speed of sound. For moving impurities, we monitor the drag force being exerted by the bosonic host to the impurity and resulting in a momentum transfer from the impurity to the emitted dispersive shock waves. This process leads to the final polaronic state possessing a reduced velocity when compared to the initial one and tending to vanish for strong repulsions as a consequence of the amplification of the drag force. The above demonstrates the crucial role of non-linear excitations in the dynamics of the Bose polaron.

This work is structured as follows. Section 2 introduces the homogeneous binary mixture setup and the concept of the Lee-Low-Pines transformation. In Section 3 we present our main theoretical approach in terms of the GA, which we apply to characterize the static and moving Bose polaron at equilibrium. In order to establish the validity of the GA approach in characterizing the 1D polaron, in Section 4 we compare our GA results with the fully correlated ML-MCTDHX approach. The dynamics of the Bose polaron, associated with the emergence of the temporal orthogonality catastrophe phenomenon is outlined in Section 5. In Section 6 we summarize our results and provide future perspectives for further study. Appendix A elaborates on the bosonic momentum renormalization in the thermodynamic limit of 1D systems, while Appendix B explores the impact of the range of the interspecies interaction potential on the nature of the emitted excitations during the dynamics. Finally, Appendix C outlines the ingredients of the employed computational approaches.

2. Polaron Hamiltonian and Lee-Low-Pines Transformation

We consider a system of N_B bosons of mass m_B interacting with a single impurity atom of mass m_I within a 1D ring of perimeter L. It is described by the Hamiltonian

$$\hat{H} = -\frac{\hbar^2}{2m_B}\sum_{k=1}^{N_B}\frac{\partial^2}{\partial x_k^2} - \frac{\hbar^2}{2m_I}\frac{\partial^2}{\partial x_I^2} + g_{BI}\sum_{k=1}^{N_B}\delta(x_k - x_I) + g_{BB}\sum_{k=1}^{N_B}\sum_{k'<k}\delta(x_k - x_{k'}), \quad (1)$$

where x_k, $k = 1, \ldots, N_B$, correspond to the coordinates of the bath particles and x_I refers to the position of the impurity. In addition, g_{BB} and g_{BI} correspond to the intraspecies interactions of the bath atoms and the interspecies coupling among the bath atom and the impurity respectively. Notice, that ring confinement of ultracold gases is experimentally feasible [108,109]. Here we are also interested in the limit $L \to \infty$, where our results converge to the thermodynamic limit of homogeneous systems and the boundary conditions become irrelevant. In this context, box potentials emulating the homogeneous thermodynamic limit results can be also realized experimentally [110–113]. In either case, the system is adequately described as 1D when it is subjected to strong confinement along with the transverse spatial directions. The transverse confinement leads to the modification of the scattering length of the atomic collisions and allows for the control of the involved interaction strengths via confinement and Fano-Feshbach resonances [114].

There are several theoretical approaches to tackle the properties of the Hamiltonian of Equation (1) for small g_{BB}. Traditionally they mainly relied on the linearization of the intraspecies interaction term of the bath via the Bogoliubov approach [43,49,50,115]. Here we will take an alternative route based on the spatial homogeneity of the system, which allows us to further simplify the Hamiltonian of Equation (1), by performing the so-called Lee-Low-Pines transformation [116–118]. The latter is a coordinate transformation to the frame-of-reference of the impurity namely $r_k = x_k - x_I$ and $r_I = x_I$. The transformed Hamiltonian reads

$$\hat{H}_{\text{LLP}} = -\frac{\hbar^2}{2m_r}\sum_{k=1}^{N_B}\frac{\partial^2}{\partial r_k^2} + g_{BI}\sum_{k=1}^{N_B}\delta(r_k) + g_{BB}\sum_{k=1}^{N_B}\sum_{k'<k}\delta(r_k - r_{k'})$$
$$-\frac{\hbar^2}{2m_I}\frac{\partial^2}{\partial r_I^2} - \frac{\hbar^2}{m_I}\sum_{k=1}^{N_B}\sum_{k'<k}\frac{\partial}{\partial r_k}\frac{\partial}{\partial r_{k'}} + \frac{\hbar^2}{m_I}\sum_{k=1}^{N_B}\frac{\partial}{\partial r_k}\frac{\partial}{\partial r_I}, \quad (2)$$

where $m_r = (m_B^{-1} + m_I^{-1})^{-1}$ is the reduced mass of the bath-impurity system. Interestingly, the momentum operator of the impurity $\hat{p}_I = -i\hbar \frac{\partial}{\partial r_I}$ commutes with the transformed Hamiltonian, Equation (2), and therefore the momentum of the impurity is conserved in the Lee-Low-Pines transformed frame. This allows us to simplify the two-species system into an effective single-species one, by replacing $\hat{p}_I = p_I \in \mathbb{R}$. This reduction comes with the expense of having to deal with an additional momentum-momentum interaction term for the bath atoms, with a coupling inversely proportional to the mass of the impurity m_I.

3. Gross Ansatz Treatment of the Lee-Low-Pines Hamiltonian

In the case $m_I \to \infty$, $\hat{H}_{\text{LLP}}$ reduces to the well-studied Lieb-Liniger model [119], with an additional δ-shaped potential at the origin $r = 0$. It is known [120] that the excitation spectrum of the Lieb-Liniger model is well described by the Bogoliubov one [121] for $\gamma_{\text{LL}} = 2m_B g_{BB}/(\hbar^2 n_0) \ll 1$, where n_0 is the density of the bath atoms, $n_0 = N_B/L$. This motivates a mean-field treatment of the Hamiltonian of Equation (2) in the case of small g_{BB}. In particular, we expand the state of the system in terms of the so-called GA, $|\Psi(t)\rangle = |\Psi_{GA}(t)\rangle$, with [3,122],

$$\Psi_{GA}(r_I, r_1, \ldots, r_{N_B}; t) = \frac{1}{\sqrt{L}} e^{\frac{i}{\hbar} p_I r_I} \prod_{k=1}^{N_B} \psi(r_k; t), \qquad (3)$$

with p_I being the momentum of the impurity in the Lee-Low-Pines frame. Additionally, $\psi(r; t)$ is the single-particle wavefunction occupied by all the bath atoms. Note here that, within GA, $\psi(r; t)$ depends only on $r_k = x_k - x_I$. Another important feature of this wavefunction ansatz, Equation (3), is that it neglects all correlations emanating among the bath particles. As a consequence, it assumes that the bath despite the presence of the impurity, remains in a BEC state. Nevertheless, the correlations among the impurity and the bath particles are properly taken into account. This can be verified by considering the two-body density of the bath and the impurity atoms

$$\rho_{IB}^{(2)}(x_I; x_1; t) = n_0 |\psi(x_1 - x_I; t)|^2 = n_0 |\psi(r_1; t)|^2 \neq \rho_B^{(1)}(x_1; t) \rho_I^{(1)}(x_I; t) = \frac{n_0}{L}. \qquad (4)$$

In summary, the GA allows us to obtain the variationally optimal two-body correlations between the impurity and the bath, by neglecting all higher-order correlations [3].

3.1. The Polaron Solution

To find the variationally optimal configuration within the GA approximation we have to minimize the energy functional stemming from $\hat{H}_{\text{LLP}}$, under the constraint of a normalized $\psi(r)$. The corresponding functional can be obtained by e.g., following the Dirac-Frenkel variational principle [123,124] and introducing the Lagrange coefficient $\mu(t)$

$$\begin{aligned} E[\psi(r;t)] &= \left\langle \Psi_{GA}(t) \middle| \hat{H}_{\text{LLP}} - i\hbar \frac{d}{dt} \middle| \Psi_{GA}(t) \right\rangle + \mu(t) N_B \left(1 - \int dr\, |\psi(r;t)|^2 \right) \\ &= \frac{p_I^2}{2m_I} + \mu(t) N_B + N_B \int dr \Bigg[-i\hbar \psi^*(r;t) \frac{\partial \psi(r;t)}{\partial t} - \frac{\hbar^2}{2m_r} \psi^*(r;t) \frac{\partial^2 \psi(r;t)}{\partial r^2} \\ &\quad + g_{BI} \delta(r) |\psi(r;t)|^2 + \frac{g_{BB}}{2}(N_B - 1)|\psi(r;t)|^4 + \frac{i\hbar p_I}{m_I} \psi^*(r;t) \frac{\partial \psi(r;t)}{\partial r} \\ &\quad - \frac{\hbar^2 (N_B - 1)}{2m_I} \left(\int dr'\, \psi^*(r';t) \frac{\partial \psi(r';t)}{\partial r'} \right) \psi^*(r;t) \frac{\partial \psi(r;t)}{\partial r} - \mu(t) |\psi(r;t)|^2 \Bigg]. \end{aligned} \qquad (5)$$

The variation of Equation (5) yields the Gross-Pitaevskii type [121] equation

$$i\hbar\frac{\partial}{\partial t}\psi(r;t) = \left[-\frac{\hbar^2}{2m_r}\frac{\partial^2}{\partial r^2} + \frac{i\hbar^2 k_0(t)}{m_I}\frac{\partial}{\partial r} + g_{BI}\delta(r) \right.$$
$$\left. + g_{BB}(N_B-1)|\psi(r;t)|^2 - \mu\right]\psi(r;t), \quad (6)$$

where $\hbar k_0(t) \equiv \left(p_I + i\hbar(N_B-1)\int dr'\, \psi^*(r';t)\frac{\partial \psi(r';t)}{\partial r'}\right)$. Notice here the non-linear dependence of Equation (6) on $\frac{\partial \psi}{\partial r}$, which goes beyond the framework of the standard Gross-Pitaevskii equation and accounts for the coupling of the impurity momentum with the state of the bath.

Herewith, let us focus on stationary solutions, $\psi(r;t) = \psi(r)$, where Equation (5) reduces to the corresponding energy functional and $k_0(t) = k_0$, $\mu(t) = \mu$. We remark that Equation (6) has already been solved in Ref. [94] for $N_B, L \to \infty$, while $n_0 = N_B/L = $ finite and in the case of a given value of k_0. Setting $\psi(r) = \sqrt{n(r)/N_B}e^{i\varphi(r)}$ the ingredients of the underlying solution read

$$n(r) = n_0\left[\beta^2 + \frac{1}{\gamma^2}\tanh^2\frac{|r|+r_0}{\sqrt{2}\gamma\xi}\right], \text{ and}$$
$$\varphi(r) = \frac{r}{|r|}\left[\tan^{-1}\left(\frac{1}{\beta\gamma}\tanh\frac{r_0}{\sqrt{2}\gamma\xi}\right) - \tan^{-1}\left(\frac{1}{\beta\gamma}\tanh\frac{|r|+r_0}{\sqrt{2}\gamma\xi}\right)\right], \quad (7)$$

with $\beta = v/c$, $\gamma = (1-\beta^2)^{-\frac{1}{2}}$, the speed of sound defined as $c = \sqrt{\varepsilon_{BB}n_0/m_r}$ and the flow velocity $v = \hbar k_0/m_I$ of the BEC relative to the impurity. The healing length is $\xi = \hbar/\sqrt{2m_r g_{BB} n_0}$ and the Lagrange coefficient, $\mu = g_{BB}n_0$, which can be identified as the chemical potential [121]. In order to express the solution belonging to Equation (7) in terms of the system parameters g_{BI} and p_I, the values of r_0 and v have to be determined self-consistently by solving the following two algebraic equations

$$g_{BI} = \frac{\hbar c}{\gamma^3}\frac{\tanh\frac{r_0}{\sqrt{2}\gamma\xi}}{\beta^2 + \sinh^2\frac{r_0}{\sqrt{2}\gamma\xi}},$$
$$p_I = \frac{\hbar\beta}{\xi}\left[-\frac{1}{\sqrt{2}}\frac{m_I}{m_r} + \frac{2n_0\xi}{\gamma}\left(1-\tanh\frac{r_0}{\sqrt{2}\gamma\xi}\right)\right] - \hbar n_0\Delta\varphi. \quad (8)$$

Here $\Delta\varphi$ is the phase difference of the BEC wavefunction, $\psi(r)$, at $r = \pm\infty$, namely

$$\Delta\varphi = \lim_{r\to\infty}\varphi(r) - \lim_{r\to-\infty}\varphi(r)$$
$$= 2\left[\tan^{-1}\left(\frac{1}{\beta\gamma}\tanh\frac{r_0}{\sqrt{2}\gamma\xi}\right) - \tan^{-1}\left(\frac{1}{\beta\gamma}\right)\right]. \quad (9)$$

Before proceeding, let us stress that the solution of Equation (7) possesses unconventional boundary conditions as the wavefunction changes by a phase factor $e^{i\Delta\varphi}$ from $r \to -\infty$ to $r \to +\infty$. This is the reason of the existence of the term $\propto \Delta\varphi$ in Equation (8). In particular, in the presence of such boundary conditions the bosonic momentum needs to be renormalized by a finite amount [121] (see also Appendix A). This implies that p_I is not connected with v via the relation $p_I = m_I v$, a fact that will become particularly important later on. Additionally, a phase difference $\Delta\varphi \neq 0$ which is realized for $p_I \neq 0$ implies a global change in the BEC wavefunction $\psi(r)$. This feature indicates that the 1D Bose polaron, within GA, possesses the character of a collective excitation of the BEC.

3.2. The Case of a Static Polaron

Recently, the properties of the Gross-Pitaevskii type Equation (6) have been intensively studied [55–62,64,65] especially in one and three spatial dimensions. Below we will briefly review the implications of the 1D solution Equation (7) on the properties of the polaron [55–59]. For $p_I = 0$ the self consistency Equation (8) can be solved exactly, yielding $\beta = 0$ and

$$r_0 = \frac{\xi}{\sqrt{2}} \sinh^{-1}\left(\frac{2\hbar c}{g_{BI}}\right). \tag{10}$$

Consequently, most of the properties of the Bose polaron depend on the ratio,

$$\frac{g_{BI}}{2\hbar c} = \sqrt{\gamma_{LL}} \frac{g_{BI}}{g_{BB}} \left(1 + \frac{m_B}{m_I}\right)^{-\frac{1}{2}}. \tag{11}$$

Recall that the GA description is expected to be valid as long as $\gamma_{LL} \ll 1$. Therefore, the behavior of the polaron is mainly tunable via the ratio of the intra and interspecies interaction strengths and the mass imbalance among the impurity and the bath particles. However, this mass ratio, m_B/m_I, affects Equation (11) only weakly since $0.18 < \left(1 + \frac{m_B}{m_I}\right)^{-\frac{1}{2}} < 0.98$ for all currently experimentally realizable ultracold setups[2], leading to the conclusion that the most important factor for characterizing the state of the polaron is the interaction strength fraction g_{BI}/g_{BB}.

A quantity that will be important for the description of the polaron dynamics is its energy, $E_p = E[\psi(r)] - E_0$, with $E_0 = g_{BB}n_0^2/2$, being the excess energy of the polaron state with respect to the energy of the system for $g_{BI} = 0$. Thus, the energy of the static polaron (see also Equation (5)) reads

$$E_p = \frac{\hbar c n_0}{3} \left\{ 4 - \left[\sqrt{1 + \left(\frac{g_{BI}}{2\hbar c}\right)^2} - \frac{g_{BI}}{2\hbar c}\right]^3 - 3\left[\sqrt{1 + \left(\frac{g_{BI}}{2\hbar c}\right)^2} - \frac{g_{BI}}{2\hbar c}\right] \right\}. \tag{12}$$

A simple Taylor expansion in terms of $\frac{g_{BI}}{2\hbar c}$, demonstrates that the energy of the polaron within GA grows linearly for small g_{BI}, as is also expected for the non-interacting BEC background, $\psi(r) = \sqrt{n_0}$. Significant deviations only appear when $g_{BI} \approx 2\hbar c$, where the energy of the polaron becomes smaller than the one of the corresponding non-interacting profile, $E_{NI} = g_{BI}n_0$, since the BEC density in the vicinity of the impurity is suppressed. For strong repulsions, namely $g_{BI}/(2\hbar c) \gg 1$, the energy of the polaron saturates to the value $4\hbar c n_0/3$, a tendency which has been shown to qualitatively agree with corresponding Quantum Monte Carlo predictions in Ref. [54].

Figure 1a, demonstrates the behavior of E_p over the characteristic energy scale $\hbar c n_0$ for increasing $g_{BI}/(2\hbar c)$. By comparing the behavior of this quantity with the first-order asymptotics of Equation (12), we can observe the emergence of the three distinct interaction regimes. Namely, for small, $g_{BI}/(2\hbar c) < 0.25$, and large values, $g_{BI}/(2\hbar c) > 2$, the impurity-medium energy, E_p, matches the results of the corresponding asymptotic expansions. In contrast, within the intermediate interaction regime $0.25 < g_{BI}/(2\hbar c) < 2$ deviations between the exact values of E_p, Equation (12), and the approximate Taylor expansions occur. Finally, let us note that the typical energy scale of the system $\hbar c n_0$ is related to the corresponding interaction-independent one $\hbar^2 n_0^2/m_B$ via

$$\hbar c n_0 = \sqrt{\frac{\gamma_{LL}}{2}\left(1 + \frac{m_B}{m_I}\right)} \frac{\hbar^2 n_0^2}{m_B}, \tag{13}$$

which is a function of the Lieb-Liniger parameter, γ_{LL}, and the mass ratio, m_B/m_I. The above indicate that the energy scale of the Bose polaron is small compared to the non-interacting energy scale, $\hbar^2 n_0^2/m_B$, at least when we focus on the case of a BEC host in which $\gamma_{LL} \ll 1$.

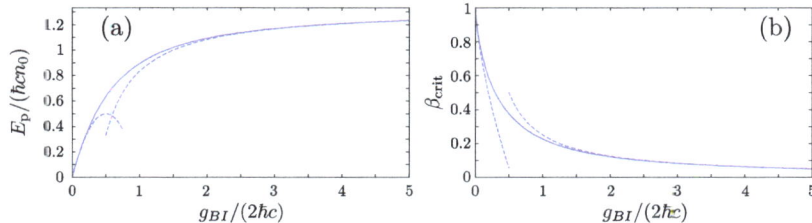

Figure 1. Analytical predictions for the energy and critical velocity of the Bose polaron within GA. (a) Polaron energy, E_p [Equation (12)] and (b) critical velocity of the polaronic solution, β_{crit}, [Equation (14)] for varying bath-impurity interaction strength, g_{BI}. In both cases the solid lines indicate the exact results while the dashed lines correspond to weak (leftmost line), $\mathcal{O}\left(\frac{g_{BI}}{2\hbar c}\right)^2$, and strong (rightmost line), $\mathcal{O}\left(\frac{2\hbar c}{g_{BI}}\right)^2$, asymptotic Taylor expansions.

3.3. Moving Polaron and the Soliton Solution

Having briefly commented on the analytic polaron solution for $p_I = 0$, let us elaborate on the case of a moving polaron with $p_I \neq 0$, where no analytic solution exists and it has been far less discussed in the literature. In that case, the parameters of the polaron need to be found numerically by solving the self-consistency Equation (8), for r_0 and β [57]. It can be easily proven that solutions of Equation (8) for r_0 exist only in the case that the velocity of the polaron β, does not exceed the critical one β_{crit} [94]. The value of the critical velocity, $v_{\text{crit}} = \beta_{\text{crit}} c$, can be obtained by finding the maximum with respect to r_0 of the right-hand side of the first self consistency equation, Equation (8), see also Ref. [94]. This process yields the following algebraic equation

$$\frac{g_{BI}}{2\hbar c} = \sqrt{2}\left(1 - \beta_{\text{crit}}^2\right) \frac{\sqrt{\sqrt{1 + 8\beta_{\text{crit}}^2} - (1 + 2\beta_{\text{crit}}^2)}}{4\beta_{\text{crit}}^2 - 1 + \sqrt{1 + 8\beta_{\text{crit}}^2}}. \tag{14}$$

Notice here, that the value of the critical velocity depends only on the ratio $g_{BI}/(2\hbar c)$. The behavior of β_{crit} along with its strong and weak asymptotics is provided in Figure 1b. It can be seen that for $g_{BI} = 0$ the critical velocity is equal to the speed of sound, $\beta_{\text{crit}} = 1$, and for increasing g_{BI} it is suppressed. For large g_{BI}, β_{crit} behaves as $\beta_{\text{crit}} \propto 1/g_{BI}$, in agreement with the predictions of Ref. [94].

At a first glance, one would expect that the value of β_{crit} can be employed for deriving an upper bound for the maximally allowed p_I, however here we will argue that this is not the case. In particular, for $p_I = \pm \hbar n_0 \pi$ the Gross-Pitaevskii type Equation (6) can be solved analytically yielding the black soliton solution

$$\psi_{p_I = \pm \hbar n_0 \pi}(r) = \mp \sqrt{n_0} \tanh \frac{r}{\sqrt{2}\xi}. \tag{15}$$

Since the impurity lies at $x_I = 0$ being the notch of the black-soliton, this solution actually corresponds to a dark-bright soliton for the composite system. It might seem contradictory that in the case of relatively large momenta, $|p_I| = \pi \hbar n_0$, a stationary BEC flow is encountered. However, this counterintuitive result can be attributed to the fact that p_I does not refer to the momentum of the impurity in the laboratory frame. In particular by inverting the Lee-Low-Pines transformation we obtain

$$\hat{p}_I^{\text{lab}} = p_I - \underbrace{\sum_{i=1}^{N_B}\left(-i\hbar \frac{\partial}{\partial r_i}\right)}_{\equiv \hat{p}_B}, \tag{16}$$

with $\hat{p}_B$ being the momentum of the bath in the impurity frame, which is invariant under the frame transformation, since $\partial/\partial r_i = \partial/\partial x_i$. Therefore, the conservation law of p_I in the impurity frame implies that the total momentum, $p_I = \langle \hat{p}_I^{lab} \rangle + \langle \hat{p}_B \rangle$, is conserved in the laboratory frame. Notice that for the black soliton solution, $\langle \hat{p}_B \rangle = \pm \hbar n_0 \pi = p_I$, which agrees with the fact that the solution is static, $\langle \hat{p}_I^{lab} \rangle = 0$.

In order to analyze the crossover from the static polaronic to the black soliton solution, we focus on the solutions of Equation (8) for $0 \leq p_I \leq \hbar n_0 \pi$. The solutions for varying p_I and g_{BI} while keeping $g_{BB} = 0.1 \hbar^2 n_0/m_B$ fixed are presented for $m_I = 0.5 m_B$ (Figure 2(a_1)–(d_1)), $m_I = m_B$ (Figure 2(a_2)–(d_2)) and $m_I = 2 m_B$ (Figure 2(a_3)–(d_3)). Independently of the impurity mass the velocity of the polaron satisfies $\beta_p \leq \beta_{crit}$ (Figure 2(a_i), $i = 1, 2, 3$), hinting towards the conclusion that the state described by Equation (7) is stable[3] for every p_I and g_{BI}. Moreover, the polaron velocity β exhibits a non-monotonic behavior since for small momenta $p_I < m_I c$, β is increasing with p_I until it reaches a maximum at a g_{BI}-dependent momentum value $p_{I,0} \geq m_I c$. Beyond that point β decreases with increasing p_I until it reaches the value of $\beta = 0$ for $p_I = \pi \hbar n_0$. In addition, it can be seen that the solution for r_0 (Figure 2(b_i), $i = 1, 2, 3$) is appreciably larger than 0 only for $p_I < m_I c$ (see dashed line) and for $g_{BI} < 0.5 \hbar^2 n_0/m_B$.

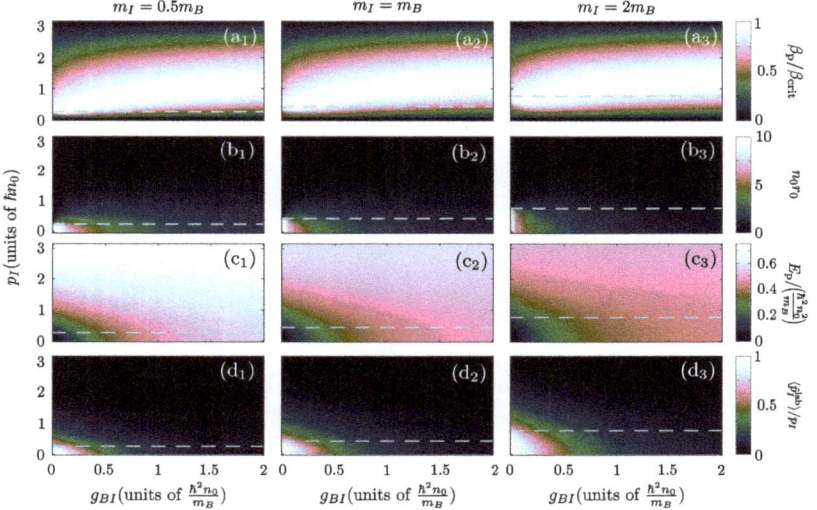

Figure 2. Characteristic properties of the moving Bose polaron within GA. (a_1–a_3) Velocity of the polaron over its critical one, β_p/β_{crit}, (b_1–b_3) offset parameter, r_0, of the polaron solution, (c_1–c_3) polaron energy, E_p and (d_1–d_3) expectation value ratio of the impurity momentum between the laboratory and the impurity frames, $\langle \hat{p}_I^{lab} \rangle/p_I$, for different values of g_{BI} and p_I. The distinct columns correspond to different impurity masses, $m_I = m_B/2$ (left panels), $m_I = m_B$ (middle panels) and $m_I = 2 m_B$ (right panels). In all cases, the data correspond to thermodynamic limit calculations, $N, L \to \infty$, with $g_{BB} = 0.1 \hbar^2 n_0/m_B$ and dashed lines represent $p_I = m_I c$.

The energy of the moving polaron is presented in Figure 2(c_i), $i = 1, 2, 3$. Here there are two notable effects. For a fixed g_{BI}, E_p depends more weakly on p_I as the value of g_{BI} increases. This is a manifestation of the increase of the effective mass, $m^* = \left(\frac{\partial^2 E_p}{\partial p_I^2} \right)^{-1}$, of the polaron with g_{BI} reported in Ref. [57]. Moreover, for momenta $p_I \to \hbar n_0 \pi$ or large interactions the energy of the polaron tends to saturate to the corresponding energy of the dark-bright soliton solution, Equation (15), $E_b = \lim_{g_{BI} \to \infty} E_p = \frac{4}{3} \hbar n_0 c$. It is evident from Figure 2(c_i), that this asymptotic value of energy decreases with increasing m_I a fact that can be understood by inspecting Equation (13).

The above indicate two distinct regimes for the behavior of the system, the polaron regime encountered for low momenta $p_I \sim 0$ and interactions, $g_{BI} \sim 0$, and the dark-bright soliton regime for high momenta, $p_I \sim \pm \hbar n_0 \pi$ and/or strong interactions, $g_{BI} \to \infty$. To characterize the crossover of these two regimes we employ the quantity $\langle \hat{p}_I^{lab} \rangle / p_I \in [0,1]$, see Figure 2($d_i$) with $i = 1, 2, 3$. This quantity compares the momentum contribution of the motion of the impurity, $\langle \hat{p}_I^{lab} \rangle$, to the induced BEC flow, $\langle \hat{p}_B \rangle = p_I - \langle \hat{p}_I^{lab} \rangle$. Therefore, values proximal to 1 indicate that the impurity motion is the dominant contribution and as a consequence, the system is in the polaron regime. On the other hand, values close to 0 signify that the dominant contribution is the BEC flow and accordingly the system behaves as a dark-bright soliton. As Figure 2(d_i) testifies, the polaron regime occurs only for $p_I < m_I c$ and $g_{BI} < 0.5 \hbar^2 n_0 / m_B$, where also $r_0 \gg 0$, see also Figure 2(a_i). Otherwise, the state of the system lies within the dark-bright soliton regime.

As already mentioned previously the mass of the impurity does not significantly alter the behavior of the system. It only affects the system quantitatively by shifting the threshold $m_I c^2$, where the velocity of the impurity becomes supersonic in the case of $g_{BI} = 0$. Indeed, this threshold is related to the crossover between the polaronic and dark-bright soliton regimes causing a shift along p_I for the structures manifested among the different observables.

Concluding, we are in a position to infer the dual character of the 1D polaron as captured by the GA approximation. For varying interaction strengths and momenta the character of impurity changes. In the case of small g_{BI} and p_I the impurity contributes to a well-defined quasiparticle associated with the local excitation of its BEC environment due to its presence. In the opposite scenario of large g_{BI} or $p_I \to \pm \pi \hbar n_0$ the impurity is embedded within a collective excitation akin to a static dark-bright soliton. The exploration of this crossover should provide an interesting perspective for future experiments.

4. Impact of Correlations and Validity of the GA Approximation

Let us now investigate the impact of correlations on the above-mentioned properties of the polaron. For this purpose we employ the Multi-Configuration Time-Dependent Hartree Method for Bosons (MCTDHB) [125,126], being a reduction of the ML-MCTDHX [106], that is able to capture all the relevant correlations emanating in the system. Since currently, the MCTDHB method can only simulate systems with a definite number of particles, here we will focus (in both the ML-MCTDHB and GA case) on a system with $N_B = 100$ confined within a ring of length $L = 100 n_0^{-1}$.

Notice that within MCTDHB we can work with the Lee-Low-Pines transformed Hamiltonian of Equation (2) by exploiting the p_I symmetry of the Hamiltonian of Equation (1). The many-body wavefunction of the system in this case can be reduced, without any loss of generality, to

$$\Psi(x_I, x_1, x_2, \ldots, x_{N_B}) = \frac{1}{\sqrt{L}} e^{\frac{i}{\hbar} p_I x_I} \Psi_B (\underbrace{x_1 - x_I}_{r_1}, \underbrace{x_2 - x_I}_{r_2}, \ldots, \underbrace{x_{N_B} - x_I}_{r_{N_B}}). \quad (17)$$

Then MCTDHB can be employed in order to variationally optimize the $\Psi_B(r_1, \ldots, r_{N_B})$ part of the many-body wavefunction in the absence of any approximation. This allows us to probe the effect of correlations between the atoms of the bath that the GA of Equation (3), neglects. For more details regarding our MCTDHB calculations see Appendix C.

The equilibrium state properties of the polaron for weak intraspecies bath repulsions, $g_{BB} = 0.1 \frac{\hbar^2 n_0}{m_B}$, in the equal mass case, $m_I = m_B$ are compared in Figure 3 within the results of the MCTDHB and the GA approaches. In order to contrast the state of a system confined in a ring of $L = 100 n_0^{-1}$ to the thermodynamic limit $N_B, L \to \infty$, we also provide the corresponding results of the GA when extrapolated to the thermodynamic limit, see Ref. [55–59].

The behaviour of the bath-impurity two-body correlations, $g_{IB}^{(2)}(0;x_B) = \frac{L}{n_0}\rho_{IB}^{(2)}(0;x_B)$, Equation (4), for different interspecies repulsions g_{BI} is demonstrated within the MCTDHB approach in Figure 3a. For increasing g_{BI} we observe a gradual depletion of $\rho_{IB}^{(2)}(0;x_B)$ in the vicinity of the impurity, $x_B \approx x_I = 0$, stemming from the repulsive bath-impurity coupling [73,82]. These anti-correlations are accompanied by bunching of bath-impurity correlations, $g_{IB}^{(2)}(0;x_B) = L\rho_{IB}^{(2)}(0;x_B)/n_0 > 1$, for $x_B > 10n_0^{-1}$ (hardly visible in Figure 3a) which originates from the conservation of the total particle number of bath atoms on the ring. To contrast our findings with the approximate GA method, in Figure 3b we compare the effect of anti-correlations between the bath and the impurity atoms captured by $\rho_{IB}^{(2)}(0;0)$ among the different approaches. Note here, that this quantity is closely related to the Tan contact [59,127–133]. We find that the GA is able to reproduce the behavior observed within the MCTDHB approach. The fully correlated approach predicts only a slightly more pronounced anti-bunching as shown in the inset of Figure 3b. Notice also that the results of the ring confined setups agree very well with the thermodynamic limit ones, indicating the insignificance of finite-size effects for $\rho_{IB}^{(2)}(0;0)$. To appreciate better the effect of the correlations and the confinement of the particles in a ring, Figure 3c compares the bath-impurity correlations, $\rho_{IB}^{(2)}(0,x_B)$, for strong repulsions, $g_{BI} = 2\frac{\hbar^2 n_0}{m_B}$, between the two approaches. As it can be easily deduced the GA results closely follow the MCTDHB ones. The only deviations occur away from the position of the impurity $x_B > 10n_0^{-1}$ (see also the inset of Figure 3c), where in the fully correlated case spatial oscillations of the $\rho_{IB}^{(2)}(0;x_B)$ profile are observed. These deviations can be explained by the fact that in the bath a correlation hole appears for two atoms being in close proximity (not shown here for brevity, see also Ref. [134] and references therein). Notice also that the results referring to the ring geometry yield $\rho_{IB}^{(2)}(0,\pm L/2) > n_0/L$. This is a consequence of the particle conservation, occurring in order to accustom for the lower density in the vicinity of the impurity. In contrast, this behavior is absent in the thermodynamic limit, where $\rho_{IB}^{(2)}(0,|r| > \xi) \approx n_0/L$.

Figure 3d reveals that the inclusion of bath-bath correlations does not significantly affect the energy of the polaron $E_p = E(g_{BI}) - E(g_{BI} = 0)$. This leads to the conclusion that the GA provides an excellent prediction for the polaronic energy, in agreement with Ref. [55]. Of course, the presence of higher-order correlations within the MCTDHB approach results in a slight reduction of the polaronic energy as illustrated in the inset of Figure 3d. In contrast, the effect of the ring confinement provides a more important kinetic energy penalty[4], which can be identified by comparing the confined results to the thermodynamic limit case.

Regarding the effective mass, m^*, depicted in Figure 3e, also a remarkable agreement among both methods and system sizes is observed, see in particular the inset of Figure 3e. Indeed, the effective mass of the polaron is related to the local correlations of the dressing cloud in the vicinity of the impurity [38], where finite-size effects are insignificant, and are well described by the GA. The last quantity of interest for the Bose-polaron is its quasi-particle residue[5], $Z_p = \sqrt{|\langle \Psi_0|\Psi_p\rangle|^2}$, with $|\Psi_0\rangle$, $|\Psi_p\rangle$ being the non-interacting and the polaronic states respectively [80,82,83]. In Figure 3f it can be seen that the results including beyond two-body bath-impurity correlations differ significantly from the GA ones. This is because the residue, Z_p, is related with the many-body wavefunction overlap of the polaronic state to the non-interacting one, and therefore correlations of all orders significantly affect this quantity. In particular, it can be verified that, while finite-size corrections seem to not be significant in the case of the GA, the presence of higher-order correlations suppresses appreciably the polaronic residue. Importantly, despite the remarkable agreement on the level of two-body correlations the overlap between the MCTDHB and the GA wavefunction for the system confined in the ring ranges from 67 to 68%, see the inset of Figure 3f. This reduction of the many-body wavefunction overlap can be explained by the fact that MCT-DHB in contrast to the GA allows for the depletion of the bath wavefunction $\Psi_B(r_1,\ldots,r_{N_B})$ due to the presence of quantum fluctuations. Notice that any depleted many-body state, where even a single bath atom is in a state orthogonal to the BEC wavefunction, $\psi(r)$, has exactly zero overlap with the fully condensed many-body wavefunction described by the GA. Nevertheless, in this case, despite the zero overlap of these two many-body states, the corresponding low-order correlation functions would be almost identical for $N_B \gg 1$.

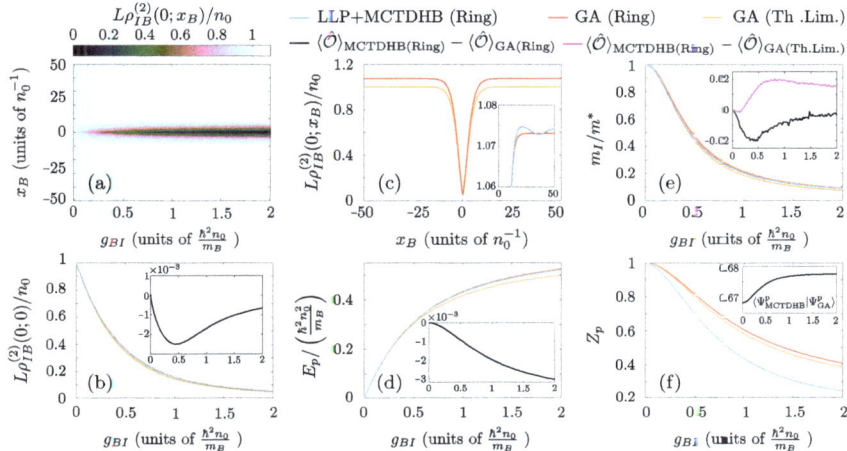

Figure 3. Comparison of the Bose polaron characteristics between the GA and the correlated MCTDHB framework. (**a**) Bath-impurity correlations, $\rho_{IB}^{(2)}(0;x_B)$, for varying interspecies interaction strength, g_{BI}, within MCTDHB. (**b**) Bath-impurity correlations at coincidence, $\rho_{IB}^{(2)}(0;0)$, for different g_{BI} and for all employed approaches (see legend). (**c**) Comparison of the correlation profile $\rho_{IB}^{(2)}(0;x_B)$ within the MCTDHB and the GA for $g_{BI} = 2\hbar^2 n_0/m_B$. The inset of (**c**) provides a magnification of $\rho_{IB}^{(2)}(0;x_B)$, showing the behavior of the system away from the impurity. Comparison of (**d**) the polaron energy, E_p, (**e**) the inverse effective mass, m_I/m^* and (**f**) the polaron residue among the different approaches and for varying g_{BI}. To elucidate the comparison between GA and MCTDHB, the insets of (**b**,**d**,**e**) provide the difference of the corresponding observables between the distinct approaches (see legend). The inset of (**f**) indicates the many-body overlap between the MCTDHB and the GA many-body states for varying g_{BI}. In all cases, $m_I = m_B$, $p_I = 0$ and $g_{BB} = 0.1\hbar^2 n_0/m_B$. The relevant ring confined setups are characterized by $N_B = 100$ and $L = 100n_0^{-1}$.

5. Dynamical Response of the System: The Temporal Orthogonality Catastrophe

Having identified the main properties of the equilibrium state of the Bose polaron in free 1D space now we proceed by considering its dynamical response. In particular, in the same manner as in Refs. [58,68,79,82,83,135], we examine the polaron generation after an abrupt quench of the interaction strength, g_{BI}, from $g_{BI} = 0$ to some final positive value $g_{BI}^f > 0$. Within the GA approximation, Equation (3), and for $g_{BI} = 0$ the lowest in energy wavefunction of the composite system with a given value of impurity momentum, p_I, reads

$$\Psi_0(x_I, x_1, \ldots, x_{N_B}; p_I) = L^{-\frac{N_B+1}{2}} \exp\left(-\frac{i}{\hbar} p_I x_I\right). \quad (18)$$

We are especially interested in observing the overlap of the time-evolved interacting state, $|\Psi(t)\rangle$ to the initial non-interacting one $|\Psi(0)\rangle = |\Psi_0\rangle$. As already discussed in Refs. [29,83,136] this observable can be directly probed in spectroscopic experiments and allows to address the polaronic properties. Another, important concept in homogeneous systems is the influence of the impurity momentum on the subsequent dynamics of the quenched, bath-impurity system, which we also consider below.

Regarding the numerical details of our simulations, we have considered $N_B = 1600$ particles, with $m_B = m_I$ confined in a ring with perimeter $L = 1600n_0^{-1}$. The increase of the ring perimeter is essential for approaching the thermodynamic limit and avoiding effects stemming from the imposed boundary conditions. In the following, we have exclusively employed the GA approach, since for such large particle numbers ensuring in general the convergence of fully correlated approaches is computationally beyond reach.

5.1. Dynamics of a Subsonic Impurity
5.1.1. Dynamics of Two-Body Correlations

Typical spatiotemporal evolution patterns of the two-body correlation function, $g_{IB}^{(2)}(0; x_B; t) = (L/n_0)\rho_{IB}^{(2)}(0; x_B; t)$, for an initial velocity of the impurity that does not exceed the speed of sound $c = \sqrt{g_{BB} n_0 / m_r} \approx 0.45 \hbar n_0 / m_B$, are presented in Figure 4a,b. The different panels correspond to varying initial impurity momenta, p_I, but in all cases the final interaction strength $g_{BI}^f = g_{BB} = 0.1 \hbar^2 n_0 / m_B$ is kept fixed.

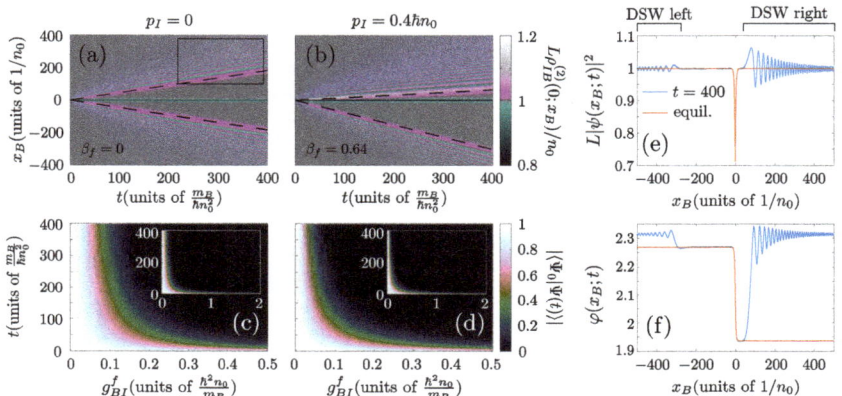

Figure 4. Quench dynamics of an impurity in a homogeneous Bose gas. (**a,b**) Spatiotemporal evolution of the two-body interspecies correlations, $\rho_{IB}^{(2)}(0; x_B)$, for different initial impurity momenta, p_I (see column labels). Here the postquench interaction is $g_{BI}^f = 0.1 \hbar^2 n_0 / m_B = g_{BB}$. The dashed lines indicate $x_B = (\pm 1 - \beta_f)ct$, with β_f the final velocity of the generated polaron provided as an inset label. (**c,d**) The time-dependent overlap, $|\langle \Psi_0 | \Psi(t) \rangle|$, of the post-quench many-body wavefunction, Equation (3), with the initial state, for varying g_{BI}. The insets of (**c,d**) provide the time-evolution of $|\langle \Psi_0 | \Psi(t) \rangle|$ within a more extensive g_{BI} range. (**e,f**) present the modulus and phase of the GA bath-wavefunction, $\psi(x_B; t)$ respectively for $g_{BI}^f = 0.1 \hbar^2 n_0 / m_B$, $p_I = 0.4 \hbar n_0$ and $t = 400 \frac{m_B}{\hbar n_0^2}$. For comparison (**e,f**) also provide the equilibrium profile of the polaron, Equation (7), with $\beta = \beta_f = 0.64$. In all cases the system is confined in a ring of $L = 1600 n_0^{-1}$ and contains $N_B = 1600$ while $m_I = m_B$.

In the case of a static impurity, $p_I = 0$, it can be seen that the quench leads to the emission of two $\rho_{IB}^{(2)}(0; x_B; t)$ disturbances for initial times ($t < 10$) that travel away from the impurity with a velocity proximal to the speed of sound, $\pm c$, see the dashed lines in Figure 4a. These disturbances subsequently break into structures, possessing an oscillatory two-body density pattern in space and being reminiscent of dispersive shock waves [91–94], see the box in Figure 4a and also Appendix B. In the vicinity of the impurity, $r = 0$, a depletion of bath atoms emerges similarly to the case of a static polaron analyzed previously, see Sections 3.2 and 4. For later times, $t \geq 300 \frac{m_B}{\hbar n_0^2}$, the two-body density $\rho_{BI}^{(2)}(0; x_B; t)$ in the spatial extent of the impurity $|x_B| < 30 n_0^{-1}$, matches very well to the expected profile for a static, $\beta = 0$, polaron whose form is given by Equation (7).

This behavior can be explained due to the instantaneous quench and the sharpness of the $\delta(r)$ interaction potential among the bath and the impurity. In particular, it is well documented in the BEC literature [137–139] that rapidly switching on the potential within the spatial extent of a BEC leads to the phenomenon of phase imprinting[6]. The resulting disturbance in the vicinity of the impurity subsequently propagates outwards leading to the excitation of the bosonic host and the formation of dispersive shock wave structures. These excitations carry away the additional energy due to the quench allowing for the polaron to be formed behind them. For more details on this mechanism see also Appendix B.

For increasing impurity momentum, $p_I = 0.4\hbar n_0 \approx m_I c$, we observe a qualitatively different system response, see Figure 4b. Here, the two-body density disturbance emitted "upstream" (i.e., towards the direction of motion of the impurity) recedes from the impurity at a much slower pace than the corresponding "downstream" disturbance while the former has a significantly larger amplitude than the latter. These observations are explained in terms of the drag experienced by the moving impurity. More specifically, it is known that if the velocity of a perturbing potential relative to a superfluid exceeds a certain critical value then the superfluidity of the environment is broken and the potential experiences a drag force. The latter is analyzed in Refs. [81,91,140] in the case that an external potential is dragged through a BEC. Note that this external potential possesses a well-defined instantaneous position, independently of the exerted drag force. However, the physical situation described here is slightly different because the impurity is a quantum particle that carries definite kinetic energy. Therefore, when a drag force emerges, it leads to the deceleration of the impurity up to the point that its velocity is so small that the drag force is nullified. Except for the reduction of the impurity velocity, the drag force leads to Cherenkov-like[7] radiation [141–143]. This leads to the amplification of the disturbances emitted "upstream" of the impurity and the emergence of an associated energy transfer process from the impurity to its bosonic environment.

The finite asymptotic velocity of the impurity is indicated in $\rho_{IB}^{(2)}(0; x_B; t)$ as a difference in the magnitude of the relative velocity of the emitted dispersive shock waves. Indeed, by assuming that the disturbances travel with a velocity $v_{DSW} \approx \pm c$ then in the impurity frame their velocities would be modified to $v_{DSW} - v_p = (\pm 1 - \beta_f)c$, where $\beta_f c$ is the velocity of the polaron. To estimate the final velocity of the polaron $\propto \beta_f$, we fit the density and phase profile of the GA wavefunction $\psi(|r| \leq 30 n_0^{-1}; t)$, after an evolution time of $t = 400 \frac{m_B}{\hbar n_0^2}$, to the corresponding analytic expression[8], Equation (7), for obtaining β_f and r_0. In Figure 4b, we demonstrate that the above approximations are in excellent agreement with the motion of the dispersive shock waves. Notice here, that the emitted structures realize a so-called "light" cone via which the correlations among the bath and the impurity are spread in the system after the quench [144,145]. In particular, by examining the modulus (Figure 4e) and phase (Figure 4f) of $\psi(r; t)$, we can verify that the corresponding profiles match the equilibrium polaron solution with $\beta = \beta_f$, Equation (7), in the spatial extent between the shock waves. Therefore, these excitations provide a means for transferring information regarding the generation of the Bose polaron throughout the BEC with a velocity equal to c, see also the dashed lines in Figure 4b.

5.1.2. Time-Dependent Overlap: Temporal Orthogonality Catastrophe

Having appreciated, the main features of the two-body correlation dynamics, we now analyze their imprint on the time-dependent overlap $|\langle \Psi_0 | \Psi(t) \rangle|$ for different g_{BI}^f. The quantity $|\langle \Psi_0 | \Psi(t) \rangle|$ is commonly referred to as the fidelity between the $|\Psi_0\rangle$ and $|\Psi(t)\rangle$ many-body states and it is related to the time-evolution of the quasi-particle residue, Z_p, of the polaron [82,83]. By inspecting the static polaron case, $p_I = 0$, presented in Figure 4c, we observe a very similar behavior as in the case of a parabolically trapped Bose-gas-impurity system examined in Ref. [83]. For interactions satisfying $g_{BI} < g_{BB} = 0.1\hbar^2 n_0 / m_B \ll 2\hbar c \approx 0.9\hbar^2 n_0/m_B$ the time-dependent overlap $|\langle \Psi_0 | \Psi(t) \rangle|$ possesses a value proximal to 1, indicating that the state of the impurity after the quench is almost equivalent to the non-interacting one (Equation (18)). Indeed, as it can be deduced from Figure 3d,f, in this regime the residue of the polaron is $Z_p \approx 1$ and also its energy is proximal to $E_p \approx g_{BI} n_0$. These imply that the quench does not result in a pronounced production of excitations such as the dispersive shock waves exhibited in Figure 4a, that would substantially affect $|\langle \Psi_0 | \Psi(t) \rangle|$

as we discuss below. For stronger interactions, $|\langle\Psi_0|\Psi(t)\rangle|$ changes drastically. Around $g_{BI} \approx g_{BB} = 0.1\hbar^2 n_0/m_B$, we find that $|\langle\Psi_0|\Psi(t)\rangle|$ is substantially depleted during the dynamics, reaching a finite value $|\langle\Psi_0|\Psi(t)\rangle| > 0$ for long times $t > 300\frac{m_B}{\hbar n_0^2}$, see Figure 4c. This behavior is inherently related to the emission of dispersive shock wave disturbances and the formation of the Bose polaron behind them as observed in Figure 4a.

To explain this behavior for intermediate interactions we have to examine the equilibrium properties of the Bose polaron and in particular its energy, Equation (12). As shown in Figure 1a, the non-linear correction terms in Equation (12) become important, leading to a sizable correction from the linear behavior observed for $g_{BI} < g_{BB}$. This leads to an energy surplus of the post-quench state, possessing $E = g_{BI}n_0$, when compared to the corresponding polaronic state that the system eventually relaxes too. Therefore, the emergence of dispersive shock waves can be explained as a mechanism that carries the excess energy away from the region of the impurity. The presence of these additional structures leads to the depletion of the time-dependent overlap $|\langle\Psi_0|\Psi(t)\rangle|$. A similar behaviour occurs also for stronger interactions, $g_{BI} > g_{BB} = 0.1\hbar^2 n_0/m_B$, where $|\langle\Psi_0|\Psi(t)\rangle|$ eventually saturates to zero. Because of this the final state of the system is almost orthogonal to the initial one, therefore leading to the phenomenon of the temporal orthogonality catastrophe [79,80,82,83].

Let us now comment on the influence of the initial impurity momentum on the time-dependent overlap $|\langle\Psi_0|\Psi(t)\rangle|$. Figure 4d, depicts $|\langle\Psi_0|\Psi(t)\rangle|$ for a finite momentum impurity $p_I = 0.4\hbar n_0$, where a similar response to the static case, Figure 4c, takes place. The most important difference is observed for $g_{BI} \approx g_{BB}$, where a larger suppression of $|\langle\Psi_0|\Psi(t)\rangle|$ occurs for $p_I = 0.4\hbar n_0$ than for $p_I = 0$. The discrepancy of the moving impurity case, when compared to the static one, can be explained in terms of the additional drag force that emerges in the former scenario. As already discussed above, the drag force leads to an impurity velocity smaller than the initial one since part of the initial momentum of the impurity is transferred to the "upstream" emitted dispersive shock wave excitation, see Figure 4b. This reduction of the impurity velocity during the dynamics leads to further suppression of $|\langle\Psi_0|\Psi(t)\rangle|$ than the one observed for $p_I = 0$, resulting in the appearance of the temporal orthogonality catastrophe phenomenon even in the case of $g_{BI} \approx g_{BB}$.

5.1.3. Drag Force and Momentum Transfer Mechanism

Let us now elaborate on the influence of the drag force in the time evolution of the polaronic state. As already mentioned for a moving polaron the drag force reduces the velocity of the impurity up to a value where the drag force is nullified. According to Refs. [81,146] the drag force can be approximated as

$$F_D = \int dr\, |\psi(r)|^2 \frac{dV_{BI}}{dr} = -g_{BI}\left.\frac{d|\psi(r)|^2}{dr}\right|_{r=0}, \quad (19)$$

where V_{BI} is the impurity potential perturbing the BEC, and it corresponds in our case to the bath-impurity interaction term, $V_{BI} = g_{BI}\delta(r)$. Equation (19) indicates that the drag force is proportional to the derivative of the density in the vicinity of the impurity standing as a material barrier. In the case of a polaron, Equation (7) reveals that $\frac{d|\psi(r)|^2}{dr} = 0$ for $r = 0$, and therefore the drag-force is zero. This implies that a trivial upper bound that the final velocity of the impurity should satisfy is $\beta_f < \beta_{\text{crit}}$, in order to allow for polaronic solutions. For impurities moving with subsonic velocities, we can get a better upper bound for the final velocity of the polaron by considering the available values of the p_I for the final equilibrium polaronic state. In the case that the polaronic state is created adiabatically, then the final state after the quench would possess a momentum p_I and the corresponding velocity $\beta_p(p_I)$, indicated in Figure 2a. However, since we are considering an interaction quench this scenario is not realized and instead we would have a final momentum for the polaron $p_I^f \leq p_I$ and a final velocity $\beta_f \leq \beta_p(p_I)$.

To justify the above let us clarify the role of the conserved quantity p_I in the dynamics. According to Equation (16), we have $p_I = \langle \Psi(t)|\hat{p}_I^{\text{lab}}|\Psi(t)\rangle + \langle \Psi(t)|\hat{p}_B|\Psi(t)\rangle$, and therefore only the sum of the impurity and bath momenta in the laboratory frame has to be conserved. Recall that, the state of the system for long times corresponds to a polaron and two dispersive shock wave excitations that are far away from one another so that they do not interact, see Figure 4b. Due to the exerted drag force on the impurity and the consequent induced Cherenkov radiation, the upstream shock wave carries a larger (in magnitude) momentum than the downstream one. Therefore, these two structures contribute a value $\Delta p > 0$ to the total momentum, equal to the corresponding difference of their momenta. This, in turn, implies that the momentum of the polaron for long times satisfies, $p_I^f = p_I - \Delta p < p_I$ and due to the increasing tendency of $\beta_p(p_I)$ with $p_I < m_I c$, see Figure 2(a$_2$), $\beta_f \leq \beta_p(p_I)$.

The above arguments can be directly verified by our numerical calculations, see Figure 5a, where we compare the velocity after the quench, β_f (obtained by the same procedure as in Figure 4a,b) to $\beta_p(p_I)$. This procedure yields that except for $g_{BI} \sim 0$, $\beta_f < \beta_p(p_I)$ holds independently of the value of p_I, demonstrating the diabatic character of the polaron formation after an interaction quench of g_{BI}. Additionally, the dynamics become more diabatic as the post-quench interaction strength is increased with the velocity of the polaron approaching a value of $\beta_f = 0$ for strong g_{BI}, independently of p_I. This more diabatic character of the dynamics with increasing g_{BI} can be understood by invoking Equation (19) implying that the amplitude of the drag force scales proportionally to the bath-impurity interaction strength. According to the above, and as Figure 5b testifies, the drag force is applied more abruptly to the impurity particle as g_{BI} increases, leading to a higher degree of excitation of the bath and hence larger momentum transfer, Δp_I. This momentum transfer can be directly probed in experiments by monitoring the momentum in the laboratory frame, $p_I^{\text{lab}}(t) = \langle \Psi(t)|\hat{p}_I^{\text{lab}}|\Psi(t)\rangle$. Figure 5c indicates the decreasing tendency of $p_I^{\text{lab}}(t)$ with time for all interaction strengths. Most importantly, even for small times $t < 50 \frac{m_B}{\hbar n_0^2}$ and $g_{BI} > g_{BB}$, $p_I^{\text{lab}}(t)$ becomes smaller than the corresponding equilibrium value for the polaron, see the corresponding lines in Figure 5b,c, demonstrating the existence of the momentum transfer mechanism.

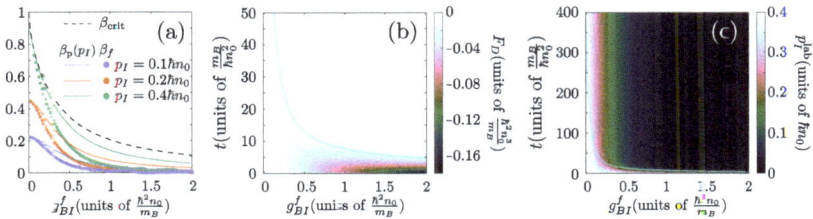

Figure 5. Characterization of the drag force exerted on the impurity by the Bose gas. (a) The critical, β_{crit} (dashed line) and equilibrium, $\beta_p(v_I)$ (solid lines) velocities of the Bose polaron with $g_{BI} = g_{BI}^f$, compared to the final velocity of the polaron formed after the quench, $\beta_f(p_I)$ (data points) for varying g_{BI}^f. The parameters of the system are as in Figure 4 and p_I is given in the legend. (b) Temporal evolution of the drag force exerted to an impurity, initially possessing $p_I = 0.4\hbar n_0$, for different values of the post-quench interspecies interaction strength, g_{BI}^f. (c) Time-evolution of the impurity momentum for $p_I = 0.4\hbar n_0$ and varying g_{BI}^f. The solid lines in (b,c) indicate the time that p_I^{lab} becomes equal to the corresponding value for the equilibrium polaron with $g_{BI} = g_B^f$.

5.2. Dynamics of a Supersonic Impurity

To conclude, we shall briefly comment on the case of a supersonically moving impurity. Figure 6 illustrates a characteristic example of the corresponding correlation dynamics, when $p_I = 1\hbar n_0$ and $g_{BI}^f = 0.07\hbar^2 n_0/m_B < g_{BB} = 0.1\hbar^2 n_0/m_B$. We observe that for small times $t < 100 \frac{m_B}{\hbar n_0^2}$ in addition to the emitted dispersive shock waves, also a density depletion takes place downstream of the impurity (see the boxed area in the inset of Figure 6a). As the impurity slows down due to the exerted drag force, the polaron starts to form at times $t \approx 100 - 200 \frac{m_B}{\hbar n_0^2}$. The depleted part of the density then collides at $t \approx 400 \frac{m_B}{\hbar n_0^2}$ (see the encircled region in the inset of Figure 6a) with the newly formed polaron lying at $x_B = 0$. Eventually the density depletion overtakes the polaron ending up in the upstream region, $x_B > 0$, for longer times, $t > 600 \frac{m_B}{\hbar n_0^2}$ (see Figure 6a). Similar to the subsonic cases the motion of the downstream shock wave (hardly visible in Figure 6a) and the large amplitude density excitation emanating in the upstream region are moving with a velocity equal to the speed of sound. Notice the agreement of the excitation trajectory with $x_{\text{DSW}} = (\pm 1 - \beta_f)ct + x_0$ for $t > 300 \frac{m_B}{\hbar n_0^2}$, here $\beta_f = 0.7464$ is the final velocity of the polaron found via fitting the polaron profile as discussed previously.

The origin of this additional excitation can be traced back to known properties for 1D BEC subjected to barrier dragging [73]. It is known that for barrier velocities exceeding a threshold $v_b > c$, stationary flow solutions (in the frame comoving with the barrier) exist, see the discussion in Ref. [93,146]. These solutions are characterized by a flat profile downstream of the barrier and a periodically modulating density in the upstream region. However, for such structures in contrast to the polaron corresponding to Equation (7), the drag force exerted to the barrier is finite. Consequently, since the impurity playing the role of the potential barrier possesses a finite momentum such flows cannot be stationary and have to decay when the velocity of the impurity becomes smaller than v_b. To substantiate the above claim, we solve the corresponding Gross-Pitaevskii equation in the frame of the potential barrier

$$i\hbar \frac{\partial}{\partial t}\psi(r) = \left[-\frac{\hbar^2}{2m_B} \frac{\partial^2}{\partial r^2} + i\hbar v_0 \frac{\partial}{\partial r} + g_{BI}\delta(r) + g_{BB}(N_B - 1)|\psi(r)|^2 \right]\psi(r), \quad (20)$$

where the constant velocity of the barrier, v_0, is set to the initial velocity of the impurity. In particular note that Equation (20) is a reduction of Equation (6) for $m_I \to \infty$ and $v_0 = p_I/m_I = $ constant. Therefore, it corresponds to the asymptotic polaron solution for an infinitely heavy impurity, $m_I \to \infty$. Figure 6b presents the spatiotemporal evolution of the BEC density after a quench from $g_{BI} = 0$ to $g_{BI}^f = 0.07\hbar^2 n_0/m_B$ and $v_0 = 1\hbar n_0/m_B$, $g_{BB} = 0.1\hbar^2 n_0/m_B$. At the initial stages of the dynamics, we observe the emission of the downstream dispersive shock wave (hardly visible in Figure 6b). However, the picture regarding the rest of the emerging structures is different than what was discussed for the $m_I = m_B$ polaron. In particular, we observe that upstream of the impurity a stationary oscillatory density pattern forms, reminiscent of the above mentioned solutions described in Refs. [93,146]. Notice also that downstream of the impurity another dispersive shock wave structure is emitted. The trajectories of the fronts of the two emitted shock waves indicate a relative velocity $v_{\text{DSW}} = (\pm c - v_0)$ with respect to the impurity. Therefore, these dispersive shock waves form a "light" cone, similar to what we have observed for subsonically moving polarons. However, since in this case $v_0 > c \approx 0.32\hbar n_0/m_B$, both shock waves lie in the downstream region of the barrier.

To relate the results of Equation (20) to the case of a polaron, we consider a massive impurity with $m_I = 10m_B$. The justification of this choice is that a massive impurity possesses larger inertia and therefore it is less susceptible to deceleration stemming from the drag force exerted by the BEC. This allows us to probe a possible intermediate-mass regime for the cases depicted in Figure 6a,b. Figure 6c shows the time evolution of $\rho_{IB}^{(2)}(0; x_B)$ for a quench with the same parameters as in Figure 6a,b. For initial times, $t < 200 \frac{m_B}{\hbar n_0^2}$, the two-body correlations exhibit the same structure as the one observed in the Gross-Pitaevskii case. In particular notice the emission of the two downstream dispersive shock waves forming a "light" cone ($v_{\text{DSW}} = (\pm c - p_I/m_I)$) and the quasi-stationary upstream oscillatory density pattern. Subsequently, due to the finite momentum of the impurity and the exerted drag force from the BEC, the impurity slows down. This can be verified by observing that for $t > 200 \frac{m_B}{\hbar n_0^2}$ the position of the fronts of the emitted shock waves does not follow $x_{\text{DSW}} = (\pm c - p_I/m_I)t$. Instead, they are shifted towards the impurity due to their reduced velocity. Turning to long times, $t > 600 \frac{m_B}{\hbar n_0^2}$, a sizable depletion of the BEC density in the vicinity of the impurity, $x_B = 0$ (see Figure 6c), appears indicating the formation of the polaron.

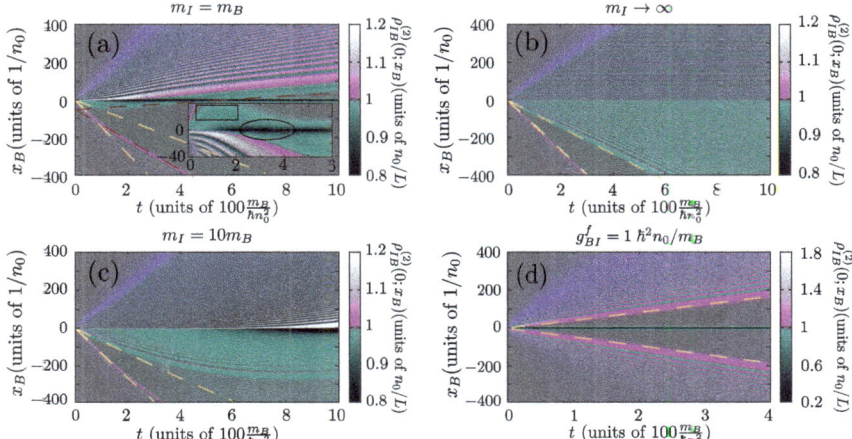

Figure 6. Dynamics of an initially supersonically moving impurity. (**a–c**) Spatiotemporal evolution of the bath-impurity correlation function $\rho_{IB}^{(2)}(0; x_B)$, for a quench to $g_{BI}^f = 0.07\hbar^2 n_0/m_3$ and $p_I = 1\hbar n_0$. The inset of (**a**) provides a magnification of the corresponding bath-impurity correlation function in the vicinity of the impurity. The mass of the impurity is provided in the corresponding labels, while $g_{BB} = 0.1\hbar^2 n_0/m_B$, $N_B = 3200$ and $L = 3200 n_0^{-1}$. The light dashed lines indicate $x_I = (\pm c - p_I/m_I)t$ and the dark dashed lines in (**a**) correspond to $x_I = (\pm 1 - \beta_f)ct + x_0$, with $\beta_f = 0.7464$ the final velocity of the polaron and $x_0 = 64 n_0^{-1}$ an offset selected for illustration purposes. (**d**) The time evolution of $\rho_{IB}^{(2)}(0; x_B)$, for the same parameters as in (**a**) except for $g_{BI}^f = 1\hbar^2 n_0/m_B$. The trajectories indicated by the dashed lines correspond to $x_I = (\pm 1 - \beta_f)ct$, with $\beta_f = 0.08$.

By invoking the results of Figure 6b,c, we can interpret the initial stages of the dynamics, $t < 100 \frac{m_B}{\hbar n_0^2}$, of Figure 6a (referring to $m_I = m_B$) as the formation of a quasi-stationary supersonic BEC flow pattern and its decay when the velocity of the impurity becomes lower than v_b. After a transient time $100 < t\frac{\hbar n_0^2}{m_B} < 400$ where the polaron forms and slows down due to the drag-force it experiences, an equilibrium polaron state is reached for $t > 400 \frac{m_B}{\hbar n_0^2}$ where the drag-force is nullified, similarly to the case of an initially subsonic impurity.

Finally, we comment that the dynamics of the system exhibit similar behavior as the one observed in Figure 6a, as long as, the interspecies interaction strength, g_{BI}, is sufficiently weak. Indeed, it is known [93,146] that for larger interspecies interactions (or equivalently the barrier heights) the velocity threshold for the formation of stationary supersonic flow, v_b, increases. In addition, the amplitude of the drag-force, Equation (19), is proportional to g_{BI}, yielding a rapid deceleration of the impurity for large interspecies interactions. Accordingly, for strong bath-impurity repulsions, no stationary supersonic flow can be approached during the dynamics, since both the threshold v_b increases and the deceleration of the impurity becomes more prominent. In this case, the dynamics of supersonically moving impurities is qualitatively similar to the regime $p_I \approx m_I c$, compare Figure 6d to Figure 4b.

6. Conclusions

We have examined the stationary and dynamical properties of the 1D Bose polaron in the absence of external confinement. It has been argued that, the stationary properties of the Bose polaron can be reliably evaluated within the GA approach for the case of a weakly interacting Bose gas [55–57,59]. Within this approximation, all non-trivial bath-bath correlations are neglected and the bath-impurity two-body correlations are variationally optimized. By comparing with the correlated MCTDHB approach, we verify that the GA adequately captures important properties of the polaron such as its energy, effective mass, and the bath-impurity two-body correlation profiles. However, it is found that the residue is overestimated within GA as it neglects the quantum depletion of the BEC background. Importantly, regarding a moving impurity, we have demonstrated that the character of the equilibrium many-body state crossovers from a polaronic quasi-particle to a collective excitation, having the form of a dark-bright soliton. Indeed, for small interactions and momenta, a polaron is generated and characterized by a localized depletion of the two-body bath-impurity correlation when the corresponding particles are in close proximity. In the opposite case of strong interactions or large momenta, the state of the mixture is similar to a stationary dark-bright soliton.

Regarding the dynamical response of the system we show that the phenomenon of the temporal orthogonality catastrophe which has been originally observed in confined polaron systems [79,80,82,83] generalizes to the homogeneous case (see also [58]). In all cases, the system approaches an equilibrium polaron state in the long-time dynamics accompanied by additional excitations induced by the quench. In particular, for a static impurity, the many-body wavefunction of the system becomes orthogonal to the corresponding non-interacting one for long timescales, despite the fact that the corresponding polaron state possesses a finite overlap to the non-interacting one [59]. For moving impurities the temporal orthogonality catastrophe is more pronounced since the drag force leads to the deceleration of the impurity. Dispersive shock wave structures play an important role in the quenched polaron dynamics as they provide the means to transfer the excess energy due to the quench away from the spatial extent of the impurity allowing for the eventual relaxation of the system to an equilibrium polaron configuration. Even in the case of a supersonically moving impurity, a final equilibrium polaron configuration is reached. However, the timescale needed for the slow-down of the impurity depends crucially on its mass. The emission of these non-linear structures in the time-evolution highlights the importance of non-linear and non-perturbative processes for understanding the dynamics of impurity systems. In addition to the above, the generality of the temporal orthogonality catastrophe mechanism for abrupt interaction quenches mandates a different experimental protocol relying on adiabatic transfer to the polaron configuration [80] for realizing strongly interacting Bose polaron states. Our results can be experimentally probed in setups employing one-dimensional gases with ring confinement [108,109] or embedded in a box potential [110–113], provided that the ring or box length is much larger than the healing length of the BEC. Note also, that the quench scheme analyzed here can be experimentally realized by employing a radiofrequency spectroscopy protocol in a similar manner to [29,79,82,83]. Here the impurity is transferred from a hyperfine state that is non-interacting to a state that is interacting with the medium by a strong $\pi/2$-pulse resonant with the corresponding transition.

There are several avenues for further research that can be pursued in future studies. In particular, all the results presented herein refer to the weak interaction regime of the Bose gas where its state can be well approximated as a BEC and its excitations treated within the Bogoliubov approximation. For stronger bath-bath interactions, where the elementary excitations of the Bose gas do not follow the Bogoliubov approximation [120], it is intriguing to examine the applicability of the GA approach and its limitations. In addition, in this interaction range particle-hole excitations, namely the type II excitations of the Lieb-Liniger model [119], become significant and it is therefore interesting to inspect whether they contribute to the modification of the polaronic quasiparticle or the emergence of a distinct type of excitations. Our findings indicating the importance of non-linear dynamics for characterizing the fate of the polaron might also be important for the case of higher dimensions, where recent studies indicate the possibility of the temporal orthogonality catastrophe

[60,51]. This is particularly important since phenomena related to pattern formation and the emergence of drag force are well known for two- and three-dimensional systems [121]. For instance, the creation and dynamics of structures such as oblique solitons and vortices [143] might be relevant for understanding the quench induced dynamics of the Bose polaron in two dimensions and the temporal orthogonality catastrophe in such systems.

Author Contributions: Conceptualization, methodology, investigation and formal analysis, G.M.K. and S.I.M.; writing—original draft preparation, G.M.K.; writing—review and editing, S.I.M. and P.S.; supervision, project administration, and funding acquisition, P.S. All authors have read and agreed to the published version of the manuscript.

Funding: This work is funded by the Cluster of Excellence 'Advanced Imaging of Matter' of the Deutsche Forschungsgemeinschaft (DFG)-EXC 2056-project ID 390715994.

Institutional Review Board Statement: Not applicable.

Informed Consent Statement: Not applicable.

Data Availability Statement: All data discussed in this study are available upon reasonable request.

Acknowledgments: S.I.M. acknowledges support from the NSF through a grant for ITAMP at Harvard University and is grateful to the Lenz-Ising Award of the University of Hamburg.

Conflicts of Interest: The authors declare no conflict of interest.

Appendix A. Bosonic Momentum Renormalization

To appreciate the physical context of the unconventional boundary conditions of Equation (7) we consider a system confined in a 1D ring of perimeter $L \gg \frac{\pi}{2}$. In this case the phase of $\psi_L(r)$ satisfies $\varphi_L(r) = \varphi_L(r+L)$ and therefore the solution of Equation (7) cannot be embedded in this finite system. However, the system for $|r| \lesssim \xi$, should behave in a similar manner to Equation (7), since the boundary conditions should not alter the behavior of the system at this spatial scale. In particular, the convergence of $\rho_{IB}^{(2)}(0;x_B)$ to the limit $L \to \infty$ is observed already for $L = 800 n_0^{-1}$, see Figure A1a. This implies that also in this setting a phase shift occurs. Indeed, such phase shifts in the vicinity of the impurity can be observed for $r \approx 0$ in the numerical solution of Equation (6) for a system confined in a ring of finite perimeter, see Figure A1b.

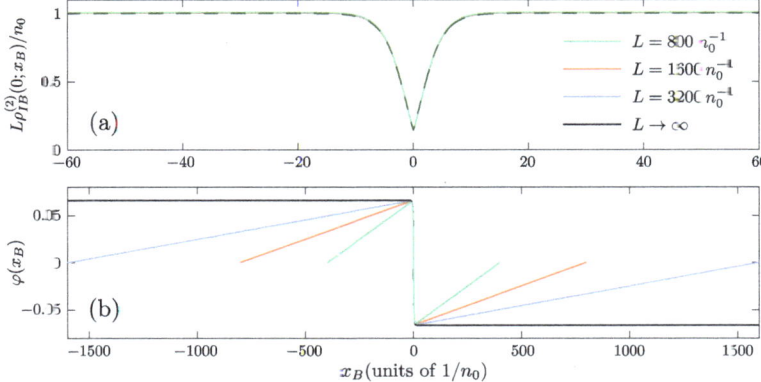

Figure A1. Convergence of the GA Bose polaron solution to the $N, L \to \infty$ limit. (a) Bath-impurity correlation function, $\rho_{IB}^{(2)}(0;x_B)$ for $g_{BI} = 1\hbar^2 n_0^{-1}/m_B$, $g_{BB} = 0.1\hbar^2 n_0/m_B$, $p_I = 0.1\hbar n_0$ and $m_I = m_B$ but different ring lengths L (see legend). In order to keep $n_0 = 1$ in our calculations, we demand $N_B = n_0 L$, while the spatial region $|x_B| > 60 n_0^{-1}$ is not depicted, since $\rho_{IB}^{(2)}(0;x_B) \approx \rho_{IB}^{(2)}(0;60 n_0^{-1})$. (b) The phase profile, $\phi(x_B) = \arg(\psi(x_E))$, of the solutions for the above mentioned parameters and for the same varying values of L.

To compensate for this phase shift a phase gradient appears in the ring solution at $r \gg \xi$ so that $\varphi_L(\pm L/2) = 0$. Notice that this phase gradient corresponds to a flow of the BEC counteracting the one stemming from the polaron and hence the former is referred to as the counterflow in the following. This effect is captured in Figure A1b by examining different values of L. In addition, it can be clearly seen that this gradient decreases for increasing L and therefore in the case that $L \to \infty$ the slope of this gradient is nullified. Importantly, this alteration of the phase profile in the case of finite systems, results in a contribution to the bath momentum since the latter is defined as

$$p_B = -i\hbar N_B \int dr\, \psi^*(r) \frac{d\psi(r)}{dr} \approx \hbar \int dr\, n(r) \frac{d\varphi(r)}{dr}, \tag{A1}$$

where we have employed that $\psi(r) = \sqrt{n(r)/N_B} e^{i\varphi(r)}$ and assumed that $\frac{dn(r)}{dr} = 0$ in the spatial extent where the counterflow occurs, $r \gg \xi$. Since the phase gradient occurs for large $r \gg \xi$, where $n(r) \to n_0$ and $\frac{d\varphi(r)}{dr} \approx$ constant, its momentum contribution is finite and characteristic of the phase difference created by the solution $\Delta\varphi = \varphi(r = L/2) - \varphi(r = -L/2)$. In particular, as evident in Figure A1b we can approximate $\frac{d\varphi(r)}{dr} = -\frac{\Delta\varphi}{L}$. The above imply that the momentum of the system in the thermodynamic limit $L \to \infty$ is shifted by a finite amount from the result obtained by integrating the wavefunction of Equation (7) such that

$$p_B = -i\hbar N_B \int_{-\infty}^{+\infty} dr\, \psi^*(r) \frac{d\psi(r)}{dr} \underbrace{-\hbar n_0 \Delta\varphi}_{\equiv p_{b.c.}}. \tag{A2}$$

The term $p_{b.c.} = -\hbar n_0 \Delta\varphi$ is a characteristic shift caused by the unconventional boundary conditions of the solution, Equation (7), and should always be added to the "bare" part stemming from the integration of the corresponding wavefunction. This "renormalization" of the bosonic momentum is well-known in the literature, for a more detailed discussion we refer the interested reader to Ref. [121].

Appendix B. The Impact of the Interspecies Interaction Potential

As discussed in the main text, dispersive shock wave excitations are emitted from the spatial regime of the impurity following an interspecies interaction quench. Here we will elaborate on the origin of such excitations by comparing the case of a zero-range δ-shaped interaction potential with finite width ones. The key to understand the emission of non-linear patterns at initial times is the concept of phase imprinting and the relation of the phase of the BEC with its flow. It is well known [43,80] that the typical time-scale for the formation of excitations in a BEC is of the order of $\xi/c \sim \hbar/\mu$, where ξ, c and μ are the healing length, speed of sound and chemical potential of the BEC respectively. Therefore, the bath atoms cannot react to any change of the system parameters occurring much faster than this time scale.

Similarly, to Ref. [80] this allows us, for $t \ll \hbar/\mu$, to neglect the effect of terms proportional to $\frac{\partial}{\partial r_k}$ appearing in the Hamiltonian $\hat{H}_{LLP}$, Equation (2). Within the GA the above imply that the equation of motion of Equation (6) reduces to

$$i\hbar \frac{\partial}{\partial t} \psi(r;t) = \left[V_{BI}(r) + \underbrace{g_{BB} |\psi(r;t)|^2}_{\approx \mu} - \mu \right] \psi(r;t), \tag{A3}$$

which can be solved yielding a time-evolution $\psi(r;t) = e^{-\frac{i}{\hbar} V_{BI}(r) t} \psi(r;0)$ for the variational single-particle wavefuction of the bath. In this solution, a spatially dependent shift of the BEC phase proportional to the local value of the interaction potential appears. The phase of the BEC wavefunction, and hence the above mentioned shift, is important because it dictates the local velocity of the BEC flow according to

$$v_{\text{superflow}}(r;t) \equiv \frac{\hbar}{m_B}\frac{\partial}{\partial r}\varphi(r;t) \stackrel{t \ll \hbar/\mu}{=} \frac{1}{m_r}\left(-\frac{\partial V_{BI}(r)}{\partial r}\right)t, \qquad (A4)$$

where $\varphi(r;t) = \arg(\psi(r;t))$. Equation (A4) indicates that steep interaction potentials, lead to large values for the flow velocity of the BEC and importantly also large gradients of the flow velocity. When this relative flow of the BEC becomes comparable to the speed of sound c then the superfluidity of the medium is broken and additional excitations emerge, according to the Landau criterion for superfluidity. This procedure for inducing non-linear excitations, commonly referred to as phase imprinting, has been widely employed experimentally for the creation of non-linear structures such as vortices and solitons [137–139]. Importantly for our discussion, the generation of dispersive shock waves by rapidly switching on a repulsive interaction potential has been demonstrated in Ref. [92] In that work, the steepness of the perturbing potential was controlled by keeping its width fixed and increasing its amplitude. Below we will take a complementary approach where the steepness is increased by keeping $g_{BI} = \int dr\, V_{BI}(r)$ fixed while reducing the overall width of the interspecies interaction potential. More specifically, we compare $V_{BI}(r) = g_{BI}\delta(r)$ with the Gaussian-shaped potential

$$V_{BI}(x) = \frac{g_{BI}}{\sqrt{2\pi}w}e^{-\frac{x^2}{2w^2}}, \qquad (A5)$$

where w parametrizes the finite width of the interaction. Note here that also Equation (A5) reduces to the δ-function limit for $w \to 0$. In this context our discussion below outlines the extrapolation of the concepts developed in [92] to the case of potentials with an infinitesimal range.

Figure A2 compares the polaron formation dynamics after a quench of the bath-impurity interaction strength to $g_{BI}^f = 0.1\hbar^2 n_0/m_B = g_{BB}$ for $N_B = 1600$ bath atoms in a ring with $L = 1600 n_0^{-1}$ for the different interaction potentials. Here, an initially static impurity, $p_I = 0$, is considered possessing $m_I = m_B$. Figure A2a presents the time-evolution of $\rho_{BI}^{(2)}(0;x_B)$ for a Gaussian interaction potential, Equation (A5), with width $w = 4n_0^{-1} \gtrsim \xi \approx 3.16 n_0^{-1}$. In particular, Figure A2a demonstrates the emission of dispersive shock waves, which are moving with velocity proximal to c (see the dashed lines in Figure A2a). The oscillatory density pattern associated with these structures can be clearly seen in Figure A2b for $t = 300\frac{m_B}{\hbar n_0^2}$ and $|x_B| > 100 n_0^{-1}$. It is associated with a corresponding oscillatory phase as demonstrated in Figure A2c. These results are in agreement with previous studies on dispersive shock wave patterns [91,94] The behavior of the system for short times, $t = 0.1\frac{m_B}{\hbar n_0^2} \ll \xi/c \approx 7.07\frac{m_B}{\hbar n_0^2}$ elucidates the mechanism for the generation of these structures, see the insets of Figure A2b,c. In particular, the expected profile

$$\varphi(x_B,t) = -\frac{t}{\hbar}V_{BI}(x) \qquad (A6)$$

describes well the phase of the system, see the inset of Figure A2c. Also as a consequence of Equation (A4), we can observe that even at such short times a small portion of the BEC atoms (notice the 10^{-6} scale in the inset of Figure A2b) have already moved away from the impurity following the gradient of the phase. The above outcomes are in line with the experiment of Ref. [92]. Indeed, due to the phase imprinting at initial times, the bath particles are forced to move away from the impurity building up the wavepackets seen at $x_B \approx 5n_0^{-1}$ in the inset of Figure A2b. Since the accumulated phase, Equation (A6), increases linearly with time the velocity of the flow-forming these wavepackets increases and can thus reach supersonic speeds, when compared to the stationary flow away from the impurity, leading to the formation of dispersive shock waves. As the steepness of the potential increases by reducing the value of w this phenomenon is amplified due to the faster increase of the superflow velocity in the spatial extent of the impurity. and therefore in the δ-potential limit it becomes maximal motivating the occurrence of dispersive shock wave structures, also in this case.

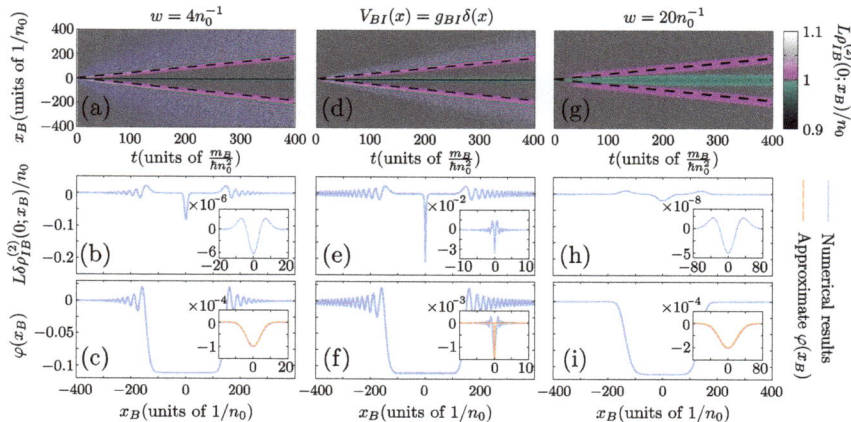

Figure A2. Emergence of dispersive shock waves for short-range interaction potentials. (**a**) Spatiotemporal evolution of $\rho_{IB}^{(2)}(0;x_B)$ for $g_{BI}^f = 0.1\hbar^2 n_0/m_B = g_{BB}$, $p_I = 0$, $L = 1600 n_0^{-1}$ and $N_B = 1600$ in the case that a Gaussian bath-impurity interaction potential with width $w = 4n_0^{-1}$ is employed. (**b**) Same as (**a**) but for the particular time instant $t = 300 m_B/(\hbar n_0^2)$. (**c**) the phase profile corresponding to (**b**). The insets of (**b**,**c**) correspond to $t = 0.1 m_B/(\hbar n_0^2)$. (**d**–**f**) correspond to the same quantities as in (**a**–**c**) respectively, calculated for the same set of parameters. However, here the bath-impurity potential corresponds to δ-function. (**g**–**i**) the same quantities as in (**a**–**c**) but for a wider Gaussian potential $w = 20n_0^{-1}$. The insets of (**c**,**f**,**i**) in addition to the GA numerical results also indicate the approximate profile expected from the phase imprinting of the impurity potential (see text).

To verify the above expectation we next focus on the case of the δ-potential. The phenomenology in that case is similar to the Gaussian-potential one (see Figure A2d), which is also supported by examining the density, Figure A2e, and phase, Figure A2f, profiles e.g., for $t = 300 \frac{m_B}{\hbar n_0^2}$. In the δ-potential case, we cannot, however, find evidence for the mechanism of phase imprinting since for $t = 0.1 \frac{m_B}{\hbar n_0^2} \ll \xi/c \approx 7.07 \frac{m_B}{\hbar n_0^2}$. Indeed, the density of the BEC in the vicinity of the impurity is significantly disturbed (see the inset of Figure A2e) while the corresponding phase does not match the expected profile of Equation (A6). To explain these apparent discrepancies one has to consider the δ-potential as the asymptotic limit of a progression of $V_{BI}(x)$ characterized by reducing width. Indeed, as the width of the potential, w, decreases, phase imprinting and the consequent generation of dispersive shock waves occur for smaller times. In the asymptotic case of a δ potential, these processes are exhibited within an extremely small timescale resulting in the signatures of the dispersive shock waves already appearing for $t = 0.1 \frac{m_B}{\hbar n_0^2}$, compare Figure A2e,f with their corresponding insets.

To make a more explicit connection to the experimental results of Ref. [92], let us briefly comment on the case of a potential with very large width, $w = 20 n_0^{-1} \gg \xi$. In this case, the behavior of the system is qualitatively different than for the previous cases, see Figure A2g, as no dispersive shock waves are produced. Indeed, the emitted excitations refer to density modulations of the BEC within a length scale much larger than ξ. Because of this and due to the linearity of the Bogoliubov dispersion relation for quasimomenta $k < 1/\xi$, we can conclude that such excitations are a superposition of sound waves, propagating away from the impurity with a group velocity given by the speed of sound [147,148]. The smoothness of the corresponding density profile can be verified by observing the density and the phase of the BEC at $t = 300 \frac{m_B}{\hbar n_0^2}$, see Figure A2h,i respectively. At first glance, the reason behind the generation of these excitations is not evident since for initial times the structures emerging in the density and phase of the BEC are qualitatively equivalent to the case of $w = 4 n_0^{-1}$, compare the insets of Figure A2b,c with Figure A2h,i respectively. Here the significant quantitative difference in the amplitude of these patterns is the cause for the qualitatively different long-time behavior that these two systems exhibit. In particular, for $w = 20n_0^{-1}$, the variation of the phase is much smoother and it increases much slower in time than in the case of $w = 4n_0^{-1}$. This allows the bath particles to travel away from the impurity at much smaller speeds than in the case of a narrower potential and therefore the velocity of the superflow can smoothly decay to zero as we get away from the impurity. Consequently, no non-linear excitations are produced since the Landau criterion is never violated and the only structure that gets emitted is a small density disturbance corresponding to the above-mentioned sound waves.

Appendix C. Details on the Computational Techniques

To examine the non-equilibrium dynamics of the system we numerically solve the GA equation of motion, Equation (6), for a finite number of particles so that $n_C = N_B/L = 1$. Recall that in this case the chemical potential, $\mu(t)$, corresponds to a Lagrange multiplier, which has to be evaluated by demanding that the particle number is conserved. The process outlined above, allows us to cast the equation-of-motion in the single-particle Schrödinger type equation

$$i\hbar \frac{\partial}{\partial t}|\psi(t)\rangle = \left(\hat{\mathcal{H}}[\psi(r;t)] - \langle\psi(t)|\hat{\mathcal{H}}[\psi(r;t)]|\psi(t)\rangle\right)|\psi(r;t)\rangle, \tag{A7}$$

with $\hat{\mathcal{H}}[\psi(r;t)] = -\frac{\hbar^2}{2m_B}\frac{\partial^2}{\partial r^2} + \frac{i\hbar^2 k_0(t)}{m_I}\frac{\partial}{\partial r} + g_{BI}\delta(r) + g_{BB}(N_B-1)|\psi(r;t)|^2$, denoting the effective single-particle Hamiltonian and $\psi(r) \equiv \langle r|\psi(t)\rangle$. Then the effective Schrödinger equation of Equation (A7) is discretized by employing an exponential discrete variable representation [149]. For the corresponding time-evolution, we use the standard fourth-order Runge-Kutta integrator. Notice here, that the employed basis set intrinsically introduces periodic boundaries at both ends of the potential. An advantage of the exponential discrete variable representation is that the first and second derivative matrices of the corresponding basis refer to the Fourier ones, allowing us to employ the Fast-Fourier-Transform algorithm for numerical efficiency. In place of the δ-potential an approximation of it is employed, namely

$$[V_{BI}]_j = \frac{g_{BI}}{\Delta x}\delta_{j,\frac{n}{2}}, \tag{A8}$$

where δ_{jk} is the Kronecker delta, $j = 0, 2, ..., n-1$ represents the index of each of the n grid points located at $x_j = -\frac{L}{2} + \frac{jL}{n}$, and $\Delta x = L/n$ is the grid spacing. Within the discrete variable representation framework, it can be shown that the approximation for the δ-potential of Equation (A8) is variationally optimal. To estimate the validity of our numerical results, we repeat the calculations for different spatial, Δx, and temporal, Δt, discretizations. We have verified that $\psi(r;t)$ for time-intervals $t < 400$ becomes independent of the discretization for $\Delta t = 0.0005$ and $\Delta x = 25/256$, where dimensionless units $\hbar = m_B = n_0 = 1$ are employed.

To estimate the impact of correlations in the ground state properties of the Bose polaron we utilize the Multi-Layer Multi-Configuration Time-Dependent Hartree method for atomic mixtures (ML-MCTDHX) [106]. The key idea of ML-MCTDHX lies in the usage of a time-dependent and variationally optimized many-body basis set, which allows for the optimal truncation of the total Hilbert space. Since here we simulate only the Bose gas part of the many-body wavefunction the ML-MCTDHX method, reduces to the simpler Multi-Configuration Time-Dependent Hartree method for bosons (MCTDHB) approach [125,126]. Within the latter the ansatz for the bath many-body wavefunction, $|\Psi_B(t)\rangle$, is taken as a linear combination of time-dependent permanents $|n_1, n_2, \ldots, n_M(t)\rangle$,

$$|\Psi_B(t)\rangle = \sum_{n_1, n_2, \ldots, n_M | \sum_{k=1}^{M} n_k = N_B} A_{\vec{n}}(t)|n_1, n_2, \ldots, n_M(t)\rangle, \tag{A9}$$

with time-dependent weights $A_{\vec{n}}(t)$. In turn, each time-dependent permanent is expanded in terms of M time-dependent variationally optimized single-particle functions $\phi_k(r;t)$, with $k = 1, \ldots, M$, as follows

$$\langle r_1, \ldots, r_{N_B} | n_1, n_2, \ldots, n_M(t) \rangle = \left(\prod_{k=1}^{M} n_k! \right)^{-\frac{1}{2}} \sum_{i=1}^{N_B!} \prod_{j=1}^{n_1} \phi_1(r_{\mathcal{P}_i(j)};t) \prod_{j=n_1+1}^{n_1+n_2} \phi_2(r_{\mathcal{P}_i(j)};t) \cdots \prod_{j=1+\sum_{k=1}^{M-1} n_k}^{N_B} \phi_M(r_{\mathcal{P}_i(j)};t), \quad \text{(A10)}$$

where $\mathcal{P}_i$ is the operator performing the ith permutation of $\{1, 2, \ldots, N_B\}$. For our numerical implementation the single-particle functions are expanded within a primitive basis corresponding to the exponential discrete variable representation that we also use in the GA case. The time-evolution of the N_B-body wavefunction under the effect of the Hamiltonian $\hat{H}_{\text{LLP}}$ reduces to the determination of the A-vector coefficients and the single-particle functions, which follow the variationally obtained equations of motion [125,126]. Let us note here that in the limiting case of $M = 1$, the method reduces to Equation (A7), while for the case of $M = M_p$, this method is equivalent to a full configuration interaction approach.

To obtain the ground state within MCTHDB we rely on the so-called improved relaxation scheme. This scheme can be summarized as follows:

1. initialize the system with an ansatz set of single-particle functions $\phi_k^{(0)}(r)$, where $k = 1, \ldots, M$,
2. diagonalize the Hamiltonian within a basis spanned by the single-particle functions,
3. set the eigenvector with the lowest energy as the $A^{(0)}$-vector,
4. propagate the single-particle functions in imaginary time within a finite time interval $d\tau$,
5. update the single-particle functions to $\phi_k^{(1)}(r)$ and
6. repeat steps 2–5 until the state coefficients converge within the prescribed accuracy.

For the diagonalization at step 2, the Lanczos approach is employed and for the propagation of $\phi_k(r; \tau)$ at step 4, we employ the Dormand-Prince integrator. For ensuring the consistency of the truncation with respect to M, we have compared our $M = 3$ and $M = 4$ calculations verifying that the results presented in Figure 3 differ at most by 0.1%. Our results shown in the main text correspond to $M = 4$.

Notes

1. To avoid confusion, since within the common Gross-Pitaevskii equation for an ideal BEC all correlations are neglected, here we will instead adopt the term GA [3] when referring to the technique employed in Refs. [55–65].
2. The lower bound corresponds to a ^{6}Li impurity immersed in a ^{176}Yb bath and the upper bound to a ^{176}Yb impurity immersed in a Bose medium of ^{7}Li.
3. Importantly, by explicitly evaluating the Hessian matrix for the numerical solutions presented in Figure 2 we can prove that $\left(H_{E_P} \right)_{ij} = \frac{\partial^2 E_P}{\partial a_i \partial a_j}$ is positive definite, where $i, j = 1, 2$, with $a_1 = \beta$, $a_2 = r_0$. This supports the stability of the solution within the subspace spanned by Equation (7).
4. The bath density is expelled from the vicinity of the impurity and accumulates in the spatial region away from it $x_B > 10 n_0^{-1}$, see also Figure 3c. This density increase leads to greater kinetic energy scaling quadratically with the bath density. However, since the number of expelled atoms is roughly constant as the perimeter of the ring L increases this correction becomes negligible for $L \to \infty$.
5. Note that the residue of polaronic quasiparticles can be monitored experimentally via radiofrequency spectroscopy [27,80].
6. This means that due to the presence of the potential, the phase of the BEC shifts, leading to a flow of the bosonic density away from the repulsive potential. Note here that the amplitude of this phase disturbance increases with the decrease of the width of the perturbing potential. This effect is maximized for a δ-shape as the one corresponding to the bath-impurity interactions.
7. This term denotes the excitation of the BEC due to the locally supersonic motion of the impurity. This effect is analogous to the emission of electromagnetic radiation when electrons move through a dielectric medium with a velocity greater than the phase velocity of light.

Note here that the phase of $\psi(r;t)$ is shifted so that $\arg[\psi(r=0;t)]=0$ and the rest of the parameters in Equation (7) are fixed to their corresponding values in the thermodynamic limit, namely $\xi = (0.1)^{-1/2} n_0^{-1}$.

References

1. Alexandrov, A.S.; Devreese, J.T. *Advances in Polaron Physics*; Springer: Berlin/Heidelberg, Germany, 2010. [CrossRef]
2. Padmore, T.C.; Fetter, A.L. Impurities in an Imperfect Bose Gas. I. the Condensate. *Ann. Phys.* **1971**, *62*, 293–319. [CrossRef]
3. Gross, E. Motion of Foreign Bodies in Boson Systems. *Ann. Phys.* **1962**, *19*, 234–253. [CrossRef]
4. Landau, L.D.; Pekar, S.I. Effective mass of a polaron. *Zh. Eksp. Tecr. Fiz.* **1948**, *18*, 419–423.
5. Pekar, S.I. Theory of Colored Crystals. *Zh. Eksp. Teor. Fiz.* **1947**, *17*, 868–882.
6. Pekar, S.I. Autolocalization of the electron in an inertially polarizable dielectric medium. *Zh. Eksp. Teor. Fiz.* **1946**, *16*, 335–340.
7. Feynman, R.P. Slow Electrons in a Polar Crystal. *Phys. Rev.* **1955**, *97*, 660–665. [CrossRef]
8. Fröhlich, H. Electrons in Lattice Fields. *Adv. Phys.* **1954**, *3*, 325–361. [CrossRef]
9. Fetherolf, J.H.; Golež, D.; Berkelbach, T.C. A Unification of the Holstein Polaron and Dynamic Disorder Pictures of Charge Transport in Organic Crystals. *Phys. Rev. X* **2020**, *10*, 021062. [CrossRef]
10. Fratini, S.; Ciuchi, S. Bandlike Motion and Mobility Saturation in Organic Molecular Semiconductors. *Phys. Rev. Lett.* **2009**, *103*, 266601. [CrossRef]
11. Kenkre, V. Finite-Bandwidth Calculations for Charge Carrier Mobility in Organic Crystals. *Phys. Lett. A* **2002**, *305*, 443–447. [CrossRef]
12. Verdi, C.; Caruso, F.; Giustino, F. Origin of the Crossover From Polarons To Fermi Liquids in Transition Metal Oxides. *Nat. Commun.* **2017**, *8*, 15769. [CrossRef]
13. Moser, S.; Moreschini, L.; Jaćimović, J.; Barišić, O.S.; Berger, H.; Magrez, A.; Chang, Y.J.; Kim, K.S.; Bostwick, A.; Rotenberg, E.; et al. Tunable Polaronic Conduction in Anatase TiO_2. *Phys. Rev. Lett.* **2013**, *110*, 196403. [CrossRef] [PubMed]
14. Davydov, A. The Theory of Contraction of Proteins Under Their Excitation. *J. Theor. Biol.* **1973**, *38*, 559–569. [CrossRef]
15. Mahani, M.R.; Mirsakiyeva, A.; Delin, A. Breakdown of Polarons in Conducting Polymers At Device Field Strengths. *J. Phys. Chem. C* **2017**, *121*, 10317–10324. [CrossRef]
16. Bredas, J.L.; Street, G.B. Polarons, Bipolarons, and Solitons in Conducting Polymers. *Acc. Chem. Res.* **1985**, *18*, 309–315. [CrossRef]
17. Bobbert, P.A.; Nguyen, T.D.; van Oost, F.W.A.; Koopmans, B.; Wohlgenannt, M. Bipolaron Mechanism for Organic Magnetoresistance. *Phys. Rev. Lett.* **2007**, *99*, 216801. [CrossRef] [PubMed]
18. Hewson, A.C. *The Kondo Problem to Heavy Fermions*; Cambridge Studies in Magnetism; Cambridge University Press: Cambridge, UK, 1993. [CrossRef]
19. Sous, J.; Chakraborty, M.; Krems, R.V.; Berciu, M. Light Bipolarons Stabilized by Peierls Electron-Phonon Coupling. *Phys. Rev. Lett.* **2018**, *121*, 247001. [CrossRef]
20. Chakraverty, B.K.; Ranninger, J.; Feinberg, D. Experimental and Theoretical Constraints of Bipolaronic Superconductivity in High T_c Materials: An Impossibility. *Phys. Rev. Lett.* **1998**, *81*, 433–436. [CrossRef]
21. Lakhno, V. Superconducting properties of a nonideal bipolaron gas. *Physics C* **2019**, *561*, 1–8. [CrossRef]
22. Alexandrov, A.S.; Kabanov, V.V.; Mott, N.F. Coherent *ab* and *c* Transport Theory of High-T_c Cuprates. *Phys. Rev. Lett.* **1996**, *77*, 4796–4799. [CrossRef] [PubMed]
23. Mott, N. Polaron models of high-temperature superconductivity. *Physics C* **1993**, *205*, 191–205. [CrossRef]
24. Lee, P.A.; Nagaosa, N.; Wen, X.G. Doping a Mott Insulator: Physics of High-Temperature Superconductivity. *Rev. Mod. Phys.* **2006**, *78*, 17–85. [CrossRef]
25. Gross, C.; Bloch, I. Quantum Simulations With Ultracold Atoms in Optical Lattices. *Science* **2017**, *357*, 995–1001. [CrossRef]
26. Schirotzek, A.; Wu, C.H.; Sommer, A.; Zwierlein, M.W. Observation of Fermi Polarons in a Tunable Fermi Liquid of Ultracold Atoms. *Phys. Rev. Lett.* **2009**, *102*, 230402. [CrossRef] [PubMed]
27. Kohstall, C.; Zaccanti, M.; Jag, M.; Trenkwalder, A.; Massignan, P.; Bruun, G.M.; Schreck, F.; Grimm, R. Metastability and Coherence of Repulsive Polarons in a Strongly Interacting Fermi Mixture. *Nature* **2012**, *485*, 615–618. [CrossRef]
28. Scazza, F.; Valtolina, G.; Massignan, P.; Recati, A.; Amico, A.; Burchianti, A.; Fort, C.; Inguscio, M.; Zaccanti, M.; Roati, G. Repulsive Fermi Polarons in a Resonant Mixture of Ultracold Li6 Atoms. *Phys. Rev. Lett.* **2017**, *118*, 083602. [CrossRef]
29. Cetina, M.; Jag, M.; Lous, R.S.; Fritsche, I.; Walraven, J.T.M.; Grimm, R.; Levinsen, J.; Parish, M.M.; Schmidt, R.; Knap, M.; et al. Ultrafast Many-Body Interferometry of Impurities Coupled To a Fermi Sea. *Science* **2016**, *354*, 96–99. [CrossRef] [PubMed]
30. Wenz, A.N.; Zurn, G.; Murmann, S.; Brouzos, I.; Lompe, T.; Jochim, S. From Few To Many: Observing the Formation of a Fermi Sea One Atom At a Time. *Science* **2013**, *342*, 457–460. [CrossRef]
31. Koschorreck, M.; Pertot, D.; Vogt, E.; Fröhlich, B.; Feld, M.; Köhl, M. Attractive and Repulsive Fermi Polarons in Two Dimensions. *Nature* **2012**, *485*, 619–622. [CrossRef]
32. Catani, J.; Lamporesi, G.; Naik, D.; Gring, M.; Inguscio, M.; Minardi, F.; Kantian, A.; Giamarchi, T. Quantum Dynamics of Impurities in a One-Dimensional Bose Gas. *Phys. Rev. A* **2012**, *85*, 023623. [CrossRef]
33. Spethmann, N.; Kindermann, F.; John, S.; Weber, C.; Meschede, D.; Widera, A. Dynamics of Single Neutral Impurity Atoms Immersed in an Ultracold Gas. *Phys. Rev. Lett.* **2012**, *109*, 235301. [CrossRef]
34. Skou, M.G.; Skov, T.G.; Jørgensen, N.B.; Nielsen, K.K.; Camacho-Guardian, A.; Pohl, T.; Bruun, G.M.; Arlt, J.J. Non-Equilibrium Quantum Dynamics and Formation of the Bose Polaron. *Nat. Phys.* **2021**, *17*, 731–735. [CrossRef]

35. Yan, Z.Z.; Ni, Y.; Robens, C.; Zwierlein, M.W. Bose Polarons Near Quantum Criticality. *Science* **2020**, *368*, 190–194. [CrossRef]
36. Hu, M.G.; de Graaff, M.J.V.; Kedar, D.; Corson, J.P.; Cornell, E.A.; Jin, D.S. Bose Polarons in the Strongly Interacting Regime. *Phys. Rev. Lett.* **2016**, *117*, 055301. [CrossRef] [PubMed]
37. Jørgensen, N.B.; Wacker, L.; Skalmstang, K.T.; Parish, M.M.; Levinsen, J.; Christensen, R.S.; Bruun, G.M.; Arlt, J.J. Observation of Attractive and Repulsive Polarons in a Bose-Einstein Condensate. *Phys. Rev. Lett.* **2016**, *117*, 055302. [CrossRef]
38. Massignan, P.; Zaccanti, M.; Bruun, G.M. Polarons, Dressed Molecules and Itinerant Ferromagnetism in Ultracold Fermi Gases. *Rep. Prog. Phys.* **2014**, *77*, 034401. [CrossRef] [PubMed]
39. Schmidt, R.; Knap, M.; Ivanov, D.A.; You, J.S.; Cetina, M.; Demler, E. Universal Many-Body Response of Heavy Impurities Coupled To a Fermi Sea: A Review of Recent Progress. *Rep. Prog. Phys.* **2018**, *81*, 024401. [CrossRef] [PubMed]
40. Kalas, R.M.; Blume, D. Interaction-Induced Localization of an Impurity in a Trapped Bose-Einstein Condensate. *Phys. Rev. A* **2006**, *73*, 043608. [CrossRef]
41. Cucchietti, F.M.; Timmermans, E. Strong-Coupling Polarons in Dilute Gas Bose-Einstein Condensates. *Phys. Rev. Lett.* **2006**, *96*, 210401. [CrossRef]
42. Astrakharchik, G.E.; Pitaevskii, L.P. Motion of a Heavy Impurity Through a Bose-Einstein Condensate. *Phys. Rev. A* **2004**, *70*, 013608. [CrossRef]
43. Grusdt, F.; Demler, E. New theoretical approaches to Bose polarons. In *Quantum Matter at Ultralow Temperatures*; Inguscio, M., Ketterle, W., Stringari, S., Roati, G., Eds.; IOS Press Amsterdam: Amsterdam, The Netherlands, 2015; Volume 191, pp. 325–411.
44. Sun, M.; Zhai, H.; Cui, X. Visualizing the Efimov Correlation in Bose Polarons. *Phys. Rev. Lett.* **2017**, *119*, 013401. [CrossRef] [PubMed]
45. Christensen, R.S.; Levinsen, J.; Bruun, G.M. Quasiparticle Properties of a Mobile Impurity in a Bose-Einstein Condensate. *Phys. Rev. Lett.* **2015**, *115*, 160401. [CrossRef]
46. Shi, Z.Y.; Yoshida, S.M.; Parish, M.M.; Levinsen, J. Impurity-Induced Multibody Resonances in a Bose Gas. *Phys. Rev. Lett.* **2018**, *121*, 243401. [CrossRef] [PubMed]
47. Levinsen, J.; Parish, M.M.; Bruun, G.M. Impurity in a Bose-Einstein Condensate and the Efimov Effect. *Phys. Rev. Lett.* **2015**, *115*, 125302. [CrossRef] [PubMed]
48. Yoshida, S.M.; Endo, S.; Levinsen, J.; Parish, M.M. Universality of an Impurity in a Bose-Einstein Condensate. *Phys. Rev. X* **2018**, *8*, 011024. [CrossRef]
49. Casteels, W.; Van Cauteren, T.; Tempere, J.; Devreese, J.T. Strong coupling treatment of the polaronic system consisting of an impurity in a condensate. *Laser Phys.* **2011**, *21*, 1480. [CrossRef]
50. Tempere, J.; Casteels, W.; Oberthaler, M.K.; Knoop, S.; Timmermans, E.; Devreese, J.T. Feynman path-integral treatment of the BEC-impurity polaron. *Phys. Rev. B* **2009**, *80*, 184504. [CrossRef]
51. Ardila, L.A.P.; Jørgensen, N.B.; Pohl, T.; Giorgini, S.; Bruun, G.M.; Arlt, J.J. Analyzing a Bose Polaron Across Resonant Interactions. *Phys. Rev. A* **2019**, *99*, 063607. [CrossRef]
52. Ardila, L.A.P.; Giorgini, S. Bose Polaron Problem: Effect of Mass Imbalance on Binding Energy. *Phys. Rev. A* **2016**, *94*, 063640. [CrossRef]
53. Ardila, L.A.P.; Giorgini, S. Impurity in a Bose-Einstein Condensate: Study of the Attractive and Repulsive Branch Using Quantum Monte Carlo Methods. *Phys. Rev. A* **2015**, *92*, 033612. [CrossRef]
54. Grusdt, F.; Astrakharchik, G.E.; Demler, E. Bose Polarons in Ultracold Atoms in One Dimension: Beyond the Fröhlich Paradigm. *New J. Phys.* **2017**, *19*, 103035. [CrossRef]
55. Jager, J.; Barnett, R.; Will, M.; Fleischhauer, M. Strong-Coupling Bose Polarons in One Dimension: Condensate Deformation and Modified Bogoliubov Phonons. *Phys. Rev. Res.* **2020**, *2*, 033142. [CrossRef]
56. Will, M.; Astrakharchik, G.E.; Fleischhauer, M. Polaron Interactions and Bipolarons in One-Dimensional Bose Gases in the Strong Coupling Regime. *Phys. Rev. Lett.* **2021**, *127*, 103401. [CrossRef] [PubMed]
57. Panochko, G.; Pastukhov, V. Mean-Field Construction for Spectrum of One-Dimensional Bose Polaron. *Ann. Phys.* **2019**, *409*, 167933. [CrossRef]
58. Jager, J.; Barnett, R. A Stochastic Fields Approach to the Quench Dynamics of a One Dimensional Bose Polaron. *Phys. Rev. Research* **2021**, *3*, 033212. [CrossRef]
59. Volosniev, A.G.; Hammer, H.W. Analytical Approach to the Bose-Polaron Problem in One Dimension. *Phys. Rev. A* **2017**, *96*, 031601. [CrossRef]
60. Guenther, N.E.; Schmidt, R.; Bruun, G.M.; Gurarie, V.; Massignan, P. Mobile Impurity in a Bose-Einstein Condensate and the Orthogonality Catastrophe. *Phys. Rev. A* **2021**, *103*, 013317. [CrossRef]
61. Drescher, M.; Salmhofer, M.; Enss, T. Theory of a Resonantly Interacting Impurity in a Bose-Einstein Condensate. *Phys. Rev. Res.* **2020**, *2*, 032011. [CrossRef]
62. Takahashi, J.; Imai, R.; Nakano, E.; Iida, K. Bose Polaron in Spherical Trap Potentials: Spatial Structure and Quantum Depletion. *Phys. Rev. A* **2019**, *100*, 023624. [CrossRef]
63. Schmidt, R.; Enss, T. Self-Stabilized Bose Polarons. *arXiv* **2021**, arXiv:2102.13616.
64. Hryhorchak, O.; Panochko, G.; Pastukhov, V. Impurity in a Three-Dimensional Unitary Bose Gas. *Phys. Lett. A* **2020**, *384*, 126934. [CrossRef]

65. Hryhorchak, O.; Panochko, G.; Pastukhov, V. Mean-Field Study of Repulsive 2d and 3d Bose Polarons. *J. Phys. B At. Mol. Opt. Phys.* **2020**, *53*, 205302. [CrossRef]
66. Mistakidis, S.I.; Volosniev, A.G. Schmelcher, P. Induced Correlations Between Impurities in a One-Dimensional Quenched Bose Gas. *Phys. Rev. Res.* **2020**, *2*, 023154. [CrossRef]
67. Mistakidis, S.I.; Volosniev, A.G.; Zinner, N.T.; Schmelcher, P. Effective Approach To Impurity Dynamics in One-Dimensional Trapped Bose Gases. *Phys. Rev. A* **2019**, *100*, 013619. [CrossRef]
68. Mistakidis, S.I.; Hilbig, L.; Schmelcher, P. Correlated Quantum Dynamics of Two Quenched Fermionic Impurities Immersed in a Bose-Einstein Condensate. *Phys. Rev. A* **2019**, *100*, 023620. [CrossRef]
69. Schecter, M.; Gangardt, D.M.; Kamenev, A. Quantum Impurities: From Mobile Josephson Junctions To Depletons. *New J. Phys.* **2016**, *18*, 065002. [CrossRef]
70. Johnson, T.H.; Clark, S.R.; Bruderer, M.; Jaksch, D. Impurity Transport Through a Strongly Interacting Bosonic Quantum Gas. *Phys. Rev. A* **2011**, *84*, 023617. [CrossRef]
71. Cai, Z.; Wang, L.; Xie, X.C.; Wang, Y. Interaction-Induced Anomalous Transport Behavior in One-Dimensional Optical Lattices. *Phys. Rev. A* **2010**, *81*, 043602. [CrossRef]
72. Theel, F.; Keiler, K.; Mistakidis, S.I.; Schmelcher, P. Entanglement-Assisted Tunneling Dynamics of Impurities in a Double Well Immersed in a Bath of Lattice Trapped Bosons. *New J. Phys.* **2020**, *22*, 023027. [CrossRef]
73. Mistakidis, S.I.; Grusdt, F.; Koutentakis, G.M.; Schmelcher, P. Dissipative Correlated Dynamics of a Moving Impurity Immersed in a Bose-Einstein Condensate. *New J. Phys.* **2019**, *21*, 103026. [CrossRef]
74. Lausch, T.; Widera, A.; Fleischhauer, M. Prethermalization in the Cooling Dynamics of an Impurity in a Bose-Einstein Condensate. *Phys. Rev. A* **2018**, *97*, 023621. [CrossRef]
75. Krönke, S.; Knörzer, J.; Schmelcher, P. Correlated Quantum Dynamics of a Single Atom Collisionally Coupled To an Ultracold Finite Bosonic Ensemble. *New J. Phys.* **2015**, *17*, 053001. [CrossRef]
76. Theel, F.; Keiler, K.; Mistakidis, S.I.; Schmelcher, P. Many-Body Collisional Dynamics of Impurities Injected Into a Double-Well Trapped Bose-Einstein Condensate. *Phys. Rev. Res.* **2021**, *3*, 023068. [CrossRef]
77. Bougas, G.; Mistakidis, S.I.; Schmelcher, P. Pattern Formation of Correlated Impurities Subjected To an Impurity-Medium Interaction Pulse. *Phys. Rev. A* **2021**, *103*, 023313. [CrossRef]
78. Mukherjee, K.; Mistakidis, S.I.; Majumder, S.; Schmelcher, P. Pulse- and Continuously Driven Many-Body Quantum Dynamics of Bosonic Impurities in a Bose-Einstein Condensate. *Phys. Rev. A* **2020**, *101*, 023615. [CrossRef]
79. Mistakidis, S.I.; Katsimiga, G.C.; Koutentakis, G.M.; Busch, T.; Schmelcher, P. Pump-Probe Spectroscopy of Bose Polarons: Dynamical Formation and Coherence. *Phys. Rev. Res.* **2020**, *2*, 033380. [CrossRef]
80. Mistakidis, S.I.; Koutentakis, G.M.; Grusdt, F.; Sadeghpour, H.R.; Schmelcher, P. Radiofrequency Spectroscopy of One-Dimensional Trapped Bose Polarons: Crossover From the Adiabatic To the Diabatic Regime. *New J. Phys.* **2021**, *23*, 043051. [CrossRef]
81. Katsimiga, G.C.; Mistakidis, S.I.; Koutentakis, G.M.; Kevrekidis, P.G.; Schmelcher, P. Many-Body Dissipative Flow of a Confined Scalar Bose-Einstein Condensate Driven By a Gaussian Impurity. *Phys. Rev. A* **2018**, *98*, 013632. [CrossRef]
82. Mistakidis, S.I.; Koutentakis, G.M.; Katsimiga, G.C.; Busch, T.; Schmelcher, P. Many-Body Quantum Dynamics and Induced Correlations of Bose Polarons. *New J. Phys.* **2020**, *22*, 043007. [CrossRef]
83. Mistakidis, S.I.; Katsimiga, G.C.; Koutentakis, G.M.; Busch, T.; Schmelcher, P. Quench Dynamics and Orthogonality Catastrophe of Bose Polarons. *Phys. Rev. Lett.* **2019**, *122*, 183001. [CrossRef] [PubMed]
84. Boudjemâa, A.; Guebli, N.; Sekmane, M.; Khlifa-Karfa, S. Breathing Modes of Repulsive Polarons in Bose-Bose Mixtures. *J. Phys. Cond. Matt.* **2020**, *32*, 415401. [CrossRef] [PubMed]
85. Johnson, T.H.; Bruderer, M.; Cai, Y.; Clark, S.R.; Bao, W.; Jaksch, D. Breathing Oscillations of a Trapped Impurity in a Bose Gas. *Europhys. Lett.* **2012**, *98*, 26001. [CrossRef]
86. Kevrekidis, P.G.; Frantzeskakis, D.J.; Carretero-González, R. *Emergent Nonlinear Phenomena in Bose-Einstein Condensates: Theory and Experiment*; Springer Science & Business Media: Berlin/Heidelberg, Germany, 2007; Volume 45. [CrossRef]
87. Kevrekidis, P.G.; Frantzeskakis, D.J.; Carretero-González, R. *The Defocusing Nonlinear Schrödinger Equation*; Society for Industrial and Applied Mathematics: Philadelphia, PA, USA, 2015; [CrossRef]
88. Weller, A.; Ronzheimer, J.P.; Gross, C.; Esteve, J.; Oberthaler, M.K.; Frantzeskakis, D.J.; Theocharis, G.; Kevrekidis, P.G. Experimental Observation of Oscillating and Interacting Matter Wave Dark Solitons. *Phys. Rev. Lett.* **2008**, *101*, 130401. [CrossRef] [PubMed]
89. Scott, T.F.; Ballagh, R.J.; Burnett, K. Formation of Fundamental Structures in Bose-Einstein Condensates. *J. Phys. B At. Mol. Opt. Phys.* **1998**, *31*, L329–L335. [CrossRef]
90. Fursa, D.V.; Bray, I. Convergent Close-Coupling Calculations of Electron—Helium Scattering. *J. Phys. B At. Mol. Opt. Phys.* **1997**, *30*, 757–785. [CrossRef]
91. Kamchatnov, A.M.; Pavloff, N. Generation of Dispersive Shock Waves By the Flow of a Bose-Einstein Condensate Past a Narrow Obstacle. *Phys. Rev. A* **2012**, *85*, 033603. [CrossRef]
92. Chang, J.J.; Engels, P.; Hoefer, M.A. Formation of Dispersive Shock Waves By Merging and Splitting Bose-Einstein Condensates. *Phys. Rev. Lett.* **2008**, *101*, 170404. [CrossRef]
93. Leboeuf, P.; Pavloff, N. Bose-Einstein Beams: Coherent Propagation Through a Guide. *Phys. Rev. A* **2001**, *64*, 033602. [CrossRef]
94. Hakim, V. Nonlinear Schrödinger Flow Past an Obstacle in One Dimension. *Phys. Rev. E* **1997**, *55*, 2835–2845. [CrossRef]

95. Dutton, Z. Observation of Quantum Shock Waves Created with Ultra-Compressed Slow Light Pulses in a Bose-Einstein Condensate. *Science* **2001**, *293*, 663–668. [CrossRef]
96. Theocharis, G.; Weller, A.; Ronzheimer, J.P.; Gross, C.; Oberthaler, M.K.; Kevrekidis, P.G.; Frantzeskakis, D.J. Multiple Atomic Dark Solitons in Cigar-Shaped Bose-Einstein Condensates. *Phys. Rev. A* **2010**, *81*, 063604. [CrossRef]
97. Burger, S.; Bongs, K.; Dettmer, S.; Ertmer, W.; Sengstock, K.; Sanpera, A.; Shlyapnikov, G.V.; Lewenstein, M. Dark Solitons in Bose-Einstein Condensates. *Phys. Rev. Lett.* **1999**, *83*, 5198–5201. [CrossRef]
98. Mistakidis, S.I.; Katsimiga, G.C.; Kevrekidis, P.G.; Schmelcher, P. Correlation Effects in the Quench-Induced Phase Separation Dynamics of a Two Species Ultracold Quantum Gas. *New J. Phys.* **2018**, *20*, 043052. [CrossRef]
99. Katsimiga, G.C.; Mistakidis, S.I.; Koutentakis, G.M.; Kevrekidis, P.G.; Schmelcher, P. Many-Body Quantum Dynamics in the Decay of Bent Dark Solitons of Bose-Einstein Condensates. *New J. Phys.* **2017**, *19*, 123012. [CrossRef]
100. Katsimiga, G.C.; Koutentakis, G.M.; Mistakidis, S.I.; Kevrekidis, P.G.; Schmelcher, P. Dark-Bright Soliton Dynamics Beyond the Mean-Field Approximation. *New J. Phys.* **2017**, *19*, 073004. [CrossRef]
101. Syrwid, A.; Zakrzewski, J.; Sacha, K. Time Crystal Behavior of Excited Eigenstates. *Phys. Rev. Lett.* **2017**, *119*, 250602. [CrossRef]
102. Delande, D.; Sacha, K. Many-Body Matter-Wave Dark Soliton. *Phys. Rev. Lett.* **2014**, *112*, 040402. [CrossRef]
103. Martin, A.D.; Ruostekoski, J. Quantum and Thermal Effects of Dark Solitons in a One-Dimensional Bose Gas. *Phys. Rev. Lett.* **2010**, *104*, 194102. [CrossRef] [PubMed]
104. Mishmash, R.V.; Danshita, I.; Clark, C.W.; Carr, L.D. Quantum Many-Body Dynamics of Dark Solitons in Optical Lattices. *Phys. Rev. A* **2009**, *80*, 053612. [CrossRef]
105. Dziarmaga, J.; Karkuszewski, Z.P.; Sacha, K. Images of the Dark Soliton in a Depleted Condensate. *J. Phys. B At. Mol. Opt. Phys.* **2003**, *36*, 1217–1229. [CrossRef]
106. Cao, L.; Bolsinger, V.; Mistakidis, S.I.; Koutentakis, G.M.; Krönke, S.; Schurer, J.M.; Schmelcher, P. A Unified Ab Initio Approach To the Correlated Quantum Dynamics of Ultracold Fermionic and Bosonic Mixtures. *J. Chem. Phys.* **2017**, *147*, 044106. [CrossRef]
107. Tajima, H.; Takahashi, J.; Nakano, E.; Iida, K. Collisional Dynamics of Polaronic Clouds Immersed in a Fermi Sea. *Phys. Rev. A* **2020**, *102*, 051302. [CrossRef]
108. Bell, T.A.; Glidden, J.A.P.; Humbert, L.; Bromley, M.W.J.; Haine, S.A.; Davis, M.J.; Neely, T.W.; Baker, M.A.; Rubinsztein-Dunlop, H. Bose-Einstein Condensation in Large Time-Averaged Optical Ring Potentials. *New J. Phys.* **2016**, *18*, 035003. [CrossRef]
109. Beattie, S.; Moulder, S.; Fletcher, R.J.; Hadzibabic, Z. Persistent Currents in Spinor Condensates. *Phys. Rev. Lett.* **2013**, *110*, 025301. [CrossRef] [PubMed]
110. Hueck, K.; Luick, N.; Sobirey, L.; Siegl, J.; Lompe, T.; Moritz, H. Two-Dimensional Homogeneous Fermi Gases. *Phys. Rev. Lett.* **2018**, *120*, 060402. [CrossRef] [PubMed]
111. Mukherjee, B.; Yan, Z.; Patel, P.B.; Hadzibabic, Z.; Yefsah, T.; Struck, J.; Zwierlein, M.W. Homogeneous Atomic Fermi Gases. *Phys. Rev. Lett.* **2017**, *118*, 123401. [CrossRef]
112. Corman, L.; Chomaz, L.; Bienaimé, T.; Desbuquois, R.; Weitenberg, C.; Nascimbène, S.; Dalibard, J.; Beugnon, J. Quench-Induced Supercurrents in an Annular Bose Gas. *Phys. Rev. Lett.* **2014**, *113*, 135302. [CrossRef]
113. Gaunt, A.L.; Schmidutz, T.F.; Gotlibovych, I.; Smith, R.P.; Hadzibabic, Z. Bose-Einstein Condensation of Atoms in a Uniform Potential. *Phys. Rev. Lett.* **2013**, *110*, 200406. [CrossRef]
114. Chin, C.; Grimm, R.; Julienne, P.; Tiesinga, E. Feshbach resonances in ultracold gases. *Rev. Mod. Phys.* **2010**, *82*, 1225–1286. [CrossRef]
115. Tajima, H.; Takahashi, J.; Mistakidis, S.; Nakano, E.; Iida, K. Polaron Problems in Ultracold Atoms: Role of a Fermi Sea Across Different Spatial Dimensions and Quantum Fluctuations of a Bose Medium. *Atoms* **2021**, *9*, 18. [CrossRef]
116. Gurari, M. XXXVI. Self Energy of Slow Electrons in Polar Materials. *Lond. Edinb. Dublin Philos. Mag. J. Sci.* **1953**, *44*, 329–336. [CrossRef]
117. Lee, T.D.; Pines, D. The Motion of Slow Electrons in Polar Crystals. *Phys. Rev.* **1952**, *88*, 960–961. [CrossRef]
118. Lee, T.D.; Low, F.E.; Pines, D. The Motion of Slow Electrons in a Polar Crystal. *Phys. Rev.* **1953**, *90*, 297–302. [CrossRef]
119. Lieb, E.H.; Liniger, W. Exact Analysis of an Interacting Bose Gas. I. the General Solution and the Ground State. *Phys. Rev.* **1963**, *130*, 1605–1616. [CrossRef]
120. Lieb, E.H. Exact Analysis of an Interacting Bose Gas. II. the Excitation Spectrum. *Phys. Rev.* **1963**, *130*, 1616–1624. [CrossRef]
121. Pitaevskii, L.; Stringari, S. *Bose-Einstein Condensation and Superfluidity*; International Series of Monographs on Physics; Oxford University Press: Oxford, UK, 2016. [CrossRef]
122. Schurer, J.M.; Negretti, A.; Schmelcher, P. Unraveling the Structure of Ultracold Mesoscopic Collinear Molecular Ions. *Phys. Rev. Lett.* **2017**, *119*, 063001. [CrossRef]
123. Dirac, P.A.M. Note on Exchange Phenomena in the Thomas Atom. *Math. Proc. Camb. Philos. Soc.* **1930**, *26*, 376–385. [CrossRef]
124. Frenkel, J. *Wave Mechanics*, 1st ed.; Claredon Press: Oxford, UK, 1934; pp. 423–428.
125. Alon, O.E.; Streltsov, A.I.; Cederbaum, L.S. Multiconfigurational Time-Dependent Hartree Method for Bosons: Many-Body Dynamics of Bosonic Systems. *Phys. Rev. A* **2008**, *77*, 033613. [CrossRef]
126. Alon, O.E.; Streltsov, A.I.; Cederbaum, L.S. Unified View on Multiconfigurational Time Propagation for Systems Consisting of Identical Particles. *J. Chem. Phys.* **2007**, *127*, 154103. [CrossRef]
127. Sant'Ana, F.T.; Hébert, F.; Rousseau, V.G.; Albert, M.; Vignolo, P. Scaling Properties of Tan's Contact: Embedding Pairs and Correlation Effect in the Tonks-Girardeau Limit. *Phys. Rev. A* **2019**, *100*, 063608. [CrossRef]

128. Olshanii, M.; Dunjko, V. Short-Distance Correlation Properties of the Lieb-Liniger System and Momentum Distributions of Trapped One-Dimensional Atomic Gases. *Phys. Rev. Lett.* **2003**, *91*, 090401. [CrossRef]
129. Werner, F.; Castin, Y. General Relations for Quantum Gases in Two and Three Dimensions. II. Bosons and Mixtures. *Phys. Rev. A* **2012**, *86*, 053633. [CrossRef]
130. Pricoupenko, L. Isotropic Contact Forces in Arbitrary Representation: Heterogeneous Few-Body Problems and Low Dimensions. *Phys. Rev. A* **2011**, *83*, 062711. [CrossRef]
131. Tan, S. Generalized Virial Theorem and Pressure Relation for a Strongly Correlated Fermi Gas. *Ann. Phys.* **2008**, *323*, 2987–2990. [CrossRef]
132. Tan, S. Large Momentum Part of a Strongly Correlated Fermi Gas. *Ann. Phys.* **2008**, *323*, 2971–2986. [CrossRef]
133. Tan, S. Energetics of a Strongly Correlated Fermi Gas. *Ann. Phys.* **2008**, *323*, 2952–2970. [CrossRef]
134. Brouzos, I. Ultracold Atoms in One Dimension: From Two to Many. Ph.D. Thesis, Universität Hamburg, Hamburg, Germany, 2012.
135. Mistakidis, S.I.; Katsimiga, G.C.; Koutentakis, G.M.; Schmelcher, P. Repulsive Fermi Polarons and Their Induced Interactions in Binary Mixtures of Ultracold Atoms. *New J. Phys.* **2019**, *21*, 043032. [CrossRef]
136. Knap, M.; Shashi, A.; Nishida, Y.; Imambekov, A.; Abanin, D.A.; Demler, E. Time-Dependent Impurity in Ultracold Fermions: Orthogonality Catastrophe and Beyond. *Phys. Rev. X* **2012**, *2*, 041020. [CrossRef]
137. Scherer, D.R.; Weiler, C.N.; Neely, T.W.; Anderson, B.P. Vortex Formation By Merging of Multiple Trapped Bose-Einstein Condensates. *Phys. Rev. Lett.* **2007**, *98*, 110402. [CrossRef] [PubMed]
138. Denschlag, J. Generating Solitons By Phase Engineering of a Bose-Einstein Condensate. *Science* **2000**, *287*, 97–101. [CrossRef]
139. Becker, C.; Stellmer, S.; Soltan-Panahi, P.; Dörscher, S.; Baumert, M.; Richter, E.M.; Kronjäger, J.; Bongs, K.; Sengstock, K. Oscillations and Interactions of Dark and Dark-Bright Solitons in Bose-Einstein Condensates. *Nat. Phys.* **2008**, *4*, 496–501. [CrossRef]
140. Khamis, E.G.; Gammal, A. Supersonic Flow of a Bose-Einstein Condensate Past an Oscillating Attractive-Repulsive Obstacle. *Phys. Rev. A* **2013**, *87*, 045601. [CrossRef]
141. Susanto, H.; Kevrekidis, P.G.; Carretero-González, R.; Malomed, B.A.; Frantzeskakis, D.J.; Bishop, A.R. Čerenkov-Like Radiation in a Binary Superfluid Flow Past an Obstacle. *Phys. Rev. A* **2007**, *75*, 055601. [CrossRef]
142. Carusotto, I.; Hu, S.X.; Collins, L.A.; Smerzi, A. Bogoliubov-Čerenkov Radiation in a Bose-Einstein Condensate Flowing Against an Obstacle. *Phys. Rev. Lett.* **2006**, *97*, 260403. [CrossRef] [PubMed]
143. El, G.A.; Gammal, A.; Kamchatnov, A.M. Oblique Dark Solitons in Supersonic Flow of a Bose-Einstein Condensate. *Phys. Rev. Lett.* **2006**, *97*, 180405. [CrossRef] [PubMed]
144. Lieb, E.H.; Robinson, D.W. The Finite Group Velocity of Quantum Spin Systems. *Commun. Math. Phys.* **1972**, *28*, 251–257. [CrossRef]
145. Cheneau, M.; Barmettler, P.; Poletti, D.; Endres, M.; Schauß, P.; Fukuhara, T.; Gross, C.; Bloch, I.; Kollath, C.; Kuhr, S. Light-Cone-Like Spreading of Correlations in a Quantum Many-Body System. *Nature* **2012**, *481*, 484–487. [CrossRef] [PubMed]
146. Pavloff, N. Breakdown of Superfluidity of an Atom Laser Past an Obstacle. *Phys. Rev. A* **2002**, *66*, 013610. [CrossRef]
147. Joseph, J.; Clancy, B.; Luo, L.; Kinast, J.; Turlapov, A.; Thomas, J.E. Measurement of Sound Velocity in a Fermi Gas Near a Feshbach Resonance. *Phys. Rev. Lett.* **2007**, *98*, 170401. [CrossRef]
148. Andrews, M.R.; Kurn, D.M.; Miesner, H.J.; Durfee, D.S.; Townsend, C.G.; Inouye, S.; Ketterle, W. Propagation of Sound in a Bose-Einstein Condensate. *Phys. Rev. Lett.* **1997**, *79*, 553–556. [CrossRef]
149. Littlejohn, R.G.; Cargo, M.; Carrington, T.; Mitchell, K.A.; Poirier, B. A General Framework for Discrete Variable Representation Basis Sets. *J. Chem. Phys.* **2002**, *116*, 8691–8703. [CrossRef]

Article

Polaritons in an Electron Gas—Quasiparticles and Landau Effective Interactions

Miguel Angel Bastarrachea-Magnani [1,2], Jannie Thomsen [2], Arturo Camacho-Guardian [3,*] and Georg M. Bruun [2,4]

[1] Departamento de Física, Universidad Autónoma Metropolitana-Iztapalapa, San Rafael Atlixco 186, Ciudad de Mexico 09340, Mexico; bastarrachea@xanum.uam.mx

[2] Department of Physics and Astronomy, Aarhus University, Ny Munkegade, DK-8000 Aarhus, Denmark; jannie-mikrochips@hotmail.com (J.T.); bruungmb@phys.au.dk (G.M.B.)

[3] T.C.M. Group, Cavendish Laboratory, University of Cambridge, JJ Thomson Avenue, Cambridge CB3 0HE, UK

[4] Shenzhen Institute for Quantum Science and Engineering and Department of Physics, Southern University of Science and Technology, Shenzhen 518055, China

* Correspondence: ac2387@cam.ac.uk

Abstract: Two-dimensional semiconductors inside optical microcavities have emerged as a versatile platform to explore new hybrid light–matter quantum states. A strong light–matter coupling leads to the formation of exciton-polaritons, which in turn interact with the surrounding electron gas to form quasiparticles called polaron-polaritons. Here, we develop a general microscopic framework to calculate the properties of these quasiparticles, such as their energy and the interactions between them. From this, we give microscopic expressions for the parameters entering a Landau theory for the polaron-polaritons, which offers a simple yet powerful way to describe such interacting light–matter many-body systems. As an example of the application of our framework, we then use the ladder approximation to explore the properties of the polaron-polaritons. Furthermore, we show that they can be measured in a non-demolition way via the light transmission/reflection spectrum of the system. Finally, we demonstrate that the Landau effective interaction mediated by electron-hole excitations is attractive leading to red shifts of the polaron-polaritons. Our work provides a systematic framework to study exciton-polaritons in electronically doped two-dimensional materials such as novel van der Waals heterostructures.

Keywords: polariton; Fermi polaron; Landau theory; quasiparticle interactions

1. Introduction

Semiconductors in optical microcavities constitute a rich setting for exploring hybrid light–matter quantum systems with potential optoelectronic applications [1,2]. An important example is the case of exciton-polaritons, which are quantum mechanical superpositions of photons and bound electron-hole pairs confined in a two-dimensional (2D) semiconductor layer inside an optical cavity [3,4]. An appealing feature of polaritons is that they inherit the properties of both their fundamental constituents, thereby providing a tunable way to transfer attributes from matter to light, and vice versa. Hence, not only can they be selectively excited, controlled and detected by optical means, but they also possess strong interactions that introduce novel non-linear optical effects [5,6]. As exciton-polaritons can be considered bosons for extended temperature and density ranges, they exhibit effects such as Bose–Einstein condensation and superfluidity [7–14], although the pump-loss nature of the experiments leads to a number of important differences compared to the equilibrium condensates.

Atomically thin transition-metal dichalcogenids (TMDs) [15–17] are among the 2D materials that have been in the spotlight in recent years. They are composed by two hexagonal planes of a transition metal atom M (Mo, W) that covalently binds with chalcogen atoms (S, Se, Te) to form an hexagonal lattice with a trigonal prismatic arrangement (MX_2) [18–20]. It has been found that atomically thin layers of TMDs are thermodynamically stable and that they are direct-gap semiconductors from the visible to the infrared spectrum [17,19,21,22]. The extrema of the bands are located at the finite momentum K^+ (K^-) points in the hexagonal Brillouin zone and connected by a broken inversion symmetry. Together with a strong spin-orbit coupling (SOC) this leads to valley-spin locking, i.e., the coupling between the valley and spin degrees of freedom [23–25]. As a result, there are valley selective optical rules [17,26,27], which, together with strong light–matter coupling [28,29] offer a promising playground for spin optoelectronics and valleytronics [24,30,31].

The large binding energy of excitons in TMDs as compared to other microcavity semiconductors such as quantum-wells [32–34], combined with the possibility to control the electron density in the different valleys, opens up exciting new venues to explore Bose–Fermi mixtures in a hybrid light–matter setting [35–37]. This has stimulated a number of studies regarding the properties electron–exciton mixtures and their coupling to light [38–48]. In particular, the emergence of new quasiparticles, the so-called Fermi-polaron-polaritons have been observed [49]. They can be roughly described as a coherent superposition of photons and Fermi polarons, which are formed by the polaritons interacting with the surrounding electron gas (2DEG) in analogy with what is observed in atomic gases [50–57].

Two recent experiments have observed large energy shifts of these polaron-polaritons due to the injection of itinerant electrons in a monolayer TMD indicating the presence of induced interactions between them [36,58], which opens the door to exploring interacting quasiparticles in a new hybrid light–matter setting. Landau's theory of quasiparticles stands out as a powerful yet simple framework to precisely describe such interacting many-body systems, including their single particle and collective properties both in and out of equilibrium [59–61]. In light of this, an important question concerns how to calculate the parameters entering such a Landau theory for polaron-polaritons.

Inspired by this, we present here a theoretical framework for polaron-polaritons in a 2DEG in terms of Green's functions. Moreover, we show how this can be used to calculate the parameters of a Landau theory of polaron-polaritons, which encompasses the strong light–matter coupling. Apart from assuming that the concentration of the polaron-polaritons is much smaller than that of the 2DEG and that equilibrium theory can be applied, our theory is completely general. We then give a concrete example of these results by employing an approximate many-body theory, the so-called ladder approximation, which includes strong two-body correlations leading to a bound state between an exciton and an electron, i.e., a trimer. Using this, we explore the different polaron-polariton branches and demonstrate how the transmission/reflection spectrum of the system offer a new experimental way to determine the energy and residue of the underlying polarons in a non-demolition way. The energy of the polaron-polaritons is then shown to decrease with their concentration corresponding to an attractive Landau quasiparticle interaction mediated by particle-hole excitations in the 2DEG.

The remainder of the manuscript is structured as follows. In Section 2, we introduce the system and discuss the formation of the hybrid light–matter polaritons. In Section 3, we turn our attention to the effects of interactions and show how this can be described microscopically. We then connect this to Landau's quasiparticle theory providing microscopic expressions for the quasiparticle energies and their effective interactions. In Section 4, we apply these results to the ladder approximation and analyse the predicted properties of the quasiparticles and the interactions between them. We also propose a new way to measure these via the light transmission/reflection spectrum. Finally, in Section 5 we present our conclusions and offer some perspectives.

2. System

We consider a 2D semiconductor in an optical microcavity. Photons in the cavity are strongly coupled to excitons in the semiconductor and the excitons in turn interact with a 2D electron gas (2DEG). The Hamiltonian for the system is $\hat{H} = \hat{H}_0 + \hat{H}_I$, where

$$\hat{H}_0 = \sum_{\mathbf{k}} \left[\varepsilon_{e\mathbf{k}} \hat{e}_{\mathbf{k}}^\dagger \hat{e}_{\mathbf{k}} + \varepsilon_{x\mathbf{k}} \hat{x}_{\mathbf{k}}^\dagger \hat{x}_{\mathbf{k}} + \varepsilon_{c\mathbf{k}} \hat{c}_{\mathbf{k}}^\dagger \hat{c}_{\mathbf{k}} \right] + \sum_{\mathbf{k}} \Omega \left(\hat{x}_{\mathbf{k}}^\dagger \hat{c}_{\mathbf{k}} + \hat{c}_{\mathbf{k}}^\dagger \hat{x}_{\mathbf{k}} \right) \tag{1}$$

are the non-interacting and the light–matter coupling terms. Here $\hat{x}_{\mathbf{k}}^\dagger$, $\hat{c}_{\mathbf{k}}^\dagger$, and $\hat{e}_{\mathbf{k}}^\dagger$, creates an exciton, photon, and electron, respectively, with two-dimensional crystal momentum $\mathbf{k}$. The energy of these particles is $\varepsilon_{x\mathbf{k}} = \mathbf{k}^2/2m_x$, $\varepsilon_{c\mathbf{k}} = \mathbf{k}^2/2m_c + \delta$, and $\varepsilon_{e\mathbf{k}} = \mathbf{k}^2/2m_e$, where m_x, m_c, and m_e are their masses and δ is the detuning between the exciton and photon energies at zero momentum. We set $\hbar = k_B = 1$ throughout. For concreteness, we take $m_c = 10^{-5} m_x$, $m_x = 2m_e$ and assume the light–matter coupling Ω to be real. The energy offset of the electrons will be absorbed into their chemical potential. It follows from the optical and valley selection rules of TMDs [15–17] that polarised photons couple to excitons in a specific spin and valley state, which in turn predominantly interacts with the 2DEG in the opposite valley. Here, we focus on a given spin and valley and therefore suppress those degrees of freedom in Equation (1) and onwards. The excitons are assumed to have a binding energy much larger than any other relevant energy scale in the system so that they can be considered as point bosons. For high exciton densities or localised excitons, their composite nature becomes important and the point boson approximation breaks down, leading to changes in the effective light–matter interaction and saturation effects [36,46].

The non-interacting Hamiltonian equation, Equation (1), is readily diagonalised by means of a Hopfield transformation [3]

$$\begin{bmatrix} \hat{x}_{\mathbf{k}} \\ \hat{c}_{\mathbf{k}} \end{bmatrix} = \begin{bmatrix} \mathcal{C}_{\mathbf{k}} & -\mathcal{S}_{\mathbf{k}} \\ \mathcal{S}_{\mathbf{k}} & \mathcal{C}_{\mathbf{k}} \end{bmatrix} \begin{bmatrix} \hat{L}_{\mathbf{k}} \\ \hat{U}_{\mathbf{k}} \end{bmatrix} \tag{2}$$

where $L_{\mathbf{k}}^\dagger$ ($U_{\mathbf{k}}^\dagger$) are the creation operators of lower and upper polaritons, respectively, with momentum $\mathbf{k}$. The corresponding Hopfield coefficients are $\mathcal{C}_{\mathbf{k}}^2 = (1 + \delta_{\mathbf{k}}/\sqrt{\delta_{\mathbf{k}}^2 + 4\Omega^2})/2$ and $\mathcal{S}_{\mathbf{k}}^2 = 1 - \mathcal{C}_{\mathbf{k}}^2$ with $\delta_{\mathbf{k}} = \varepsilon_{c\mathbf{k}} - \varepsilon_{x\mathbf{k}}$, and

$$\varepsilon_{\sigma\mathbf{k}} = \frac{1}{2} \left(\varepsilon_{c\mathbf{k}} + \varepsilon_{x\mathbf{k}} \pm \sqrt{\delta_{\mathbf{k}}^2 + 4\Omega^2} \right), \tag{3}$$

giving the energy of the standard upper $\sigma = U$ and lower $\sigma = L$ exciton-polaritons in the absence of the Fermi sea. Interactions between the excitons and electrons in opposite valleys are described by the term

$$\hat{H}_I = \frac{1}{\mathcal{A}} \sum_{\mathbf{q},\mathbf{k},\mathbf{k}'} V_{\mathbf{q}} \hat{e}_{\mathbf{k}+\mathbf{q}}^\dagger \hat{x}_{\mathbf{k}'-\mathbf{q}}^\dagger \hat{x}_{\mathbf{k}'} \hat{e}_{\mathbf{k}}, \tag{4}$$

where $\mathcal{A}$ is the area of the system. For small Fermi energies and relevant momenta the electron–exciton interaction can be approximated as a contact one $V_{\mathbf{q}} \simeq T_0$ [49]. This is equivalent to treating the exciton-polaritons as point-like bosons. Additionally, we assume that the Coulomb interaction between the electrons are included by a renormalisation of their dispersion using Fermi liquid theory [62,63], and we furthermore neglect the direct interaction between excitons. For small densities, the latter is rather weak due to the large binding energy of the excitons, which is typically two orders of magnitude larger than the rest of energy scales [32–34,64], and it can easily be included at the mean-field level.

3. Fermi Polaron-Polaritons

We now consider the situation where the density of exciton-polaritons is small compared to the electron density. In this case, the effects of the exciton-polaritons on the 2DEG can be neglected and the problem reduces to that of mobile bosonic impurities in an electron gas. The interaction between the exciton-polaritons and the surrounding electron gas then gives rise to the formation of quasiparticles denoted Fermi polaron-polaritons or, in short, polaron-polaritons. Apart from the presence of strong light coupling this has strong similarities to the formation of Fermi polarons in atomic gases [65]. In this section we will describe their generic properties both from a microscopic point of view as well as using Landau's quasiparticle framework. We will furthermore provide precise links between the two descriptions when appropriate. While these results are general, we will illustrate them by using a microscopic approximated many-body theory as an example.

3.1. Microscopic Theory

Despite the fact that polariton systems are driven by external lasers, many of their steady-state properties can be accurately described using equilibrium theory with a few modifications, such as chemical potentials being determined by the external laser frequencies [6]. We therefore employ finite temperature quantum field theory to analyse the problem microscopically [66]. Since the electrons are unaffected by the excitons, we can focus on the cavity photons and excitons described by the 2 × 2 exciton-photon finite-temperature Green's function $\mathcal{G}(\mathbf{k}, \tau) = -\langle T_\tau \{\hat{\Psi}_\mathbf{k}(\tau) \hat{\Psi}_\mathbf{k}^\dagger(0)\}\rangle$, where $\hat{\Psi}_\mathbf{k} = [\hat{x}_\mathbf{k}, \hat{c}_\mathbf{k}]^T$ and T_τ denotes the imaginary time ordering. By Fourier transformation, it can be written in terms of the free propagator $\mathcal{G}_0(k)$ and the proper self-energy $\blacksquare(k)$ as

$$\mathcal{G}^{-1}(k) = \mathcal{G}_0^{-1}(k) - \blacksquare(k) = \begin{bmatrix} i\omega_l - \varepsilon_{x\mathbf{k}} & 0 \\ 0 & i\omega_l - \varepsilon_{c\mathbf{k}} \end{bmatrix} - \begin{bmatrix} \Sigma_{xx}(k) & \Omega \\ \Omega & 0 \end{bmatrix}. \tag{5}$$

where $k = (\mathbf{k}, \omega_l)$, $\omega_l = 2\pi l T$ with $l = 0, \pm 1, \dots$ is a bosonic Matsubara frequency, T is the temperature, and $\Sigma_{xx}(k)$ is the exciton self-energy. As usual, one can obtain the retarded Green's function by analytic continuation $\mathcal{G}(\mathbf{k}, \omega) = \mathcal{G}(\mathbf{k}, i\omega_l)|_{i\omega_l \to \omega + i0^+}$.

In the absence of light, the problem is equivalent to impurity particles interacting with a Fermi sea, which is known to lead to the formation quasiparticles called Fermi polarons [65,67,68]. The coupling to light turns these polarons into polaron-polaritons, and in analogy with Equation (3), the energy of these quasiparticles is given by the self-consistent solutions of

$$\varepsilon_{\sigma \mathbf{k}} = \frac{1}{2}\left[\varepsilon_{c\mathbf{k}} + \varepsilon_{x\mathbf{k}} + \Sigma_{xx}(\mathbf{k}, \varepsilon_{\sigma \mathbf{k}}) \pm \sqrt{[\delta_\mathbf{k} - \Sigma_{xx}(\mathbf{k}, \varepsilon_{\sigma \mathbf{k}})]^2 + 4\Omega^2}\right]. \tag{6}$$

Here, the subindex σ denotes the different quasiparticle branches emerging in the system. Also, a new set of Hopfield coefficients arise giving the matter and photon components of the polaron-polaritons. As in Equation (2) they are

$$\mathcal{C}_{\mathbf{k}\sigma}^2 = \frac{1}{2} + \frac{\varepsilon_{c\mathbf{k}} - \varepsilon_{x\mathbf{k}} - \Sigma_{xx}(\mathbf{k}, \varepsilon_{\sigma \mathbf{k}})}{2\sqrt{[\varepsilon_{c\mathbf{k}} - \varepsilon_{x\mathbf{k}} - \Sigma_{xx}(\mathbf{k}, \varepsilon_{\sigma \mathbf{k}})]^2 + 4\Omega^2}} \quad \text{and} \quad \mathcal{S}_{\mathbf{k}\sigma}^2 = 1 - \mathcal{C}_{\mathbf{k}\sigma}^2. \tag{7}$$

3.2. Landau Theory

Landau's description of macroscopic systems in terms of quasiparticles is a highlight in theoretical physics and provides a remarkably simple yet accurate description of otherwise complex many-body systems [59,60]. This includes both their single-particle and collective equilibrium and non-equilibrium properties, and it is therefore important to understand how it can be applied to polaron-polaritons. We now address this question and provide precise links between Landau's framework and the microscopic theory in the previous section.

The foundation of Landau's theory idea is to write the energy E of a system in powers of its low energy excitations, which have particle-like properties, i.e., the quasiparticles as [61]

$$E = E_g + \sum_{\mathbf{q},\sigma} \varepsilon_{\mathbf{k}\sigma}^0 n_{\mathbf{k}\sigma} + \frac{1}{2\mathcal{A}} \sum_{\mathbf{k},\mathbf{k}',\sigma,\sigma'} f_{\mathbf{k}\sigma,\mathbf{k}'\sigma'} n_{\mathbf{k}\sigma} n_{\mathbf{k}'\sigma'} + \dots, \tag{8}$$

where E_g is the ground state energy of the system and $\varepsilon^0_{\mathbf{k}\sigma}$ is the quasiparticle energy. The distribution function in a given quasiparticle branch σ is given by $n_{\mathbf{k}\sigma}$, and $f_{\mathbf{k}\sigma,\mathbf{k}'\sigma'}$ is the interaction between quasiparticles in branches σ and σ' with momenta $\mathbf{k}$ and $\mathbf{k}'$. In principle, there are terms of higher order in $n_{\mathbf{k}\sigma}$ in Equation (8), which correspond to three-body interaction terms and higher. However, such terms are usually not important for realistic densities and it is standard in Landau's quasiparticle theory to truncate the series at quadratic order corresponding to including two-body interactions, as we do here.

In the present case, the quasiparticles are the polaron-polaritons and their energy $\varepsilon^0_{\mathbf{k}\sigma}$ are given by solutions of Equation (6) taking the zero impurity limit. i.e., a vanishing quasiparticle distribution function $n_{\mathbf{k}\sigma} = 0$. The ground state of the system is simply the 2DEG with no polaron-polaritons present with the energy $\mathcal{A}n_e\varepsilon_F/2$ where n_e is the density of the 2DEG with Fermi energy ε_F. When the number of quasiparticles is non-zero, it follows from Equation (8) that their energy is

$$\varepsilon_{\mathbf{k}\sigma} = \varepsilon^0_{\mathbf{k}\sigma} + \frac{1}{\mathcal{A}} \sum_{\mathbf{k}'\sigma'} f_{\mathbf{k}\sigma,\mathbf{k}'\sigma'} n_{\mathbf{k}'\sigma'}. \tag{9}$$

It follows from Equation (9) that the interaction between the quasiparticles can be found as [69]

$$\frac{f_{\mathbf{k}\sigma,\mathbf{k}'\sigma'}}{\mathcal{A}} = \frac{d\varepsilon_{\mathbf{k}\sigma}}{dn_{\mathbf{k}'\sigma'}} = Z_{\mathbf{k}\sigma} \mathcal{X}^2_{\mathbf{k}\sigma} \frac{\partial \Sigma_{xx}(\mathbf{k},\varepsilon_{\mathbf{k}\sigma})}{\partial n_{\mathbf{k}'\sigma'}}, \tag{10}$$

where

$$Z^{-1}_{\mathbf{k}\sigma} = 1 - \mathcal{X}^2_{\mathbf{k}\sigma} \partial_\omega \Sigma_{xx}(\mathbf{k},\varepsilon_{\mathbf{k}\sigma}) \tag{11}$$

is the residue of a polaron-polariton in branch σ with momentum $\mathbf{k}$ and we have used Equation (6) in the second equality. Here, $\mathcal{X}_{\mathbf{k}\sigma} = \mathcal{S}_{\mathbf{k}\sigma}$ when the quasiparticle energy is determined using the $+\sqrt{\ldots}$ version of the upper polariton poles in Equation (6), whereas $\mathcal{X}_{\mathbf{k}\sigma} = \mathcal{C}_{\mathbf{k}\sigma}$ when the $-\sqrt{\ldots}$ version of the lower polariton in Equation (6) is used. Compared to the usual microscopic many-body formula for Landau's quasiparticle interaction [70,71], Equation (10) has the additional feature of containing the many-body Hopfield coefficients. They reflect that it is only the excitonic part of the quasiparticles which interact with the surrounding 2DEG.

Equations (5)–(10) provide a framework for describing polaron-polaritons in a 2DEG microscopically and moreover show how to connect this to Landau's quasiparticle theory. The main assumptions are that the concentration of polaron-polaritons is much smaller than that of the electrons so that their effects on the 2DEG can be neglected, and that we can use equilibrium theory to describe its steady state properties. We now illustrate these results using an approximate many-body theory.

4. The Ladder Approximation

To give a concrete example of the results in the previous section, we apply the much used ladder approximation to describe polaritons interacting with a 2DEG. This theory has turned out to be surprisingly accurate for mobile impurities in atomic Fermi gases [65], which is a problem with many similarities to the one at hand. The basic idea is to include the two-body scattering physics exactly in a many-body environment and it is thus particularly suited to describe systems with strong two-body correlations such as molecule formation or hard core repulsion [66]. In the present context, the molecules correspond to bound states of an exciton and an electron, i.e., a trion, which indeed have been observed in TMDs [35,72–78] motivating the use of this approximation. In the ladder approximation, the exciton self-energy is given by

$$\Sigma_{xx}(k) = \frac{T}{\mathcal{A}} \sum_q \mathcal{G}_e(q) \mathcal{T}(k+q), \tag{12}$$

where $k = (\mathbf{k}, i\omega_l)$, $\mathcal{G}_e^{-1}(\mathbf{k}, i\omega_j) = i\omega_j - \xi_{\mathbf{k}}^e$ is the electron propagator with $i\omega_j = (2j+1)\pi T$ a fermionic Matsubara frequency, and $\sum_q$ denotes a sum over both Matsubara frequencies and 2D momentum. The electron energy is taken with respect to the Fermi energy of the 2DEG, i.e., $\xi_{e\mathbf{k}} = \varepsilon_{e\mathbf{k}} - \varepsilon_F$. In Equation (12), we have introduced the exciton–electron scattering matrix given by [79–81]

$$\mathcal{T}(k) = \frac{1}{\text{Re}\Pi_V(\mathbf{k}=0,\varepsilon_T) - \Pi(k)}, \qquad (13)$$

where $\Pi(k)$ is the in-medium exciton–electron pair-propagator

$$\Pi(k) = -\frac{T}{\mathcal{A}} \sum_q \mathcal{G}_{xx}^{(0)}(k+q)\mathcal{G}_e(-q) = \sum_\sigma \int \frac{d^2\mathbf{q}}{(2\pi)^2} \mathcal{X}_{\sigma \mathbf{k+q}}^2 \frac{1 + n_B(\xi_{\mathbf{k+q}\sigma}) - n_F(\xi_{e-\mathbf{q}})}{i\omega_j - \xi_{\mathbf{k+q}\sigma} - \xi_{-\mathbf{q}}^e}. \qquad (14)$$

Here, $\mathcal{G}_{xx}^{(0)}(k) = \sum_\sigma \mathcal{X}_{\sigma \mathbf{k}}^2 / (i\omega_l - \xi_{\mathbf{k}\sigma})$ is the exciton Green's function in the absence of interactions expressed in terms of the upper $\sigma = U$ and lower polariton $\sigma = L$ with $\xi_{\mathbf{k}\sigma} = \varepsilon_{\mathbf{k}\sigma} - \mu_\sigma$ where $\varepsilon_{\mathbf{k}\sigma}$ is given by Equation (3). In this way, we include the hybridisation of the exciton and the photon in the scattering matrix. Note that we have introduced the chemical potentials μ_σ to account for a non-zero concentration of the polaritons described by the Bose–Einstein distribution $n_B(x) = [\exp(\beta x) - 1]^{-1}$, whereas $n_F(x) = [\exp(\beta x) + 1]^{-1}$ is the Fermi–Dirac distribution for the electrons.

In deriving Equation (13) we have assumed a momentum independent exciton–electron interaction, which is accurate for $k_F a_B^x \ll 1$, where a_B^x is the Bohr radius giving the typical size of the exciton. Additionally, the bare coupling strength has been expressed in terms of the energy ε_T of the trion in the absence of the 2DEG as $\text{Re}\Pi_V(0,\varepsilon_T) = \mathcal{T}_0^{-1}$ [79–81]. At the level of a single impurity and zero temperature, the $\mathcal{T}$-matrix formalism is equivalent to Chevy's variational ansatz [67], which has recently been employed to explore Fermi polaron-polaritons in TMD monolayers [49]. As we shall demonstrate below, our field-theoretical approach is readily extended to include the effects of temperature and a non-zero quasiparticle concentration. Such effects are usually challenging to incorporate in a variational approach.

4.1. Zero Polaron-Polariton Density

We now discuss the properties of polaron-polaritons in the limit where their density vanishes, which corresponds to taking $n_B(\xi_{\sigma \mathbf{k+q}}) \to 0$ in Equation (14). In this case, the Matsubara sum in Equation (12) yields

$$\Sigma_{xx}(k) = \int \frac{d^2\mathbf{q}}{(2\pi)^2} n_F(\xi_{e\mathbf{q}}) \mathcal{T}(\mathbf{k}+\mathbf{q}, i\omega_\nu + \xi_{e\mathbf{q}}). \qquad (15)$$

In Figure 1, we show the zero momentum photonic spectral density $A_{cc}(\omega) = -2\text{Im}G_{cc}(\mathbf{k}=0,\omega)$ as a function of the detuning δ obtained by inverting Equation (5). We use the experimentally realistic values $\Omega = 8$ meV and $\varepsilon_T = -25$ meV [35,82]. In Figure 1a,b we show the spectral function for increasing electron densities with $\varepsilon_F/\varepsilon_T = 0.015$ ($n_e = 8.0 \times 10^{10}$) and 0.19 ($n_e = 1.0 \times 10^{12}$), respectively. For a typical experimental temperature $T \approx 1K$ [58], the thermal energy remains much smaller than the Rabi coupling ($k_B T/\Omega \approx 0.05$), the trion binding energy, and the Fermi energy of the system. Temperature effects are therefore expected to be negligible.

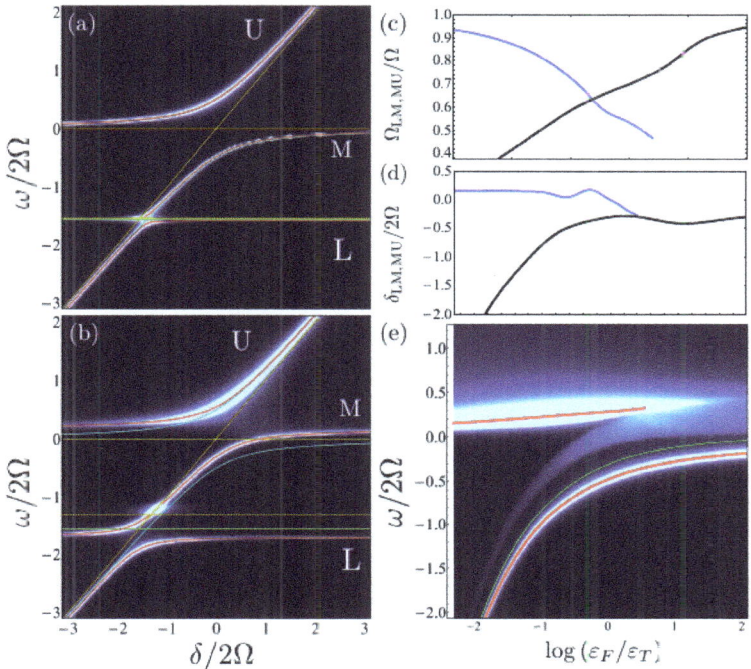

Figure 1. Photon spectral distribution $A_{cc}(\mathbf{k}=0,\omega)$ for $n_e = 8.0 \times 10^{10}$ ($\varepsilon_F/\varepsilon_T = 0.015$) (**a**) and $n_e = 1.0 \times 10^{12}$ ($\varepsilon_F/\varepsilon_T = 0.19$) (**b**). We observe three quasiparticle branches L, M and U of exciton-polaron-polaritons (red curves). The yellow solid curves correspond to the uncoupled photon and exciton energies, while the cyan lines give the polariton branches in absence of electron–exciton interactions. The horizontal green solid line indicates the bare binding energy of the trion ε_T and the dashed yellow the binding energy in the presence of many-body correlations. (**c**) Size of the Rabi coupling for the L-M branches (attractive polaron) Ω_{LM} (blue) and the M-U branches (repulsive polaron) Ω_{MU} (black) as a function of the ratio $\varepsilon_F/\varepsilon_T$. (**d**) Value of the detuning where the avoided crossings between the polaron-polariton branches occur with the same color coding as in (c). The background colors show the 2D polaron spectral function in the absence of light. For the calculations we employ an additional artificial broadening $\eta/2\Omega = 0.01$. (**e**) Spectral function of the Fermi polaron as a function of $\varepsilon_F/\varepsilon_T$ for $\Omega = 0$.

Let us first focus on the limit $\delta \gg |\Omega|$, where the photon is decoupled from the excitons and electrons. In addition to the photon, there are two quasiparticle branches in this limit: The so-called attractive polaron corresponding to the exciton attracting the electrons around it giving a quasiparticle energy below the trion energy, and the repulsive polaron corresponding to the electron repelling the electrons around it giving an energy above zero. We see that the repulsive polaron has the most spectral weight for low electron density with $\varepsilon_F/\varepsilon_T = 0.015$, whereas the attractive branch starts to gain more spectral weight for a high electron density with $\varepsilon_F/\varepsilon_T = 0.19$. This is consistent with what it is found for polarons in atomic gases since a small electron density with $\varepsilon_F \ll \varepsilon_T$ corresponds to the so-called BEC limit and a large electron density $\varepsilon_F \gg \varepsilon_T$ corresponds to the BCS limit. For atomic gases, one indeed has that the residue of the attractive polaron approaches unity in the BCS limit, whereas that of the repulsive polaron vanishes and vice versa in the BEC limit [65,83].

When $\delta/|\Omega|$ decreases, the photon starts to couple to the attractive and repulsive polarons resulting in three hybrid light–matter quasiparticle branches, which we have denoted as the upper U, middle M, and lower L polaron-polaritons. There are two prominent avoided crossings between these branches as it can be seen in Figure 1a,b, and their size and position can be understood as follows. In absence of any light–matter coupling, the impurity forms an attractive (repulsive) polaron with energy $\omega_{\mathbf{k}}^{a(r)}$ and residue $Z_{\mathbf{k}}^{a(r)}$ [44,65,83]. The coupling of these polarons to the photon can be described by the photon Green's function

$$G_{cc}^{-1}(\mathbf{k},\omega) \approx \omega - \varepsilon_{c\mathbf{k}} - \Omega^2 \left[\frac{Z_{\mathbf{k}}^a}{\omega - \omega_{\mathbf{k}}^a} + \frac{Z_{\mathbf{k}}^r}{\omega - \omega_{\mathbf{k}}^r} \right], \qquad (16)$$

which is illustrated in Figure 2. It describes the repeated transitions between the photon and the polarons by the Rabi coupling as the polaron-polariton propagates through the medium. Equation (16) includes only the quasiparticle peaks of the exciton propagator and ignores any many-body continuum of states in the spirit of Landau theory. From Equation (16), we see that the matrix element giving the size of the avoided crossing of the photon branch with the repulsive and attractive polarons is

$$\Omega_{\mathrm{UM}} = \Omega \sqrt{Z_{\mathbf{k}}^r} \qquad \text{and} \qquad \Omega_{\mathrm{LM}} = \Omega \sqrt{Z_{\mathbf{k}}^a}, \qquad (17)$$

respectively. This explains why the avoided crossing for the repulsive/attractive polaron is large/small for small electron density $\varepsilon_F/\varepsilon_T = 0.015$ in Figure 1a, since this corresponds to the BEC limit where the residue of the repulsive polaron approaches unity [65,83]. In the same fashion, the avoided crossing of the repulsive/attractive polaron is small/large for large electron density in Figure 1b, since this corresponds to the BCS limit where the attractive polaron has a residue close to unity and the residue of the repulsive polaron vanishes.

$G_{cc}(\mathbf{k},\omega) = $

Figure 2. Feynman diagram for the coupling of the photon propagator (black, wavy line) to the exciton (red line). The dotted lines represent the Rabi coupling.

To explore this further, we plot in Figure 1c the size of the two avoided crossings extracted as the minimum energy difference between the polaron-polariton branches as a function of the electron density. This clearly shows how Ω_{UM} decreases with increasing electron density, reflecting the decreasing weight of the repulsive polaron. As the BCS limit is approached, the repulsive polaron becomes ill-defined and we cannot determine Ω_{UM}. Mirroring this, Ω_{LM} increases with increasing electron density since the residue of the attractive polaron increases as the BCS limit is approached. Since the avoided crossing of the photon with the exciton in the absence of electrons is given by Ω, we conclude from this that the residues of the repulsive and attractive polarons can be extracted by measuring the size of their avoided crossings.

Furthermore, from Equation (17) we see that the position of the avoided crossings is determined by when the energies of the attractive and repulsive polarons cross the photon branch. To illustrate this, we plot in Figure 1d the value of the detuning where the avoided crossings occur as a function of the electron density. We also plot the spectral function of the polaron in a 2D Fermi gas in the absence of light coupling determined from Equation (5) setting $\Omega = 0$ [83] in Figure 1e. The good agreement between the peaks of this spectral function giving the energies of the attractive and repulsive polarons in a Fermi gas and the positions of the two avoided crossings confirms that the underlying physics is indeed driven by the coupling of polarons to light.

In conclusion, these results unfold a new experimental way to determine the energy and residue of the polaron in a non-demolition way by detecting the light transmission/reflection spectrum of the system. This method represents an important alternative to earlier approaches based on Rabi-oscillations in radio-frequency (RF) spectroscopy [51,55,84,85]. We note that these avoided crossings have already been observed experimentally [49,58,86].

4.2. Non-Zero Polaron-Polariton Density

We now consider the case of a non-zero polaron-polariton density focusing on how this affects their energy. From this, we will derive a microscopic expression for Landau's quasiparticle interaction within the ladder approximation.

Our starting point is Equation (12) for the exciton self-energy. For a non-zero density of excitons, evaluating the Matsubara sum yields [69]

$$\Sigma_{xx}(\mathbf{k}, i\omega_\nu) = \int \frac{d^2\mathbf{q}}{(2\pi)^2} \Big[n_F(\xi_{e\mathbf{q}}) \mathcal{T}(\mathbf{k}+\mathbf{q}, i\omega_\nu + \xi_{e\mathbf{q}})$$
$$+ \int_{-\infty}^{\infty} \frac{d\omega'}{\pi} \frac{n_F(\omega') \mathrm{Im}\mathcal{T}(\mathbf{k}+\mathbf{q}, \omega' + i0^+)}{i\omega_\nu - \omega' + \xi_{e\mathbf{q}}} - \frac{n_F(\omega^{tr}_{\mathbf{k}+\mathbf{q}}) Z^{tr}_{\mathbf{k}+\mathbf{q}}}{i\omega_\nu - \omega^{tr}_{\mathbf{k}+\mathbf{q}} + \xi_{e\mathbf{q}}} \Big]. \quad (18)$$

Compared to Equation (15), the finite exciton density gives rise to the two new terms in the second line of Equation (18). The last term is a contribution coming from a non-zero population of the trion state, which appears as a pole in the many-body scattering matrix at the energy $\omega^{tr}_\mathbf{k}$ with residue $Z^{tr}_\mathbf{k}$. This results in an interaction between the trions and the excitons mediated by the exchange of an electron [69], which has been observed to give rise to large optical non-linearities. We neglect this term in the following assuming a zero population of trions and refer the reader to Ref. [36] for an analysis of the interesting interaction between excitons and trions mediated by electron exchange.

A non-zero exciton density enters the self-energy explicitly via the second term in Equation (18), which comes from the branch-cut of the exciton–electron scattering matrix. Physically, it corresponds to the propagation of an electron and an exciton with population $n_F(\omega)$. The exciton density also enters the scattering matrix $\mathcal{T}$ via the exciton-electron pair propagator given by Equation (14). In Figure 3, we plot the energy shift of the lowest polaron-polariton branch $\Delta\varepsilon_{\mathbf{q}L} = \varepsilon_{\mathbf{q}L} - \varepsilon^0_{\mathbf{q}L}$ for $\mathbf{q} = 0$ as a function of its density $n_L = \mathcal{A}^{-1} \sum_\mathbf{q} n_B(\xi_{\mathbf{q}L})$ for several values of the cavity detuning. Here, $\varepsilon^0_{\mathbf{q}L}$ denotes the energy of the lower polaron-polariton branch in the limit of vanishing density consistent with the notation in Section 3.2. The energy shift is obtained by solving Equation (6) for a varying chemical potential of the polaritons. We see that the energy shift is *negative* and depends approximately linearly on density n_L. From Landau theory, this negative shift corresponds to an *attractive interaction* between the quasiparticles as can be seen explicitly from Equation (9).

To derive a microscopic expression for the interaction between the polaron-polaritons, it follows from Equation (10) that we must evaluate the derivative of the exciton self-energy with respect to their distribution $n_{\mathbf{q}\sigma} = n_B(\xi_{\mathbf{q}\sigma})$. We thus expand Equation (18) as $\Sigma_{xx}(\mathbf{k}, \omega) = \Sigma_{n_\sigma = 0}(\mathbf{k}, \omega) + \delta\Sigma(\mathbf{k}, \omega) + \mathcal{O}(n_\sigma^2)$, and by evaluating this on-shell with $\omega = \xi_{\mathbf{k}\sigma}$ one obtains [69]

$$\frac{\partial \Sigma_{xx}(\mathbf{k}, \xi_{\mathbf{k}\sigma})}{\partial n_{\mathbf{k}'\sigma'}} = \mathcal{X}^2_\mathbf{k} c_{c'} \int \frac{d^2\mathbf{p}}{(2\pi)^2} \frac{1}{\xi_{\mathbf{k}\sigma} - \xi_{\mathbf{k}'\sigma'} + \xi_{\mathbf{p}e} - \xi_{\mathbf{k}-\mathbf{k}'+\mathbf{p}e}} \times$$
$$\Big[n_F(\xi^e_\mathbf{p}) \mathcal{T}^2(\mathbf{k}' - \mathbf{p}, \xi_{\mathbf{k}\sigma} + \xi^e_\mathbf{p}) - n_F(\xi^e_{\mathbf{k}-\mathbf{k}'+\mathbf{p}}) \mathcal{T}^2(\mathbf{k}' - \mathbf{p}, \xi^e_{\mathbf{k}-\mathbf{k}'+\mathbf{p}} + \xi_{\mathbf{k}'\sigma'}) \Big]. \quad (19)$$

Here, it is understood that all energies $\xi_{\mathbf{k}\sigma}$ as well as the $\mathcal{T}$ matrix are evaluated for vanishing quasiparticle density. This expression can be generalised to a non-zero density by using the full density-dependent $\mathcal{T}$-matrix as shown in Appendix A. Note that since we are using a non self-consistent approximation, it is the density of the bare upper and polaritons that enter inside the exciton self-energy. To derive Equation (19), we have identified these densities with those of the polaron-polaritons, which corresponds to the first step in a self-consistent calculation.

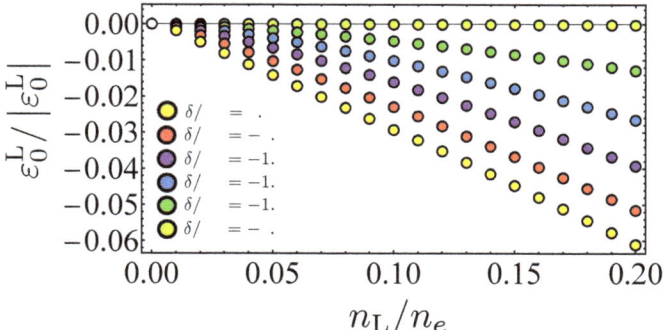

Figure 3. Energy shift of the L polaron-polariton branch as a function of their concentration for representative values of the cavity detuning from $\delta/2\Omega = -3.0$ to 2.0. The color coding is indicated in the figure. We employ a finite but small temperature $\beta\varepsilon_F = 0.1$

The effective interaction between polaron-polaritons in branches σ and σ' with momenta $\mathbf{k}$ and $\mathbf{k}'$ can now be obtained by inserting Equation (19) in Equation (10). Equation (19) is illustrated diagrammatically in Figure 4, which shows that it corresponds to an induced interaction between two polaron-polaritons mediated by particle-hole excitations of the electron gas. Indeed, when the polaron-polariton energy is detuned far from the trion energy one can approximate the scattering matrices in Equation (19) by the constant $\mathcal{T} \simeq \mathcal{T}(\mathbf{0}, \xi_{\mathbf{k}\sigma})$, and the interaction becomes proportional to the 2D Lindhard function [69], which is characteristic of a particle-hole mediated interaction [71]. For stronger interactions between the excitons and the electrons, one must retain the full energy and momentum dependence of the scattering matrix in Equation (19).

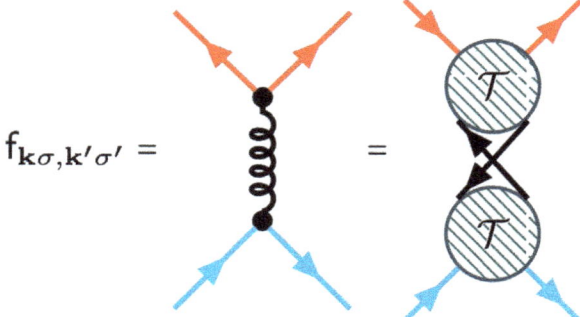

Figure 4. Feynman diagram of the interaction between quasiparticles σ (red lines) and σ' (cyan lines) mediated by the 2DEG. The wiggly line corresponds to the induced interaction which translates to a $\mathcal{T}$-matrix repeated scattering mediated by an electron-hole pair (black lines) in the 2DEG.

We now return to Figure 3 where the energy shift of the lowest polaritonic branch ($\sigma' = L$) is shown as a function of the same lowest polariton concentration ($\sigma = L$). We can understand it in terms of the effective interaction between the lowest polaron-polaritons. The interaction is attractive since the energy shift is negative, and it increases in strength with the detuning δ. The reason for this is two-fold. First, it is the excitonic component that interacts with the electrons and this component increases with the detuning for the lowest polaron-polariton. Second, the energy of the lowest polaron-polariton approaches the trion energy with increasing δ, which gives rise to strong resonant effects in the electron–exciton scattering. As a result, we see from Figure 3 that there can be a sizeable negative energy shift of the polaron-polariton due the attractive interaction mediated by particle-hole excitations in the 2DEG. So far, one has instead observed a temporary positive energy shift corresponding to a repulsive interaction, which has been attributed to a non-equilibrium phase filling effect [58]. It would thus be very interesting to investigate this further experimentally as the effective interaction between quasiparticles is a key component of Landau's quasiparticle theory and because it may give rise to strong non-linear optical effects [69,87].

5. Conclusions

We presented a theoretical framework for describing polaron-polaritons in 2D semiconductors inside optical microcavities. Microscopic expressions for the parameters entering a Landau quasiparticle theory were given, which provides a simple yet accurate way to describe this new system of interacting hybrid light–matter quasiparticles. Our framework is general apart from assuming that the concentration of the quasiparticles is much smaller than the surrounding electron gas and that equilibrium theory can be applied. To illustrate the results, the ladder approximation was then used to explore the system. We also proposed a new non-demolition scheme to probe the energy and residue of the polaron-polaritons via the Rabi splittings in the light transmission/reflection spectrum. Finally, we showed that the Landau effective interaction between the polaron-polaritons mediated by particle-hole excitations in the electron gas is attractive.

Our theoretical framework provides a systematic way to analyse current experiments exploring exciton-polaritons in monolayer TMDs [49,58]. It can moreover be extended to study a new class of exciton-polaritons in van der Waals heterostructures with interlayer Feshbach resonances [88,89], hybridised inter- and inter-layer excitons [90], dipolaritons [91], and spatially localised excitons [92,93]. The rich features predicted in these systems [94,95] open the door to using polaritons as quantum probes in strongly correlated electronic states [96] and to realising and controlling strongly interacting photons. An exciting development is to explore the regime of higher polaron-polariton concentrations, where many intriguing phases, such as a Bose–Einstein condensate of polaron-polaritons [37], superconductivity, and supersolidity [97] have been predicted.

Author Contributions: All authors contributed equally to the manuscript. All authors have read and agreed to the published version of the manuscript.

Funding: This work has been supported by the Danish National Research Foundation through the Center of Excellence "CCQ" (Grant agreement no.: DNRF156), and the Independent Research Fund Denmark-Natural Sciences (Grant No. DFF-8021-00233B).

Institutional Review Board Statement: Not applicable.

Informed Consent Statement: Not applicable.

Data Availability Statement: The data that support the findings of this study are available from the corresponding author upon reasonable request.

Conflicts of Interest: The authors declare no conflict of interest.The funders had no role in the design of the study; in the collection, analyses, or interpretation of data; in the writing of the manuscript, or in the decision to publish the results.

Abbreviations

The following abbreviations are used in this manuscript:

TMD   Transition Metal Dicalchogenid
2DEG   Two-Dimensional Electron Gas

Appendix A. Strong Coupling Polariton Interactions

We take the self-energy as calculated in Equation (18), but without considering the $\mathcal{T}$-matrix real pole,

$$\Sigma_{xx}(\mathbf{k},i\omega_\nu) = \int \frac{d^2\mathbf{q}}{(2\pi)^2} n_F(\xi_{e\mathbf{q}}) \mathcal{T}(\mathbf{k}+\mathbf{q},i\omega_\nu + \xi_{e\mathbf{q}}) \quad (A1)$$
$$+ \int \frac{d^2\mathbf{q}}{(2\pi)^2} \int_{-\infty}^{\infty} \frac{d\omega'}{\pi} \frac{n_F(\omega')\mathrm{Im}\mathcal{T}(\mathbf{k}+\mathbf{q},\omega'+i0^+)}{i\omega_\nu - \omega' + \xi_{e\mathbf{q}}},$$

Next, we employ the following relationships

$$\mathrm{Im}\mathcal{T} = \left[(\mathrm{Re}\mathcal{T})^2 + (\mathrm{Im}\mathcal{T})^2\right]\mathrm{Im}\Pi\left[(\mathcal{T}-i\mathrm{Im}\mathcal{T})^2 + (\mathrm{Im}\mathcal{T})^2\right]\mathrm{Im}\Pi = \quad (A2)$$
$$\left[\mathcal{T}^2 - 2i\mathcal{T}\mathrm{Im}\mathcal{T} - (\mathrm{Im}\mathcal{T})^2 + (\mathrm{Im}\mathcal{T})^2\right]\mathrm{Im}\Pi = \left[\mathcal{T}^2 - 2i\mathcal{T}\mathrm{Im}\mathcal{T}\right]\mathrm{Im}\Pi.$$

This becomes a series over the imaginary part of the pair propagator. We separate the principal and imaginary parts of the pair propagator in Equation (14) as

$$\Pi(\mathbf{q},\omega) = \sum_\sigma \int \frac{d^2\mathbf{p}}{(2\pi)^2} \mathcal{X}^2_{\sigma\mathbf{q}+\mathbf{p}}[1 - n_F(\xi_{e-\mathbf{p}}) + n_B(\xi_{\sigma\mathbf{q}+\mathbf{p}})] \times \quad (A3)$$
$$\left[\mathcal{P}\frac{1}{\omega - \xi_{e-\mathbf{p}} - \xi_{\sigma\mathbf{q}+\mathbf{p}}} - i\pi\delta(\omega - \xi_{e-\mathbf{p}} - \xi_{\sigma\mathbf{q}+\mathbf{p}})\right],$$

inserting it in Equation (A2), we obtain

$$\mathrm{Im}\mathcal{T}(\mathbf{q},\omega) = -\pi\left[\mathcal{T}^2 - 2i\mathcal{T}\mathrm{Im}\mathcal{T}\right] \times \quad (A4)$$
$$\sum_\sigma \int \frac{d^2\mathbf{p}}{(2\pi)^2} \mathcal{X}^2_{\sigma\mathbf{q}+\mathbf{p}}[1 - n_F(\xi_{e-\mathbf{p}}) + n_B(\xi_{\sigma\mathbf{q}+\mathbf{p}})]\delta(\omega - \xi_{e-\mathbf{p}} - \xi_{\sigma\mathbf{q}+\mathbf{p}}).$$

Substituting this result in the second term of Equation (A1) and using that $n_F(x+y)(1 - n_F(x) + n_B(y)) = n_F(x)n_B(y)$; therefore, the self-energy reads

$$\Sigma_{xx}(\mathbf{k},\omega) = \int \frac{d^2\mathbf{q}}{(2\pi)^2} \left\{ n_F(\xi_{e\mathbf{q}})\mathcal{T}(\mathbf{k}+\mathbf{q},\omega + \xi_{e\mathbf{q}}) \right. \quad (A5)$$
$$-\sum_\sigma \int \frac{d^2\mathbf{p}}{(2\pi)^2} \frac{\mathcal{X}^2_{\sigma\mathbf{k}+\mathbf{q}+\mathbf{p}} n_B(\xi_{\sigma\mathbf{k}+\mathbf{q}+\mathbf{p}}) n_F(\xi_{e-\mathbf{p}})}{\omega - \xi_{\sigma\mathbf{k}+\mathbf{q}+\mathbf{p}} + \xi_{e\mathbf{q}} - \xi_{e-\mathbf{p}} + i0^+} \times$$
$$\left[\mathcal{T}^2(\mathbf{k}+\mathbf{q},\xi_{e-\mathbf{p}} + \xi_{\sigma\mathbf{k}+\mathbf{q}+\mathbf{p}} + i0^+) - 2i\mathcal{T}(\mathbf{k}+\mathbf{q},\xi_{e-\mathbf{p}} + \xi_{\sigma\mathbf{k}+\mathbf{q}+\mathbf{p}} + i0^+)\mathrm{Im}\mathcal{T}(\mathbf{k}+\mathbf{q},\xi_{e-\mathbf{p}} + \xi_{\sigma\mathbf{k}+\mathbf{q}+\mathbf{p}} + i0^+)\right]\Big\}.$$

As explained in the main text, the quasiparticle interactions are given by the functional derivative of Equations (10) with respect to the quasiparticle distribution [61,70]

$$\frac{f_{\sigma\mathbf{k},\sigma'\mathbf{k}'}}{\mathcal{A}} = Z_{\sigma'\mathbf{k}'}\frac{\partial \xi_{\sigma\mathbf{k}}}{\partial n_{\sigma'\mathbf{k}'}} = Z_{\sigma'\mathbf{q}'}\mathcal{X}^2_{\sigma'\mathbf{k}'}\frac{\partial \Sigma(\mathbf{k},\xi_{\sigma\mathbf{k}})}{\partial n_{\sigma'\mathbf{k}'}}, \quad (A6)$$

this entails the calculation of the derivative of the second part of the self-energy

$$\frac{\delta}{\delta n_B(\xi_{\sigma'\mathbf{k}'})}\left[n_B(\xi_{\sigma\mathbf{k}})\left(\mathcal{T}^2(\mathbf{k},\omega) - 2i\mathcal{T}(\mathbf{k},\omega)\mathrm{Im}\mathcal{T}(\mathbf{k},\omega)\right)\right] = \quad (A7)$$
$$\frac{\delta n_B(\xi_{\sigma\mathbf{k}})}{\delta n_B(\xi_{\sigma'\mathbf{k}'})}\left\{\mathcal{T}^2(\mathbf{k},\omega) - 2i\mathcal{T}(\mathbf{k},\omega)\mathrm{Im}\mathcal{T}(\mathbf{k},\omega) + \right.$$
$$n_B(\xi_{\sigma\mathbf{k}})[2\mathcal{T}(\mathbf{k},\omega) - 2i\mathrm{Im}\mathcal{T}(\mathbf{k},\omega)]\frac{\partial \mathcal{T}(\mathbf{k},\omega)}{\delta n_B(\xi_{\sigma'\mathbf{k}'})} - n_B(\xi_{\sigma\mathbf{k}})\mathcal{T}(\mathbf{k},\omega)\left(\frac{\partial \mathcal{T}(\mathbf{k},\omega)}{\delta n_B(\xi_{\sigma'\mathbf{k}'})} - \frac{\partial \mathcal{T}^*(\mathbf{k},\omega)}{\delta n_B(\xi_{\sigma'\mathbf{k}'})}\right)\Big\}.$$

The functional derivative of the $\mathcal{T}$-matrix is given by

$$\frac{\delta}{\delta n_B(\xi_{\sigma'\mathbf{k}'})}\mathcal{T}(\mathbf{k},\omega) = \frac{\mathcal{T}_0^2}{[1-\mathcal{T}_0\Pi(\mathbf{k},\omega)]^2}\frac{\delta\Pi(\mathbf{k},\omega)}{\delta n_B(\xi_{\sigma'\mathbf{k}'})} = \quad (A8)$$

$$\mathcal{T}^2(\mathbf{k},\omega)\sum_\sigma \int \frac{d^2\mathbf{p}}{(2\pi)^2}\mathcal{X}^2_{\sigma\mathbf{k}+\mathbf{p}}\frac{1}{\omega-\xi_{e-\mathbf{p}}-\xi_{\sigma\mathbf{k}+\mathbf{p}}}\frac{\delta n_B(\xi_{\sigma\mathbf{k}+\mathbf{p}})}{\delta n_B(\xi_{\sigma'\mathbf{k}'})} =$$

$$= \mathcal{T}^2(\mathbf{k},\omega)\int \frac{d^2\mathbf{p}}{(2\pi)^2}\mathcal{X}^2_{\sigma\mathbf{k}+\mathbf{p}}\frac{\delta_{\sigma,\sigma'}\delta(\mathbf{k}'-(\mathbf{k}+\mathbf{p}))}{\omega-\xi_{e-\mathbf{p}}-\xi_{\sigma\mathbf{k}+\mathbf{p}}+i0^+} = \frac{\mathcal{X}^2_{\sigma'\mathbf{k}'}\mathcal{T}^2(\mathbf{k},\omega)}{\omega-\xi_{e\mathbf{k}-\mathbf{k}'}-\xi_{\sigma\mathbf{k}'}+i0^+}.$$

As the derivative is of the order $\mathcal{T}^2$, if we keep only terms associated to second-order diagrammatic contributions, we can approximate

$$\frac{\delta}{\delta n_B(\xi_{\sigma'\mathbf{k}'})}\left[n_B(\xi_{\sigma\mathbf{k}})\left(\mathcal{T}^2(\mathbf{k},\omega)-2i\mathcal{T}(\mathbf{k},\omega)\mathrm{Im}\mathcal{T}(\mathbf{k},\omega)\right)\right] \simeq \mathcal{T}^2(\mathbf{k},\omega)\delta(\mathbf{k}-\mathbf{k}')\delta_{\sigma,\sigma'}. \quad (A9)$$

In this way, after substituting the derivative of the $\mathcal{T}$-matrix into the derivative of the self-energy, the mediated potential on-shell, up to second order diagrams, reads

$$\frac{\partial\Sigma(\mathbf{k},\xi_{\sigma\mathbf{k}})}{\partial n_{\sigma'\mathbf{k}'}} = \mathcal{X}^2_{\sigma'\mathbf{k}'}\int \frac{d^2\mathbf{q}}{(2\pi)^2}\frac{1}{\xi_{\sigma\mathbf{k}}-\xi_{\sigma'\mathbf{k}'}+\xi_{e\mathbf{q}}-\xi_{e\mathbf{k}-\mathbf{k}'+\mathbf{q}}+i0^+}\times \quad (A10)$$

$$\left[n_F(\xi_{e\mathbf{q}})\mathcal{T}^2(\mathbf{k}'-\mathbf{q},\xi_{\sigma\mathbf{k}}+\xi_{e\mathbf{q}}+i0^+)-n_F(\xi_{e\mathbf{k}-\mathbf{k}'+\mathbf{q}})\mathcal{T}^2(\mathbf{k}'-\mathbf{q},\xi_{e\mathbf{k}-\mathbf{k}'+\mathbf{q}}+\xi_{\sigma'\mathbf{k}'}+i0^+)\right].$$

which is identical to Equation (19) from the main text.

References

1. Sanvitto, D.; Kéna-Cohen, S. The road towards polaritonic devices. *Nat. Mater.* **2016**, *15*, 1061–1073. [CrossRef] [PubMed]
2. Kavokin, A.V.; Baumberg, J.J.; Malpuech, G.; Laussy, F.P. *Microcavities*; Series on Semiconductor Science and Technology; Oxford University Press: New York, NY, USA, 2017.
3. Hopfield, J.J. Theory of the Contribution of Excitons to the Complex Dielectric Constant of Crystals. *Phys. Rev.* **1958**, *112*, 1555–1567. [CrossRef]
4. Weisbuch, C.; Nishioka, M.; Ishikawa, A.; Arakawa, Y. Observation of the coupled exciton-photon mode splitting in a semiconductor quantum microcavity. *Phys. Rev. Lett.* **1992**, *69*, 3314–3317. [CrossRef] [PubMed]
5. Laussy, F.P. Quantum Dynamics of Polariton Condensates. In *Exciton Polaritons in Microcavities. New Frontiers*; Sanvitto, D., Timofeev, V., Eds.; Springer Series in Solid-State Sciences; Springer: Berlin/Heidelberg, Germany, 2012; pp. 1–37.
6. Carusotto, I.; Ciuti, C. Quantum fluids of light. *Rev. Mod. Phys.* **2013**, *85*, 299–366. [CrossRef]
7. Kasprzak, J.; Richard, M.; Kundermann, S.; Baas, A.; Jeambrun, P.; Keeling, J.M.J.; Marchetti, F.M.; Szymańska, M.H.; André, R.; Staehli, J.L.; et al. Bose-Einstein condensation of exciton polaritons. *Nature* **2006**, *443*, 409–414. [CrossRef]
8. Balili, R.; Hartwell, V.; Snoke, D.; Pfeiffer, L.; West, K. Bose-Einstein Condensation of Microcavity Polaritons in a Trap. *Science* **2007**, *316*, 1007–1010. [CrossRef]
9. Amo, A.; Lefrère, J.; Pigeon, S.; Adrados, C.; Ciuti, C.; Carusotto, I.; Houdré, R.; Giacobino, E.; Bramati, A. Superfluidity of polaritons in semiconductor microcavities. *Nat. Phys.* **2009**, *5*, 805–810. [CrossRef]
10. Amo, A.; Sanvitto, D.; Laussy, F.P.; Ballarini, D.; Valle, E.d.; Martin, M.D.; Lemaître, A.; Bloch, J.; Krizhanovskii, D.N.; Skolnick, M.S.; et al. Collective fluid dynamics of a polariton condensate in a semiconductor microcavity. *Nature* **2009** *457*, 291–295. [CrossRef]
11. Kohnle, V.; Léger, Y.; Wouters, M.; Richard, M.; Portella-Oberli, M.T.; Deveaud-Plédran, B. From Single Particle to Superfluid Excitations in a Dissipative Polariton Gas. *Phys. Rev. Lett.* **2011**, *106*, 255302. [CrossRef]
12. Kohnle, V.; Léger, Y.; Wouters, M.; Richard, M.; Portella-Oberli, M.T.; Deveaud, B. Four-wave mixing excitations in a dissipative polariton quantum fluid. *Phys. Rev. B* **2012**, *86*, 064508. [CrossRef]
13. Lagoudakis, K.G.; Wouters, M.; Richard, M.; Baas, A.; Carusotto, I.; André, R.; Dang, L.S.; Deveaud-Plédran, B. Quantized vortices in an excitonâ??polariton condensate. *Nat. Phys.* **2008**, *4*, 706–710. [CrossRef]
14. Sanvitto, D.; Marchetti, F.M.; Szymańska, M.H.; Tosi, G.; Baudisch, M.; Laussy, F.P.; Krizhanovskii, D.N.; Skolnick, M.S.; Marrucci, L.; Lemaître, A.; et al. Persistent currents and quantized vortices in a polariton superfluid. *Nat. Phys.* **2010**, *6*, 527–533. [CrossRef]
15. Radisavljevic, B.; Radenovic, A.; Brivio, J.; Giacometti, V.; Kis, A. Single-layer MoS2 transistors. *Nat. Nanotechnol* **2011**, *6*, 147–150. [CrossRef]
16. Mak, K.F.; Shan, J. Photonics and optoelectronics of 2D semiconductor transition metal dichalcogenides. *Nat. Photonics* **2016**, *10*, 216–226. [CrossRef]

17. Wang, G.; Chernikov, A.; Glazov, M.M.; Heinz, T.F.; Marie, X.; Amand, T.; Urbaszek, B. Colloquium: Excitons in atomically thin transition metal dichalcogenides. *Rev. Mod. Phys.* **2018**, *90*, 021001. [CrossRef]
18. Bromley, R.A.; Murray, R.B.; Yoffe, A.D. The band structures of some transition metal dichalcogenides. III. Group VIA: Trigonal prism materials. *J. Phys. C Solid State Phys.* **1972**, *5*, 759–778. [CrossRef]
19. Mak, K.F.; Lee, C.; Hone, J.; Shan, J.; Heinz, T.F. Atomically Thin MoS_2: A New Direct-Gap Semiconductor. *Phys. Rev. Lett.* **2010**, *105*, 136805. [CrossRef]
20. Zhu, Z.Y.; Cheng, Y.C.; Schwingenschlögl, U. Giant spin-orbit-induced spin splitting in two-dimensional transition-metal dichalcogenide semiconductors. *Phys. Rev. B* **2011**, *84*, 153402. [CrossRef]
21. Novoselov, K.S.; Jiang, D.; Schedin, F.; Booth, T.J.; Khotkevich, V.V.; Morozov, S.V.; Geim, A.K. Two-dimensional atomic crystals. *Proc. Natl. Acad. Sci. USA* **2005**, *102*, 10451–10453. [CrossRef]
22. Splendiani, A.; Sun, L.; Zhang, Y.; Li, T.; Kim, J.; Chim, C.Y.; Galli, G.; Wang, F. Emerging Photoluminescence in Monolayer MoS2. *Nano Lett.* **2010**, *10*, 1271–1275. [CrossRef]
23. Ramasubramaniam, A. Large excitonic effects in monolayers of molybdenum and tungsten dichalcogenides. *Phys. Rev. B* **2012**, *86*, 115409. [CrossRef]
24. Xiao, D.; Liu, G.B.; Feng, W.; Xu, X.; Yao, W. Coupled Spin and Valley Physics in Monolayers of MoS_2 and Other Group-VI Dichalcogenides. *Phys. Rev. Lett.* **2012**, *108*, 196802. [CrossRef]
25. Echeverry, J.P.; Urbaszek, B.; Amand, T.; Marie, X.; Gerber, I.C. Splitting between bright and dark excitons in transition metal dichalcogenide monolayers. *Phys. Rev. B* **2016**, *93*, 121107. [CrossRef]
26. Cao, T.; Wang, G.; Han, W.; Ye, H.; Zhu, C.; Shi, J.; Niu, Q.; Tan, P.; Wang, E.; Liu, B.; et al. Valley-selective circular dichroism of monolayer molybdenum disulphide. *Nat. Commun.* **2012**, *3*, 887. [CrossRef]
27. Yu, H.; Cui, X.; Xu, X.; Yao, W. Valley excitons in two-dimensional semiconductors. *Natl. Sci. Rev.* **2015**, *2*, 57–70. [CrossRef]
28. Dufferwiel, S.; Schwarz, S.; Withers, F.; Trichet, A.A.P.; Li, F.; Sich, M.; Del Pozo-Zamudio, O.; Clark, C.; Nalitov, A.; Solnyshkov, D.D.; et al. Excitonâ??polaritons in van der Waals heterostructures embedded in tunable microcavities. *Nat. Commun.* **2015**, *6*, 8579. [CrossRef]
29. Liu, X.; Galfsky, T.; Sun, Z.; Xia, F.; Lin, E.c.; Lee, Y.H.; Kéna-Cohen, S.; Menon, V.M. Strong light-matter coupling in two-dimensional atomic crystals. *Nat. Photonics* **2015**, *9*, 30–34. [CrossRef]
30. Xu, X.; Yao, W.; Xiao, D.; Heinz, T.F. Spin and pseudospins in layered transition metal dichalcogenides. *Nat. Phys.* **2014**, *10*, 343. [CrossRef]
31. Schaibley, J.R.; Yu, H.; Clark, G.; Rivera, P.; Ross, J.S.; Seyler, K.L.; Yao, W.; Xu, X. Valleytronics in 2D materials. *Nat. Rev. Mater.* **2016**, *1*, 16055. [CrossRef]
32. Chichibu, S.; Azuhata, T.; Sota, T.; Nakamura, S. Spontaneous emission of localized excitons in InGaN single and multiquantum well structures. *Appl. Phys. Lett.* **1996**, *69*, 4188–4190. [CrossRef]
33. Qiu, D.Y.; da Jornada, F.H.; Louie, S.G. Optical Spectrum of MoS_2: Many-Body Effects and Diversity of Exciton States. *Phys. Rev. Lett.* **2013**, *111*, 216805. [CrossRef] [PubMed]
34. He, K.; Kumar, N.; Zhao, L.; Wang, Z.; Mak, K.F.; Zhao, H.; Shan, J. Tightly Bound Excitons in Monolayer WSe_2. *Phys. Rev. Lett.* **2014**, *113*, 026803. [CrossRef] [PubMed]
35. Mak, K.F.; He, K.; Lee, C.; Lee, G.H.; Hone, J.; Heinz, T.F.; Shan, J. Tightly bound trions in monolayer MoS2. *Nat. Mater.* **2012**, *12*, 207. [CrossRef] [PubMed]
36. Emmanuele, R.P.A.; Sich, M.; Kyriienko, O.; Shahnazaryan, V.; Withers, F.; Catanzaro, A.; Walker, P.M.; Benimetskiy, F.A.; Skolnick, M.S.; Tartakovskii, A.I.; et al. Highly nonlinear trion-polaritons in a monolayer semiconductor. *Nat. Commun.* **2020**, *11*, 3589. [CrossRef]
37. Julku, A.; Bastarrachea-Magnani, M.A.; Camacho-Guardian, A.; Bruun, G.M. Bose-Einstein condensation of exciton polaron-polaritons. *arXiv* **2021**, arXiv:2103.16313.
38. Suris, R.; Kochereshko, V.; Astakhov, G.; Yakovlev, D.; Ossau, W.; Nürnberger, J.; Faschinger, W.; Landwehr, G.; Wojtowicz, T.; Karczewski, G.; et al. Excitons and Trions Modified by Interaction with a Two-Dimensional Electron Gas. *Phys. Status Solidi* **2001**, *227*, 343–352. [CrossRef]
39. Suris, R.A. Correlation Between Trion and Hole in Fermi Distribution in Process of Trion Photo-Excitation in Doped QWs. In *Optical Properties of 2D Systems with Interacting Electrons*; Ossau, W.J., Suris, R., Eds.; Springer: Dordrecht, The Netherlands, 2003; pp. 111–124.
40. Rapaport, R.; Cohen, E.; Ron, A.; Linder, E.; Pfeiffer, L.N. Negatively charged polaritons in a semiconductor microcavity. *Phys. Rev. B* **2001**, *63*, 235310. [CrossRef]
41. Qarry, A.; Rapaport, R.; Ramon, G.; Cohen, E.; Ron, A.; Pfeiffer, L.N. Polaritons in microcavities containing a two-dimensional electron gas. *Semicond. Sci. Technol.* **2003**, *18*, S331–S338. [CrossRef]
42. Bajoni, D.; Perrin, M.; Senellart, P.; Lemaître, A.; Sermage, B.; Bloch, J. Dynamics of microcavity polaritons in the presence of an electron gas. *Phys. Rev. B* **2006**, *73*, 205344. [CrossRef]
43. Pimenov, D.; von Delft, J.; Glazman, L.; Goldstein, M. Fermi-edge exciton-polaritons in doped semiconductor microcavities with finite hole mass. *Phys. Rev. B* **2017**, *96*, 155310. [CrossRef]
44. Efimkin, D.K.; MacDonald, A.H. Exciton-polarons in doped semiconductors in a strong magnetic field. *Phys. Rev. B* **2018**, *97*, 235432. [CrossRef]

45. Glazov, M.M. Optical properties of charged excitons in two-dimensional semiconductors. *J. Chem. Phys.* **2020**, *153*, 034703. [CrossRef]
46. Kyriienko, O.; Krizhanovskii, D.N.; Shelykh, I.A. Nonlinear Quantum Optics with Trion Polaritons in 2D Monolayers: Conventional and Unconventional Photon Blockade. *Phys. Rev. Lett.* **2020**, *125*, 197402. [CrossRef]
47. Rana, F.; Koksal, O.; Manolatou. C. Many-body theory of the optical conductivity of excitons and trions in two-dimensional materials. *Phys. Rev. B* **2020**, *102*, 085304. [CrossRef]
48. Efimkin, D.K.; Laird, E.K.; Levinsen, J.; Parish, M.M.; MacDonald, A.H. Electron-Exciton Interactions in the Exciton-Polaron Problem. *Phys. Rev. B* **2021**, *103*, 075417. [CrossRef]
49. Sidler, M.; Back, P.; Cotlet, O.; Srivastava, A.; Fink, T.; Kroner, M.; Demler, E.; Imamoglu, A. Fermi polaron-polaritons in charge-tunable atomically thin semiconductors. *Nat. Phys.* **2016**, *13*, 255. [CrossRef]
50. Schirotzek, A.; Wu, C.H.; Sommer, A.; Zwierlein, M.W. Observation of Fermi Polarons in a Tunable Fermi Liquid of Ultracold Atoms. *Phys. Rev. Lett.* **2009**, *102*, 230402. [CrossRef]
51. Kohstall, C.; Zaccanti, M.; Jag, M.; Trenkwalder, A.; Massignan, P.; Bruun, G.M.; Schreck, F.; Grimm, R. Metastability and coherence of repulsive polarons in a strongly interacting Fermi mixture. *Nature* **2012**, *485*, 615–618. [CrossRef]
52. Koschorreck, M.; Pertot, D.; Vogt, E.; Fröhlich, B.; Feld, M.; Köhl, M. Attractive and repulsive Fermi polarons in two dimensions. *Nature* **2012**, *485*, 619–622. [CrossRef]
53. Cetina, M.; Jag, M.; Lous, R.S.; Walraven, J.T.M.; Grimm, R.; Christensen, R.S.; Bruun, G.M. Decoherence of Impurities in a Fermi Sea of Ultracold Atoms. *Phys. Rev. Lett.* **2015**, *115*, 135302. [CrossRef]
54. Cetina, M.; Jag, M.; Lous, R.S.; Fritsche, I.; Walraven, J.T.M.; Grimm, R.; Levinsen, J.; Parish, M.M.; Schmidt, R.; Knap, M.; et al. Ultrafast many-body interferometry of impurities coupled to a Fermi sea. *Science* **2016**, *354*, 96–99. [CrossRef] [PubMed]
55. Scazza, F.; Valtolina, G.; Massignan, P.; Recati, A.; Amico, A.; Burchianti, A.; Fort, C.; Inguscio, M.; Zaccanti, M.; Roati, G. Repulsive Fermi Polarons in a Resonant Mixture of Ultracold ^{6}Li Atoms. *Phys. Rev. Lett.* **2017**, *118*, 083602. [CrossRef] [PubMed]
56. Adlong, H.S.; Liu, W.E.; Scazza, F.; Zaccanti, M.; Oppong, N.D.; Fölling, S.; Parish, M.M.; Levinsen, J. Quasiparticle Lifetime of the Repulsive Fermi Polaron. *Phys. Rev. Lett.* **2020**, *125*, 133401. [CrossRef] [PubMed]
57. Fritsche, I.; Baroni, C.; Dobler, E.; Kirilov, E.; Huang, B.; Grimm, R.; Bruun, G.M.; Massignan, P. Stability and breakdown of Fermi polarons in a strongly interacting Fermi-Bose mixture. *Phys. Rev. A* **2021**, *103*, 053314. [CrossRef]
58. Tan, L.B.; Cotlet, O.; Bergschneider, A.; Schmidt, R.; Back, P.; Shimazaki, Y.; Kroner, M.; İmamoğlu, A.M.C. Interacting Polaron-Polaritons. *Phys. Rev. X* **2020**, *10*, 021011. [CrossRef]
59. Landau, L. The theory of a Fermi liquid. *J. Exp. Theor. Phys.* **1957**, *3*, 920–925.
60. Landau, L. Oscillations in a Fermi Liquid. *J. Exp. Theor. Phys.* **1957**, *5*, 101–108.
61. Baym, G.; Pethick, C. *Landau Fermi-Liquid Theory: Concepts and Applications*; Wiley-VCH: Mörlenbach, Germany 1991.
62. Shankar, R. Renormalization-group approach to interacting fermions. *Rev. Mod. Phys.* **1994**, *66*, 129–192. [CrossRef]
63. Ahn, S.; Sarma, S.D. Fragile Versus Stable Two-Dimensional Fermionic Quasiparticles. 2021. *Phys. Rev. B* **2021**, *104*, 125118. [CrossRef]
64. Zhu, B.; Chen, X.; Cui, X. Exciton Binding Energy of Monolayer WS2. *Sci. Rep.* **2015**, *5*, 9218. [CrossRef]
65. Massignan, P.; Zaccanti, M.; Bruun, G.M. Polarons, dressed molecules and itinerant ferromagnetism in ultracold Fermi gases. *Rep. Prog. Phys.* **2014**, *77*, 034401. [CrossRef]
66. Fetter, A.; Walecka, J. *Quantum Theory of Many-Particle Systems*; Dover Books on Physics Series; Dover Publications: New York, NY, USA, 1971.
67. Chevy, F. Universal phase diagram of a strongly interacting Fermi gas with unbalanced spin populations. *Phys. Rev. A* **2006**, *74*, 063628. [CrossRef]
68. Levinsen, J.; Parish, M.M. Strongly Interacting Two-Dimensional Fermi Gases. In *Annual Review of Cold Atoms and Molecules*; World Scientific: Singapore, 2015; Chapter 1; pp. 1–75. [CrossRef]
69. Bastarrachea-Magnani, M.A.; Camacho-Guardian, A.; Bruun, G.M. Attractive and Repulsive Exciton-Polariton Interactions Mediated by an Electron Gas. *Phys. Rev. Lett.* **2021**, *126*, 127405. [CrossRef]
70. Camacho-Guardian, A.; Bruun, G.M. Landau Effective Interaction between Quasiparticles in a Bose-Einstein Condensate. *Phys. Rev. X* **2018**, *8*, 031042. [CrossRef]
71. Giuliani, G.F.; Vignale, G. *Quantum Theory of the Electron Liquid*; Cambridge University Press: New York, NY, USA, 2005.
72. Lampert, M.A. Mobile and Immobile Effective-Mass-Particle Complexes in Nonmetallic Solids. *Phys. Rev. Lett.* **1958**, *1*, 450–453. [CrossRef]
73. Thilagam, A. Two-dimensional charged-exciton complexes. *Phys. Rev. B* **1997**, *55*, 7804–7808. [CrossRef]
74. Esser, A.; Zimmermann, R.; Runge, E. Theory of Trion Spectra in Semiconductor Nanostructures. *Phys. Status Solidi* **2001**, *227*, 317–330. [CrossRef]
75. Courtade, E.; Semina, M.; Manca, M.; Glazov, M.M.; Robert, C.; Cadiz, F.; Wang, G.; Taniguchi, T.; Watanabe, K.; Pierre, M.; et al. Charged excitons in monolayer WSe$_2$: Experiment and theory. *Phys. Rev. B* **2017**, *96*, 085302. [CrossRef]
76. Zhu, C.R.; Zhang, K.; Glazov, M.; Urbaszek, B.; Amand, T.; Ji, Z.W.; Liu, B.L.; Marie, X. Exciton valley dynamics probed by Kerr rotation in WSe$_2$ monolayers. *Phys. Rev. B* **2014**, *90*, 161302. [CrossRef]
77. Ganchev, B.; Drummond, N.; Aleiner, I.; Fal'ko, V. Three-Particle Complexes in Two-Dimensional Semiconductors. *Phys. Rev. Lett.* **2015**, *114*, 107401. [CrossRef]

78. Sie, E.J.; Lui, C.H.; Lee, Y.H.; Kong, J.; Gedik, N. Observation of Intervalley Biexcitonic Optical Stark Effect in Monolayer WS2. *Nano Lett.* **2016**, *16*, 7421–7426. [CrossRef]
79. Wouters, M. Resonant polariton-polariton scattering in semiconductor microcavities. *Phys. Rev. B* **2007**, *76*, 045319. [CrossRef]
80. Carusotto, I.; Volz, T.; Imamoğlu, A. Feshbach blockade: Single-photon nonlinear optics using resonantly enhanced cavity polariton scattering from biexciton states. *EPL Europhys. Lett.* **2010**, *90*, 37001. [CrossRef]
81. Bastarrachea-Magnani, M.A.; Camacho-Guardian, A.; Wouters, M.; Bruun, G.M. Strong interactions and biexcitons in a polariton mixture. *Phys. Rev. B* **2019**, *100*, 195301. [CrossRef]
82. Wang, G.; Marie, X.; Gerber, I.; Amand, T.; Lagarde, D.; Bouet, L.; Vidal, M.; Balocchi, A.; Urbaszek, B. Giant Enhancement of the Optical Second-Harmonic Emission of WSe$_2$ Monolayers by Laser Excitation at Exciton Resonances. *Phys. Rev. Lett.* **2015**, *114*, 097403. [CrossRef]
83. Schmidt, R.; Enss, T.; Pietilä, V.; Demler, E. Fermi polarons in two dimensions. *Phys. Rev. A* **2012**, *85*, 021602. [CrossRef]
84. Nascimbène, S.; Navon, N.; Jiang, K.J.; Tarruell, L.; Teichmann, M.; McKeever, J.; Chevy, F.; Salomon, C. Collective Oscillations of an Imbalanced Fermi Gas: Axial Compression Modes and Polaron Effective Mass. *Phys. Rev. Lett.* **2009**, *103*, 170402. [CrossRef]
85. Camacho-Guardian, A.; Nielsen, K.K.; Pohl, T.; Bruun, G.M. Polariton dynamics in strongly interacting quantum many-body systems. *Phys. Rev. Res.* **2020**, *2*, 023102. [CrossRef]
86. Efimkin, D.K.; MacDonald, A.H. Many-body theory of trion absorption features in two-dimensional semiconductors. *Phys. Rev. B* **2017**, *95*, 035417. [CrossRef]
87. Camacho-Guardian, A.; Bastarrachea-Magnani, M.A.; Bruun, G.M. Mediated Interactions and Photon Bound States in an Exciton-Polariton Mixture. *Phys. Rev. Lett.* **2021**, *126*, 017401. [CrossRef]
88. Schwartz, I.; Shimazaki, Y.; Kuhlenkamp, C.; Watanabe, K.; Taniguchi, T.; Kroner, M.; Imamoğlu, A. Observation of electrically tunable Feshbach resonances in twisted bilayer semiconductors. *arXiv* **2021**, arXiv:2105.03997.
89. Kuhlenkamp, C.; Knap, M.; Wagner, M.; Schmidt, R.; Imamoglu, A. Tunable Feshbach resonances and their spectral signatures in bilayer semiconductors. *arXiv* **2021**, arXiv:2105.01080.
90. Alexeev, E.M.; Ruiz-Tijerina, D.A.; Danovich, M.; Hamer, M.J.; Terry, D.J.; Nayak, P.K.; Ahn, S.; Pak, S.; Lee, J.; Sohn, J.I.; et al. Resonantly hybridized excitons in moirésuperlattices in van der Waals heterostructures. *Nature* **2019**, *567*, 81–86. [CrossRef] [PubMed]
91. Togan, E.; Lim, H.T.; Faelt, S.; Wegscheider, W.; Imamoglu, A. Enhanced Interactions between Dipolar Polaritons. *Phys. Rev. Lett.* **2018**, *121*, 227402. [CrossRef]
92. Zhang, L.; Wu, F.; Hou, S.; Zhang, Z.; Chou, Y.H.; Watanabe, K.; Taniguchi, T.; Forrest, S.R.; Deng, H. Van der Waals heterostructure polaritons with moiré-induced nonlinearity. *Nature* **2021**, *591*, 61–65. [CrossRef]
93. Camacho-Guardian, A.; Cooper, N.R. Moiré-induced optical non-linearities: Single and multi-photon resonances. *arXiv* **2021**, arXiv:2108.06177.
94. Shimazaki, Y.; Schwartz, I.; Watanabe, K.; Taniguchi, T.; Kroner, M.; Imamoğlu, A. Strongly correlated electrons and hybrid excitons in a moiréheterostructure. *Nature* **2020**, *580*, 472–477. [CrossRef]
95. Kennes, D.M.; Claassen, M.; Xian, L.; Georges, A.; Millis, A.J.; Hone, J.; Dean, C.R.; Basov, D.N.; Pasupathy, A.N.; Rubio, A. Moiréheterostructures as a condensed-matter quantum simulator. *Nat. Phys.* **2021**, *17*, 155–163. [CrossRef]
96. Shimazaki, Y.; Kuhlenkamp, C.; Schwartz, I.; Smoleński, T.; Watanabe, K.; Taniguchi, T.; Kroner, M.; Schmidt, R.; Knap, M.; Imamoğlu, A.M.C. Optical Signatures of Periodic Charge Distribution in a Mott-like Correlated Insulator State. *Phys. Rev. X* **2021**, *11*, 021027. [CrossRef]
97. Cotleţ, O.; Zeytinoğlu, S.; Sigrist, M.; Demler, E.; Imamoğlu, A.M.C. Superconductivity and other collective phenomena in a hybrid Bose-Fermi mixture formed by a polariton condensate and an electron system in two dimensions. *Phys. Rev. B* **2016**, *93*, 054510. [CrossRef]

Article

Emergence of Anyons on the Two-Sphere in Molecular Impurities

Morris Brooks [1,*], **Mikhail Lemeshko** [1], **Douglas Lundholm** [2] **and Enderalp Yakaboylu** [1,3,*]

[1] IST Austria (Institute of Science and Technology Austria), Am Campus 1, 3400 Klosterneuburg, Austria; mikhail.lemeshko@ist.ac.at
[2] Department of Mathematics, Uppsala University, P.O. Box 480, SE-751 06 Uppsala, Sweden; douglas.lundholm@math.uu.se
[3] Max Planck Institute of Quantum Optics, 85748 Garching, Germany
* Correspondence: morris.brooks@ist.ac.at (M.B.); enderalp.yakaboylu@ist.ac.at (E.Y.)

Abstract: Recently it was shown that anyons on the two-sphere naturally arise from a system of molecular impurities exchanging angular momentum with a many-particle bath (Phys. Rev. Lett. 126, 015301 (2021)). Here we further advance this approach and rigorously demonstrate that in the experimentally realized regime the lowest spectrum of two linear molecules immersed in superfluid helium corresponds to the spectrum of two anyons on the sphere. We develop the formalism within the framework of the recently experimentally observed angulon quasiparticle.

Keywords: anyons; quasiparticles; Quantum Hall Effect; topological states of matter

1. Introduction

The discovery of the fractional Quantum Hall Effect and the advent and application of topological quantum field theories have revolutionized our understanding of the quantum properties of matter [1–8]. Among the prospective applications, the notion of topological quantum computation has recently emerged as one of the most exciting approaches for constructing a fault-tolerant quantum computer by seeking to exploit the emergent properties of many-particle systems to encode and manipulate quantum information in a manner which is resistant to error [9–12]. One simple such proposal for topological quantum computing and information storage relies on the existence of topological states of matter whose quasiparticle excitations are anyons.

An anyon is a type of quasiparticle that can arise in systems confined to two dimensions and whose exchange properties interpolate between bosons and fermions [13–15]. Because of the topological peculiarities of two spatial dimensions, the world lines of anyons can braid nontrivially around each other [13,16,17], and therefore, unlike fermions or bosons, exchanging two anyons twice is not topologically equivalent to leaving them alone. This opens up a whole new domain of quantum statistics known as intermediate or fractional statistics. Even though the realization of anyons in experimentally feasible systems has been subject of recent research [18–25], all these works concern particles moving on the Euclidean plane $\mathbb{R}^2$, or a subset thereof. However, since the statistical behaviour of anyons depends on the topology, and even more importantly on the geometry and symmetry, of the underlying space, investigations on curved spaces can demonstrate novel properties of quantum statistics [2,26–32] (see also graph geometries [33,34]). Indeed it has been recently demonstrated that the emerging fractional statistics for particles restricted to move on the sphere, instead of on the plane, arises naturally in the context of quantum impurity problems, particularly, in the context of molecular impurities [35]. There, it has been shown that the emerging statistical interaction manifests itself in the alignment of molecules, which could also be of use as a powerful technique to measure the statistics parameter. This paves the way towards experimental realization as well as detection of anyons on the sphere using molecular impurities.

In the present manuscript, we explicitly show how the angulon Hamiltonian [36–38] gives rise to a system of two interacting anyons on the two-sphere $\mathbb{S}^2$. The angulon represents a quantum impurity exchanging orbital angular momentum with a many-particle bath, and serves as a reliable model for the rotation of molecules in superfluids [39–42]. In particular, we demonstrate that, under appropriate time-reversal symmetry breaking conditions, restricting the angulon Hamiltonian to states in the first Born–Oppenheimer approximation gives rise to the anyon Hamiltonian. Time-reversal symmetry is broken by using an additional external magnetic field and applying rotation, while the Born–Oppenheimer approximation is satisfied by considering heavy molecules. We further discuss and supply some technical details of the argument that had been left out in [35]. Note that the phenomenon of quantum statistics transmutation typically involves emergent scalar interaction potentials and non-statistical gauge fields as well, and it is necessary to have sufficient control of these effects in order to provide robust signatures of anyons.

2. Anyon Hamiltonian

Anyons are identical particles described by wave functions Ψ which acquire a phase factor $e^{i\alpha\pi}$, respectively $e^{-i\alpha\pi}$, under permutation of two sets of coordinates. In contrast to fermions and bosons, we do not assume that the statistics parameter α is an integer. Namely, it could be any real number, say between 0 and 1, or between -1 and 0, i.e., a fraction of an integer (thereby 'fractional statistics'). Consequently, we have to distinguish between the continuous exchange processes where two particles make an elementary anti-clockwise braid around each other, in which case the wave function gains a factor $e^{i\alpha\pi}$, and processes where they braid clockwise around each other, in which case the wave function has to acquire the inverse factor $e^{-i\alpha\pi}$. Here we however see a difference on the sphere compared to the plane, since e.g., the 2-particle braid group reduces from $\mathbb{Z}$ on the plane to $\mathbb{Z}_2$ on the sphere, due to a double exchange being topologically trivial. This also means that we cannot determine topologically which way the particles braided, and thus reduces the whole problem to the ordinary case of bosons or fermions, $\alpha \in \{0,1\}$. In fact, this conclusion is a manifestation of the symmetry of the full sphere, and indeed the existence of anyons necessarily requires the breaking of time-reversal or orientation symmetry (corresponding to the choice of sign of α and the handedness of braids in our braid group representation). A similar analysis for the N-particle case leads to the condition $(N-1)\alpha \in \mathbb{Z}$, analogous to the well-known Dirac quantization condition [26,28,30]. We can overcome this issue, by instead considering the punctured sphere $\mathbb{S}^2 \setminus \{\mathcal{N}\}$, where $\mathcal{N}$ denotes the north pole (and $\mathcal{S}$ will denote the south pole), i.e., we consider anyons which are no longer invariant under the action of $O(3)$ but only with respect to rotations in the polar angle. Clearly, $\mathbb{S}^2 \setminus \{\mathcal{N}\}$ is topologically equivalent to the plane. Nevertheless, the analysis of anyons living on the sphere (or a subset thereof) requires novel ideas and techniques. The first reason for this is that $\mathbb{S}^2 \setminus \{\mathcal{N}\}$ carries a non-flat geometry, i.e., the free dynamics of two anyons is given by the Hamiltonian

$$H_{\text{Anyon}}^{\text{sing}} := -\sum_{j=1}^{2} \nabla_j^2 := -\sum_{j=1}^{2} g_{ab} \nabla_j^a \nabla_j^b,$$

where g_{ab} is the metric tensor of the sphere, and we put suitable conditions at $\mathcal{N}$ and on the coincidence set for the particles (for simplicity, we may consider functions Ψ vanishing on the diagonal of the configuration space $(\mathbb{S}^2 \setminus \{\mathcal{N}\})^2$; cf. [43–45].) The second difference to the plane is that the natural orientation-preserving symmetry group of the full sphere is given by the three dimensional rotations $SO(3)$, while the symmetry group of the plane consists of a rotation around a single axis and translations in the plane. As one might expect, and we will see explicitly below, the symmetry group plays a crucial role in deriving the emergence of anyons from suitable impurity problems.

It will be convenient to represent the anyonic wave function as $\Psi = e^{i\alpha\phi}\psi$, where ψ is a bosonic wave function and ϕ is a fixed smooth multivalued function with the property $\phi(q_2, q_1) = \phi(q_1, q_2) \pm \pi$ under simple continuous exchange of the two coordinates $q_j \in \mathbb{S}^2$, in order that Ψ acquires a correct phase factor $e^{\pm i\alpha\pi}$. A concrete example of such a function ϕ is given in complex stereographic coordinates $z_1, z_2 \in \mathbb{C}$ by $\frac{1}{i}\log\left(\frac{z_1 - z_2}{|z_1 - z_2|}\right)$. Applying the unitary transformation $e^{i\alpha\phi}$ to the free anyon dynamics yields

$$H_{\text{Anyon}} := e^{-i\alpha\phi} H_{\text{Anyon}}^{\text{sing}} e^{i\alpha\phi} = -\sum_{j=1}^{2}(\nabla_j + i\alpha\nabla_j\phi)^2 = -\sum_{j=1}^{2}(\nabla_j + iA_j)^2, \quad (1)$$

with the anyon statistics gauge field A_j given by $A_j := \alpha\nabla_j\phi$. Note that H_{Anyon}, which is unitarily equivalent to the free anyon dynamics (although by a *singular* gauge transformation, thereby changing the reference geometry) has the advantage of acting on bosonic (single-valued) wave functions ψ.

3. Emerging Gauge Field from the Angulon Hamiltonian

The angulon Hamiltonian for two rotors/impurities is defined by

$$H_{\text{angulon}} := -\sum_{j=1}^{2}\nabla_j^2 + \sum_{l,m}\omega_l\, b_{l,m}^\dagger b_{l,m} + b_{Z(q_1,q_2)}^\dagger + b_{Z(q_1,q_2)}, \quad (2)$$

where $-\nabla_j^2 = \mathbf{L}_j^2 = L_{jx}^2 + L_{jy}^2 + L_{jz}^2$ is the rotor Hamiltonian, $q_j \in \mathbb{S}^2$ is the position of the j-th impurity on the sphere, $b_{l,m}$ are collective rotation modes of the bath, and $b_{Z(q_1,q_2)}^{(\dagger)} = \sum_{l,m} Z_{l,m}(q_1, q_2)^{(*)} b_{l,m}^{(\dagger)}$ defines the coupling between these systems at the Fröhlich level [36–38]. Note that this Hamiltonian is typically fully invariant under the action of $O(3)$, so that we cannot expect any non-trivial anyons to emerge.

Instead, in the following, we aim to derive the statistics gauge field A_j as emergent from the following *modified* angulon Hamiltonian:

$$H'_{\text{angulon},\Omega} := H_{\text{angulon}} + \Omega^2 V(q_1, q_2) + \Omega \sum_{l,m_1,m_2}(\Lambda_{\bar{q}})_{l,m_1,m_2} b_{l,m_1}^\dagger b_{l,m_2}, \quad (3)$$

where $\bar{q} := (q_1 + q_2)/|q_1 + q_2|$ is the normalized center of mass of the two impurities,

$$(\Lambda_{\bar{q}})_{l,m_1,m_2} := \sum_m m\, \overline{D_{m,m_2}^l(\alpha, \beta, \gamma)} D_{m,m_1}^l(\alpha, \beta, \gamma)$$

is the momentum operator aligned in the direction of $-\bar{q}$ which we define with the help of the Wigner matrix $D_{m,m_2}^l(\alpha, \beta, \gamma)$ where α, β, γ are the Euler angles of a rotation $R_{\alpha,\beta,\gamma}$ with the property $R_{\alpha,\beta,\gamma}(S) = \bar{q}$, V is an additional quadratic potential, and the parameter Ω, which will describe the strength of a simultaneous magnetic field and a rotation, is assumed to be large. With the convention above, the momentum operator Λ_z aligned with the z-axis reads $\Lambda_z = \Lambda_S$. Note that having the momentum operator $\Lambda_{\bar{q}}$ aligned in the direction $\bar{q}$ will simplify our computation significantly. In the next section we will discuss a model where we take the operator $\Lambda_z = \Lambda_S$ aligned with the z-axis as usual, and argue that as $\Omega \to \infty$ they describe the same limit within a certain setup. We will also discuss how one can realize the modified operator $H'_{\text{angulon},\Omega}$ by coupling H_{angulon} to an additional constant magnetic field. In this concrete realization of Equation (3) the scaling on V comes naturally.

We refer to Hamiltonian (3) as modified, since it has a dispersion relation $\sum_{l,m}\omega_l\, b_{l,m}^\dagger b_{l,m} + \Omega \sum_{l,m_1,m_2}(\Lambda_{\bar{q}})_{l,m_1,m_2} b_{l,m_1}^\dagger b_{l,m_2}$ which is not invariant under a change of orientation. Furthermore, the introduction of a suitably chosen potential V punctures the sphere and therefore breaks the $SO(3)$ invariance as well. Let us denote with θ_j the azimuthal angle of the impurity position q_j and with φ_j its polar angle w.r.t. the laboratory reference frame. The q_1, q_2-dependent coefficients of $Z(q_1, q_2)$ are then given by

$$Z_{l,m} := \sum_j c_l \, Y_{l,m}(\theta_j, \varphi_j),$$

where $Y_{l,m}$ are the spherical harmonics and c_l are real coefficients. We will occasionally suppress the q_1, q_2-dependency of $Z(q_1, q_2)$, and simply write Z. Note that we may instead of Equation (3) consider a symmetry-breaking interaction such as $\tilde{Z} := (1 + \Omega \Lambda_{\hat{q}} \omega^{-1})^{-1} Z(q_1, q_2)$ leading to the emergence of anyons with the same statistical gauge field. As stated, however, we here aim for a simplest possible realization of anyons, as a first step.

The full Hamiltonian (3) acts on an appropriate dense domain in the tensor product Hilbert space of the impurities $L^2_{\text{sym/asym}}(\mathbb{S}^2 \times \mathbb{S}^2)$, where $L^2_{\text{sym}}(\mathbb{S}^2 \times \mathbb{S}^2)$ is the bosonic Hilbert space and $L^2_{\text{asym}}(\mathbb{S}^2 \times \mathbb{S}^2)$ the fermionic one, with the Fock space $\mathcal{F}(L^2(\mathbb{S}^2))$ of the bath. Following the analysis for impurity problems in the planar case [25], the statistics gauge field emerges from $H'_{\text{angulon},\Omega}$, by restricting it to the ground state of its pure many-body part $\sum_{l,m} \omega_l \, b^\dagger_{l,m} b_{l,m} + \Omega \sum_{l,m_1,m_2} (\Lambda_{\hat{q}})_{l,m_1,m_2} b^\dagger_{l,m_1} b_{l,m_2} + b^\dagger_{Z(q_1,q_2)} + b_{Z(q_1,q_2)}$ which acts only on the Fock space $\mathcal{F}(L^2(\mathbb{S}^2))$ of the bath. Namely, with the help of a coherent state transformation, we can write the ground state as (we use the notation $b_x = \sum_{l,m} x_{lm} b_{lm}$ and : for action or composition)

$$\Phi(q_1, q_2) := \exp\left[b_{(\omega + \Omega \Lambda_{\hat{q}})^{-1} Z(q_1,q_2)} - b^\dagger_{(\omega + \Omega \Lambda_{\hat{q}})^{-1} Z(q_1,q_2)}\right] \cdot |0\rangle. \qquad (4)$$

Explicitly, by completing the square,

$$b^\dagger \cdot (\omega + \Omega \Lambda_{\hat{q}}) \cdot b + b^\dagger_Z + b_Z = (b + \xi)^\dagger \cdot (\omega + \Omega \Lambda_{\hat{q}}) \cdot (b + \xi) - c,$$

with $\xi := (\omega + \Omega \Lambda_{\hat{q}})^{-1} Z$ and $c := \xi^\dagger (\omega + \Omega \Lambda_{\hat{q}}) \xi$. We see that the non-symmetric dispersion relation $\omega + \Omega \Lambda_{\hat{q}}$ leads to a breaking of symmetry in the vacuum section $\Phi(q_1, q_2)$, since the coefficients $(\omega + \Omega \Lambda_{\hat{q}})^{-1} \cdot Z(q_1, q_2)$ are no longer invariant under the action of $O(3)$.

In the following, we consider a gapped dispersion $\omega_l \to \infty$ and heavy impurities such that the ground state decouples from the rest of the Hamiltonian. In this regime, the low energy spectrum of Hamiltonian (3) can be described by the first Born–Oppenheimer approximation

$$\langle \psi | H_{\text{Emerg}} | \psi \rangle := \langle \psi \Phi | H'_{\text{angulon},\Omega} | \psi \Phi \rangle,$$

where $\psi(q_1, q_2)$ is an impurity wave function (bosonic or fermionic). By applying the coherent state transformation $S_0 := \exp\left[b_{(\omega + \Omega \Lambda_{\hat{q}})^{-1} Z(q_1,q_2)} - b^\dagger_{(\omega + \Omega \Lambda_{\hat{q}})^{-1} Z(q_1,q_2)}\right]$ as above, we see that, formally,

$$H_{\text{Emerg}} = \langle 0 | - \sum_j (\nabla_j + S_0^{-1}(\nabla_j S_0))^2 | 0 \rangle + \Omega^2 V - Z^\dagger (\omega + \Omega \Lambda_{\hat{q}})^{-1} Z.$$

The issue with this representation is that we do not have a nice expression for the quantity $S_0^{-1} \nabla_j S_0$. This is due to the fact that the following family of operators is non-commuting:

$$\{b_{(\omega + \Omega \Lambda_{\hat{q}})^{-1} Z(q_1,q_2)} - b^\dagger_{(\omega + \Omega \Lambda_{\hat{q}})^{-1} Z(q_1,q_2)} : q_1, q_2 \in \mathbb{S}^2\},$$

and therefore we cannot apply the usual chain rule $\nabla_j \exp[F] = \nabla_j F \exp[F]$. In order to arrive at an explicit expression, we will apply two unitary transformations, which should map the non-commuting family to a commuting one. Note that this transformation has to be

q_1, q_2-dependent, since a single fixed unitary transformation always maps non-commuting families to non-commuting ones.

We first need to transform the whole system to a fixed reference point, such that $\bar{q} \mapsto \bar{q}' = S$, i.e., such that the middlepoint $\bar{q}$ between q_1 and q_2 stays fixed at the south pole S. For an arbitrary position $q \neq \mathcal{N}$ which is not the north pole, let $T \in SO(3)$ be a rotation which maps q into the south pole, i.e., $T(q) = S$. Clearly there are many rotations which satisfy $T(q) = S$. Therefore, we demand further that T leaves the axis $S \times q$ invariant for $q \neq S$ and define T to be the identity if $q = S$. The conditions $T(q) = S$ and $T(S \times q) = S \times q$ uniquely determine the map T. Since T is q-dependent, we will write $T_q = T$. In the following, we will always use the center of mass $\bar{q}$ as the argument, i.e., we consider $T_{\bar{q}}$. In order to promote $T_{\bar{q}}$ to a transformation on the whole Hilbert space, note that we can write it as

$$T_{\bar{q}} = \exp\left[\begin{pmatrix} 0 & -z_{\bar{q}} & y_{\bar{q}} \\ z_{\bar{q}} & 0 & -x_{\bar{q}} \\ -y_{\bar{q}} & x_{\bar{q}} & 0 \end{pmatrix}\right],$$

with coefficients $(x_{\bar{q}}, y_{\bar{q}}, z_{\bar{q}}) := d(\bar{q}, S)(S \times \bar{q})/|S \times \bar{q}|$, where $d(\bar{q}, S)$ is the geodesic distance of $\bar{q}$ to the south pole S. Let us furthermore denote transformed points as $q' := T_{\bar{q}} \cdot q$. With this at hand, we can define the transformation of a Fock space valued state $\Psi(q_1, q_2)$ as

$$\hat{T}(\Psi)(q_1, q_2) := \exp\left[ib^\dagger \cdot (x_{\bar{q}}\Lambda_x + y_{\bar{q}}\Lambda_y + z_{\bar{q}}\Lambda_z) \cdot b\right] \cdot \Psi(q_1, q_2)$$

Recall that the transformation $T_{\bar{q}}$ only makes sense as long as $\bar{q} \neq \mathcal{N}$. Therefore, we only consider this transformation $\hat{T}$ for confined states Ψ, for example only for states which have a support contained in an open set $O \subset \overline{O} \subset \{q \in \mathbb{S}^2 : q_3 < 0\}$. Note that this is not necessarily a real restriction, since the modified operator $H'_{\text{angulon},\Omega}$ contains a confining potential V anyway, which we will assume to have its minimum close to S.

We can write the transformed Hamiltonian $\hat{T}^{-1} H'_{\text{angulon},\Omega} \hat{T}$ as

$$-\sum_j \left(\nabla_j + \hat{T}^{-1}(\nabla_j \hat{T})\right)^2 + \Omega^2 V(q_1, q_2) + b^\dagger \cdot (\omega + \Omega \Lambda_z) \cdot b + b^\dagger_{Z(q'_1, q'_2)} + b_{Z(q'_1, q'_2)}.$$

Note that after the transformation, the angular momentum operator Λ_z is aligned with respect to the z-axis instead of the direction $\bar{q}$. Let us denote with $\phi = \phi(q_1, q_2)$ the polar angle of q'_1, which is the position of the first impurity after the rotation T. Furthermore, let $R = R_\phi$ be a rotation around the z-axis by an amount of ϕ. Then, the polar angle of the transformed point $q''_1 := R^{-1}(q'_1)$ is zero, while the polar angle of $q''_2 := R^{-1}(q'_2)$ equals π. Both points q''_1, q''_2 have the same azimuthal angle θ. We promote $R = R_\phi$ to an operation on the whole Hilbert space by

$$\hat{R}(\Psi)(q_1, q_2) = \exp\left[i\phi\, b^\dagger \cdot \Lambda_z \cdot b\right] \cdot \Psi(q_1, q_2).$$

The transformed operator $\hat{R}^{-1} \hat{T}^{-1} H'_{\text{angulon},\Omega} \hat{T} \hat{R}$ then reads

$$-\sum_j \left(\nabla_j + \hat{R}^{-1}\hat{T}^{-1}(\nabla_j \hat{T})\hat{R} + i(\nabla\phi)\sum_{l,m} m\, b^\dagger_{l,m} b_{l,m}\right)^2 + \Omega^2 V(q_1, q_2) + b^\dagger \cdot (\omega + \Omega \Lambda_z) \cdot b$$
$$+ b^\dagger_{Z(q''_1, q''_2)} + b_{Z(q''_1, q''_2)},$$

In the final step, we diagonalize the pure many body part $b^\dagger \cdot (\omega + \Omega \Lambda_z) \cdot b + b^\dagger_{Z(q_1'',q_2'')} + b_{Z(q_1'',q_2'')}$, by applying the coherent state transformation

$$S := \exp\left[b_{(\omega+\Omega\Lambda_z)^{-1}Z(q_1'',q_2'')} - b^\dagger_{(\omega+\Omega\Lambda_z)^{-1}Z(q_1'',q_2'')}\right].$$

Since the coefficients at the transformed points $Z_{l,m}(q_1'',q_2'') = (1+(-1)^m)c_l Y_{l,m}(\theta,0)$ are all real valued and the expressions only dependent on θ, we know that the collection

$$\left\{b_{(\omega+\Omega\Lambda_z)^{-1}Z(q_1'',q_2'')} - b^\dagger_{(\omega+\Omega\Lambda_z)^{-1}Z(q_1'',q_2'')} : q_1, q_2 \in O\right\}$$

is a family of commuting operators. Consequently, we can finally apply the chain rule and compute $S^{-1}(\nabla_j S)$ quite explicitly as

$$S^{-1}(\nabla_j S) = b_{(\omega+\Omega\Lambda_z)^{-1}\nabla_j Z(q_1'',q_2'')} - b^\dagger_{(\omega+\Omega\Lambda_z)^{-1}\nabla_j Z(q_1'',q_2'')}.$$

We can express the transformed Hamiltonian $S^{-1}\hat{R}^{-1}\hat{T}^{-1}H'_{\text{angulon},\Omega}\hat{T}\hat{R}S$ as

$$-\sum_j \left(\nabla_j + i\alpha(\theta)(\nabla_j\phi) + Y_j + S^{-1}(\nabla_j S) - i(\nabla_j\phi)\left(b_W + b^\dagger_W\right) + i(\nabla_j\phi)\sum_{l,m} m\, b^\dagger_{l,m}b_{l,m}\right)^2$$
$$+ \Omega^2 V(q_1, q_2) - E_0 + b^\dagger \cdot (\omega + \Omega\Lambda_z) \cdot b,$$

with the abbreviations

$$W := \Lambda_z(\omega + \Omega\Lambda_z)^{-1}Z(q_1'',q_2''),$$
$$Y_j := S^{-1}\hat{R}^{-1}\hat{T}^{-1}(\nabla_j \hat{T})\hat{R}S,$$
$$E_0 := Z(q_1'',q_2'')^T(\omega+\Omega\Lambda_z)^{-1}Z(q_1'',q_2''),$$

and

$$\alpha(\theta) := Z(q_1'',q_2'')^T(\omega+\Omega\Lambda_z)^{-1}\Lambda_z(\omega+\Omega\Lambda_z)^{-1}Z(q_1'',q_2'').$$

Observe that the vacuum expectation of $i\nabla_j\phi(b_W + b^\dagger_W)$ and $i\nabla_j\phi\sum_{l,m} m\, b^\dagger_{l,m}b_{l,m}$ is zero. Therefore these terms will only contribute to the emergent scalar potential but not to the emergent gauge field. Let us recall the definition of the vacuum section Φ in Equation (4). With the help of the unitary maps T, R and S we can write $\Phi = \hat{T}\hat{R}S\,|0\rangle$ and consequently

$$H_{\text{Emerg}} := \langle\Phi|H'_{\text{angulon},\Omega}|\Phi\rangle = \langle 0|S^{-1}\hat{R}^{-1}\hat{T}^{-1}H'_{\text{angulon},\Omega}\hat{T}\hat{R}S|0\rangle$$
$$= -\langle 0|\sum_j\left(\nabla_j + i\alpha(\theta)(\nabla_j\phi) + Y_j + S^{-1}(\nabla_j S) - i(\nabla_j\phi)\left(b_W + b^\dagger_W\right)\right.$$
$$\left. + i(\nabla_j\phi)\sum_{l,m}m\, b^\dagger_{l,m}b_{l,m}\right)^2|0\rangle + \langle 0|\Omega^2 V - E_0 + b^\dagger \cdot (\omega+\Omega\Lambda_z)\cdot b|0\rangle.$$

The second expectation is simply $\langle 0|\Omega^2 V - E_0 + b^\dagger \cdot (\omega + \Omega\Lambda_z)\cdot b|0\rangle = \Omega^2 V - E_0$. In order to compute the first one, let us define the magnetic potential $A_j := \alpha(\theta)\nabla_j\phi$ and the gauge covariant derivative $\nabla_j^A := \nabla_j + iA_j$. Let us further abbreviate

$$U_j := (\omega+\Omega\Lambda_z)^{-1}\left[\nabla_j Z(q_1'',q_2'') - i\nabla_j\phi\Lambda_z Z(q_1'',q_2'')\right].$$

Then we can rewrite the first vacuum expectation as

$$\langle 0| - \sum_j \left(\nabla_j^A + Y_j + \left(b_{U_j} + b_{U_j}^\dagger \right) + i(\nabla_j \phi) \sum_{l,m} m\, b_{l,m}^\dagger b_{l,m} \right)^2 |0\rangle$$

$$= -\sum_j \left[\left(\nabla_j^A + \langle 0|Y_j|0\rangle \right)^2 - \langle 0|Y_j|0\rangle^2 + \langle 0| (Y_j + b_{U_j} + b_{U_j}^\dagger + i(\nabla_j \phi) \sum_{l,m} m\, b_{l,m}^\dagger b_{l,m})^2 |0\rangle \right].$$

Let us define the magnetic background potential $\tilde{A}_j := -i \langle 0|Y_j|0\rangle$ and the modified scalar potential

$$\tilde{V} := \Omega^2 V + \sum_j \langle 0|Y_j|0\rangle^2 - \sum_j \langle 0| (Y_j + b_{U_j} + b_{U_j}^\dagger + i(\nabla_j \phi) \sum_{l,m} m\, b_{l,m}^\dagger b_{l,m})^2 |0\rangle - E_0,$$

then we can compactly express the emergent Hamiltonian as

$$H_{\text{Emerg}} = -\sum_j \left(\nabla_j^A + i\tilde{A}_j \right)^2 + \tilde{V}.$$

In case of constant $\alpha(\theta) = \alpha$, the operator $-\sum_j (\nabla_j^A)^2$ corresponds to the anyon Hamiltonian (1) with statistics parameter α, i.e.,

$$H_{\text{Emerg}} = H_{\text{Anyon}} + \sum_j \left(\tilde{A}_j^2 - i(\nabla_j \cdot \tilde{A}_j) - 2i\tilde{A}_j \cdot \nabla_j^A \right) + \tilde{V}. \quad (5)$$

In reference [35], approximately constant α (depending on Ω) is indeed realized for a suitable, and experimentally feasible, choice of ω and c_l. Particularly, ω is chosen at the roton minimum of the dispersion relation of superfluid helium, which allows us to achieve a gapped dispersion, and the coupling c_l is described by the model interaction used in order to describe angulon instabilities and oscillations observed in the experiment. Therefore, the Hamiltonian $H'_{\text{angulon},\Omega}$ gives rise to a system of two anyons, coupled to an additional magnetic potential $\tilde{A}_j$ and an additional scalar potential $\tilde{V}$.

In the following let us verify that the magnetic potential $\tilde{A}_j$ is regular, which on a suitable scale means that curl $\tilde{A}_j$ can be treated as a background field and thus does not influence the statistics. First of all, we can write it as

$$\tilde{A}_j = -i \langle 0|S^\dagger \hat{R}^\dagger \hat{T}^{-1} \nabla_j(\hat{T}) \hat{R} S|0\rangle = -i \langle \Phi | \hat{T}^{-1} \nabla_j(\hat{T}) | \Phi \rangle.$$

where Φ is as usual the vacuum section. First we want to compute the Lie algebra element $T_{\bar{q}}^{-1} \nabla_j T_{\bar{q}}$. In order to verify that $T_{\bar{q}}$ is a matrix-valued C^∞ (smooth) function, so especially that its derivative exists and is a continuous function, recall the explicit representation

$$T_{\bar{q}} = \exp\left[\frac{d(\bar{q}, \mathcal{S})}{|\mathcal{S} \times \bar{q}|} \begin{pmatrix} 0 & -(\mathcal{S} \times \bar{q})_3 & (\mathcal{S} \times \bar{q})_2 \\ (\mathcal{S} \times \bar{q})_3 & 0 & -(\mathcal{S} \times \bar{q})_1 \\ -(\mathcal{S} \times \bar{q})_2 & (\mathcal{S} \times \bar{q})_1 & 0 \end{pmatrix} \right].$$

As long as $\mathcal{S} \times \bar{q} \neq 0$, i.e., as long as $\bar{q} \neq \mathcal{S}$ and $\bar{q} \neq \mathcal{N}$, $T_{\bar{q}}$ is clearly C^∞. Since we want to investigate the limit $q_1, q_2 \to \mathcal{S}$ anyway, we do not have to worry about the case $\bar{q} = \mathcal{N}$. Regarding the south pole itself, observe that the function $d(\bar{q}, \mathcal{S})/|\mathcal{S} \times \bar{q}|$ is C^∞, even for $\bar{q} = \mathcal{S}$. Consequently, we know that $T_{\bar{q}}^{-1}(\nabla_j T_{\bar{q}})$ exists and it is a smooth function as long as $\bar{q} \neq \mathcal{N}$. Note that $T_{\bar{q}}^{-1}(\nabla_j T_{\bar{q}})$ is an element of the Lie algebra of $SO(3)$, and therefore we can write it as

$$T_{\bar{q}}^{-1}(\nabla_j T_{\bar{q}}) = \begin{pmatrix} 0 & -\gamma(q_1, q_2) & \beta(q_1, q_2) \\ \gamma(q_1, q_2) & 0 & -\alpha(q_1, q_2) \\ -\beta(q_1, q_2) & \alpha(q_1, q_2) & 0 \end{pmatrix},$$

with continuous and real functions $\alpha(q_1, q_2), \beta(q_1, q_2)$ and $\gamma(q_1, q_2)$. Consequently, we can write the operator $\hat{T}^{-1}(\nabla_j \hat{T})$ as

$$\hat{T}^{-1}(\nabla_j \hat{T}) = b^\dagger \cdot (\alpha_j(q_1, q_2) i \Lambda_x + \beta_j(q_1, q_2) i \Lambda_y + \gamma_j(q_1, q_2) i \Lambda_z) \cdot b.$$

From the representation above we see that the additional magnetic field $\tilde{A}_j$ is regular and therefore does not contribute to the statistics, i.e., H_{Emerg} describes anyons subject to an additional magnetic gauge field $\tilde{A}_j(q_1, q_2)$ as well as an additional electric potential field $\tilde{V}(q_1, q_2)$. Let us now describe a set-up, where the additional magnetic background field $\tilde{A} = (\tilde{A}_1, \tilde{A}_2)$ can be neglected entirely, i.e., we look for reasonable conditions such that $\tilde{A} \xrightarrow[q_1, q_2 \to \mathcal{S}]{} 0$. Since T and Φ are compatible with rotations around the z axis, we know that $\tilde{A}(q_1 = \mathcal{S}, q_2 = \mathcal{S}) = 0$. It is therefore enough to verify that the vector field $\tilde{A}$ is continuous. By our representation of $\hat{T}^{-1}(\nabla_j \hat{T})$ above, the continuity of $\tilde{A}$ follows from the continuity of $\langle \Phi(q_1, q_2) | b^\dagger \cdot \Lambda_e \cdot b | \Phi(q_1, q_2) \rangle$, $e \in \mathbb{S}^2$, in q_1, q_2. A sufficient condition for $\langle \Phi(q_1, q_2) | b^\dagger \cdot \Lambda_e \cdot b | \Phi(q_1, q_2) \rangle$ being continuous would be the following growth condition on the coefficients: $|c_l| \leq \frac{C}{l}$ and $\omega_l \pm \Omega l \geq l^{1+\epsilon}$ with $\epsilon > 0$. While the former condition can be fulfilled with the model parameter describing the molecule-helium interaction, see reference [35], the latter condition can be satisfied by considering a strong magnetic field. Then, $\tilde{A} \xrightarrow[q_1, q_2 \to \mathcal{S}]{} 0$ vanishes for q_1, q_2 close to the south pole, in contrast to the singular gauge field $\nabla_j \phi$ which has a pole at $\mathcal{S}$.

With the convergence $\tilde{A} \xrightarrow[q_1, q_2 \to \mathcal{S}]{} 0$ at hand, we can verify that the coupling to the background field $\nabla_j^A \mapsto \nabla_j^A + i \tilde{A}_j$ can be neglected in the limit of large Ω. In order to do this, let us define the dilatation operator

$$D_\ell : \begin{cases} L^2(\ell \mathbb{S}^2) \otimes L^2(\ell \mathbb{S}^2) \to L^2(\mathbb{S}^2) \otimes L^2(\mathbb{S}^2), \\ \Psi \mapsto D_\ell(\Psi)(q_1, q_2) := \Psi(\ell q_1, \ell q_2). \end{cases}$$

Note that the statistics gauge field A transforms exactly like the derivative operator as $D_\ell^{-1} A D_\ell = \ell A$. Therefore, $D_\ell^{-1} \nabla_j^A D_\ell = \ell \nabla_j^A$ and $D_\ell^{-1} H_{\text{Anyon}} D_\ell = \ell^2 H_{\text{Anyon}}$. Transforming the emerging Hamiltonian yields

$$D_\ell^{-1}\left(\ell^{-2} H_{\text{Emerg}}\right) D_\ell = -\sum_j \left(\nabla_j^A + i \ell^{-1} \tilde{A}\left(\ell^{-1} q_1, \ell^{-1} q_2\right)\right)^2 + \ell^{-2} \tilde{V}(\ell^{-1} q_1, \ell^{-1} q_2).$$

Using the assumption that the confining potential V is quadratic, we see that the natural length scale of the confinement is given by the equation $\ell^{-4} \Omega^2$, i.e., $\ell := \sqrt{\Omega}$. In the next section we will see that a quadratic potential comes naturally, however different choices for V could yield other interesting limits. Since $\ell \to \infty$ in the limit of large Ω, we conclude $\tilde{A}(\ell^{-1} q_1, \ell^{-1} q_2) \to 0$. With the abbreviation $V_\Omega(q_1, q_2) := \frac{1}{\sqrt{\Omega}} \tilde{V}(\frac{q_1}{\sqrt{\Omega}}, \frac{q_2}{\sqrt{\Omega}})$ we then have the asymptotic result

$$D_{\sqrt{\Omega}}^{-1}\left(\frac{1}{\sqrt{\Omega}} H_{\text{Emerg}}\right) D_{\sqrt{\Omega}} \xrightarrow[\Omega \to \infty]{} \sqrt{\Omega} H_{\text{Anyon}} + V_\Omega.$$

Hence, in the limit of large Ω the emerging Hamiltonian corresponds to a system of two anyons living on a sphere of radius $\ell = \sqrt{\Omega}$, with no additional magnetic field but coupled only to an additional scalar potential V_Ω.

4. Realization of a Modified Quantum Dispersion Relation

We now come back to the standard angulon Hamiltonian (2), and modify it by coupling it to an external magnetic potential $A_j^\Omega := \Omega(-y_j, x_j, 0)$, i.e., we consider the operator

$$H_{\text{angulon},\Omega} := -\sum_j (\nabla_j - iA_j^\Omega)^2 + \sum_{l,m} \omega_l\, b_{l,m}^\dagger b_{l,m} + b_Z^\dagger + b_{\bar Z}. \tag{6}$$

Let $J_z = L_{z,1} + L_{z,2} + b^\dagger \cdot \Lambda_z \cdot b$ be the total angular momentum of the two particles together with the many body environment. By rotating the system in the $x - y$ plane at the cyclotron frequency Ω we obtain

$$\tilde H_{\text{angulon},\Omega} := e^{-it\Omega J_z}\left(H_{\text{angulon},\Omega} - i\partial_t\right)e^{it\Omega J_z} + i\partial_t$$

$$= -\sum_j \left(\left(\nabla_j - iA_j^\Omega\right)^2 + \Omega L_{z,j}\right) + b^\dagger \cdot (\omega + \Omega\Lambda_z) \cdot b - b_{\bar Z}^- + b_Z$$

$$= -\sum_j \nabla_j^2 + \Omega^2 \sum_j (x_j^2 + y_j^2) + b^\dagger \cdot (\omega + \Omega\Lambda_z) \cdot b + b_Z^\dagger + b_Z,$$

where we used $\Omega L_{z,j} = -iA_j^\Omega \cdot \nabla_j$. With the definition $V(q_1, q_2) := \sum_j (x_j^2 + y_j^2)$, we see that $\tilde H_{\text{angulon},\Omega}$ almost coincides with

$$H'_{\text{angulon},\Omega} = -\sum_j \nabla_j^2 + \Omega^2 V(q_1, q_2) + b^\dagger \cdot (\omega + \Omega\Lambda_{\bar q}) \cdot b + b_Z^\dagger + b_Z,$$

except that the angular momentum operator Λ_z in $\tilde H_{\text{angulon},\Omega}$ is aligned in the z direction, while for $H'_{\text{angulon},\Omega}$ the operator $\Lambda_{\bar q}$ is aligned in the center of mass direction $\bar q$.

In the previous section we have seen that the modified angulon Hamiltonian $H'_{\text{angulon},\Omega}$ gives rise to a system of two interacting anyons in the limit of large Ω. In the following, we want to argue why the same conclusion holds for the slightly different operator $\tilde H_{\text{angulon},\Omega}$, i.e., we are going to justify that anyons emerge in the low energy regime of $\tilde H_{\text{angulon},\Omega}$ as well. Let us define the Fock space valued function

$$\Psi := \exp\left[b_{(\omega+\Omega\Lambda_z)^{-1}Z} - b^\dagger_{(\omega+\Omega\Lambda_z)^{-1}Z}\right] \cdot |0\rangle,$$

which is the vacuum state of the many-body part of $\tilde H_{\text{angulon},\Omega}$, i.e., it is the ground state of

$$\mathbb{H}_\Omega := b^- \cdot (\omega + \Omega\Lambda_z) \cdot b + b_Z^\dagger + b_Z.$$

In order to observe the emergence of anyons, let us define the alternative section

$$\Phi := \exp\left[b_{(\omega+\Omega\Lambda_{\bar q})^{-1}Z} - b^\dagger_{(\omega+\Omega\Lambda_{\bar q})^{-1}Z}\right] \cdot |0\rangle,$$

which gives rise to the correct gauge field A_z. The issue is that Φ is no longer the vacuum section of $\mathbb{H}_\Omega$. However, if we can show that $E_\Phi := \langle\Phi|\mathbb{H}_\Omega|\Phi\rangle$ approximates the true ground state energy of $\mathbb{H}_\Omega$

$$\tilde E_0 := -Z^\dagger(\omega + \Omega\Lambda_z)^{-1} Z,$$

and if there is a spectral gap from a nondegenerate ground state, then we can argue that the states (considered as rays of the Hilbert space) are close.

Let us now verify that the energy deviation $\epsilon := E_\Phi - \tilde{E}_0$ is small in the limit of large Ω. First of all, we can express ϵ as

$$\epsilon = Z^\dagger \Big[(\omega + \Omega \Lambda_{\bar{q}})^{-1} \Omega(\Lambda_z - \Lambda_{\bar{q}})(\omega + \Omega \Lambda_{\bar{q}})^{-1} - (\omega + \Omega \Lambda_z)^{-1} \Omega(\Lambda_z - \Lambda_{\bar{q}})(\omega + \Omega \Lambda_{\bar{q}})^{-1}\Big] Z.$$

Let us make the reasonable assumption that $\omega + \Omega \Lambda_{\bar{q}}$ is non degenerate, i.e., for simplicity let us assume that $\omega_l \pm \Omega l \geq \delta \Omega(l+1)$ for some $0 < \delta < 1$. Furthermore, we assume that $|Z_{l,m}| \leq \frac{C}{l+1}$ for some C. We define the operator ν by $\nu_l := \sqrt{\delta(l+1)}$ in the diagonalizing basis of Λ_z. Since $\Lambda_{\bar{q}}$ is block-diagonal with respect to l, $\Lambda_{\bar{q}}$ commutes with ν and consequently we can rewrite the first part of the error $\epsilon = \epsilon_1 - \epsilon_2$ (the second part can be rewritten in the same way)

$$\epsilon_1 = (\nu^{-1}Z)^\dagger \Big[\Omega \nu^2 (\omega + \Omega \Lambda_{\bar{q}})^{-1} \Omega^{-1} \nu^{-1}(\Lambda_z - \Lambda_{\bar{q}}) \nu^{-1} (\omega + \Omega \Lambda_{\bar{q}})^{-1} \nu^2\Big] (\nu^{-1}Z).$$

Note that we have the bound on the operator norm $\|\Omega \nu^2 (\omega + \Omega \Lambda_{\bar{q}})^{-1}\| \leq 1$, as well as $\|\nu^{-1}(\Lambda_z - \Lambda_{\bar{q}})\nu^{-1}\| \leq \frac{2}{\delta}$ and $\|\chi^{<L} \nu^{-1}(\Lambda_z - \Lambda_{\bar{q}})\nu^{-1}\| \ll 1$ for $\bar{q} \to \mathcal{S}$, where we define $\chi_l^{<L} := 1$ for $l < L$ and $\chi_l^{<L} := 0$ otherwise. By our assumption $|Z_{l,m}| \leq \frac{C}{l}$, we know that $\|\nu^{-1}Z\|^2 =: \tilde{C} < \infty$, therefore we obtain $\|(1 - \chi_\ell^{<L})\nu^{-1}Z\| \xrightarrow[L\to\infty]{} 0$ and

$$\lim_{\bar{q}\to\mathcal{S}} \Omega \epsilon_1 \leq \lim_{\bar{q}\to\mathcal{S}} 2\left(\tilde{C}\|\chi^{<L}\nu^{-1}(\Lambda_z - \Lambda_{\bar{q}})\nu^{-1}\| + \frac{2}{\delta}\|(1-\chi_\ell^{<L})\nu^{-1}Z\|^2\right)$$

$$= \frac{4}{\delta}\|(1-\chi_\ell^{<L})\nu^{-1}Z\|^2 \xrightarrow[L\to\infty]{} 0.$$

Applying a similar argument for ϵ_2 yields the estimate for the total error $\epsilon \ll \frac{1}{\Omega}$. Note that the ground state energy itself satisfies $\tilde{E}_0 \approx \frac{1}{\Omega}$. Consequently, the error term ϵ is negligibly small even compared to the ground state energy $\tilde{E}_0$, i.e.,

$$\epsilon \ll \tilde{E}_0.$$

We conclude that $E_\Phi := \langle \Phi | \mathbb{H}_\Omega | \Phi \rangle$ approximates the ground state energy $\tilde{E}_0 = \langle \Psi | \mathbb{H}_\Omega | \Psi \rangle$ of $\mathbb{H}_\Omega$, and since $\mathbb{H}_\Omega$ has a uniform spectral gap this especially means that there exists $\theta_{\bar{q}} \in [-\pi, \pi)$ such that $\|\Phi - e^{i\theta_{\bar{q}}}\Psi\| \ll 1$. This justifies the usage of the section Φ instead of Ψ in the Born–Oppenheimer approximation.

Lastly, we stress that the Born–Oppenheimer approximation itself and the emergence of the exact anyonic spectrum, i.e., the spectrum of the Hamiltonian (1), was justified both analytically and numerically for simpler but highly representative models in [25,35].

5. Conclusions

In conclusion, we explicitly show that in the Born–Oppenheimer approximation the many-particle bath manifests itself as the statistics gauge field on the two-sphere with respect to the molecular impurities immersed into it.

The analysis of anyons on the sphere becomes much more difficult than the well-studied planar case, mainly because of non separation of center of mass from relative variables. This problem has also been stressed and tackled in recent studies of anyons on the two-sphere [30,31,35], which have been successful in computing the spectrum of two anyons subject to a homogeneous magnetic field (technically a monopole such that the Dirac quantization condition is satisfied). Our result in this work cannot be directly compared with the explicit spectrum for two anyons computed in [31,35] since it involves additional scalar interactions and a not completely homogeneous magnetic field, and, even more crucially, an effective trapping potential due to the specific rotation setup. Analytical and numerical analyses of the spectra in the present situation are subjects of future work.

We further demonstrate that a possible experimental realization is feasible within the framework of the angulon quasiparticle by applying an external magnetic field to the molecular impurities and rotating the impurity-bath system. This lays the foundations for realizing anyons on the two-sphere in terms of molecular impurities in superfluid helium. We finally note that although the dispersion relation of superfluid helium nanodroplets is continuous, the interaction between the molecule and the helium droplet is dominated at a finite excitation momentum, see reference [38]. This allows us to explore the problem with a gapped dispersion relation so that the Born–Oppenheimer approximation can be achieved by considering heavy impurities as discussed in reference [35].

Author Contributions: Writing, M.B. and M.L. and D.L. and E.Y.; funding acquisition, D.L. All authors have read and agreed to the published version of the manuscript.

Funding: This research was funded by Göran Gustafsson Foundation grant number 1804.

Institutional Review Board Statement: Not applicable.

Informed Consent Statement: Not applicable.

Data Availability Statement: Not applicable.

Acknowledgments: D. Lundholm acknowledges financial support from the Göran Gustafsson Foundation (grant no. 1804).

Conflicts of Interest: The authors declare no conflict of interest.

References

1. Tsui, D.C.; Stormer, H.L.; Gossard, A.C. Two-Dimensional Magnetotransport in the Extreme Quantum Limit. *Phys. Rev. Lett.* **1982**, *48*, 1559–1562. [CrossRef]
2. Laughlin, R.B. Anomalous Quantum Hall Effect: An Incompressible Quantum Fluid with Fractionally Charged Excitations. *Phys. Rev. Lett.* **1983**, *50*, 1395–1398. [CrossRef]
3. Arovas, D.; Schrieffer, J.R.; Wilczek, F. Fractional Statistics and the Quantum Hall Effect. *Phys. Rev. Lett.* **1984**, *53*, 722–723. [CrossRef]
4. Thouless, D.J.; Kohmoto, M.; Nightingale, M.P.; den Nijs, M. Quantized Hall Conductance in a Two-Dimensional Periodic Potential. *Phys. Rev. Lett.* **1982**, *49*, 405–408. [CrossRef]
5. Kane, C.L.; Mele, E.J. Z_2 topological order and the quantum spin Hall effect. *Phys. Rev. Lett.* **2005**, *95*, 146802. [CrossRef] [PubMed]
6. Fu, L.; Kane, C.L.; Mele, E.J. Topological Insulators in Three Dimensions. *Phys. Rev. Lett.* **2007**, *98*, 106803. [CrossRef]
7. Haldane, F.D.M. Model for a Quantum Hall Effect without Landau Levels: Condensed-Matter Realization of the "Parity Anomaly". *Phys. Rev. Lett.* **1988**, *61*, 2015–2018. [CrossRef]
8. Lundholm, D.; Rougerie, N. Emergence of Fractional Statistics for Tracer Particles in a Laughlin Liquid. *Phys. Rev. Lett.* **2016**, *116*, 170401. [CrossRef]
9. Kitaev, A. Fault-tolerant quantum computation by anyons. *Ann. Phys.* **2003**, *303*, 2–30. [CrossRef]
10. Lloyd, S. Quantum computation with abelian anyons. *Quantum Inf. Process.* **2002**, *1*, 13–18. [CrossRef]
11. Freedman, M.; Kitaev, A.; Larsen, M.; Wang, Z. Topological quantum computation. *Bull. Am. Math. Soc.* **2003**, *40*, 31–38. [CrossRef]
12. Nayak, C.; Simon, S.H.; Stern, A.; Freedman, M.; Das Sarma, S. Non-Abelian anyons and topological quantum computation. *Rev. Mod. Phys.* **2008**, *80*, 1083–1159. [CrossRef]
13. Leinaas, J.M.; Myrheim, J. On the theory of identical particles. *Il Nuovo Cimento B* **1977**, *37*, 1–23. [CrossRef]
14. Wilczek, F. Magnetic Flux, Angular Momentum, and Statistics. *Phys. Rev. Lett.* **1982**, *48*, 1144–1146. [CrossRef]
15. Wilczek, F. Quantum Mechanics of Fractional-Spin Particles. *Phys. Rev. Lett.* **1982**, *49*, 957–959. [CrossRef]
16. Goldin, G.A.; Menikoff, R.; Sharp, D.H. Representations of a local current algebra in nonsimply connected space and the Aharonov–Bohm effect. *J. Math. Phys.* **1981**, *22*, 1664–1668. [CrossRef]
17. Wu, Y.S. General Theory for Quantum Statistics in Two Dimensions. *Phys. Rev. Lett.* **1984**, *52*, 2103–2106. [CrossRef]
18. Cooper, N.R.; Simon, S.H. Signatures of Fractional Exclusion Statistics in the Spectroscopy of Quantum Hall Droplets. *Phys. Rev. Lett.* **2015**, *114*, 106802. [CrossRef]
19. Zhang, Y.; Sreejith, G.J.; Gemelke, N.D.; Jain, J.K. Fractional angular momentum in cold atom systems. *Phys. Rev. Lett.* **2014**, *113*, 160404. [CrossRef]
20. Zhang, Y.; Sreejith, G.J.; Jain, J.K. Creating and manipulating non-Abelian anyons in cold atom systems using auxiliary bosons. *Phys. Rev. B* **2015**, *92*, 075116. [CrossRef]
21. Morampudi, S.C.; Turner, A.M.; Pollmann, F.; Wilczek, F. Statistics of Fractionalized Excitations through Threshold Spectroscopy. *Phys. Rev. Lett.* **2017**, *118*, 227201. [CrossRef]

22. Umucalılar, R.O.; Macaluso, E.; Comparin, T.; Carusotto, I. Time-of-Flight Measurements as a Possible Method to Observe Anyonic Statistics. *Phys. Rev. Lett.* **2018**, *120*, 230403. [CrossRef] [PubMed]
23. Correggi, M.; Duboscq, R.; Lundholm, D.; Rougerie, N. Vortex patterns in the almost-bosonic anyon gas. *EPL* **2019**, *126*, 20005. [CrossRef]
24. Yakaboylu, E.; Lemeshko, M. Anyonic statistics of quantum impurities in two dimensions. *Phys. Rev. B* **2018**, *98*, 045402. [CrossRef]
25. Yakaboylu, E.; Ghazaryan, A.; Lundholm, D.; Rougerie, N.; Lemeshko, M.; Seiringer, R. Quantum impurity model for anyons. *Phys. Rev. B* **2020**, *102*, 144109. [CrossRef]
26. Thouless, D.J.; Wu, Y.S. Remarks on fractional statistics. *Phys. Rev. B* **1985**, *31*, 1191–1193. [CrossRef] [PubMed]
27. Einarsson, T. Fractional statistics on a torus. *Phys. Rev. Lett.* **1990**, *64*, 1995–1998. [CrossRef] [PubMed]
28. Comtet, A.; McCabe, J.; Ouvry, S. Some remarks on anyons on the two-sphere. *Phys. Rev. D* **1992**, *45*, 709–712. [CrossRef]
29. Einarsson, T. Fractional statistics on compact surfaces. *Mod. Phys. Lett. B* **1991**, *5*, 675–686. [CrossRef]
30. Ouvry, S.; Polychronakos, A.P. Anyons on the sphere: analytic states and spectrum. *Nucl. Phys. B* **2019**, *949*, 114797. [CrossRef]
31. Polychronakos, A.P.; Ouvry, S. Two anyons on the sphere: Nonlinear states and spectrum. *Nucl. Phys. B* **2020**, *951*, 114906. [CrossRef]
32. Haldane, F.D.M. Fractional Quantization of the Hall Effect: A Hierarchy of Incompressible Quantum Fluid States. *Phys. Rev. Lett.* **1983**, *51*, 605–608. [CrossRef]
33. Harrison, J.M.; Keating, J.P.; Robbins, J.M.; Sawicki, A. *n*-particle quantum statistics on graphs. *Comm. Math. Phys.* **2014**, *330*, 1293–1326. [CrossRef]
34. Maciazek, T.; Sawicki, A. Non-abelian Quantum Statistics on Graphs. *Commun. Math. Phys.* **2019**, *371*, 921–973. [CrossRef]
35. Brooks, M.; Lemeshko, M.; Lundholm, D.; Yakaboylu, E. Molecular Impurities as a Realization of Anyons on the Two-Sphere. *Phys. Rev. Lett.* **2021**, *126*, 015301. [CrossRef]
36. Schmidt, R.; Lemeshko, M. Rotation of Quantum Impurities in the Presence of a Many-Body Environment. *Phys. Rev. Lett.* **2015**, *114*, 203001. [CrossRef] [PubMed]
37. Schmidt, R.; Lemeshko, M. Deformation of a Quantum Many-Particle System by a Rotating Impurity. *Phys. Rev. X* **2016**, *6*, 011012. [CrossRef]
38. Lemeshko, M.; Schmidt, R. Molecular Impurities Interacting with a Many-Particle Environment: From Ultracold Gases to Helium Nanodroplets. In *Low Energy and Low Temperature Molecular Scattering*; Osterwalder, A., Dulieu, O., Eds.; Royal Society of Chemistry: London, UK, 2016.
39. Lemeshko, M. Quasiparticle Approach to Molecules Interacting with Quantum Solvents. *Phys. Rev. Lett.* **2017**, *118*, 095301. [CrossRef]
40. Shchadilova, Y. Viewpoint: A New Angle on Quantum Impurities. *Physics* **2017**, *10*, 20. [CrossRef]
41. Shepperson, B.; Söndergaard, A.A.; Christiansen, L.; Kaczmarczyk, J.; Zillich, R.E.; Lemeshko, M.; Stapelfeldt, H. Laser-induced alignment of iodine molecules in He-nanodroplets: Long-time coherence, revivals, and breaking-free. *arXiv* **2017**, arXiv:1702.01977.
42. Shepperson, B.; Chatterley, A.S.; Søndergaard, A.A.; Christiansen, L.; Lemeshko, M.; Stapelfeldt, H. Strongly aligned molecules inside helium droplets in the near-adiabatic regime. *J. Chem. Phys.* **2017**, *147*, 013946. [CrossRef] [PubMed]
43. Bourdeau, M.; Sorkin, R.D. When can identical particles collide? *Phys. Rev. D* **1992**, *45*, 687–696. [CrossRef] [PubMed]
44. Lundholm, D.; Solovej, J.P. Local exclusion and Lieb-Thirring inequalities for intermediate and fractional statistics. *Ann. Henri Poincaré* **2014**, *15*, 1061–1107. [CrossRef]
45. Correggi, M.; Oddis, L. Hamiltonians for Two-Anyon Systems. *Rend. Mat. Appl.* **2018**, *39*, 277–292.

Review

One-Dimensional Disordered Bosonic Systems

Chiara D'Errico [1,2,*] and Marco G. Tarallo [3]

1. Istituto per la Protezione Sostenibile Delle Piante, CNR-IPSP, 10135 Torino, Italy
2. European Laboratory for Non-Linear Spectroscopy, LENS, 50019 Sesto Fiorentino, Italy
3. Istituto Nazionale di Ricerca Metrologica, 10135 Torino, Italy; m.tarallo@inrim.it
* Correspondence: chiara.derrico@cnr.it

Abstract: Disorder is everywhere in nature and it has a fundamental impact on the behavior of many quantum systems. The presence of a small amount of disorder, in fact, can dramatically change the coherence and transport properties of a system. Despite the growing interest in this topic, a complete understanding of the issue is still missing. An open question, for example, is the description of the interplay of disorder and interactions, which has been predicted to give rise to exotic states of matter such as quantum glasses or many-body localization. In this review, we will present an overview of experimental observations with disordered quantum gases, focused on one-dimensional bosons, and we will connect them with theoretical predictions.

Keywords: Bose–Einstein condensates; cold gases in optical lattices; quantum phase transitions; disordered systems

1. Introduction

Ultracold atoms platforms are able to mimic the physics of other quantum many-body systems [1–3]. Thanks to the high degree of tunability of many important parameters, they have been used to study the low-temperature quantum phases and the transport properties of neutral particles with short-range interaction [4,5]. Their strong versatility allows researchers to use these platforms to investigate the physics of disorder [6–8], mainly using two different kinds of optical disordered potentials: laser speckles [9–20] and quasiperiodic lattices [21–34], both allowing for the first observation of Anderson localization in matter-waves [15,24]. Although the present review is devoted to one-dimensional (1D) bosons, it is important to mention that the possibility to control the dimensionality of the systems allowed experimentalists to also study 2D diffusion [35] and coherence [36], coherent backscattering [37,38], and 3D Anderson localization with both fermions [39] and bosons [40,41].

Despite many years of investigation and the many efforts that have been undertaken, both from the experimental and theoretical point of view, a clear and complete characterization of the effect of disorder on transport and coherence of a quantum system is still missing. An open issue, for example, is the description of the non-trivial interplay between disorder and interactions, which has been predicted to give rise to exotic states of matter such as quantum glasses [42,43] or many-body localization [44,45]. In particular, a transition between a superfluid phase for weakly repulsive bosons and a localized Bose glass phase for strong repulsion has been predicted both for one-dimensional [42] and higher-dimensional [43] bosons. However, the first experimental attempts to insert weak interactions in Anderson-localized disordered systems have clearly shown that the interaction energy can compete with disorder and induce delocalization by restoring coherence [25,26] or transport [27–30]. The quest for the effect of strong interactions requires to freeze the radial degrees of freedom, for example, by reducing the dimensionality of the system. One-dimensional bosons are the prototype disordered systems, with an established theoretical framework, useful to answer to some of the fundamental questions about the quantum phases and the transport properties of low-temperature matter.

In this review, we will focus on the experimental observations obtained with ultracold quantum gases [21–23,31–34]. In particular, after a brief survey of the theoretical background of 1D disordered systems, we review the experimental results achieved to detect and study disordered interacting quantum phases, analyzing their signature on coherence, transport, and energy excitation properties.

2. Theoretical Background of 1D Disordered Systems

Let us consider a disordered Bose gas in a discrete 1D space, whose space dependence is described by the site index j. This system is described by a modified Bose–Hubbard Hamiltonian:

$$H = -J\sum_j (b^\dagger_{j+1} b_j + b^\dagger_j b_{j+1}) + \frac{U}{2}\sum_j n_j(n_j - 1) + \sum_j (\epsilon_j + V_j^{HO}) n_j \quad (1)$$

where b_j denotes the boson annihilation operator at site j, while the site occupation quantified by the usual operator $n_j = b^\dagger_j b_j$. The first two terms on the right-hand side of Equation (1) represent the usual Bose–Hubbard interactions, corresponding to site-to-site tunneling with a rate J and the on-site repulsion ($U > 0$). The third term in Equation (1) accounts for the presence of both the harmonic trap V_j^{HO} and the disorder potential ϵ_j.

The disorder potential ϵ_j can be generated in several ways, resulting in a specific spectral distribution. Both theoretically and experimentally, two cases are the most relevant: (a) random distribution of energies $\epsilon_j \in [-\Delta, \Delta]$ and (b) quasiperiodic distribution $\epsilon_j = \Delta \cos(2\pi j\sigma)$ with σ being an irrational number [46]. The latter can be experimentally generated by superimposing to a main periodic potential an auxiliary lattice one with incommensurate wavelength ($\lambda_2 = \lambda_1/\sigma$). Hence, the three main energy scales characterizing the Hamiltonian, i.e., the tunneling energy J, the quasidisorder strength Δ, and the interaction energy U, can be controlled by tuning the depth of the main lattice S_1, the depth of the secondary one S_2 (being $\Delta = \sigma^2 S_2/2$), or the interparticle scattering length on a Feshbach resonance [47], respectively. The simultaneous presence of disorder and commensurate potential generates a competition between the three possible quantum phases, namely the superfluid (SF) phase, the Mott insulator (MI), which occurs at large interactions for commensurate fillings, and the so-called Bose glass (BG) phase, which is induced by disorder. Figure 1 shows the zero-temperature ($T = 0$) phase diagram of 1D bosons in the quasiperiodic lattice as a function of the ratios Δ/J and U/J, obtained by numerically solving the Bose–Hubbard problem [48].

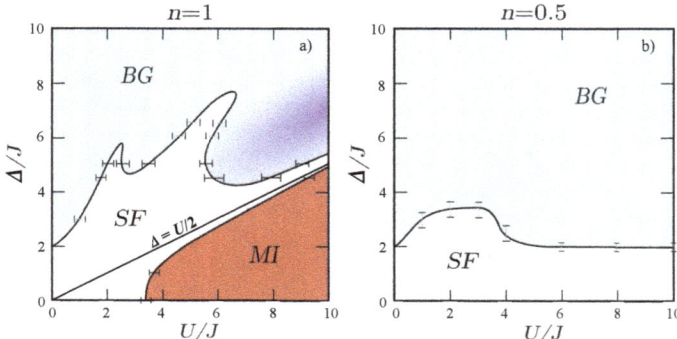

Figure 1. Phase diagrams for a quasiperiodic Bose–Hubbard model for densities $n = 1$ (**a**) and $n = 0.5$ (**b**). Figure adapted from Reference [48].

We must distinguish between two physically different situations depending on the average boson occupation number $n = N/M$, where N is the number of bosons and M is the length of the 1D system. For incommensurate fillings ($n < 1$), the system is similar to the continuum case [49], with a SF phase replaced by a BG phase by increasing the disorder strength Δ. On the other hand, for unit filling ($n = 1$), the ground state is a MI with a gap. Adding disorder, such a gapped phase persists up to the value $\Delta = U/2$ (dashed line) where the excitation spectrum becomes gapless and the system first becomes a SF and then a BG

One-dimensional disordered bosonic systems, as described by Equation (1), provide an ideal platform for testing and developing precise theoretical methods for studying many-body physics, which yields useful predictions about the position of quantum phase transitions and the indications on the most appropriate observables for their detection. In the case of pseudorandom quasiperiodic disorder, phase diagrams have been obtained by exact numerical results on the Bose–Hubbard model in small systems [50,51]. However, they suffer a limited accuracy in locating the points of phase transition. More detailed results have been found by means of quantum Monte Carlo methods [52] and the density-matrix renormalization group (DMRG) algorithm [48]. These theoretical works represent the groundwork for the experimental detection of disordered quantum phases, and they also point out the experimental tools to detect the quantum phase transitions of these systems. In particular, beside the compressibility, Reference [48] points out to the measurement of *coherence* of the quantum gas, which is detected by time-of-flight imaging from the width of the momentum distribution (see for results Section 3.1). Another interesting tool for detecting phase transition is the observation of *excitation spectrum* (see Section 3.3). The excitation spectrum of strongly repulsive 1D bosons in a disordered or quasiperiodic optical lattice has been computed [53]. The predicted excitation spectrum shows a peculiar behavior with two excitation peaks, one as expected around the repulsion energy scale U with width $\sim 2\Delta$ and the other one centered at Δ with the same width. The prediction of the presence of an absorption feature in the low-frequency band appears as a consequence of the formation of a Bose glass at incommensurate filling, thus making the excitation spectrum measurement an important tool of investigation. Experimentally, it can be easily assessed by coherent lattice modulation spectroscopy [21,54].

3. Experimental Results

The experimental realization of a 1D bosonic system with ultracold gases is schematically shown in Figure 2. Starting from a 3D Bose–Einstein condensate (BEC), the atoms are typically loaded in a strong 2D optical lattice [55]. This traps the atoms to an array of tightly confining 1D potential tubes, thus generating a set of many quasi-1D systems. Along the 1D tubes, another optical lattice is employed to produce a set of disordered quasi-1D systems, which are described by the disordered Bose–Hubbard Hamiltonian in Equation (1). Here, the disorder is introduced either with a secondary optical lattice, generating the quasiperiodic disordered lattice [21], or by a second atomic species as system impurity [31].

A systematic experimental study of the many-body properties of such a system can be performed by momentum distribution or by excitation energy measurements. The coherence (Section 3.1) and transport (Section 3.2) properties of the tubes can be studied by measuring the momentum distribution of the system, achieved through absorption imaging after a free expansion. These measurements correspond to an average over all the tubes of the systems, and thus over its different densities. In the case of transport measurements, to induce a dynamics on the atoms along the tubes, the system is brought out of equilibrium by a sudden change of the harmonic trap. The excitation spectra of the system are obtained by modulating the amplitude of the main lattice depth. The amount of energy absorbed by the system can be extracted by temperature measurements of the 3D BEC, which is recreated after an adiabatic switch-off of the 1D confinement [33]. Alternatively, the modulation heating effect can be detected by phase coherence measurements. Phase coherence is restored by reducing the depths of the trapping lattices to less than five recoil energies [56], while phase interference is imaged after a time-of-flight. Typically, the amount of heating can be quantified either by the visibility $\mathcal{V}$ of the interference peaks [31], which is defined analogously to the optical case as a function of the atomic density ρ

$$\mathcal{V} = \frac{\rho_{max} - \rho_{min}}{\rho_{max} + \rho_{min}},$$

or by the width of the central peak [21,22] (see Section 3.3).

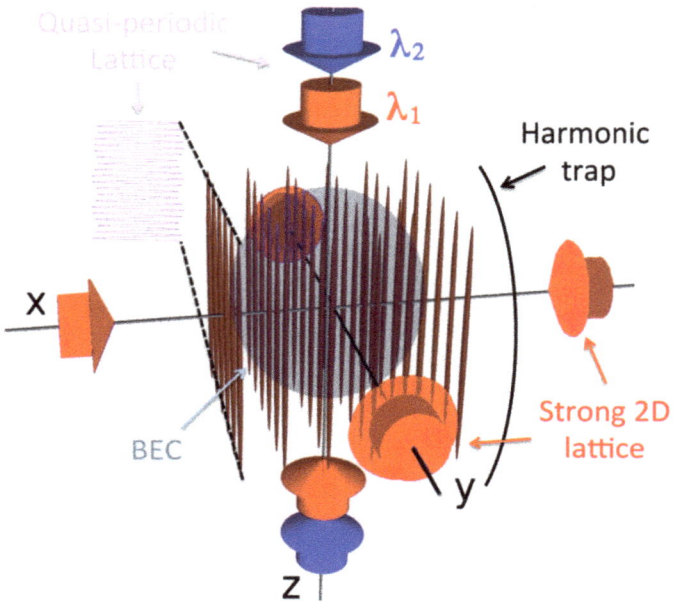

Figure 2. Schematic drawing of the typical experimental realization of a 1D disordered bosonic system. Two strong optical lattices are used to provide a tight confinement and form an array of 1D potential tubes. The axial quasiperiodic potential is formed by superimposing two incommensurate optical lattices of wavelengths λ_1 and λ_2. The harmonic trap results from the intensity gradient of the Gaussian laser beams.

3.1. Coherence

An overview of the nature of a disordered interacting system has been provided by measurements of the momentum distribution $P(k)$ in an array of 1D tubes of ^{39}K atoms in a quasiperiodic lattice. An experimental measurement of the coherence of the system is shown in Figure 3, where the width Γ of $P(k)$ is plotted as function of the interaction strength U and the disorder strength Δ. At small Δ and U, the observation of a narrow $P(k)$ is a signature of a coherent regime (blue zone). For increasing values of the two energy scales, the coherent regime is progressively replaced by a more incoherent regime (green, yellow, and red zones). The observed increase of Γ can be attributed to either the emergence of an insulating phase or to an increase in the temperature. The latter effect on Γ has been experimentally excluded by entropy measurements [33]. In fact, the measured entropy does not show any increase with increasing disorder strength. This suggests that the increased Γ is due to the emergence of an insulating phase, as predicted for the $T = 0$ temperature case. Despite the finite T and the inhomogeneity of the experimental tubes, the diagram behavior resembles that of the $T = 0$ theoretical predictions for homogeneous systems, where the existence of a BG phase is predicted [42,43,48,52].

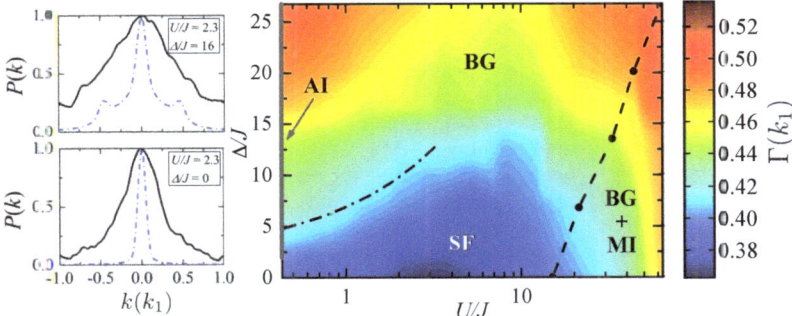

Figure 3. Measured rms width Γ of the momentum distribution $P(k)$ of arrays of quasi-1D samples of ^{39}K atoms in the $U-\Delta$ diagram. Γ is reported in units of k_1, where $k_1 = 2\pi/\lambda_1$ is the main lattice wavevector. The dashed line indicates the upper bound for the existence of the MI, according with $T=0$ DMRG calculations. Left panels show the measured momentum distribution (solid black line) for two points of the diagram in the SF (bottom) and BG (top) regions, compared with the $T=0$ DMRG calculations (dashed-dotted blue line). Figure adapted from Reference [33].

Comparing the experimental diagram with the theory in Figure 1, we see that for increasing interaction along the $\Delta = 0$ line, Γ increases due to the progressive formation of an incoherent MI. For increasing disorder along the $U = 0$ line, the system forms an Anderson insulator for $\Delta > 2J$ [57]. For weak disorder and interaction, the system is in a SF regime, surrounded by a re-entrant insulating regime extending from small to large U. In the weakly interacting regime, a crossover from the incoherent disorder-induced insulator toward more coherent regimes is observed when the interaction energy $nU \gtrsim \Delta - 2J$ (see dashed-dotted line in Figure 3). In the strongly interacting regime, disorder and interactions cooperate to localize the system and a second crossover towards less coherent regimes occurs. The interaction induced MI, which for a homogeneous system with $n=1$ is expected to survive in the disordered potentials only for moderate disorder $\Delta < U/2$, is expected to exist in the experimental inhomogeneous one only below the dashed black line shown in Figure 3. In this region, as an effect of the inhomogeneous density of the experimental system, for $\Delta < 2J$, the MI coexists with a SF fraction, which is localized by the disorder in a BG phase for $\Delta > 2J$.

For a complete comparison of the experimental phase diagram with theoretical predictions, it would be necessary to include both finite temperature and inhomogeneity of the experimental system into numerical simulations. This would result in costly numerical calculations. If only system inhomogeneity is included, zero-temperature DMRG calculations (left panels in Figure 3) find a diagram with a general behavior close to the experimental one but with a SF Γ much smaller than that observed in the experiments [33]. To include the finite temperature of the experimental system, two different DMRG schemes have been developed: (i) a direct simulation of the thermal density matrix in the form of a matrix-product purification and (ii) a less costly phenomenological method based on DMRG ground-state data that are extended to finite temperatures by introducing an effective thermal correlation length [34]. These simulations have shown that, while in the weakly interacting regime thermal effects can be rather strong, they are significantly less relevant in the strongly interacting one. There, the scaling of the correlation length with T shows a weak dependence below a crossover temperature, indicating that the strongly correlated quantum phases predicted by the $T=0$ theory can persist at finite temperatures.

3.2. Transport

The insulating nature of the incoherent region has been confirmed by transport measurements. The mobility can be measured by observing the system evolution after an impulse has been applied to it. In Figure 4a,b, the results from the first experiments with ^{87}Rb atoms are shown. The clean case ($\Delta = 0$) is compared with two different disordered configurations: atomic impurities (Figure 4a) and quasiperiodic potential (Figure 4b). When a variable impulse is applied to the system, the velocity acquired by the atoms can be fitted with a linear function whose slope defines the mobility coefficient. In the absence of disorder, the mobility coefficient decreases with the increasing in the potential lattice depth S_1 and reaches zero mobility when entering in the MI region. When disorder is present, the behavior is analogous, suggesting the system is entering in an insulating regime. Nevertheless, while with impurities the transition to the zero-mobility was shifted towards smaller values of S_1, in the case of the quasiperiodic potential (with constant S_2), no shift of the critical depth is measured. Such different behavior could be due to the fact that increasing S_1 towards the insulating regime, the disorder Δ/J is decreasing, thus pushing the critical interaction to enter the BG regime to larger values of U/J, where the BG phase coexists with the MI one. This problem has been bypassed in ^{39}K experiments by using Feshbach resonances to tune the interaction independently from the value of S_1 [58,59].

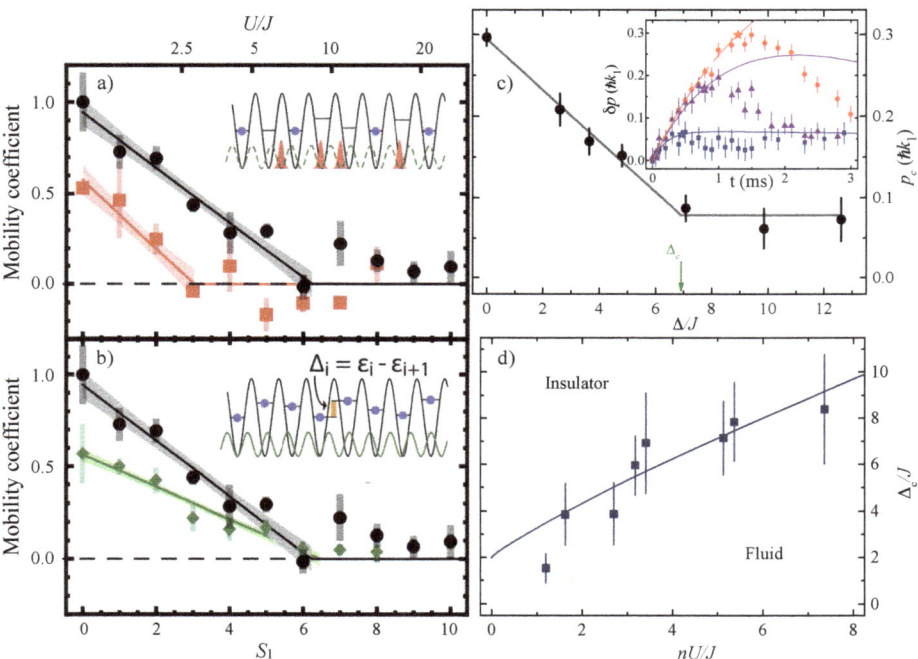

Figure 4. (**a**,**b**) Mobility coefficient of ^{87}Rb after impulse excitation versus lattice depth S_1 without disorder (black circles) compared with different disorder configurations: (**a**) atomic impurities ($f_{imp} = 0.5$, red squares) and (**b**) an incommensurate lattice ($S_2 = 3$, green diamonds). The lattice depths are defined in units of recoil energies, $S_i = V_i/E_{ri}$ with $i = 1, 2$. Figure adapted from Reference [31]. (**c**,**d**) Transport after trap excitation of an array of quasi-1D samples of weakly interacting ^{39}K atoms: (**c**) critical momentum p_c for weak interaction ($U/J = 1.26$) as a function of the disorder strength and (**d**) critical Δ_c/J at the fluid–insulator transition in the disorder-interaction plane, extracted by several piecewise fits of p_c as a function of Δ for different values of fixed U (solid line in panel (**c**)). In the inset of panel **c**, the time evolution of δp, from which p_c has been extracted (stars), is shown for three values of Δ: $\Delta = 0$ (red circles), $\Delta = 3.6J$ (purple triangles), and $\Delta = 10J$ (blue squared). Figure adapted from Reference [32].

Figure 4c,d shows momentum dependent transport measurements in the weakly interacting regime. The experimental protocol consists of tracking the time evolution of the momentum δp acquired by the system for different values of the disorder strength Δ and the interaction energy U, tuned via Feshbach resonance. Typical datasets of such measurements are plotted in the inset of Figure 4c, where Δ is different for each dataset, while U is kept constant. Here, we can observe that the system explores a sharp transition from a weakly dissipative regime (at small δp), well fitted with a damped oscillation function (solid lines), to a strongly unstable one (at large δp). The critical momentum p_c separating the two regimes has been identified as the momentum value, where the experimental data deviate from the fitting curve used in the first regime (stars in the inset of Figure 4c). The measured critical momentum p_c at each Δ, similarly to the previously described mobility coefficient, linearly decreases until it reaches a plateau value, corresponding to the insulating regime of the system. With a piecewise fit of p_c, one can extract the critical disorder strength Δ_c to enter in the insulating regime at fixed interaction energy U (Figure 4c). Repeating the measurements for different interactions, it has been observed that the critical disorder to enter the insulating regime increases with U/J (Figure 4d), at least for weak interaction. By employing the vanishing of p_c for the observed instability the fluid–insulator transition driven by disorder has been located, across the interaction-disorder plane in the weakly interacting regime. In fact, while the experiments with [87]Rb atoms are limited to the strongly interacting regime, the momentum-dependent measurements with [39]K samples allow researchers to investigate the weakly interacting one.

In order to confirm the insulating nature of the observed incoherent regimes in the full diagram of Figure 3, the momentum δp acquired by the [39]K system after a fixed time from its excitation has been measured (Figure 5). This effective mobility is shown in Figure 5a for the clean case and for two fixed values of the disorder strength. With no disorder and small U the system is conductive, while the mobility decreases when approaching the MI region. With finite disorder, instead, the system is insulating for both very weak and strong interactions, while a finite mobility can be recovered for moderate values of U. These results indicate that the incoherent regimes at both weak and strong U are also insulating, thus confirming the re-entrant behavior of the insulating regime observed in the coherence diagram. An additional measurement performed at a higher temperature indicates that, as expected by theory [44], the mobility for intermediate disorder strength is essentially T-independent in the explored range $k_B T = (3.1$–$4.5)J$ (Figure 5b).

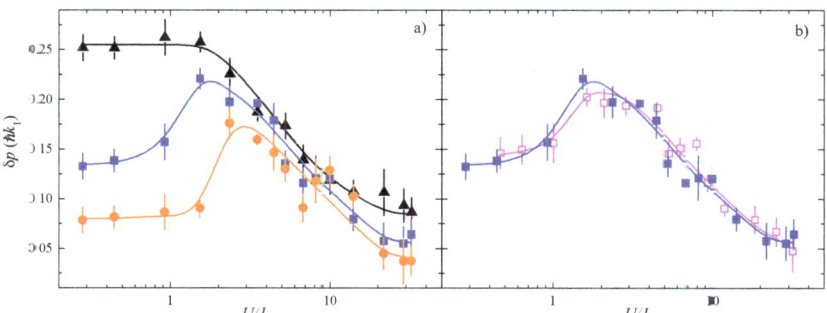

Figure 5. Effective mobility as a function of disorder and interactions. (**a**) Momentum δp acquired by the system after a fixed evolving time $t = 0.9$ ms in the tilted potential for three different disorder strengths, $\Delta = 0$ (black triangles), $\Delta = 6.2J$ (blue squares), and $\Delta = 8.8J$ (orange circles). (**b**) The $\Delta = 6.2J$ measurements are acquired for two temperatures of the SF component, $k_B T = 3.1(4)J$ (full blue) and $k_B T = 4.5(7)J$ (empty magenta). Figure adapted from Reference [33].

3.3. Excitation Spectra

To probe the nature of the insulating phases, it is necessary to investigate the excitation properties of the system. This can be undertaken by performing lattice modulation spectroscopy, i.e., by measuring the energy absorbed by the system after a sinusoidal amplitude modulation of the main lattice at fixed frequency ν. While the MI is known to be gapped, the BG phase is predicted to be a gapless insulator. First experiments with [87]Rb observed the broadening of the typical MI spectrum (Figure 6), with both quasiperiodic potentials [21,31] and localized impurity atoms [31]. Despite showing signatures of BG formation, they do not permit to distinguish a specific signature of the BG spectrum due to the strong interaction ($U > 50J$) and the strong disorder ($\Delta > 50J$) regime. Moreover, noise correlation spectroscopy allowed experimentalists to monitor the destruction of the MI ordered structure in the presence of an additional secondary lattice potential (Figure 6g), but not to highlight a specific feature due to the BG phase.

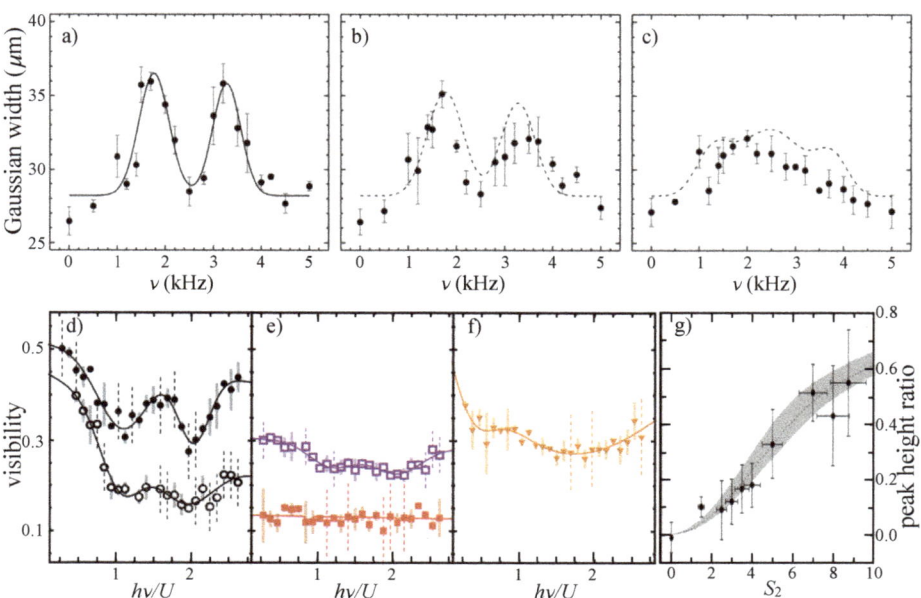

Figure 6. Excitation spectra (**a**–**f**) and noise correlations spectroscopy (**g**) of arrays of quasi-1D samples of ^{87}Rb atoms. (**a**–**c**) Spectra in a quasiperiodic potential for a depth $S_1 = 25$ of the main lattice and increasing depths of the secondary lattice: (**a**) $S_2 = 0$, (**b**) $S_2 = 0.2$, and (**c**) $S_2 = 0.5$. Here, the spectra have been quantified by measuring the Gaussian width of the central peak of the momentum distribution of atoms released from the lattices with reduced intensity ($S_1 = 5$, $S_2 = 0$). Figure adapted from Reference [22]. (**d**–**f**) Visibility of excitation gap for different disorder configurations: (**d**) in the absence of disorder for $S_1 = 9$ and $S_1 = 14$ (open and filled black circles), (**e**) for $S_1 = 14$ with atomic impurity fractions $f_{imp} = 0.1$ (open purple squares) and $f_{imp} = 0.5$ (filled red squares), and (**f**) for $S_1 = 14$, with no impurities and an incommensurate lattice of depth $S_2 = 1$ (orange triangles). Here, the spectra have been quantified by measuring the interference peak visibility in the momentum distribution of atoms released from the lattice with reduced intensity ($S_1 = 4$, $S_2 = 0$) [60]. Figure adapted from Reference [31]. (**g**) Noise correlation spectroscopy in a quasiperiodic potential: the ratio between the height of the k_2 and k_1 correlation peaks as a function of S_2. Figure adapted from Reference [23]. The lattice depths are defined in units of recoil energies, $S_i = V_i / E_{ri}$ with $i = 1, 2$.

Experiments with ^{39}K permit to explore the excitation spectrum in the full range of interaction and disorder diagram and to find regions where it is possible to distinguish the gapless spectrum of the BG from the gapped one of the MI. In these experiments, the absorbed energy has been quantified by measuring the temperature of the BEC after the adiabatic switch-off of the 1D confinement. Depending on the amount of acquired energy, the time-of-flight atomic distribution can be fitted either by a two-component function (a Thomas–Fermi profile plus a Gaussian distribution) or by a Gaussian function. In the former case, the heating is related to the BEC fraction; in the latter, it is related to the width σ of the Gaussian distribution. Let us start from the strongly interacting regime, where, in the presence of moderate disorder, the BG phase should coexist with the MI (Figure 7). In the clean case, the spectrum is characterized by the double peak shape typical of the trapped MI, with a first peak centered at $h\nu = U$ due to excitation between sites in the

MI domains with the same filling. In addition, a second peak is centered at $h\nu = 2U$ due to excitation between sites in the MI domains with different occupations. Adding a finite disorder, the spectrum shows a clear change. First, there is a broadening of the MI peaks, as already observed with ^{87}Rb experiments at strong disorder. Second, at low frequencies, it appears an extra peak filling the Mott gap, centered around $h\nu = \Delta$, which can be ascribed to the regions with incommensurate filling, i.e., to the BG phase.

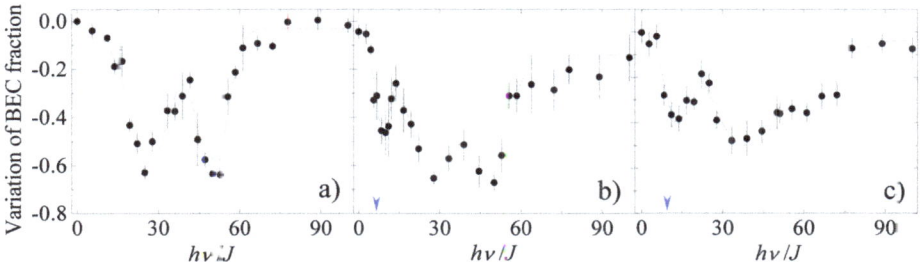

Figure 7. Excitation spectra of arrays of quasi-1D samples of ^{39}K atoms with strong interactions. (**a**–**c**) Experimental spectra for $U = 26J$ and $\Delta = 0$ (**a**), $\Delta = 6.5J$ (**b**), and $\Delta = 9.5J$ (**c**). The spectra have been quantified by measuring the relative variation of the BEC fraction with respect to the unexcited value ($\nu = 0$). The blue arrows are at $h\nu = \Delta$, the dashed-dotted line in (**a**) is at $h\nu = U$, and the continuous lines are fits with multiple Gaussians. Figure adapted from Reference [33].

The agreement between BG theory and experiment is best understood once the MI background is subtracted from the experimental data. Figure 8 shows a zoom of the excitation spectra around the disorder strength energy Δ after the Gaussian background of the MI peak has been subtracted, and the resulting peak response has been normalized to unity. We can see that the experimental spectra of the BG are reasonably well reproduced by theory calculations, where a fermionized-boson model has been used [53,61].

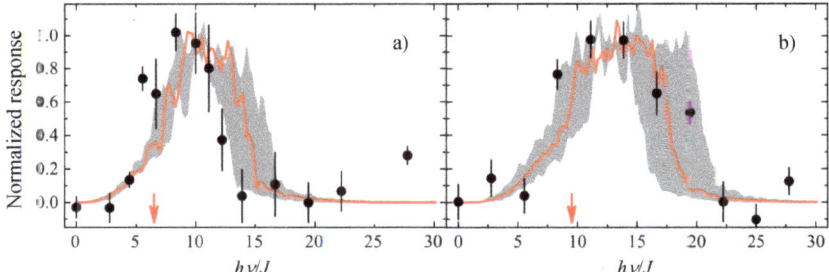

Figure 8. Excitation spectrum of the strongly interacting BG. The experimental data (black circles) for the low-frequency part of the spectra in Figure 7 are compared with theory (red solid line) for two disorder strengths: (**a**) $\Delta = 6.5J$ and (**b**) $\Delta = 9.5J$. The grey region shows the effect of a 20% uncertainty on Δ. The red arrows are at $h\nu = \Delta$. Figure adapted from Supplemental Materials of Reference [33].

We now analyze the spectral properties of the system across the phase diagram. In Figure 9, the behavior of the excitation spectrum moving from weak to strong interaction at a given finite disorder is shown. In the case of weak interaction, the excitation spectra at $\Delta = 8.9J$ are shown for three increasing values of U (Figure 9a–c). For vanishing U, a weak excitation peak centered at Δ has been observed, consistent with the presence of an Anderson insulator. The experimental excitation spectrum is well reproduced by a non-interacting bosonic model (Figure 9a). Increasing U, the system response progressively enhances and broadens (Figure 9b), ending up with an excitation spectrum that is undistinguishable from that of a clean SF (Figure 9c). This behavior is thus consistent with the system crossing the BG–SF transition.

In the case of strong interaction, the excitation spectra at the $\Delta = 6.5J$ are shown for three increasing values of U (Figure 9d–f). The peak centered at Δ is the signature of the strongly correlated BG. Such "Δ-peak" can be observed only in a limited region of Δ and U values. When U is comparable with Δ, the MI and BG peaks overlap, the former being typically larger and covering the latter (Figure 9d). When U is much larger than Δ, the fraction of sites with incommensurate density that can form a BG becomes negligible and, again, only the MI peaks are clearly detectable (Figure 9f). Furthermore, for very large disorder strengths ($\Delta > 20J$), the spectrum becomes very broad and is only weakly affected by interaction, indicating that the system behavior is dominated by disorder, and any feature is observable.

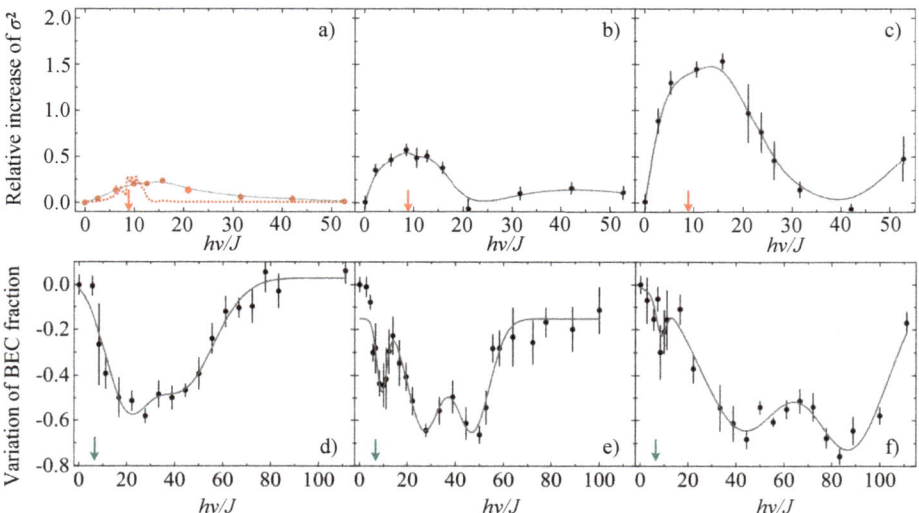

Figure 9. Excitation spectra of ^{39}K atoms from weak to strong interactions. (**a–c**) Excitation spectra for fixed disorder, $\Delta = 8.9J$, and small increasing interactions: $U = 0.35J$ (**a**), $U = 1.4J$ (**b**), or $U = 2.1J$ (**c**). The spectra have been quantified by measuring the relative increase of σ with respect to the unexcited value ($\nu = 0$). (**d–f**) Excitation spectra for fixed disorder, $\Delta = 6.5J$, and large increasing interactions: $U = 20J$ (**d**), $U = 26J$ (**e**), or $U = 58J$ (**f**). The arrows mark Δ/J. The spectra have been quantified by measuring the relative variation of the BEC fraction with respect to the unexcited value ($\nu = 0$). Figure adapted from Reference [33].

The measurements of the excitation spectra, together with those of coherence (Figure 3) and transport (Figure 5), confirm an opposite nature of the two regimes of weak and strong U, respectively, bosonic and fermionic, and an opposite role of the interactions. In the low-U bosonic case, small repulsive interactions compete with disorder and screen the disorder-induced localization, favoring the coupling of single-particle states and gradually restoring coherence between particles and superfluidity. In the large-U fermionic case, instead, strong interactions induce fermonization of the bosonic sample, thus favoring, in the presence of disorder, Anderson localization.

4. Outlook and Perspectives

In this brief review, we discuss the experiments with 1D bosons where the effect of disorder has been investigated in the disorder-interaction plane. The topic of quantum matter in the presence of disorder is very complex, in particular, when dealing with experimental systems being inhomogeneous and at finite temperature. The coexistence of fractions with different densities, in fact, transforms the theoretical sharp quantum phase transitions into broad crossovers. A way to overcome this limit in future experiments could be to use a flat-top beam shaper providing homogeneous trapped systems [62–66]. This should also allow, in the strongly interacting regime, for a better discrimination of the BG and the MI phases. Concerning the problem of the finite temperature, it would be very important to reduce the actual temperature of the atomic 1D systems. The main source of heating is typically the phase noise affecting the 2D strong radial lattices and the main axial one. Recent theoretical calculations suggest to use a shallow quasiperiodic potential to reduce the lattice heating effect without losing information about the underlying quantum phases [67]. Another possibility could be to apply a phase stabilization on the lattices [68].

An intriguing direction of investigation would be the direct study of the effect of temperature on 1D disordered phases. A possible experimental implementation consists of using a second BEC insensitive to the lattices as a thermal bath [69,70]. This would ensure both the thermal equilibrium in the 1D system and to have an independent measure of its temperature.

Another interesting question related to disordered systems is whether the existence of the finite temperature insulating phase in the weakly interacting regime could be related to the hot topic of many-body localization [71]. Different experiments with ultracold atoms recently investigated the many-body localization phenomenon, mainly for fermions [72–75], and only later for a disordered Bose–Hubbard system [76–78], but its existence is still under debate [79].

Author Contributions: Both authors contributed to the writing of the text. All authors have read and agreed to the published version of the manuscript.

Funding: This research received no external funding.

Conflicts of Interest: The authors declare no conflict of interest.

Abbreviations

The following abbreviations are used in this manuscript:

1D	One-dimensional
MI	Mott insulator
SF	Superfluid
BG	Bose glass
BEC	Bose–Einstein condensate

References

1. Bloch, I.; Dalibard, J.; Nascimbène, S. Quantum simulations with ultracold quantum gases. *Nat. Phys.* **2012**, *8*, 267–276. [CrossRef]
2. Gross, C.; Bloch, I. Quantum simulations with ultracold atoms in optical lattices. *Science* **2017**, *357*, 995–1001. [CrossRef] [PubMed]
3. Schäfer, F.; Fukuhara, T.; Sugawa, S.; Takasu, Y.; Takahashi, Y. Tools for quantum simulation with ultracold atoms in optical lattices. *Nat. Rev. Phys.* **2020**, *2*, 411–425. [CrossRef]
4. Lewenstein, M.; Sanpera, A.; Ahufinger, V.; Damski, B.; Sen(De), A.; Sen, U. Ultracold atomic gases in optical lattices: Mimicking condensed matter physics and beyond. *Adv. Phys.* **2007**, *56*, 243–379. [CrossRef]
5. Bloch, I.; Dalibard, J.; Zwerger, W. Many-body physics with ultracold gases. *Rev. Mod. Phys.* **2008**, *80*, 885–954. [CrossRef]
6. Sanchez-Palencia, L.; Lewenstein, M. Disordered quantum gases under control. *Nat. Phys.* **2010**, *6*, 87–95. [CrossRef]
7. Modugno, G. Anderson localization in Bose–Einstein condensates. *Rep. Prog. Phys.* **2010**, *73*, 102401. [CrossRef]
8. Shapiro, B. Cold atoms in the presence of disorder. *J. Phys. Math. Theor.* **2012**, *45*, 143001. [CrossRef]
9. Lye, J.E.; Fallani, L.; Modugno, M.; Wiersma, D.S.; Fort, C.; Inguscio, M. Bose-Einstein Condensate in a Random Potential. *Phys. Rev. Lett.* **2005**, *95*, 070401. [CrossRef] [PubMed]
10. Clément, D.; Varón, A.F.; Hugbart, M.; Retter, J.A.; Bouyer, P.; Sanchez-Palencia, L.; Gangardt, D.M.; Shlyapnikov, G.V.; Aspect, A. Suppression of Transport of an Interacting Elongated Bose-Einstein Condensate in a Random Potential. *Phys. Rev. Lett.* **2005**, *95*, 170409. [CrossRef]
11. Fort, C.; Fallani, L.; Guarrera, V.; Lye, J.E.; Modugno, M.; Wiersma, D.S.; Inguscio, M. Effect of Optical Disorder and Single Defects on the Expansion of a Bose-Einstein Condensate in a One-Dimensional Waveguide. *Phys. Rev. Lett.* **2005**, *95*, 170410. [CrossRef] [PubMed]

12. Schulte, T.; Drenkelforth, S.; Kruse, J.; Ertmer, W.; Arlt, J.; Sacha, K.; Zakrzewski, J.; Lewenstein, M. Routes Towards Anderson-Like Localization of Bose-Einstein Condensates in Disordered Optical Lattices. *Phys. Rev. Lett.* **2005**, *95*, 170411. [CrossRef]
13. Clément, D.; Varón, A.F.; Retter, J.A.; Sanchez-Palencia, L.; Aspect, A.; Bouyer, P. Experimental study of the transport of coherent interacting matter-waves in a 1D random potential induced by laser speckle. *New J. Phys.* **2006**, *8*, 165–165. [CrossRef]
14. Chen, Y.P.; Hitchcock, J.; Dries, D.; Junker, M.; Welford, C.; Hulet, R.G. Phase coherence and superfluid-insulator transition in a disordered Bose-Einstein condensate. *Phys. Rev. A* **2008**, *77*, 033632. [CrossRef]
15. Billy, J.; Josse, V.; Zuo, Z.; Bernard, A.; Hambrecht, B.; Lugan, P.; Clément, D.; Sanchez-Palencia, L.; Bouyer, P.; Aspect, A. Direct observation of Anderson localization of matter waves in a controlled disorder. *Nature* **2008**, *453*, 891–894. [CrossRef]
16. White, M.; Pasienski, M.; McKay, D.; Zhou, S.Q.; Ceperley, D.; DeMarco, B. Strongly Interacting Bosons in a Disordered Optical Lattice. *Phys. Rev. Lett.* **2009**, *102*, 055301. [CrossRef] [PubMed]
17. Pasienski, M.; McKay, D.; White, M.; DeMarco, B. A disordered insulator in an optical lattice. *Nat. Phys.* **2010**, *6*, 677–680. [CrossRef]
18. Dries, D.; Pollack, S.E.; Hitchcock, J.M.; Hulet, R.G. Dissipative transport of a Bose-Einstein condensate. *Phys. Rev. A* **2010**, *82*, 033603. [CrossRef]
19. Volchkov, V.V.; Pasek, M.; Denechaud, V.; Mukhtar, M.; Aspect, A.; Delande, D.; Josse, V. Measurement of Spectral Functions of Ultracold Atoms in Disordered Potentials. *Phys. Rev. Lett.* **2018**, *120*, 060404. [CrossRef]
20. Richard, J.; Lim, L.K.; Denechaud, V.; Volchkov, V.V.; Lecoutre, B.; Mukhtar, M.; Jendrzejewski, F.; Aspect, A.; Signoles, A.; Sanchez-Palencia, L.; et al. Elastic Scattering Time of Matter Waves in Disordered Potentials. *Phys. Rev. Lett.* **2019**, *122*, 100403. [CrossRef]
21. Fallani, L.; Lye, J.E.; Guarrera, V.; Fort, C.; Inguscio, M. Ultracold Atoms in a Disordered Crystal of Light: Towards a Bose Glass. *Phys. Rev. Lett.* **2007**, *98*, 130404. [CrossRef] [PubMed]
22. Guarrera, V.; Fallani, L.; Lye, J.E.; Fort, C.; Inguscio, M. Inhomogeneous broadening of a Mott insulator spectrum. *New J. Phys.* **2007**, *9*, 107. [CrossRef]
23. Guarrera, V.; Fabbri, N.; Fallani, L.; Fort, C.; van der Stam, K.M.R.; Inguscio, M. Noise Correlation Spectroscopy of the Broken Order of a Mott Insulating Phase. *Phys. Rev. Lett.* **2008**, *100*, 250403. [CrossRef]
24. Roati, G.; D'Errico, C.; Fallani, L.; Fattori, M.; Fort, C.; Zaccanti, M.; Modugno, G.; Modugno, M.; Inguscio, M. Anderson localization of a non-interacting Bose–Einstein condensate. *Nature* **2008**, *453*, 895–898. [CrossRef]
25. Deissler, B.; Zaccanti, M.; Roati, G.; D'Errico, C.; Fattori, M.; Modugno, M.; Modugno, G.; Inguscio, M. Delocalization of a disordered bosonic system by repulsive interactions. *Nat. Phys.* **2010**, *6*, 354–358. [CrossRef]
26. Deissler, B.; Lucioni, E.; Modugno, M.; Roati, G.; Tanzi, L.; Zaccanti, M.; Inguscio, M.; Modugno, G. Correlation function of weakly interacting bosons in a disordered lattice. *New J. Phys.* **2011**, *13*, 023020. [CrossRef]
27. Lucioni, E.; Deissler, B.; Tanzi, L.; Roati, G.; Zaccanti, M.; Modugno, M.; Larcher, M.; Dalfovo, F.; Inguscio, M.; Modugno, G. Observation of Subdiffusion in a Disordered Interacting System. *Phys. Rev. Lett.* **2011**, *106*, 230403. [CrossRef] [PubMed]
28. D'Errico, C.; Moratti, M.; Lucioni, E.; Tanzi, L.; Deissler, B.; Inguscio, M.; Modugno, G.; Plenio, M.B.; Caruso, F. Quantum diffusion with disorder, noise and interaction. *New J. Phys.* **2013**, *15*, 045007. [CrossRef]
29. Lucioni, E.; Tanzi, L.; D'Errico, C.; Moratti, M.; Inguscio, M.; Modugno, G. Modeling the transport of interacting matter waves in a disordered system by a nonlinear diffusion equation. *Phys. Rev. E* **2013**, *87*, 042922. [CrossRef]
30. D'Errico, C.; Chaudhuri, S.; Gori, L.; Kumar, A.; Lucioni, E.; Tanzi, L.; Inguscio, M.; Modugno, G. Transport of an interacting Bose gas in 1D disordered lattices. *AIP Conf. Proc.* **2014**, *1610*, 24–33. [CrossRef]
31. Gadway, B.; Pertot, D.; Reeves, J.; Vogt, M.; Schneble, D. Glassy Behavior in a Binary Atomic Mixture. *Phys. Rev. Lett.* **2011**, *107*, 145306. [CrossRef] [PubMed]
32. Tanzi, L.; Lucioni, E.; Chaudhuri, S.; Gori, L.; Kumar, A.; D'Errico, C.; Inguscio, M.; Modugno, G. Transport of a Bose Gas in 1D Disordered Lattices at the Fluid-Insulator Transition. *Phys. Rev. Lett.* **2013**, *111*, 115301. [CrossRef] [PubMed]
33. D'Errico, C.; Lucioni, E.; Tanzi, L.; Gori, L.; Roux, G.; McCulloch, I.P.; Giamarchi, T.; Inguscio, M.; Modugno, G. Observation of a Disordered Bosonic Insulator from Weak to Strong Interactions. *Phys. Rev. Lett.* **2014**, *113*, 095301. [CrossRef] [PubMed]
34. Gori, L.; Barthel, T.; Kumar, A.; Lucioni, E.; Tanzi, L.; Inguscio, M.; Modugno, G.; Giamarchi, T.; D'Errico, C.; Roux, G. Finite-temperature effects on interacting bosonic one-dimensional systems in disordered lattices. *Phys. Rev. A* **2016**, *93*, 033650. [CrossRef]
35. Robert-de Saint-Vincent, M.; Brantut, J.P.; Allard, B.; Plisson, T.; Pezzé, L.; Sanchez-Palencia, L.; Aspect, A.; Bourdel, T.; Bouyer, P. Anisotropic 2D Diffusive Expansion of Ultracold Atoms in a Disordered Potential. *Phys. Rev. Lett.* **2010**, *104*, 220602. [CrossRef]
36. Allard, B.; Plisson, T.; Holzmann, M.; Salomon, G.; Aspect, A.; Bouyer, P.; Bourdel, T. Effect of disorder close to the superfluid transition in a two-dimensional Bose gas. *Phys. Rev. A* **2012**, *85*, 033602. [CrossRef]
37. Jendrzejewski, F.; Müller, K.; Richard, J.; Date, A.; Plisson, T.; Bouyer, P.; Aspect, A.; Josse, V. Coherent Backscattering of Ultracold Atoms. *Phys. Rev. Lett.* **2012**, *109*, 195302. [CrossRef]
38. Müller, K.; Richard, J.; Volchkov, V.V.; Denechaud, V.; Bouyer, P.; Aspect, A.; Josse, V. Suppression and Revival of Weak Localization through Control of Time-Reversal Symmetry. *Phys. Rev. Lett.* **2015**, *114*, 205301. [CrossRef]
39. Kondov, S.S.; McGehee, W.R.; Zirbel, J.J.; DeMarco, B. Three-Dimensional Anderson Localization of Ultracold Matter. *Science* **2011**, *334*, 66–68. [CrossRef] [PubMed]

40. Jendrzejewski, F.; Bernard, A.; Müller, K.; Cheinet, P.; Josse, V.; Piraud, M.; Pezzé, L.; Sanchez-Palencia, L.; Aspect, A.; Bouyer, P. Three-dimensional localization of ultracold atoms in an optical disordered potential. *Nat. Phys.* **2012**, *8*, 398–403. [CrossRef]
41. Semeghini, G.; Landini, M.; Castilho, P.; Roy, S.; Spagnolli, G.; Trenkwalder, A.; Fattori, M.; Inguscio, M.; Modugno, G. Measurement of the mobility edge for 3D Anderson localization. *Nat. Phys.* **2015**, *11*, 554–559. [CrossRef]
42. Giamarchi, T.; Schulz, H.J. Anderson localization and interactions in one-dimensional metals. *Phys. Rev. B* **1988**, *37*, 325–340. [CrossRef] [PubMed]
43. Fisher, M.P.A.; Weichman, P.B.; Grinstein, G.; Fisher, D.S. Boson localization and the superfluid-insulator transition. *Phys. Rev. B* **1989**, *40*, 546–570. [CrossRef] [PubMed]
44. Aleiner, I.L.; Altshuler, B.L.; Shlyapnikov, G.V. A finite-temperature phase transition for disordered weakly interacting bosons in one dimension. *Nat. Phys.* **2010**, *6*, 900–904. [CrossRef]
45. Iyer, S.; Oganesyan, V.; Refael, G.; Huse, D.A. Many-body localization in a quasiperiodic system. *Phys. Rev. B* **2013**, *87*, 134202. [CrossRef]
46. Aubry, S.; André, G. Analyticity breaking and Anderson localization in incommensurate lattices. *Ann. Israel. Phys. Soc.* **1980**, *3*, 133.
47. Chin, C.; Grimm, R.; Julienne, P.; Tiesinga, E. Feshbach resonances in ultracold gases. *Rev. Mod. Phys.* **2010**, *82*, 1225–1286. [CrossRef]
48. Roux, G.; Barthel, T.; McCulloch, I.P.; Kollath, C.; Schollwöck, U.; Giamarchi, T. Quasiperiodic Bose-Hubbard model and localization in one-dimensional cold atomic gases. *Phys. Rev. A* **2008**, *78*, 023628. [CrossRef]
49. Ristivojevic, Z.; Petković, A.; Le Doussal, P.; Giamarchi, T. Phase Transition of Interacting Disordered Bosons in One Dimension. *Phys. Rev. Lett.* **2012**, *109*, 026402. [CrossRef]
50. Roth, R.; Burnett, K. Phase diagram of bosonic atoms in two-color superlattices. *Phys. Rev. A* **2003**, *68*, 023604. [CrossRef]
51. Bar-Gill, N.; Pugatch, R.; Rowen, E.; Katz, N.; Davidson, N. Quantum Phases of Ultra Cold Bosons in Incommensurate 1D Optical Lattices. *arXiv* **2006**, arXiv:0603513.
52. Roscilde, T. Bosons in one-dimensional incommensurate superlattices. *Phys. Rev. A* **2008**, *77*, 063605. [CrossRef]
53. Orso, G.; Iucci, A.; Cazalilla, M.A.; Giamarchi, T. Lattice modulation spectroscopy of strongly interacting bosons in disordered and quasiperiodic optical lattices. *Phys. Rev. A* **2009**, *80*, 033625. [CrossRef]
54. Tarallo, M.G.; Alberti, A.; Poli, N.; Chiofalo, M.L.; Wang, F.Y.; Tino, G.M. Delocalization-enhanced Bloch oscillations and driven resonant tunneling in optical lattices for precision force measurements. *Phys. Rev. A* **2012**, *86*, 033615. [CrossRef]
55. Bloch, I. Ultracold quantum gases in optical lattices. *Nat. Phys.* **2005**, *1*, 23–30. [CrossRef]
56. Gerbier, F.; Widera, A.; Fölling, S.; Mandel, O.; Gericke, T.; Bloch, I. Phase Coherence of an Atomic Mott Insulator *Phys. Rev. Lett.* **2005**, *95*, 050404. [CrossRef] [PubMed]
57. Modugno, M. Exponential localization in one-dimensional quasi-periodic optical lattices. *New J. Phys.* **2009**, *11*, 033023. [CrossRef]
58. Roati, G.; Zaccanti, M.; D'Errico, C.; Catani, J.; Modugno, M.; Simoni, A.; Inguscio, M.; Modugno, G. ^{39}K Bose-Einstein Condensate with Tunable Interactions. *Phys. Rev. Lett.* **2007**, *99*, 010403. [CrossRef]
59. D'Errico, C.; Zaccanti, M.; Fattori, M.; Roati, G.; Inguscio, M.; Modugno, G.; Simoni, A. Feshbach resonances in ultracold 39K. *New J. Phys.* **2007**, *9*, 223–223. [CrossRef]
60. Gadway, B.; Pertot, D.; Reimann, R.; Schneble, D. Superfluidity of Interacting Bosonic Mixtures in Optical Lattices. *Phys. Rev. Lett.* **2010**, *105*, 045303. [CrossRef]
61. Pupillo, G.; Rey, A.M.; Williams, C.J.; Clark, C.W. Extended fermionization of 1D bosons in optical lattices. *New J. Phys.* **2006**, *8*, 161. [CrossRef]
62. Veldkamp, W.B. Laser beam profile shaping with interlaced binary diffraction gratings. *Appl. Opt.* **1982**, *21*, 3209–3212. [CrossRef] [PubMed]
63. Hoffnagle, J.A.; Jefferson, C.M. Design and performance of a refractive optical system that converts a Gaussian to a flattop beam. *Appl. Opt.* **2000**, *39*, 5488–5499. [CrossRef]
64. Tarallo, M.G.; Miller, J.; Agresti, J.; D'Ambrosio, E.; DeSalvo, R.; Forest, D.; Lagrange, B.; Mackowsky, J.M.; Michel, C.; Montorio, J.L.; et al. Generation of a flat-top laser beam for gravitational wave detectors by means of a nonspherical Fabry–Perot resonator. *Appl. Opt.* **2007**, *46*, 6648–6654. [CrossRef]
65. Liang, J.; Rudolph N. Kohn, J.; Becker, M.F.; Heinzen, D.J. 1.5% root-mean-square flat-intensity laser beam formed using a binary-amplitude spatial light modulator. *Appl. Opt.* **2009**, *48*, 1955–1962. [CrossRef] [PubMed]
66. Gaunt, A.L.; Schmidutz, T.F.; Gotlibovych, I.; Smith, R.P.; Hadzibabic, Z. Bose-Einstein Condensation of Atoms in a Uniform Potential. *Phys. Rev. Lett.* **2013**, *110*, 200406. [CrossRef]
67. Yao, H.; Giamarchi, T.; Sanchez-Palencia, L. Lieb-Liniger Bosons in a Shallow Quasiperiodic Potential: Bose Glass Phase and Fractal Mott Lobes. *Phys. Rev. Lett.* **2020**, *125*, 060401. [CrossRef]
68. Li, M.D.; Lin, W.; Luo, A.; Zhang, W.Y.; Sun, H.; Xiao, B.; Zheng, Y.G.; Yuan, Z.S.; Pan, J.W. High-powered optical superlattice with robust phase stability for quantum gas microscopy. *Opt. Express* **2021**, *29*, 13876–13886. [CrossRef] [PubMed]
69. Catani, J.; Barontini, G.; Lamporesi, G.; Rabatti, F.; Thalhammer, G.; Minardi, F.; Stringari, S.; Inguscio, M. Entropy Exchange in a Mixture of Ultracold Atoms. *Phys. Rev. Lett.* **2009**, *103*, 140401. [CrossRef]

70. McKay, D.C.; Meldgin, C.; Chen, D.; DeMarco, B. Slow Thermalization between a Lattice and Free Bose Gas. *Phys. Rev. Lett.* **2013**, *111*, 063002. [CrossRef] [PubMed]
71. Abanin, D.A.; Altman, E.; Bloch, I.; Serbyn, M. Colloquium: Many-body localization, thermalization, and entanglement. *Rev. Mod. Phys.* **2019**, *91*, 021001. [CrossRef]
72. Schreiber, M.; Hodgman, S.S.; Bordia, P.; Lüschen, H.P.; Fischer, M.H.; Vosk, R.; Altman, E.; Schneider, U.; Bloch, I. Observation of many-body localization of interacting fermions in a quasirandom optical lattice. *Science* **2015**, *349*, 842–845. [CrossRef]
73. Bordia, P.; Lüschen, H.P.; Hodgman, S.S.; Schreiber, M.; Bloch, I.; Schneider, U. Coupling Identical one-dimensional Many-Body Localized Systems. *Phys. Rev. Lett.* **2016**, *116*, 140401. [CrossRef]
74. Smith, J.; Lee, A.; Richerme, P.; Neyenhuis, B.; Hess, P.W.; Hauke, P.; Heyl, M.; Huse, D.A.; Monroe, C. Many-body localization in a quantum simulator with programmable random disorder. *Nat. Phys.* **2016**, *12*, 907–911. [CrossRef]
75. Lüschen, H.P.; Bordia, P.; Scherg, S.; Alet, F.; Altman, E.; Schneider, U.; Bloch, I. Observation of Slow Dynamics near the Many-Body Localization Transition in One-Dimensional Quasiperiodic Systems. *Phys. Rev. Lett.* **2017**, *119*, 260401. [CrossRef]
76. Rispoli, M.; Lukin, A.; Schittko, R.; Kim, S.; Tai, M.E.; Léonard, J.; Greiner, M. Quantum critical behaviour at the many-body localization transition. *Nature* **2019**, *573*, 385–389. [CrossRef]
77. Lukin, A.; Rispoli, M.; Schittko, R.; Tai, M.E.; Kaufman, A.M.; Choi, S.; Khemani, V.; Léonard, J.; Greiner, M. Probing entanglement in a many-body–localized system. *Science* **2019**, *364*, 256–260. [CrossRef]
78. Léonard, J.; Rispoli, M.; Lukin, A.; Schittko, R.; Kim, S.; Kwan, J.; Sels, D.; Demler, E.; Greiner, M. Signatures of bath-induced quantum avalanches in a many-body–localized system. *arXiv* **2020**, arXiv:2012.15270.
79. Panda, R.K.; Scardicchio, A.; Schulz, M.; Taylor, S.R.; Žnidarič, M. Can we study the many-body localisation transition? *EPL (Europhys. Lett.)* **2020**, *128*, 67003. [CrossRef]

Article

Fragmentation of Identical and Distinguishable Bosons' Pairs and Natural Geminals of a Trapped Bosonic Mixture

Ofir E. Alon [1,2]

[1] Department of Mathematics, University of Haifa, Haifa 3498838, Israel; ofir@research.haifa.ac.il
[2] Haifa Research Center for Theoretical Physics and Astrophysics, University of Haifa, Haifa 3498838, Israel

Abstract: In a mixture of two kinds of identical bosons, there are two types of pairs: identical bosons' pairs, of either species, and pairs of distinguishable bosons. In the present work, the fragmentation of pairs in a trapped mixture of Bose–Einstein condensates is investigated using a solvable model, the symmetric harmonic-interaction model for mixtures. The natural geminals for pairs made of identical or distinguishable bosons are explicitly contracted by diagonalizing the intra-species and inter-species reduced two-particle density matrices, respectively. Properties of pairs' fragmentation in the mixture are discussed, the role of the mixture's center-of-mass and relative center-of-mass coordinates is elucidated, and a generalization to higher-order reduced density matrices is made. As a complementary result, the exact Schmidt decomposition of the wave function of the bosonic mixture is constructed. The entanglement between the two species is governed by the coupling of their individual center-of-mass coordinates, and it does not vanish at the limit of an infinite number of particles where any finite-order intra-species and inter-species reduced density matrix per particle is 100% condensed. Implications are briefly discussed.

Keywords: Bose–Einstein condensates; mixtures; identical-boson pairs; distinguishable-boson pairs; natural geminals; natural orbitals; reduced density matrices; intra-species reduced density matrices; inter-species reduced density matrices; fragmentation; condensation; infinite-particle-number limit; harmonic-interaction models; pair fragmentation; Schmidt decomposition; center-of-mass; relative center-of-mass

1. Introduction

Condensation and fragmentation are basic and widely-studied concepts of Bose–Einstein condensates emanating from the properties of the reduced one-particle density matrix [1–5]. The bosons are said to be condensed if there is a single macroscopic eigenvalue of the reduced one-particle density matrix [6] and fragmented if there are two or more such macroscopic eigenvalues [7]. These eigenvalues are commonly called natural occupation numbers, and the respective eigenfunctions of the reduced one-particle density matrix are referred to as natural orbitals. The fragmentation of Bose–Einstein condensates has been investigated, e.g., in [8–27].

The condensation and especially fragmentation of the reduced two-particle density matrix of interacting identical bosons is less studied; see, e.g., [28]. Here, the analysis of the reduced two-particle density matrix would determine whether pairs of bosons are condensed or fragmented. The respective eigenfunctions of the reduced two-particle density matrix are often called natural geminals. We note that natural geminals in electronic systems have long been explored, see, e.g., [29–40].

Consider now a mixture of two kinds of identical bosons, which are labeled species 1 and species 2. Mixtures of Bose–Einstein condensates is a highly investigated topic; see, e.g., [41–70]. One may ask, just like for the single-species bosons, about the condensation or fragmentation of each of the species and how, for instance, one species is affected by the presence of the other species and vice versa. To answer this question, the intra-species reduced one-particle density matrices of species 1 and 2 are required, i.e., analyzing the intra-species occupation numbers and natural orbitals. Following the above line, one could also investigate the fragmentation of higher-order intra-species reduced density matrices in the mixture. For instance, to investigate whether pairs of identical bosons, of either species 1 or species 2, are fragmented, diagonalizing the intra-species reduced two-particle density matrices is needed. In summary, the fragmentation of identical bosons and its manifestation in higher-order reduced density matrices stem from the properties of intra-species quantities.

However, a mixture of Bose–Einstein condensates offers a degree-of-freedom or many-particle construction which does not exist for single-species bosons, namely, inter-species reduced density matrices. Now, if the fragmentation of identical bosons and pairs is defined as the macroscopic occupation of respective eigenvalues following the diagonalization of intra-species reduced density matrices, we may analogously define the fragmentation of distinguishable bosons' pairs as a macroscopic occupation of the eigenvalues of the inter-species reduced two-particle density matrix. Obviously, the latter is the lowest-order inter-species quantity, since at least one particle of each species is needed to build an inter-species entity.

The above discussion defines the goals of the present work, which are: (i) to investigate the fragmentation of pairs of identical bosons and establish the fragmentation of pairs of distinguishable bosons in a mixture of Bose–Einstein condensates; (ii) to construct the respective natural geminals of the mixture, for identical pairs and for distinguishable pairs; (iii) to show that the fragmentation of distinguishable bosons' pairs in the mixture persists with higher-order inter-species reduced density matrices; (iv) to construct the Schmidt decomposition of the mixture's wave function and discuss some of its properties at the limit of an infinite-number of particles where the mixture is 100% condensed; and (v) to achieve the first four goals analytically, using an exactly solvable model.

To this end, we recruited the harmonic-interaction model for mixtures [71–76], or, more precisely here, a symmetric version of which [77]. The harmonic-interaction model for single-species bosons (and fermions) has been used extensively in the literature, including for investigating the properties of Bose–Einstein condensates [78–92]. In our work, we built on results obtained and techniques used for the reduced density matrices of single-species bosons within the harmonic-interaction model [78–82], and, among others, generalized and extended them for the intra-species and particularly the inter-species reduced density matrices of mixtures [74].

The structure of the paper is as follows: In Section 2, we construct and investigate the fragmentation of intra-species and inter-species pair functions in the mixture. In Section 3, we extend the results and explore the fragmentation of pairs of distinguishable pairs. Furthermore, a complementary result for the Schmidt decomposition of the mixture's wavefucntion at the limit of an infinite number of particles is offered. In Section 4, a summary of the results and an outlook of some prospected research topics are provided. Finally, Appendix A collects the details of fragmentation of bosons and pairs in the single-species system for a comparison with the mixture.

2. Intra-Species and Inter-Species Natural Pair Functions

2.1. The Symmetric Two-Species Harmonic-Interaction Model

We consider a mixture of two Bose–Einstein condensates described by the Hamiltonian of the symmetric two-species harmonic-interaction model [74,77]:

$$\hat{H}(x_1,\ldots,x_N,y_1,\ldots,x_N) = \sum_{j=1}^{N}\left(-\frac{1}{2m}\frac{\partial^2}{\partial x_j^2} + \frac{1}{2}m\omega^2 x_j^2\right) + \lambda \sum_{1\leq j<k}^{N}(x_j - x_k)^2 + \\ + \sum_{j=1}^{N}\left(-\frac{1}{2m}\frac{\partial^2}{\partial y_j^2} + \frac{1}{2}m\omega^2 y_j^2\right) + \lambda \sum_{1\leq j<k}^{N}(y_j - y_k)^2 + \lambda_{12}\sum_{j=1}^{N}\sum_{k=1}^{N}(x_j - y_k)^2. \quad (1)$$

There are N bosons of type 1, N bosons of type 2, and the mass of each boson is m. λ is the intra-species interaction strength, either between two bosons of type 1 or two bosons of type 2, and λ_{12} is the inter-species interaction strength between type 1 and type 2 bosons. Dimensionality plays no role in the present work; hence, we work in one spatial dimension. $\hbar = 1$ is used throughout. Employing Jacoby coordinates for the mixture and translating back to the laboratory frame, the $2N$-boson wave function and corresponding many-particle density matrix are given by

$$\Psi(x_1,\ldots,x_N,y_1,\ldots,y_N) = \left(\frac{m\Omega}{\pi}\right)^{\frac{N-1}{2}} \left(\frac{M_{12}\Omega_{12}}{\pi}\right)^{\frac{1}{4}} \left(\frac{M\omega}{\pi}\right)^{\frac{1}{4}} \quad (2a)$$
$$\times e^{-\frac{\alpha}{2}\sum_{j=1}^{N}(x_j^2+y_j^2) - \beta \sum_{1\leq j<k}^{N}(x_jx_k+y_jy_k) + \gamma \sum_{j=1}^{N}\sum_{k=1}^{N} x_jy_k},$$

$$\Psi(x_1,\ldots,x_N,y_1,\ldots,y_N)\Psi^*(x_1',\ldots,x_N',y_1',\ldots,y_N') = \left(\frac{m\Omega}{\pi}\right)^{N-1}\left(\frac{M_{12}\Omega_{12}}{\pi}\right)^{\frac{1}{2}}\left(\frac{M\omega}{\pi}\right)^{\frac{1}{2}} \quad (2b)$$
$$\times e^{-\frac{\alpha}{2}\sum_{j=1}^{N}(x_j^2+x_j'^2+y_j^2+y_j'^2) - \beta \sum_{1\leq j<k}^{N}(x_jx_k+x_j'x_k'+y_jy_k+y_j'y_k') + \gamma \sum_{j=1}^{N}\sum_{k=1}^{N}(x_jy_k+x_j'y_k')},$$

with

$$\Omega = \sqrt{\omega^2 + \frac{2N}{m}(\lambda + \lambda_{12})}, \qquad \Omega_{12} = \sqrt{\omega^2 + \frac{4N}{m}\lambda_{12}}, \quad (2c)$$
$$\alpha = m\Omega + \beta, \qquad \beta = \frac{m}{2N}(\Omega_{12} + \omega - 2\Omega), \qquad \gamma = \frac{m}{2N}(\Omega_{12} - \omega),$$

and the relative center-of-mass $M_{12} = \frac{m}{2N}$ and center-of-mass $M = 2mN$ masses. The wave function and similarly the many-particle density of the mixture depend on two dressed frequencies, Ω and Ω_{12}, and consist of three parts: One-body part with coefficient α, intra-species two-body coupling with coefficient β, and inter-species two-body coupling with coefficient γ, whereas α and β depend on the intra-species and inter-species interactions, γ depends on the inter-species interaction only.

Another issue worth mentioning is the stability region of the mixture, namely when the mixture is bound. The condition that a bound solution of the mixture exists requires that all $2N$ degrees-of-freedom (oscillators after diagonalization with the Jacoby coordinates) are bound. Namely, the $2(N-1)$ relative-coordinate oscillators, which depend on both the intra-species and the inter-species interactions λ and λ_{12}, should be bound; the relative center-of-mass oscillator, which depends on the inter-species interaction λ_{12} only, should be bound; and the center-of-mass oscillator which does not depend on any of the two interactions and is always bound. Thus, for a bound mixture, both dressed frequencies Ω and Ω_{12} must be positive. This implies the conditions $\lambda + \lambda_{12} > -\frac{m\omega^2}{2N}$ and $\lambda_{12} > -\frac{m\omega^2}{4N}$, respectively, on the interactions. In other words, the inter-species interaction λ_{12} is bound from below, implying that the mutual repulsion between the two species cannot be too strong but is not bound from above, meaning that the mutual attraction between the two species can be unlimitedly strong. Furthermore, the intra-species interaction λ can take any value as long as the inter-species interaction is sufficiently attractive, i.e., $\lambda > -\frac{m\omega^2}{2N} - \lambda_{12}$. We shall return to the dressed frequencies Ω and Ω_{12} below. Note that in our work, we use the notions bound and stable interchangeably. For example, the border of stability of the mixture is the above-described border of parameters within which the ground state exists.

2.2. Intra-Species Natural Pair Functions

The intra-species reduced density matrices are defined when all bosons of the other type are integrated out. We concentrate in what follows on the reduced one-particle and in particular the two-particle density matrices of species 1,

$$\rho_1^{(1)}(x,x') = N \int dx_2 \cdots dx_N dy_1 \cdots dy_N \Psi(x,x_2,\ldots,x_N,y_1,\ldots,y_N)$$
$$\times \Psi^*(x',x_2,\ldots,x_N,y_1,\ldots,y_N), \quad (3)$$
$$\rho_1^{(2)}(x_1,x_2,x_1',x_2') = N(N-1) \int dx_3 \cdots dx_N dy_1 \cdots dy_N \Psi(x_1,x_2,x_3,\ldots,x_N,y_1,\ldots,y_N)$$
$$\times \Psi^*(x_1',x_2',x_3,\ldots,x_N,y_1,\ldots,y_N).$$

In a symmetric mixture, the corresponding reduced density matrices of species 2, $\rho_2^{(1)}(y,y')$ and $\rho_2^{(2)}(y_1,y_2,y_1',y_2')$, are the same and need not be repeated.

The reduction of the many-particle density (2b) to its finite-order reduced density matrices is somewhat lengthy and given in [74]. We start from the final expression for the intra-species reduced one-particle density matrix, which is given by

$$\rho_1^{(1)}(x,x') = N\left(\frac{\alpha+C_{1,0}}{\pi}\right)^{\frac{1}{2}} e^{-\frac{\alpha}{2}(x^2+x'^2)} e^{-\frac{1}{4}C_{1,0}(x+x')^2}$$

$$= N\left(\frac{\alpha+C_{1,0}}{\pi}\right)^{\frac{1}{2}} e^{-\frac{\alpha+\frac{C_{1,0}}{2}}{2}(x^2+x'^2)} e^{-\frac{1}{2}C_{1,0}xx'}, \quad (4)$$

$$\alpha + C_{1,0} = (\alpha - \beta)\frac{[(\alpha-\beta)+N\beta]^2 - N^2\gamma^2}{[(\alpha-\beta)+N\beta][(\alpha-\beta)+(N-1)\beta] - N(N-1)\gamma^2}.$$

The coefficient $C_{1,0}$ governs the properties of the intra-species reduced one-particle density matrix and reminds one that all bosons of type 2 and all but a single boson of type 1 are integrated out. As might be expected, $\rho_1^{(1)}(x,x')$ depends on the three parts of the many-boson wave function, i.e., on the α, β, and γ terms (2a). In the absence of inter-species interaction, i.e., for $\gamma = 0$, the coefficient $C_{1,0}$ boils down to that of the single-species harmonic-interaction model; see Appendix A for further discussion.

Just as for the case of single-species bosons [81,82], the intra-species reduced one-particle density matrix (4) can be diagonalized using Mehler's formula. Mehler's formula can be written as follows:

$$\left[\frac{(1-\rho)s}{(1+\rho)\pi}\right]^{\frac{1}{2}} e^{-\frac{1}{2}\frac{(1+\rho^2)s}{1-\rho^2}(x^2+x'^2)} e^{+\frac{2\rho s}{1-\rho^2}xx'}$$

$$= \sum_{n=0}^{\infty}(1-\rho)\rho^n \frac{1}{\sqrt{2^n n!}}\left(\frac{s}{\pi}\right)^{\frac{1}{4}} H_n(\sqrt{s}x)e^{-\frac{1}{2}sx^2} \frac{1}{\sqrt{2^n n!}}\left(\frac{s}{\pi}\right)^{\frac{1}{4}} H_n(\sqrt{s}x')e^{-\frac{1}{2}sx'^2}, \quad (5)$$

with $s > 0$ and, generally, for intra-species and inter-species reduced density matrices as well as later on for Schmidt decomposition of the wave function, $1 > \rho \geq 0$. H_n are the Hermite polynomials.

Comparing the structure of the intra-species reduced one-particle density matrix $\rho_1^{(1)}(x,x')$ with that of Mehler's formula one readily has

$$s_1^{(1)} = \sqrt{\alpha(\alpha+C_{1,0})} = \sqrt{\frac{\alpha(\alpha-\beta)\{[(\alpha-\beta)+N\beta]^2-N^2\gamma^2\}}{[(\alpha-\beta)+N\beta][(\alpha-\beta)+(N-1)\beta]-N(N-1)\gamma^2}},$$

$$\rho_1^{(1)} = \frac{\alpha-s_1^{(1)}}{\alpha+s_1^{(1)}} = \frac{\sqrt{\frac{\alpha\{[(\alpha-\beta)+N\beta][(\alpha-\beta)+(N-1)\beta]-N(N-1)\gamma^2\}}{(\alpha-\beta)\{[(\alpha-\beta)+N\beta]^2-N^2\gamma^2\}}}-1}{\sqrt{\frac{\alpha\{[(\alpha-\beta)+N\beta][(\alpha-\beta)+(N-1)\beta]-N(N-1)\gamma^2\}}{(\alpha-\beta)\{[(\alpha-\beta)+N\beta]^2-N^2\gamma^2\}}}+1}, \quad (6)$$

$$1 - \rho_1^{(1)} = \frac{2s_1^{(1)}}{\alpha+s_1^{(1)}},$$

where $1 - \rho_1^{(1)}$ is the condensate fraction of species 1 (and of species 2), i.e., the fraction of condensed bosons, and $\rho_1^{(1)}$ is the depleted fraction, namely, the fraction of bosons residing outside the lowest, condensed mode. $s_1^{(1)}$ is the scaling, or effective frequency, of the intra-species natural orbitals. The condensate fraction, depleted fraction, and scaling of the natural orbitals are all given in closed form as a function of the number of bosons N, and the intra-species λ and inter-species λ_{12} interaction strengths. A specific application of the general expressions (6) for the mixture appears below.

For the intra-species two-particle reduced density matrix, we have:

$$\rho_1^{(2)}(x_1,x_2,x_1',x_2') = N(N-1)\left(\frac{\alpha+C_{1,0}}{\pi}\right)^{\frac{1}{2}}\left(\frac{\alpha+C_{2,0}}{\pi}\right)^{\frac{1}{2}} \times$$
$$\times e^{-\frac{\alpha}{2}\left(x_1^2+x_2^2+x_1'^2+x_2'^2\right)}e^{-\beta\left(x_1x_2+x_1'x_2'\right)}e^{-\frac{1}{4}C_{2,0}\left(x_1+x_2+x_1'+x_2'\right)^2}, \quad (7)$$
$$\alpha+\beta+2C_{2,0} = (\alpha-\beta)\frac{[(\alpha-\beta)+N\beta]^2-N^2\gamma^2}{[(\alpha-\beta)+N\beta][(\alpha-\beta)+(N-2)\beta]-N(N-2)\gamma^2},$$

where $C_{1,0}$ is the coefficient of the intra-species reduced one-particle density matrix (4), and the combination $(\alpha+\beta+2C_{2,0})$ would appear shortly after.

To obtain the natural geminals of $\rho_1^{(2)}(x_1,x_2,x_1',x_2')$, we define the variables $q_1 = \frac{1}{\sqrt{2}}(x_1+x_2)$, $q_2 = \frac{1}{\sqrt{2}}(x_1-x_2)$ and $q_1' = \frac{1}{\sqrt{2}}(x_1'+x_2')$, $q_2' = \frac{1}{\sqrt{2}}(x_1'-x_2')$, i.e., the center-of-mass and relative coordinate of two identical bosons. With this rotation of coordinates, we have for the different terms in (7):

$$\begin{aligned} x_1^2+x_2^2+x_1'^2+x_2'^2 &= q_1^2+q_1'^2+q_2^2+q_2'^2, \\ x_1x_2+x_1'x_2' &= \tfrac{1}{2}\left(q_1^2+q_1'^2-q_2^2-q_2'^2\right), \\ (x_1+x_2+x_1'+x_2')^2 &= 2\left(q_1^2+q_1'^2+2q_1q_1'\right). \end{aligned} \quad (8)$$

Consequently, one readily finds the diagonal form

$$\rho_1^{(2)}(q_1,q_1',q_2,q_2') = N(N-1)\left(\frac{\alpha-\beta}{\pi}\right)^{\frac{1}{2}}e^{-\frac{\alpha-\beta}{2}\left(q_2^2+q_2'^2\right)} \times$$
$$\times \left(\frac{\alpha+\beta+2C_{2,0}}{\pi}\right)^{\frac{1}{2}}e^{-\frac{\alpha+\beta+C_{2,0}}{2}\left(q_1^2+q_1'^2\right)}e^{-C_{2,0}q_1q_1'}, \quad (9)$$

where the normalization coefficients before and after diagonalization are, of course, equal and satisfy $(\alpha+C_{1,0})(\alpha+C_{2,0}) = (\alpha-\beta)(\alpha+\beta+2C_{2,0})$.

After the transformation (8), the first term of $\rho_1^{(2)}(q_1,q_1',q_2,q_2')$ is separable as a function of q_2 and q_2', whereas by using Mehler's formula onto the variables q_1 and q_1', the second term can be diagonalized. Thus, comparing the second term in (9) and Equation (5), we find

$$s_1^{(2)} = \sqrt{(\alpha+\beta)(\alpha+\beta+2C_{2,0})} = \sqrt{\frac{(\alpha^2-\beta^2)\left\{[(\alpha-\beta)+N\beta]^2-N^2\gamma^2\right\}}{[(\alpha-\beta)+N\beta][(\alpha-\beta)+(N-2)\beta]-N(N-2)\gamma^2}},$$

$$\rho_1^{(2)} = \frac{(\alpha+\beta)-s_1^{(2)}}{(\alpha+\beta)+s_1^{(2)}} = \frac{\sqrt{\frac{(\alpha+\beta)\{[(\alpha-\beta)+N\beta][(\alpha-\beta)+(N-2)\beta]-N(N-2)\gamma^2\}}{(\alpha-\beta)\{[(\alpha-\beta)+N\beta]^2-N^2\gamma^2\}}}-1}{\sqrt{\frac{(\alpha+\beta)\{[(\alpha-\beta)+N\beta][(\alpha-\beta)+(N-2)\beta]-N(N-2)\gamma^2\}}{(\alpha-\beta)\{[(\alpha-\beta)+N\beta]^2-N^2\gamma^2\}}}+1}, \quad (10)$$

$$1-\rho_1^{(2)} = \frac{2s_1^{(2)}}{\alpha+s_1^{(2)}}.$$

With expressions (10), the decomposition of the intra-species reduced two-particle density matrix in terms of its natural geminals is explicitly given by

$$\rho_1^{(2)}(x_1,x_2,x_1',x_2') = N(N-1)\sum_{n=0}^{\infty}\left(1-\rho_1^{(2)}\right)\left(\rho_1^{(2)}\right)^n \Phi_{1,n}^{(2)}(x_1,x_2)\Phi_{1,n}^{(2),*}(x_1',x_2'),$$

$$\Phi_{1,n}^{(2)}(x_1,x_2) = \frac{1}{\sqrt{2^n n!}}\left(\frac{s_1^{(2)}}{\pi}\right)^{\frac{1}{4}}H_n\left(\sqrt{\frac{s_1^{(2)}}{2}}(x_1+x_2)\right)e^{-\frac{1}{4}s_1^{(2)}(x_1+x_2)^2} \quad (11)$$

$$\times \left(\frac{\alpha-\beta}{\pi}\right)^{\frac{1}{4}}e^{-\frac{1}{4}(\alpha-\beta)(x_1-x_2)^2}.$$

Equation (11) is a general result on the intra-species natural geminals of the mixture. Together with (10), they imply that $1-\rho_2^{(1)}$ is the fraction of condensed pairs of species 1 (and of species 2), $\rho_1^{(2)}$ is the fraction of depleted pairs, i.e., the fraction of pairs residing outside the lowest, condensed natural geminal, and $s_1^{(2)}$ is the scaling, or effective frequency, of the intra-species natural pair functions. The intra-species natural geminals along with their condensate and depleted fractions are prescribed as explicit functions of the number of bosons N, and the intra-species λ and inter-species λ_{12} interactions. A specific application of the general decomposition (10) and (11) to natural geminals of the mixture is provided below. Finally, we point out that the generalization to higher-order intra-species reduced density matrices and corresponding natural functions follow the above pattern and are not discussed further here.

Let us work out an explicit application where we shall find and analyze fragmentation of identical boson's pairs. Consider the specific scenario where $\lambda + \lambda_{12} = 0$, i.e., that the intra-species interaction is inverse to and 'compensates' the effect of the inter-species interaction on each of the species in the manner that the intra-species frequency is that of non-interacting particles, $\Omega = \omega$. This implies that the frequency of $2N - 1$ oscillators, the $2(N-1)$ relative-coordinate oscillators, and the center-of-mass oscillator is ω, and that only the relative center-of-mass oscillator carries an interaction-dressed frequency which is Ω_{12}. We would see the consequences below. Then, the coefficients of the three parts of the wave function simplify, and one has $\alpha = m\omega + \beta = m\omega\left[1 + \frac{1}{2N}\left(\frac{\Omega_{12}}{\omega} - 1\right)\right]$ and $\beta = \gamma = \frac{m}{2N}(\Omega_{12} - \omega)$. Consequently, the expressions (6) and (10) simplify, and the intra-species reduced one-particle and two-particle density matrices can be evaluated further. Thus, we readily find

$$s_1^{(1)} = m\omega\sqrt{\frac{1+\frac{1}{2N}\left(\frac{\Omega_{12}}{\omega}-1\right)}{1+\frac{1}{2N}\left(\frac{\omega}{\Omega_{12}}-1\right)}},$$

$$\rho_1^{(1)} = \frac{\sqrt{\left[1+\frac{1}{2N}\left(\frac{\Omega_{12}}{\omega}-1\right)\right]\left[1+\frac{1}{2N}\left(\frac{\omega}{\Omega_{12}}-1\right)\right]}-1}{\sqrt{\left[1+\frac{1}{2N}\left(\frac{\Omega_{12}}{\omega}-1\right)\right]\left[1+\frac{1}{2N}\left(\frac{\omega}{\Omega_{12}}-1\right)\right]}+1}, \quad (12a)$$

$$1 - \rho_1^{(1)} = \frac{2}{\sqrt{\left[1+\frac{1}{2N}\left(\frac{\Omega_{12}}{\omega}-1\right)\right]\left[1+\frac{1}{2N}\left(\frac{\omega}{\Omega_{12}}-1\right)\right]}+1}$$

for the intra-species reduced one-particle density matrix, where $\alpha + C_{1,0} = m\omega\frac{1}{1+\frac{1}{2N}\left(\frac{\omega}{\Omega_{12}}-1\right)}$ is used, and

$$s_1^{(2)} = m\omega\sqrt{\frac{1+\frac{1}{N}\left(\frac{\Omega_{12}}{\omega}-1\right)}{1+\frac{1}{N}\left(\frac{\omega}{\Omega_{12}}-1\right)}},$$

$$\rho_1^{(2)} = \frac{\sqrt{\left[1+\frac{1}{N}\left(\frac{\Omega_{12}}{\omega}-1\right)\right]\left[1+\frac{1}{N}\left(\frac{\omega}{\Omega_{12}}-1\right)\right]}-1}{\sqrt{\left[1+\frac{1}{N}\left(\frac{\Omega_{12}}{\omega}-1\right)\right]\left[1+\frac{1}{N}\left(\frac{\omega}{\Omega_{12}}-1\right)\right]}+1}, \quad (12b)$$

$$1 - \rho_1^{(2)} = \frac{2}{\sqrt{\left[1+\frac{1}{N}\left(\frac{\Omega_{12}}{\omega}-1\right)\right]\left[1+\frac{1}{N}\left(\frac{\omega}{\Omega_{12}}-1\right)\right]}+1}$$

for the intra-species reduced two-particle density matrix, where $\alpha + \beta = m\omega\left[1 + \frac{1}{N}\left(\frac{\Omega_{12}}{\omega} - 1\right)\right]$ and $\alpha + \beta + 2C_{2,0} = m\omega\frac{1}{1+\frac{1}{N}\left(\frac{\omega}{\Omega_{12}}-1\right)}$ are utilized. We see that the fragmentation of identical pairs and bosons are governed by the ratio $\frac{\Omega_{12}}{\omega}$ and its inverse $\frac{\omega}{\Omega_{12}}$, meaning that it takes place both at the attractive and repulsive sectors of interactions. Moreover, the condensed and depleted fractions of the pairs and bosons are symmetric to interchanging $\frac{\Omega_{12}}{\omega}$ and $\frac{\omega}{\Omega_{12}}$; see discussion below.

Let us analyze explicitly macroscopic fragmentation of geminals, i.e., when there is a macroscopic occupation of more than a single intra-species natural pair function of $\rho_1^{(2)}(x_1, x_2, x_1', x_2')$. As a reference, we also refer to the corresponding and standardly defined macroscopic fragmentation of the intra-species natural orbitals of $\rho_1^{(1)}(x,x')$. The structure of the eigenvalues, emanating from Mehler's formula and its applicability to the various reduced density matrices, suggests that, say, the 'middle' value $\rho = 1 - \rho = \frac{1}{2}$, i.e., when the condensed and depleted fractions are equal, is a convenient manifestation of macroscopic fragmentation. Indeed, for this value the first few natural occupation fractions $(1-\rho)\rho^n$, $n = 0, 1, 2, 3, 4, \ldots$ are

$$\frac{1}{2}, \frac{1}{4}, \frac{1}{8}, \frac{1}{16}, \frac{1}{32}, \ldots, \tag{13}$$

namely, there is 50% occupation of the first natural geminal, 25% occupation of the second, 12.5% of the third, 6.25% of the fourth, 3.125% of the fifth, and so on. For brevity, we refer to the fragmentation values in (13) as 50% fragmentation.

Now, one can compute for which ratio $\frac{\Omega_{12}}{\omega}$, or, equivalently, for which inter-species interaction $\lambda_{12} = \frac{m\omega^2}{4N}\left[\left(\frac{\Omega_{12}}{\omega}\right)^2 - 1\right]$, the intra-species reduced two-particle and one-particle density matrices are macroscopically fragmented as in (13). Thus, solving (12a) for 50% natural-orbital fragmentation, we find

$$\rho_1^{(1)} = \frac{1}{2} \implies \frac{\Omega_{12}}{\omega} = \left(1 + \frac{8N^2}{N - \frac{1}{2}}\right) \pm \sqrt{\left(1 + \frac{8N^2}{N - \frac{1}{2}}\right)^2 - 1}, \tag{14}$$

and working out (12b) for 50% natural-geminal fragmentation, we obtain

$$\rho_1^{(2)} = \frac{1}{2} \implies \frac{\Omega_{12}}{\omega} = \sqrt{1 + \frac{4N}{m\omega^2}\lambda_{12}} = \left(1 + \frac{4N^2}{N-1}\right) \pm \sqrt{\left(1 + \frac{4N^2}{N-1}\right)^2 - 1}. \tag{15}$$

There are two 'reciprocate' solutions for both the natural geminals and natural orbitals: We see that 50% fragmentation occurs for strong attractions, i.e., when $\frac{\Omega_{12}}{\omega}$ is large, or near the border of stability for repulsions, which is when $\frac{\Omega_{12}}{\omega}$ is close to zero. In addition, to achieve the same degree of 50% with a larger number N of species 1 (and species 2) bosons, a stronger attraction or repulsion is needed. Finally, comparing the natural-geminal with the natural-orbital fragmentation at the same 50% value, one sees from (15) and (14) that slightly weaker interactions, attractions or repulsions, are needed for the former.

It is also useful to register the one-particle and two-particle densities, i.e., the diagonal parts $\rho_1^{(1)}(x) = \rho_1^{(1)}(x, x' = x)$ and $\rho_1^{(2)}(x_1, x_2) = \rho_1^{(2)}(x_1, x_2, x_1' = x_1, x_2' = x_2)$, which read

$$\rho_1^{(1)}(x) = N\left(\frac{\alpha + C_{1,0}}{\pi}\right)^{\frac{1}{2}} e^{-(\alpha + C_{1,0})x^2} = N\left(\frac{m\omega}{\pi\left[1 + \frac{1}{2N}\left(\frac{\omega}{\Omega_{12}} - 1\right)\right]}\right)^{\frac{1}{2}} e^{-\frac{m\omega}{1 + \frac{1}{2N}\left(\frac{\omega}{\Omega_{12}} - 1\right)}x^2},$$

$$\rho_1^{(2)}(x_1, x_2) = N(N-1)\left(\frac{\alpha - \beta}{\pi}\right)^{\frac{1}{2}} e^{-\frac{\alpha-\beta}{2}(x_1-x_2)^2}\left(\frac{\alpha + \beta + 2C_{2,0}}{\pi}\right)^{\frac{1}{2}} e^{-\frac{\alpha+\beta+2C_{2,0}}{2}(x_1+x_2)^2} \tag{16}$$

$$= N(N-1)\left(\frac{m\omega}{\pi}\right)^{\frac{1}{2}} e^{-\frac{m\omega}{2}(x_1-x_2)^2}\left(\frac{m\omega}{\pi\left[1 + \frac{1}{N}\left(\frac{\omega}{\Omega_{12}} - 1\right)\right]}\right)^{\frac{1}{2}} e^{-\frac{m\omega}{2\left[1 + \frac{1}{N}\left(\frac{\omega}{\Omega_{12}} - 1\right)\right]}(x_1+x_2)^2}.$$

From the densities (16), we can infer a measure for the size of identical pairs' and bosons' clouds using the widths of the respective Gaussian functions therein. Thus, we have

$$\sigma_{1,x}^{(1)} = \sqrt{\frac{1 + \frac{1}{2N}\left(\frac{\omega}{\Omega_{12}} - 1\right)}{2m\omega}},$$

$$\sigma_{1,\frac{x_1+x_2}{\sqrt{2}}}^{(2)} = \sqrt{\frac{1 + \frac{1}{N}\left(\frac{\omega}{\Omega_{12}} - 1\right)}{2m\omega}}, \quad \sigma_{1,\frac{x_1-x_2}{\sqrt{2}}}^{(2)} = \sqrt{\frac{1}{2m\omega}}. \tag{17a}$$

We can understand intuitively why the width $\sigma^{(2)}_{1,\frac{x_1-x_2}{\sqrt{2}}}$ is the typical length of the harmonic trap. For this, recall that $\sigma^{(2)}_{1,\frac{x_1-x_2}{\sqrt{2}}}$ is associated with the relative two-boson coordinate q_2, q'_2. The general intra-species two-particle reduced density matrix (9) is diagonal in this relative coordinate. The respective exponent is $\alpha - \beta = m\Omega$. Then, since for the specific case studied $\lambda + \lambda_{12} = 0$ the exponent boils down to that of the bare harmonic potential, i.e., $\Omega = \omega$, we readily obtain the result.

To assess the combined impact of the intra-species and inter-species interactions atop the fragmentation of the reduced density matrices, it is useful to compute the sizes (17a) for large inter-species attractions or inter-species repulsions at the border of stability. One finds, respectively,

$$\lim_{\frac{\Omega_{12}}{\omega} \to \infty} \sigma^{(1)}_{1,x} = \sqrt{\frac{1-\frac{1}{2N}}{2m\omega}}, \quad \sigma^{(1)}_{1,x} \longrightarrow \infty \quad \text{for} \quad \frac{\Omega_{12}}{\omega} \to 0^+,$$

$$\lim_{\frac{\Omega_{12}}{\omega} \to \infty} \sigma^{(2)}_{1,\frac{x_1+x_2}{\sqrt{2}}} = \sqrt{\frac{1-\frac{1}{N}}{2m\omega}}, \quad \sigma^{(2)}_{1,\frac{x_1+x_2}{\sqrt{2}}} \longrightarrow \infty \quad \text{for} \quad \frac{\Omega_{12}}{\omega} \to 0^+, \quad (17b)$$

where $\sigma^{(2)}_{1,\frac{x_1-x_2}{\sqrt{2}}}$ as discussed above is independent of the interactions. Interestingly, the size of the densities for strong inter-species attractions, which is accompanied by strong intra-species repulsions because $\lambda + \lambda_{12} = 0$, saturates at about the trap's size and does not depend on the strengths of interactions. In other words, a high degree of fragmentation is possible in the mixture without shrinking of the density due to strong inter-species attractive interaction or expansion of the intra-species densities due to strong intra-species repulsive interaction. For the sake of comparative analysis, it is instructive to make contact with the fragmentation of single-species bosons in the harmonic-interaction model; see Appendix A.

2.3. Inter-Species Natural Pair Functions

As mentioned above, in a mixture of two types of identical bosons, there are other kinds of pairs, namely, pairs of distinguishable particles. If we are to examine the lowest-order inter-species reduced density matrix, we can ask regarding distinguishable pairs questions analogous to those asked concerning identical pairs. The purpose of this subsection is to derive the relevant tools and answer such questions.

The inter-species reduced two-particle density matrix, i.e., the lowest-oder inter-species quantity, is defined from the all-particle density matrix as

$$\rho^{(2)}_{12}(x,x',y,y') = N^2 \int dx_2 \cdots dx_N dy_2 \cdots dy_N \Psi(x,x_2,\ldots,x_N,y,y_2,\ldots,y_N)$$
$$\times \Psi^*(x',x_2,\ldots,x_N,y',y_2,\ldots,y_N). \quad (18)$$

For the harmonic-interaction model of the symmetric mixture, it can be computed analytically and, starting from (2b), is given by [74]

$$\rho^{(2)}_{12}(x,x',y,y') = N^2 \left[\frac{(\alpha_1+C_{1,1})^2 - D^2_{1,1}}{\pi^2} \right]^{\frac{1}{2}} \times$$
$$\times e^{-\frac{\alpha_1}{2}(x^2+x'^2+y^2+y'^2)} e^{-\frac{1}{4}C_{1,1}\left[(x+x')^2+(y+y')^2\right]} e^{+\frac{1}{2}D_{1,1}(x+x')(y+y')} e^{+\frac{1}{2}D'_{1,1}(x-x')(y-y')}, \quad (19a)$$

where

$$\alpha + C_{1,1} \mp D_{1,1} = (\alpha - \beta)\frac{(\alpha-\beta)+N(\beta\mp\gamma)}{(\alpha-\beta)+(N-1)(\beta\mp\gamma)},$$
$$D'_{1,1} = \gamma. \quad (19b)$$

We see that the structure of the inter-species reduced two-particle density matrix is more involved than that of the intra-species reduced two-particle density matrix, as well as that of the product of the two, species 1 and species 2 intra-species reduced one-particle density matrices. Nonetheless, it can be diagonalized.

To diagonalize $\rho_{12}^{(2)}(x, x', y, y')$, one must couple and make linear combinations of coordinates associated with distinguishable bosons. Defining $u = \frac{1}{\sqrt{2}}(x+y)$, $v = \frac{1}{\sqrt{2}}(x-y)$ and $u' = \frac{1}{\sqrt{2}}(x'+y')$, $v' = \frac{1}{\sqrt{2}}(x'-y')$, we have for the different terms in (19):

$$x^2 + y^2 + x'^2 + y'^2 = u^2 + u'^2 + v^2 + v'^2,$$

$$(x+x')^2 + (y+y')^2 = (u+u')^2 + (v+v')^2 = u^2 + u'^2 + v^2 + v'^2 + 2(uu' + vv'), \quad (20)$$

$$(x \pm x')(y \pm y') = \tfrac{1}{2}\left[(u \pm u')^2 - (v \pm v')^2\right] = \tfrac{1}{2}\left(u^2 + u'^2 - v^2 - v'^2\right) \pm (uu' - vv').$$

Consequently, we readily find the decomposition

$$\rho_{12}^{(2)}(u, u', v, v') = N^2 \left(\frac{\alpha_1 + C_{1,1} - D_{1,1}}{\pi}\right)^{\frac{1}{2}} e^{-\frac{\alpha_1 + \frac{C_{1,1}}{2} - \frac{D_{1,1} + D'_{1,1}}{2}}{}} \left(u^2 + u'^2\right) e^{-\frac{1}{2}[C_{1,1} - (D_{1,1} - D'_{1,1})]uu'} \quad (21)$$

$$\times \left(\frac{\alpha_1 + C_{1,1} + D_{1,1}}{\pi}\right)^{\frac{1}{2}} e^{-\frac{\alpha_1 + \frac{C_{1,1}}{2} - \frac{D_{1,1} + D'_{1,1}}{2}}{}} \left(v^2 + v'^2\right) e^{-\frac{1}{2}[C_{1,1} + (D_{1,1} - D'_{1,1})]vv'},$$

where the normalizations after and before diagonalization are, of course, equal. As might be expected, since the structure of $\rho_{12}^{(2)}(x, x', y, y')$ is more involved than that of $\rho_1^{(2)}(x_1, x_2, x'_1, x'_2)$, the diagonalization of the former is more intricate. Fortunately, we can do that using the application of Mehler's formula twice, on the appropriately-constructed inter-species 'mixed' coordinates u, u' and v, v'. We thus obtain

$$s_{12,\pm}^{(2)} = \sqrt{\left(\alpha \mp D'_{1,1}\right)(\alpha + C_{1,1} \mp D_{1,1})} = \sqrt{(\alpha \mp \gamma)(\alpha - \beta)\frac{(\alpha - \beta) + N(\beta \mp \gamma)}{(\alpha - \beta) + (N-1)(\beta \mp \gamma)}},$$

$$\rho_{12,\pm}^{(2)} = \frac{(\alpha \mp D'_{1,1}) - s_{12,\pm}^{(2)}}{(\alpha \mp D'_{1,1}) + s_{12,\pm}^{(2)}} = \frac{\frac{(\alpha \mp \gamma)[(\alpha - \beta) + (N-1)(\beta \mp \gamma)]}{(\alpha - \beta)[(\alpha - \beta) + N(\beta \mp \gamma)]} - 1}{\frac{(\alpha \mp \gamma)[(\alpha - \beta) + (N-1)(\beta \mp \gamma)]}{(\alpha - \beta)[(\alpha - \beta) + N(\beta \mp \gamma)]} + 1}, \quad (22)$$

$$1 - \rho_{12,\pm}^{(2)} = \frac{2 s_{12,\pm}^{(2)}}{(\alpha \mp D'_{1,1}) + s_{12,\pm}^{(2)}},$$

where the "+" terms quantify the fragmentation in the u, u' part of the inter-species reduced two-particle density matrix and the "−" terms quantify the fragmentation in the v, v' part of the inter-species reduced two-particle density matrix; also see below. Equation (22) is one of the main results of the present work and bears a clear and appealing physical meaning: that pairs made of distinguishable bosons can be fragmented and that this fragmentation is governed by the center-of-mass and by a relative coordinate of distinguishable bosons. We shall return to this point in what follows.

We can now prescribe the decomposition of the inter-species reduced two-particle density matrix to its distinguishable natural pair functions, which is given by

$$\rho_{12}^{(2)}(x, x', y, y')$$
$$= N^2 \sum_{n_+=0}^{\infty} \sum_{n_-=0}^{\infty} \left(1 - \rho_{12,+}^{(2)}\right)\left(1 - \rho_{12,-}^{(2)}\right)\left(\rho_{12,+}^{(2)}\right)^{n_+}\left(\rho_{12,-}^{(2)}\right)^{n_-} \Phi_{12,n_+,n_-}^{(2)}(x, y) \Phi_{12,n_+,n_-}^{(2),*}(x', y'),$$

$$\Phi_{12,n_+,n_-}^{(2)}(x, y) = \frac{1}{\sqrt{2^{n_+} n_+!}} \left(\frac{s_{12,+}^{(2)}}{\pi}\right)^{\frac{1}{4}} H_{n_+}\left(\sqrt{\frac{s_{12,+}^{(2)}}{2}}(x+y)\right) e^{-\frac{1}{4} s_{12,+}^{(2)} (x+y)^2} \quad (23)$$

$$\times \frac{1}{\sqrt{2^{n_-} n_-!}} \left(\frac{s_{12,-}^{(2)}}{\pi}\right)^{\frac{1}{4}} H_{n_-}\left(\sqrt{\frac{s_{12,-}^{(2)}}{2}}(x-y)\right) e^{-\frac{1}{4} s_{12,-}^{(2)} (x-y)^2}.$$

All in all, (23) implies that the distinguishable-pair 'condensed fraction' is given by $\left(1 - \rho^{(2)}_{12,+}\right)\left(1 - \rho^{(2)}_{12,-}\right)$ and the respective depleted fraction by $1 - \left(1 - \rho^{(2)}_{12,+}\right)\left(1 - \rho^{(2)}_{12,-}\right) = \rho^{(2)}_{12,+} + \rho^{(2)}_{12,-} - \rho^{(2)}_{12,+}\rho^{(2)}_{12,-}$. Each of the inter-species 'mixed' coordinates $\frac{x \pm y}{\sqrt{2}}$ carries its own scaling, $s^{(2)}_{12,\pm}$. The distinguishable natural geminals $\Phi^{(2)}_{12,n_+,n_-}(x,y)$ are, needless to say, orthonormal to each other.

We proceed now for an application. We considered above the specific case of $\lambda + \lambda_{12} = 0$, which leads to $\Omega = \omega$, $\alpha = m\omega \left[1 + \frac{1}{2N}\left(\frac{\Omega_{12}}{\omega} - 1\right)\right]$, and $\beta = \gamma = \frac{m}{2N}(\Omega_{12} - \omega)$. Recall that this implies that the frequency of $2N - 1$ coordinates, the $2(N-1)$ relative coordinates, and the center-of-mass coordinate is ω and that only the relative center-of-mass coordinate has an interaction-dressed frequency, Ω_{12}. To evaluate $\rho^{(2)}_{12}(x, x', y, y')$, we also need the combinations $(\alpha + C_{1,1} - D_{1,1}) = m\omega$ and $\left(\alpha - D'_{1,1}\right) = m\omega$ for the "+" branch, as well as $(\alpha + C_{1,1} + D_{1,1}) = m\omega \frac{1}{1 + \frac{1}{N}\left(\frac{\omega}{\Omega_{12}} - 1\right)}$ and $\left(\alpha + D'_{1,1}\right) = m\omega\left[1 + \frac{1}{N}\left(\frac{\Omega_{12}}{\omega} - 1\right)\right]$ for the "−" branch.

Thus, expressions (22) can readily be evaluated, and the following picture of inter-species fragmentation is found:

$$s^{(2)}_{12,+} = m\omega, \qquad \rho^{(2)}_{12,+} = 0, \qquad 1 - \rho^{(2)}_{12,+} = 1, \tag{24a}$$

indicating that there is no contribution to fragmentation from the symmetric 'mixed' coordinate u, u'. On the other end,

$$s^{(2)}_{12,-} = m\omega \sqrt{\frac{1 + \frac{1}{N}\left(\frac{\Omega_{12}}{\omega} - 1\right)}{1 + \frac{1}{N}\left(\frac{\omega}{\Omega_{12}} - 1\right)}},$$

$$\rho^{(2)}_{12,-} = \frac{\sqrt{\left[1 + \frac{1}{N}\left(\frac{\Omega_{12}}{\omega} - 1\right)\right]\left[1 + \frac{1}{N}\left(\frac{\omega}{\Omega_{12}} - 1\right)\right]} - 1}{\sqrt{\left[1 + \frac{1}{N}\left(\frac{\Omega_{12}}{\omega} - 1\right)\right]\left[1 + \frac{1}{N}\left(\frac{\omega}{\Omega_{12}} - 1\right)\right]} + 1}, \tag{24b}$$

$$1 - \rho^{(2)}_{12,-} = \frac{2}{\sqrt{\left[1 + \frac{1}{N}\left(\frac{\Omega_{12}}{\omega} - 1\right)\right]\left[1 + \frac{1}{N}\left(\frac{\omega}{\Omega_{12}} - 1\right)\right]} + 1},$$

namely, that the fragmentation fully originates from the asymmetric 'mixed' coordinate v, v'. We conclude that, whereas the fragmentation of identical pairs is associated with their center-of-mass coordinate, the fragmentation of distinguishable pairs is linked, in this explicit case, only with a relative coordinate between two distinguishable bosons. Interestingly, the degree of intra-species and inter-species pair fragmentation is the same in the specific case considered, despite pertaining to different parts of the mixtures' many-boson wave function. Furthermore, there are different numbers of pairs: $\frac{N}{2}$ intra-species identical pairs (for each of the species) and N inter-species pairs of distinguishable bosons.

Now, one can compute the ratio $\frac{\Omega_{12}}{\omega} = \sqrt{1 + \frac{4N}{m\omega^2}\lambda_{12}}$ for which the inter-species reduced two-particle density matrix is 50% fragmented as in (13). Since $\rho^{(2)}_{12,+} = 0$ does not contribute, the only contribution to fragmentation comes from $\rho^{(2)}_{12,-}$. Thus, solving (24b) for 50% distinguishable-pair-function fragmentation, we obtain

$$\rho^{(2)}_{12,-} = \frac{1}{2} \quad \Longrightarrow \quad \frac{\Omega_{12}}{\omega} = \left(1 + \frac{4N^2}{N-1}\right) \pm \sqrt{\left(1 + \frac{4N^2}{N-1}\right)^2 - 1}. \tag{25}$$

As above, there are two 'reciprocate' solutions: one for strong inter-species attraction and the second close to the border of stability for intermediate-strength inter-species repulsion. We remind that since $\lambda + \lambda_{12} = 0$ in our example, the respective intra-species interaction is opposite in sign. In addition, to achieve the same degree of 50% fragmentation with a larger number N of distinguishable pairs, a stronger inter-species attraction or repulsion is needed. Furthermore, as discussed above, comparing distinguishable-pair and identical-pair fragmentation at the same 50% value in this example, one sees from (25) and (15) that the same interaction is needed.

Finally, we prescribe the inter-species two-particle density, namely, the diagonal part $\rho_{12}^{(2)}(x,y) = \rho_{12}^{(2)}(x,x'=x,y,y'=y)$, which is given by

$$\rho_{12}^{(2)}(x,y) = N^2 \left(\frac{\alpha_1+C_{1,1}-D_{1,1}}{\pi}\right)^{\frac{1}{2}} e^{-\frac{\alpha_1+C_{1,1}-D_{1,1}}{2}(x+y)^2}$$

$$\times \left(\frac{\alpha_1+C_{1,1}+D_{1,1}}{\pi}\right)^{\frac{1}{2}} e^{-\frac{\alpha_1+C_{1,1}+D_{1,1}}{2}(x-y)^2} \quad (26)$$

$$= N^2 \left(\frac{m\omega}{\pi}\right)^{\frac{1}{2}} e^{-\frac{m\omega}{2}(x+y)^2} \left(\frac{m\omega}{\pi\left[1+\frac{1}{N}\left(\frac{\omega}{\Omega_{12}}-1\right)\right]}\right)^{\frac{1}{2}} e^{-\frac{m\omega}{2\left[1+\frac{1}{N}\left(\frac{\omega}{\Omega_{12}}-1\right)\right]}(x-y)^2}.$$

Next, the size of the distinguishable pairs' cloud can be assessed from the density (26) using the widths of the respective Gaussian functions. Accordingly, we find

$$\sigma_{12,\frac{x+y}{\sqrt{2}}}^{(2)} = \sqrt{\frac{1}{2m\omega}}, \quad \sigma_{12,\frac{x-y}{\sqrt{2}}}^{(2)} = \sqrt{\frac{1+\frac{1}{N}\left(\frac{\omega}{\Omega_{12}}-1\right)}{2m\omega}}. \quad (27a)$$

The explanation why the width $\sigma_{12,\frac{x+y}{\sqrt{2}}}^{(2)}$ is also the typical length of the harmonic potential is somewhat less intuitive. The distinguishable pair center-of-mass coordinate u, u' appears in the general inter-species reduced two-particle density matrix (21) in a coupled form which requires diagonalization via Mehler's formula. We find in the specific case $\lambda + \lambda_{12} = 0$ that $\gamma = \beta$. This leads to a neat cancellation of terms, and the retaining of a single term in the Mehler's expansion with the typical length of the harmonic potential.

To show the combined effect of the intra-species and inter-species interactions accompanying the fragmentation of $\rho_{12}^{(2)}(x, x', y, y')$, it is useful to compute the sizes (27a) for large inter-species attractions or inter-species repulsions at the border of stability. We obtain, respectively,

$$\lim_{\frac{\Omega_{12}}{\omega} \to \infty} \sigma_{12,\frac{x-y}{\sqrt{2}}}^{(2)} = \sqrt{\frac{1-\frac{1}{N}}{2m\omega}}, \quad \sigma_{12,\frac{x-y}{\sqrt{2}}}^{(2)} \longrightarrow \infty \quad \text{for} \quad \frac{\Omega_{12}}{\omega} \to 0^+, \quad (27b)$$

where $\sigma_{12,\frac{x+y}{\sqrt{2}}}^{(2)}$ as discussed above is independent of the interactions. We see that the size of the inter-species density saturates as does the trap's size and does not depend on the strengths of interactions in the limit of strong inter-species attractions. Analogously to identical pairs, a strong fragmentation of distinguishable pairs is possible in the mixture without the shrinking of the inter-species density due to strong inter-species attractive interaction. At the other end, when the inter-species repulsion is close to the border of stability, the inter-species density expands boundlessly. Summarizing, inter-species fragmentation is governed by the ratio $\frac{\Omega_{12}}{\omega}$ and takes place both at the attractive and repulsive sectors of interactions. For the sake of analysis, we compared the results for inter-species pair fragmentation with intra-species pair fragmentation and discussed the similarity and differences between the respective two-particle densities (16) and (26).

3. Pair of Distinguishable Pairs and Schmidt Decomposition of the wave function

Following the results of the previous section on the fragmentation of distinguishable pairs, there are two questions that warrant answers. The first is whether inter-species fragmentation persists beyond distinguishable pairs, say, to pairs of distinguishable pairs? Inasmuch as single-species and intra-species fragmentations take place at the lowest-level reduced one-particle density matrix and persist at higher-level single-species reduced density matrices, we wish to establish the result of inter-species fragmentation at the level of higher-order reduced density matrices. After all, the reduced two-particle density matrix is the lowest-order inter-species one. The second question deals with the nature of the inter-species coordinates governing fragmentation. At the level of distinguishable-pair fragmentation, i.e., within the inter-species reduced two-particle density matrix, one cannot unambiguously tell whether the relative center-of-mass coordinate of the two species is involved or whether other relative inter-species coordinates govern fragmentation. This is because in a pair of distinguishable particles, one cannot distinguish between the two types of coordinates.

As seen in the previous section, the inter-species reduced two-particle density matrix is more intricate than the intra-species ones, and consequently, its diagonalization is more involved. We derive now the inter-species reduced four-particle density matrix and examine which 'normal coordinates' govern its diagonalization. Then, the natural four-particle functions are obtained explicitly and investigated.

Finally, and as a complementary result of the techniques used for inter-species fragmentation, we carry the connection between inter-species and intra-species center-of-mass coordinates, in conjunction with the usage of Mehler's formula within a mixture, further. This is performed by constructing the Schmidt decomposition of the mixture's wave function and discussing the consequences of this decomposition at the limit of an infinite number of particles.

3.1. Inter-Species Fragmentation in Higher-Order Reduced Density Matrices

The inter-species reduced four-particle density matrix is defined as

$$\rho_{12}^{(4)}(x_1, x_2, x_1', x_2', y_1, y_2, y_1', y_2') = N^2(N-1)^2 \int dx_3 \cdots dx_N dy_3 \cdots dy_N \qquad (28)$$
$$\times \Psi(x_1, x_2, x_3, \ldots, x_N, y_1, y_2, y_3, \ldots, y_N) \Psi^*(x_1', x_2', x_3, \ldots, x_N, y_1', y_2', y_3, \ldots, y_N).$$

Note that here we only treat the four-particle quantity with two identical bosons per each species. Integrating the harmonic interaction-model for symmetric mixtures, we find the final expression explicitly

$$\rho_{12}^{(4)}(x_1, x_2, x_1', x_2', y_1, y_2, y_1', y_2') = N^2(N-1)^2 \left[\frac{(\alpha+C_{1,1})^2 - D_{1,1}^2}{\pi^2}\right]^{\frac{1}{2}} \left[\frac{(\alpha+C_{2,2})^2 - D_{2,2}^2}{\pi^2}\right]^{\frac{1}{2}}$$
$$\times e^{-\frac{\alpha}{2}\left(x_1^2 + x_2^2 + x_1'^2 + x_2'^2 + y_1^2 + y_2^2 + y_1'^2 + y_2'^2\right)} e^{-\beta(x_1 x_2 + x_1' x_2' + y_1 y_2 + y_1' y_2')} \qquad (29a)$$
$$\times e^{-\frac{1}{4}C_{2,2}\left[(x_1+x_2+x_1'+x_2')^2 + (y_1+y_2+y_1'+y_2')^2\right]} \times$$
$$\times e^{+\frac{1}{2}D_{2,2}(x_1+x_2+x_1'+x_2')(y_1+y_2+y_1'+y_2')} e^{+\frac{1}{2}D_{2,2}'(x_1+x_2-x_1'-x_2')(y_1+y_2-y_1'-y_2')},$$

where

$$\alpha + \beta + 2(C_{2,2} \mp D_{2,2}) = (\alpha - \beta) \frac{(\alpha-\beta) + N(\beta \mp \gamma)}{(\alpha-\beta) + (N-2)(\beta \mp \gamma)}, \qquad (29b)$$
$$D_{2,2}' = \gamma,$$

and $\alpha + C_{1,1} \mp D_{1,1}$ are given in (19b). The combinations of parameters $\alpha + \beta + 2(C_{2,2} \mp D_{2,2})$ would appear below shortly.

To diagonalize $\rho_{12}^{(4)}(x_1, x_2, x_1', x_2', y_1, y_2, y_1', y_2')$, we need to mix and rotate the coordinates of the two species into new coordinates appropriately. Thus, defining the new coordinates as the center-of-mass, relative center-of-mass, and relative coordinates of two identical pairs, one for each of the species, $u_1 = \frac{1}{2}[(x_1+x_2)+(y_1+y_2)]$, $v_1 = \frac{1}{2}[(x_1+x_2)-(y_1+y_2)]$, $u_2 = \frac{1}{\sqrt{2}}(x_1-x_2)$, $v_2 = \frac{1}{\sqrt{2}}(y_1-y_2)$ and $u_1' = \frac{1}{2}[(x_1'+x_2')+(y_1'+y_2')]$, $v_1' = \frac{1}{2}[(x_1'+x_2') - (y_1'+y_2')]$, $u_2' = \frac{1}{\sqrt{2}}(x_1'-x_2')$, $v_2' = \frac{1}{\sqrt{2}}(y_1'-y_2')$, we have for the different terms in (29a):

$$x_1^2 + x_2^2 + y_1^2 + y_2^2 + x_1'^2 + x_2'^2 + y_1'^2 + y_2'^2 = u_1^2 + u_1'^2 + v_1^2 + v_1'^2 + u_2^2 + u_2'^2 + v_2^2 + v_2'^2,$$

$$x_1 x_2 + x_1' x_2' + y_1 y_2 + y_1' y_2' = \tfrac{1}{2}\left(u_1^2 + u_1'^2 + v_1^2 + v_1'^2 - u_2^2 - u_2'^2 - v_2^2 - v_2'^2\right),$$

$$(x_1 + x_2 + x_1' + x_2')^2 + (y_1 + y_2 + y_1' + y_2')^2 = 2\left[(u_1 + u_1')^2 + (v_1 + v_1')^2\right],$$

$$[(x_1 + x_2) \pm (x_1' + x_2')][(y_1 + y_2) \pm (y_1' + y_2')] = (u_1 \pm u_1')^2 - (v_1 \pm v_1')^2. \tag{30}$$

Relations (30) imply that one could equally define inter-species linear combinations of the relative coordinates, since $u_2^2 + v_2^2 = \left[\frac{(x_1-x_2)+(y_1-y_2)}{2}\right]^2 + \left[\frac{(x_1-x_2)-(y_1-y_2)}{2}\right]^2$ and $u_2'^2 + v_2'^2 = \left[\frac{(x_1'-x_2')+(y_1'-y_2')}{2}\right]^2 + \left[\frac{(x_1'-x_2')-(y_1'-y_2')}{2}\right]^2$. We chose the former combinations.

Plugging (30) into (29), we readily find for the transformed inter-species reduced four-particle density matrix

$$\rho_{12}^{(4)}(u_1, u_1', v_1, v_1', u_2, u_2', v_2, v_2') = N^2(N-1)^2$$
$$\times \left(\frac{\alpha-\beta}{\pi}\right)^{\frac{1}{2}} e^{-\frac{\alpha-\beta}{2}\left(u_2^2+u_2'^2\right)} \left(\frac{\alpha-\beta}{\pi}\right)^{\frac{1}{2}} e^{-\frac{\alpha-\beta}{2}\left(v_2^2+v_2'^2\right)}$$
$$\times \left[\frac{\alpha+\beta+2(C_{2,2}-D_{2,2})}{\pi}\right]^{\frac{1}{2}} e^{-\frac{\alpha+\beta+C_{2,2}-\left(D_{2,2}+D_{2,2}'\right)}{2}\left(u_1^2+u_1'^2\right)} e^{-[C_{2,2}-(D_{2,2}-D_{2,2}')]u_1 u_1'} \tag{31}$$
$$\times \left[\frac{\alpha+\beta+2(C_{2,2}+D_{2,2})}{\pi}\right]^{\frac{1}{2}} e^{-\frac{\alpha+\beta+C_{2,2}+\left(D_{2,2}+D_{2,2}'\right)}{2}\left(v_1^2+v_1'^2\right)} e^{-[C_{2,2}+(D_{2,2}-D_{2,2}')]v_1 v_1'},$$

where the normalization coefficients before and after diagonalization are, naturally, equal and fulfill $[\alpha + (C_{1,1} \mp D_{1,1})][\alpha + (C_{2,2} \mp D_{2,2})] = (\alpha - \beta)[\alpha + \beta + 2(C_{2,2} \mp D_{2,2})]$.

As can be seen in (31) and (21), the similarities and differences between the structures of $\rho_{12}^{(4)}(u_1, u_1', v_1, v_1', u_2, u_2', v_2, v_2')$ and $\rho_{12}^{(2)}(u, u', v, v')$ clarify the issue of which coordinates are coupled and identify the coordinates that are not. In particular, just like for the two-particle quantity, we can apply Mehler's formula twice, on the appropriately constructed inter-species 'mixed coordinates' u_1, u_1' and v_1, v_1', to diagonalize the inter-species reduced four-particle density matrix. When this is performed, one obtains

$$s_{12,\pm}^{(4)} = \sqrt{\left(\alpha + \beta \mp 2D_{2,2}'\right)[\alpha + \beta + 2(C_{2,2} \mp D_{2,2})]}$$
$$= \sqrt{(\alpha + \beta \mp 2\gamma)(\alpha - \beta)\frac{(\alpha-\beta)+N(\beta\mp\gamma)}{(\alpha-\beta)+(N-2)(\beta\mp\gamma)}},$$
$$\rho_{12,\pm}^{(4)} = \frac{\left(\alpha+\beta\mp 2D_{2,2}'\right)-s_{12,\pm}^{(4)}}{\left(\alpha+\beta\mp 2D_{2,2}'\right)+s_{12,\pm}^{(4)}} = \frac{\frac{(\alpha+\beta\mp 2\gamma)[(\alpha-\beta)+(N-2)(\beta\mp\gamma)]}{(\alpha-\beta)[(\alpha-\beta)+N(\beta\mp\gamma)]}-1}{\frac{(\alpha+\beta\mp 2\gamma)[(\alpha-\beta)+(N-2)(\beta\mp\gamma)]}{(\alpha-\beta)[(\alpha-\beta)+N(\beta\mp\gamma)]}+1}, \tag{32}$$
$$1 - \rho_{12,\pm}^{(4)} = \frac{2 s_{12,\pm}^{(4)}}{\left(\alpha+\beta\mp 2D_{2,2}'\right)+s_{12,\pm}^{(4)}},$$

where the "+" terms quantify, the fragmentation in the u_1, u_1' part of the inter-species reduced four-particle density matrix and the "−" terms determine the fragmentation in the v_1, v_1' part of the inter-species reduced four-particle density matrix. As found and shown in (31), there is no fragmentation due to the relative-coordinate parts u_2, u_2' and v_2, v_2'. Equation (32) adds to the main results of the present work and bears a transparent and appealing physical meaning: in the mixture, inter-species fragmentation is quantified by the eigenvalues obtained from Mehler's formula when the latter is applied to the mixture's center-of-mass and relative center-of-mass coordinates of distinguishable pairs of pairs. Extensions to larger distinguishable aggregates of species 1 and species 2 identical bosons in the mixture is possible along the above lines and are not pursued further here.

We can now prescribe the decomposition of the inter-species reduced four-particle density matrix, inasmuch as the reduced two-particle density matrix was decomposed, into its natural four-particle functions made of distinguishable particles. The final result is given by

$$\rho_{12}^{(4)}(x_1, x_2, x_1', x_2', y_1, y_2, y_1', y_2') = N^2(N-1)^2 \sum_{n_+=0}^{\infty} \sum_{n_-=0}^{\infty} \left(1 - \rho_{12,+}^{(4)}\right)\left(1 - \rho_{12,-}^{(4)}\right)$$
$$\times \left(\rho_{12,+}^{(4)}\right)^{n_+} \left(\rho_{12,-}^{(4)}\right)^{n_-} \Phi_{12,n_+,n_-}^{(4)}(x_1, x_2, y_1, y_2) \Phi_{12,n_+,n_-}^{(4),*}(x_1', x_2', y_1', y_2'),$$

$$\Phi_{12,n_+,n_-}^{(4)}(x_1, x_2, y_1, y_2)$$

$$= \frac{1}{\sqrt{2^{n_+} n_+!}} \left(\frac{s_{12,+}^{(4)}}{\pi}\right)^{\frac{1}{4}} H_{n_+}\left(\frac{\sqrt{s_{12,+}^{(4)}}}{2}[(x_1+x_2)+(y_1+y_2)]\right) e^{-\frac{1}{8}s_{12,+}^{(4)}[(x_1+x_2)+(y_1+y_2)]^2} \qquad (33)$$

$$\times \frac{1}{\sqrt{2^{n_-} n_-!}} \left(\frac{s_{12,-}^{(4)}}{\pi}\right)^{\frac{1}{4}} H_{n_-}\left(\frac{\sqrt{s_{12,-}^{(4)}}}{2}[(x_1+x_2)-(y_1+y_2)]\right) e^{-\frac{1}{8}s_{12,-}^{(4)}[(x_1+x_2)-(y_1+y_2)]^2}$$

$$\times \left(\frac{\alpha-\beta}{\pi}\right)^{\frac{1}{4}} e^{-\frac{\alpha-\beta}{4}(x_1-x_2)^2} \left(\frac{\alpha-\beta}{\pi}\right)^{\frac{1}{4}} e^{-\frac{\alpha-\beta}{4}(y_1-y_2)^2}.$$

Equation (33) means that the pair-of-distinguishable-pairs 'condensed fraction' is given by the product $\left(1 - \rho_{12,+}^{(4)}\right)\left(1 - \rho_{12,-}^{(4)}\right)$ and the respective depleted fraction is $1 - \left(1 - \rho_{12,+}^{(4)}\right)\left(1 - \rho_{12,-}^{(4)}\right) = \rho_{12,+}^{(4)} + \rho_{12,-}^{(4)} - \rho_{12,+}^{(4)}\rho_{12,-}^{(4)}$. The center-of-mass and relative center-of-mass coordinates of the two pairs, $\frac{(x_1+x_2)\pm(y_1+y_2)}{2}$, carry the respective scalings $s_{12,\pm}^{(4)}$. The natural four-particle functions $\Phi_{12,n_+,n_-}^{(4)}(x_1, x_2, y_1, y_2)$ are enumerated by the two quantum numbers n_+, n_- and are obviously orthonormal to each other.

We proceed now to examine the fragmentation in this higher-order inter-species reduced density matrix. We investigate, as mentioned above, the specific case of $\lambda + \lambda_{12} = 0$. To compute $\rho_{12}^{(4)}(x_1, x_2, x_1', x_2', y_1, y_2, y_1', y_2')$, we require the quantities $[\alpha + \beta + 2(C_{2,2} - D_{2,2})] = m\omega$ and $\left(\alpha + \beta - 2D_{2,2}'\right) = m\omega$ for the "+" branch, as well as $[\alpha + \beta + 2(C_{2,2} + D_{2,2})] = m\omega \frac{1}{1+\frac{2}{N}\left(\frac{\omega}{\Omega_{12}}-1\right)}$ and $\left(\alpha + \beta + 2D_{2,2}'\right) = m\omega\left[1 + \frac{2}{N}\left(\frac{\Omega_{12}}{\omega}-1\right)\right]$ for the "−" branch.

Now, expressions (32) can readily be evaluated, and the following picture of higher-order inter-species fragmentation is found:

$$s_{12,+}^{(4)} = m\omega, \qquad \rho_{12,+}^{(4)} = 0, \qquad 1 - \rho_{12,+}^{(4)} = 1, \qquad (34a)$$

indicating that there is no contribution to fragmentation from the center-of-mass 'mixed coordinate' u_1, u_1'. This is additional to the no contribution to fragmentation coming from the relative coordinates u_2, u_2' and v_2, v_2'; see (31). For the relative center-of-mass 'mixed coordinate' v_1, v_1', on the other end, one finds

$$s_{12,-}^{(4)} = m\omega \sqrt{\frac{1+\frac{2}{N}\left(\frac{\Omega_{12}}{\omega}-1\right)}{1+\frac{2}{N}\left(\frac{\omega}{\Omega_{12}}-1\right)}},$$

$$\rho_{12,-}^{(4)} = \frac{\sqrt{\left[1+\frac{2}{N}\left(\frac{\Omega_{12}}{\omega}-1\right)\right]\left[1+\frac{2}{N}\left(\frac{\omega}{\Omega_{12}}-1\right)\right]}-1}{\sqrt{\left[1+\frac{2}{N}\left(\frac{\Omega_{12}}{\omega}-1\right)\right]\left[1+\frac{2}{N}\left(\frac{\omega}{\Omega_{12}}-1\right)\right]}+1}, \qquad (34b)$$

$$1 - \rho_{12,-}^{(4)} = \frac{2}{\sqrt{\left[1+\frac{2}{N}\left(\frac{\Omega_{12}}{\omega}-1\right)\right]\left[1+\frac{2}{N}\left(\frac{\omega}{\Omega_{12}}-1\right)\right]}+1},$$

namely, that the fragmentation of pairs of distinguishable pairs fully originates from the relative center-of-mass 'mixed coordinate' v_1, v_1'. We see that also the higher-order inter-species fragmentation is governed by the ratio $\frac{\Omega_{12}}{\omega}$ and takes place both at the attractive and repulsive sectors of interactions. In conclusion, the higher-order inter-species fragmentation is proved.

Now, one can compute the ratio $\frac{\Omega_{12}}{\omega} = \sqrt{1 + \frac{4N}{m\omega^2}\lambda_{12}}$ for which the inter-species reduced four-particle density matrix is 50% fragmented, as in (13). Since $\rho_{12,+}^{(4)} = 0$ does not contribute in this specific case, the only contribution to fragmentation comes from $\rho_{12,-}^{(4)}$. Thus, solving (34b) for 50% distinguishable-four-particle-function fragmentation, we obtain

$$\rho_{12,-}^{(4)} = \frac{1}{2} \implies \frac{\Omega_{12}}{\omega} = \left(1 + \frac{2N^2}{N-2}\right) \pm \sqrt{\left(1 + \frac{2N^2}{N-2}\right)^2 - 1}. \quad (35)$$

As for distinguishable pairs, there are two 'reciprocate' solutions: one for strong attractions and the second close to the border of stability for repulsions. In addition, to achieve the same degree of 50% fragmentation with a larger number $\frac{N}{2}$ of distinguishable four-boson aggregates, a stronger attraction or repulsion is needed. Furthermore, comparing distinguishable-four-boson and distinguishable-two-boson fragmentation at the same 50% value, one sees from (35) and (25) that slightly weaker interactions–attractions or repulsions–are needed for the former. This behavior of the fragmentation of increasing orders of inter-species reduced density matrices is analogous to and generalizes that of intra-species and single-species reduced density matrices; see the previous section and the appendix, respectively.

Finally, we present for completeness the inter-species four-particle density, i.e., the diagonal part $\rho_{12}^{(4)}(x_1, x_2, y_1, y_2) = \rho_{12}^{(4)}(x_1, x_2, x_1' = x_1, x_2' = x_2, y_1, y_2, y_1' = y_1, y_2' = y_2)$, which is given by

$$\rho_{12}^{(4)}(x_1, x_2, y_1, y_2) = N^2(N-1)^2 \left(\frac{\alpha-\beta}{\pi}\right) e^{-\frac{\alpha-\beta}{2}(x_1-x_2)^2} e^{-\frac{\alpha-\beta}{2}(y_1-y_2)^2}$$

$$\times \left[\frac{\alpha+\beta+2(C_{2,2}-D_{2,2})}{\pi}\right]^{\frac{1}{2}} e^{-\frac{\alpha+\beta+2(C_{2,2}-D_{2,2})}{4}[(x_1+x_2)+(y_1+y_2)]^2}$$

$$\times \left[\frac{\alpha+\beta+2(C_{2,2}+D_{2,2})}{\pi}\right]^{\frac{1}{2}} e^{-\frac{\alpha+\beta+2(C_{2,2}+D_{2,2})}{4}[(x_1+x_2)-(y_1+y_2)]^2} \quad (36)$$

$$= N^2(N-1)^2 \left(\frac{m\omega}{\pi}\right)^{\frac{3}{2}} e^{-\frac{m\omega}{2}(x_1-x_2)^2} e^{-\frac{m\omega}{2}(y_1-y_2)^2} e^{-\frac{m\omega}{4}[(x_1+x_2)+(y_1+y_2)]^2}$$

$$\times \left(\frac{m\omega}{\pi\left[1+\frac{2}{N}\left(\frac{\omega}{\Omega_{12}}-1\right)\right]}\right)^{\frac{1}{2}} e^{-\frac{m\omega}{4\left[1+\frac{2}{N}\left(\frac{\omega}{\Omega_{12}}-1\right)\right]}[(x_1+x_2)-(y_1+y_2)]^2}.$$

To proceed, the size of the distinguishable four-boson cloud can be estimated from the widths of the respective Gaussian functions in the density (36). Thus, we obtain

$$\sigma_{12,\frac{x_1-x_2}{\sqrt{2}}}^{(4)} = \sqrt{\frac{1}{2m\omega}}, \quad \sigma_{12,\frac{y_1-y_2}{\sqrt{2}}}^{(4)} = \sqrt{\frac{1}{2m\omega}}, \quad \sigma_{12,\frac{(x_1+x_2)+(y_1+y_2)}{2}}^{(4)} = \sqrt{\frac{1}{2m\omega}}, \quad (37a)$$

$$\sigma_{12,\frac{(x_1+x_2)-(y_1+y_2)}{2}}^{(4)} = \sqrt{\frac{1 + \frac{2}{N}\left(\frac{\omega}{\Omega_{12}}-1\right)}{2m\omega}}.$$

The explanations why the widths $\sigma_{12,\frac{x_1-x_2}{\sqrt{2}}}^{(4)}, \sigma_{12,\frac{y_1-y_2}{\sqrt{2}}}^{(4)}$ with intra-species relative coordinates and, separately, the width $\sigma_{12,\frac{(x_1+x_2)-(y_1+y_2)}{2}}^{(4)}$ with inter-species center-of-mass coordinate are all the typical length of the harmonic potential follow those given above, alongside Equations (17a) and (27a), respectively, and are not reproduced here.

To show the combined effect of the inter-species and intra-species interactions accompanying the fragmentation of $\rho_{12}^{(4)}(x_1, x_2, x_1', x_2', y_1, y_2, y_1', y_2')$, it is instrumental to compute the sizes (37a) for large inter-species attractions or inter-species repulsions at the border of stability. We obtain, respectively,

$$\lim_{\frac{\Omega_{12}}{\omega} \to \infty} \sigma^{(4)}_{12, \frac{(x_1+x_2)-(y_1+y_2)}{2}} = \sqrt{\frac{1-\frac{2}{N}}{2m\omega}}, \quad \sigma^{(4)}_{12, \frac{(x_1+x_2)-(y_1+y_2)}{2}} \longrightarrow \infty \quad \text{for} \quad \frac{\Omega_{12}}{\omega} \to 0^+, \tag{37b}$$

where $\sigma^{(4)}_{12, \frac{x_1-x_2}{\sqrt{2}}}$, $\sigma^{(4)}_{12, \frac{y_1-y_2}{\sqrt{2}}}$, and $\sigma^{(4)}_{12, \frac{(x_1+x_2)+(y_1+y_2)}{2}}$, as mentioned above, do not depend on the interactions. We see that the size of the inter-species four-boson density also saturates at about the trap's size, and does not depend on the strengths of interactions in the limit of strong inter-species attractions. As for the pair of distinguishable bosons, a strong fragmentation is possible in the mixture with hardly any shrinking of the density in comparison with that of the bare trap due to the condition $\lambda + \lambda_{12} = 0$, namely when strong inter-species attractive interaction is accompanied by strong intra-species repulsion of equal magnitude. In summary, inter-species fragmentation in higher-order reduced density matrices is also governed by the ratio $\frac{\Omega_{12}}{\omega}$ and takes place both at the attractive and repulsive sectors of interactions.

3.2. Inter-Species Entanglement and the Limit of an Infinite Number of Particles

In the previous sections, the reduced density matrices for identical and distinguishable pairs of bosons were diagonalized, and the intra-species and inter-species fragmentations explored. Both kinds of fragmentations are critical phenomena in the sense that, going to the limit of an infinite number of particles while keeping the interaction parameters (products of the number of particles times the interaction strengths) constant, the respective reduced density matrix per particle becomes 100% condensed [74]. This can be easily found from the leading natural eigenvalues of the natural functions explicitly obtained above; see the general (6), (10), (22), (32) and specific (12), (24), (34) expressions, which are all equal to 1 in this limit.

In the present, concluding subsection, we touch upon a property of the mixture which does not diminish at the limit of an infinite number of particles. Classifying properties of Bose–Einstein condensates and their mixtures at the limit of an infinite number of particles, and especially when many-body and mean-field theories do not coincide, is an active field of research, where variances of observables and the overlap between the many-body and mean-field wave functions are discussed elsewhere; see [75–77,93–101]. Here, combining the techniques used in the previous sections, we apply Mehler's formula to perform the Schmidt decomposition of the wave function.

Let us examine the mixture's wave function, for which the coordinates of the two species are coupled to each other owing to the inter-species interaction; see the last term in (2a). As a reminder, the wave function is obtained by representing the Hamiltonian (1) with the mixture's Jacoby coordinates, for which it is fully diagonalized, and translating it back to the laboratory frame. To decouple the coordinates of each species, in the sense of prescribing the Schmidt decomposition of the wave function, it is useful to go 'half a step' backward, and express (2a), using the individual species' Jacoby coordinates.

The Jacoby coordinates of each species are given by

$$\begin{aligned} X_k &= \tfrac{1}{\sqrt{k(k+1)}} \sum_{j=1}^{k} (x_{k+1} - x_j), \quad 1 \le k \le N-1, \quad X_N = \tfrac{1}{\sqrt{N}} \sum_{j=1}^{N} x_j, \\ Y_k &= \tfrac{1}{\sqrt{k(k+1)}} \sum_{j=1}^{k} (y_{k+1} - y_j), \quad 1 \le k \le N-1, \quad Y_N = \pm \tfrac{1}{\sqrt{N}} \sum_{j=1}^{N} y_j, \end{aligned} \tag{38}$$

where, for the derivation given below, it is useful to distinguish between the two cases for the definition of, say, Y_N: The plus sign is assigned to positive γ, namely, to attractive inter-species interactions for which $\Omega_{12} > \omega$, and the minus sign is assigned to negative γ, i.e., to repulsive inter-species interactions where $\Omega_{12} < \omega$.

For the symmetric mixture, given the above Jacobi coordinates of each species, Equation (38), the wave function reads

$$\Psi(X_1,\ldots,X_N,Y_1,\ldots,Y_N) = \left(\frac{m\Omega}{\pi}\right)^{\frac{N-1}{2}} \left(\frac{M_{12}\Omega_{12}}{\pi}\right)^{\frac{1}{4}} \left(\frac{M\omega}{\pi}\right)^{\frac{1}{4}} \quad (39a)$$
$$\times e^{-\frac{1}{2}m\Omega \sum_{k=1}^{N-1}(X_k^2+Y_k^2)} e^{-\frac{1}{2}m(\Omega_{12}+\omega)}(X_N^2+Y_N^2) e^{\pm\frac{1}{2}m(\Omega_{12}-\omega)X_N Y_N}.$$

Indeed, all relative coordinates are decoupled, and the only coupling due to the inter-species interaction is between the center-of-mass X_N of species 1 bosons and the center-of-mass Y_N of species 2 bosons. Consequently, applying Mehler's formula to the terms with the intra-species center-of-mass Jacoby coordinates X_N and Y_N the Schmidt decomposition of (39a) is readily performed and given by

$$\Psi(X_1,\ldots,X_N,Y_1,\ldots,Y_N) = \sum_{n=0}^{\infty} \sqrt{1-\rho_{SD}^2}\,\rho_{SD}^n \Phi_{1,n}(X_1,\ldots,X_N)\Phi_{2,n}(Y_1,\ldots,Y_N),$$

$$\Phi_{1,n}(X_1,\ldots,X_N) = \left(\frac{m\Omega}{\pi}\right)^{\frac{N-1}{4}} e^{-\frac{1}{2}m\Omega\sum_{k=1}^{N-1}X_k^2} \frac{1}{\sqrt{2^n n!}}\left(\frac{s_{SD}}{\pi}\right)^{\frac{1}{4}} H_n(\sqrt{s_{SD}}X_N) e^{-\frac{1}{2}s_{SD}X_N^2},$$

$$\Phi_{2,n}(Y_1,\ldots,Y_N) = \left(\frac{m\Omega}{\pi}\right)^{\frac{N-1}{4}} e^{-\frac{1}{2}m\Omega\sum_{k=1}^{N-1}Y_k^2} \frac{1}{\sqrt{2^n n!}}\left(\frac{s_{SD}}{\pi}\right)^{\frac{1}{4}} H_n(\sqrt{s_{SD}}Y_N) e^{-\frac{1}{2}s_{SD}Y_N^2}, \quad (39b)$$

$$\sqrt{1-\rho_{SD}^2} = \frac{2\sqrt{\frac{\Omega_{12}}{\omega}}}{1-\frac{\Omega_{12}}{\omega}}, \qquad \rho_{SD} = \frac{\left(\frac{\Omega_{12}}{\omega}\right)^{\pm 1}-1}{\left(\frac{\Omega_{12}}{\omega}\right)^{\pm 1}+1}, \qquad s_{SD} = m\sqrt{\omega\Omega_{12}}.$$

We repeat that the plus sign is for attraction and the minus for repulsion, which is what guarantees that ρ_{SD} and consequently the Schmidt coefficients $\sqrt{1-\rho_{SD}^2}\rho_{SD}^n$, $n=0,1,2,3,\ldots$ are always positive. s_{SD} defines the inverse width of the individual species' center-of-mass Gaussians in the Schmidt basis $\Phi_{1,n}(X_1,\ldots,X_N)$ and $\Phi_{2,n}(Y_1,\ldots,Y_N)$.

Let us concisely discuss the properties of the Schmidt decomposition of the mixture, Equation (39b). Clearly and interestingly, the Schmidt coefficients are independent of the intra-species dressed frequency Ω, which only appears in conjunction with intra-species relative coordinates, i.e., the Schmidt coefficients depend solely on the inter-species interaction. Furthermore, there is a kind of symmetry between respective attractive and repulsive inter-species interactions, as one obtains the same Schmidt coefficients for the inter-species frequency $\frac{\Omega_{12}}{\omega} = \sqrt{1+\frac{4N\lambda_{12}}{m\omega^2}}$ and inverse frequency $\frac{\omega}{\Omega_{12}} = \frac{1}{\sqrt{1+\frac{4N\lambda_{12}}{m\omega^2}}}$.

Last but not least, the same Schmidt coefficients are obtained when the product of the number of bosons in each species times the inter-species interaction strength, $N\lambda_{12}$, is held fixed, and N is increased to infinity. In other words, whereas identical and distinguishable bosons, pairs, four-particle aggregates, etc. are 100% condensed at the limit of an infinite number of particles, i.e., the leading eigenvalue of all finite-order intra-species and inter-species reduced density matrices per particle is 1, the mixture's wave function exhibits a fixed amount of entanglement at the infinite-particle-number limit. This is a good place to bring the present study to an end.

4. Summary and Outlook

The present work aims at developing and combining concepts from quantum theory of many-particle systems with novel results on the physics of trapped mixtures of Bose–Einstein condensates. The notions of natural orbitals and natural geminals are fundamental to many-particle systems made of identical particles. These natural functions entail the diagonalization of the reduced one-particle and two-particle density matrices, respectively. In a mixture of two kinds of identical particles—here explicitly two types of bosons—there are, naturally, identical bosons and pairs made of indistinguishable bosons of either species. To find their natural orbitals and natural geminals, the construction and subsequent diagonalization of respective intra-species reduced density matrices is necessary. In the mixture, there are, additionally, pairs made of distinguishable bosons. Analogously, their theoretical description would require assembling, diagonalizing, and analyzing the interspecies reduced two-particle density matrix. In the present work, we have investigated pairs made of identical or distinguishable bosons in a mixture of Bose–Einstein condensates, covering both the structure of the respective natural pair functions, on the more formal theoretical side, and the exploration of pairs' fragmentation. Like identical bosons, which can, depending on whether the reduced one-particle density matrix has one or more macroscopic eigenvalues, be condensed or fragmented, so do the pairs of bosons. We showed in the present work that, in the mixture, both pairs made of identical bosons and pairs consisting of distinguishable bosons can be condensed and moreover fragmented.

To tackle the above and other questions, we employed a solvable model, the symmetric harmonic-interaction model for mixtures. The natural geminals for pairs made of identical or distinguishable bosons were explicitly contracted as a function of the inter-species and intra-species interactions. This was performed by diagonalizing the corresponding intra-species and inter-species reduced two-particle density matrices using applications of Mehler's formula on appropriately constructed linear combinations of intra-species and inter-species coordinates. Here, the role of the mixture's center-of-mass and relative center-of-mass coordinates was identified and explained. The structure of identical and distinguishable pairs in the mixture was discussed, and a generalization to pairs of distinguishable pairs using the inter-species reduced four-body density matrix was made. A particular case, where attractive and repulsive inter-species and intra-species interactions are (opposite in sign and) equal in magnitude, was worked out explicitly. The fragmentation of bosons, pairs, and pairs of pairs in the mixture was proven, and the size of the respective densities analyzed. Last but not least, as a complementary investigation, the exact Schmidt decomposition of the mixture's wave function was performed. The entanglement between the two species was shown to be governed by the coupling of their individual center-of-mass coordinates and, consequently, not to vanish at the limit of an infinite number of particles where any finite-order intra-species and inter-species reduced density matrix per particle is 100% condensed.

The results reported in this work were obtained analytically, because the one-body trapping potential and the two-body inter-particle interactions are all harmonic. It is relevant to inquire whether the results would be robust in general. We know that fragmentation of single-species bosons takes place in traps of various shapes; see, e.g., [13], for the inter-particle interactions of various ranges [24], and at the level of the one-particle and two-particle reduced density matrices [28]. Furthermore, as seen in Appendix A, fragmentation of bosons and pairs occurs, respectively, at the level of the one-particle and two-particle reduced density matrices within the single-species harmonic-interaction model. We can therefore quite confidently foresee that the results obtained here analytically, of intra-species and inter-species pairs' fragmentation using the (symmetric) harmonic-interaction model for mixtures, would persist for trapped interacting bosonic mixtures in general. Demonstrating that explicitly we would have to resort to many-body numerical tools, see, e.g., in [50,59,62,67]. Similarly, our analytical and numerical experience for studying single-species trapped bosons at the limit of an infinite-number of particles [95,96,99,101], along with the corresponding analytical results for variances and overlaps in mixtures [75,77], strongly suggest that a similar generality would hold true for the Schmidt decomposition of trapped interacting mixtures at the infinite-particle-number limit.

The present investigations suggest several directions for further developments. We have treated the symmetric mixture, and an anticipated extension to generic trapped mixtures, with different numbers of bosons, masses, and interaction strengths for each species, would be in place. In what capacity can the fragmentation of identical pairs in the different species be made to differ, and to what extent would the fragmentation of distinguishable pairs become more complex? Do the center-of-mass and relative center-of-mass coordinates keep their role in the diagonalization of inter-species reduced density matrices for a generic mixture? It also makes sense, in a generic mixture, to investigate the fragmentation of aggregates with unequal numbers of bosons from each species, such as, for instance, the analysis of inter-species reduced three-particle density matrices. Another foreseen extension is about mixtures with more species and, if feasible, about generic multi-species mixtures where, e.g., one species could serve as a bridge between two baths. Take for instance the (symmetric) three-species harmonic-interaction model. The diagonalization of the Hamiltonian would require relative coordinates for each of the species, the center-of-mass coordinate of all bosons, and two relative center-of-mass coordinates to be determined [71]. The major challenge would be the reduction of the all-particle density matrix to the various intra-species and inter-species reduced density matrices. Recall that, for single-species bosons, the reduction of the all-particle density matrix leads to 'vector' recursive relations (the coefficients of the reduced density matrices depend on one index) [78] and that for a two-species mixture, the reduction of the all-particle density matrix results in 'matrix' recursive relations (the coefficients of the various intra-species and inter-species reduced density matrices depend on two indices) [74]. It is thus reasonable to expect that in the three-species mixture, the reduction of the all-particle density matrix would require 'tensor' recursive relations. Finally, for a three-species mixture, the question whether an extended or general Schmidt decomposition [102] is at all feasible would become relevant, and if the answer is positive, whether in conjunction, the three individual species' center-of-mass coordinates would become disentangled. Surely, exciting generalizations are awaiting for further investigations.

Finally, one could forecast that the topic of Bose–Einstein condensates and mixtures in the limit of an infinite number of particles would be enriched by exploring the Schmidt decomposition of the wave function. Recall that at the infinite-particle-number limit, any finite-order intra-species and inter-species reduced density matrix per particle is 100% condensed. Here, studying the variances of observables and overlaps of wave functions has deepened our understanding of the differences between many-body and mean-field theories of Bose–Einstein condensates and mixtures at the limit of an infinite number of particles. However, these properties are already defined for single-species bosons. The Schmidt decomposition, on the other hand, is a property that enters the topic of the infinite-particle-number limit starting, obviously, only from a two-species mixture—all of which paves the way for further intriguing investigations to come.

Funding: This research was supported by the Israel Science Foundation (Grant No. 1316/19).

Data Availability Statement: Not applicable.

Conflicts of Interest: The author declares no conflict of interest. .

Appendix A. Comparison to Fragmentation in the Single-Species System

The Hamiltonian of the single-species harmonic-interaction model is given by [78]

$$\hat{H}(x_1,\ldots,x_N) = \sum_{j=1}^{N}\left(-\frac{1}{2m}\frac{\partial^2}{\partial x_j^2} + \frac{1}{2}m\omega^2 x_j^2\right) + \lambda \sum_{1\leq j<k}^{N}(x_j - x_k)^2. \tag{A1}$$

Employing single-species Jacoby coordinates and translating back to the laboratory frame, the N-boson wave function and corresponding density matrix are given by

$$\Psi(x_1,\ldots,x_N) = \left(\frac{m\Omega}{\pi}\right)^{\frac{N-1}{4}}\left(\frac{m\omega}{\pi}\right)^{\frac{1}{4}} e^{-\frac{\alpha}{2}\sum_{j=1}^{N} x_j^2 - \beta \sum_{1\leq j<k}^{N} x_j x_k},$$

$$\Psi(x_1,\ldots,x_N)\Psi^*(x_1',\ldots,x_N') = \left(\frac{m\Omega}{\pi}\right)^{\frac{N-1}{2}}\left(\frac{m\omega}{\pi}\right)^{\frac{1}{2}} e^{-\frac{\alpha}{2}\sum_{j=1}^{N}\left(x_j^2+x_j'^2\right)-\beta\sum_{1\leq j<k}^{N}\left(x_j x_k + x_j' x_k'\right)}, \tag{A2}$$

$$\alpha = m\Omega + \beta = m\Omega\left[1 + \frac{1}{N}\left(\frac{\omega}{\Omega}-1\right)\right], \quad \beta = m\Omega\frac{1}{N}\left(\frac{\omega}{\Omega}-1\right), \quad \Omega = \sqrt{\omega^2 + \frac{2\lambda N}{m}}.$$

The stability of the system, i.e., the condition that a bound solution exists, means that the interaction satisfies $\lambda > -\frac{m\omega^2}{2N}$.

The reduced one-particle density matrix reads

$$\rho^{(1)}(x,x') = N\left(\frac{\alpha+C_1}{\pi}\right)^{\frac{1}{2}} e^{-\frac{\alpha+\frac{C_1}{2}}{2}\left(x^2+x'^2\right)} e^{-\frac{1}{2}C_1 xx'},$$

$$\alpha + C_1 = (\alpha-\beta)\frac{(\alpha-\beta)+N\beta}{(\alpha-\beta)+(N-1)\beta} = m\Omega \frac{1}{1+\frac{1}{N}\left(\frac{\Omega}{\omega}-1\right)}. \quad (A3)$$

Comparing the structure of the reduced single-particle density matrix that of Mehler's formula [81,82], one readily has

$$s^{(1)} = \sqrt{\alpha(\alpha+C_1)} = m\Omega\sqrt{\frac{1+\frac{1}{N}\left(\frac{\omega}{\Omega}-1\right)}{1+\frac{1}{N}\left(\frac{\Omega}{\omega}-1\right)}},$$

$$\rho^{(1)} = \frac{\alpha-s^{(1)}}{\alpha+s^{(1)}} = \frac{\sqrt{\left[1+\frac{1}{N}\left(\frac{\omega}{\Omega}-1\right)\right]\left[1+\frac{1}{N}\left(\frac{\Omega}{\omega}-1\right)\right]}-1}{\sqrt{\left[1+\frac{1}{N}\left(\frac{\omega}{\Omega}-1\right)\right]\left[1+\frac{1}{N}\left(\frac{\Omega}{\omega}-1\right)\right]}+1}, \quad (A4)$$

$$1-\rho^{(1)} = \frac{2s^{(1)}}{\alpha+s^{(1)}} = \frac{2}{\sqrt{\left[1+\frac{1}{N}\left(\frac{\omega}{\Omega}-1\right)\right]\left[1+\frac{1}{N}\left(\frac{\Omega}{\omega}-1\right)\right]}}.$$

The reduced two-particle density matrix $\rho^{(2)}(x_1, x_2, x'_1, x'_2)$ reads, after the rotation of coordinates,

$$\rho^{(2)}(q_1, q'_1, q_2, q'_2) = N(N-1)\left(\frac{\alpha-\beta}{\pi}\right)^{\frac{1}{2}} e^{-\frac{\alpha-\beta}{2}\left(q_2^2+q_2'^2\right)}$$

$$\times \left(\frac{\alpha+\beta+2C_2}{\pi}\right)^{\frac{1}{2}} e^{-\frac{\alpha+\beta+C_2}{2}\left(q_1^2+q_1'^2\right)} e^{-C_2 q_1 q'_1}, \quad (A5)$$

$$\alpha + \beta + 2C_2 = (\alpha-\beta)\frac{(\alpha-\beta)+N\beta}{(\alpha-\beta)+(N-2)\beta} = m\Omega\frac{1}{1+\frac{2}{N}\left(\frac{\Omega}{\omega}-1\right)},$$

where $q_1 = \frac{1}{\sqrt{2}}(x_1+x_2)$, $q_2 = \frac{1}{\sqrt{2}}(x_1-x_2)$ and $q'_1 = \frac{1}{\sqrt{2}}(x'_1+x'_2)$, $q'_2 = \frac{1}{\sqrt{2}}(x'_1-x'_2)$. Comparing the structure of the reduced two-particle density matrix with that of Mehler's Formula (5), we readily find

$$s^{(2)} = \sqrt{(\alpha+\beta)(\alpha+\beta+2C_2)} = m\Omega\sqrt{\frac{1+\frac{2}{N}\left(\frac{\omega}{\Omega}-1\right)}{1+\frac{2}{N}\left(\frac{\Omega}{\omega}-1\right)}},$$

$$\rho^{(2)} = \frac{(\alpha+\beta)-s^{(2)}}{(\alpha+\beta)+s^{(2)}} = \frac{\sqrt{\left[1+\frac{2}{N}\left(\frac{\omega}{\Omega}-1\right)\right]\left[1+\frac{2}{N}\left(\frac{\Omega}{\omega}-1\right)\right]}-1}{\sqrt{\left[1+\frac{2}{N}\left(\frac{\omega}{\Omega}-1\right)\right]\left[1+\frac{2}{N}\left(\frac{\Omega}{\omega}-1\right)\right]}+1}, \quad (A6)$$

$$1-\rho^{(2)} = \frac{2s^{(2)}}{(\alpha+\beta)+s^{(2)}} = \frac{2}{\sqrt{\left[1+\frac{2}{N}\left(\frac{\omega}{\Omega}-1\right)\right]\left[1+\frac{2}{N}\left(\frac{\Omega}{\omega}-1\right)\right]}},$$

where $\alpha + \beta = m\Omega\left[1+\frac{2}{N}\left(\frac{\omega}{\Omega}-1\right)\right]$. We see from (A4) and (A6) that fragmentation of bosons and pairs is governed, in the single-species harmonic-interaction model, by the ratio $\frac{\Omega}{\omega}$ and takes place both at the attractive and repulsive sectors of the interaction.

Similarly to the main text, we compute for which ratio $\frac{\Omega}{\omega}$, or, equivalently, for which interaction $\lambda = \frac{m\omega^2}{2N}\left[\left(\frac{\Omega}{\omega}\right)^2 - 1\right]$, the two-particle and one-particle reduced density matrices are macroscopically fragmented as in (13). Note the difference that, here, $\frac{\Omega}{\omega}$ is the single-species interaction and in the main text, for the mixture, $\frac{\Omega_{12}}{\omega}$ is the inter-species interaction. Thus, solving (A4) for 50% natural-orbital fragmentation, we find

$$\rho^{(1)} = \frac{1}{2} \implies \frac{\Omega}{\omega} = \left(1+\frac{4N^2}{N-1}\right) \pm \sqrt{\left(1+\frac{4N^2}{N-1}\right)^2 - 1}, \quad (A7)$$

and working out (A6) for 50% natural-geminal fragmentation, we obtain

$$\rho_1^{(2)} = \frac{1}{2} \implies \frac{\Omega}{\omega} = \sqrt{1 + \frac{2N\lambda}{m\omega^2}} = \left(1 + \frac{2N^2}{N-2}\right) \pm \sqrt{\left(1 + \frac{2N^2}{N-2}\right)^2 - 1}. \quad (A8)$$

There are two 'reciprocate' solutions for both the natural geminals and natural orbitals: Indeed, 50% fragmentation occurs for strong attractions, namely, when $\frac{\Omega}{\omega}$ is large, or in the vicinity of the border of stability for repulsions, i.e., when $\frac{\Omega}{\omega}$ is close to zero. In addition, to achieve the same degree of 50% fragmentation with a larger number of bosons N, a stronger attraction or repulsion is needed. Finally, comparing the natural-geminal with natural-orbital fragmentation at the same 50% value, one sees from (A8) and (A7) that slightly weaker interactions attractions or repulsions are needed for the former, in a similar manner to intra-species fragmentation in the mixture discussed in the main text.

Finally, we prescribe the one-particle and two-particle densities, i.e., the diagonal parts $\rho^{(1)}(x) = \rho^{(1)}(x, x' = x)$ and $\rho^{(2)}(x_1, x_2) = \rho^{(2)}(x_1, x_2, x_1' = x_1, x_2' = x_2)$ which read

$$\rho^{(1)}(x) = N\left(\frac{\alpha + C_1}{\pi}\right)^{\frac{1}{2}} e^{-(\alpha+C_1)x^2} = N\left(\frac{m\Omega}{\pi[1+\frac{1}{N}(\frac{\Omega}{\omega}-1)]}\right)^{\frac{1}{2}} e^{-\frac{m\Omega}{1+\frac{1}{N}(\frac{\Omega}{\omega}-1)}x^2},$$

$$\rho^{(2)}(x_1, x_2) = N(N-1)\left(\frac{\alpha - \beta}{\pi}\right)^{\frac{1}{2}} e^{-\frac{\alpha-\beta}{2}(x_1-x_2)^2} \left(\frac{\alpha + \beta + 2C_2}{\pi}\right)^{\frac{1}{2}} e^{-\frac{\alpha+\beta+2C_2}{2}(x_1+x_2)^2} \quad (A9)$$

$$= N(N-1)\left(\frac{m\Omega}{\pi}\right)^{\frac{1}{2}} e^{-\frac{m\Omega}{2}(x_1-x_2)^2} \left(\frac{m\Omega}{\pi[1+\frac{2}{N}(\frac{\Omega}{\omega}-1)]}\right)^{\frac{1}{2}} e^{-\frac{m\Omega}{2[1+\frac{2}{N}(\frac{\Omega}{\omega}-1)]}(x_1+x_2)^2}.$$

Here, in the single-species case, λ governs the size of the densities which, as we now show, depending on the interaction stronger than for the mixture; also see the main text for comparison and further discussion.

We can deduce the size of pairs' and bosons' clouds using the widths of the corresponding Gaussian functions in the densities (A9). Hence, we have

$$\sigma_x^{(1)} = \sqrt{\frac{1+\frac{1}{N}(\frac{\Omega}{\omega}-1)}{2m\Omega}},$$

$$\sigma_{\frac{x_1+x_2}{\sqrt{2}}}^{(2)} = \sqrt{\frac{1+\frac{2}{N}(\frac{\Omega}{\omega}-1)}{2m\Omega}}, \quad \sigma_{\frac{x_1-x_2}{\sqrt{2}}}^{(2)} = \sqrt{\frac{1}{2m\Omega}}. \quad (A10a)$$

To describe further effects of the interaction λ accompanying fragmentation of the reduced density matrices (A4) and (A6), we compute the sizes (A10a) for strong attractions or repulsions at the border of stability. We obtain, respectively,

$$\lim_{\frac{\Omega}{\omega}\to\infty} \sigma_x^{(1)} = \sqrt{\frac{1}{2m\omega N}}, \quad \sigma_x^{(1)} \longrightarrow \infty \quad \text{for} \quad \frac{\Omega}{\omega} \to 0^+,$$

$$\lim_{\frac{\Omega}{\omega}\to\infty} \sigma_{\frac{x_1+x_2}{\sqrt{2}}}^{(2)} = \sqrt{\frac{1}{m\omega N}}, \quad \sigma_{\frac{x_1+x_2}{\sqrt{2}}}^{(2)} \longrightarrow \infty \quad \text{for} \quad \frac{\Omega}{\omega} \to 0^+, \quad (A10b)$$

$$\lim_{\frac{\Omega}{\omega}\to\infty} \sigma_{\frac{x_1-x_2}{\sqrt{2}}}^{(2)} = 0, \quad \sigma_{\frac{x_1-x_2}{\sqrt{2}}}^{(2)} \longrightarrow \infty \quad \text{for} \quad \frac{\Omega}{\omega} \to 0^+,$$

as all widths (A10a) depend on the interaction strength. The size of the densities for strong attractions diminishes to much smaller values than the trap's size, values that depend on the number of bosons but not on the strength of interaction. Thus, a high degree of fragmentation due to the strong attractive interaction is possible in the single-species system only together with the shrinking of the density. Alternatively, toward the edge of stability region, the density of the single-species system expands due to repulsive interaction unlimitedly as the degree of fragmentation increases. These should be compared to and contrasted with the results in the main text for the intra-species densities and the interplay between inter-species and intra-species interactions within intra-species fragmentation in the mixture.

References

1. Löwdin, P.-O. Quantum Theory of Many-Particle Systems. I. Physical Interpretations by Means of Density Matrices, Natural Spin-Orbitals, and Convergence Problems in the Method of Configurational Interaction. *Phys. Rev.* **1955**, *97*, 1474. [CrossRef]
2. Yang, C.N. Concept of Off-Diagonal Long-Range Order and the Quantum Phases of Liquid He and of Superconductors. *Rev. Mod. Phys.* **1962**, *34*, 694. [CrossRef]
3. Davidson, E. *Reduced Density Matrices in Quantum Chemistry*; Academic Press: New York, NY, USA, 1976.
4. Coleman, A.J.; Yukalov, V.I. *Reduced Density Matrices: Coulson's Challenge*; Lectures Notes in Chemistry; Springer: Berlin, Germany, 2000; Volume 72.
5. Mazziotti, D.A. (Ed.) *Reduced -Density-Matrix Mechanics: With Application to Many-Electron Atoms and Molecules*; Advances in Chemical Physics; Wiley: New York, NY, USA, 2007; Volume 134.
6. Penrose, O.; Onsager, L. Bose-Einstein Condensation and Liquid Helium. *Phys. Rev.* **1956**, *104*, 576. [CrossRef]
7. Mueller, E.J.; Ho, T.-L.; Ueda, M.; Baym, G. Fragmentation of Bose-Einstein condensates. *Phys. Rev. A* **2006**, *74*, 033612. [CrossRef]
8. Girardeau, M. Simple and Generalized Condensation in Many-Boson Systems. *Phys. Fluids* **1962**, *5*, 1468. [CrossRef]
9. Pollock, F. Quantization of Circulation in a Non-Ideal Bose Gas. *Phys. Fluids* **1967**, *10*, 473. [CrossRef]
10. Noziéres, P.; Saint James, D. Particle vs. pair condensation in attractive Bose liquids. *J. Phys.* **1982**, *43*, 1133. [CrossRef]
11. Noziéres, P. *Bose-Einstein Condensation*; Griffin, A., Snoke, D.W., Stringari, S., Eds.; Cambridge University Press: Cambridge, UK, 1996; p. 15.
12. Spekkens, R.W.; Sipe, J.E. Spatial fragmentation of a Bose-Einstein condensate in a double-well potential. *Phys. Rev. A* **1999**, *59*, 3868. [CrossRef]
13. Streltsov, A.I.; Cederbaum, L.S.; Moiseyev, N. Ground-state fragmentation of repulsive Bose-Einstein condensates in double-trap potentials. *Phys. Rev. A* **2004**, *70*, 053607. [CrossRef]
14. Streltsov, A.I.; Cederbaum, L.S. Properties of fragmented repulsive condensates. *Phys. Rev. A* **2005**, *71*, 063612. [CrossRef]
15. Alon, O.E.; Cederbaum, L.S. Pathway from Condensation via Fragmentation to Fermionization of Cold Bosonic Systems. *Phys. Rev. Lett.* **2005**, *95*, 140402. [CrossRef]
16. Bader, P.; Fischer, U.R. Fragmented Many-Body Ground States for Scalar Bosons in a Single Trap. *Phys. Rev. Lett.* **2009**, *103*, 060402. [CrossRef]
17. Fischer, U.R.; Bader, P. Interacting trapped bosons yield fragmented condensate states in low dimensions. *Phys. Rev. A* **2010**, *82*, 013607. [CrossRef]
18. Zhou, Q.; Cui, X. Fate of a Bose-Einstein Condensate in the Presence of Spin-Orbit Coupling. *Phys. Rev. Lett.* **2013**, *110*, 140407. [CrossRef]
19. Kawaguchi, Y. Goldstone-mode instability leading to fragmentation in a spinor Bose-Einstein condensate. *Phys. Rev. A* **2014**, *89*, 033627. [CrossRef]
20. Song, S.-W.; Zhang, Y.-C.; Zhao, H.; Wang, X.; Liu, W.-M. Fragmentation of spin-orbit-coupled spinor Bose-Einstein condensates. *Phys. Rev. A* **2014**, *89*, 063613. [CrossRef]
21. Kang, M.-K.; Fischer, U.R. Revealing Single-Trap Condensate Fragmentation by Measuring Density-Density Correlations after Time of Flight. *Phys. Rev. Lett.* **2014**, *113*, 140404. [CrossRef]
22. Jen, H.H.; Yip, S.-K. Fragmented many-body states of a spin-2 Bose gas. *Phys. Rev. A* **2015**, *91*, 063603. [CrossRef]
23. Fischer, U.R.; Kang, M.-K. "Photonic" Cat States from Strongly Interacting Matter Waves. *Phys. Rev. Lett.* **2015**, *115*, 260404. [CrossRef]
24. Fischer, U.R.; Lode, A.U.J.; Chatterjee, B. Condensate fragmentation as a sensitive measure of the quantum many-body behavior of bosons with long-range interactions. *Phys. Rev. A* **2015**, *91*, 063621. [CrossRef]
25. Lode, A.U.J. Multiconfigurational time-dependent Hartree method for bosons with internal degrees of freedom: Theory and composite fragmentation of multicomponent Bose-Einstein condensates. *Phys. Rev. A* **2016**, *93*, 063601. [CrossRef]
26. Kolovsky, A.R. Bogoliubov depletion of the fragmented condensate in the bosonic flux ladder. *Phys. Rev. A* **2017**, *95*, 033622. [CrossRef]
27. Tomchenko, M. On a Fragmented Condensate in a Uniform Bose System. *J. Low Temp. Phys.* **2020**, *198*, 100. [CrossRef]
28. Sakmann, K.; Streltsov, A.I.; Alon, O.E.; Cederbaum, L.S. Reduced density matrices and coherence of trapped interacting bosons. *Phys. Rev. A* **2008**, *78*, 023615. [CrossRef]
29. Kutzelnigg, W. Direct Determination of Natural Orbitals and Natural Expansion Coefficients of Many-Electron Wavefunctions. I. Natural Orbitals in the Geminal Product Approximation. *J. Chem. Phys.* **1964**, *40*, 3640. [CrossRef]
30. Smith, D.W.; Fogel, S.J. Natural Orbitals and Geminals of the Beryllium Atom. *J. Chem. Phys.* **1965**, *43*, S91. [CrossRef]
31. Coleman, A.J. Structure of Fermion Density Matrices. II. Antisymmetrized Geminal Powers. *J. Math. Phys.* **1965**, *6*, 1425. [CrossRef]
32. McWeeny, R.; Kutzelnigg, W. Symmetry properties of natural orbitals and geminals I. Construction of spin- and symmetry-adapted functions. *Int. J. Quantum Chem.* **1968**, *2*, 187. [CrossRef]
33. Kutzelnigg, W. A relation between the angular moments of natural orbitals and natural geminals. *Chem. Phys. Lett.* **1969**, *4*, 449. [CrossRef]
34. Surján, P.R. (Ed.) *An Introduction to the Theory of Geminals*; Correlation and Localization. Topics in Current Chemistry; Springer: Berlin, Germany, 1999; Volume 203, p. 63.

35. Casula, M.; Attaccalite, C.; Sorella, S. Correlated geminal wave function for molecules: An efficient resonating valence bond approach. *J. Chem. Phys.* **2004**, *121*, 7110. [CrossRef]
36. Werner, H.-J.; Knizia, G.; Manby, F.R. Explicitly correlated coupled cluster methods with pair-specific geminals. *Mol. Phys.* **2011**, *109*, 407. [CrossRef]
37. Surjan, P.R.; Szabados, A.; Jeszenszki, P.; Zoboki, T. Strongly orthogonal geminals: size-extensive and variational reference states. *J. Math. Chem.* **2012**, *50*, 534. [CrossRef]
38. Makkonen, I.; Ervasti, M.M.; Siro, T.; Harju, A. Enhancement models of momentum densities of annihilating electron-positron pairs: The many-body picture of natural geminals. *Phys. Rev. B* **2014**, *89*, 041105(R). [CrossRef]
39. Henderson, T.M.; Scuseria, G.E. Geminal-based configuration interaction. *J. Chem. Phys.* **2019**, *151*, 051101. [CrossRef]
40. Genovese, C.; Shirakawa, T.; Nakano, K.; Sorella, S. General Correlated Geminal Ansatz for Electronic Structure Calculations: Exploiting Pfaffians in Place of Determinants. *J. Chem. Theory Comput.* **2020**, *16*, 10. [CrossRef] [PubMed]
41. Myatt, C.J.; Burt, E.A.; Ghrist, R.W.; Cornell, E.A.; Wieman, C.E. Production of Two Overlapping Bose-Einstein Condensates by Sympathetic Cooling. *Phys. Rev. Lett.* **1997**, *78*, 586. [CrossRef]
42. Stamper-Kurn, D.M.; Andrews, M.R.; Chikkatur, A.P.; Inouye, S.; Miesner, H.-J.; Stenger, J.; Ketterle, W. Optical Confinement of a Bose-Einstein Condensate. *Phys. Rev. Lett.* **1998**, *80*, 2027. [CrossRef]
43. Ho, T.-L.; Shenoy, V.B. Binary Mixtures of Bose Condensates of Alkali Atoms. *Phys. Rev. Lett.* **1996**, *77*, 3276. [CrossRef]
44. Esry, B.D.; Greene, C.H.; Burke, J.P., Jr.; Bohn, J.L. Hartree-Fock Theory for Double Condensates. *Phys. Rev. Lett.* **1997**, *78*, 3594. [CrossRef]
45. Pu, H.; Bigelow, N.P. Properties of Two-Species Bose Condensates. *Phys. Rev. Lett.* **1998**, *80*, 1130. [CrossRef]
46. Timmermans, E. Phase Separation of Bose-Einstein Condensates. *Phys. Rev. Lett.* **1998**, *81*, 5718. [CrossRef]
47. Altman, E.; Hofstetter, W.; Demler, E.; Lukin, M.D. Phase diagram of two-component bosons on an optical lattice. *New J. Phys.* **2003**, *5*, 113. [CrossRef]
48. Kuklov, A.B.; Svistunov, B.V. Counterflow Superfluidity of Two-Species Ultracold Atoms in a Commensurate Optical Lattice. *Phys. Rev. Lett.* **2003**, *90*, 100401. [CrossRef]
49. Eckardt, A.; Weiss, C.; Holthaus, M. Ground-state energy and depletions for a dilute binary Bose gas. *Phys. Rev. A* **2004**, *70*, 043615. [CrossRef]
50. Alon, O.E.; Streltsov, A.I.; Cederbaum, L.S. Multiconfigurational time-dependent Hartree method for mixtures consisting of two types of identical particles. *Phys. Rev. A* **2007**, *76*, 062501. [CrossRef]
51. Sakhel, A.R.; DuBois, J.L.; Glyde, H.R. Condensate depletion in two-species Bose gases: A variational quantum Monte Carlo study. *Phys. Rev. A* **2008**, *77*, 043627. [CrossRef]
52. Zöllner, S.; Meyer, H.D.; Schmelcher, P. Composite fermionization of one-dimensional Bose-Bose mixtures. *Phys. Rev. A* **2008**, *78*, 013629. [CrossRef]
53. Oleś, B.; Sacha, K. N-conserving Bogoliubov vacuum of a two-component Bose-Einstein condensate: density fluctuations close to a phase-separation condition. *J. Phys. A* **2008**, *41*, 145005. [CrossRef]
54. Hao, Y.; Chen, S. Density-functional theory of two-component Bose gases in one-dimensional harmonic traps. *Phys. Rev. A* **2009**, *80*, 043608. [CrossRef]
55. Girardeau, M.D. Pairing, Off-Diagonal Long-Range Order, and Quantum Phase Transition in Strongly Attracting Ultracold Bose Gas Mixtures in Tight Waveguides. *Phys. Rev. Lett.* **2009**, *102*, 245303. [CrossRef] [PubMed]
56. Smyrnakis, J.; Bargi, S.; Kavoulakis, G.M.; Magiropoulos, M.; Kärkkäinen, K.; Reimann, S.M. Mixtures of Bose Gases Confined in a Ring Potential. *Phys. Rev. Lett.* **2009**, *103*, 100404. [CrossRef]
57. Girardeau, M.D.; Astrakharchik, G.E. Ground state of a mixture of two bosonic Calogero-Sutherland gases with strong odd-wave interspecies attraction *Phys. Rev. A* **2010**, *81*, 043601. [CrossRef]
58. Gautam, S.; Angom, D. Ground state geometry of binary condensates in axissymmetric traps. *J. Phys. B* **2010**, *43*, 095302. [CrossRef]
59. Krönke, S.; Cao, L.; Vendrell, O.; Schmelcher, P. Non-equilibrium quantum dynamics of ultra-cold atomic mixtures: the multi-layer multi-configuration time-dependent Hartree method for bosons. *New J. Phys.* **2013**, *15*, 063018. [CrossRef]
60. García-March, M.Á.; Busch, T. Quantum gas mixtures in different correlation regimes. *Phys. Rev. A* **2013**, *87*, 063633. [CrossRef]
61. Anoshkin, K.; Wu, Z.; Zaremba, E. Persistent currents in a bosonic mixture in the ring geometry. *Phys. Rev. A* **2013**, *88*, 013609. [CrossRef]
62. Cao, L.; Krönke, S.; Vendrell, O.; Schmelcher, P. The multi-layer multi-configuration time-dependent Hartree method for bosons: Theory, implementation, and applications. *J. Chem. Phys.* **2013**, *139*, 134103. [CrossRef] [PubMed]
63. Peña Ardila, L.A.; Giorgini, S. Impurity in a Bose-Einstein condensate: Study of the attractive and repulsive branch using quantum Monte Carlo methods. *Phys. Rev. A* **2015**, *92*, 033612. [CrossRef]
64. Petrov, D.S. Quantum Mechanical Stabilization of a Collapsing Bose-Bose Mixture. *Phys. Rev. Lett.* **2015**, *115*, 155302. [CrossRef]
65. Schurer, J.M.; Negretti, A.; Schmelcher, P. Unraveling the Structure of Ultracold Mesoscopic Collinear Molecular Ions. *Phys. Rev. Lett.* **2017**, *119*, 063001 [CrossRef]
66. Chen, J.; Schurer, J.M.; Schmelcher, P. Entanglement Induced Interactions in Binary Mixtures. *Phys. Rev. Lett.* **2018**, *121*, 043401. [CrossRef]

67. Lévêque, C.; Madsen, L.B. Multispecies time-dependent restricted-active-space self-consistent-field-theory for ultracold atomic and molecular gases. *J. Phys. B* **2018**, *51*, 155302. [CrossRef]
68. Sowiński, T.; García-March, M.Á. One-dimensional mixtures of several ultracold atoms: A review. *Rep. Prog. Phys.* **2019**, *82*, 104401. [CrossRef]
69. Mistakidis, S.I.; Volosniev, A.G.; Schmelcher, P. Induced correlations between impurities in a one-dimensional quenched Bose gas. *Phys. Rev. Res.* **2020**, *2*, 023154. [CrossRef]
70. Andriati, A.; Brito, L.; Tomio, L.; Gammal, A. Stability of a Bose condensed mixture on a bubble trap. *Phys. Rev. A* **2021**, *104*, 033318. [CrossRef]
71. Osadchii, M.S.; Muraktanov, V.V. The System of Harmonically Interacting Particles: An Exact Solution of the Quantum-Mechanical Problem. *Int. J. Quantum Chem.* **1991**, *39*, 173. [CrossRef]
72. Bouvrie, P.A.; Majtey, A.P.; Tichy, M.C.; Dehesa, J.S.; Plastino, A.R. Entanglement and the Born-Oppenheimer approximation in an exactly solvable quantum many-body system. *Eur. Phys. J. D* **2014**, *68*, 346. [CrossRef]
73. Armstrong, J.R.; Volosniev, A.G.; Fedorov, D.V.; Jensen, A.S.; Zinner, N.T. Analytic solutions of topologically disjoint systems. *J. Phys. A* **2015**, *48*, 085301. [CrossRef]
74. Alon, O.E. Solvable model of a generic trapped mixture of interacting bosons: reduced density matrices and proof of Bose-Einstein condensation. *J. Phys. A* **2017**, *50*, 295002. [CrossRef]
75. Klaiman, S.; Streltsov, A.I.; Alon, O.E. Solvable Model of a Generic Trapped Mixture of Interacting Bosons: Many-Body and Mean-Field Properties. *J. Phys. Conf. Ser.* **2018**, *999*, 012013. [CrossRef]
76. Alon, O.E. Solvable Model of a Generic Driven Mixture of Trapped Bose-Einstein Condensates and Properties of a Many-Boson Floquet State at the Limit of an Infinite Number of Particles. *Entropy* **2020**, *22*, 1342. [CrossRef]
77. Klaiman, S.; Streltsov, A.I.; Alon, O.E. Solvable model of a trapped mixture of Bose-Einstein condensates. *Chem. Phys.* **2017**, *482*, 362. [CrossRef]
78. Cohen, L.; Lee, C. Exact reduced density matrices for a model problem. *J. Math. Phys.* **1985**, *26*, 3105. [CrossRef]
79. Pruski, S.; Maćkowiak, J.; Missuno, O. Reduced density matrices of a system of N coupled oscillators. 2. Eigenstructure of the 1-particle matrix for the canonical ensemble. *Rep. Math. Phys.* **1972**, *3*, 227. [CrossRef]
80. Pruski, S.; Maćkowiak, J.; Missuno, O. Reduced density matrices of a system of N coupled oscillators. 3. The eigenstructure of the p-particle matrix for the ground state. *Rep. Math. Phys.* **1972**, *3*, 241. [CrossRef]
81. Robinson, P.D. Coupled oscillator natural orbitals. *J. Chem. Phys.* **1977**, *66*, 3307. [CrossRef]
82. Schilling, C. Natural orbitals and occupation numbers for harmonium: Fermions versus bosons. *Phys. Rev. A* **2013**, *88*, 042105. [CrossRef]
83. Hall, R.L. Some exact solutions to the translation-invariant N-body problem. *J. Phys. A* **1978**, *11*, 1227. [CrossRef]
84. Hall, R.L. Exact solutions of Schrödinger's equation for translation-invariant harmonic matter. *J. Phys. A* **1978**, *11*, 1235. [CrossRef]
85. Załuska-Kotur, M.A.; Gajda, M.; Orłowski, A.; Mostowski, J. Soluble model of many interacting quantum particles in a trap. *Phys. Rev. A* **2000**, *61*, 033613. [CrossRef]
86. Yan, J. Harmonic Interaction Model and Its Applications in Bose-Einstein Condensation. *J. Stat. Phys.* **2003**, *113*, 623. [CrossRef]
87. Gajda, M. Criterion for Bose-Einstein condensation in a harmonic trap in the case with attractive interactions. *Phys. Rev. A* **2006**, *73*, 023603. [CrossRef]
88. Armstrong, J.R.; Zinner, N.T.; Fedorov, D.V.; Jensen, A.S. Analytic harmonic approach to the N-body problem. *J. Phys. B* **2011**, *44*, 055303. [CrossRef]
89. Armstrong, J.R.; Zinner, N.T.; Fedorov, D.V.; Jensen, A.S. Virial expansion coefficients in the harmonic approximation. *Phys. Rev. E* **2012**, *86*, 021115.
90. Kościk, P.; Okopińska, A. Correlation effects in the Moshinsky model. *Few-Body Syst.* **2013**, *54*, 1637. [CrossRef]
91. Benavides-Riveros, C.L.; Toranzo, I.V.; Dehesa, J.S. Entanglement in N-harmonium: bosons and fermions. *J. Phys. B* **2014**, *47*, 195503. [CrossRef]
92. Schilling, C.; Schilling, R. Number-parity effect for confined fermions in one dimension. *Phys. Rev. A* **2016**, *93*, 021601(R). [CrossRef]
93. Lieb, E.H.; Seiringer, R.; Yngvason, J. Bosons in a trap: A rigorous derivation of the Gross-Pitaevskii energy functional. *Phys. Rev. A* **2000**, *61*, 043602. [CrossRef]
94. Lieb, E.H.; Seiringer, R. Proof of Bose-Einstein Condensation for Dilute Trapped Gases. *Phys. Rev. Lett.* **2002**, *88*, 170409. [CrossRef]
95. Klaiman, S.; Alon, O.E. Variance as a sensitive probe of correlations. *Phys. Rev. A* **2015**, *91*, 063613. [CrossRef]
96. Klaiman, S.; Cederbaum, L.S. Overlap of exact and Gross-Pitaevskii wave functions in Bose-Einstein condensates of dilute gases. *Phys. Rev. A* **2016**, *94*, 063648. [CrossRef]
97. Anapolitanos, I.; Hott, M.; Hundertmark, D. Derivation of the Hartree equation for compound Bose gases in the mean field limit. *Rev. Math. Phys.* **2017**, *29*, 1750022. [CrossRef]
98. Michelangeli, A.; Olgiati, A. Mean-field quantum dynamics for a mixture of Bose-Einstein condensates. *Anal. Math. Phys.* **2017**, *7*, 377. [CrossRef]
99. Cederbaum, L.S. Exact many-body wave function and properties of trapped bosons in the infinite-particle limit. *Phys. Rev. A* **2017**, *96*, 013615. [CrossRef]

100. Sakmann, K.; Schmiedmayer, J. Conserving symmetries in Bose-Einstein condensate dynamics requires many-body theory. *arXiv* **2018**, arXiv:1802.03746v2.
101. Alon, O.E. Analysis of a Trapped Bose-Einstein Condensate in Terms of Position, Momentum, and Angular-Momentum Variance. *Symmetry* **2019**, *11*, 1344. [CrossRef]
102. Peres, A. Higher order Schmidt decompositions. *Phys. Lett. A* **1995**, *202*, 16. [CrossRef]

Article

Asymmetric Lineshapes of Efimov Resonances in Mass-Imbalanced Ultracold Gases

Panagiotis Giannakeas [1,*] and Chris H. Greene [2,3]

1. Max-Planck-Institut für Physik Komplexer Systeme, Nöthnitzer Str. 38, D-01187 Dresden, Germany
2. Department of Physics and Astronomy, Purdue University, West Lafayette, IN 47907, USA; chgreene@purdue.edu
3. Purdue Quantum Science and Engineering Institute, Purdue University, West Lafayette, IN 47907, USA
* Correspondence: pgiannak@pks.mpg.de

Abstract: The resonant profile of the rate coefficient for three-body recombination into a shallow dimer is investigated for mass-imbalanced systems. In the low-energy limit, three atoms collide with zero-range interactions, in a regime where the scattering lengths of the heavy–heavy and the heavy–light subsystems are positive and negative, respectively. For this physical system, the adiabatic hyperspherical representation is combined with a fully semi-classical method and we show that the shallow dimer recombination spectra display an asymmetric lineshape that originates from the coexistence of Efimov resonances with Stückelberg interference minima. These asymmetric lineshapes are quantified utilizing the Fano profile formula. In particular, a closed-form expression is derived that describes the width of the corresponding Efimov resonances and the Fano lineshape asymmetry parameter q. The profile of Efimov resonances exhibits a q–reversal effect as the inter- and intra-species scattering lengths vary. In the case of a diverging asymmetry parameter, i.e., $|q| \to \infty$, we show that the Efimov resonances possess zero width and are fully decoupled from the three-body and atom–dimer continua, and the corresponding Efimov metastable states behave as bound levels.

Keywords: few-body collisions; Efimov effect; mass-imbalanced systems; recombination

1. Introduction

The Efimov effect is one of the most counter-intuitive phenomena in few-body physics, where an infinity of three-body bound states is formed even when the scattering length of the two-body subsystems is negative [1–4]. This phenomenon was theoretically predicted by V. Efimov to occur for three equal-mass particles that interact via zero-range potentials, with trimer binding energies that scale geometrically [5]. The existence of these exotic trimer states was experimentally confirmed by Kraemer et al. in an ultracold gas of Cs atoms [6]. This suggested new possibilities for theoretical and experimental investigations [1–3,7–12] to address various physical aspects of the Efimov states, such as the discrete-scale invariance of the trimer binding energies [13] or the sensitivity of the ground-state energy on the short-range physics. In particular, the latter stems from the fact that, within the zero-range model, the trimer spectrum is unbound from below due to *Thomas collapse* [14] and an auxiliary parameter, i.e., three-body parameter, was introduced in order to specify the ground-state energy rendering the entire spectrum system dependent [5]. However, experimental and theoretical advances demonstrated that, for ultracold atoms, the Efimov spectrum exhibits a certain class of universality, i.e., van der Waals universality [15–25]. Namely, it was shown that the lowest Efimov state appears at scattering lengths $a_-^{(1)} \approx -10\ell_{vdW}$, with ℓ_{vdW} being the length scale of van der Waals interactions between two neutral atoms.

Mass-imbalanced ultracold gases are an ideal platform to explore more deeply the idiosyncrasies of Efimov spectra. In particular, three-body collisions of ultracold atoms with unequal masses offer more favorable experimental conditions that enable observation of multiple successive trimer states and measurement of their geometrical energy scaling, i.e., the smoking gun of Efimov physics [26–28]. Apart from this, mass-imbalanced ensembles offer a large parameter space, such as the particles' mass ratio, the sign and magnitude of the inter- and intra-species scattering lengths, which provide fertile ground to investigate the pristine attributes of the Efimov states. Specifically, theoretical and experimental efforts have mapped out a large portion of the parameter space, addressing the underlying physics of recombination processes in heavy–heavy–light (HHL) systems [26,27,29–32]. The particular case that stands out corresponds to HHL systems that possess inter- and intra-species scattering lengths of opposite sign, i.e., $a_{HL} < 0$ and $a_{HH} > 0$, respectively. For example, in the experimental works of Refs. [29,33], it was demonstrated in the regime of broad Fano–Feshbach resonances [34] that the lowest Efimov state is in good agreement with the predictions of the universal zero-range and van der Waals theory. However, subsequent experimental investigations show that deviations from the universal theory are more pronounced for narrow Fano–Feshbach resonances [35]. Furthermore, within the zero-range theory, Ref. [36] illustrated that the diabaticity of the three-body collisions imposes additional limitations on the universal properties of the Efimov spectrum, where mostly adiabatic collisions yield trimer states independent of the three-body parameter, as was pointed out in the case of Refs. [29,33].

Additionally, Ref. [36] showed that three-body recombination into a shallow heavy–heavy dimer possesses a unique property that only mass-imbalanced systems exhibit, namely the co-existence of Efimov resonances with Stückelberg suppression effects in the same range of scattering lengths. In this work, we further study this particular attribute of HHL systems and demonstrate that the corresponding Efimov resonances in the recombination rate coefficient plotted versus scattering length can display an asymmetric profile, which can be quantified by the Fano profile formula. In particular, our analysis employs the adiabatic hyperspherical framework for zero-range two-body interactions, which is combined with a fully semi-classical theory [36]. Moreover, a simplified version of the semi-classical approach is shown, where the lowest hyperspherical curves are approximated by universal potential tails at large hyperradii, as in Ref. [37]. This permits us to derive closed-form relations for the S-matrix elements, which are expressed in terms of the width of the Efimov resonance and Fano's lineshape asymmetry parameter q. As an example, the asymmetric profiles of the Efimov resonances in the recombination coefficient of ^{6}Li-^{133}Cs-^{133}Cs and ^{6}Li-^{87}Rb-^{87}Rb are analyzed, both of which showcase a q-reversal phenomenon as a function of the inter- and intra-species scattering length ratio. Furthermore, we observe that, for a diverging q parameter, the Efimov resonances behave as bound states that are embedded in the continuum [38]. This occurs since the decay width of the resonances vanishes as $|q| \to \infty$ and the corresponding Efimovian quasi-bound states decouple from the three-body and atom–dimer continua.

The structure of this work is as follows: in Section 2, the Hamiltonian of the three-body system and the parameters of interest are given. Sections 2.1 and 2.2 provide a detailed review of the methods that are employed in our analysis. More specifically, Section 2.1 discusses the adiabatic hyperspherical representation and the fully semi-classical treatment of the coupled hyperradial equations. In Section 2.2, a simplified version of the semi-classical theory is given that permits us to express the S-matrix elements of recombination processes into shallow dimers in terms of the inter- and intra-species scattering lengths. Finally, Section 3 focuses on the asymmetric profile of Efimov resonances in the spectrum of the three-body recombination coefficient for HHL systems.

2. General Considerations and Methods

Consider a three-body system that consists of two heavy (H) alkali atoms and a light (L) one at low energies. The particles mutually interact through s-wave pairwise interactions that are modeled via Fermi–Huang's zero-range pseudopotential. Our greatest interest here is in the regime where the mass-imbalanced system can recombine into a shallow heavy–heavy dimer with a recoiling light atom. This scenario arises for inter- and intra-species interactions of opposite sign, meaning that the scattering length between a heavy–light or heavy–heavy pair of particles is $a_{HL} < 0$ or $a_{HH} > 0$, respectively. Furthermore, relaxation and recombination processes into deep dimer channels are neglected, and we focus on the physics that arises due to energies near the break-up threshold, i.e., the zero-energy limit. For this purpose, we focus on the two lowest potential curves of HHL systems, which suffice to describe three-body recombination processes into shallow dimers, as was shown in Ref. [36], permitting the derivation of closed-form expressions for the S-matrix.

2.1. The Adiabatic Hyperspherical Representation and the Semi-Classical Approach

The total three-body Hamiltonian for the HHL system of interest is given by the following expression:

$$H_{\text{tot}} = \sum_{i=1}^{3} -\frac{\hbar^2}{2m_i}\nabla_i^2 + \sum_{i>j} V_{ij}(r_{ij}), \text{ with}$$

$$V_{ij}(r_{ij}) = \frac{4\pi\hbar^2 a_{ij}}{2\mu_{ij}}\delta(r_{ij})\partial_{r_{ij}}[r_{ij}\times], \quad (1)$$

where V_{ij} represents the Fermi–Huang pseudopotential. a_{ij} and μ_{ij} refer to the scattering length and two-body reduced mass of the ij-pair of particles, respectively. ∇_i^2 denotes the Laplacian for r_i, and m_i indicates the mass of the i-th particle. Note that the scattering lengths a_{ij} between the atoms are chosen to be larger than any other length scale of the system, permitting us to focus on the universal characteristics of the three-body system under consideration.

Utilizing the Jacobi vector choice of Ref. [39], Equation (1) can be separated into the Hamiltonians of center of mass and relative degrees of freedom. Since the s-wave interactions involve only the relative distance between a pair of particles, the center-of-mass Hamiltonian is fully decoupled, meaning that the relative one retains all the relevant information of the three-body system. Therefore, we focus only on the relative Hamiltonian, which gives, after transforming it into hyperspherical coordinates (for details, see [2]), the following expression:

$$H_{\text{rel}} = -\frac{\hbar^2}{2\mu R^{5/2}}\frac{\partial^2}{\partial R^2}R^{5/2} + H_{\text{ad}}(R;\Omega), \quad (2)$$

where $\mu = \sqrt{m_1 m_2 m_3/(m_1+m_2+m_3)} \equiv m_H/\sqrt{1+2m_H/m_L}$ indicates the three-body reduced mass, R is the hyperradius, and Ω is a collective coordinate denoting the five hyperangles [40,41]. $H_{\text{ad}}(R;\Omega)$ represents the part of the Hamiltonian that contains the hyperangular centrifugal potential as well as the two-body interactions expressed in the hyperspherical coordinates.

$$H_{\text{ad}}(R;\Omega) = \frac{\hbar^2}{2\mu}\hat{\Lambda}^2 + \frac{15\hbar^2}{8\mu R^2} + \sum_{i>j} V_{ij}(R;\Omega), \quad (3)$$

where $\hat{\Lambda}$ denotes the grand angular momentum operator.

In the spirit of the adiabatic hyperspherical representation, the properly symmetrized three-body wave function is provided by the following ansatz:

$$\Psi(R,\Omega) = \frac{1}{R^{5/2}}\sum_{\nu}\phi_{\nu}(R;\Omega)F_{\nu}(R), \quad (4)$$

where $F_{\nu}(R)$ and $\phi_{\nu}(R;\Omega)$ indicate the ν-th hyperradial and hyperangular part of the wave function, respectively. In particular, $\phi_{\nu}(R;\Omega)$ components of $\Psi(R,\Omega)$ are obtained by diagonalizing Equation (3) at a fixed hyperradius R.

$$H_{\text{ad}}(R;\Omega)\phi_{\nu}(R;\Omega) = U_{\nu}(R)\phi_{\nu}(R;\Omega), \quad (5)$$

where the eigenvalues $U_\nu(R)$ are the so-called *adiabatic hyperspherical potential curves*.

Substitution of Equations (4) and (5) into the Schrödinger equation of the Hamiltonian $H_{\rm rel}$ and integration over all the hyperangles Ω yields a set of coupled ordinary second-order differential equations that solely depend on the hyperradius R.

$$\left[-\frac{d^2}{dR^2} + \frac{2\mu}{\hbar^2}(U_\nu(R) - E)\right]F_\nu(R) = \sum_{\nu'} V_{\nu\nu'}(R)F_{\nu'}(R), \qquad (6)$$

where $V_{\nu\nu'}(R)$ indicate the non-adiabatic coupling matrix elements/operators that are given by the following expressions:

$$V_{\nu\nu'}(R) = 2P_{\nu\nu'}(R)\frac{d}{dR} + Q_{\nu\nu'}(R) \text{ with} \qquad (7)$$

$$P_{\nu\nu'}(R) = \langle \phi_\nu(R;\Omega)|\frac{\partial}{\partial R}\phi_{\nu'}(R;\Omega)\rangle_\Omega \qquad (8)$$

$$Q_{\nu\nu'}(R) = \langle \phi_\nu(R;\Omega)|\frac{\partial^2}{\partial R^2}\phi_{\nu'}(R;\Omega)\rangle_\Omega, \qquad (9)$$

where $\langle\ldots\rangle_\Omega$ denotes the integration over the hyperangles only.

Owing to the zero-range interactions, the non-adiabatic coupling matrix elements, $P_{\nu\nu'}(R)$ and $Q_{\nu\nu'}(R)$, as well as the hyperspherical potential curves, $U_\nu(R)$, can be calculated semi-analytically [1,39,42,43]. However, the resulting hyperspherical potential curves $U_\nu(R)$, especially the lowest one, possess attractive singularities at the origin, i.e., the Thomas collapse. Therefore, an auxiliary parameter is introduced in order to truncate the attractive singularity in the potential curves, which, in its simplest form, consists of a hard wall placed at a small hyperradius, $R \approx r_{3b}$. The three-body parameter r_{3b} is arbitrary (from the point of view of zero-range theory) and is usually fixed via experimental observations. In addition, the zero-range approximation greatly simplifies the computational cost since only hyperradial equations in Equation (6) require a numerical solution using standardized R-matrix methods [44–46].

Figure 1 depicts the two lowest hyperspherical potential curves $U_\nu^{1/3}(R/a_{HH})$ as obtained from zero-range approximation: the upper (blue) potential that vanishes at large hyperradii R in the break-up threshold and the lower (red) potential, which, in the limit of large R, approaches the energy of the HH dimer. The light blue region denotes the hard wall boundary condition at r_{3b}/a_{HH} that removes the attractive singularity of the lower curve. The potential curves of Figure 1 suffice in order to intuitively understand the recombination of three free particles into a universal pair of atoms with a recoiling one. Consider the three-body system at a collisional energy $\bar{E}$ (in units of $\frac{\hbar^2}{m_H a_{HH}^2}$) indicated by the dotted line in Figure 1. In particular, we are interested in the low-energy limit in order to validate the two-channel approximation and highlight the threshold behavior of three-body collisions in HHL settings. Viewing this three-body system heuristically as a time-dependent collision, starting from infinite long distances, the three particles propagate inwards in the upper potential curve and tunnel with some probability under the repulsive barrier and then probe the corresponding classical allowed region at short hyperradii. In this region, the non-adiabatic P-matrix element P_{12} between the upper and lower potential curve plays a key role in inducing transitions. More specifically, at distances R_{LZ}/a_{HH} (vertical dashed line), the corresponding P-matrix maximizes, indicating the strong coupling regime. This means that the particles transition with a certain probability from the upper to the lower curve and subsequently propagate outwards, fragmenting into a two-body molecule plus a spectator atom. This recombination process is quantified mainly by evaluating the $|S_{12}|^2$ element of the scattering S-matrix.

As was shown in Ref. [36], the $|S_{12}|^2$ matrix element can be obtained analytically within the two-channel approximation by combining the Landau–Zener physics with the Jeffreys–Wentzel–Kramers–Brillouin (JWKB) approach. The main constituents of this semi-classical approach are depicted in Figure 1. More specifically, we assume that the P-matrix element of the potential curves in Figure 1 possesses a Lorentzian lineshape in the vicinity or $R \approx R_{LZ}$, and we include the Langer correction in JWKB integrals [47]. Under these considerations, the $|S_{12}|^2$ matrix element for the hyperspherical potential curves in Figure 1 reads:

$$|S_{12}|^2 = e^{-2\tau} p(1-p) \cos^2(\Phi_L^U - \Phi_L^L - \frac{\pi}{4} + \lambda) \left\{ (1 - \frac{e^{-4\tau}}{16})[p \cos^2(\Phi_L^L + \Phi_R^U - \frac{\pi}{4}) \right.$$
$$+ (1-p) \cos^2(\Phi_L^U + \Phi_R^U + \lambda)] - (1 - \frac{e^{-2\tau}}{4})^2 p(1-p) \cos^2(\Phi_L^U - \Phi_L^L - \frac{\pi}{4} + \lambda)$$
$$\left. + \frac{e^{-4\tau}}{16} \right\}^{-1}, \qquad (10)$$

where $e^{-2\tau}$ indicates the tunneling probability in a single collision with the repulsive barrier of the upper potential curve in Figure 1.

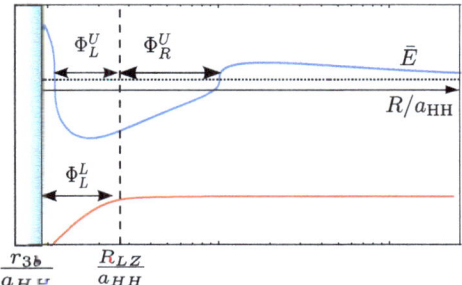

Figure 1. An illustration of the lowest hyperspherical potential curves $U_\nu^{1/3}(R/a_{HH})$ with $a_{HH} > 0$ and $c_{HL} < 0$. The red (blue) line saturates at large hyperradii in the atom–dimer (three-body break-up) threshold. The quantities Φ_L^U and Φ_R^U indicate the JWKB phase accumulation in the upper potential curve. For the lower potential, the corresponding phase is denoted by Φ_L^L. The vertical dashed line represents the hyperradius where the non-adiabatic coupling P-matrix element P_{12} maximizes. The horizontal dotted line refers to the three-body collisional energy $\bar{E}$ in units of $\frac{\hbar^2}{m_H a_{HH}^2}$, and the three-body parameter, $\frac{r_{3b}}{a_{HH}}$, depicted by the blue region.

The JWKB phases in the upper curve are indicated by the terms Φ_L^U and Φ_R^U. More specifically, Φ_L^U is the phase accumulation from the far-left classical turning point up to $R \approx R_{LZ}$, whereas Φ_R^U is the JWKB integral from $R \approx R_{LZ}$ up to the inner classical turning point of the repulsive barrier. Similarly, in the lower potential curve, Φ_L^L corresponds to the phase accumulation between the hard wall (blue shaded region) located at $\frac{r_{3b}}{a_{HH}}$ and $R \approx R_{LZ}$. Furthermore, p corresponds to the Landau–Zener non-adiabatic probability to transition from the upper to the lower hyperspherical potential curve in a single pass through the avoided crossing region. The non-adiabatic probability p is evaluated from the P-matrix elements, which, as we mentioned above, are approximated to have a Lorentzian lineshape versus the hyperradius and a maximum at $R \approx R_{LZ}$ [48]. λ is the Stokes phase and it is a correction added to the components of the hyperradial wave function, i.e., $F_\nu(R)$ with $\nu = 1, 2$, as they propagate through the non-adiabatic transition region [49,50]. The Stokes correction phase depends on the non-adiabatic probability p and it obeys the relation

$$\lambda = \arg\Gamma\left(i\frac{\delta}{\pi}\right) - \frac{\delta}{\pi}\ln\frac{\delta}{\pi} + \frac{\delta}{\pi} + \frac{\pi}{4}, \qquad (11)$$

where $\delta = -\frac{\ln p}{2}$. Figure 2 shows the Stokes phase versus p, where, in the diabatic (adiabatic) limit, i.e., $p = 1$ (0), the Stokes phase tends to $\lambda = -\pi/4$ (0). Equation (10) captures the two main effects that occur in HHL systems. More specifically, the roots of the numerator of Equation (10) indicate the Stückelberg suppression effects minimizing the probability of the HHL system to recombine into a shallow dimer. On the other hand, the roots of the denominator in Equation (10) denote the Efimov resonance phenomenon that enhances the recombination into a shallow dimer. An additional insight obtained by Equation (10) is that the Stückelberg suppression effects depend on the three-body parameter due to the phase Φ_L^L accumulation in the lower potential curve. In principle, also the Efimov resonances depend on r_{3b}; however, as Equation (10) suggests, in the limit of adiabatic collisions, i.e., $p \ll 1$, only the phase accumulation in the upper potential curve survives, which is independent of the three-body parameter, meaning that such collisions possess a universal character.

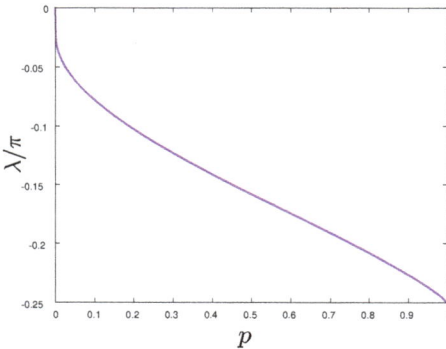

Figure 2. The Stokes correction phase as a function of the non-adiabatic probability p.

The *degree of diabaticity* p is depicted in Figure 3, in the zero-energy limit, as a function of $a_{HH}/|a_{HL}|$ for different mass ratios m_H/m_L, covering, in this manner, the regime from strong-to-weak mass-imbalanced atomic ensembles. Note that we consider values of the ratio $a_{HH}/|a_{HL}|$ that correspond to $|a_{HL}|$ and a_{HH}, both being larger than the van der Waals length scales of the HL and HH pairs of atoms, respectively, ensuring the validity of the zero-range theory. In particular, we observe in Figure 3 that, for a large mass ratio, i.e., $m_H/m_L = 21$, the corresponding three-body collision is more diabatic than in the case of weak mass imbalance, i.e., $m_H/m_L = 6.3$. This means that HHL systems with strong mass imbalance, i.e., $m_H/m_L > 21$, can easily transition from the three-body continuum to the shallow dimer–atom channel, implying that the corresponding recombination process is strongly affected by the three-body parameter r_{3b}. This behavior of the non-adiabatic probability p on m_H/m_L can be understood in terms of the ratio of the P-matrix elements and the energy difference of the hyperspherical potential curves, i.e., Δ, at $R = R_{LZ}$. According to Ref. [48], the probability p is given by the relation $p = e^{-\pi \Delta/[4v P_{12}(R_{LZ})]}$, where v refers to the semi-classical velocity of the particles at $R = R_{LZ}$. Thus, for $a_{HL} \to -\infty$, the ratio of the energy gap Δ and $P_{12}(R_{LZ})$ increases as m_H/m_L decreases, yielding, in return, a decreasing probability p and vice versa.

As an example, Figure 4 illustrates the scaled S-matrix element $\frac{|S_{12}|^2}{(ka_{HL})^4}$ for the ^{6}Li-^{87}Rb-^{87}Rb three-body system at low energies $E = \frac{\hbar^2 k^2}{2\mu}$. Figure 4a corresponds to the semi-classical model using Equation (10), and Figure 4b refers to the case where the hyperradial equations are solved numerically within the R-matrix approach. Both panels are in excellent agreement and the qualitative features, i.e., the enhancement and suppression of $\frac{|S_{12}|^2}{(ka_{HL})^4}$, are similar to those shown in Ref. [36]. In particular, as discussed in Ref. [36], the enhancement of $\frac{|S_{12}|^2}{(ka_{HL})^4}$ is associated with an Efimov resonance. Namely, the upper potential curve in Figure 1 can support a quasi-bound state behind the repulsive barrier at specific values of the ratios $\frac{|a_{HL}|}{a_{HH}}$ and $\frac{r_{3b}}{a_{HH}}$. Therefore, for colliding energies E that match the energy of the quasi-bound three-body state, the atoms can easily tunnel under the barrier, where they can probe the non-adiabatic transition region and eventually hop with some probability to the $\bar{x}b_2$ + Li channel. Therefore, the presence of a quasi-bound state in the upper potential curve in Figure 1 causes $\frac{|S_{12}|^2}{(ka_{HL})^4}$ to be more pronounced. On the other hand, the suppression of $\frac{S_{12}}{(ka_{HL})^4}$ is a manifestation of Stückelberg physics due to the destructive interference of the alternative pathways, which prevents the three particles from exiting to infinity along the $\bar{x}b_2$ + Li channel. However, in Ref. [36], the ^{6}Li-^{133}Cs-^{133}Cs system was investigated and the corresponding $\frac{|S_{12}|^2}{(ka_{HL})^4}$ possesses one main qualitative difference from ^{6}Li-^{87}Rb-^{87}Rb. Specifically, the ^{6}Li-^{133}Cs-^{133}Cs system exhibits narrower Efimov resonances (see Figure 2b,c in Ref. [36]) than those shown Figure 4 for ^{6}Li-^{87}Rb-^{87}Rb. This difference mainly arises from the fact that the collisions in ^{6}Li-^{133}Cs-^{133}Cs are more diabatic than in ^{6}Li-^{87}Rb-^{87}Rb. As Figure 3 suggests, the non-adiabatic probability p for ^{6}Li-^{133}Cs-^{133}Cs is much closer to the unit than for the case of ^{6}Li-^{87}Rb-^{87}Rb. The lower values of p for ^{6}Li-^{87}Rb-^{87}Rb indicate the weak coupling of the quasi-bound Efimov state to the atom–dimer continuum, which, in return, is manifested as a broad resonance in the $\frac{|S_{12}|^2}{(ka_{HL})^4}$ matrix element.

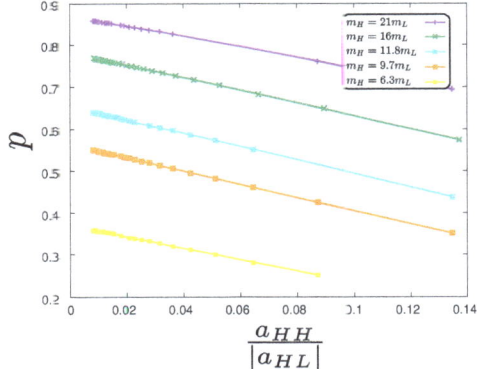

Figure 3. The degree of diabaticity p as a function of the scattering length ratio a_{HH}/a_{HL} for different mass ratios m_H/m_L, covering the regime of strong-to-weak mass-imbalanced three-body systems.

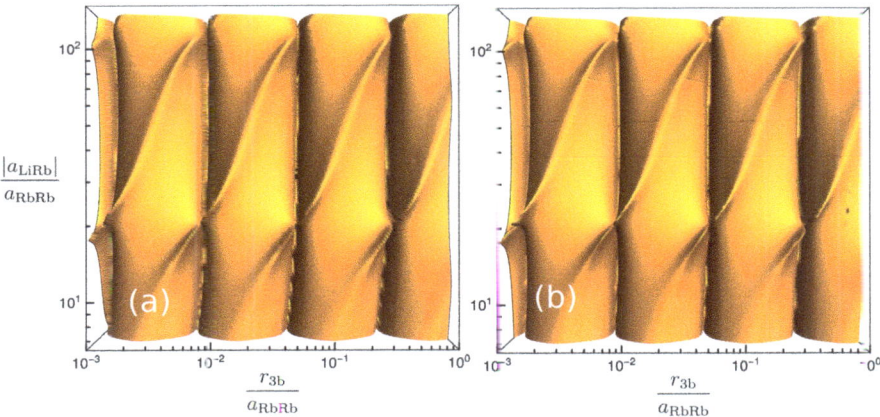

Figure 4. The scaled $\frac{|S_{12}|^2}{(ka_{HL})^4}$ matrix element versus the ratios $\frac{a_{HL}}{a_{HH}}$ and $\frac{r_{3b}}{a_{HH}}$ for the ^{6}Li-^{87}Rb-^{87}Rb system at low energy $E = \frac{\hbar^2 k^2}{2\mu}$. (a) Semi-classical approach and (b) R-matrix numerical calculations.

2.2. A Simplified Semi-Classical Model

In the following, we focus on the derivation of a simplified semi-classical model based on the prescription given in Ref. [37]. Our goal is to unveil the scaling behavior of the S_{12} matrix element with respect to the length scales and the degree of diabaticity p that govern HHL systems by incorporating only the necessary approximations. Therefore, for our purposes, from this point on, we assume that the colliding energy of the three atoms tends to zero, i.e., $E = \hbar^2 k^2 / 2\mu \to 0$.

As in Figure 1, Figure 5 illustrates the two lowest hyperspherical potential curves, which are properly parameterized using only the limiting tails of the curves of Figure 1 in a piecewise manner. Namely, for the upper potential curve (blue line) in Figure 5, the universal tail $U_1(R) = -\frac{\hbar^2}{2\mu R^2}(s_0^2 + 1/4)$ is shown for hyperradii ranging from the non-adiabatic transition region, i.e., R_{LZ}, up to $R \sim \gamma |a_{HL}|$. Moreover, for $R > \gamma |a_{HL}|$, we consider only the tail of the repulsive barrier of the potential curve shown in Figure 1, which falls off as $U_1(R) \sim \frac{\hbar^2}{2\mu R^2}(15/4)$, with the outer classical turning point being located at $R \sim 2/k$. In addition, the effects of motion along the upper potential curve for $R < R_{LZ}$ are mapped to an arbitrary phase Φ. For the lower curve, at small hyperradii, we employ the universal tail $U_2(R) = -\frac{\hbar^2}{2\mu R^2}[(s_0^*)^2 + 1/4]$, whereas, for $R > R_{LZ}$, we assume that the potential curve is constant, with energy equal to the heavy–heavy dimer. Note that the parameters s_0 and s_0^* correspond to the universal Efimov scaling coefficients for two and three resonant two-body interactions, respectively, and they are tabulated in Ref. [51] for several HHL systems.

Based on the piecewise potential curves of Figure 5 and considering the low-energy limit, i.e., $k \to 0$, the tunneling amplitude $e^{-\tau}$ and the semi-classical phases Φ_L^U, Φ_R^U and Φ_L^L are given by the following expressions:

$$e^{-\tau} \approx \int_{\gamma|a_{HL}|}^{2/k} \sqrt{4/R^2} \approx (\gamma k a_{HL}/2)^2, \quad \Phi_L^U = \Phi, \tag{12}$$

$$\Phi_R^U \approx \int_{\beta|a_{HL}|}^{\gamma|a_{HL}|} \sqrt{s_0^2/R^2} \approx s_0 \ln \frac{\gamma|a_{HL}|}{\beta a_{HH}} \tag{13}$$

$$\text{and } \Phi_L^L \approx \int_{r_{3b}}^{\beta|a_{HL}|} \sqrt{(s_0^*)^2/R^2} \approx s_0^* \ln \frac{\beta a_{HH}}{r_{3b}}. \tag{14}$$

where the dimensionless parameters β and γ define the interval of hyperradius R such that the upper potential curve has the form $U_1(R) = -\frac{\hbar^2}{2\mu R^2}(s_0^2 + 1/4)$. In general, β and γ are considered free parameters and they can be fixed by a fitting procedure to experimental or numerical data. Moreover, recall that the above JWKB integrals include the Langer corrections. After substitution of Equation (12)–(14) into Equation (10), the S-matrix element S_{12} reads

$$\frac{|S_{12}|^2}{(ka_{HL})^4} = \frac{\gamma^4}{16} p \cos^2\left(s_0^* \ln \frac{r_{3b}}{a_{HH}} + \psi_1 + \lambda\right) \left\{ \frac{p}{1-p} \right.$$
$$\times \sin^2[s_0 \ln \frac{|a_{HL}|}{a_{HH}} + \psi_2 - (s_0^* \ln \frac{r_{3b}}{a_{HH}} + \psi_1)]$$
$$+ \cos^2(s_0 \ln \frac{|a_{HL}|}{a_{HH}} + \psi_2 + \lambda)$$
$$\left. - p \cos^2(s_0^* \ln \frac{r_{3b}}{a_{HH}} + \psi_1 + \lambda) \right\}^{-1}, \tag{15}$$

where the terms $(1 - (\gamma k a_{HL}/2)^8/16) \approx 1$ and $(1 - (\gamma k a_{HL}/2)^4/4) \approx 1$ since we focus on the low-energy regime, i.e., $k \to 0$. The phases ψ_1 and ψ_2 obey the expressions $\psi_1 = \Phi - s_0^* \ln \beta - \pi/4$ and $\psi_2 = \Phi + s_0 \ln(\gamma/\beta)$, respectively.

Equation (15) captures the main properties of the S-matrix element S_{12} shown in Figure 4. The numerator of Equation (15) describes the positions of the Stückelberg interference minima, which, as shown in Figure 4, scale logarithmically with respect to the ratio r_{3b}/a_{HH}. Moreover, the spacing between successive minima is constant on a logarithmic scale and related to the universal Efimov scaling coefficient s_0^*. On the other hand, the roots of the denominator of Equation (15) trace out the maxima of $\frac{|S_{12}|^2}{(ka_{HL})^4}$ in Figure 4, i.e., the Efimov resonances, where the position of the successive resonances is defined by the s_0 universal factor. We note that Equation (15), due to its simple structure, can be used as a fitting formula for experimental measurements by treating the (ψ_1, ψ_2, γ) or (Φ, β, γ) as fitting parameters.

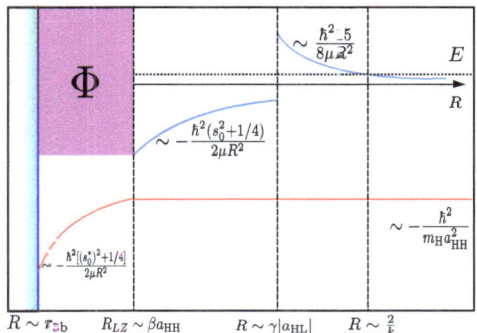

Figure 5. An illustration of the approximate hyperspherical potential curves shown in Figure 1, where s_0 and s_0^* are the universal Efimov scaling coefficients. These piecewise curves are used in Equations (12), (13) and (15).

3. Asymmetric Lineshapes in Three-Body Recombination Coefficients

Figure 4 demonstrates that recombination resonant features are intertwined with Stückelberg interference minima. This constitutes a unique feature of mass-imbalanced systems since, for homonuclear three-body collisions, the corresponding S-matrix element exhibits either Efimov resonances or Stückelberg suppression effects for negative or positive scattering lengths, respectively. Therefore, this section focuses on the lineshape of the $|S_{12}|^2$ squared matrix element plotted as a function of the ratio $\frac{r_{3b}}{a_{HH}}$ at fixed values of $\frac{|a_{HL}|}{a_{HH}}$. In order to demonstrate the asymmetric lineshape of the Efimov resonances in HHL systems, it suffices to consider a range of $\frac{r_{3b}}{a_{HH}}$ values in the neighborhood of a Stückelberg minimum, assuming a total colliding energy $E \approx 0$.

Under these considerations, utilizing the Fano profile formula, Equation (15) can be expressed in terms of the width of the resonance, Γ, and the Fano q-parameter, which describes the asymmetry of the profile of the $|S_{12}|^2$.

$$\frac{|S_{12}|^2}{(ka_{HL})^4} = A \frac{(x+q)^2}{x^2+1}, \text{ with} \qquad (16)$$

$$A = \frac{\gamma^4(1-p)}{16} \sin^2(s_0^* x_r + \psi_1 + \lambda) \left\{ \cos\left[2(s_0 \ln \frac{|a_{HL}|}{a_{HH}} - s_0^* x_r + \psi_2 - \psi_1)\right] + (1-p)\cos\left[2(s_0^* x_r + \psi_1 + \lambda)\right] \right\}^{-1},$$

where $x = 2(\ln \frac{r_{3b}}{a_{HH}} - x_r)/\Gamma$, with x_r referring to the values of the ratio $\ln \frac{r_{3b}}{a_{HF}}$ that minimize the denominator of Equation (15) at fixed $\frac{|a_{HL}|}{a_{HH}}$. Note that Equation (16) has the same functional form as the conventional Fano formula, i.e., $\sigma = \sigma_0(\epsilon+q)^2/(\epsilon^2-1)$ [52], where the ratio $\ln \frac{r_{3b}}{a_{HH}}$ is the independent variable instead of the energy. For Equation (16), the Fano lineshape asymmetry parameter q and the width Γ are given by the following expressions:

$$q = -\frac{2}{s_0^* \Gamma} \cot(s_0^* x_r + \psi_1 + \lambda) \text{ and} \tag{17}$$

$$\left(\frac{\Gamma}{2}\right)^2 = \frac{1-p}{(s_0^*)^2 p} \left[\cos^2\left(s_0 \ln \frac{|a_{HL}|}{a_{HH}} + \psi_2 + \lambda\right) - p \cos^2(s_0^* x_r \right.$$
$$\left. + \psi_1 + \lambda) + \frac{p}{1-p} \sin^2\left(s_0 \ln \frac{|a_{HL}|}{a_{HH}} - s_0^* x_r + \psi_2 - \psi_1\right) \right]$$
$$\times \left\{ \cos[2(s_0 \ln \frac{|a_{HL}|}{a_{HH}} - s_0^* x_r + \psi_2 - \psi_1)] \right.$$
$$\left. + (1-p) \cos[2(s_0^* x_r + \psi_1 + \lambda)] \right\}^{-1}. \tag{18}$$

Note that Γ is dimensionless here, in contrast to the usual Fano lineshape, where Γ has units of energy (or frequency).

The three-body recombination coefficient of HHL systems can be expressed in terms of the S_{12} matrix element, yielding the relation

$$K_3 = \frac{64 \hbar \pi^2}{\mu k^4} |S_{12}|^2, \tag{19}$$

where $k = \sqrt{2\mu E/\hbar^2}$, with E being the total colliding energy of the three-body system.

For a total colliding energy $E \approx 0$, Figure 6a,b depict the scaled recombination coefficient $\frac{m_H K_3}{\hbar a_{HL}^4}$ versus the ratio $\ln \frac{r_{3b}}{a_{HH}}$ in the vicinity of a Stückelberg minimum for two three-body systems, i.e., ^{6}Li–^{133}Cs–^{133}Cs and ^{6}Li–^{87}Rb–^{87}Rb, respectively. More specifically, the symbols in both panels correspond to the full semi-classical calculations, whereas the solid lines are obtained by Equation (15), i.e., the simplified semi-classical model, using γ, ψ_1 and ψ_2 as fitting parameters.

Note that Table 1 summarizes the values of these parameters for both HHL systems exhibiting universal characteristics, since they are independent of scattering length ratio $\frac{|a_{HL}|}{a_{HH}}$. Therefore, in order to extract the values of the γ, ψ_1 and ψ_2 parameters, it suffices to fit only the semi-classical calculations for $|a_{HL}|/a_{HH} = 47.4$ and $|a_{HL}|/a_{HH} = 101.1$ in panels (a) and (b), respectively. However, the phases ψ_1 and ψ_2 and the amplitude γ depend on the mass ratio of the HHL system since the corresponding hyperspherical potential curves are strongly influenced by variations in m_H/m_L. Evidently, both panels showcase the asymmetric profile of the Efimov resonance as a distinctive feature of HHL systems, where Equation (15) is in excellent agreement with the corresponding semi-classical calculations. In particular, in Figure 6a, we observe that, for scattering length ratios in the range $55 < \frac{|a_{HL}|}{a_{HH}} < 69$, the Efimov resonance occurs to the left of the Stückelberg minimum and its width decreases towards $\frac{|a_{HL}|}{a_{HH}} \to 70$. For $\frac{|a_{HL}|}{a_{HH}} > 70$, the Efimov resonance emerges to the right of the Stückelberg minimum with an increasing width. This behavior of the resonant structure as a function of the ratio $\frac{|a_{HL}|}{a_{HH}}$ is known as the q-reversal effect, where the asymmetry parameter q changes sign at $\frac{|a_{HL}|}{a_{HH}} \sim 70$. For ^{6}Li-^{87}Rb-^{87}Rb shown in Figure 6b, a similar behavior is observed, demonstrating that the occurrence of q-reversal is independent of the particles' mass ratio. The q-reversal phenomenon is a manifestation of quantum interference, and, in HHL systems, it occurs when $s_0^* x_r + \psi_1 + \lambda = n\pi/2$, with n being an integer.

Table 1. A summary of the universal parameters used in Equations (16)–(18) for the systems of ^{6}Li–^{133}Cs–^{133}Cs and ^{6}Li–^{87}Rb–^{87}Rb. Note that the values of s_0 and s_0^* are calculated in Ref. [51].

HHL System	s_0	s_0^*	γ	ψ_1	ψ_2
^{6}Li-^{133}Cs-^{133}Cs	1.983	2.003	4.42	0.46	0.13
^{6}Li-^{87}Rb-^{87}Rb	1.633	1.682	3.13	0.8	0.4

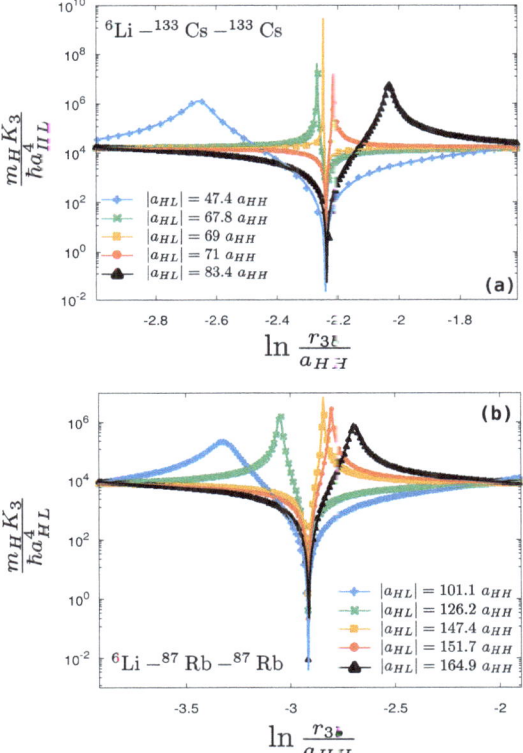

Figure 6. In the limit of $E \to 0$, the scaled recombination coefficient $\frac{m_H K_3}{\hbar a_{HL}^4}$ is shown as a function of $\ln \frac{r_{3b}}{a_{HH}}$ for (a) ^{6}Li-^{133}Cs-^{133}Cs and (b) ^{6}Li-^{87}Rb-^{87}Rb. The symbols refer to the corresponding calculations in the semi-classical approach. The solid lines indicate the fitting of Equation (15) using the universal parameters shown in Table 1.

Additionally, Figure 7 demonstrates the validity of the Fano lineshape formula given in Equation (16). More specifically, Figure 7 illustrates a comparison of the scaled recombination coefficient between the fitting of Equation (15) (red and black dots) and the Fano lineshape formula from Equation (16) (red and black solid lines) at low collisional energies. In particular, the red (black) symbols and lines refer to the ^{6}Li-^{133}Cs-^{133}Cs (^{6}Li-^{87}Rb-^{87}Rb) for a scattering length ratio $\frac{|a_{CsLi}|}{a_{CsCs}} = 67.8$ ($\frac{|a_{RbLi}|}{a_{RbRb}} = 126.2$). We observe that the Fano lineshape formula from Equation (16) is in good agreement with the corresponding semi-classical calculations of Equation (15).

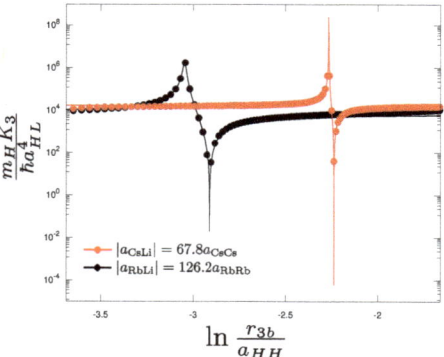

Figure 7. A comparison of the scaled recombination coefficient obtained via the fitting of Equation (15) (points) and the Fano lineshape formula (solid lines) from Equation (16) for two HHL systems. The red points and lines correspond to ^{6}Li-^{133}Cs-^{133}Cs for a scattering length ratio $\frac{|a_{CsLi}|}{a_{CsCs}} = 67.8$. The black points and lines denote the ^{6}Li-^{87}Rb-^{87}Rb system at $\frac{|a_{RbLi}|}{a_{RbRb}} = 126.2$. Note that the total colliding energy is set to zero.

The width Γ of the Efimov resonances and the lineshape asymmetry q are shown in Figure 8 for ^{6}Li–^{133}Cs–^{133}Cs (see panels (a) and (b)) and ^{6}Li–^{87}Rb–^{87}Rb (see panels (c) and (d)). Γ and q are obtained via Equations (17) and (18) using the universal parameters of Table 1. In panels (b) and (d), we observe the q-reversal effect, where, at $\frac{|a_{HL}|}{a_{HH}} = 70$ and $\frac{|a_{HL}|}{a_{HH}} = 140$, the lineshape asymmetry q diverges. This implies that, for large q parameters, the recombination coefficient approaches a symmetric lineshape that is centered at x_r. Furthermore, we observe that, at $|q| \to \infty$, the corresponding widths of the Efimov resonances tend to zero, i.e., $\Gamma \to 0$, as is illustrated in Figure 8a for ^{6}Li-^{133}Cs-^{133}Cs and Figure 8c for ^{6}Li-^{87}Rb-^{87}Rb. This means that, in this range of parameters, the Efimovian quasi-bound state stabilizes into a bound one that is fully decoupled from the three-body and the atom–dimer continua. This counter-intuitive phenomenon is known as a bound state in the continuum and such states have been observed in various fields of physics [38].

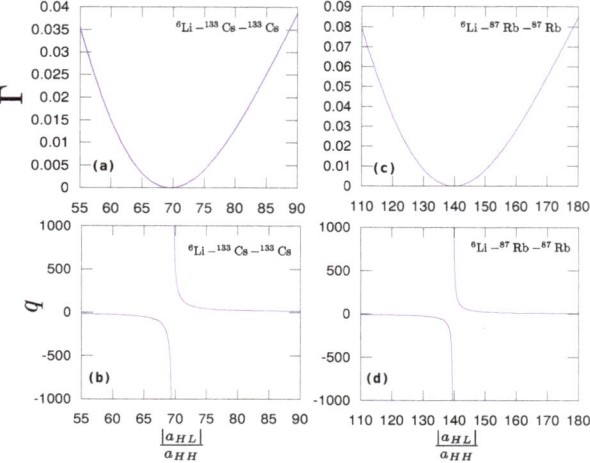

Figure 8. Panels (a–d) show the width of the Efimov resonance Γ and the asymmetry parameter q versus the scattering length ratio $\frac{|a_{HL}|}{a_{HH}}$ for the ^{6}Li-^{133}Cs-^{133}Cs (^{6}Li-^{87}Rb-^{87}Rb) system, respectively. Note that the total colliding energy is set to zero. Moreover, Γ and q are obtained via Equations (17) and (18), respectively, using the universal parameters shown in Table 1.

4. Summary

In summary, the properties of three-body recombination processes into shallow dimers for HHL systems are investigated. Focusing on the low-energy regime, we consider inter- and intra-species interactions that possess negative and positive scattering lengths, respectively, thereby highlighting the threshold behavior of such HHL systems. For this three-body system, we have reviewed the theoretical methods used in Ref. [36] and, in particular, the semi-classical approach, providing additional details on the Stokes phase and the degree of diabaticity p. Furthermore, a simplified version of the semi-classical method is derived by approximating the hyperspherical curves with piecewise potential tails, as in Ref. [37]. The simplified semi-classical model provides closed-form expressions of the S-matrix elements that describe the process of three free particles recombining into the shallow dimer–atom channel. Namely, we show that Equation (15) captures all the main attributes of the recombination spectra for HHL systems, such as the asymmetric lineshape in the three-body recombination coefficient, the logarithmic scaling of the Efimov resonances and Stückelberg interference minima. In particular, Figure 6 demonstrates that Equation (15) can be used as a fitting formula for the recombination spectra in HHL systems since the parameters ψ_1, ψ_2 and γ are insensitive to the scattering length ratio $\frac{|a_{HL}|}{a_{HH}}$. Focusing on the resonant profile of the recombination coefficient, Equation (15) is parameterized in terms of the width of the resonance Γ and the lineshape asymmetry q. This parameterization enables us to identify two emergent phenomena that occur only in heteronuclear three-body collisions: (i) the q-reversal effect, which describes the change in the asymmetry of the profile of the three-body recombination coefficient as a function of the scattering length ratio $\frac{|a_{HL}|}{a_{HH}}$, and (ii) the modification of an Efimov resonance into a bound state embedded in the three-body and atom–dimer continua for $|q| \to \infty$.

Author Contributions: All authors contributed equally to the manuscript. All authors have read and agreed to the published version of the manuscript.

Funding: The work of CHG was supported in part by the U.S. National Science Foundation, Grant No. PHY-1912350. The numerical calculations were performed using NSF XSEDE Resource Allocation No. TG-PHY150003.

Data Availability Statement: The data that support the findings of this study are available from the corresponding author upon reasonable request.

Acknowledgments: The authors would like to thank M.T. Eiles for fruitful discussions.

Conflicts of Interest: The authors declare no conflict of interest.

References

1. Nielsen, E.; Fedorov, D.V.; Jensen, A.S.; Garrido, E. The three-body problem with short-range interactions. *Phys. Rep.* **2001**, *347*, 373–459. [CrossRef]
2. Greene, C.H.; Giannakeas, P.; Pérez-Ríos, J. Universal few-body physics and cluster formation. *Rev. Mod. Phys.* **2017**, *89*, 035006. [CrossRef]
3. Naidon, P.; Endo, S. Efimov Physics: A Review. *Rep. Prog. Phys.* **2017**, *80*, 056001. [CrossRef] [PubMed]
4. D'Incao, J.P. Few-Body Physics in Resonantly Interacting Ultracold Quantum Gases. *J. Phys. B At. Mol. Opt. Phys.* **2018**, *51*, 043001. [CrossRef]
5. Efimov, V. Hard-core interaction and the three-nucleon problem. *Sov. J. Nucl. Phys.* **1970**, *10*, 62.
6. Kraemer, T.; Mark, M.; Waldburger, P.; Danzl, J.G.; Chin, C.; Engeser, B.; Lange, A.D.; Pilch, K.; Jaakkola, A.; Nägerl, H.C.; et al. Evidence for Efimov quantum states in an ultracold gas of caesium atoms. *Nature* **2006**, *440*, 315–318. [CrossRef]
7. Riisager, K. Nuclear halo states. *Rev. Mod. Phys.* **1994**, *66*, 1105–1115. [CrossRef]
8. Braaten, E.; Hammer, H.W. Universality in few-body systems with large scattering length. *Phys. Rep.* **2006**, *428*, 259–390. [CrossRef]
9. Rittenhouse, S.T.; von Stecher, J.; D'Incao, J.; Mehta, N.; Greene, C.H. The hyperspherical four-fermion problem. *J. Phys. B At. Mol. Opt. Phys.* **2011**, *44*, 172001. [CrossRef]
10. Blume, D. Few-body physics with ultracold atomic and molecular systems in traps. *Rep. Prog. Phys.* **2012**, *75*, 046401. [CrossRef]
11. Wang, Y.; D'Incao, J.P.; Esry, B.D. Chapter 1—Ultracold Few-Body Systems. In *Advances in Atomic, Molecular, and Optical Physics*; Ennio Arimondo, P.R.B., Lin, C.C., Eds.; Academic Press: Berlin/Heidelberg, Germany, 2013; Volume 62, 115p.

12. Wang, Y.; Julienne, P.; Greene, C.H. Few-body physics of ultracold atoms and molecules with long-range interactions. In *Annual Review of Cold Atoms and Molecules*; Madison, K.W., Bongs, K., Carr, L.D., Rey, A.M., Zhai, H., Eds.; World Scientific Press: Singapore, 2015; Volume 3, pp. 77–134.
13. Huang, B.; Sidorenkov, L.A.; Grimm, R.; Hutson, J.M. Observation of the second triatomic resonance in Efimov's scenario. *Phys. Rev. Lett.* **2014**, *112*, 190401. [CrossRef] [PubMed]
14. Thomas, L.H. The interaction between a neutron and a proton and the structure of H^3. *Phys. Rev.* **1935**, *47*, 903–909. [CrossRef]
15. Wang, Y.; Julienne, P.S. Universal van der Waals physics for three cold atoms near Feshbach resonances. *Nat. Phys.* **2014**, *10*, 768–773. [CrossRef]
16. Roy, S.; Landini, M.; Trenkwalder, A.; Semeghini, G.; Spagnolli, G.; Simoni, A.; Fattori, M.; Inguscio, M.; Modugno, G. Test of the Universality of the Three-Body Efimov Parameter at Narrow Feshbach Resonances. *Phys. Rev. Lett.* **2013**, *111*, 053202. [CrossRef] [PubMed]
17. Wang, J.; D'Incao, J.; Esry, B.; Greene, C.H. Origin of the three-body parameter universality in Efimov physics. *Phys. Rev. Lett.* **2012**, *108*, 263001. [CrossRef]
18. Gross, N.; Shotan, Z.; Kokkelmans, S.; Khaykovich, L. Observation of universality in ultracold ^{7}Li three-body recombination. *Phys. Rev. Lett.* **2009**, *103*, 163202. [CrossRef] [PubMed]
19. Naidon, P.; Endo, S.; Ueda, M. Microscopic Origin and Universality Classes of the Efimov Three-Body Parameter. *Phys. Rev. Lett.* **2014**, *112*, 105301. [CrossRef]
20. Naidon, P.; Endo, S.; Ueda, M. Physical origin of the universal three-body parameter in atomic Efimov physics. *Phys. Rev. A* **2014**, *90*, 022106. [CrossRef]
21. Ferlaino, F.; Grimm, R. Forty years of Efimov physics: How a bizarre prediction turned into a hot topic. *Physics* **2010**, *3*, 9. [CrossRef]
22. Giannakeas, P.; Greene, C.H. Van Der Waals Universality in Homonuclear Atom-Dimer Elastic Collisions. *Few-Body Syst.* **2017**, *58*, 20. [CrossRef]
23. Mestrom, P.M.A.; Wang, J.; Greene, C.H.; D'Incao, J.P. Efimov–van Der Waals Universality for Ultracold Atoms with Positive Scattering Lengths. *Phys. Rev. A* **2017**, *95*, 032707. [CrossRef]
24. Mestrom, P.M.A.; Colussi, V.E.; Secker, T.; Groeneveld, G.P.; Kokkelmans, S.J.J.M.F. Van Der Waals Universality near a Quantum Tricritical Point. *Phys. Rev. Lett.* **2020**, *124*, 143401. [CrossRef] [PubMed]
25. Kunitski, M.; Zeller, S.; Voigtsberger, J.; Kalinin, A.; Schmidt, L.P.H.; Schoeffler, M.; Czasch, A.; Schoellkopf, W.; Grisenti, R.E.; Jahnke, T.; et al. Observation of the Efimov state of the helium trimer. *Science* **2015**, *348*, 551–555. [CrossRef] [PubMed]
26. Pires, R.; Ulmanis, J.; Häfner, S.; Repp, M.; Arias, A.; Kuhnle, E.D.; Weidemüller, M. Observation of Efimov Resonances in a Mixture with Extreme Mass Imbalance. *Phys. Rev. Lett.* **2014**, *112*, 250404. [CrossRef] [PubMed]
27. Ulmanis, J.; Häfner, S.; Pires, R.; Kuhnle, E.D.; Weidemüller, M.; Tiemann, E. Universality of weakly bound dimers and Efimov trimers close to Li–Cs Feshbach resonances. *New J. Phys.* **2015**, *17*, 055009. [CrossRef]
28. Tung, S.K.; Jiménez-García, K.; Johansen, J.; Parker, C.V.; Chin, C. Geometric Scaling of Efimov States in a ^{6}Li-^{133}Cs. *Phys. Rev. Lett.* **2014**, *113*, 240402. [CrossRef]
29. Häfner, S.; Ulmanis, J.; Kuhnle, E.D.; Wang, Y.; Greene, C.H.; Weidemüller, M. Role of the intraspecies scattering length in the Efimov scenario with large mass difference. *Phys. Rev. A* **2017**, *95*, 062708. [CrossRef]
30. Petrov, D.S.; Werner, F. Three-body recombination in heteronuclear mixtures at finite temperature. *Phys. Rev. A* **2015**, *92*, 022704. [CrossRef]
31. Zhao, C.Y.; Han, H.L.; Wu, M.S.; Shi, T.Y. Universal three-body parameter of heavy-heavy-light systems with a negative intraspecies scattering length. *Phys. Rev. A* **2019**, *100*, 052702. [CrossRef]
32. Sun, M.; Liu, C.; Shi, Z.Y. Efimov physics in the complex plane. *arXiv* **2021**, arXiv:2109.11206.
33. Ulmanis, J.; Häfner, S.; Pires, R.; Kuhnle, E.D.; Wang, Y.; Greene, C.H.; Weidemüller, M. Heteronuclear Efimov Scenario with Positive Intraspecies Scattering Length. *Phys. Rev. Lett.* **2016**, *117*, 153201. [CrossRef] [PubMed]
34. Chin, C.; Grimm, R.; Julienne, P.; Tiesinga, E. Feshbach resonances in ultracold gases. *Rev. Mod. Phys.* **2010**, *82*, 1225. [CrossRef]
35. Johansen, J.; DeSalvo, B.J.; Patel, K.; Chin, C. Testing universality of Efimov physics across broad and narrow Feshbach resonances. *Nat. Phys.* **2017**, *13*, 731–735. [CrossRef]
36. Giannakeas, P.; Greene, C.H. Ultracold Heteronuclear Three-Body Systems: How Diabaticity Limits the Universality of Recombination into Shallow Dimers. *Phys. Rev. Lett.* **2018**, *120*, 023401. [CrossRef] [PubMed]
37. D'Incao, J.P.; Esry, B.D. Scattering Length Scaling Laws for Ultracold Three-Body Collisions. *Phys. Rev. Lett.* **2005**, *94*, 213201. [CrossRef] [PubMed]
38. Hsu, C.W.; Zhen, B.; Stone, A.D.; Joannopoulos, J.D.; Soljačić, M. Bound States in the Continuum. *Nat. Rev. Mater.* **2016**, *1*, 16048. [CrossRef]
39. Rittenhouse, S.T.; Mehta, N.P.; Greene, C.H. Green's functions and the adiabatic hyperspherical method. *Phys. Rev. A* **2010**, *82*, 022706. [CrossRef]
40. Avery, J. *Hyperspherical Harmonics: Applications in Quantum Theory*; Kluwer Academic Publishers: Norwell, MA, USA, 1989.
41. Smirnov, Y.F.; Shitikova, K.V. Method of K harmonics and the shell model. *Sov. J. Part. Nucl.* **1977**, *8*, 44.
42. Kartavtsev, O.I.; Malykh, A.V. Low-energy three-body dynamics in binary quantum gases. *J. Phys. B* **2007**, *40*, 1429–1441. [CrossRef]

43. Kartavtsev, O.I.; Malykh, A.V. Universal low-energy properties of three two-dimensional bosons. *Phys. Rev. A* **2006**, *74*, 042506. [CrossRef]
44. Aymar, M.; Greene, C.H.; Luc-Koenig, E. Multichannel Rydberg spectroscopy of complex atoms. *Rev. Mod. Phys.* **1996**, *68*, 1015. [CrossRef]
45. Mehta, N.; Esry, B.; Greene, C.H. Three-body recombination in one dimension. *Phys. Rev. A* **2007**, *76*, 022711 [CrossRef]
46. Burke, J.P., Jr. Theoretical Investigation of Cold Alkali Atom Collisions. Ph.D. Thesis, University of Colorado, Boulder, CO, USA, 1999.
47. Nielsen, E.; Macek, J. Low-energy recombination of identical bosons by three-body collisions. *Phys. Rev. Lett.* **1999**, *83*, 1566. [CrossRef]
48. Clark, C.W. Calculation of Non-adiabatic Transition Probabilities. *Phys. Lett. A* **1979**, *70*, 295. [CrossRef]
49. Child, M. Semiclassical theory of tunneling and curve-crossing problems: A diagrammatic approach. *J. Mol. Spectrosc.* **1974**, *53*, 280–301. [CrossRef]
50. Zhu, C.; Nakamura, H. Theory of nonadiabatic transition for general two-state curve crossing problems. I. Nonadiabatic tunneling case. *J. Chem. Phys.* **1994**, *101*, 10630–10647. [CrossRef]
51. Wang, Y.; Wang, J.; D'Incao, J.P.; Greene, C.H. Universal Three-Body Parameter in Heteronuclear Atomic Systems. *Phys. Rev. Lett.* **2012**, *109*, 243201. [CrossRef]
52. Fano, U. Effects of Configuration Interaction on Intensities and Phase Shifts. *Phys. Rev.* **1961**, *124*, 1866–1878. [CrossRef]

Article

Dynamics of the Creation of a Rotating Bose–Einstein Condensation by Two Photon Raman Transition Using a Laguerre–Gaussian Laser Pulse

Koushik Mukherjee [1,*], Soumik Bandyopadhyay [2,3,†], Dilip Angom [2], Andrew M. Martin [4] and Sonjoy Majumder [1]

[1] Indian Institute of Technology Kharagpur, Kharagpur 721302, West Bengal, India; sonjoym@phy.iitkgp.ac.in
[2] Physical Research Laboratory, Ahmedabad 380009, Gujarat, India; soumik@prl.res.in (S.B.); angom@prl.res.in (D.A.)
[3] Indian Institute of Technology Gandhinagar, Palaj, Gandhinagar 382355, Gujarat, India
[4] School of Physics, University of Melbourne, Melbourne, VIC 3010, Australia; martinam@unimelb.edu.au
* Correspondence: koushikphysics21@gmail.com
† Current address: INO-CNR BEC Center and Department of Physics, University of Trento, Via Sommarive 14, 38123 Trento, Italy.

Abstract: We present numerical simulations to unravel the dynamics associated with the creation of a vortex in a Bose–Einstein condensate (BEC), from another nonrotating BEC using two-photon Raman transition with Gaussian (G) and Laguerre–Gaussian (LG) laser pulses. In particular, we consider BEC of Rb atoms at their hyperfine ground states confined in a quasi two dimensional harmonic trap. Optical dipole potentials created by G and LG laser pulses modify the harmonic trap in such a way that density patterns of the condensates during the Raman transition process depend on the sign of the generated vortex. We investigate the role played by the Raman coupling parameter manifested through dimensionless peak Rabi frequency and intercomponent interaction on the dynamics during the population transfer process and on the final population of the rotating condensate. During the Raman transition process, the two BECs tend to have larger overlap with each other for stronger intercomponent interaction strength.

Keywords: Bose–Einstein condensate; Laguerre–Gaussian; Raman transition; cold atoms; light–matter interaction; particle transfer; density pattern

1. Introduction

Creation of vortex states in atomic Bose–Einstein condensates (BECs) has been the subject of quite intensive research with particular focus on superfluid properties [1–3] and quantum turbulence [4–10]. A number of theoretical and experimental studies have considered the properties of vortex states in single and multicomponent BECs [11–16], their stability [17–24] and collective excitations [25–29], thus opening up an avenue of opportunities to explore and develop quantum state engineering in a macroscopic system [21,30,31]. Owing to the highly controllable state-of-the-art BEC experiments, the presence of a vortex in BECs can be detected and their dynamics can be monitored with good spatial and temporal resolution [31–36]. Numerous techniques, which mainly rely upon two distinct physical situations, have been proposed theoretically [37–44] and developed experimentally [45–48] to generate vortices in BECs. In rotating traps, vortices are the thermodynamic ground states with quantized angular momentum, but in stationary traps, the creation of vortices requires other dynamical means. Various methods to create vortices include the perturbation of the system with a time-dependent boundary. In particular, such time-dependent boundaries can be created either by moving a blue detuned laser through the condensate [43,49] or by rotating the trap anisotropy [46]. In the other scheme, the so-called phase imprinting technique [37,42,45,50–54], one can engineer the macroscopic wavefunctions of BECs by coupling the internal atomic levels with either an optical field

or a magnetic field. Remarkably, the topological phase pattern of the coupling field is imprinted into the condensate wavefunctions. This topological phase, which is independent of the field strength, is uniquely determined by the spatial structure of the coupling field.

The helical phase front of Laguerre–Gaussian (LG) laser beams has been associated with its orbital angular momentum (OAM) in the paraxial regime [55]. A photon of such an LG laser modes has phase profile $e^{il\phi}$, and carries $l\hbar$ unit OAM in the transverse plane, where ϕ is the angular coordinate and l is an integer, known as the winding number of the beam. Such LG modes are known to transfer OAM from an optical field to the Rydberg atom [56], BECs [57–60], and to create a mechanical rotation of particles [61,62]. It was shown that a coherent coupling between the ground state of condensate with a rotating condensate in vortex state, can be achieved by the transfer of OAM of photons to the condensed atoms through Raman transitions [37]. Quantum dynamics of such vortex coupler using LG beam was studied, and an off-axis motion of the quantized vortex cores was interpreted as the collapse and revival of the atoms of the condensate [63]. Besides, a pair of LG laser modes with unequal phase windings couple internal atomic states of BEC through Raman transitions, and thus giving rise to spin and orbital angular momentum coupling in the ground states of a spinor BEC [64,65]. Moreover, it has been shown that almost all the atoms in the non-rotating BEC can be transferred to the BEC with vortex, by employing LG beams [66,67].

Although an impressive volume of literature has been devoted to this subject, few of its vital aspects remain further to be explored. One such aspect constitutes the role played by the interaction between two BEC components on the population transfer. Indeed, during the transfer process, atoms of two condensates are present in two different hyperfine states, one with vorticity and another without vorticity. Thus, not only the atom–laser coupling, but also the atom–atom interaction between two different components is expected to influence the population transfer process. Note that the focus of the majority of the previous studies has been on the complete particle transfer from one quantum state to another. However, it is expected that by maneuvering atom-light coupling and inter-component interaction one could achieve a population transfer of any desired value. In this way it equips us to realize a binary-mixture where one component contains a vortex, and the other does not, thus emulating the so-called vortex-bright-soliton structure [16,68]. Additionally, it is also desirable to know, through the miscibility parameter [15,69,70], how atoms in the condensate with a vortex penetrate into atoms of the condensate without any vortex during the transfer process [15,69,70]. Therefore, motivated by experimental accessibility [71,72] and theoretical novelty of the problem, we theoretically address these important aspects of the transfer mechanism in this paper.

We investigate the dynamics of population transfer from a nonrotating BEC to a Raman coupled rotating BEC by employing LG and Gaussian (G) pulses. In this process, the atoms in rotating BEC gain angular momentum from the LG laser pulse. We consider pulsed G and LG beams as the pump and Stokes beams, respectively, to transfer the atoms from one hyperfine level to another. In particular, we choose the temporal width of the pulses to be in the same time scale determined by the trap frequency. This consideration provides us the framework to understand the dynamics during the transfer process. Numerically integrating the Raman coupled multicomponent Gross-Pitaevskii equations, we point out the following key points: (i) the sign of the vorticity of the condensate as well as the initial growth region of the vortex state, captured within the density patterns, depend upon which laser mode is chosen as pump or Stokes beam and (ii) the repulsive inter-component atomic interaction and peak Rabi frequency of laser beams determine the number of atoms transferred to the non-rotating BEC. By calculating the overlap integral between the two condensates we also quantify how two condensates penetrate into each other during the transfer process.

We have organized the remainder of this paper as follows. In Section 2 we describe the theory of transfer mechanism. Section 3 provides a brief description of the numerical schemes used. In Section 4 we present results of the complete particle transfer and effects of the inter-particle interactions and the Raman coupling parameter on the final population of the rotating BEC. In Section 5, we discuss the implication and possible future extensions associated with the results presented. Appendix A presents the effects of trap frequencies and the time-delay between the pulses on the population transfer. Finally, in Appendix B we briefly outline the Hamiltonian and the derivation of the equations of motions.

2. Theoretical Methods

In our study, we consider BEC of alkali atoms trapped in a quasi two-dimensional harmonic trap confined in the $x-y$ plane with z axis being the quantization axis. In order to transfer OAM from the optical beam to the BEC, we consider three electronic levels of the alkali atoms are coupled by a pair of laser pulses in Λ-type configuration as shown in Figure 1. Atoms of initially prepared BEC are at the state $|1\rangle$, one of the hyperfine levels of the electronic ground state of atoms. The state $|3\rangle$ is an intermediate non-resonant excited state. The final state is considered to be $|2\rangle$, another hyperfine level of the electronic ground state of the atoms. The atoms are irradiated by two laser pulses propagating collinearly parallel to the quantization axis [73]. We remark that with the dipole approximation of the atomic transitions, the changes in the internal spin states of atoms are dictated by polarizations of two light fields. However, the changes in external orbital motion of the atoms of BEC around the quantization axis are determined by the difference of the orbital angular momentum (OAM) of two light fields [57]. Let us consider that the OAM of the twisted laser pulses for the transition from state $|1\rangle$ to state $|3\rangle$ is l_1 and for $|3\rangle$ to $|2\rangle$ transition is l_2. Then, the electric field vectors involved in this absorption or emission transitions can be written as (for $i = 1$ and 2)

$$\mathbf{E}_i(x,y,t) = \hat{e}_i \mathcal{E}_i(t)(x^2+y^2)^{\frac{|l_i|}{2}} e^{-(\frac{x^2+y^2}{w_i^2})} e^{-i(k_i z - \omega_i t)}, \quad (1)$$

where $\mathcal{E}_i(t)$, $\hat{e}_i$, k_i and ω_i are the corresponding time dependent amplitude profile, polarization vector, wave number and frequency of the i-th pulse, respectively. We consider the temporal amplitude profiles of both pulses have the same form [74]:

$$\mathcal{E}_{1(2)}(t) = \mathcal{E}_{\max} e^{-(\frac{t-\tau_{1(2)}}{T})^2}, \quad (2)$$

where $\tau_{1(2)}$ is the temporal position of the peak value of electric field $\mathcal{E}_{1(2)}$. Maximum amplitude $\mathcal{E}_{\max}$ and pulse duration T are the same for both pulses. The optical absorption-emission cycle imparts OAM onto the atoms in final state $|2\rangle$ and creates a vortex in the BEC with charge $(l_1 - l_2)$ unit. Because of collinearity of the E_1 and E_2 pulses, no additional linear momentum is generated in the final state. In addition to such two-photon transitions in atomic BEC, these lasers also create extra confining potential, namely optical dipole potentials for the atoms in the states $|1\rangle$ and $|2\rangle$ [75]. In practice the value of detuning Δ is large, which ensures the negligible populations in state $|3\rangle$. This allows us to eliminate the state $|3\rangle$ adiabatically. During the transfer process, atoms are present in both the hyperfine states, $|1\rangle$ and $|2\rangle$. Therefore, coherent evolution of the condensates of atoms in these two states, characterized by wavefunctions $\Psi_1(x,y,t)$ and $\Psi_2(x,y,t)$ respectively, are governed by two Raman coupled Gross-Pitaevskii equations (see Appendix B for the derivation)

$$i\frac{\partial \Psi_1}{\partial t} = \left[-\frac{1}{2}\nabla_\perp^2 + \frac{r^2}{2} + \sum_j \mathcal{G}_{1j}|\Psi_j|^2 + \mathcal{V}_1(t) r^{2|l_1|} e^{-\frac{2r^2}{w_1^2}}\right]\Psi_1 + \mathcal{V}'(x,y,t)\Psi_2 e^{-i(l_1-l_2)\phi}, \quad (3)$$

and,

$$i\frac{\partial \Psi_2}{\partial t} = \left[-\frac{1}{2}\nabla_\perp^2 + \frac{r^2}{2} + \sum_j \mathcal{G}_{2j}|\Psi_j|^2 + \mathcal{V}_2(t) r^{2|l_2|} e^{-\frac{2(r^2)}{w_2^2}}\right]\Psi_2 + \mathcal{V}'(x,y,t)\Psi_1 e^{i(l_1-l_2)\phi}, \quad (4)$$

where $r^2 = x^2 + y^2$, $\mathcal{V}' = \sqrt{\mathcal{V}_1 \mathcal{V}_2}(r^2)^{(|l_1|+|l_2|)/2} \exp[-2r^2(1/w_1^2 + 1/w_2^2)]$, and $\mathcal{V}_{1(2)}(t) = \mathcal{V}_{\max} \exp\left[-(t - \tau_{1(2)})^2/T^2\right]$ with $\mathcal{V}_{\max} = \mathcal{E}_{\max}^2 d^2/\hbar^2 \omega \Delta$. $\mathcal{E}_{\max}^2$ is maximum light intensity of both pulses and d is the atomic transition dipole moment and $w_{1(2)}$ is the beam waist of the corresponding laser pulse. Therefore, the effective trap potentials felt by atoms of the condensates are

$$V_{\text{eff},1(2)} = \frac{r^2}{2} + \mathcal{V}_{1(2)}(t) r^{2|l_1|(|l_2|)} e^{-\frac{2(r^2)}{w_{1(2)}^2}}. \tag{5}$$

We derive Equations (3) and (4) by nondimensionalizing Equations (A11) and (A12) respectively. For this, we scale the spatial coordinates by oscillator length $a_{\text{osc}} = \sqrt{\hbar/m\omega}$, time by $1/\omega$ and condensate wavefunctions by $\sqrt{N/a_{\text{osc}}^3}$. Here, m is the mass of the atoms and N is the total number of atoms in the system, and ω is the trapping frequencies along x and y directions of the harmonic trap. We denote N_1 and N_2 as the number of atoms in condensates Ψ_1 and Ψ_2 respectively, and consider the total number, $N = N_1 + N_2$, is conserved during and after the transfer process. We point out that initially $N_1 = N$ and $N_2 = 0$. Note that, the parameter associated with the peak Rabi frequency, $\mathcal{V}_{\max}$, contains parameters from the considered atomic transition, laser pulses and the trap of the condensate. The quasi-2D configuration of the trap is achieved by ensuring large trapping frequency in z direction, that is, $\omega_z \gg \omega$. The intra and inter-component coupling strengths are $\mathcal{G}_{ii} = 2N\sqrt{2\pi\lambda} a_{ii}/a_{\text{osc}}$ and $\mathcal{G}_{ij} = \mathcal{G}_{ji} = 2N\sqrt{2\pi\lambda} a_{ij}/a_{\text{osc}}$, respectively, and $\lambda = \omega_z/\omega$ is the anisotropy parameter. The intra-component and inter-component scattering lengths are denoted by a_{ii} and a_{ij}, respectively. Initially, only the condensate Ψ_1 is present within the trap. With two photon Raman transitions, the condensate Ψ_2 grows by gaining atoms from the condensate Ψ_1. During this process atoms in Ψ_2 gain $(l_1 - l_2)$ unit orbital angular momentum, which is manifested as a phase factor $e^{i(l_1-l_2)\phi}$ in the condensate wavefunction Ψ_2. The phase factor $e^{-i(l_1-l_2)\phi}$ in the coupling term of Equation (3) ensures that no angular momentum is transferred back to the atoms in condensate Ψ_1. Transfer of this angular momentum to the condensate Ψ_2 results in generating quantized vortex in the condensate. A quantized vortex in a BEC is point like topological defect which is manifested in the phase profile of the condensate wavefunction Ψ_2. Around the vortex the phase of the condensate wavefunction changes by $\kappa \times 2\pi$, where κ is an integer, which is referred to as the winding number or charge of the vortex.

A system of two component BECs can exhibit two phases, miscible or immiscible, depending on the the strengths of intracomponent and intercomponent interactions. At zero temperature, two defect free condensates in a homogeneous trap are miscible when $a_{12}^2 \leq a_{11} a_{22}$, and immiscible for $a_{12}^2 \geq a_{11} a_{22}$ [76]. However, these conditions are modified when the condensates are considered in inhomogeneous trap [77]. Effects of finite temperature [70] and topological defects [15] on the miscible-immiscible transition have been reported. A well known measure to characterize these two phases is the overlap integral defined as [15,69,70]

$$\Lambda = \frac{\left[\iint dx\, dy\, n_1(x,y)\, n_2(x,y)\right]^2}{\left[\iint dx\, dy\, n_1^2(x,y)\right]\left[\iint dx\, dy\, n_2^2(x,y)\right]}, \tag{6}$$

where $n_{1(2)}(x,y) = \left|\Psi_{1(2)}(x,y)\right|^2$ are the densities of the condensates. $\Lambda = 0$ corresponds that the two condensates are spatially separated, that is, the system is in immiscible phase. Whereas, $\Lambda = 1$ implies maximal spatial overlap between the condensates, that is, the system is in complete miscible phase.

To this end, by utilizing two-photon Raman transition, we transfer the atoms from one initially populated quantum state to another unpopulated state via an intermediate state, see Figure 1. A pump field links state $|1\rangle$ to electronically excited state $|3\rangle$, and Stokes field links state $|3\rangle$ to another low energy state $|2\rangle$. We perform a one-way controlled particle transfer from one hyperfine state to another, where atoms of the daughter state carries one unit vorticity, either positive or negative, thus enabling us to create a rotating BEC. In this context, coherent population transfer is possible if the Stokes field precedes, but temporally overlaps with, the pump field, and the pulses are applied adiabatically.

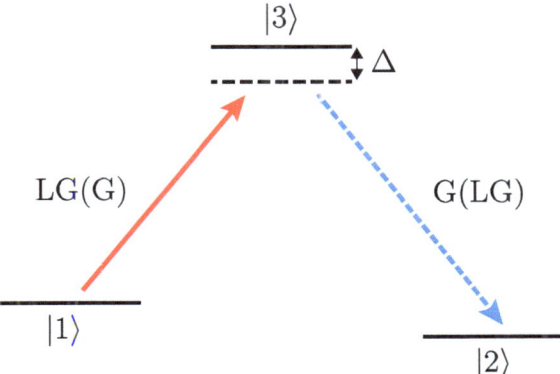

Figure 1. Schematic of the electronic states considered, in a Λ configuration. Specifically, the states of interest are $|1\rangle$ and $|2\rangle$ which represent the states associated with the two-component Bose–Einstein Condensate (BEC). These two states are coupled, via $|3\rangle$, through detuned Guassian (G) and Laguerre–Gaussian (LG) laser pulses. In this work two laser pulse sequences are considered: (i) G-LG where the Gaussian is the pulse ($|1\rangle \to |3\rangle$) beam and the Laguerre–Gaussian is the Stokes ($|3\rangle \to |2\rangle$) beam and (ii) LG-G where the Laguerre–Gaussian is the pulse ($|1\rangle \to |3\rangle$) beam and the Gaussian is the Stokes ($|3\rangle \to |2\rangle$) beam.

3. Numerical Methods

We start with a BEC of N atoms at state $|1\rangle$, in the absence of laser pulses. Therefore, we set terms associated with laser pulses in Equation (3) to be zero to obtain the initial solution. Then, the wavefunction of the initial BEC, Ψ_1, is generated by solving Equation (3) in imaginary time using split-time Crank–Nicolson method [78]. The initial wavefunction of BEC of the atoms in state $|2\rangle$, Ψ_2, is considered to be zero. Using these two initial wave functions, we evolve the system in presence of laser pulses. For this, we solve the coupled GP equations in Equations (3) and (4) in real time. The phase imprinting in the Ψ_2 occurs dynamically due to the two photon Raman transitions, which is obtained by considering,

$$\Psi_1(x,y,t_{n+1}) = \cos\left(\frac{\mathcal{V}'dt}{2}\right)\Psi_1(x,y,t_n) - ie^{-i(l_1-l_2)\phi}\sin\left(\frac{\mathcal{V}'dt}{2}\right)\Psi_2(x,y,t_n), \quad (7)$$

and

$$\Psi_2(x,y,t_{n+1}) = \cos\left(\frac{\mathcal{V}'dt}{2}\right)\Psi_2(x,y,t_n) - ie^{i(l_1-l_2)\phi}\sin\left(\frac{\mathcal{V}'dt}{2}\right)\Psi_1(x,y,t_n). \quad (8)$$

Since Ψ_2 is zero at the initial time t_0, $l_1 - l_2$ unit vortex is imprinted on Ψ_2 at $t_1 = t_0 + \delta t$ and vorticity of Ψ_1 remains zero. This transfer of angular momentum continues, as long as both pulses are present. However, since the process is one-way, it stops when all the atoms in condensate Ψ_1 are transferred to the rotating condensate. For simulations, we choose a square grid of 300 × 300 grid points with a grid spacing $\delta_x = \delta_y = 0.05a_{osc}$ and time step $\Delta_t = 0.0001\omega^{-1}$. In our study, we consider hyperfine states of ^{87}Rb with $|1,-1\rangle$ as $|1\rangle$ and $|2,+1\rangle$ as $|2\rangle$. The intracomponent scattering lengths a_{11} and a_{22} of these two states are $100.4a_0$ and $95.44a_0$ [79] respectively, where a_0 is the Bohr radius. The trap frequency $\omega = 2\pi \times 30.832$ Hz [80] and the anisotropy parameter $\lambda = 40$ are the same for both condensates. For this system the oscillator length $a_{osc} = 1.94$ μm. Furthermore, the relation

$\mu_{1(2)} \ll \hbar\omega_z$ holds throughout the time evolution indicating that quasi-2D configuration is maintained always. Total number of atoms in the system is $N = 10^4$. To create a BEC with a vortex of charge -1 unit, we use G pulse as "pump" of which $l_1 = 0$, and LG Pulse as "Stokes" with $l_2 = 1$. If we interchange the "pump" and "Stokes" laser pulses, a vortex of charge $+1$ unit will be created in the BEC. For simulations, we use the pulses with same temporal duration of $T = 4.9$ ms.

4. Results and Discussion

4.1. Creation of Vortex in the BEC

In G-LG pulse sequence, we employ G pulse as pump and LG pulse as Stokes, for which $l_1 = 0$ and $l_2 = 1$ respectively. For this arrangement, we consider $\tau_1 = 1.4$ and $\tau_2 = 1.0$ in the units of $1/\omega$. During the Raman transitions of atoms from state $|1\rangle$ to $|2\rangle$ an amount of -1 unit OAM is transferred to the atoms in state $|2\rangle$. Here, we describe the transfer process. First, a photon from the G laser pulse which has zero OAM is absorbed by the atom in $|1\rangle$. As a result, the atom is excited to an intermediate excited state $|3\rangle$. Then, a photon with $+1$ unit OAM is emitted by the atom at the state $|3\rangle$ onto the LG beam. After this emission process the atom comes back to another ground state $|2\rangle$. The conservation of the total angular momentum of the system, that is, the total angular momentum of atom plus light pulses, ensures that atom at the state $|2\rangle$ gains -1 unit OAM. Thus, -1 unit vorticity is created in the condensate Ψ_2. Similarly, $+1$ unit vorticity can be created in the condensate Ψ_2 through LG-G pulse sequence, where we use LG pulse as pump and G pulse as Stokes of which $l_1 = 1$ and $l_2 = 0$ respectively.

4.2. Density Evolution of the Condensates

We have discussed that the sign of the vorticity in condensate Ψ_2 depends on the laser modes chosen as pump and Stokes beam. Here, we point out how the sign of the vorticity can be inferred from the changes of density patterns of the condensates during the transfer process. Furthermore, these density patterns serve as promising candidates to elucidate the residual excitations created during the light–matter interaction, since these excitations leave their foot-prints on the density profiles creating additional humps and dips [81,82]. Figure 2(a_1–a_6,b_1–b_6) illustrate the density profiles of the condensates during the Raman transitions, when the vortex of charge -1 unit is generated in the condensate Ψ_2. Whereas, Figure 2(c_1–c_6,d_1–d_6) illustrate the density profiles when $+1$ unit vortex is created. In the lower-left corner of each density profile we mention the fraction of atoms in the condensate with respect total number of atoms in the system.

From the comparison between the Figure 2(a_1–a_6,b_1–b_6,c_1–c_6,d_1–d_6), it is evident that density patterns of the condensates during the creation of -1 unit vortex are different from the case of creation of $+1$ unit vortex. During the initial growth of the condensate Ψ_2, the atoms occupy the central region of the trap when the vortex of charge -1 unit is created, whereas the atoms occupy the peripheral region of the trap when the $+1$ unit vortex created. At $t = 0$, the laser pulses are absent and the condensate Ψ_1 is populated by all the atoms in the system, hence, the condensate Ψ_2 is empty. It is important to mention that for the coherent population transfer, we apply the Stokes beam first. Therefore, in the early stage of the dynamics population of condensate Ψ_2 remains zero. Once the pump beam is applied, condensate Ψ_2 starts growing at the expense of atoms being transferred from the condensate Ψ_1. At the same time, a vortex of either -1 or $+1$ unit is imprinted on condensate Ψ_2 depending on the angular momenta of the pump and Stokes beams. For the case of LG-G pulse sequence, which is illustrated in Figure 2(c_1–c_6,d_1–d_6), we observe that 11% of atoms has been transferred in the first 10.84 ms, but 68% of atoms are transferred in the next 1.96 ms. In contrast to this, we observe that fewer numbers of atoms are transferred to condensate Ψ_2 at the same time instants when compared to the G-LG pulse sequence, which is also evident from Figure 2(b_1–b_6). In both the cases, the generated vortex appears with core, that is, zero density region at the center of condensate Ψ_2, which is visible in the density profiles of Ψ_2 shown in Figure 2(b_1–b_6,d_1–d_6). It is worth noting that density depleted region at the center of the trap is also observed in the density profiles of condensate Ψ_1 during the creation of -1 unit vortex in Ψ_2 (Figure 2(a_1–a_6)). However, such a hole is absent in the condensate Ψ_1, when $+1$ unit vortex is created. To understand the nature of the density depleted regions, we study the phase profiles of the condensates. We confirm the presence of phase discontinuity at the center of condensate Ψ_2 for both the cases. It is mentioned earlier that the phase of the condensate wavefunction changes by $\kappa \times 2\pi$ around a quantized vortex, where κ is the winding-number or charge of the vortex. We compute the winding number κ to be -1 when we use G as pulse and LG as Stokes beam, whereas $\kappa = +1$ when we consider LG-G pulse sequence. On the other hand, the phase profile of the condensate Ψ_1 does not possess phase discontinuity during the transfer process for both cases. Thus, the hole in condensate Ψ_1 which is generated during the application of G-LG pulse sequence, is not a vortex.

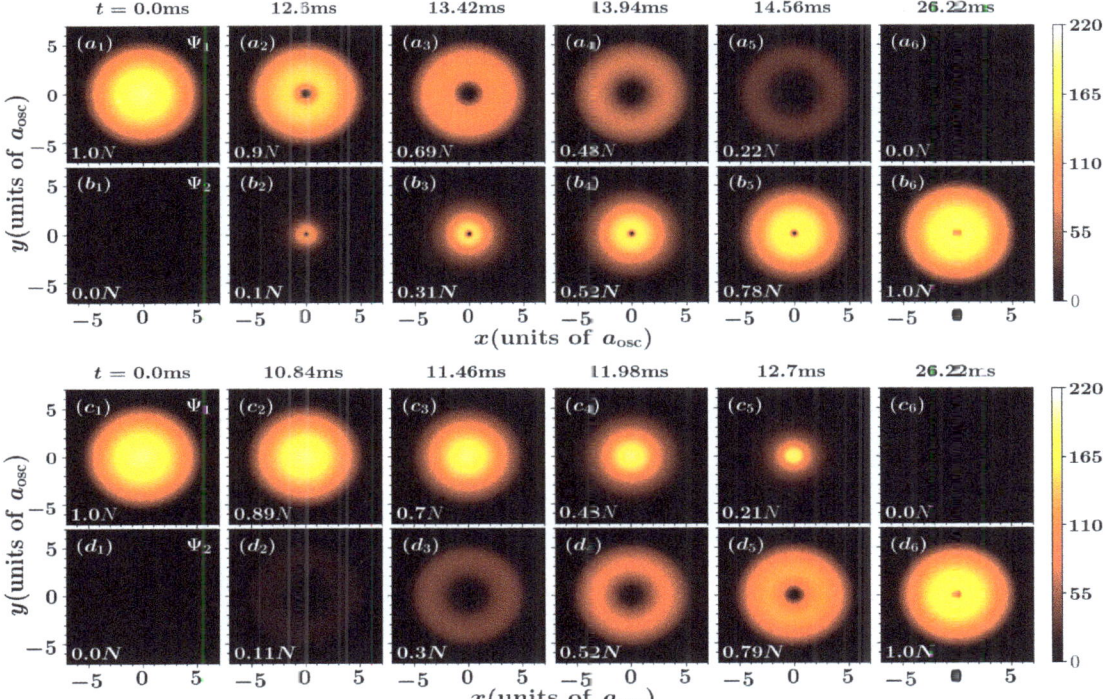

Figure 2. (Color online) Shows the time evolution of density profiles of the condensates of (a_1–a_6), (c_1–c_6) atoms in $|1\rangle$ and (b_1–b_6), (d_1–d_6) those in $|2\rangle$, when -1 unit [(b_1–b_6)] and $+1$ [(d_1–d_6)] unit vortex is created in the condensate Ψ_2. In the course of time, the condensate Ψ_2 gets populated. The fraction of atoms in the condensate with respect to total number of atoms $N = 10^4$, is mentioned at the bottom left corner of each figure. Atoms are kick-started to be transferred from the condensate Ψ_1 to the condensate Ψ_2 in the central region of the trap for -1 unit vortex transfer, but in the peripheral region of the trap for $+1$ unit vortex transfer. Almost 100% atoms get transferred to state $|2\rangle$ for both the cases.

Focusing our discussion on G-LG pulse sequence, we ascribe the presence of hole in condensate Ψ_1 to the distortion of harmonic trap potential by the optical dipole potential. In this case, the optical dipole potential is induced by the G laser pulse for the condensate Ψ_1 and by the LG laser pulse for the condensate Ψ_2. Note that, at $t = 0$ ms the laser pulses are absent and the minimum of the harmonic oscillator occurs at the center of the trap. Hence, we obtain a pancake-shaped density profile of the condensate Ψ_1, which has maximum density at the trap center to minimize trap potential energy. Then, during the application of laser pulse, the G-pulse gradually creates a rotationally symmetric "hump" at the center of the trap, which increases the potential energy at the trap center. Therefore, the minimum of the effective trap potential $V_{\text{eff},1}$ gets shifted radially away from the center, resulting in a rotationally symmetric annular region as the new minimum of the potential. It is important to mention that the density profile of a condensate in a binary mixture depends on the effective trap potential in conjunction with the number of atoms in the condensate, intra and intercomponent scattering length. Therefore, the atoms of the condensate Ψ_1 move away from center of the trap and settle at the annular region to minimize the trap potential energy. This creates a hole at the center of the density profile of the condensate Ψ_1. Since the optical dipole potential induced by LG pulse has parabolic form around the center of the trap, the position of the minimum of the effective potential $V_{\text{eff},2}$ does not change over time. However, the steepness of this effective potential changes with time. It increases up to time $t = \tau_1$ and then gradually decreases back to its initial value which is determined by the considered harmonic potential. Therefore, the atoms in the condensate Ψ_2 are always pushed towards the center of the trap to minimize trap potential energy. As a result, during the growth of Ψ_2, the central region of the trap is occupied by the transferred atoms first, and then rest of the region is occupied.

For LG-G pulse sequence, laser modes of pump and Stokes beam are interchanged. Now the optical dipole potential is induced by the LG laser pulse for the condensate Ψ_1 and by the G laser pulse for the condensate Ψ_2. Therefore, with the increase of the steepness of the parabolic potential, which is generated by the LG pulse, the atoms in the condensate Ψ_1 are pushed towards the central region of the trap. The atoms that are transferred to condensate Ψ_2 experience the "hump" in the trap potential at the center, which is created by the G pulse. Thus, the atoms in condensate Ψ_2 are pushed towards an annular minimum region of the effective trap potential. This results in larger core of the vortex in condensate Ψ_2 during the transfer process, which is to be contrasted with the previous case.

4.3. Root-Mean-Square Radius of the Condensates

The growth rate of condensate Ψ_2 can be inferred from the rate of change of rms radii of the condensates. In Figure 3 we illustrate the evolution of the r_{rms} of both condensates during the transfer process for the cases when G-LG and LG-G pulse sequences are considered. From the comparison between the considered cases, we can infer that the growth rate of the condensate Ψ_2 is faster in the case of LG-G pulse sequence than the case of G-LG pulse sequence. Note that, for the chosen pulses, the strength of the Raman interaction term $\mathcal{V}'$ is always maximum, at the boundary of the trap. However, atoms in the condensate try to occupy the minimum of the trap potential to minimize the trap potential energy. In particular, the effective trap potential $V_{\text{eff},2}$ of condensate Ψ_2 has a minimum at the center of trap for G-LG pulse sequence, but at a distance $r = w_0\sqrt{\ln(4\mathcal{V}_2(t)/w_0^2)/2}$ from the center, for LG-G pulse sequence. Therefore, in the later case, the minimum of the effective trap potential is closer to the trap boundary where the Raman coupling $\mathcal{V}'$ term is maximum.

This suggests that the growth rate of the condensate Ψ_2 depends on the distance between the position of the minimum of effective trap potential and the position of maximum Raman coupling. After the transfer process, the rms radius of Ψ_2 oscillates around a mean value. The frequency of such residual radial oscillations, as can be seen from Figure 3, is approximately $\omega' = \omega/3$ for both pulse sequences. The amplitude of oscillation is much smaller than the mean radius of condensate. Most importantly, such a small amplitude of oscillation indicates that negligible amount residual excitations have been activated during the population transfer. However, detail analysis of such excitations is out of the scope of this work.

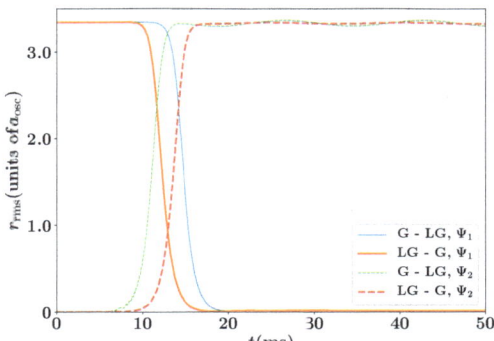

Figure 3. (Color online) Shows the time evolution root mean square radius r_{rms} of BEC Ψ_1 and Ψ_2 for different pulse sequences(see legends). The BECs are confined harmonic trapping potential with frequency $\omega = 2\pi \times 30.832$ Hz and the intra-and interspecies interactions are taken as $a_{11} = 100.04a_0$, $a_{22} = 95.44a_0$, and $a_{12} = 100a_0$ respectively. The dynamics is triggered by employing LG[G]-G[LG] pulse sequence, where LG[G] is the pump beam and G[LG] is the stokes beam.

4.4. Effects of Intercomponent Interaction

We now discuss the effects of intercomponent interaction between the two condensates, during the transfer process and the final population of the condensate Ψ_2. We consider the LG-G pulse sequence as the representative example.

The scattering length a_{12}, which quantifies interactions between the atoms of the two different components, plays an important role in determining spatial wavefunctions and the energy of the condensates. Indeed, for certain temporal duration of pulses and intercomponent scattering length, the strength of the atom-light interaction V_{max} have to be monitored to get the desired population of atoms in the state $|2\rangle$. In the Figure 4, we present the number of atoms in condensate Ψ_2 at the end of the transfer process as a function of a_{12} and V_{max}. We vary peak Rabi frequency V_{max} from 1 to 100 and intercomponent atomic scattering length a_{12} from $70a_0$ to $110a_0$. Peak Rabi frequency can be controlled either by changing peak light intensity of the pulse or by changing the detuning. Whereas, the scattering length can be varied through the magnetic Feshbach resonance [83]. We observe complete population transfer from condensate Ψ_1 to condensate Ψ_2 when V_{max} is greater than 100 (not shown in the diagram). Intercomponent interactions merely affect the transfer process. In this region, atom–light interaction is strong enough to affect any density distribution determined by a_{12}. However, this situation does not hold for intermediate values of V_{max}, predominantly between 100 and 10. In this region, stronger is the intercomponent interaction, larger is the number of atoms transferred to condensate Ψ_2. For small values of V_{max}, larger values of a_{12} suppresses the transfer process, which is evident from Figure 4. It is important to mention that in this limit, we observe the growth of condensate Ψ_2 is different for different values of intercomponent atomic scattering length. That is, depending on the strength of the atom-light interaction, a_{12} affects the population transfer in different manner. For example, for $V_{max} = 1$, the final population of Ψ_2 is suppressed for larger a_{12}, whereas, for $V_{max} = 10$, strong interaction increases the population in Ψ_2 (see Figure 5a,b).

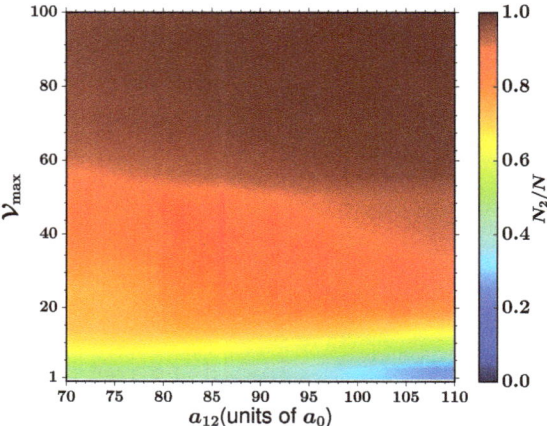

Figure 4. (Color online) Illustrates the number of atoms transferred to the condensate Ψ_2 as a function of intercomponent scattering length a_{12} and the light–matter interaction parameter $\mathcal{V}_{\max}$. The colorbar shows the fraction of atoms in condensate Ψ_2 with respect to the total number of atoms $N = 10^4$ in the system at the end of the transfer process. The population transfer from Ψ_1 to Ψ_2 is carried-out using LG(pump)-G(stokes) pulse sequence. The system is confined in a harmonic trapping potential with frequency $\omega = 2\pi \times 30.832$ Hz and the intraspecies scattering lengths are $a_{11} = 100.04 a_0$ and $a_{22} = 95.44 a_0$.

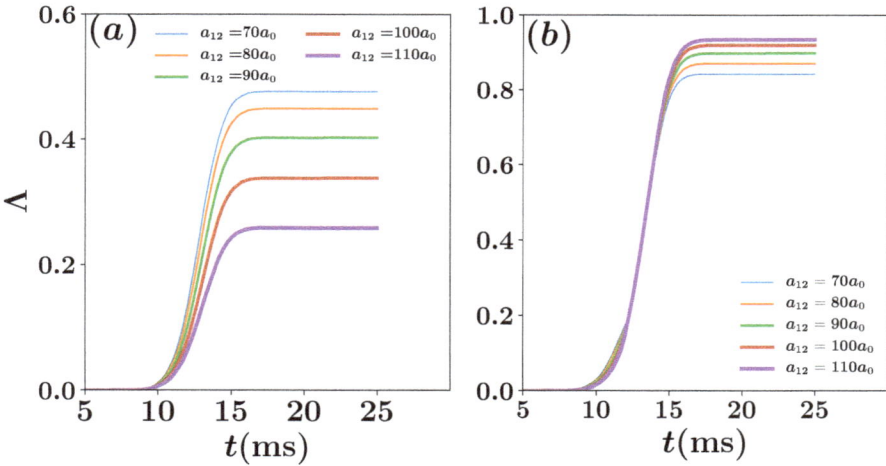

Figure 5. (Color online) Shows the time evolution of the population in the condensate Ψ_2 for a fixed Rabi frequency, with (a) $\mathcal{V}_{\max} = 1$ and (b) $\mathcal{V}_{\max} = 10$, and different interspecies scattering lengths a_{12} [see legends]. The dynamics is triggered by employing LG(pump)-G(stokes) pulse sequence. The BEC Ψ_2 is confined in a harmonic trapping potential with frequency $\omega = 2\pi \times 30.832$ Hz. The total number of atoms in the system is $N = 10^4$ and the intraspecies scattering lengths are given by $a_{11} = 100.04 a_0$ and $a_{22} = 95.44 a_0$. For $\mathcal{V}_{\max} = 1$, larger a_{12} suppresses the population transfer processes, but favors the same for $\mathcal{V}_{\max} = 10$.

In order to gain further intuition regarding the combined effect of the atom-light coupling and inter-component interaction we resort to the density evolution. Figure 6 presents few representative snapshots of the density profiles for $\mathcal{V}_{\max} = 1$ and $a_{12} = 80 a_0$. Note that this particular parameter set corresponds to 45% particle transfer to Ψ_2 (see Figure 5), therefore, enabling the creation of binary mixture of almost equal particles. This, in particular, is better comprehended from the density profiles depicted in Figure 6. Preparing the initial state characterized by all the atoms residing at the state $|1\rangle$ (Figure 6(a_1,b_1)), the light–matter interaction is initiated by employing LG-and G beams as pump and stokes beam, respectively. Note that the large vortex core of Ψ_2 during the early stage of population transfer is caused by the presence of the Gaussian potential barrier at its center (see Figure 6(b_2)). However, the same vortex core gradually shrinks as more number of particles are transferred and the Gaussian barrier gradually diminishes (see Figure 6(b_3,b_4)). Finally, the BEC at $|2\rangle$ possess 45% of the total number of particles. A close inspection of Figure 6(a_4–a_6,b_4–b_6) reveals that a breathing motion characterized by expansion and contraction of the density profiles has been triggered in both Ψ_1 and Ψ_2. Another observation is that Ψ_2, after the population transfer, exhibits larger vortex core when compared to the case of complete particle transfer, see Figure 2(d_6) and Figure 6(b_6).

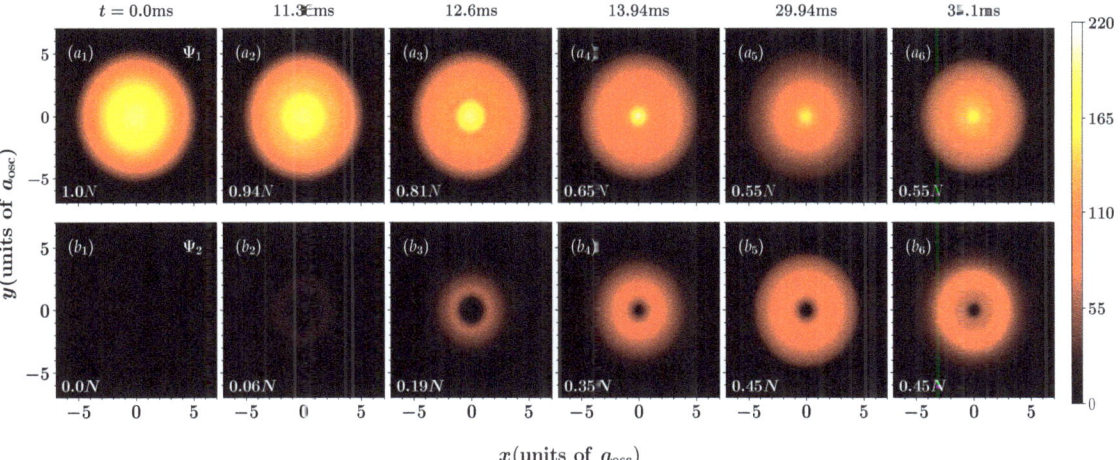

Figure 6. (Color online) Shows the time evolution (see the legends) of the density profiles of the BEC Ψ_1 at (a_1–a_6) $|1\rangle$ and those of BEC Ψ_2 at (b_1–b_6) $|2\rangle$. The population transfer from Ψ_1 to Ψ_2 is triggered by utilizing a LG(pump)–G(stokes) pulse sequence and setting the light–matter interaction parameter $V_{max} = 1$ and the interspecies scattering length $a_{12} = 80a_0$, while all other parameters are the same as before. The fraction of atoms the condensate with respect to the total number of atoms $N = 10^4$, is mentioned at the bottom left corner of each figure.

In addition, we observe the peak Rabi frequency plays an important role in determining the miscibility between the two components during light–matter interaction. This is in contrast to the case when the light field is absent, that is, miscibility of two condensates is determined by the intra and intercomponent interactions. To illustrate this, we have considered Rabi frequencies, $V_{max} = 1$ and $V_{max} = 10$, for which both the condensates Ψ_1 and Ψ_2 have finite number of atoms N_1 and N_2, even after the light–matter interaction. For these two cases, we show the variation of the miscibility parameter Λ with time in Figure 7. Note that just after the initiation of the transfer process, condensate Ψ_2 grows within the condensate Ψ_1, resulting in gradual increase of Λ. However, when a sufficient number of atoms have been transferred to condensate Ψ_2 and both the pulses have significant temporal overlap, mutual repulsion between the condensates and the optical dipole potential tend to push the two condensates away from each other. This results in decrease of Λ. Again, the overlap between the condensates and hence Λ increases as pulses gradually die down. It is important to notice that during the light–matter interaction we obtain larger values of Λ for larger values of a_{12}. This indicates, the stronger the intercomponent repulsion between the two condensates, the larger the overlap between them is. This is to be contrasted with the case when light–matter interaction is absent, in which, larger intercomponent repulsion separates the condensates spatially. After the light–matter interaction, that is, when the optical dipole potentials disappear, the miscibility between the condensates is determined by intra- and inter-component interactions.

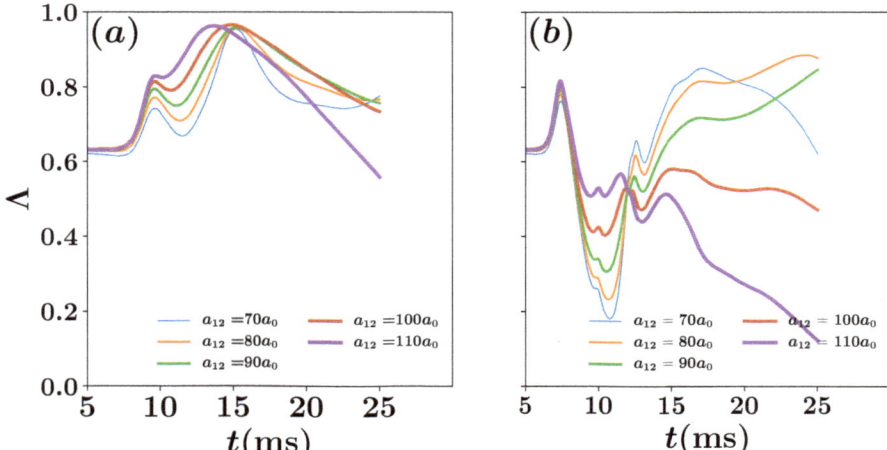

Figure 7. (Color online) Shows the time evolution of the overlap integral Λ for a fixed Rabi frequency, with (**a**) $\mathcal{V}_{\max} = 1$ and (**b**) $\mathcal{V}_{\max} = 10$, and different interspecies scattering lengths a_{12} [see legends]. The dynamics is initiated by employing LG(pump)-G(stokes) pulse sequence. The binary BECs are confined in harmonic trapping potential with frequency $\omega = 2\pi \times 30.832$ Hz. The total number of atoms in the system is $N = 10^4$ and the intraspecies scattering lengths are given by $a_{11} = 100.04 a_0$ and $a_{22} = 95.44 a_0$.

5. Conclusions

In conclusion, we have shown that how two-photon Raman transition can be used to generate a rotating BEC with vorticity of either sign, by transferring atoms from another condensate. In this transition, atoms gain angular momentum from the LG laser pulse before being transferred to a rotating condensate. Density patterns of the condensates during the light–matter interaction depend on sign of the vorticity of the rotating condensate.

In particular, we have show that how a specific choice of pump and stokes beams can alter the locations, within the trap, where the transferred particles start accumulating. Notably, this result stems form the optical potentials felt by the atoms of each individual state. Most importantly, the interchange of pump and stokes laser beams not only changes the sign of vorticity, but also gives rise different dipole potentials influencing both the growth rate and growth region of the new Bose–Eintein condensate. The growth of the new condensate with -1 unit vorticity is started from the central region of the trap, but a condensate with $+1$ unit vorticity starts to grow from the peripheral region of the same. Furthermore, the "smoothness" of the density profiles and the temporal evolution of rms radius imply that there are very few excitations emerging during the light–matter interaction.

Moreover, we have shown that the number of transferred atoms can be monitored by tuning the intercomponent interaction, if the peak Rabi frequency of light–matter interaction is low and in particular, large intercomponent interaction subdues this transfer process. In this way, by maneuvering the atom-light interaction strength and the intercomponent scattering length one can create binary mixture of condensates.

Another major finding from our investigation is that intercomponent interaction kind of plays an opposite role in the process of phase separation during the Raman transition process, in contrast to literature [84] when such dynamical perturbation is absent. We find that a stronger intercomponent interaction favors greater miscibility between the condensates during the light–matter interaction.

Finally, we point out that the storage of a photon pair entangled in OAM space through Raman transition in the cold atomic ensemble has served as a sandbox to study information processing [85]. Besides, because atoms can have higher spin manifolds than light, the extension of our work to the spinor BEC would be an important study. Various topological properties can be developed in the ground state depending on Rabi frequency and atom-atom interaction strength, for example, a Mermin-Ho vortex or a meron pair phase [86], and might lead to the exhibition of non-Abelian braiding statistics [87] which is particularly interesting for topological quantum computing protocols [88]. We expect our study will shed light for further research in this direction.

Author Contributions: Conceptualization, K.M., A.M.M. and S.M.; methodology, K.M., S.B. and D.A.; software, K.M. and S.B.; validation, K.M.; formal analysis, K.M.; investigation, K.M.; resources, S.M.; data curation, K.M.; writing—original draft preparation, K.M.; writing—review and editing, K.M., S.B., D.A., A.M.M. and S.M.; visualization, K.M.; supervision, S.M.; project administration, S.M.; funding acquisition, K.M. and S.M. All authors have read and agreed to the published version of the manuscript.

Funding: K.M. acknowledges MHRD, Govt of India for the research fellowship.

Institutional Review Board Statement: Not applicable.

Informed Consent Statement: Not applicable.

Data Availability Statement: All the data that support the plots within this paper are available from the corresponding author upon reasonable request.

Acknowledgments: K.M. is thankful to Subrata Das for technical assistance. K.M. is also grateful to Physical Research Laboratory, Ahmedabad for the hospitality during the initial stages of this work. S.B. and D.A. gratefully thank Arko Roy and Pekko Kuopanportti for insightful discussions.

Conflicts of Interest: The authors declare no conflict of interest. The funders had no role in the design of the study; in the collection, analyses, or interpretation of data; in the writing of the manuscript, or in the decision to publish the results.

Appendix A. Effects of Harmonic Trap and Time-Delay between the Pulses

Here we discuss the effects of the trapping frequencies of the harmonic potentials and the time-delay between two pulses during the particle transfer and on the final population of the component Ψ_2. In particular, we are interested in the weak atom-light coupling regime where both components contain finite number of particles. To that purpose we set $\mathcal{V}_{max} = 1$, also the interspecies scattering length is $a_{12} = 80a_0$. Figure A1a presents time evolution of the fraction of total number of particles in Ψ_2 for different trapping frequencies ω. It is evident that consideration of a different trapping frequency only changes the time scale of the relevant phenomenology. Remarkably, it does not alter the final population of the Ψ_2 to a great extent. The onset and the growth rate of the population transfer are influenced by the trapping frequency. For instance, for $\omega/(2\pi) = 30.832$ Hz, the transfer starts at earlier time instant and occurs at a faster rate when compared to the others.

Next we inspect the effect of varying time-delay between the two pulses on the population transfer in the weak light–matter coupling regime (see Figure A1b). We fix the peak location (τ_2) of the stokes pulse at $\tau_2 = 10.33$ ms and vary the peak location (τ_1) of the pump pulse. We notice that maximum particle transfer is approximately 45% of the total population, which is achieved when τ_1 lies in the range 11.36–12.39 ms. However, when the time delay is too large ($\tau_1 = 15.49$ ms) or too small ($\tau_1 = 10.36$ ms) the number of particles in Ψ_2 decreases. Besides, when the time delay is very small, in other words temporal peaks of the two pulses are very close to each other, the growth of the population shows a very different behavior, see the blue curve in Figure A1b. The noticeable swell, during the light–matter interaction, in the curve corresponding to $\tau_1 = 10.36$ ms can be related to the creation of significant amount of excitations in both components. These excitations stemming from the interactions with laser pulses also remain in both components after the interaction is over. We remark that such residual excitations leave their finger-prints onto the density profiles of the components (not shown here for the brevity), and bear the signatures of the break-down of coherent population transfer.

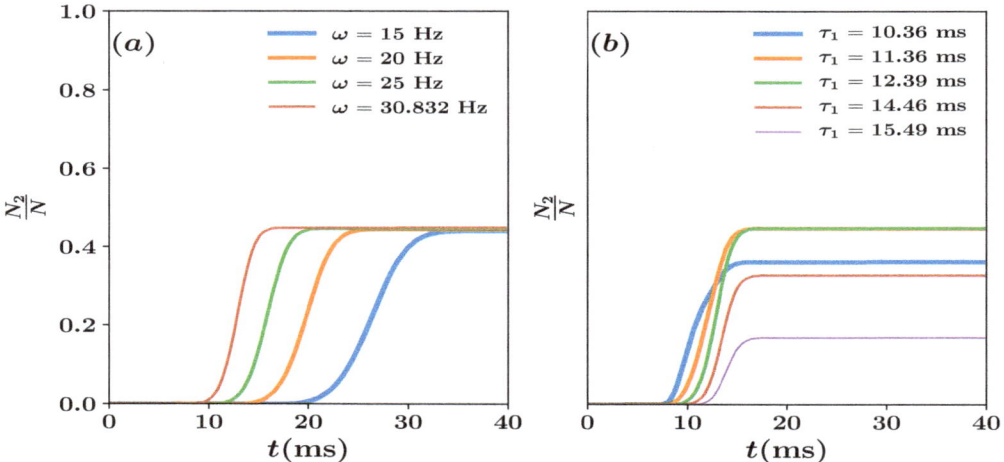

Figure A1. (Color online) Time evolution of the fraction of particle number transferred to the BEC Ψ_2 for (**a**) various trapping frequencies ω and (**b**) various peak positions of the (τ_1) of the pump laser pulse. A LG-G pulse sequence is used to trigger the dynamics in the weak light–matter interaction regime characterized by $V_{\max} = 1$. While studying the effect of the trapping frequencies [(a)], τ_2 and τ_1 are fixed at 10.33 ms and 13.43 ms, respectively. On the other, the rapping frequency $\omega = 2\pi \times 30.832$ Hz and peak position $\tau_2 = 10.33$ of stokes pulse are kept fixed when studying the variation of τ_1 [(b)]. The total number of particles in the system is $N = 10^4$, and the intra-and interspecies interactions are $a_{11} = 99a_0$, $a_{22} = 95.44a_0$ and $a_{12} = 80a_0$.

Appendix B. Hamiltonian and Derivation of Equation of Motions

Let $\hat{\Psi}_j^\dagger$ and $\hat{\Psi}_j$ be the creation and annihilation operators respectively for atoms at state $|j\rangle$. The Hamiltonian for interacting boson alkali atoms in a trap potential, with respect to a frame rotating at the frequency of applied laser fields in the rotating wave approximation can be written as

$$H = \int d\mathbf{r}_1 \hat{\Psi}_1^\dagger(\mathbf{r}_1,t) \hat{h}_1 \hat{\Psi}_1(\mathbf{r}_1,t) + \int d\mathbf{r}_2 \hat{\Psi}_2^\dagger(\mathbf{r}_2,t) \hat{h}_2 \hat{\Psi}_2(\mathbf{r}_2,t) + \hbar\Delta \int d\mathbf{r}_3 \hat{\Psi}_3^\dagger(\mathbf{r}_3,t) \hat{\Psi}_3(\mathbf{r}_3,t)$$
$$+ \frac{U_{11}}{2} \int d\mathbf{r}_1 \hat{\Psi}_1^\dagger(\mathbf{r}_1,t) \hat{\Psi}_1^\dagger(\mathbf{r}_1,t) \hat{\Psi}_1(\mathbf{r}_1,t) \hat{\Psi}_1(\mathbf{r}_1,t) + \frac{U_{22}}{2} \int d\mathbf{r}_2 \hat{\Psi}_2^\dagger(\mathbf{r}_2,t) \hat{\Psi}_2^\dagger(\mathbf{r}_2,t) \hat{\Psi}_1(\mathbf{r}_2,t) \hat{\Psi}_1(\mathbf{r}_2,t)$$
$$+ U_{12} \int d\mathbf{r}' \hat{\Psi}_1^\dagger(\mathbf{r}',t) \hat{\Psi}_2^\dagger(\mathbf{r}',t) \hat{\Psi}_1(\mathbf{r}',t) \hat{\Psi}_2(\mathbf{r}',t) + \hbar \int d\mathbf{r}' \Omega_1(\mathbf{r}',t) e^{il_1\phi} \hat{\Psi}_3^\dagger(\mathbf{r}',t) \hat{\Psi}_1(\mathbf{r}',t)$$
$$+ \hbar \int d\mathbf{r}' \Omega_2(\mathbf{r}',t) e^{il_2\phi} \hat{\Psi}_3^\dagger(\mathbf{r}',t) \hat{\Psi}_2(\mathbf{r}',t) + H.c$$

we have following commutation relations for the bosonic operators:

$$[\hat{\Psi}_j(\mathbf{r},t), \hat{\Psi}_k^\dagger(\mathbf{r}',t)] = \delta(\mathbf{r}-\mathbf{r}')\delta_{jk},$$
$$[\hat{\Psi}_j(\mathbf{r},t), \hat{\Psi}_k(\mathbf{r}',t)] = 0,$$
$$[\hat{\Psi}_j^\dagger(\mathbf{r},t), \hat{\Psi}_k^\dagger(\mathbf{r}',t)] = 0$$
(A1)

Now Heisenberg equation of motion gives

$$i\hbar \frac{\partial \hat{\Psi}_1(\mathbf{r},t)}{\partial t} = [\hat{\Psi}_1(\mathbf{r},t), H] \quad \text{(A2)}$$

$$i\hbar\frac{\partial \hat{\Psi}_2(\mathbf{r},t)}{\partial t} = [\hat{\Psi}_2(\mathbf{r},t), H] \tag{A3}$$

$$i\hbar\frac{\partial \hat{\Psi}_3(\mathbf{r},t)}{\partial t} = [\hat{\Psi}_3(\mathbf{r},t), H] \tag{A4}$$

Using bosonic commutation relation and Heisenberg equation of motion we get

$$i\hbar\frac{\partial \hat{\Psi}_1(\mathbf{r},t)}{\partial t} = \hat{h}_1\hat{\Psi}_1(\mathbf{r},t) + U_{11}\hat{\Psi}_1^\dagger(\mathbf{r},t)\hat{\Psi}_1(\mathbf{r},t)\hat{\Psi}_1(\mathbf{r},t) \tag{A5}$$
$$+ U_{12}\hat{\Psi}_2^\dagger(\mathbf{r},t)\hat{\Psi}_2(\mathbf{r},t)\hat{\Psi}_1(\mathbf{r},t) + \Omega_1^*(\mathbf{r},t)e^{-il_1\phi}\hat{\Psi}_3(\mathbf{r},t),$$

$$i\hbar\frac{\partial \hat{\Psi}_2(\mathbf{r},t)}{\partial t} = \hat{h}_2\hat{\Psi}_2(\mathbf{r},t) + U_{22}\hat{\Psi}_2^\dagger(\mathbf{r},t)\hat{\Psi}_2(\mathbf{r},t)\hat{\Psi}_2(\mathbf{r},t) \tag{A6}$$
$$+ U_{21}\hat{\Psi}_1^\dagger(\mathbf{r},t)\hat{\Psi}_1(\mathbf{r},t)\hat{\Psi}_2(\mathbf{r},t) + \hbar\Omega_1^*(\mathbf{r},t)e^{-il_2\phi}\hat{\Psi}_3(\mathbf{r},t),$$

and

$$i\hbar\frac{\partial \hat{\Psi}_3(\mathbf{r},t)}{\partial t} = \hbar\Delta\hat{\Psi}_3(\mathbf{r},t) + \hbar\Omega_1(\mathbf{r},t)e^{il_1\phi}\hat{\Psi}_1(\mathbf{r},t) \tag{A7}$$
$$+ \hbar\Omega_2(\mathbf{r},t)e^{il_2\phi}\hat{\Psi}_2(\mathbf{r},t).$$

Eliminating of the field operator $\hat{\Psi}_3(r,t)$ adiabatically,

$$i\hbar\frac{\partial \hat{\Psi}_3(\mathbf{r},t)}{\partial t} = 0 \tag{A8}$$

$$\hat{\Psi}_3(\mathbf{r},t) = -(\Omega_1(\mathbf{r},t)e^{il_1\phi}\hat{\Psi}_1(\mathbf{r},t) + \Omega_2(\mathbf{r},t)e^{il_2\phi}\hat{\Psi}_2(\mathbf{r},t))/\Delta \tag{A9}$$

Putting (A9) into (A5) and (A6) we get,

$$i\hbar\frac{\partial \hat{\Psi}_1(\mathbf{r},t)}{\partial t} = \hat{h}_1\hat{\Psi}_1(\mathbf{r},t) + U_{11}\hat{\Psi}_1^\dagger(\mathbf{r},t)\hat{\Psi}_1(\mathbf{r},t)\hat{\Psi}_1(\mathbf{r},t) + \tag{A10}$$
$$U_{12}\hat{\Psi}_2^\dagger(\mathbf{r},t)\hat{\Psi}_2(\mathbf{r},t)\hat{\Psi}_1(\mathbf{r},t) - \frac{\hbar|\Omega_1(\mathbf{r},t)|^2}{\Delta}\hat{\Psi}_1(\mathbf{r},t) -$$
$$\frac{\hbar\Omega_2(\mathbf{r},t)\Omega_1^*(\mathbf{r},t)}{\Delta}\hat{\Psi}_2(\mathbf{r},t)e^{-i(l_1-l_2)\phi}$$

and

$$i\hbar\frac{\partial \hat{\Psi}_2(\mathbf{r},t)}{\partial t} = \hat{h}_2\hat{\Psi}_2(\mathbf{r},t) + U_{22}\hat{\Psi}_2^\dagger(\mathbf{r},t)\hat{\Psi}_2(\mathbf{r},t)\hat{\Psi}_2(\mathbf{r},t) + \tag{A11}$$
$$U_{21}\hat{\Psi}_1^\dagger(\mathbf{r},t)\hat{\Psi}_1(\mathbf{r},t)\hat{\Psi}_2(\mathbf{r},t) - \frac{\hbar|\Omega_2(\mathbf{r},t)|^2}{\Delta}\hat{\Psi}_2(\mathbf{r},t) -$$
$$\frac{\hbar\Omega_1(\mathbf{r},t)\Omega_2^*(\mathbf{r},t)}{\Delta}\hat{\Psi}_1(\mathbf{r},t)e^{i(l_1-l_2)\phi}$$

where $\Omega_1(r)$ and $\Omega_2(r)$, Rabi frequencies of the transitions $|1\rangle \to |3\rangle$ and $3\rangle \to |2\rangle$, are given by $\mathbf{E}_1(\mathbf{r},t)\cdot \mathbf{d}_{13}/\hbar$ and $\mathbf{E}_2(\mathbf{r},t)\cdot \mathbf{d}_{32}/\hbar$ with d_{13} and d_{32} being the corresponding transition dipole moments. we consider $d_{13} = d_{23} = d$. At $T = 0$, in limit of low energy s-wave scattering, and neglecting quantum fluctuation, the field operator $\hat{\Psi}_j$ can be replaced by a complex valued wavefunction Ψ_j. Therefore, (A3) and (A4) become

$$i\hbar\frac{\partial \Psi_1(\mathbf{r},t)}{\partial t} = \left[-\frac{\hbar^2}{2m}\nabla^2 + V(\mathbf{r}) - \frac{\hbar|\Omega_1(\mathbf{r},t)|^2}{\Delta}\right]\Psi_1 + U_{11}|\Psi_1|^2\Psi_1 + U_{12}|\Psi_2|^2\Psi_1 \quad \text{(A12)}$$
$$- \frac{\hbar\Omega_2(\mathbf{r},t)\Omega_1^*(\mathbf{r},t)}{\Delta}\Psi_2(\mathbf{r},t)e^{-i(l_1-l_2)\phi}$$

and

$$i\hbar\frac{\partial \Psi_2(\mathbf{r},t)}{\partial t} = \left[-\frac{\hbar^2}{2m}\nabla^2 + V(\mathbf{r}) - \frac{\hbar|\Omega_2(\mathbf{r},t)|^2}{\Delta}\right]\Psi_2 + U_{11}|\Psi_2|^2\Psi_2 + U_{12}|\Psi_1|^2\Psi_2 \quad \text{(A13)}$$
$$- \frac{\hbar\Omega_1(\mathbf{r},t)\Omega_2^*(\mathbf{r},t)}{\Delta}\Psi_2(\mathbf{r},t)e^{i(l_1-l_2)\phi}$$

Using (1) and (4)

$$\left|\Omega_{(1)2}\right|^2 = \left(\frac{\mathcal{E}_{max}d_{32}}{\hbar\Delta}\right)^2 e^{-\left(\frac{t-\tau_{1(2)}}{T}\right)^2}(x^2+y^2)^{|l_{1(2)}|}e^{-2\left(\frac{x^2+y^2}{w_{1(2)}^2}\right)} \quad \text{(A14)}$$

and

$$\Omega_2^*\Omega_1 = \left(\frac{\mathcal{E}_{max}d_{32}}{\hbar\Delta}\right)^2 e^{-\left(\frac{t-\tau_1}{T}\right)^2 - \left(\frac{t-\tau_2}{T}\right)^2}(x^2+y^2)^{\frac{|l_1|+|l_2|}{2}}$$
$$\times e^{-\frac{2(x^2+y^2)}{\left(\frac{1}{w_1^2}+\frac{1}{w_2^2}\right)}} \quad \text{(A15)}$$

Here the BEC is considered to be confined at $z = 0$ plane and $\omega_1 \approx \omega_2$.

References

1. Rokhsar, D.S. Vortex Stability and Persistent Currents in Trapped Bose Gases. *Phys. Rev. Lett.* **1997**, *79*, 2164. [CrossRef]
2. Mueller, E.; Goldbart, P.M.; Lyanda-Geller, Y. Multiply connected Bose-Einstein-condensed alkali-metal gases: Current-carrying states and their decay. *Phys. Rev. A* **1998**, *57*, R1505(R). [CrossRef]
3. Onofrio, R.; Raman, C.; Abo-Shaeer, J.; Chikkatur, A.; Ketterle, W. Observation of Superfluid Flow in a Bose-Einstein Condensed Gas and their decay. *Phys. Rev. Lett.* **2000**, *85*, 2228. [CrossRef]
4. Kobayashi, M.; Tsubota, M. Quantum turbulence in a trapped Bose-Einstein condensate. *Phys. Rev. A* **2007**, *76*, 045603. [CrossRef]
5. White, A.C.; Proukakis, N.P.; Youd, A.J.; Wacks, D.H.; Baggaley, A.W.; Barenghi, C.F. Turbulence in a Bose-Einstein condensate. *J. Phys. Conf. Ser.* **2011**, *318*, 062003. [CrossRef]
6. Neely, T.W.; Bradley, A.S.; Samson, E.C.; Rooney, S.J.; Wright, E.M.; Law, K.J.H.; Carretero-González, R.; Kevrekidis, P.G.; Davis, M.J.; Anderson, B.P. Characteristics of Two-Dimensional Quantum Turbulence in a Compressible Superfluid. *Phys. Rev. Lett.* **2013**, *111*, 235301. [CrossRef]
7. Barenghi, C.F.; Skrbek, L.; Sreenivasan, K.R. Introduction to quantum turbulence. *Proc. Natl. Acad. Sci. USA* **2014**, *111*, 4647–4652. [CrossRef]
8. White, A.C.; Anderson, B.P.; Bagnato, V.S. Vortices and turbulence in trapped atomic condensates. *Proc. Natl. Acad. Sci. USA* **2014**, *111*, 4719–4726. [CrossRef]
9. Kwon, W.J.; Moon, G.; Choi, J.Y.; Seo, S.W.; Shin, Y.I. Relaxation of superfluid turbulence in highly oblate Bose-Einstein condensates. *Phys. Rev. A* **2014**, *90*, 063627. [CrossRef]
10. Seo, S.W.; Ko, B.; Kim, J.H.; Shin, Y. Observation of vortex-antivortex pairing in decaying 2D turbulence of a superfluid gas. *Sci. Rep.* **2017**, *7*, 4587. [CrossRef]
11. Fedichev, P.O.; Shlyapnikov, G.V. Dissipative dynamics of a vortex state in a trapped Bose-condensed gas. *Phys. Rev. A* **1999**, *60*, R1779–R1782. [CrossRef]
12. Fetter, A.L.; Svidzinsky, A.A. Vortices in a trapped dilute Bose-Einstein condensate. *J. Phys. Condens. Matter* **2001**, *13*, R135. [CrossRef]
13. Koens, L.; Martin, A.M. Perturbative behavior of a vortex in a trapped Bose-Einstein condensate. *Phys. Rev. A* **2012**, *86*, 013605. [CrossRef]
14. Kevrekidis, P.G.; Wang, W.; Carretero-González, R.; Frantzeskakis, D.J.; Xie, S. Vortex precession dynamics in general radially symmetric potential traps in two-dimensional atomic Bose-Einstein condensates. *Phys. Rev. A* **2017**, *96*, 043612. [CrossRef]
15. Bandyopadhyay, S.; Roy, A.; Angom, D. Dynamics of phase separation in two-species Bose-Einstein condensates with vortices. *Phys. Rev. A* **2017**, *96*, 043603. [CrossRef]

16. Mukherjee, K.; Mukherjee, K.; Mistakidis, S.; Kevrekidis, P.G.; Schmelcher, P. Quench induced vortex-bright-soliton formation in binary Bose-Einstein condensates. *J. Phys. B At. Mol. Opt. Phys.* **2020**. [CrossRef]
17. Isoshima, T.; Machida, K. Vortex stabilization in Bose-Einstein condensate of alkali-metal atom gas. *Phys. Rev. A* **1999**, *59*, 2203–2212. [CrossRef]
18. Virtanen, S.M.M.; Salomaa, M.M. Effect of the thermal gas component on the stability of vortices in trapped Bose–Einstein condensates. *J. Phys. B At. Mol. Opt. Phys.* **2002**, *35*, 3967. [CrossRef]
19. García-Ripoll, J.J.; Pérez-García, V.M. Stable and Unstable Vortices in Multicomponent Bose-Einstein Condensates *Phys. Rev. Lett.* **2000**, *84*, 4264–4267. [CrossRef]
20. Coddington, I.; Haljan, P.C.; Engels, P.; Schweikhard, V.; Tung, S.; Cornell, E.A. Experimental studies of equilibrium vortex properties in a Bose-condensed gas. *Phys. Rev. A* **2004**, *70*, 063607. [CrossRef]
21. Shin, Y.; Saba, M.; Vengalattore, M.; Pasquini, T.A.; Sanner, C.; Leanhardt, A.E.; Prentiss, M.; Pritchard, D.E.; Ketterle, W. Dynamical Instability of a Doubly Quantized Vortex in a Bose-Einstein Condensate. *Phys. Rev. Lett.* **2004**, *93*, 160406. [CrossRef]
22. Isoshima, T.; Okano, M.; Yasuda, H.; Kasa, K.; Huhtamäki, J.A.M.; Kumakura, M.; Takahashi, Y. Spontaneous Splitting of a Quadruply Charged Vortex. *Phys. Rev. Lett.* **2007**, *99*, 200403. [CrossRef]
23. Kuopanportti, P.; Lundh, E.; Huhtamäki, J.A.M.; Pietilä, V.; Möttönen, M. Core sizes and dynamical instabilities of giant vortices in dilute Bose-Einstein condensates. *Phys. Rev. A* **2010**, *81*, 023603 [CrossRef]
24. Kuopanportti, P.; Möttönen, M. Splitting dynamics of giant vortices in dilute Bose-Einstein condensates. *Phys. Rev. A* **2010**, *81*, 033627. [CrossRef]
25. Dodd, R.J.; Burnett, K.; Edwards, M.; Clark, C.W. Excitation spectroscopy of vortex states in dilute Bose-Einstein condensed gases. *Phys. Rev. A* **1997**, *56*, 587–590. [CrossRef]
26. Choi, S.; Baksmaty, L.O.; Woo, S.J.; Bigelow, N.P. Excitation spectrum of vortex lattices in rotating Bose-Einstein condensates. *Phys. Rev. A* **2003**, *68*, 031605. [CrossRef]
27. Skryabin, D.V. Instabilities of vortices in a binary mixture of trapped Bose-Einstein condensates: Role of collective excitations with positive and negative energies. *Phys. Rev. A* **2000**, *63*, 013602. [CrossRef]
28. Middelkamp, S.; Kevrekidis, P.G.; Frantzeskakis, D.J.; Carretero-González, R.; Schmelcher, P. Bifurcations, stability, and dynamics of multiple matter-wave vortex states. *Phys. Rev. A* **2010**, *82*, 013646. [CrossRef]
29. Kuopanportti, P.; Bandyopadhyay, S.; Roy, A.; Angom, D. Splitting of singly and doubly quantized composite vortices in two-component Bose-Einstein condensates. *arXiv* **2018**, arXiv:1803.08223.
30. Mateo, A.M.N.; Delgado, V. Dynamical Evolution of a Doubly Quantized Vortex Imprinted in a Bose-Einstein Condensate. *Phys. Rev. Lett.* **2006**, *97*, 180409. [CrossRef]
31. Neely, T.W.; Samson, E.C.; Bradley, A.S.; Davis, M.J.; Anderson, B.P. Observation of Vortex Dipoles in an Oblate Bose-Einstein Condensate. *Phys. Rev. Lett.* **2010**, *104*, 160401. [CrossRef]
32. Bolda, E.L.; Walls, D.F. Detection of Vorticity in Bose-Einstein Condensed Gases by Matter-Wave Interference. *Phys. Rev. Lett.* **1998**, *81*, 5477–5480. [CrossRef]
33. Chevy, F.; Madison, K.W.; Bretin, V.; Dalibard, J. Interferometric detection of a single vortex in a dilute Bose-Einstein condensate. *Phys. Rev. A* **2001**, *64*, 031601. [CrossRef]
34. Freilich, D.V.; Bianchi, D.M.; Kaufman, A.M.; Langin, T.K.; Hall, D.S. Real-Time Dynamics of Single Vortex Lines and Vortex Dipoles in a Bose-Einstein Condensate. *Science* **2010**, *329*, 1182–1185. [CrossRef]
35. Navarro, R.; Carretero-González, R.; Torres, P.J.; Kevrekidis, P.G.; Frantzeskakis, D.J.; Ray, M.W.; Altuntaş, E.; Hall, D.S. Dynamics of a Few Corotating Vortices in Bose-Einstein Condensates. *Phys. Rev. Lett.* **2013**, *110*, 225301. [CrossRef]
36. Wilson, K.E.; Newman, Z.L.; Lowney, J.D.; Anderson, B.P. In situ imaging of vortices in Bose-Einstein condensates. *Phys. Rev. A* **2015**, *91*, 023621. [CrossRef]
37. Marzlin, K.P.; Zhang, W.; Wright, E.M. Vortex Coupler for Atomic Bose-Einstein Condensates. *Phys. Rev. Lett.* **1997**, *79*, 4728–4731. [CrossRef]
38. Dum, R.; Cirac, J.I.; Lewenstein, M.; Zoller, P. Creation of Dark Solitons and Vortices in Bose-Einstein Condensates. *Phys. Rev. Lett.* **1998**, *80*, 2972–2975. [CrossRef]
39. Jackson, B.; McCann, J.F.; Adams, C.S. Vortex Formation in Dilute Inhomogeneous Bose-Einstein Condensates. *Phys. Rev. Lett.* **1998**, *80*, 3903–3906. [CrossRef]
40. Dobrek, L.; Gajda, M.; Lewenstein, M.; Sengstock, K.; Birkl, G.; Ertmer, W. Optical generation of vortices in trapped Bose-Einstein condensates. *Phys. Rev. A* **1999**, *60*, R3381–R3384. [CrossRef]
41. Petrosyan, K.G.; You, L. Topological phases and circulating states of Bose-Einstein condensates. *Phys. Rev. A* **1999**, *59*, 639–642. [CrossRef]
42. Ruostekoski, J. Topological phase preparation in a pair of atomic Bose-Einstein condensates. *Phys. Rev. A* **2000**, *61*, 041603. [CrossRef]
43. Damski, B.; Sacha, K.; Zakrzewski, J. Stirring a Bose-Einstein condensate. *J. Phys. B At. Mol. Opt. Phys.* **2002**, *35*, 4051. [CrossRef]
44. Shibayama, H.; Yasaku, Y.; Kuwamoto, T. Vortex nucleation in Bose-Einstein condensates confined in a QUIC trap by topological phase imprinting. *J. Phys. B At. Mol. Opt. Phys.* **2011**, *44*, 075302. [CrossRef]
45. Matthews, M.R.; Anderson, B.P.; Haljan, P.C.; Hall, D.S.; Wieman, C.E.; Cornell, E.A. Vortices in a Bose-Einstein Condensate. *Phys. Rev. Lett.* **1999**, *83*, 2498–2501. [CrossRef]

46. Madison, K.W.; Chevy, F.; Wohlleben, W.; Dalibard, J. Vortex Formation in a Stirred Bose-Einstein Condensate. *Phys. Rev. Lett.* **2000**, *84*, 806–809. [CrossRef]
47. Raman, C.; Abo-Shaeer, J.R.; Vogels, J.M.; Xu, K.; Ketterle, W. Vortex Nucleation in a Stirred Bose-Einstein Condensate. *Phys. Rev. Lett.* **2001**, *87*, 210402. [CrossRef] [PubMed]
48. Henn, E.A.L.; Seman, J.A.; Roati, G.; Magalhães, K.M.F.; Bagnato, V.S. Generation of Vortices and Observation of Quantum Turbulence in an Oscillating Bose-Einstein Condensate. *J. Low Temp. Phys.* **2009**, *158*, 435. [CrossRef]
49. Raman, C.; Köhl, M.; Onofrio, R.; Durfee, D.S.; Kuklewicz, C.E.; Hadzibabic, Z.; Ketterle, W. Evidence for a Critical Velocity in a Bose-Einstein Condensed Gas. *Phys. Rev. Lett.* **1999**, *83*, 2502–2505. [CrossRef]
50. Burger, S.; Bongs, K.; Dettmer, S.; Ertmer, W.; Sengstock, K.; Sanpera, A.; Shlyapnikov, G.V.; Lewenstein, M. Dark Solitons in Bose-Einstein Condensates. *Phys. Rev. Lett.* **1999**, *83*, 5198–5201. [CrossRef]
51. Caradoc-Davies, B.M.; Ballagh, R.J.; Burnett, K. Coherent Dynamics of Vortex Formation in Trapped Bose-Einstein Condensates. *Phys. Rev. Lett.* **1999**, *83*, 895–898. [CrossRef]
52. Leanhardt, A.E.; Görlitz, A.; Chikkatur, A.P.; Kielpinski, D.; Shin, Y.; Pritchard, D.E.; Ketterle, W. Imprinting Vortices in a Bose-Einstein Condensate using Topological Phases. *Phys. Rev. Lett.* **2002**, *89*, 190403. [CrossRef] [PubMed]
53. Möttönen, M.; Pietilä, V.; Virtanen, S.M.M. Vortex Pump for Dilute Bose-Einstein Condensates. *Phys. Rev. Lett.* **2007**, *99*, 250406. [CrossRef] [PubMed]
54. Xu, Z.F.; Zhang, P.; Raman, C.; You, L. Continuous vortex pumping into a spinor condensate with magnetic fields. *Phys. Rev. A* **2008**, *78*, 043606. [CrossRef]
55. Allen, L.; Beijersbergen, M.W.; Spreeuw, R.J.C.; Woerdman, J.P. Orbital angular momentum of light and the transformation of Laguerre-Gaussian laser modes. *Phys. Rev. A* **1992**, *45*, 8185–8189. [CrossRef] [PubMed]
56. Mukherjee, K.; Majumder, S.; Mondal, P.K.; Deb, B. Interaction of a Laguerre–Gaussian beam with trapped Rydberg atoms. *J. Phys. B At. Mol. Opt. Phys.* **2017**, *51*, 015004. [CrossRef]
57. Mondal, P.K.; Deb, B.; Majumder, S. Angular momentum transfer in interaction of Laguerre-Gaussian beams with atoms and molecules. *Phys. Rev. A* **2014**, *89*, 063418. [CrossRef]
58. Bhowmik, A.; Mondal, P.K.; Majumder, S.; Deb, B. Interaction of atom with nonparaxial Laguerre-Gaussian beam: Forming superposition of vortex states in Bose-Einstein condensates. *Phys. Rev. A* **2016**, *93*, 063852. [CrossRef]
59. Bhowmik, A.; Majumder, S. Tuning of non-paraxial effects of the Laguerre-Gaussian beam interacting with the two-component Bose–Einstein condensates. *J. Phys. Commun.* **2018**, *2*, 125001. [CrossRef]
60. Das, S.; Bhowmik, A.; Mukherjee, K.; Majumder, S. Transfer of orbital angular momentum superposition from asymmetric Laguerre–Gaussian beam to Bose–Einstein Condensate. *J. Phys. B At. Mol. Opt. Phys.* **2020**, *53*, 025302. [CrossRef]
61. Tabosa, J.W.R.; Petrov, D.V. Optical Pumping of Orbital Angular Momentum of Light in Cold Cesium Atoms. *Phys. Rev. Lett.* **1999**, *83*, 4967–4970. [CrossRef]
62. He, H.; Friese, M.E.J.; Heckenberg, N.R.; Rubinsztein-Dunlop, H. Direct Observation of Transfer of Angular Momentum to Absorptive Particles from a Laser Beam with a Phase Singularity. *Phys. Rev. Lett.* **1995**, *75*, 826–829. [CrossRef]
63. Kanamoto, R.; Wright, E.M.; Meystre, P. Quantum dynamics of Raman-coupled Bose-Einstein condensates using Laguerre-Gaussian beams. *Phys. Rev. A* **2007**, *75*, 063623. [CrossRef]
64. DeMarco, M.; Pu, H. Angular spin-orbit coupling in cold atoms. *Phys. Rev. A* **2015**, *91*, 033630. [CrossRef]
65. Chen, L.; Pu, H.; Zhang, Y. Spin-orbit angular momentum coupling in a spin-1 Bose-Einstein condensate. *Phys. Rev. A* **2016**, *93*, 013629. [CrossRef]
66. Nandi, G.; Walser, R.; Schleich, W.P. Vortex creation in a trapped Bose-Einstein condensate by stimulated Raman adiabatic passage. *Phys. Rev. A* **2004**, *69*, 063606. [CrossRef]
67. Simula, T.P.; Nygaard, N.; Hu, S.X.; Collins, L.A.; Schneider, B.I.; Mølmer, K. Angular momentum exchange between coherent light and matter fields. *Phys. Rev. A* **2008**, *77*, 015401. [CrossRef]
68. Law, K.J.H.; Kevrekidis, P.G.; Tuckerman, L.S. Stable Vortex–Bright-Soliton Structures in Two-Component Bose-Einstein Condensates. *Phys. Rev. Lett.* **2010**, *105*, 160405. [CrossRef]
69. Jain, P.; Boninsegni, M. Quantum demixing in binary mixtures of dipolar bosons. *Phys. Rev. A* **2011**, *83*, 023602. [CrossRef]
70. Roy, A.; Angom, D. Thermal suppression of phase separation in condensate mixtures. *Phys. Rev. A* **2015**, *92*, 011601. [CrossRef]
71. Andersen, M.F.; Ryu, C.; Cladé, P.; Natarajan, V.; Vaziri, A.; Helmerson, K.; Phillips, W.D. Quantized Rotation of Atoms from Photons with Orbital Angular Momentum. *Phys. Rev. Lett.* **2006**, *97*, 170406. [CrossRef] [PubMed]
72. Ramanathan, A.; Wright, K.C.; Muniz, S.R.; Zelan, M.; Hill, W.T.; Lobb, C.J.; Helmerson, K.; Phillips, W.D.; Campbell, G.K. Superflow in a Toroidal Bose-Einstein Condensate: An Atom Circuit with a Tunable Weak Link. *Phys. Rev. Lett.* **2011**, *106*, 130401. [CrossRef] [PubMed]
73. Wright, K.; Leslie, L.; Bigelow, N. Optical control of the internal and external angular momentum of a Bose-Einstein condensate. *Phys. Rev. A* **2008**, *77*, 041601(R). [CrossRef]
74. Kamsap, M.R.; Ekogo, T.B.; Pedregosa-Gutierrez, J.; Hagel, G.; Houssin, M.; Morizot, O.; Knoop, M.; Champenois, C. Coherent internal state transfer by a three-photon STIRAP-like scheme for many-atom samples. *J. Phys. B At. Mol. Opt. Phys.* **2013**, *46*, 145502. [CrossRef]
75. Wright, E.M.; Arlt, J.; Dholakia, K. Toroidal optical dipole traps for atomic Bose-Einstein condensates using Laguerre-Gaussian beams. *Phys. Rev. A* **2000**, *63*, 013608. [CrossRef]

76. Timmermans, E. Phase Separation of Bose-Einstein Condensates. *Phys. Rev. Lett.* **1998**, *81*, 5718–5721. [CrossRef]
77. Wen, L.; Liu, W.M.; Cai, Y.; Zhang, J.M.; Hu, J. Controlling phase separation of a two-component Bose-Einstein condensate by confinement. *Phys. Rev. A* **2012**, *85*, 043602. [CrossRef]
78. Vudragović, D.; Vidanović, I.; Balaž, A.; Muruganandam, P.; Adhikari, S.K. C programs for solving the time-dependent Gross–Pitaevskii equation in a fully anisotropic trap. *Comput. Phys. Commun.* **2012**, *183*, 2021. [CrossRef]
79. Egorov, M.; Opanchuk, B.; Drummond, P.; Hall, B.V.; Hannaford, P.; Sidorov, A.I. Measurement of s-wave scattering lengths in a two-component Bose-Einstein condensate. *Phys. Rev. A* **2013**, *87*, 053614. [CrossRef]
80. Mertes, K.; Merrill, J.; Carretero-Gonzalez, R.; Frantzeskakis, D.; Kevrekidis, P.; Hall, D. Nonequilibrium Dynamics and Superfluid Ring Excitations in Binary Bose-Einstein Condensates. *Phys. Rev. Lett.* **2007**, *99*, 190402. [CrossRef] [PubMed]
81. Pethick, C.J.; Smith, H. *Bose-Einstein Condensation in Dilute Gases*; Cambridge University Press: Cambridge, UK, 2002.
82. Stringari, S.; Pitaevskii, L. *Bose-Einstein Condensation*; Oxford University Press: Oxford, UK, 2003.
83. Tojo, S.; Taguchi, Y.; Masuyama, Y.; Hayashi, T.; Saito, H.; Hirano, T. Controlling phase separation of binary Bose-Einstein condensates via mixed-spin-channel Feshbach resonance. *Phys. Rev. A* **2010**, *82*, 033609. [CrossRef]
84. Trippenbach, M.; Góral, K.; Rzazewski, K.; Malomed, B.; Band, Y.B. Structure of binary Bose-Einstein condensates. *J. Phys. B At. Mol. Opt. Phys.* **2000**, *33*, 4017. [CrossRef]
85. Ding, D.S.; Zhang, W.; Zhou, Z.Y.; Shi, S.; Xiang, G.Y.; Wang, X.S.; Jiang, Y.K.; Shi, B.S.; Guo, G.C. Quantum Storage of Orbital Angular Momentum Entanglement in an Atomic Ensemble. *Phys. Rev. Lett.* **2015**, *114*, 050502. [CrossRef] [PubMed]
86. Hu, Y.X.; Miniatura, C.; Grémaud, B. Half-skyrmion and vortex-antivortex pairs in spinor condensates. *Phys. Rev. A* **2015**, *92*, 033615. [CrossRef]
87. Semenoff, G.W.; Zhou, F. Discrete Symmetries and 1/3–Quantum Vortices in Condensates of $F = 2$ Cold Atoms. *Phys. Rev. Lett.* **2007**, *98*, 100401. [CrossRef]
88. Nayak, C.; Simon, S.H.; Stern, A.; Freedman, M.; Das Sarma, S. Non-Abelian anyons and topological quantum computation. *Rev. Mod. Phys.* **2008**, *80*, 1083–1159. [CrossRef]

MDPI
St. Alban-Anlage 66
4052 Basel
Switzerland
Tel. +41 61 683 77 34
Fax +41 61 302 89 18
www.mdpi.com

Atoms Editorial Office
E-mail: atoms@mdpi.com
www.mdpi.com/journal/atoms

www.ingramcontent.com/pod-product-compliance
Lightning Source LLC
LaVergne TN
LVHW070047120526
838202LV00101B/1506